CW01064225

Not What I Signed Up For

An autobiographical account
of family love, loss, betrayal, travel,
empowerment and resilience – and
on-line dating for the over-50s

by

Lorna Johnson

Grosvenor House
Publishing Limited

This book is published by
Grosvenor House Publishing Ltd
Link House
140 The Broadway, Tolworth, Surrey, KT6 7HT.
www.grosvenorhousepublishing.co.uk

A CIP record for this book
is available from the British Library

ISBN 978-1-83975-746-4

In loving memory of my mother,
Kathleen Mary Johnson (1901 – 1985)

And for my family:

Penny, Kieron, Annabel and my six grandchildren;

Also, for Ray Candlish, some of whose advice
I have followed and whose continued friendship and
support for my writing I value very highly.

Preface

Travel, for the thinking person, raises questions. Sometimes, it provides answers too.

Like many others, I had taken for granted that the way in which I was brought up and the priorities within my family, were common within other families that I knew.

It is sometimes only when something or someone challenges this or displays different behaviour that one questions those childhood values, expectations, beliefs and behaviours.

In my case, it had not occurred to me that my classmates at school might not be subject to the same religious pressures and expectations at home. This 'norm' of mine was also compounded by the aura I encountered as a student at a Church of England teacher training college, with students from both sexes and with backgrounds similar to mine.

Nor did societal change and the behaviour of having coffee in someone's college room (which depended on who had sufficient milk) and with someone with the opposite sex, strike me as being anything that could be misconstrued – until one of my daughters pointed this out to me in 2021 and made me aware of a possible different interpretation.

No wonder I was surprised by some of the alternative expectations that I encountered with online dating, that made me feel indignant that I should be regarded as a sexual facility.

I was still in the 20th Century while some of my dates had moved on or had values quite different from mine. Their responses were not, to quote myself, what I had signed up for or had assumed.

I am now more wary and in conversation with others, I try to ask myself whether what I mean by what I say and do, is the same as the way in which others may receive it.

Misinterpretation can happen so easily and the outcome can be so difficult to address. I assumed that my ‘online dates’, being of an age similar to mine, had similar expectations; that it was a site for getting to know other people rather than a free brothel. However, judging from my recent experience, the introductory handshake as a greeting seems to have been replaced by an early expectation of sex as an excellent way of getting to know each other.

Although I had originally intended to make this into a novel, this has developed as a memoir, an autobiography because there are things that I wanted to say and explain before it’s too late – because of a possible stroke, the pandemic, the possibility of further cancers, and the unexpected, the things we do not yet know that are on the horizon. And, as one of my children so aptly suggested, it could contribute to my eulogy – or, as one of my neighbours said, to my urology.

For the sake of those who may not wish to be identified or their part in my story to be told, I have changed the names, addresses and titles of many of those mentioned who are still alive.

Other than that, the episodes and details are as I personally remember them.

Acknowledgements

I would like to thank the following people for their encouragement and support in helping me compose this account:

Kieron Bradley, for his technical assistance with the cover photographs,

Anna Bradley for her belief in my ability to write this and for her regular support and encouragement,

Raymond Candlish, for his interest and encouragement,

Alan Dale, Cortijo Romero owner, for allowing me additional time and providing me with the necessary facilities,

Writers Kathryn Hughes, Helen Smith and Ian Thomson, my tutors on the University of East Anglia Biography and Creative Non-Fiction Masters course, for their professional advice and encouragement over two years,

John Moss, previous Dean of Education at Canterbury Christ Church University, for his suggestion that I might apply to U.E.A. for the post-graduate course.

Acknowledgements

Contents

> 'The stark truth is, of course, that grief never dies. The American counsellor Lois Tonkin reminds us that loss isn't something we 'get over', and it doesn't necessarily lessen, either. It remains at the core of us and we just expand our lives around it, burying it deeper from the surface. So with time it may become more distant, more compartmentalised and therefore easier to manage, but it does not go away.' *All That Remains, A Life in Death* by Sue Black, 2018

Chapter 1

My First Online Date

'Would you like another drink?' Brian asks me. 'Or shall we go to bed straight away?'

Brian and I are strangers. We have only just met each other, for the first time ever, introduced ourselves. For about an hour. This evening. I don't think we have even shaken hands.

I am nearly seventy and he is almost the same age. It is summer 2011 and we are in his living room. I have an overall impression of bare walls painted in pale green emulsion, and sumptuous red velvet on curtains or upholstery. We are standing almost at right angles to each other and I know that any drink I accept will be a mug of freshly ground coffee, given that I am due to drive myself home quite soon and we have already enjoyed a glass of wine at the pub.

After encounters with other dates from the 'Likewise' website, I will make notes, I'm not sure why, but for this first one, I don't. My memory is usually pretty good but perhaps it lapses when his suggestion of bed (and I assume he means 'have sex'), completely floors me: we hardly know each other.

This is not why I went onto the dating site, not at all. I am tempted to give Brian a flippant response, something about not being ill or tired, but I see he is serious and my subconscious mind and mouth refuse to collaborate to help me out.

'I see we are both here' Brian wrote in his message sent a week earlier, direct to me via the 'Likewise' dating site, 'so, since neither of us has had much luck so far, shall we chat on line? Let me know, Ryan B.'

It's a long story as to how I come to be featured on a dating site, with my photograph and profile describing myself and 'my ideal match'. I'll come to all that in a while. It has taken two marriages, three children plus a few others, something akin to coercive control, several betrayals, a custody case, legal separation, divorce, homelessness, two deaths and widowhood to get me here. And I am still not confident about what I am doing or why, I am holding a huge amount of self-doubt, self-questioning and considerable embarrassment. I have been looking for, hoping for, male friends rather as I had at school and at college. Now I feel a sense of shame about this and about the way by which I'm seeking a companion.

Although my children are now adults and I have no obligations towards anyone else, I do have moral standards and expectations. However, too often I've stood and watched opportunities go by – and wondered what might have happened had I taken a risky decision, done something different, acted out of character. I usually watch a situation developing from the safety of non-involvement. Rarely do I have regrets, only 'what if' wonderings. But it has been a long time since my husband Danny died, since anyone displayed any physical or emotional interest in me - so perhaps I feel almost flattered as well as extremely wary, because this just isn't the sort of thing I do.

I have got myself into this current position in Brian's house so it is up to me to get myself out of it, one way or another. Politely and, I trust, safely. In my mind I can hear my mother's voice, saying 'Upon your own head be it, Dear' or some other apt cliché. Or my older sister Valerie's words to me, when looking warily down into unfamiliar deep water, unsure of its temperature, nervous of what might lurk at the bottom, advising me 'Oh, for goodness's sake, stop thinking about it. Just hold your nose and jump'.

At his invitation and following his slightly desperate message of 'since we're both still here, shall we chat on line?' I have met Brian, by arrangement, in the garden of a riverside pub in Norwich. I admit to a certain sense of excitement, of venturing into the unknown. I notice how I rather too often put myself into a situation in which I can only just cope. I wonder whether I subconsciously do that to test myself, to see what I will do, how I will handle it.

After the initial uncertainties in the public house garden about how best to behave, what to say or ask when meeting a complete stranger, we have talked comfortably for some time, until the mosquitoes began to make their presence known.

As a child, I was painfully shy. I seem to be getting over that now. At least, I think I am. Or am I just more confident, or becoming less inhibited? After some of the life situations I've been through, that wouldn't be surprising.

According to what we know about each other from what we have written and before actually meeting, we think we might get on well: we are more or less the same age, each of us has several near grown-up children and has had previous long-term relationships.

From his photograph, where he uses 'Ryan B' as his user name, and on meeting him in person, I don't find him physically attractive, but he seems bright, intelligent, sociable.

We have both declared an interest in classical music; and an irreverent sense of humour which, on meeting, makes itself known. We both have similar colouring, are of similar height and he doesn't appear to be any physical threat. Both of us own our own homes, both live a similar distance from Norwich, both have driven our own cars to the pub. At some time in our lives, we have both been teachers, Brian in a secondary school and I in the primary phase – so I assume we each understand the educational system, its strength and its constraints. And we even find out, later, that we are both acquainted with the same people within the Local Education Authority. The 'Likewise' website determines that we are a nearly 100% match – but the website hasn't met either of us, doesn't know us and probably doesn't extract information from our different narratives, in order to calculate the match percentage. But it's a start.

After visual recognition, the initial face-to-face introductions in the pub garden and confirmation of shared interests and a glass or two of wine, Brian has invited me this evening back to his house for coffee; it seems to me to be the normal friendly thing to do.

I have written, in the opening words of my narrative in my dating site profile, that my husband died some seven years ago and that there is 'someone missing in my life, a soul-mate'. In his description, Brian has stated that he is looking for someone with 'integrity, intelligence and a sense of the ridiculous'. I can try to match up to that. Not to please Brian of course, whom I don't know and towards whom I feel no obligation, but because it seems to me to be a good set of values or pre-dispositions. And I think, or I hope, that it describes me.

But I don't know why he has made the suggestion that he has just made. I have done nothing that I can think of that could possibly be considered provocative, nothing to make him think this is what I want, the reason why I'm here. And I don't think I've used an inappropriate word or phrase that I think means what I imagine it to mean but apparently, according to my sniggering son and grandson, now means something totally different. When I was at the grammar school, there was a girl there called Marion who gained the reputation and the nickname of being a 'cock-tease', because after school she worked in a local stable and I was told that she used to lie down on the straw, undo her school blouse and invite the local boys to kiss her. And perhaps more? I don't know. She was known as a flirt and perhaps as a result, other girls would steer away from her, because they didn't trust her. So what messages, if any, have I inadvertently given out by agreeing to a coffee at Brian's house? Am I incredibly unaware, naive?

I have to think very fast, weigh up the current situation and check in with my feelings, motivation, ethics. As far as I can recall, I haven't heard the term 'friendship plus benefits' before, except perhaps from my eldest grandson – and if I have, I would assume it refers to some sort of social security. 'With benefits', as it is very patiently explained to me, is not what I have envisaged, not at all. It might work if I loved the person concerned and if he loved and cared deeply about me . . .

And now Brian has posed this 'bed' invitation, made a totally unexpected suggestion. I am fast approaching seventy, far too old for dating. So is Brian. And it has been a long, long time since anyone found me attractive, or wanted to be that close to me . . . And I have wondered, although not often, whether there was anything I could have done better, could have provided, to deter my husbands from wandering off and seeking their physical pleasures elsewhere.

A cock-tease I have never been. At least, I don't think so. I weigh up the pros and cons of accepting this invitation. I'm not usually indecisive. Have I led him on in any way, sent out completely unintentional signals and am I now honour-bound to do something about that? Have I been in this situation or one similar before? I know I take risks sometimes, because they make me feel more alive and in control of myself. Is this something I want to do? But what could be the harm?Or have I forgotten what to do, what goes where and what it feels like? And what about STDs, sexually transmitted diseases? I am clean, or I assume I am since I've been celibate since Danny died; and if Danny had been carrying anything nasty and had passed it on to me, then I assume it would have manifested itself before now.

But what of Brian, who may have had several partners through the dating site - and posed the same 'what about bed' question to them? He doesn't suggest a condom. But is he the sort of man to carry a stock of condoms and if he is, what does that tell me about him? And if he doesn't, what does that also say?

I feel no chemistry with Brian, no lust or physical pull, but on the other hand, no dislike or distaste. I am impartial, almost embarrassingly so. But I need to respond, make up my mind almost immediately, prove I am not like Marion. Taking a deep breath, I decide to accept his offer – which for him, appears less of an offer, more an expectation. I hold my nose . . . and jump.

The sex proves completely meaningless, it lacks vital components. Vital to me, anyway. Like a boiled egg without salt and pepper. Or soldiers. Bland, pointless. I don't feel anything emotionally, my emotional responses appear numb, dormant or even dead, although my physical reactions are certainly alive and kicking. How embarrassing. Something to do with loss of privacy, my privacy. Possibly my integrity as well. And now I feel exposed, vulnerable, but I'm not sure why, or in what way. Maybe it's a relief to know that parts of me still appear to be in good working order. However, I reflect that, on balance, I would have preferred just the coffee or even a back massage. But it was clearly not meaningless for Brian, who seems to expect a repeat performance, or performances. Whatever his needs were or are, he appears to think I can meet them. And that I will do so, at some time or another in the near future, if encouraged. 'You'll enjoy it,' he tells me. I find the whole encounter to have been sexually satisfactory but emotionally sterile.

In the months since our initial meeting, Brian takes to backing his shiny silver Toyota into my driveway and appearing at my door clutching a cellophane-wrapped bouquet of gladioli, drawing the next-door neighbours' attention to 'How often,' they say in passing over the leylandii hedge 'he visits – so what a good friend he must be.' And then 'Or is he a relative?'

I want to respond with 'No, he bloody well is not. And have you nothing better to do than check up on who is visiting me?' but I don't. Because it would be discourteous. And I have been brought up by my parents to be polite or at least, to try to be polite as well as truthful - and if possible, tactful. I suppose it is better that I just smile, look over the dividing hedge and deflect with 'Aren't your roses looking nice now. Do you feed them with anything?'

My children refer to him as E.H.B. or 'ever hopeful Brian'. I encourage them to show me more respect. Only years later does Lallo, my younger daughter, think it is appropriate to suggest 'Perhaps he actually likes you?'

Chapter 2

About Me, Family, Adults' Advice and a bit about God

According to my birth certificate, I was born in a nursing home in Romford, Essex in February 1944. War time, black-out curtains, air-raid wardens and nightly bombing of the East End of London. No National Health Service yet to provide any accident treatment free, no free ante-natal or post-natal care.

I was christened at Howard Congregational Church in Bedford; I remember seeing my christening certificate some years ago. But although we lived in Essex, Bedford's Howard Congregational Church makes sense because that was where Mrs Partridge, my maternal grandmother, had been the organist. And my National Registration Identity Card gives my address in July 1944 as 37 St Johns, Bedford where my grandmother lived and to where my mother escaped temporarily with her three children when the bombing in London was at its worst. My father had had to stay behind in Romford as he was employed by the Borough Council and involved in some sort of Civil Defence.

We returned to our house in Essex by May 1945. I can just remember the three-bedroom semi-detached house in which we lived at that time in Gidea Park, just outside Romford; it backed onto the playing field of a school that none of the family ever attended. Two doors up from our house towards Balgores Lane and on the pavement outside Number 50 or 42, an air-raid siren stood on a metal pole.

I was scared of that pole and its siren. Even when it wasn't sounding, it scared me. Because of what it might suddenly do and mean, even though the War was over; and the fear that would seep through my mother and into me.

Moo, my mother, mentioned that her first child Howard, had he survived, would have been my brother. But he was premature and died three days after he was born in 1934. According to the death certificate, he had had a weak heart. Howard's death was the first and only time at which, Moo said, she had seen my father cry.

My brother Colin was born in April the following year. He was found to be suffering from rickets, caused by some vitamin or calcium deficiency and had to wear callipers to support his legs for the first two years of his life. Two years later in July 1937, Val arrived. Colin was the delicate one with fair curls who wasn't to over-exert himself, with Val younger, tough and healthy with thick dark hair - and wilful.

I was christened Lorna, Lorna Felicity. My conception and arrival were when my mother was well into her 40s. My mother told me that it was unplanned and, without thinking about her choice of words for her young impressionable daughter, that she had become 'cocksure' about any need for contraception. My conception and birth were not wanted by my paternal grandmother. 'I can help you out of your trouble,' she had told my mother, who was normally compliant, 'because having another child at this stage in his career isn't fair on Son. There's a lady I know who lives just around the corner who can help you.'

'This child has come from God,' my mother had responded, 'it's not a trouble and I intend to keep it.'

When my mother told me this, I thought that, as parentage, it was a lot for me to live up to. Or, as she would wish me to have said, 'up to which to live.' Apart from Christian morals and classical music, some of the most important things in my mother's life were good speech - by which she meant having an accent not unlike the king's, - standard grammar as taught in grammar schools ('It's different from, Dear, and opposite to'; and 'one centres on, not around), an education at a good school – by which she usually meant at a private or better still, a public school.

The correct use of cutlery was a vital component in my upbringing, even if the cutlery was mostly E.P.N.S., (letters which I learned stood for 'electro-plated nickel silver',) an appreciation of 'classical literature' even if Moo didn't read much herself for pleasure, and good manners. Knowing the right word to use was also very important, it denoted our family's position in society. So, 'It's 'lavatory', Dear. Never 'toilet'. And we do not possess a lounge, we have a 'drawing room' or, if you need to use a different term, it's a 'sitting room'.

Finding my mother was pregnant again during the autumn before I was born, my parents had travelled to North Devon by car using my father's petrol allowance, to stay with relatives in Ilfracombe and visit the Doone Valley, which they said they thought was beautiful. On account of this, when I was born, they named me 'Lorna' in defiance rather than 'Shirley' after child actress Shirley Temple, 'Shirley' being the name that my paternal grandmother had wanted. And 'Felicity', I was told, 'means great happiness'. More for me to live up to. Or up to which . . . etcetera.

A big family assumption or rather a requirement, at least among my parents and grandparents, was that we would all be brought up as obedient God-fearing regular Congregational Church-goers. And an expectation that we three children, like the rest of my mother's relations, would each be musical. Moo's Leppard uncles would hum the base or tenor lines to any hymns they heard on the wireless, she told me, and from that she would know which hymn was being sung.

Daddy's parents had met as members of the South London Mission at The Elephant and Castle, established by the London Congregational Union. My mother and father had married at The Howard Chapel in Bedford, where my grandmother worshipped. As identical twin girls, my mother and her sister Dorothy were well-known in the Bedford area for being competent string players.

Hence the two strong threads running throughout the family were music and the Congregational Church. Coupled with that had been an abstinence from any alcohol (my mother's and Dorothy's grandfather Thomas Richard Holt had been a member of the Temperance Society and therefore a teetotaller) and a disapproval of any form of gambling - which seemed to extend to card games such as Snap, whether or not any betting was involved.

At Christmas time when the family gathered together, we would have a jug of orange squash on the table and, once the older members of the family had died out, if we were lucky there might be one bottle of non-alcoholic grape juice.

We called our mother 'Moo' simply because, as my brother Colin said, it suited her. And perhaps the title started after we had two Austrian boys staying with us through the Rotary

Club exchange scheme. Those boys had referred to their mother, any mother, as 'Mutti'; which became 'Mu'.

Moo took the nickname linking her to a cow as a compliment rather than any insult, and she was almost bovine in several ways.

She was placid, warm by nature, she liked the company of others in her herd, she was a life-giver and a steadying influence, even stoic, certainly not easily roused to anger or argument. And she was accustomed to standing motionless in doorways, gazing into the middle-distance. I never had any doubt that she loved me.

Apart from her family both nuclear and wider, there were three other very important things in Moo's life, each beginning with the letter 'B'. Bach, Beethoven and The Beatitudes[i].

My parents and grandparents worshipped at their respective 'Free' or 'Congregational' churches so I was brought up with strong non-conformist Christian values such as honesty, faithfulness, kindness, forgiveness and meekness – although I was never quite sure what 'meek' meant or how it might manifest itself. At the girls' 'Crusader' class on a Sunday afternoon, run by a couple of Baptist women, we were taught the values of 'The Sermon on the Mount'. Moo endorsed these so wholeheartedly that it was almost as if the Beatitudes had been her own idea. They were certainly a useful guide on expected behaviour - and survival.

In the face of my sister Valerie at home, who took great delight in teasing or mocking me or being annoying, lying about something or blaming me for some misdeed that she herself had done, I would be encouraged by Moo not to react, but to cling to 'Blessed are they who are persecuted for righteousness's sake; for theirs is the kingdom of heaven'. Or if I were tempted to make a sharp verbal response, then to resist because 'Blessed are the peacemakers: for they shall be called the children of God.'

Val would mock me for my evangelical attitude. On one occasion, on the morning I was due to sit an 'O' level exam and had been up past midnight the night before swotting, she woke me up before 6am by banging on my bedroom door and singing 'Christians, awake, Salute the Happy Dawn' at the top of her voice. I would have enjoyed an hour or two more's sleep.

Moo's advice to me on the many times when Val was being deliberately difficult or controversial, was 'Don't argue or contradict, just go along with anything she says or let it pass over your head. And don't be roused to anger. Just swallow your feelings and don't remonstrate; don't let people see you're hurt or upset. It won't make the situation any better and will probably make it worse,' because Val could be violent.

I do remember her being kind once; I remember it as having been kind although she may not have liked Colin receiving a present better than hers. Our grandparents in Kent had sent Moo a ten-shilling note as a Christmas present, to be divided between the three of us children in ways that Grandpa and TCP Grandma specified. Five shillings were for Colin because he was the eldest, three shillings and ninepence were for Val, leaving one shilling and thruppence for me.

I was old enough by that stage to wonder aloud whether TCP Grandma thought that sweets or a cinema ticket cost less for me because I was the youngest, or whether the divide was based on favouritism because Colin was a boy. Val 'persuaded'

Colin and Moo that the redistribution should be done more fairly, by Colin giving up six pence of his money so that Val received four shillings and I was given one shilling and sixpence. I could quickly appreciate how I, as well as Val, benefitted from this, and Colin had a strong sense of fairness. Moo said it would be fine by her as long as we all agreed, didn't argue and remembered to say 'thank you for the money' to Grandma rather than specifying the exact amount in our thank-you letters.

I challenged my father only once, told him I thought he was being unkind to my sister when he had climbed in through Val's upstairs bedroom window after she had locked her bedroom door and refused to come out, and he had thrown milk over her head because she was being rude and difficult and . . . well, being herself, only on that occasion, even worse. That was the only time that I can remember him getting cross with Val and making any physical response. That might also have been the time when Val deliberately smashed a light bulb on her solid bedroom floor and began to walk across the broken glass with bare feet. Dad had been worried about her state of mind as well as about the soles of her feet.

Dad did once get angry with me at the meal table because he thought I had said something disrespectful about Moo's father. I was hurt and bewildered about that and I asked Moo why Daddy was so cross. She explained, told me what Daddy thought I had said, that my grandfather was a madman, and 'I didn't,' I told her some hours later, 'Daddy was completely wrong, he didn't hear properly.'

I didn't argue with him or stand my ground, instead I crumpled inside from the injustice of it all. I think Moo told him what I had actually said but he didn't apologise to me, he didn't admit he was in the wrong. I learnt then that Daddy didn't apologise, ever. It was rarely necessary because he was nearly always right and he could be very authoritative. And, as Moo said to me then, TCP Grandma never apologised for anything so perhaps she had not shown Dad how to say he was sorry or when it might be necessary - because admitting she, or in this case he, was in the wrong, TCP Grandma would have considered to be 'losing face'.

In this way I was strongly persuaded to believe that any negative reaction or contrary opinion, should I be sufficiently presumptuous as to have one at all, would be disputed or disregarded, because it was considered morally wrong, even inflammatory, or just plain rude. I was encouraged to consider myself to be, as the New Testament said, 'unworthy', 'a miserable sinner'; to believe rather than to question, always to be obedient, never to disagree especially with anyone older than myself because that would be very rude. And to squash any feelings of pride or self-confidence.

When my hair was growing longer and I needed to tie it away from my face and into a pony tail, as was the fashion at the time, Daddy said I ought to leave it loose because 'Otherwise you look like a scraped carrot'. And when I was wearing an ill-fitting dress and attempted to wear a belt with it, Daddy told me not to, because 'You look like a sack of spuds tied in the middle'.

I don't think he meant to be unkind, it was just that his mind was focused on the vegetable garden. But at least he noticed me.

I knew, because Christian teaching told me several times, that as a human being I was worthless.

Val tried once, when I was about seven and we were standing in the hallway with our mother, to stab me with a pair of scissors - until Moo took them away from her. I have no idea what I had done or said to make her want to do this, except exist.

Years later, when I was twelve or thirteen and on the point of not doing something that Val wanted me to do in our kitchen, from the broom cupboard Val grabbed our father's shot gun, the one he used to shoot rabbits or pigeons from our vegetable patch. She levelled it at me and pulled the trigger.

Fortunately for both of us, it wasn't loaded, Daddy wasn't stupid. Instead, she took hold of the stock and brought the barrel down heavily on my left arm. It did no long-term damage; the bone did not break although I expect I was left with a nasty bruise. I told Moo what had happened but I don't remember any repercussions. Perhaps by that time Moo had given up trying to amend Val's behaviour, it was just too much like hard work.

Val did not see the need to take responsibility for her actions or be truthful. As an example of this, Moo told me 'Once, when Val came home from school one day with one of her long plaits missing, I asked her what had happened. 'Nothing,' Val had replied. 'Did someone at school cut it off?' Moo asked her. Val shook her head. 'Well, was it you who cut it?' Moo asked, feeling either angry or puzzled. 'No,' Val replied, looking slightly shame-faced. Then she explained, 'It wasn't me; it was the scissors what did it.'

Although Moo's family was brought up to be tea-total, Grandma and Grandpa on my father's side didn't drink any alcohol either and the only alcohol in our house might be a bottle of amontillado sherry at Christmas, (barely touched and intended, I was told, for visitors). Val had taken to walking down to The Fox Public House in Willian and having a pint of beer.

On one occasion, I remember seeing her apparently under the influence of alcohol and threatening to push our mongrel dog Kim off the roof of the balcony outside her bedroom. She might have been hamming it up, of course, play-acting because that was the sort of thing she would do in order to generate anxiety in others, or it might have been a serious threat. I knew she was unlikely to want to hurt Kim, because she loved him as much as we all did. But as Moo said, alcohol can do strange things to people, which is why Moo and her twin sister, when they were children, were taught to run past a public house in case the pub door were to be opened and they would be affected by the fumes.[ii] In her turn Moo brought me up to know what we should shun in order to stay fit, healthy and upright, and destined for heaven when the time came. Most of it was based on fear gained with a smattering of historic experience - and hearsay. And the possibility of not going to heaven.

At some time before I was born, Val had been referred to the Tavistock Clinic[iii] in London on account of her disobedience, what Moo called Val's 'wayward behaviour'. I'm not sure how often she attended the clinic, nor what the consultants there advised Moo and Daddy to do or how to behave except, I was told, 'we must show Val that we love her', an instruction which Moo passed on to me. I found obeying that requirement difficult. It was hard to show love to someone who was being, from my point of view, what Moo might call 'an absolute pain in the neck' - and anyway, wasn't I being hypocritical in pretending to love Val when I wasn't sure what I felt about her? 'Love' certainly wasn't the first emotion that came to mind.

My main ploy was to try to avoid her, to go along with whatever she suggested or said, even if I totally disagreed and thought she was being unkind, judgmental or simply nasty. At least doing that avoided a row and pacifying, avoiding a row or an argument was what was most important to Moo. 'Agreeing will take the wind out of her sails,' was Moo's forecast. I don't think she knew how to handle disagreement, perhaps she had never encountered disagreement when she and Aunty Dorothy were girls. And I never saw or heard her disagreeing with or contradicting my father.

Sometimes Val would self-harm, she would jab the point of a pair of compasses or dividers into her leg to make it bleed. Then she would watch the blood trickle down her skin, wipe it with her finger and lick it. Then encourage me to do the same with my legs, or to spread transparent Youhoo glue on to my skin, watch it dry, then pick it off. It was Val who encouraged me to pick the crust off my scabs and never to look at my face in the mirrors that hung on chains in the hall and dining room because if I did, she would accuse me, loudly, of admiring myself.

We children were not encouraged to be self-confident. Being confident or self-assured would have been regarded as cocky, getting above oneself. Perhaps that is why I have no recollection of being offered overt praise or reassurance by either of my parents or a grandparent. Moo would show her absolute disapproval of anyone, particularly female, if she were to refer to her as a being 'a terrible extrovert'. Being an extrovert was close to damnation in Moo's eyes. She considered it 'terribly vulgar'. Like tap dancing.

In the afternoons at Christmas, members of the family would gather round the piano to sing carols. I can recall the poignancy, the thumped-out message of that verse from 'Once in Royal David's City' that says

'Christian children all must be

Mild, obedient, good as He:'

at which point Moo would look straight at me, almost glaring through her pink-framed National Health spectacles, raise an eyebrow and lower her chin to check that the message had been received.

On these festive celebrations Val would play the violin, Moo the viola or the piano, either Moo's twin sister Dorothy or Colin would pick up the 'cello. I would be handed a comb and a section of our 'Izal' lavatory paper to play against. 'Izal', being crisp, would vibrate against the comb and produce a buzzing sound as I blew, the best accompaniment that they thought I was capable of offering because, musically speaking, I was a disappointment. Moo had tried me on the violin, then the piano where my hands proved to have no left/right co-ordination, after which I was given cello lessons after school and funded by Hertfordshire Rural Music Society. No use, playing music really wasn't what I was about.

Colin and Val both had perfect pitch and although I gained a good mark in my music 'O' level exam, particularly in composition and the aural part, it was more through concentration rather than by any innate ability.

Having heard Leon Goussens play the oboe in Hitchin Parish Church, I abandoned the idea of mastering a stringed instrument and was inspired to try my luck on a borrowed oboe - but the breath control required for the oboe resulted in my fainting during several lessons and making a spectacle of myself by crashing to the floor, on the final occasion shaking the timbers of the ancient building in Canterbury being used by Kent Rural Music School - at which point I gave up any hope of relieving my parents' disappointment. I knew I couldn't live up to their musical hopes or expectations. But they, especially Moo, also wanted me, expected me, to be hard-working, bright and intelligent. I managed some of this.

At Hare Park School in Gidea Park, run by tall Miss Norman and short Miss Pluck, I was taught to read using a primer printed in black and red and featuring two little Scotty dogs called 'Mac' and 'Tosh'. I worked out for myself that if I could read the words 'wind' and 'mill', then I could read the word 'windmill', which was a much longer word in a story about a Dutchman, 'Dutchman' being a word which I realised I could also break into its parts and read.

The disadvantage was that when I left Hare Park and was sent to Westbury Infant and Junior School in Letchworth, I wasn't given one of the 'Janet and John' workbooks that were handed out to the other pupils but was told to sit and read, while the rest of the class were allowed to colour in the black-and-white line drawings of Janet and John.

No wonder that Moo was informed by my class teacher Miss Fendly (and whose name I mispronounced as Miss Friendly) that I spent most of my day at school 'happily reading in a corner'. In the twice-yearly exams, I was surprised to find that I came almost top of the class: only Joyce L. and Roger B. did better.

Apart from inconveniently arriving unplanned into the world and during wartime too, I was also very aware that I cost the family money, time and ration coupons, so I had better behave as my parents and my maternal grandmother wished. If I were not musical, then I had better be a credit to the family by working hard and passing the eleven plus exam. I asked my mother more than once what would happen if I didn't pass, to which secondary school I would go. She said 'Pixmore probably. Or Norton, because Daddy knows the headmaster there. Or, if we could afford it, we would send you to Queenswood School as a boarder. It's not far from where Aunty Dorothy lives.' My opinion, my preference, wasn't asked.

I was a keen reader of Enid Blyton and had digested that boarding-school life at a place like Malory Towers must be a constant round of pranks, wearing disguises and midnight feasts, so the idea of attending the, for us, financially completely-unattainable Queenswood appealed to me. It remained out of reach and as it happened, quite unnecessary. Aunty Dorothy, who taught at her two-teacher village primary school, sent me previous years' eleven plus exam papers to practise, with verbal reasoning puzzles such as 'if a fish is to water, a bicycle is to __?' and numerous arithmetic papers. I passed the eleven plus exam without a problem and in September 1955, I began at Letchworth Grammar School.

I was about eleven and out shopping with my mother when, approaching the public rose garden in Letchworth, we met one of Moo's fellow players from the orchestra which she had joined. Having greeted Moo, the player looked questioningly at me standing by Moo's side and asked Moo 'And this is . .? Is this your baby?'

'Yes, this is my baby,' Moo responded. She didn't say 'this is Lorna'. I was defined by my mother by my age, my late arrival after Moo's other children, and my position in the family. By this age I was over 5ft tall and weighing almost seven stone. Some baby!

Unlike the two Grammar Schools in nearby Hitchin, Letchworth's was co-educational or, as they used to say, 'mixed'. Many of my classmates from Westbury transferred there too, along with pupils from local villages, Baldock and other Letchworth primary schools. Starting at a new school should have been a happy time. But when Val had been expelled from Hitchin Girls Grammar for some misdemeanour – shutting the Music Mistress in a cupboard on a Friday afternoon, Val had said – she was accepted into the sixth form at Letchworth Grammar to allow her to take her English and Music 'A' level exams.

When I started school at Letchworth Grammar as a new eleven-year-old, Val would encourage her new sub-prefect friends to call me names or tell me off for climbing up the wrong side of the stairs or suggest that my handed-down woollen jumper didn't comply with the uniform requirements. I thought it almost did, it was near enough and Moo had said it would be acceptable. It had been Val's when she started at Hitchin Grammar so the stripe around the V-neck was yellow rather than Letchworth's bottle green.

Instead of buying a new school-uniform jumper or asking TCP Grandma to knit one (we referred to our paternal grandmother as 'Grandma' or even 'TCP Grandma' behind her back because she liked to dab the antiseptic TCP, letters which Daddy irreverently said stood for 'Tom Cats' Piss', on her wrists and behind her ears, because she liked the smell,) Moo had dyed Val's Hitchin Grammar jumper at home with dark blue dye so that the yellow turned green but a sludge colour rather than bottle green. Val seemed to gain a few female friends of her own year by encouraging them to pick on me, call me 'Loony' or 'Loopy'. And my new classmates who had transferred from other primary schools cottoned on to this, thought it was fun.

I remember telling Colin about it rather than Moo, because Colin understood how hurtful Val could be with her unkind remarks and bullying behaviour. Moo would have been worried that she had done the wrong thing by not managing to afford a complete set of new uniform for me. Or a new leather satchel such as some of my classmates from Wilbury Primary had. Mine, although new, was made of canvas and it didn't last very long. The local cobbler had to repair it by stitching it, more than once.

Colin had an excellent baritone singing voice and our parents paid for him to receive singing lessons from Arthur Reckless, a professional vocal tutor in London. Because he focussed on his singing, Colin abandoned the practice of playing a stringed instrument and he brought the family cello back to our house. When he was in his late teens, Colin and my father formed an amateur operatic company in Letchworth called 'The Arcadians'. Daddy had been involved with Romford Civil Defence Dramatic and Operatic Society, also known as 'The Red Triangle'. It was started in Romford in 1941 to bring people together and relieve some of the tensions caused by the Second World War.

Our father was not an accomplished singer but he enjoyed the humour and dramatic side of Gilbert and Sullivan operettas, where his strength was in his rendition of patter songs. As a member of 'The Red Triangle' group, he played a good Jack Point in 'The Yeomen of the Guard'. I saw him give a memorable portrayal of King Gama as 'a disagreeable man' in 'Princess Ida' with a similar amateur operatic group based in Stevenage and he played an excellent Koko in 'The Mikado'.

'You would be far too self-conscious to appear on a stage in front of an audience,' Daddy once told me, 'however forgiving people might be towards an embarrassed and nervous adolescent.'

My father rarely engaged with me. Not, I hope, because he didn't like me or disapproved of me but because his mind was absorbed elsewhere, mostly in either learning lines for a forthcoming operatic performance, in his work or in the garden. So, when he asked me, a gawky teenager, to accompany him to the international badminton championships being held somewhere in London, I was ecstatic, felt deeply honoured. He was actually seeking my company.

Only later did I learn to play badminton, rather badly. Daddy had played when he had been a pupil at The Simon Langton School in Canterbury and I suspect he was probably quite good at the game. He was able, when we were among the spectators, to explain the rules to me and to comment on the different strokes, strategies and skill levels. I listened and accepted everything he told me. He was my father so he would know.

I learned, at quite an early age, that doing what I was told and generally agreeing was the best way of ensuring my mother's love and approval. Once, after Val had been particularly rude or disruptive, Moo warned me 'If you ever behave like your sister, I shall just leave'. In this way, any arguing, disagreement, lack of obedience or non-compliance became equated, for me, with rejection, with the imminent loss of love. My identity was established, defined even, by my acquiescence, by my being what my parents and others around me wanted and by what they were unable to find in my siblings.

Colin was considered to be the lazy one, the one who was physically inactive except on a bicycle. Val was considered, and with some cause, to be the naughty one, the one who would ignore any rules and gain stimulus by provoking others into retaliation. I was regarded as hard-working, obedient, thought of as the 'good' one, as much by innate disposition than from any other reason - except, perhaps, because it was an unfilled niche and I probably knew it would pay off. What a creep I must have seemed to my siblings.

At first, when I was just a baby, I slept in a cot in my parents' bedroom, next to the door onto the landing. I can vaguely remember the navy-and-white ticking stripe of the mattress cover, a crumpled sheet and having no nappy on. Once I was slightly older, I shared a bedroom and a 2foot 6inch single bed with my sister. My sister Valerie, nearly seven years old when I was born, wet the bed every night, often more than once. A warm damp patch at first, then soggy, cold, unpleasant, difficult to curve my body around while at the same time trying to avoid her wet pyjama bottom and the harsh central ridge of the sides-to-middle bottom sheet.

This reconstructed bed linen had been put together by my mother's twin sister (my mother was hopeless at sewing or at anything much using her hands, except playing the piano or the viola) by cutting vertically right down the threadbare centre of a cotton sheet and with a run-and-fell seam, sewing together the unworn and rough selvedge edges. An economical solution when new bed linen, even if it were available in the shops, had to be bought with our precious ration coupons as well as money.

The Repton Avenue house had an upstairs bathroom with art deco frosted window glass; a china potty, which we were expected to use, was kept under our bed. Val was a heavy sleeper so the need to pee wouldn't wake her or perhaps she couldn't be bothered to move from the warm fug of our blanketed single bed. After a few years, my mother divided the bedroom in half so that Val and I each had our own space. My area was beside the boarded-up tiled fireplace. Our father erected a khaki camp bed alongside the chimney breast, for me to sleep on. Its wooden legs would wobble and creak alarmingly when I clambered into it and wriggled into the homemade sheet sleeping bag. This was covered by three brown army blankets with hairs that poked unpleasantly at me through the cotton sleeping bag and itched against my skin. The camp bed had no mattress, there was nowhere for the blankets to tuck in, but it was my space, just mine. And with a stone hot water bottle, warm and dry.

As a present on my fifth birthday, my mother picked a bunch of snowdrops from the garden. She stood them in water in a Shippams paste pot and placed it on a tiled shelf at the right-hand side of the mantelpiece. 'To show that I love you,' she said. They were just for me. Ever since then, I have regarded snowdrops as my flowers, I have picked or been given them every year in time for my birthday. Beautiful resilient snowdrops, white petals with a green stripe and fresh green leaves; fragile spears fighting against the odds, refusing to be beaten by the weather, daring to poke their heads out of the cold earth well before winter has lost its frosty grip. Snowdrops set the bar of life very high for me.

My brother Colin had a bedroom of his own, near the top of the stairs in the Repton Avenue house. He was almost nine years older than I, and my mother and maternal grandmother were very proud of his rhythmic and musical ability. Although we didn't have much contact when I was young except on holiday, he was very kind to me as his little sister.

Peddling alongside me on the road on his bicycle, he would push me on my tricycle all the way from Hitchin up the pavement of Harkness Hill, past the fields of roses, past the entrance to 'Briar Patch' that was Hertfordshire County Council Children's Home, past the fever hospital near the top of the hill, towards Letchworth. I liked and trusted him.

When I was struggling with Latin at the grammar school, he would sometimes help me. He had studied Latin at Hitchin Boys Grammar whereas neither of my parents was able to advise me. And sometimes he let me construct something from his metal Meccano that he kept in a small leather suitcase, explaining what was a nut and what was a bolt, and which flat pieces might do which job. He bought me a record once, a 78, with 'The Little White Duck' song on one side and 'The Laughing Policeman' on the other. I loved listening to those songs.

I missed Colin after he left school and moved to London to be trained as an accountant. I enjoyed his company; he took care of me and he seemed to understand my likes and any dislikes. Sometimes he would come home for a weekend, often with a friend from another country whom he had met in London. On one occasion, he brought an Indian man home, who gave us all some Indian desserts or sweets as a gift. Moo's reactions were interesting, she was stuck between honesty and politeness. 'Those sweets are not unpleasant', she advised me, looking at the brown paper bag which contained what looked like sections of string dipped in toffee or syrup 'but just a trifle odd.' The only foreign food she had met before, and to which she often resorted, was pasta. Her version of macaroni cheese was dry and very boring.

At meal times before I was a teenager and while Colin was still living at home, he would eat the pastry part of any pudding or tart, the anaemic pastry made with lard which I hated but which I wasn't permitted to leave or waste, and I would consume the lemon meringue part of his dessert, because he didn't like lemon or the egg white. And he loathed tomatoes, which were my favourite teatime filling in sandwiches. I thought he was an excellent big brother.

We both found our sister Valerie very hard work. She seemed to love to annoy or do something we would find hurtful, it made her almost smirk with pleasure. Colin was also a teenage bed-wetter but that didn't matter to me, I didn't have to share a bed or a room with him. On holiday, when the rest of us slept in a four-berth caravan, Colin would bed down on the leather back seat on our Austin 16, parked just beside the hired caravan. And with him he would have Kim, our beloved black mongrel dog.

Downstairs, in the drawing room at the front of the Repton Avenue house, stood a black baby grand piano which my mother would sometimes play whenever she could find the time. The upright piano, with its walnut marquetry panels and candle holders, stood in the dining room against the wall, leaving little room for the dining table or the Morrison shelter. Our kitchen at the back of the house, was small and narrow, there was just room for a metal painted dresser, a pre-war refrigerator that hummed and leaked, and a Hoover washing machine with a hand-turned wringer.

This had been a present to my mother from Nenna, my maternal grandmother after she had observed my mother having to wash and wring out my towelling nappies by hand. We called this grandmother 'Nenna' rather than Nan or Nanny because, as she said more than once, 'the term 'Nanny' refers to a member of staff and I certainly do not regard myself as staff'. Instead, perhaps because before Leppard, her family surname in earlier generations had been 'Howard' and her family came from Petworth in Sussex, not far from Arundel where the castle was the family home of the Howards, the Dukes of Norfolk, both Nenna and certainly Moo had illusions of being from a fallen branch of the aristocracy.

Despite her fondness for 'Oh Little Town of Bethlehem' and its verse about children being 'mild' and 'obedient', Moo was willing to be less obedient towards a verse in the Victorian hymn 'All Things Bright and Beautiful', the verse that mentions one's social class and position as having been ordained by God.

'The rich man in his castle,

The poor man at his gate,

God made them high and lowly,

And ordered their estate.'

This verse has since been removed from some modern hymn books, its conservative views that suggest that one's social position is intended by God, could be taken, Moo said, to advocate against social and economic self-improvement.

Moo, having been born in 1901, still talked about and hankered after many of the values and practices of Victorian and Edwardian society. I remember asking her whether I would 'come out', which meant something in those days quite different from its current meaning.

She patiently explained to me, as if it weren't already obvious, that we didn't live or move in the social circles that produced debutantes. But it appeared to be part of her background, she understood and valued a social class hierarchy that unfortunately placed our family towards the lower part of the middle stratum.

We had codes of understanding within the family. Moo would occasionally refer to someone as being NOCD, meaning 'not our class, Dear'. On one occasion I suggested that Moo could be 'a bit posh'. She said something to the effect that 'being posh, or having money for that matter, has nothing to do with it. It's about having and maintaining high standards.'

It was vital that she should bake at least one large cake and some smaller cupcakes ready for teatime on a Sunday, in case 'someone should call.' And that the dining room table be set with our best 'Frost Pine' tea-set, tea-pot and silver cutlery, even if it were made of electro-plated nickel silver – although there were a couple of solid silver dessert spoons that had belonged to Nenna, with the letter 'P' engraved on the handle.

To cover the possibility of weekend visitors further, Moo would send me to Letchworth Corner Post Office in the morning to buy a four-fingered KitKat, so that we had chocolate biscuits to offer in addition to the inevitable oblong bridge rolls, digestives and cake. On the rare occasions when someone did drop in at teatime, we children would be cautioned in the kitchen with Moo's *sotto voce* to 'F.H.B.' regarding the KitKat fingers and anything else in short supply - meaning 'family hold back'.

On one occasion when I was about ten or eleven, I questioned why my mother had told a lie, or what I considered to be a lie. Someone had called at the front door – only tradesmen came to the back door – and asked to speak to Mr Johnson.

'I'm afraid he is not at home' Moo had replied and firmly closed the front door. I told her afterwards that Daddy was in the back garden, cutting the grass 'and you knew that, so why did you say that he was not in?' I felt very daring in questioning her.

She explained that when adults were willing to receive unexpected visitors, they were said to be 'at home'. 'And your father will not welcome visitors at the weekend when he is in his shirt sleeves and not wearing a tie, so he is not 'at home' to visitors. They understand that, even if you don't. It isn't a lie, it's a courtesy, a convention.'

I had my doubts about this, it seemed to me to be playing with the truth and adhering to a Victorian or Edwardian convention from Bedford that was no longer applicable in the reign of Queen Elizabeth ll in Letchworth Garden City. Anyway, our visitors, whosoever they may have been, could have heard the sound of a lawn mower quite clearly coming from the back garden. But I didn't say any of that, I had learned that it was far more prudent to keep quiet. 'My job as a wife,' Moo told me more than once 'is to support your father, because he's my husband. That's what a wife is there to do, to be loyal and supportive.'

Our upright Hoover washing machine, with an integral drum on one side to turn and agitate the water, had to be filled with warm water from the tap, using a length of hose pipe that frequently proved to be too short. If anyone tried to brush past it in order to reach the back door, the hose would detach itself from either the machine or the tap, squirting out soap suds and leaving a pool of water and bubbles on the red-tiled kitchen floor. It was emptied in almost the same way, using a length of hose from an outlet at the base of the machine and into a bucket. That pipe too, if disturbed, could leave the floor covered in warm soapy water.

The half-glazed rear kitchen door led into the Repton Avenue back garden with its sunken Andersen shelter, a hen house and a vegetable garden. Both my parents tended the garden to provide us with fresh food and in order to save money and precious ration coupons. One year, my father tried to raise a couple of ducks. He provided them with a very small bathing pool by filling an old baby bath with water, positioning it on the back lawn and placing a plank for the ducklings to walk up so that they could access the water. But they didn't seem to think much of that and the following year the ducks and the bath were gone.

The main restriction that I can remember from my early childhood was my not being allowed to visit a funfair or public recreation ground. 'That's the sort of place where you could easily catch a nasty illness,' Moo warned 'and I love you far too much to let that happen.' Then she would give me one of her all-enveloping hugs to compensate for my disappointment. I longed for a ride on a roundabout or one of those coloured swing boats with a furry pull that I could see from the car window.

Sometimes this fear of certain illnesses would be the reason given for not allowing me to mix with certain people, to go to a friend's house or a birthday party. This fear of infection or contagion was backed up by Moo's concern that I might catch smallpox and scarlet fever. Catching mumps, chicken pox, measles or German measles did not seem to worry her; in fact, she told me and other mothers 'the sooner you get those common diseases over and done with, the better.' She regarded the four illnesses as a rite of passage from babyhood into childhood. One of the other common childhood complaints was threadworm, a parasitic infection of the intestines.

I remember, aged four or five in the Repton Avenue bathroom, having to lean face downwards across Moo's knees so that she could inspect my bottom after I'd had a warm bath. Had I been much older, I might have been embarrassed by such lack of dignity but the usual treatment in those days for threadworms was gentian violet, as something to be swallowed. It was also used as a general antiseptic. So, when at school I saw other children having a purple colour on their grazed knees, I assumed that they too suffered from threadworms. The prevalence of threadworms may have added to Moo's insistence on hygiene and regular handwashing.

On one occasion, she told Colin to 'go and run your hands under the tap', only to discover later that he had done just that; Colin, who could be verbally pedantic and who avoided contact with water whenever he could, had obediently run his hands under the tap but, as he told her some time afterwards, she hadn't told him to turn the tap on first. She learned then to be more specific in her instructions.

In the November after my fifth birthday, my father was appointed as 'municipal engineer and surveyor' for Letchworth Garden City Urban District Council, a step up from his post in Romford Borough Council. This meant that we needed to leave our current schools including Brentwood School that Colin was attending, The Ursuline, a girls' Roman Catholic school also in Brentwood where Valerie had just started and seemed happy, and Hare Park for me, a small co-educational private school in Gidea Park where our mother taught music and was therefore permitted to pay reduced fees. We had to move house and go to the Hertfordshire Local Authority state schools.

We needed to rent the house into which we first moved because the owners didn't want to sell and most of the houses in Letchworth were leasehold, a system which my father distrusted. Having five bedrooms and both a front and a back garden, to me our new house appeared huge. It was in the Broadway, a long wide boulevard lined with trees - mature limes, fragrant when in flower, that stood on grassy verge banks with broad pavements on either side, leading down to the town's central rose garden.

My mother was delighted to find that 100 Broadway had an established asparagus bed as well as a scullery. Number 100, pebble-dashed and painted white, stood confidently back from the road. There was a roundabout, the first roundabout in England, at the top of our end of 'The Broadway', with a double streetlight on a concrete post in the centre.

Our house, technically semi-detached but co-joined to next door only by high beam across a side garden, had a sweeping staircase that ran from the front door and hall, curving up to the semi-circular landing, the five bedrooms and the main bathroom. It was equipped with brass stair-rods to hold the stair carpet in place in the centre of the stairs.

I remember thinking how 100 Broadway was a good place to live. Built before car transport was in any way common, there was nowhere for my father to park his car under cover so he rented a garage at the end of Sollershott East Road, where the road met Baldock Road with a slip road and a triangle of grass.

Walking down the pavement to collect the car each morning gave him the opportunity to give Kim a walk too. Sometimes, when it wasn't a school day, I was allowed to go with them and to ride back in the car, before Daddy had to leave for the Council Offices, taking Kim with him. Kim would ride on the front passenger seat, looking out of the open car window. Kim had a very special place in our family and in my life. He became my closest companion when he and I went for a walk at the weekends, down Letchworth Lane towards the village of Willian. In time we moved into our new house that Dad had designed and had built, at the bottom of Garth Road. Kim was never on a lead. He was obedient and had road-sense. And showed amazing understanding of us as separate members of the family.

With my siblings so much older than I, I was almost an 'only' child. My parents focussed much of their attention on the older two, on their behaviour and any problems, and seemed to take quite a relaxed, almost detached view of me and of my progress. I was grateful for this. Apart from the need to be back home by a specified time or meal, by the time I was seven and in the junior school, I appeared to have more or less a free-rein. I rode my tricycle on the pavements around the nearby roads and quickly learned my way around the part of the town between our house, Westbury Primary School and the shops including Letchworth Corner Post Office where I bought most of my sweets on Tuesdays and Saturdays; these were the week's designated 'two ounces' and 'four ounces' coupon days.

One Saturday as I was riding my tricycle on the pavement of Field Lane in Letchworth, I was stopped by a curly-headed girl whom I later knew as Fiona. She seemed friendly but she looked a year older and taller than I was and I didn't recognise her as being from my primary school. 'Hello' she said, 'I haven't seen you round here before. Is your name Susan?'

I knew it was rude to correct or disagree with my elders, much worse than a white lie, so I said 'Yes', partly because I was shy and also because it seemed the politest and most expedient way to respond. I wasn't happy with my own name which my parents didn't often use to address me, and I quite liked the name Susan so I didn't mind if it became true. It was also easier to spell than Lorna, less embarrassing for people who might otherwise ask me to repeat it, and it couldn't be misheard as 'Laura' or 'Nora'; or even 'Loony', which was what Val had begun to call me. So, Fiona and I became friends and I told her my real name. In fact, we were such close friends that for many years she became almost a surrogate sister.

Her mother was an invalid who spent much of her time in bed. I never knew exactly what was wrong with her and I saw her only once through a gap in her bedroom door. Fiona's father and my father were both Rotarians so that meant that they approved of our friendship. And when her mother's health deteriorated, Fiona became a weekly boarder at St Francis, the local girls' Roman Catholic School. She would come to my house at the weekends while her father was working as manager of 'Russell's', the local chemist shop, and Fiona would stay with us until she had to be returned to St Francis' School on a Sunday evening. Moo would give us both some pocket money each Saturday morning and together we would walk up to Letchworth Corner Post Office to buy our sweets or into the town centre to get some crayons or borrow the latest Enid Blyton 'Famous Five' book from the public library.

Moo disapproved of playing cards because she considered playing cards was akin to betting, even though there was never any money involved. I noticed that Daddy would sometimes receive an envelope from 'Littlewoods' and would spend an hour or two at the weekend completing the football pools. I didn't hear Moo ever object to him doing this. Moo had acquired her principles by osmosis from her wider Liberal Non-conformist family, but these principles as she expressed them didn't always stand up to scrutiny or logic. I was grown up before I realised that Moo hadn't been the academic high-flier that I had previously assumed, or that had been implied. She admitted that spelling wasn't her main strength. Nor was drawing, nor any form of fine-art appreciation. But she encouraged me to be self-reliant. She cited two incidents to back this up.

'Once' she related 'when Colin was little and going to Hare Park School, he was told to go into the cloakroom and get changed ready for P.E. outside in the playground. He put his plimsoles on his feet but he hadn't learned by that stage how to tie his laces. Passing the cloakroom, one of the cooks heard Colin say aloud to himself 'There's no point in me trying to tie these. If I sit here for long enough, someone is bound to come and help me.'

Moo also told me how, after Grandpa (my father's father) had died, TCP Grandma complained to her how cold the flat in Sandgate had been. Their main form of heating in that flat had been by the open fire. 'I had to explain to your grandma how to lay a fire, how to crumple some newspaper, how and where to collect twigs and when to put a few lumps of coal in the fireplace. She had never done it herself or watched anyone do it, she had always let your grandfather lay the fire. She seemed quite surprised how easy it was.'

Fiona and I started going together to the Free Church Sunday School, where I learned how to cope with boredom during a sermon by counting the number of red hats among the female congregation, imagining how I might swing from one chandelier to another without touching the ground, or trying to work out, if three Smarties laid side by side were an inch across, how many Smarties it would take to reach from my chair to the entrance doors. But then Fiona was encouraged by her father to start at Crusaders, a sort of Sunday School run by a Baptist woman whose husband was a colleague of Fiona's father. I went with Fiona to Crusaders as well, because although we were given pretty pictures of Jesus and Bible stories to lick and stick in a book at the Free Church Sunday School, at Crusaders we sang joyful choruses and sometimes stayed for tea at Mrs G's house, Mrs G. being of one of the ladies who ran the group.

If the prayers became too long while we sat cross-legged on the carpet, then we could make little teddy bears from the fluff we would surreptitiously pick and gather from the new wool carpet in their sitting room. It was at Crusaders and in Mrs G's large house where I first tasted Earl Grey tea and Roka crispy cheese biscuits. From that, Fiona and I started attending the local Baptist Church and both avoided being baptised by Reverend Smart, which seemed to both of us to be 'a step too far' - although I did think that wearing white and descending into the baptismal bath could have dramatic appeal. I had been baptised when I was christened, Moo had shown me the certificate to prove it.

But this ceremony at the Baptist Church would have been an adult baptism, making a public testimony to belonging to God by what they called 'opening my heart', declaring my belief in Jesus and the power of his love. I avoided the subject. It seemed all too personal, too intrusive with all this talk about hearts and body parts. My being expected to 'bear witness' at a Billy Graham Rally in Hitchin had been quite sufficient public exposure. We would be asked to stand up in front of everyone else, to say out loud how much we loved Jesus and what a difference he had made to our lives.

Then the whole audience was asked to 'Put money into the collection plate, to promote the good work and help spreading the message about Jesus.' I put in some coppers, then stayed sitting and silent. Val came once with a friend to a Billy Graham rally. She told me afterwards that rather than 'putting whatever you can afford into the collection plate,' as the preacher suggested, she had helped herself so that she had the bus fare back to Letchworth. I was shocked at such profanity within my family, and she might have been lying – Val quite often told lies to provoke a reaction – but it might well have been true.

One evening, when I was about ten or eleven years old, after I'd had my tea and had been sent to bed at around half past seven, I came down stairs again an hour later for something I'd forgotten and realised that the others were all in the dining room tucking into a cooked supper, whereas I had had only a sort of nursery tea with sandwiches. I was bewildered and very left out of the family, I felt that I was an unwelcome appendage, dismissed from the adults' company because I was 'the baby'.

Fiona and I fulfilled each other's sibling companionship need. Other than Fiona, my main weekend companion was Kim, our black long-haired dog. He was named 'Kim' by Dad because he and Moo had chosen him as a puppy in the dogs' rescue centre in Kimpton and had brought him home. I felt secure with Kim, at least with people from outside the family.

As Kim grew older, Colin and I assigned the 'Mr' label to him out of respect. Mr Kim and I used to go for long walks together along the back road to Great Wymondley or across Willian fields where cows grazed, rubbed their backs against horizontal hawthorn branches until the underside of bark shone as if it had been polished, and yellow cowslips grew in abundance.

I was puzzled by some of the things I heard in the Baptist Church and from the Elders at Crusaders. Fiona became quite friendly with eighteen-year-old Graham whose mother and younger sister regularly attended the Baptist Church. Graham's family did not fully approve of his friendship with Fiona. Graham apparently told Fiona that his mother had informed him that they could hold hands occasionally but shouldn't kiss because 'kissing can lead to other things.' I didn't understand what he or Fiona meant, and I'm not sure Fiona did either. We came to the conclusion that it had something to do with catching a nasty cold or a sore throat.

After church one day, I was laughing about something or other when Graham's mother walked up to me. 'You shouldn't laugh so much,' she said rather abruptly 'because Jesus had nothing to laugh about.' How did she know, I wondered? I was beginning to question some of the adults around me and not feel bad about doing so. And at the same time, I thought that trying to behave like Jesus might be rather tricky, and not have a favourable outcome – although I had to suppress the latter idea, because likening myself to Jesus was sacrilegious, even as a thought, and I feared I might be blasted for all eternity, which would be for a very long while.

I knew, because I had been told by Reverend Smart, the Baptist Minister, that 'Jesus knows everything you are thinking, every desire and every impure thought.' And he or God might, as a result, strike me dead. But we should, Revd Smart told the congregation 'Consider the leaves of the fig tree' although I had no idea why or what a fig tree looked like, although Aunty Dorothy had a greengage tree in her garden and a fig tree might be similar, I supposed. I simply didn't understand much of the evangelical language that Rev. Smart used, I wasn't sure why I was 'unworthy' and 'a miserable sinner' because most of the time, if I could avoid Val, dodge her sarcasm and her barbed tongue, I felt quite happy and certainly not miserable.

The Minister also told the congregation that we should be, or perhaps we already were, 'bathed in the blood of the lamb.' Moo's stand-by meat for us was breast of mutton because it was cheap. She would roast it slowly in a green Denby dish in the lower oven of our Rayburn in the kitchen – and I hated it, the taste, the fiddliness of dealing with it on my plate, separating out the meat from thick ribbons of fat, and the smell. And the absolute stench when Kim would vomit up the redundant fat that had been scraped into his bowl at the end of the meal. Lamb, rather than mutton, was something we rarely ate, so what had its blood . . .?

And in more than one of his lengthy sermons, the Minister also said we should 'stand in the shadow of the cross' which I thought we obviously couldn't because I knew the crucifixion had happened two thousand years before. The evangelical language confused me, I half understood that it was figurative – but I still didn't know what it all meant. It was considered totally unacceptable and 'unworthy' to question, to ask for an explanation or suggest - (to whom?) - that the message be put in plain language. Instead, we were told to watch and pray and to have faith.

The 'faith' bit was that Jesus loved us and would look after us always and forever. I tried hard to believe this, and in the power of prayer, and I could see that the Church Elders believed it completely. But the Elders appeared horrified when one autumn evening, after being taken to a Bible study class in nearby

Walsworth, I said I didn't have the bus fare home. I told them instead that it would be quicker for me to walk home in the dark along the back road towards Willian, and then cut across the golf course to our back fence. I had the firm belief that not only could I easily find my way and avoid falling into a ditch or sandy bunker on Letchworth Golf Course but also that it was extremely unlikely that I would be set upon by some stranger who might, according to the horrified looks on the Elders' faces, lie lurking in wait behind a tree for a fourteen-year-old nubile girl to be passing, clutching her Bible.

My suggested quick route home was not underpinned by fervent religious faith on my part, but was a practical approach to a problem and the confidence to deal with it, both attributes learned not from church but from my parents. And, as I was to discover, a clear sense of direction and surprisingly good eyesight in the dark. This may have been the first time that I began to have doubts about the benefits of faith. I felt that expecting Jesus or God to take responsibility for my welfare and my decisions might be a bit of a cop out, especially when the Elders failed 'to show faith' or offer to lend me the bus fare, although Moo disapproved of any lending. Or borrowing, except from the Public Library.

From then on, I would endeavour to rely more on myself to feel safe. And on Mr Kim – and Colin, when he was at home. Because of Val and her teasing friends. I didn't feel secure or settled at home unless Moo and Daddy were around. Even then, there were times when I would feel decidedly insecure, uneasy. Not sure who I was, what I believed and where, if at all, I fitted in. Or with whom.

During summer weekends, my father would quite often hand me some coins and tell me 'Be a good girl and cycle down to

Finlay's, would you? Buy a family-sized Neapolitan ice-cream as a surprise to save your mother having to cook a dessert for lunch. Wrap it up in a copy of 'The News of the World' to keep it cool, and pop it into your saddle bag. If they've run out of copies of News of the World, then get a cheaper paper like 'Reveille' or 'Weekend', either of those will do the job.'

We would have already had 'The Sunday Telegraph' delivered and I did once suggest to Dad that I could take a towel with me to avoid having to buy another newspaper but he said 'No, it'll keep cool far better wrapped in a clean newspaper. Just nip down into the town now and do as I ask. And when you get back, put the ice-cream into the top compartment of the fridge.'

When I came back, I did as I was told with the ice-cream and would settle down on the sitting room floor on my stomach, with the 'News of the World' spread out on the carpet. There I would pick out any articles or columns about murder, rape or anything vaguely titillating or naughty – until it was time to close the paper, refold it and carry it up to my parents' bedroom and place it on my father's side of their double bed. I knew nothing at that age about any male desire for visual stimulus so it didn't occur to me until fifty years later, that my father might have had an ulterior motive.

Chapter 3

The Right Words

It was August 1952 so I must have been eight when I discovered Overy Staithe.

I was on holiday with my parents, my brother Colin and my sister Valerie. Our father had planned to tow the caravan he had hired, from Hertfordshire up the east coast of England almost as far as Scotland, then across the country to the Lake District and then down the west side, across the Midlands. I thought Scotland sounded exciting, a place for adventures. I knew it had castles.

We spent the first night on a caravan site outside Scratby, near Great Yarmouth where each previous year in September, we used to rent a wooden chalet on the clifftop. After Scratby, with the three of us travelling seated at the back of our fawn-coloured Austin 16 and a large home-made shrimping net tied on to the roof, we followed our journey on a map and town by town, sticking as far as possible to the coast.

Our next possible stopping place had a strange name – Burnham Overy Staithe. It looked small on the map and when we came to it, we passed only one shop on the right-hand side of the road. The only big building appeared to be a public house, which stood robustly on the left at a rough-surfaced crossroad, its sign swinging precariously in the east wind.

As the light was failing and after Daddy made some enquiries, we were allowed to park the caravan and the car on a grassy field beside 'The Hero' Public House. My mother started to prepare our supper while Daddy, Valerie, Colin and I set off to explore, to find the beach and the sea.

But we didn't, not on that first day. At the end of a dirt track across the road from 'The Hero', we came to a 'creek'. That was a new word for me with a different spelling, I collected words, still do. My father explained what it meant, Val all the time pulling faces from behind his back and mouthing 'dimwit' at me. She was seven years older than I, could play 'Fur Elise' on the piano with both hands and thought she knew everything.

Down on a shingle shore where the water ebbed sideways and was the same grey as my school skirt, I breathed in the salty, nose-penetrating tang of the sea. My hair smelled of the salt-carrying breeze, the ends tasted of it as they whipped across my face and lips. Everything smelled of possibilities, of potential.

The grey creek ran between two banks and disappeared somewhere on the horizon, where Daddy said he could see a huge sand dune in the distance. 'But supper will be ready soon, then it would be your bedtime,' he said 'and anyway, it is getting dark.'

Back at the caravan, my parents agreed that we would explore straight after we had done the breakfast washing-up the following day and not set off with the car and caravan until mid-morning.

We discovered two routes to the sea proper. One was along the 'Hard', another new use of the word for me although I asked several times 'hard what?' and for over half the long walk the next day, insisted with all the pseudo-assurance of an eight-year-old with a grammatically pedantic mother, that 'hard' was 'a describing word'.

More tongue sticking out from Val. My mother said that I should ignore her, that she was just trying to annoy me and that I shouldn't react. My mother issued that advice quite frequently, I think she found Valerie as difficult as I did.

The route along the sand-topped Hard, the raised causeway that ran between the marshes of Burnham Overy Staithe and the sea, zigzagged frustratingly and to my young legs, it seemed that the distant bank of sand dunes would never grow closer. Instead, the main river spread out into multiple tidal creeks that eeled their way through the stretches of black mud, the black of the salt marshes, mud banks that were covered with tough-stalked purple sea lavender, some coarse green stuff called, according to the leaflet that Moo found in a rack next to the tide tables, 'sea purslane'.

Here and there where the sides of the Hard met the sand of the creek, were weathered branches of driftwood and rounded clumps of pink sea thrift that hunched themselves like frightened hedgehogs against the wind and tide.

A second and faster route that we were told about and later discovered for ourselves, was the Cockle Path. To access this, it was first necessary to wade across the river at low tide to reach a small area of sand at the foot of the black mud banks. Then, placing our steps carefully to avoid slipping on the mud still wet and oozing from the previous high tide, we could weave our way from one high point to another across solid bridges of land between the ditches where tidal water trickled conversationally from the banks down to the lower-level furrows. In a few places, where the land bridges had been washed away or eroded, some kind local person had dumped a pile of bricks and rubble that we could wobble across and that offered the mud some purchase as it was licked and nudged by the next oncoming tide.

After a twenty-minute walk among the sometimes coal-black, at other times almost indigo mud banks that were topped with the coarse green vegetation and waving lilac sea lavender, we would come to a regimented line of coarse sage-green sea purslane shrubs. We could push our way through without scraping our bare legs - because those were the days when I could wear shorts without feeling embarrassed - and then . . to a wide damp stretch of glistening sand punctuated only by the curly casts of burrowing cockles and lugworm spoils, fragments of ridged half cockle shells or protruding from the sand, giant mid-to-deep purple mussel shells, shells far larger and more prolific than any shells I had found on Dymchurch beach while staying with my grandparents; and these were intact, not chipped or broken. Such excitement! 'Overy Staithe,' I informed my parents, 'is my idea of paradise.'

There were few footprints here on the flat clean yellow strand or one or two signs of raking, scratching and digging left by those locals who, perhaps only an hour before us, had scrabbled for fresh cockles and the bottom ridge of their buckets had left shallow circles in the sand. Then, after hurrying across this stretch of beach, we would come to a very shallow stream, clear all but for the occasional strand of bright green or maroon seaweed that flowed listlessly out towards the main creek and the distant sea, the sea that we could now hear and just see, its on-coming waves tussling with the force of the out-flowing river.

Splashing across that last stream, surprisingly warm as it meandered across the sun-soaked sand, and we were on Scolt Head, a small secluded offshore barrier island of sand and marram grass and small intricately-patterned snail shells; a Nature Reserve protected, as the black and white metal sign told us and anyone else who chose to land there from the sea, by the National Trust.

The pub landlord told us that there was a community of artists living or working on Scolt Head that year, that we could recognise them if they came into the pub, because they would probably be wearing fishermen's smocks covered in blobs of paint.

On one occasion only a couple of days later when I was trying to find my way to 'The Hero' public lavatories, I got lost and plucked up courage to ask a long-haired man in a smock, while not being quite sure of the correct terminology to use on such an occasion.

'Could you please tell me the way to the, erm . . sanitorium?'

He didn't laugh, look astonished or ask 'to the what?' He understood and directed me very kindly to the right place.

Val sniggered when I told my family what words I had used and said 'You probably do need a sanatorium, Stupid.' I vowed then that I liked artists because they were kind and understanding, the man hadn't laughed at me, and that at some time in the future I would introduce everyone and anyone who was important in my life, to Overy Staithe.

Chapter 4

Friends, Loyalties, Family and the Teenage Years

It wasn't home itself that didn't feel safe but there was an under-current of potential disruption or disapproval, a lack of peace, a tension as if we were all waiting for the next thing to erupt. And I sensed that there were other things, important but private things, that I wasn't being told.

My friendship with Fiona had lessened, not because we had fallen out in any way but for two separate reasons. She had developed closer friendships with two sisters, Anne and Evelyn Bergman who were also boarders at St Francis R.C. School. Their father often worked and lived abroad for several months at a time and had invited Fiona to spend the summer holiday with him and the girls in Beirut.

Fiona and I didn't lose touch afterwards but she and her father moved house, though still within Letchworth. Fiona's mother had died, her father had married Peggy, a woman who worked with him at the chemist shop and there was no longer any need for Fiona to spend her weekends being looked after by Moo at our house. Her family's domestic arrangements had also changed so that after lunch on a Sunday, Fiona was needed to help at home while her step-mother assisted Fiona's father with the shop accounts. And when I called for her at their new house in Hitchin Road on a Sunday afternoon, she would not usually have finished the washing-up in time to leave for Crusaders with me, she would be told she had to stay and finish the job because that was more important. I gained the impression that Peggy felt that Fiona was becoming rather too religious.

I went to Crusaders for a while on my own without Fiona, and it wasn't as much fun without her being there. Fiona was fifteen months older than I and in the academic year above mine. She was still attending St Francis School but as a day pupil only. We would meet but irregularly during school lunchtimes, when we would both leave our respective educational institutions and walk down to 'Ruth's Pantry' for a half-price 1s. 3d children's lunch.

It was insubstantial but occasionally affordable from the dinner money that Moo gave me and supplemented by my monthly clothing allowance of thirty shillings. We stopped meeting in this way once Fiona had left school to begin her secretarial training. I missed her. Weekends weren't as much fun, either. So, I learned to work hard, it filled the time. And I would go on long walks with Mr Kim.

I felt secure at the grammar school, once Val had left. My school friendships were safe although my friend Rhoda's father, who was a local solicitor, showed some behaviour towards his adolescent daughter that I thought was strange – he would run his hands under her blouse and up her chest - so I didn't like playing at her house. Instead, she and I would meet before school at the tennis courts on Letchworth Common and do our best to play a game although she was far better at tennis than I was. I lacked the arm strength. I didn't much enjoy team games such as netball or hockey, I didn't want to feel I was just one of the gang nor to incur the wrath of other team-players if I missed a shot or was found to be offside. I preferred sports in which I could be an individual, matching and pitting myself against my previous best.

My *forte* was athletics, particularly high jump and the 100 and 150 yards running. I was also a keen and proficient swimmer, representing both Neville school house and the school on several occasions including the North Herts District sports events. At school, with the teachers and the people within the building, on the sports field or in the town's swimming pool, I felt comfortable, secure. Nothing unexpected was likely to happen, nothing that I felt I couldn't handle. And I was quite used to coming second or third in races and felt quite pleased with that. First place evaded me simply because other people were better.

There were ninety pupils in my first year at the grammar school. The large year groups were split into three forms according to a 'house' system named Neville, Howard and Gorst. Apart from during the Wednesday afternoon games lessons when we were divided into boys and girls, according to the sport activity considered appropriate for our gender, we met others of the same age only if we were in the same subject or ability level classes. Once or twice a week, the boys had woodwork lessons while the girls had domestic science, which involved being told how to make a pair of knickers out of a length of cotton fabric.

I can still remember the pair I made out of green check material: I wore them only once, they felt very uncomfortable, particularly where the elastic was threaded through the waist band; the whole operation seemed to me to be a complete waste of time. I would have much preferred woodwork but girls weren't allowed into the woodwork room. My navy-blue school regulation knickers usually came from Spinks', the local draper's shop in Leys Avenue and although they were not attractive - every pair had a pocket for a handkerchief, which seemed a stupid idea to me, especially immodest for use in a mixed school - they were comfortable, even when Moo told me it would be more hygienic if I were to wear a white pair underneath.

Moo, unlike TCP Grandma who was all for appearances, was a stickler for cleanliness and hygiene. She would often slip into the conversation that 'cleanliness is next to godliness' and she insisted that we children washed our bodies very thoroughly every day from top to toe and if not, then at least 'face, neck, crotch and armpits', using the bars of green Palmolive soap that she always bought. She would pad barefooted and naked along the upstairs landing towards the bathroom on a weekend morning, ready for her morning wash. Considering her upbringing and the values of the Victorian era into which she had only just avoided been born (she and Dorothy were born in late September 1901), Moo showed no concerns about female nudity, whether her own or mine.

On holiday at Burnham Overy Staithe one summer, Dad hired a rowing boat for half a day and took us out in it along the creek at high tide. I don't remember whether Colin or Val were with us but I know I had a small fishing line that I dropped over the side of the boat in the hope of catching something. After a while, I grew impatient with the lack of success so I suggested that I might like a swim before we reached the stretch where the tidal water ran fast between Scolt Head and the Gun Hill dunes. Dad pulled on the oars so the boat was level with Scolt Head and in gentler water. I slipped off my shorts and white aertex shirt, ignored any swimsuit and slithered head first over the side of the rowing boat and into the water.

It was beautifully cool. It was only when I saw a couple of people waving vigorously from the shore of Scolt Head Island, that I realised they had been cut off by the rising tide and were trying to attract our attention. They were shouting that they hoped we might give them a lift by boat back to the village or at least to the Cockle Path on the mainland. From the water, I called to Moo and Daddy that I understood what was going to happen, but that I had no clothes on and felt in no state to come out of the water in front of people whom I didn't know. Moo told me either to swim alongside and 'don't worry, they won't notice you, Dear' or, if she threw my swimsuit towards me, I could try to put it on while in the water, she said, and I knew just how difficult it could be to do that.

I remained in the water while Dad pushed the boat into the sand, the two strangers took off their sandals and clambered in. Dad rowed them across to where the Cockle Path led back across the black mud, the purple sea lavender, the coarse purslane shrubs and the marsh, towards the village. 'At the other end, you will have to wade back across the creek again but there it should be fairly shallow,' Daddy explained to his new passengers, 'and the in-coming tidal water should reach only your knees.'

During these manoeuvres, I stayed well behind the boat, treading water and hoping the rest of my body stayed out of sight. Once I was back in the boat and wrapped in a towel, Moo asked me 'Why were you so worried about having no clothes on? I don't understand why you were making such an issue out of it.' I was a well-developed twelve- or thirteen-year-old at the time.

During the autumn term when I was in the fourth form at school, one of the teachers arranged a visit to a London theatre. I don't remember whether it was Eugene O'Neill's 'Mourning Becomes Electra' or 'The Caretaker' by Harold Pinter because I saw both plays that year, but anyone in my form or the year above could ask to go. We were to travel by coach each way and the cost was far lower than if we had gone as private individuals. Moo found the extra money I needed, so I went. There were two boys from my year, Chris W. and John B., neither of whom I knew at all but who both sat in the row in front of me on the coach. Because they both lived in Salisbury Road in Baldock and belonged to Gorst House, I hadn't had the opportunity to meet either of them face to face before, but the journey from North Hertfordshire to central London gave me time to overcome my reserve and provided us with time to chat.

Partly to earn some pocket money but also to help me address my shyness, my diffidence which I recognised as a problem, I found myself a Saturday job in Letchworth, working behind the till in Sudbury's Cycles shop in Eastcheap.

The shop dealt with repairs and sales of motor bikes as well as pedal cycles, so I knew, when I applied to work there on sales, that I would have to deal with customers' queries and requests for items such as 'cotter pins' or 'gaskets', the appearance and functions of which I neither knew nor understood. That would mean that I had to display my ignorance to Mrs Stacey, who managed the shop, and to the men in the repair shop at the back, ask for their guidance, all of which should help me to engage with strangers and, I hoped, feel less embarrassed.

This part-time job also had, in a round-about way, an impact on my future career as a teacher, particular as a teacher for children with learning needs or who had gaps in their education. Mrs Stacey asked me whether I could help her son Greg, who intermittently attended a school the name of which I didn't recognise and whom she thought was not making sufficient progress. And, she told me, she was finding it almost impossible to explain our money coinage to him. So, at her request, I would work with Greg for an hour on a Sunday in her house, helping him to see the link between a one penny and a halfpenny coin; and appreciating how difficult it was to find an example by which he could understand the relationship of a half to a whole, especially using those metal coins. In the end, I took a large sponge cake and a sharp knife to explain fractions.

Talking with Chris W. and John B. in the coach to London, I discovered that John and I both worked in bicycle shops on a Saturday, John in one in Baldock and I in the one in Letchworth. We realised that we both enjoyed cycling, we both had racing bikes fitted with toe-clips and dropped handlebars, we enjoyed exploring the villages and parts of countryside that were unknown to us. With this shared interest, John became my closest friend.

After school, we would cycle from the school to my house. Moo would provide us with ginger biscuits and cups of tea, then we would sit in the drawing room listening to the latest song by Adam Faith or Cliff Richard, or playing a board game . . . until Moo would appear in the doorway, announce that it was nearly six o'clock and 'John, you must go, Dear'.

On a Sunday afternoon we would cycle to a local village in the hills and run the very small Sunday School, until the numbers dropped to nil. Perhaps influenced by my evangelistic approach, John joined the boys' Sunday Crusaders class in

Letchworth for a while. He came with me a few times to the Baptist Church and was welcomed. However, I incurred considerable disapproval, as by proxy did my mother, from the Elders at the church by my being absent one Easter Sunday from morning service.

I explained the following Sunday that since it had been the school holidays, John and I had spent a few days away together, with our parents' permission of course. We had cycled from Letchworth to Cambridge Youth Hostel, stayed there for one night and ridden on as far as the Youth Hostel on the corner of Earlham Road in Norwich. We then continued towards the coast to stay two or three nights in Sheringham Youth Hostel before returning by the same route to Letchworth. We were both just fourteen.

Moo had been ambivalent about this cycling trip when I had suggested it to her. Colin and Val had both been away for several weeks separately cycling around the country and staying at Youth Hostels in the West Country, Colin on his own and Val with her best friend Hazel. So this proposed trip in East Anglia was nothing new to my parents. A cycling holiday had been undertaken before by my older siblings and apart from Val phoning home once to report that she had lost Hazel, and Colin wrapping a half-opened tin of Nestle's sweetened condensed milk up in his trousers and stuffing them into his saddlebag, they had encountered no major problem.

Moo had been concerned for our general safety but simply said 'I know I can trust you to be sensible, Dear' and asked on what day we intended to return home. As we pedalled back from Norfolk, the wind along the Newmarket Straight was fierce, it was a 'Fen Blow' wind that picked up the dry soil and flung it in our faces. John rode up close behind me, put his hand on my back and pushed, and continued to push to help propel me and my bike forward against the wind. That level of support was, for me, a sign of true friendship.

Once back in Letchworth, the Elders at the Baptist Church considered it the height of irresponsibility for Moo to have allowed her teenage daughter to spend several days unchaperoned and away from home with a boy. I don't think Daddy would have noticed I was missing from home for that week. The Church Elders would look at me in such a way afterwards that I felt ashamed but I wasn't sure for or of what. I felt accused of something I hadn't done and that no one would actually come out and say what it was.

The idea of sex, illicit or otherwise, hadn't cross my mind, either during the cycle trip or afterward. I had been told that sexual intercourse and whatever physical processes that might entail because I wasn't at all sure, was for people who were married. And it was morally wrong for people who weren't married. And it had something to do with where babies came from and how they were created.

I knew the female anatomical part of that because Moo had told me. I remember asking Val if she knew how twins were made and she said, with all the assurance of an older sister completely devoid of any knowledge, that 'they do it twice quickly, Silly, once after the other'. I was no wiser. At school, the boys might sometimes refer to 'shagging' or 'having a shag' and Moo, who always thought the best of people, said that the word 'shag' was the name of a bird. But apart from anything else, John and I put too much thought and energy into our cycling, pressing down on the pedals, pumping up our tyres and buying provisions and cooking our meals at the different Youth Hostels.

John was simply my best friend and that was all there was to it.

Moo instructed me more than once to make my friendship with John less obvious in front of Val because, she said, 'Your sister has very few friends apart from Hazel who lives a long way away, and she seems to find making friends quite difficult. She might easily resent your closeness with John; it could upset her and disturb the family peace.'

I felt my bicycle holiday with John was regarded with such disapproval by the other Baptists that I was quite relieved when John's mother suggested to me that perhaps I might like to accompany her and John to Baldock Parish Church one Sunday for Matins. I could see what a morning service was like there, she said, what they did, which hymns from the 'Ancient and Modern' hymn book I might already know.

I had had very little experience of a regular Church of England service - I had once or twice been with Moo to an Easter Service at the 13th century church near Letchworth Hall Hotel - and Moo said that my going to a Matins or an Evensong Service in Baldock Parish Church would add to my general knowledge.

Moo explained that Aunty Dorothy, who was also my godmother, attended Northaw Parish Church every week because Northaw School where Aunty Dorothy taught, was a Church of England School and she felt duty-bound to support the parish church. So, I pondered, did that somehow make it all right then, Moo's sister's temporary switch from Congregational to C. of E? 'What matters most to me,' Moo said, 'is that you should go to church at all - and to Sunday school - because it is', she suggested, 'a way of ensuring that you will be brought up with firm Christian beliefs and Christian morals.'

Wary of pressure from Rev. Smart and the Baptist Church Elders to undergo adult baptism, I showed more interest in confirmation into the Church of England. I mentioned this to Moo and Daddy. My father was disapproving, he would rather I didn't turn 'all popish', he said. I knew I would be expected to wear white and since neither parent was willing to provide me with the money to buy a suitable white skirt, Moo suggested I might ask Aunty Dorothy for her help. With Aunty Dorothy's financial assistance, I managed to equip myself suitably - I was concerned that my teeth looked rather yellow and suggested I might paint them with white enamel, until Moo told me that it would be a bad idea and that the paint probably wouldn't dry anyway.

At Easter that year, I was confirmed. Neither Moo nor Daddy wanted to attend but John and his mother were there and John gave me a gold cross and chain to mark the occasion. I was disappointed by my parents' absence and felt that yet again, I wasn't doing what they wanted, I hadn't conformed to their wishes or met their ideals.

At the end of that year, I asked for a white Bible as a present from the family. I still have that much-used white-leather-covered gold-leafed Bible. In his best hand-writing it bears the inscription 'To Lorna, with love and best wishes from Daddy. Christmas 1959'.

Although we were studying different subjects for our main 'O' level and later our 'A' level exams - John leaned towards the sciences whereas I was keener on the arts and humanities - we were both due to sit the requisite English and Maths exams. However, I was encouraged by the school to take my English and Maths exams while I was in the fourth form, a year earlier than John and most of my classmates. This was in order that, so the school's logic went, I could get those subjects out of the way and could spend more time concentrating on my other subjects in the fifth form. I did well in my 'O' level results with eight or nine good passes. Then came the question of 'what next?'

I chose French, German and Latin as my 'A' level subjects. Moo would have liked me to have been sufficiently academically able to get into Cambridge University. But Moo didn't seem to understand the difference between a 'high-flyer' and me, as someone who would be fortunate if she even made it onto the academic bird table. No one in the immediate family had been to university, the closest relatives who had been to one were the children of Moo's cousins. Most of my relatives had opted for vocational training of some sort.

Staff at the school thought I might just be able to get to Cambridge, if I stayed for a third year in the sixth form. I had my doubts and anyway, I didn't want to spend another year at school, studying with pupils I didn't know from the year below mine. I would have preferred to have studied English rather than Latin, although I enjoyed the logic of Latin as a language, but I was advised that Cambridge would require me to have Latin 'A' level if I were to apply to a Cambridge college.

Moo also advised me not to study English at 'A' level. She warned me against it. 'Just think how Val would react' Moo warned with her left eyebrow raised 'if you either passed the exam when she didn't, or if you failed it.' I knew Val had failed her English 'A' level exam. 'She would probably make life unpleasant for you whatever your result, if you took the English 'A' level exam course,' Moo said. Moo might have been correct; I decided not to find out.

John's family were accustomed to going somewhere interesting on an afternoon at the weekend - which my parents never did 'because we need to do important things in the garden' they would both say. I was often invited to go along too with John and his parents, to a local historic house or in February, to Bygrave Church where snowdrops grew in profusion.

'Be here by three o'clock', his mum would state 'and we'll get going as soon as you arrive.' Except it was usually four o'clock by the time we all set off from their house, and sometimes even later if their car refused to start, which it did only too often. Then we would cancel plans and play a game or have what they called 'tea' early, which would be ham and tinned peaches. And I felt safe with them because John's mother and father always seemed kind and pleased to see me, they expected nothing from me except politeness and my appreciation. The inevitable uncertainties that surrounded them and their weekend plans were certain uncertainties, ones I knew from experience to expect and could handle one way or another - and the outcome was always pleasant.

John's Mum taught me to sew, how to lay out a Simplicity or Butterick paper pattern, where and what to cut, and how to use a sewing machine, all of which proved to be valuable skills in my later years and when I needed to make my own clothes, sew shirts for my husband and clothes for the children. One year, she gave me a pair of pinking shears as a present.

As we grew older, I joined John's family on a week's holiday near Torquay and the following year, John came to Overy

Staithe with Moo, Daddy and me on holiday in a four-berth touring caravan. John and I had sleeping bags on single bunks, side by side at one end of the caravan, while Moo and Daddy slept on the double bed at the other end. Kim slept either on the floor by the cooker or in the car.

John and I were like brother and sister, we were the same height and similar build, we supported each other, we could read each other's thoughts and people who didn't already know us assumed we were twins. With John, I felt secure and valued, although he expressed some disgust when I skipped happily along the pavement near his house. 'Please stop doing that, because' he said, 'you look ridiculous.'

Across all the years, Daddy had kept in touch with Frances, one of his old friends from Romford. She had been a singer for the B.B.C. and had been 'Dear Little Buttercup' in Gilbert and Sullivan's operetta 'HMS Pinafore'. Daddy had performed with her in 'Pinafore' as fellow members of the Red Triangle Group and they got on well together. She had the same surname as Moo's maiden name of Partridge, which could have made the situation more complicated and, Moo told me, his car would often be seen parked outside Frances's house in the evening before he came home.

Other people in Romford had told her that this was unwise, would start rumours, but Moo trusted that Daddy wouldn't do anything improper, she said, and that they were just rehearsing together.

In the days before we holidayed with a caravan, Daddy used to rent 'Barton', the wooden bungalow at Scratby from Norman Meadmore, a D'Oyly Carte colleague. Sometimes Frances would join us there.

Neither Val nor I looked forward to her visit, we felt she slightly resented our spending time with our father and would have preferred more time with him on her own. Frances didn't swim but she was happy to don a bathing costume and sit on a towel spread out on the sand.

Before Daddy retired and he and Moo moved to a village in Kent, he used to invite Frances to come to stay with us for a few days in Letchworth. Moo didn't exactly look forward to having her as a visitor but she and Daddy would do their best to clean and tidy the house and make the spare room look welcoming. Frances would arrive by train, clutching a huge bunch of chrysanthemums grown by her family in their small Romford garden. She presumably didn't realise that chrysanthemums are considered in some cultures to be the appropriate flowers for a funeral.

Moo would do her best to place the heavy-headed blooms in a hefty vase that stood on the windowsill halfway up the stairs; and appear grateful. I have viewed chrysanthemums with suspicion ever since. But at a later time, Daddy admitted that Frances was good company and that her appearance – not as tall as Moo, with ginger curly hair and fashionably dressed - was exactly as his mother would have wished for him in a wife. Nevertheless, Frances lacked Daddy's sense of humour and Moo's pragmatic common sense. Val and I did sometimes wonder what the relationship between Frances and our father really was. Or what Moo imagined it was - or wasn't.

There was no negative emotional undercurrent that I could detect at my grandparents' house in Sandgate except TCP Grandma's unexplained reluctance for me to play with Virginia who lived next door. I was often sent or taken to Sandgate so that I could spend at least a week of my Easter school holidays at Number 2, Wellington Terrace where, if the weather were warm enough, I might be seen safely across the road by Grandpa, drop down over the seawall and onto the shingle beach.

On that stretch of beach when the tide was out, I would find tiny crabs under the stones, see any red or green sea anemones open in the rock pools or try to prise whelks off the black rocks. Winkles, which we sometimes cooked and ate in a sandwich, were more plentiful on the rocks nearer towards Folkestone. Sometimes I played on the metal railings with the Robinson girls, twins slightly younger than I and who lived at number 8 in the same block of flats in Wellington Terrace.

My father would take me by train from Letchworth as far as Victoria Coach Station and find me a seat on the East Kent coach bound for Folkestone. I would wave goodbye to him from the coach window and off I would go. My only concern on the journey would be about our half-way stop. The coach was scheduled to pull off the main road and wait for twenty minutes for refreshments and toilets at the Bull Hotel, near Ashford. My small and unvoiced anxiety was that the coach might set off again without me. It never did, the coach driver would give us a five-minute warning of departure. Then we would be driven for another hour, reach Hythe, trundle through the town and slowly into Seabrook, then along the front until I could see Sandgate, and Folkestone cliffs in the distance.

And with the sea and its shingle beach and breakwaters on the right-hand side of the coach, I could spot the white paint of the first house of Wellington Terrace, Number One and Virginia's house - and the veranda of Number Two, my grandparents' first floor flat - and Grandpa standing on the pavement beside the steps up to the house, waiting for me, waiting in his brown trilby hat and his pipe in his mouth.

There I would spend a week away from the tensions of our house in Letchworth, away from Val and any disruptions she might cause, away from worrying whether the house were sufficiently tidy and clean for the paying guests or unexpected visitors, away from my parents' concerns and Moo fretting whether she could pay the grocery bill every week and what Dad would say if she couldn't (although she always did), away from something else intangible, a worry that I couldn't yet identify, away from living as if on the slopes of a grumbling volcano.

The only tension at my grandparents' house would be about what I was to wear to church, did I have any money for the collection - although TCP Grandma always pressed some pennies into my hand before wrapping her boot-button-eyed fox-fur around her neck - and we would walk together down the steps to the pavement. TCP Grandma's concerns were whether I was still wearing my liberty bodice because 'It's still April, Lovey, and a young girl like you needs a liberty bodice as well as a vest so close to the sea'. But TCP Grandma and Grandpa were predictable, safe and almost comforting, despite Grandma's general odour of mothballs from her beady eyed fox-fur with its small claws - and the unavoidable TCP.

But I loved the smell of Grandpa's Digger Mix tobacco, the sucking noises he would make while trying to get the bowl of his pipe to glow, playing bagatelle with him which was their only board game that rested on a brass table alongside a vase containing purple everlasting flowers; standing or even sitting in a deckchair on the veranda with him, watching boats on the horizon through binoculars that I couldn't properly adjust.

Very occasionally there might be a loud bang at sea and a plume of water, as a sea mine left from the Second World War was spotted and blown up.

Grandpa would lend me his library tickets so I could walk down to Sandgate Public Library and take out several books (only hard-back in those days) and carry them home. Then I could immerse myself in the safe worlds of Angela Brazil and her school days at St Chad's, meet up again with Jon and Penny Warrender in Malcolm Saville's books set in Shropshire and on Wenlock Edge, or even sink into the writing of Captain W.E. Johns, where I would join Biggles, Algy, Ginger and Smyth in another adventure in the air or on land somewhere; or choose Lorna Hill, who set some of her books in Northumbria. And my safety net, in any story I was reading and any fictional situation I was experiencing, was that I always knew that things would turn out all right in the end.

Every weekday, Grandma would bake a Victoria sponge cake, fill it with strawberry jam and the mock cream that she made herself from butter, boiled milk and hot water - she didn't own a Bel cream maker - and serve slices of cake after the main meal in her repertoire that was always fried fish and chips with tomato ketchup. Or she would catch a bus into Hythe, and return with the previous days' half-price cakes - cream horns (which she pronounced as cream 'orns) or something round, brown and cream-coloured with a circle of brown on top, called japs. The only surprise at TCP Grandma's house when I woke each morning was whether the tide was in or out, high or low, and even that was calculable.

Sometimes, if I asked nicely and there was nothing else planned, Grandpa would take me on the top deck of a red double decker bus to Dover and despite being nearly eighty years old, he would willingly climb up and down all those flights of steps so that, once again, I could explore Dover Castle and its dungeons.

The first book I wrote was a guide to Dover Castle, even though there were several books already written and published on the subject and by people who knew far more about it than I. Not surprisingly, my account was never published. In fact, I don't think I gave a thought to publishing or printing, it was sufficient to have it and see it written in my eleven-year-old inky handwriting. It was only long after my annual Easter visits to Kent that I realised I had been despatched to stay there for a week with my grandparents for the convenience of my parents rather than for my own enjoyment or at my request.

Occasionally, my father was required to attend a conference about something connected with his job. 'Street furniture' he told me, which meant lamp posts, bollards, rubbish bins, bench seats and anything else likely to enhance the shopping experience or the enjoyment and safety of public spaces. These conferences were held in hotels in holiday places such as Scarborough or Morecambe. And there was a chance for Moo to go with him, it would give her a break at no particular expense, and an opportunity for Moo and Dad to spend time together without needing to worry about Val and what trouble she might get herself into.

The very idea of leaving me behind and in Val's apparent care was fraught with potential problems, it was better to pack me off to stay with my grandparents. I don't know who, if anyone, kept an eye on Val. Perhaps by that stage she was in the student nurses' hostel or had been taken to stay with Aunty Dorothy or Aunty Jocelyn, each of whom appeared to handle her better than Moo. Val seemed to get on well with either aunt. 'She respects each of them more than she appears to respect her own mother', Moo once said, with resignation.

While Val was training to be a nurse and living in student nurses' accommodation, she continued to wet the bed. To try to stop this, I was told that she had been prescribed a series of different drugs – I have no idea which, maybe they were drugs intended to prevent her from sleeping so deeply – and rather than take one each evening, she would keep the pills and would sometimes store them in a tin by her bed. For some reason, they didn't prevent her bed-wetting but she apparently took them all at once and caused some concern among the other nurses because she didn't and couldn't wake up at the right time.

In some way that I don't remember or perhaps I was never told but it was implied, the overdose of drugs or the wounds she would inflict on her skin had a damaging effect on her blood stream; she developed sepsis and septicaemia, a blood infection. I wasn't given any detail but I remember her being sent home, seeing scars on Val's legs from huge boils she had had, and her needing to have several blood transfusions.

At one point, Daddy was very afraid Val was going to die. I saw him downstairs in the dining room one evening with his painting easel and oil paints, he was looking at a recent 'Polyphoto' picture of Val, sketching it onto canvas board and trying to paint her. I made some comment to him and he explained he was painting her portrait 'in case I lose her'.

Val had always been Daddy's favourite. They both had quick tempers but seemed to get on well with each other whereas Colin and I, with our larger build, hair and skin colouring and temperament, were more placid, pliable even, had much more in common with Moo. It is not to my credit that I remember thinking that if Val were to die, things would not be all bad - because perhaps I could then move from my little bedroom which was barely 9ft by 9ft and I could take over Val's room which was positioned over the garage. It was much larger than mine, had a door onto the balcony and even its own wash basin.

Moo used to ride her bicycle several times a week, often up the hill of Letchworth Lane to the post box. On the afternoons when she wasn't giving music lessons, Moo would sit at the dining room table in Elm Hollow composing articles for women's magazines and writing short stories for children. Occasionally, one of her typed stories would be accepted for publication and appear in a magazine for children called 'Sunny Stories'; or an article about something such as 'caravanning with elderly parents' would be published in 'Women's Own', 'House Wife' or 'Good Housekeeping' magazines under her pen name of 'Mary Bedford'. For these submissions, she would receive a modest sum.

She would pay this into her personal building society account that she called her 'savings'. I didn't ask her if there was anything for which she was especially saving but once a term after I became a student in Canterbury, she might send me a letter in her trundly writing, wrapped around a ten-shilling note with the P.S of 'and please don't mention the enclosed to your father.'

When she was much older and my father had retired, Moo was asked to broadcast her articles on local radio about being a twin or holidaying with an elderly grandparent. Dad always listened to these broadcasts, with pride. She also gave piano lessons to a couple of girls, so on those days I had to stay out of the sitting room.

I don't remember how Moo damaged her spine. She told me that the doctor had diagnosed a slipped disk and told her not to ride her bicycle any more. Instead, if Moo required it and I were at home, I was to walk up to the post office with a large unsealed envelope containing any manuscript that she wanted to send, buy the necessary stamps and put one extra stamp on an enclosed self-addressed envelope in case the magazine or publisher needed to return her manuscript. Once assured that her article or story was on its way, she would wait patiently, hoping not to have it returned but eager instead to receive an acceptance letter and a cheque or postal order.

Moo's back was found to be weak and she was prescribed corsets to support her spine and back muscles. This utilitarian undergarment came from the local Spirella factory. It was designed and made-to-measure especially for Moo. It provided two heavy metal bars, reminiscent of the old whalebone corsets except these bars were each a couple of inches wide, quite thick and heavy; they slotted into the back of her corsets and ran vertically from the top to the bottom. Sitting on the edge of the double bed that she and my father shared, she would wrap the corsets around her body and lace them up. She called her corsets her 'railings'.

She was reticent to make her way to the bathroom until she had donned them, in case her back should give way and she might end up as an immoveable, unwashed, crumpled, squidgy pink jellyfish heap on the landing floor carpet runner. Having to wear this support meant that she was no longer able to swim in the sea or swimming pool. Even in the hottest weather, I never once heard her complain about those corsets. Moo was reluctant to complain about anything, she was always stoic with a positive outlook.

Whatever the situation, however demanding or desperate it appeared to be, her response was either 'Never mind, I'll cope,

Dear' or, if physical effort were required, 'I'll be fine so long as I can just take my time.'

In her life, Moo had had to be resilient. She told me very little about her father Frank, who was my grandfather, except that he had been a tailor and draper with a stock of fabric from which either he or his assistants would make men's clothing. I never met him, he died long before I was born. But in my wardrobe, I still have a black wooden coat hanger inscribed in gold lettering with his name 'Frank Partridge, Tailor. Bond Gate Nuneaton'.

Moo told me 'Once, when Nenna, Dorothy and I were living in Bedford, the river burst its banks and flooded my father's premises including the basement where he had kept his stock of fabric - and it was all completely ruined.'

I asked her 'What about compensation?'

'He had no insurance,' she told me. I took that in.

She also said that her father had died of something caused during the war. I assumed, from the date of his death and since he had not been present at my parents' wedding, that she had been referring to the First World War. Wondering if he had been shot or had caught something in the trenches, I asked her what had caused his death.

She said something to the effect that many men experienced shell shock during the war and it affected their minds. 'Your grandfather Frank, who was my father' she explained 'died in Fairfield Three Counties Mental Hospital.' She went on to tell me 'After I was married and before having any children, I went to the doctor to ask whether any children might inherit my father's mental disability. And he assured me,' she said, 'that they could not.'

That was all she would tell me about my grandfather Frank, it seemed to be a subject that still caused her some pain. But I was puzzled, it didn't make sense to me. Surely, I wondered, no one inherits shell shock?

Moo's father had also been a travelling salesman so he was often away from home. Presumably he had earned a reasonable amount of money at some stage because the gold engagement ring that he had given my grandmother was set with several diamonds.

Nellie, Moo's mother, had often been the sole parent in the home while Frank was away and had managed the house in addition to her music-teaching role; but she was still able to employ Elsie, the maid who, according to Moo, would brush the girls' hair every morning when they were young. Moo wasn't aware if Elsie had any other duties within the house. On my parents' marriage certificate in July 1932, Frank is recorded as a 'woollen merchant (deceased)'.

Moo and her sister Dorothy had not been the only children, Moo said. My grandmother, herself the eldest of twelve, had apparently had a third daughter called Margaret or Peggy, who had been born after the twins, but who died at the age of three, Moo thought.

But she could find no photographs of Peggy although there were several of the twins with their long hair secured with wide bows - and one with a dog, the name of which she couldn't recall, nor to whom it belonged. And, Moo had thought, her mother might have given birth to a second batch of twins sometime after that, that had been stillborn.

I was thirteen or fourteen when my father suffered what was called 'a nervous breakdown'. According to what I understood from Moo, it was brought about in part by tensions between the independent Letchworth Garden City Company and the town council. Concerns about Val added to Dad's stress.

Daddy always seemed to be worried about something. He would even worry about what it might be that he didn't yet know but that he knew he ought to be anxious about, once he became aware of it. He would worry about having woodworm in the furniture or in the structure of the house, about damp, or wet rot or dry rot, about having leaks in the roof, about death-watch beetle. And a great deal about the weather. We would all tell him it was pointless, that worrying about rain or heat or snow wouldn't change the climate in any way.

But he sometimes did have cause for concern, because if he detected the likelihood of snow the following morning, he would be up and dressed by 6am in time to drive to the local depot to assure himself that the snowploughs had turned out and lorries were gritting the main roads around Letchworth. He had a very strong sense of responsibility, did our father.

On one occasion he became really upset. When visiting the sewage works, a colleague had slipped and fallen into the sludge. Another colleague, not Daddy because Daddy couldn't swim, had dived in to try to find his body – but he wasn't able to locate him. Daddy's colleague, the workman, drowned. I sensed Daddy felt partly responsible, not for any oversight or negligence on Daddy's part, but just because it had happened and he hadn't been there to do anything to prevent it.

He looked very sad for a long time afterwards, wouldn't take Mr Kim with him in the car. Just sat in an armchair in the dining room, staring at the floor with his head in his hands. I think he must have gone to the funeral.

I have no recollection of there having been any particular gender stereotyping, expectation or discrimination at home, despite my parents having presumably ingested many Victorian notions regarding what boys and girls might do, how they might or should behave. I knew I was a girl because I had the same female lower parts as Fiona (she and I checked while sharing a bath) and because my name was called with the other girls' names in alphabetical order in the school register, the register where the boys' names always came first. And at one school, I entered the playground through the entrance arch marked 'Girls'.

This gender equality was frequently displayed at home. There was never any 'just wait till your father gets home' nonsense, each parent seemed to us to carry equal responsibility for our welfare and either parent might deliver a necessary reprimand - although Moo would occasionally administer a smack to a hand, whereas Dad didn't. It was similar with household tasks and responsibilities. Dad would often cook our breakfasts, whether boiled kippers or a conventional fry-up, fried roes on toast, the roes being either hard or soft, or fried sweetbreads, chitterlings – or as he would say, 'chitlins'.

After he retired, he and Moo might entertain a few friends and Dad would make a large black forest gateau or some small choux pastry eclairs that he had cooked and filled with his own sweet fillings. He was also responsible for making the coffee and he took more trouble over it. Moo was often the one to use the heavy petrol mower to cut the 'Elm Hollow' grass in Garth Road - which was hard work because much of the back lawn comprised a steep slope from the house to the flatter badminton court. And when we first bought the land for Elm Hollow, local people had thought that the hollow bowl in the land might be a pond. We found it wasn't, it was full of elm saplings, elm saplings much taller than I, which Colin, Val and I were required to pull up by their roots - although I was considered to be quite tough physically, I was only ten or eleven when we moved into that house - and carry across to the bonfire area. I was never considered to be less physically able because I was a girl. And Moo and Dad would work in partnership on any painting or wallpapering. Dad was a better painter; he was far more meticulous than Moo about presentation as well as being more skilful. Moo had never learned to drive a car but each of us was taught how to sew on buttons, use a washing machine, iron our clothes, paint and wall-paper a room and as we grew older, to use sandpaper or an electric sanding machine.

One year, when she was approaching her twenties, I remember Val asking for a Black and Decker electric drill for her birthday, her being given it and using it. The downside of this was that I had no idea what 'being ladylike' or 'feminine' meant or how, if or when young girls or women might be expected to behave differently from boys or enjoy different activities. Moo did own a pot of Pond's face cream but I don't think she ever used it. It stood undusted and forlorn just in front of the mirror on her dressing table.

Only occasionally, if accompanying my father to a Rotarian dinner and dance, would Moo apply any make-up or face power. And when she did, she would keep her spectacles on in order to see what she was doing and thus get face powder on both sides of her glasses so it looked to anyone else as if Moo suffered from very bad dandruff.

My infant desire to answer any enquiry politely, honestly and undramatically was reported to Moo by Miss Fendly, my class teacher in Westbury Infant School. Aware that Nenna had had a stroke, was bed-ridden and would live with us for six months of the year and then with Aunty Dorothy for a further six-month stretch, Miss Fendly asked me one Monday morning, how my grandmother was. According to what Miss Fendly reported to Moo, I cheerfully replied 'She's very well, thank you. She died last night' as indeed she had, sleeping in our spare room in 100 Broadway in 1951, aged 74. I had known Nenna only as an elderly lady in bed all day, with long grey hair done up in a bun at the back of her neck, around whom we must all be very quiet.

While the funeral was being planned and taking place, I was packed off to stay with Aunty Katie, one of Nenna's younger sisters who lived in Welwyn Garden City. A funeral, even of a parent or grandparent, was considered to be an event not suitable for a child to attend. I don't know whether Colin or Val was allowed to attend but they certainly weren't staying with me at Auntie Katie and Uncle Arthur's house. I remember being there and probably spending the night there because I have a memory of being provided with a potty placed on the carpeted bedroom floor and being told, very firmly, to make sure I aimed straight and none of the drops of wee were to spill over onto the sandy-coloured wool carpet. I liked Aunty Katie, she was very particular and exact, an absolute pedant over language and its usage. She and Arthur had no children.

Uncle Arthur was a balding schoolmaster who had taught at Loughborough College. He had been a conscientious objector during the war and was also a vegetarian, which Moo considered to be very strange. It was Aunty Katie who introduced me as a teenager to cashew nuts after Arthur retired and he and Aunty Katie moved to live near Bognor Regis.

Aunty Katie must have attended Nenna's funeral since Nellie was her older sister, so I wonder now, did she leave me aged seven or eight, in Uncle Arthur's care for the whole day, a man whom I hardly knew who had had no experience of young children, particularly girls? Or did Aunty Katie miss her sister's funeral in order to look after me? And why was I provided with a potty rather than shown where the bathroom was? Their house was in Welwyn Garden City which was planned and built as a garden city after Letchworth was completed: so, it must have been relatively new and the house must have had a bathroom and possibly a separate loo. Recording my memories now raises so many questions that I'm unable to answer.

Colin had avoided National Service on account of his recurrent hay fever. By this time, he was working for a company called Mothercat that had something to do with construction for oil and gas. He had been offered a job in Lebanon. He rented a small flat and lived for two years in Beirut, where he also kept a dog, a stray that he named 'Norman'. By then Colin was out of the immediate picture so I couldn't rely on him for support. Our main family communication with him was by recording messages, sending them by post and exchanging tapes destined for his tape-recorder and for Dad's Grundig player.

When he returned from Beirut and later from Multan in Pakistan, Colin rented a flat in Ealing and worked in London. He would sometimes invite me to London to watch a 'Brian Rix' Whitehall farce in the theatre. My parents were quite content for me to travel for an hour on my own, to and from the capital city. Colin would buy a couple of tickets for an early evening performance, meet me off the train from Letchworth at King's Cross, make sure I had something for lunch and then take me to a Pathé cinema to watch first the News with its introductory music and image of circles travelling around broadcasting towers, then a 'Tom and Jerry' cartoon film which Colin loved.

After that and perhaps something else to eat, he would take me by tube or bus to the Whitehall Theatre. There we would laugh until we cried at ridiculous goings-on and dialogue, the doors on the set opening and closing, actors' mouths dropping open without them saying anything - until it was time for me to set off for home. Colin would accompany me on the tube as far as Finsbury Park and ensure that I boarded the correct train that stopped at Letchworth, where Dad would meet me in the car. I must have been no older than eleven or twelve, possibly even younger.

I have three other memories relating to Val and Letchworth. One concerns our father's worry about the correct course of action to take.

Dad had received a telephone call from our General Practitioner. Apparently, Val had been to see him about something and after the end of the appointment, the doctor had noticed that his prescription pad or some sheets from it, were missing. It came to light a day or so later that someone, presumably Val, had forged the doctor's signature on a prescription, filled in what drug or drugs she wanted and had presented it to a local chemist. Dad was worried that by doing this, Val had committed a criminal offence, and wondered what action he, as her father, should take.

Should he try to persuade the doctor not to report it, to take no action in order to protect Val from the consequences and likely legal action and/or prosecution? Should he safeguard his own reputation as Val's father and a prominent and respected member of the local community? As far as I could tell, Dad was upright and honest, responsible with a sense of duty towards himself, members of his family and the law.

Dad went to talk to the doctor in question and, I suspect, leaned either on the 'Rotarian old boys' network or invoked his 'all Freemasons together' support and understanding. Either way, I knew of no action being taken against Val but it did cause Dad considerable self-questioning and ethical anxiety, as well as concern that Val appeared to have no sense of right or wrong - and a concern that he, as a father, had failed or was failing in his duty towards her to bring her up to behave correctly.

It is little wonder then, that Moo had said to me, perhaps more than once, 'If you behave like your sister, I shall just leave'; although it is questionable as to where Moo might have gone, if to anywhere at all.

Sometime after this, Val had a further appointment at the doctor's surgery. She was, she apparently told the practitioner, seeing things and hearing strange voices in her head. The voices were telling her to do or think certain things. I don't remember this ever having been linked to religion or suggested that the voice belonging to God but the doctor appeared to take it quite seriously and got in touch with my parents.

Moo told me that Val appeared to be suffering from hallucinations and the mental health condition known as schizophrenia, that she had also threatened suicide. This may have been while Val was living and training at Guy's Hospital, because I think it was to St George's Mental Health Hospital in London that which she was first admitted.

Moo and Dad had to travel to London one evening to see her as soon as possible and talk with the relevant doctors. My parents got in touch with Rev. Smart, the Minister at the Baptist Church, to ask for his help - and the next thing I knew was that I was being asked to collect together my washing things, nightdress and school uniform for the morning. I was taken by car and delivered with my belongings to the Smarts' family home in Broadwater Avenue, to spend the night there while Moo and Dad were away in London.

Mrs Smart met me and Dad at their front door and said that I could slip upstairs and into their daughter Faith's bed because, she said, Faith had only spent a couple of hours in her sheets so they were quite clean. I have no idea where Faith slept that night, I knew her only from seeing her at church. I assume that I had breakfast there, then walked from the Smarts' home to school the next morning.

By the time I arrived at our house after school that afternoon, Moo and Dad had come back from London, Dad returning to his office in the Council Offices and Moo to the kitchen or working on the dining room table. Moo didn't tell me much about what had happened, what the doctors had said or what they had found, except that she and Dad hated walking along the corridors of St George's Hospital and every so often, they had to pass through a barred gate which had to be unlocked and locked behind them. It was not, she told me, like any other hospital they had ever visited. 'It was horrible,' she said.

Val was kept at St George's for some time. She told me something about the walls of her room being covered with padded mattresses but I thought she was probably making that up. Val was given to melodrama to attract attention, and to what Moo politely called 'embellishment'.

At some stage, either Val, one of the nurses or Moo told me 'Val managed to get hold of her case notes and read them. She began acting up the symptoms and behaviour that the notes described.' It seemed to me unlikely that her case notes were so accessible but Val was crafty and quite unscrupulous so this wasn't impossible. And she was a nurse so could have bluffed her way into doing this. And, I thought at the time, if this were the case, it was very silly of her. Because Val ended up being transferred and admitted to Fairfield Three Counties Mental Hospital[iv] just outside Letchworth, the very same mental hospital to which our grandfather had been admitted and in which he had died all those years before.

Poor Moo, however did she cope with that, her elder daughter being taken to where her own father had been treated unsuccessfully - and died.

In Fairfield Mental Hospital, which my schoolmates would ignorantly refer to as 'the local loony bin', Val was being subjected to ECT.[v]

Val's time at Fairfield Mental Hospital did produce one benefit as well as her mental recovery - well, if not exactly a benefit, at least it offered a plausible explanation for something which for years had not made sense to me nor to her. She somehow managed to access details of our grandfather's death (I said she was crafty) which gave the date as 8th March 1930, registered on 14th March 1930 and listed two causes as '1a Cardiac failure' and '1b General Paralysis of the Insane, 2 years and 9m.'

With Val's medical knowledge and a little research, it was easy to determine the most likely cause of mental paralysis was damage to the brain from untreated syphilis. That would explain why Moo had visited her doctor before deciding to have any children - and why, if in fact she already knew the reason, she decided against telling any of us the cause of our grandfather's death. And why Aunty Jocelyn, Moo's cousin and a bridesmaid at Moo's wedding, would say only that our grandfather Frank was considered by the family to have been 'a bit of a bad lot' and implied some sexual impropriety, which also reflected on Nenna, Moo's mother and Aunty Jocelyn's mother's older sister. And why, quite apart from any religious beliefs, Moo was so emphatic to the three of us children about the need for sexual morality in case, though she never mentioned it, immorality should lead to a debilitating sexually-transmitted disease.

Syphilis might also have explained the cause of Moo's sister Peggy's early death. I don't know if she knew the underlying reason for her father's mental illness. I have no record of what he was doing, of whether or not he was called up to serve in the armed services during the First World War. But even Moo, whose thinking was not always very logical, must have realised that he was unlikely to be suffering from shell shock if he was not serving abroad in the army during her childhood. And that even if he had been, she was unlikely to have inherited his 'shell shocked' mental state.

I think she knew, and was content to imply something quite different to us three children to protect us, and herself and her father's reputations. In that case, she would have reasoned that what she told us was not a lie, simply an obfuscation of the truth and essential loyalty towards her parents.

Chapter 5

Teacher Training College, Canterbury

It was August 1961, the day that the 'A' level exam results were due. I had recovered from the glandular fever that had kept me stuck in bed for weeks. It started quite suddenly. I had ached all over for several days, been tired and listless which was not like me at all, and Moo suggested, almost impatiently, that I should go to bed after I had fed a neighbour's hens, both of which I agreed to do. After that, for almost a month during that summer term, I was away from school and confined to bed. The doctor visited me regularly at home, my muscles ached. I had a continuously high temperature and for a week I was talking gibberish. I was unable to focus my eyes or my mind. I had no appetite and was allowed no visitors.

Hearing that I was ill and likely to miss a considerable amount of school in such an important term, Miss Gare, my French teacher, lent me a book, delivered it herself to my house. It had nothing to do with French, just something she thought I might like to look at, she said, with very little text, just pictures. It was a book of paintings by Botticelli.

So-called 'culture' in our house was connected to music and literature, it had nothing to do with the visual arts. I had no knowledge of paintings or sculpture: no experience of looking at paintings, let alone appreciating them. But I looked through that book, page after page and then again for several weeks until I was able to hand it back to Miss Gare, in person. And to thank her, from the bottom of my heart.

Neither of us was to know that in a few years' time, I would become the part-owner and part-manager of an art gallery.

Now that I was better, Dad was driving Moo and me across Salisbury Plain on our way to visit Aunty Marian, one of Moo's friends whom we called 'Aunt' out of courtesy. After Aunty Marian retired, she had moved to a bungalow in Charmouth. She was not a relation, although her surname was 'Howard' but she had lodged with Moo in Bedford while she was training to be a teacher. Aunty Marian became the head of a girls' secondary school in Chelmsford. She never married but kept in touch with Moo and she looked upon me almost as her niece. Moo always tried to keep in contact with friends and relatives, she was good like that, saw it as her role.

I wasn't particularly fond of Aunty Marian, I thought she lacked physical warmth, but I appreciated her and was grateful to her. A couple of years before this current visit, after she had retired and when I was about fourteen, Aunty Marian had wanted to spend two weeks in Switzerland during the summer holidays. She had asked Moo whether she would allow me to accompany her, as Marian's companion, she said. Moo agreed, knowing probably that she and Dad would never be able to afford a holiday abroad, especially not one that included me; and anyway, Dad was very doubtful about the idea of him going abroad at all.

He said that foreigners ate strange food like onions and garlic - and pizza, which he had never tasted but pronounced the word with assumed disgust, wrinkling his nose, his mouth in a grimace and the double zz pronounced as in 'jazz' and the letter 'i' short, to rhyme with 'whizzer'. Dad also told me 'I think the French are an indecisive bunch, they can't make up their minds about anything.'

I must have looked puzzled because he went on to explain 'I realised this at school during my once-a-week French lessons because, when I and the other boys had to say in class what we were doing that day, we were told to start with something that sounded like 'Oh, should we' - just as French boys would do', he said. I wasn't sure if he was being serious, once I realised to which French expression he was referring. Dad had very limited understanding of the French language but he also had a wicked sense of humour and would often tease me, and other people.

Aunty Marian and I had flown from an airport in Hampshire called Blackbushe. I already had a passport because that Easter I had been to stay with my foreign exchange student near Versailles, where I had felt quite homesick; but I had not travelled by plane before, nor stayed in a hotel. I don't know where the plane landed but I remember having breakfast in Basel station, warm crusted bread rolls with real butter and black cherry jam, before we caught the train to Lucerne and crossed the lake.

I loved the little Swiss town of Engelberg, nestling in a hanging valley between two ranges of mountains. I was amazed by the strident blue of the gentians, by discovering, once the clouds cleared, how very far up into the sky the mountains tops reached - and the workings of the funicular railway that hauled visitors as far as Gerschnialp, with the cable car that would take people on and upwards from there. And I treasured the illustrated map of the area that I had bought, showing all the paths and cable cars, and their routes.

As the coach entered Engelberg, I saw the word 'zimmer' written on several signs near wooden chalets, signs which I took to indicate that the owners had a room there that visitors could rent. I don't know how I knew that – unless Aunty Marian told me - because I don't think that at that stage, I had started to learn German. If I ever come across my school record book, I must check on that because reading and understanding the word 'zimmer' may even have triggered my interest in the language.

Long after this visit to Switzerland with Aunty Marian, years later and during the year after my first husband Richard had left us and perhaps to assert my new-found ability to make my own decisions, I decided to put together what little money I had, pack the car and take my three children camping to Yugoslavia. They were teenagers by then and my desire, almost my need to travel, augmented by the family annual caravan touring holidays and that visit to Switzerland with Aunty Marian, had become ingrained in me. Travel equated to stimulus. Travel raised questions in any thinking person.

Years later, on our return journey from Yugoslavia, I and the children would visit Engelberg out of nostalgia. I wanted to show them a place that had had such a huge effect on me, to know if it had changed, whether the pine inside the wooden boxes that the gift shops sold still smelled the same, whether the bells on the leather collars around the cows' necks still rang out in the same comforting sound. And whether the locals would greet us as they had greeted Aunty Marian and me, with a smiling 'grüezi' when we encountered each other on a path through the hay meadows. I was not disappointed. And by then, I would use my school-acquired German to respond, and to ask for things in shops and in the café.

Before taking the German 'A' level exam, I had applied to read German and Philosophy at University and been offered a place, subject to satisfactory grades. I don't remember which university but somewhere non-prestigious, not Cambridge, certainly. I had enjoyed studying German at school more than I had French, despite the German teacher writing in my school report that he found my behaviour to be, in his word, 'girlish'. I had no idea what he meant by that. And although I had no real idea either what the German and Philosophy course might involve, it sounded interesting.

As a back-up application, just in case something went wrong, I had put down 'Christ Church Teacher Training College' as my last choice, purely because it was in Canterbury, a city that was vaguely familiar and where, years before, Dad had gone to school. It was advertised as a completely new college, due to open in September 1962 and founded by the Church of England.

Dad stopped the car somewhere after Salisbury Plain and I telephoned the grammar school from a public phone box.

When they told me my 'A' level results, I felt sick. German? Failed. Latin? Failed. How I wished I had stuck to what I had really wanted to study, forgotten Latin and any preposterous idea of my applying to Cambridge, ignored Moo and Val and her possible response to my success or failure, and instead of all that, had taken 'A' level English. I had scraped only a pass in French. I was bewildered, empty. My chance of university had gone, completely. I was in floods of tears and shock. I had never failed an exam before, I couldn't take it in, couldn't believe it.

All the comforting that my mother offered was lost on me. I had worked hard over the two years, I knew I had. But glandular fever had hit me just at the time when I should have been revising early each morning, re-reading the German and French novels and plays, re-reading Part IV of The Aeneid, swotting really hard each day, just as I had done for 'O' levels.

Instead, I had been stuck in bed, unable to move, unable to eat, unable even to think for several weeks. Completely debilitated.

I had taken my first exam, the 'general paper' that all candidates were obliged to take, sitting at a table on my own in the school's sick room, in case I was still infectious. I was thought to have sufficiently recovered to take my chosen subjects with my class mates a fortnight later, in the school hall sitting in rows. My result for the 'general paper', the compulsory exam I had taken in isolation, was excellent. But that didn't count, it didn't count at all. I was in despair, in tears, in disbelief.

Whatever, I asked, could I do with one miserable French 'A' level? Absolutely nothing, I concluded. I didn't possess the emotional or mental resources to cope with this level of failure. I had failed my parents and let myself down. Utterly.

When we reached Charmouth, Moo explained to Aunty Marian why I looked so upset, red-eyed. All the 'never mind, Dear' placatory soothing bounced off me. Then I was asked what my second and third choices had been, still were. My second choice of university was irrelevant, I explained, because it was still a university and still required more than one measly French pass. And my third, Aunty Marian asked? 'A teacher training college,' I almost spat out, 'and I don't want to become a teacher. There are too many of them in our family, in the world.'

Hardly a tactful remark in front of an ex-headmistress but I meant it. I wanted to do something different, to be something different.

I had never wanted to be a teacher. I was the youngest in the family, had no cousins, I didn't know anything about children, had no experience of them. I wanted to do something as an occupation that would use my hands and my head together. At one time I had liked the idea of becoming an occupational therapist, like Dad's distant cousin Joan. And Joan had been able, within her profession, to work abroad and in her case, Denmark.

I fancied that occupational therapy might allow me to make willow baskets or something like that, and earn a reasonable salary in doing so, and helping other people to get better. I liked using my hands, making things. But I hadn't taken any 'O' level science subjects so I lacked any of the knowledge of human biology that I assumed I would need for occupational therapy.

Reluctantly, I resigned myself to attending at least an interview at this new teacher training college. I could see whether there was anything I could do there with my French 'A' level that could help me find an occupation I might enjoy. I didn't even possess the College prospectus, if there were one.

The next hurdle was that Dad hadn't realised that Christ Church College was a Church of England institution. 'Could you not have found a college supported by a non-conformist church', he wondered, 'if you had to put down a training college at all, done something more in keeping with family expectations?' To counter his objection, he went on 'But I suppose Christ Church College is situated in Canterbury, the same city in which I was educated years ago at Simon Langton Boys School.'

Somehow, for Dad, that made it all right. Or if not all right, a little less wrong. It was a city he knew, one he liked, it was familiar. We had once or twice driven through Canterbury on our way by car to Sandgate to visit my grandparents and I remembered seeing the walls, ancient and thick, that enclosed the city, and being very impressed by them and by Westgate Towers as an entrance into the main street. They furthered my interest in history, the same interest that had taken me, and Grandpa, several times to Dover Castle. So perhaps, at this Christ Church place and in the city itself, there would be plenty of history to inspire me?

The interview took place during the summer of 1962 in St Martin's Priory. The College had no buildings of its own except the Priory. Moo said that an interview was a formal occasion so she advised me to dress formally. And to wear a hat. I didn't have a hat, other than my green corduroy prefect's beret with a silk tassel, and a hand-knitted bobble hat purchased at some church bazaar. So, I borrowed, and wore, a navy one that Moo had sometimes worn to church. I don't remember what else, a coat probably if I had one, or a mac of some sort.

Miss Young, who introduced herself as the Vice-Principal and who conducted the interview, asked me about my exam results and so on. She then explained that the college didn't offer

French as one of its main subjects, it offered only English, Divinity, Science, Geography or Maths - so which of these would I choose, were I to be accepted?

While I was at Letchworth Grammar School, I had taken 'O' levels in all of these except science and obtained good pass marks in each; therefore, science was out of the question. There had been a timetable clash at the Grammar School which had meant that I had been unable to study both English Literature and Religious Education in the same year. That had disappointed me, as I valued both.

So, Moo had kindly offered to find, and pay for, a private tutor for me after school hours for English Literature and had negotiated with the school that I could take the English Literature 'O' level exam if my external tutor thought I would pass it. And I had passed it with quite good marks, despite having only skim-read Thomas Hardy's 'Under the Greenwood Tree', which was one of the set books.

Now, at interview, I was presented with the possibility of being taught English Literature at the college and discussing it in a group along with other people.

I immediately opted for English as my main subject. And, although I had no experience of young children, I liked even less the idea of teaching classes of secondary school children who might behave like my sister Val. Instead, I selected 'infant/junior' as my preferred age range. Choices made, then. All I had to do was to wait to see whether I was accepted.

I had selected this particular college rather than Homerton in Cambridge which would have been nearer, partly because

Christ Church was to be mixed. I had never stayed in a house or attended any school that didn't include both genders, it seemed peculiar to me to do otherwise.

My best friend John B. was going to St Mark and St John's College, known as 'Marjon,' in Chelsea but that was for men only. Perhaps John and I would be able to meet sometimes in London. We could still be best friends, and tell each other about our teaching experiences, about life in college. Except that I wasn't to be, as he would be, living 'in college'.

A letter from Miss Young, the Vice-Principal, received a week later informed me formally that I was accepted by the college, and that unless I planned to live at home and travel to Canterbury daily (out of the question), I would be spending my first year in digs in Ethelbert Road, near the hospital in Canterbury. Although there would be about seventy-five of us, mainly women, in that first-year cohort, there was no college living accommodation, no hall or gender-specific block due to be built until the following year.

However forceful Miss Young had been in her previous post in charge of a women's training college in London, she had been completely out-gunned by Mrs Stevens, the person who was to be my landlady. I later learned that Mrs Stevens had told Miss Young that she wouldn't accept students unless they would be in equal numbers and from both genders.

All other digs in that first year were single-gender lodgings, spread across Canterbury, the outskirts and surrounding villages. So, there were to be six of us lodging together, three young men and three young women, almost straight out of school and in the college's only mixed digs.

As it transpired, I was to live there along with Kanchana from Thailand who suggested we should call her 'Karn', Janet from the Lake District, Mick from the Isle of Sheppey, Anthony from Halifax in Yorkshire and a dark-haired John from the Southampton area.

Karn and Anthony each had a single room while Janet and I, and John and Mick, were given twin rooms. We would all eat breakfast and our evening meal together with Mrs Stevens in the formal dining room but lunch, we were told, would be provided somewhere closer to The Priory.

Looking back, I am now embarrassed and ashamed to realise how self-centred I was and how unempathetically I behaved towards Karn. There she was, in a strange country, not able to speak English very fluently, separated by thousands of miles from her family, with no close friends and no one from her own country to talk to. As far as we were aware, coming to England and going to a teacher training college hadn't been her choice.

It appeared, from what Karn said, that it had been her parents' idea, mainly to help her find a husband, we supposed. We did try to befriend Karn, of course. But not very hard and with hindsight, certainly not hard enough - and it was difficult to relate to Karn.

Mrs Stevens once suggested that Karn might help her to cook and serve a Thai evening meal, to give us an example of the sort of food that Thai people might enjoy, and to make her feel more at home. But I gathered that Karn didn't know how to cook, that the servants in her family had always done the food shopping and the cooking.

I was keen to stay in contact with my school-friend John partly because there were many women's teacher training colleges in the vicinity of Marjon. Although he was my best friend, I didn't trust he would be able to resist exploring the field once he had left home, especially if he and a group of lads went out together for the evening.

John had admitted kissing a girl from the farm during one family holiday in Devon and I had been quite upset by such 'infidelity', as I thought, on his part.

My first experiment with sex had been on the rear seat of their family car that year in a darkened farmyard, strongly encouraged by John.

At the time, we referred to this as 'sexual intercourse', the longer description seemed to indicate a more protracted, more considered process than did the rather snappy over-in-a-flash word 'sex' – or 'shag'. Most of my knowledge about sex came from John. Not that he had had any experience himself as a teenager but, as my best friend, I could ask him things and even discuss with him what we both didn't know.

My mother had told me where babies came from when I was quite young but hadn't gone into any detail as to how that embryo got there in the first place. It all seemed very strange, almost like magic and just as exciting; and naughty.

I had acquired a sketchy idea of some of this from delving into the pages of a third-year biology text book. It featured both the horseshoe pattern beneath a horse chestnut twig, which was our subject for study during that term and further on, well-thumbed pages showing the reproduction of the rabbit, with labelling and line drawings of the organs.

As a D.I.Y guide, it wasn't much help. I knew some of the words, though. According to my class-mates, all 'rude' words, the ones we shouldn't know about and mustn't mention out loud during lessons, began with the letter 'P'.

These were 'pregnancy', 'pubic', 'puberty', 'penis', 'periods', 'pants' plus, rather oddly 'pelvis', presumably because it was also located in the same region of the body. More well-thumbed pages in the school-issued and non-illustrated dictionaries.

Val said she thought the term 'district nurse' also signified something rude that we should not know about, presumably because a district nurse had been in the habit of visiting Nenna regularly for personal care and for those visit, we children were instructed to stay downstairs and well out of the way.

Although Moo was happy to parade her naked body in the upstairs of our house, my father and Colin were always well covered up. I needed to ask John, and in the privacy of our garage under the pretence of fiddling with our bikes, to feel him through his school trousers, in order to understand the topography of the male human body. And, if I felt hard enough, its responses.

The question of actual 'sexual intercourse' came up when we were on holiday in Devon with John's parents and younger brother Gerald. With as much a need to investigate as any physical desire and coerced by John, we thought that the rear seat of John's father's car, parked in the darkened farmyard, was the ideal place. It was dry, comfortable (or so we thought – so much for theory), private and we would hear anyone coming.

But the width and lack of space in the car rear compartment resulted in a need to wind down one of the rear side windows in order to stick the calves of my legs out of it – and even in that uncomfortable and exposed position, full intercourse still wasn't achievable - which I had found quite a relief because John and I were still afraid of pregnancy, of the shame and embarrassment it would cause us and both our families.

No one had told us anything much about contraception, only that sex, unless we were married, was wrong and un-Christian. So, what might John do in his own private room in Chelsea for three whole years, I wondered?

For Anthony, one of my fellow students and fellow lodgers who had been a pupil at Batley Grammar and whose family had only recently moved to Halifax, the south of England was totally new. When he had travelled by train from Yorkshire to Canterbury, it was, he told us, the first time he had been to London. Anthony, Janet, dark-haired John and I all enjoyed walking in the nearby Kent countryside, snug in our recently-purchased navy duffle coats. We would spend many an afternoon exploring the local villages in pairs, Janet with John, Anthony with me, until the snow came that winter of 1962-63.

The snow was thick. Temperatures had started to plummet during the previous December, with a large amount of snowfall on Boxing Day in parts of Kent, turning green to white.

I travelled back from Letchworth to London by train, crossed London on the Underground, then caught a train to Canterbury East and heaved my suitcase in the snow up the Old Dover Road and into Ethelbert Road.

At first, the city and the buildings were pretty but the novelty of snow soon wore off as the six of us had to trudge in cold wellingtons along the snowy paths from Ethelbert

Road, across snowy roads, through snowy alleyways, up snowy rises, coming into the Priory through the front door, kicking the snow from our boots, shaking the snow off our duffle coats, warming our wet gloves and freezing fingers as best we could in the oak-panelled main room and the library.

Towards the end of the second week of freezing temperatures, we heard that the sea at Herne Bay was frozen.

Catching a bus, Anthony and I travelled to Herne Bay to see this phenomenon. Making our way through the snow to the beach, we saw frozen foam in long drifts lying on the shingle just above the water line. The sea was milky grey, with patches of ice moving lethargically with the tide. On the promenade, shards of ice that had been cleared from the shore became jagged mounds, piled up like fallen brick rubble. I took a couple of photographs with my Kodak Brownie camera because I wanted to remember how extraordinary it was. And how biting the cold.

The big freeze lasted until March 1963. The snow didn't melt away. Slowly, little by little, it evaporated until the concrete slabs on the pavements appeared pale and dry, with grey edging like Victorian funeral cards, where only a thin frame of dirty snow remained.

During the spring and summer terms, Anthony and I would hitchhike to places of interest in Kent, quite often to the coast. We joined the rambling society which Hilary organised; a group of about fifteen of us would be taken to a fixed point and make our way from there back to Canterbury.

I met John B. a couple of times in London during our first year as college students. He was keen to show me proudly around Soho as if it were his local area and assumed a detailed knowledge of the fashionable places to go, and which celebrity could be seen and where. I didn't think John had ever been inside 'Les Enfants Terribles' in Dean Street but if he had, it would have been only for a cup of coffee or as a gesture of rebellion, a sign that he was becoming his own man, because, in his preaching, Rev. Smart had spoken more than once against coffee bars, referring to them as 'dens of iniquity'.

From his grant, John had managed to afford contact lenses. He hated being prescribed spectacles for reading and he rarely wore them. He didn't like my wearing glasses either, said they spoiled my face, so I took the opportunity while in London to visit an optician who prescribed contact lenses for me too.

These were hard lenses, quite small, no bigger than the iris of an eye that needed to be inserted and removed with a tiny device rather like a minute sink plunger. Getting any grit behind a lens was excruciatingly painful so having paid out what to me was almost a term's grant, I resorted to wearing my spectacles unless I were meeting John or at a college social event.

Living and studying now in different places, John and I were growing apart. He was finding new friends among the women from Whitelands Training College that stood on King's Road, Chelsea.

I invited Anthony to stay at our house for a couple of days one Easter on his return journey to Canterbury. I introduced John and Anthony to each other, but I don't think either of them thought much of the other. John made it quite clear to me afterwards that he disapproved of Anthony coming into his local area, guest or not.

Christ Church being a new college, with no history, no social or Students' Union infra-structure, we students needed to decide and devise this for ourselves. With permission gained through the college authorities, we used the Red Cross Hall that stood on the corner of Longport and Littlebourne Road for any social events.

Realising that we needed a fellow student to take charge to make day-to-day decisions on our behalf, during the first term we agreed that Mike Wagg and Gillian Wills would be President and Vice-President, with a secretary, treasurer and social secretary to help get college life going. Mike was a good leader and did a great deal of ground work with the Students' Union.

As the snow dissipated, we were able to watch the foundations being laid for the buildings that were to become the women's hostel block. This was so close to the prison that once the blocks were built and the women had moved in, if we dared, we and the male prisoners could wave at each other from the upper rooms.

At the lower end of the site stood the men's smaller hostel block. Then came the 'junior common room' with the refectory above, the senior common room for our lecturers, toilets, an entrance hall, a main hall where we would be able to hold future social events, a room that was to become the library, lecture rooms and offices for tutors, a corridor of music practice rooms and a chapel with tall, triangular windows that let in plenty of light. There was also a quadrangle planned and a small pond for fish.

As the end of my first year at college approached and a second intake of students was due in September 1963, several initiatives were abandoned. One of the first to go was the attempt by our Mathematics lecturer, Alf Flight, to introduce a sung mass by composer Healey Willan. We gave it a try for several Sundays in St Martin's Church and at evening rehearsals but it either proved too difficult for a bunch of non-music students or required too many rehearsals. Both probably. We resorted to a more familiar sung mass.

The second initiative had also been introduced to us by Alf Flight. This was an approach to maths that involved looking at segmented windows, especially those semi-circular windows above doorways, and from the number of sections, considering the various angles, computations and sizes of each pane of glass. I can't remember exactly what the mathematical purpose was except to make us look, take notice and think, but I cannot even now see a semi-circular window above an entrance door without remembering Dr Flight.

A third initiative that I think began with Dr Mason, the college Principal, was to try to bring together science and religion. That didn't work either, so a new course was introduce for our second year, called 'Civilisation'. In a word, this appeared to incorporate almost everything anyone knew about anything, from the history of Sudan to the different varieties of cheese that was first mentioned by our tutor Dr Armstrong-James in his introductory education lesson. We students liked Dr Armstrong-James but he left after the first year in college. Apparently, he and Dr Mason had had a row about something and the following year, A-J as he was known, was gone.

If this all sounds very hit-and-miss, a hotchpotch curriculum, then yes, it was. But the good thing about that was that we were able to give feedback, to say that so-and-so wasn't working, long before students at the London School of

Economics began complaining about the content of their courses. And things at Christ Church College changed, there was a general sharpening up.

I was extremely happy there both in my accommodation and in the lectures and seminars. It was somewhere where I felt able to contribute, my views were listened to, my opinion seemed to matter and I could make certain choices about my own life and how I might wish to lead it.

I had a good social life. With such a limited number of students, everybody knew everyone else, at least by name, although the men seemed to stick together and most of the women did the same. There were restrictions, of course. But not many and in general, it was a free-and-easy place.

I didn't cut any lectures, I found the books or plays we were reading in English were interesting, I didn't miss a deadline for handing in work and it was given back to me on time, marked clearly and helpfully. By the second year, I had a room on the first floor of 'Temple' within the women's block, among fellow students whom I liked, and several freshers, new women just starting as part of the college's second year intake.

During the summer vacation, I was offered a paid job in Normandy, speaking English to the grandchildren of Mme Jacquinot, wife of the then French Minister of State. Mme Jacquinot was very keen that seven-year-old Emmanuel and Inès, aged five or six, should learn to speak English. My sister Val had had this job a year earlier and had even travelled with the family to Verbier for skiing. The children had a Polish nanny called Toya, who took care of them while they were staying in Normandy, where Mme. Jacquinot rented the 'Chateau des Roches' on the edge of Trouville.

The chateau, a building with turrets in traditional Loire valley style, stood on a slight outcrop overlooking the sandy beach and the sea. The children ate breakfast somewhere separate with Toya in their own quarters.

I would sit alone in the dining room at the end of a very long wooden table and my breakfast was served to me each morning by Guy, the butler. By eleven o'clock, Toya, the children and I would be on the beach, normally regardless of the weather. If it were raining too hard, then we would all don our waterproofs and set out to walk along the beach towards Deauville for some fresh air. We had our own blue beach umbrella, which offered shelter in sunny weather and a location point on the sand.

Most of the time, Emmanuel would build a sand castle or, if he were not getting his own way, would sit rocking forwards and back on the concrete step where the walkway ended and the beach began. Toya didn't like him being there on his own for very long, although he was well within sight and only fifty yards away. She was concerned he might sustain some injury or be kidnapped. I could see that the latter might be a blessing, especially when he was in a thunderous mood.

Inès was lovely, with a sunny nature. There were two other children, Sylvie and Patrique, almost the same ages and with whom they were allowed to play because they were Guy's children and were living in the basement of the same building.

I saw the parents of Emmanuel and Inès only once in the two months I was at the Chateau des Roches. Their father André de Seignard, Marquis de La Fressange, was from old French nobility and their mother had been an Argentinian model. They arrived at the beach unexpectedly and left the same day. Since those days, Inès[vi] has become famous.

I was in touch by letter with Anthony while I was in France. I missed him, I missed having anyone else English with whom I could hold a proper conversation, there was little in the evenings to amuse me or keep me busy once formal dinner was over. One evening, I took myself to the cinema in Deauville to watch a film about an invasion of ants on the march across parts of Africa, which was slightly unsettling.

If I walked as far as Deauville along the beach after lunch while the children were having their rest, I would read the headlines of the French newspapers on the stand. I saw some of the accounts of national concerns regarding John Profumo, Christine Keeler, Mandy Rice-Davis and Dr Steven Ward but it made little impact on me, except to see that there were goings-on in London that were unexplained, and that somehow sexual intercourse and modelling were involved. Other than that, I read a series of novels in either English or translated into French but without a companion, I often felt lonely.

Because I knew he was good company, I wrote to Anthony suggesting that once he had finished his holiday job with Crossley Carpets in Halifax, he might hitchhike to Normandy and join me, then the two of us could spend the rest of our vacation hitching across France, Germany and Switzerland until it was time to return to college.

We both had rucksacks hung on metal frames, sheet sleeping bags and membership of the Youth Hostel Association. We would be free to travel until we ran out of time and money.

In late August or early September, Anthony arrived at the main door of the Chateau des Roches. I had warned Guy that I might have a visitor and asked if that would be all right. It would, he said, and should he make up a separate room or would Anthony be sleeping in my room? He said something about love and sleeping together being wonderful. I told him 'I won't be doing that, we English behave quite differently - so please could Anthony have his own room, but not far from mine as he doesn't speak French? And we will be leaving together tomorrow to start on our travels.'

Guy offered to give us a lift into Paris as he and his wife Minette would be returning to work in the Jacquinots' main home in the avenue Charles Floquet, not far from the Eiffel Tower. He said he would find us somewhere in the apartment to sleep, which he did, downstairs on a couple of couches. Anthony and I left the apartment the following morning, having thanked Guy.

Donning our rucksacks, we made for the nearest Metro station that would take us out of central Paris and as far as the southern suburbs of the city. From there, with maps in hands, we would start hitching.

I don't remember much of that trip. I know we went to Troyes and stayed at the Youth Hostel there. I think it was there where, by torchlight, I encountered strange black creatures climbing up the walls of the outside unlit lavatories. I thought they might be scorpions but I didn't know if scorpions lived that far north. But I used the facilities very carefully after seeing them.

I know we travelled close to the Swiss and German borders, visiting Strasbourg and Mulhouse, then Basel and on into Switzerland, where we spent several nights at Engelberg Youth Hostel. I wondered whether it would be possible to plan a trip for a group of us students the following year, to spend a week or so at the Youth Hostel, so that other people could have as much enjoyment as Anthony and I were having, exploring the area, walking in the hay meadows and riding in the cable cars to the mountain slopes.

On our journey across Switzerland and back north, we certainly got to Geneva, because I remember seeing the Palace of Nations, the United Nations building on a hill, and finding how difficult it was to get a lift from there, how far out of Geneva we had to walk before anyone would stop. I remember that journey particularly because it was during that drive towards Paris that we saw a sign near an area of cleared land that read 'Chantier interdit au public'[vii]. Anthony and I puzzled over what that meant, until our English driver worked it out and confidently informed us that it must mean 'no singing in public' - an instruction that puzzled us even more.

As a relationship, the friendship between Anthony and me worked quite well. We didn't fall out at all and we didn't argue. But partly because of circumstances, I seemed to be the one taking the lead. I wasn't sure what Anthony was contributing in terms of my own development, whereas John B, with his father and his brother Gerald, had taught me about their hobby of photography, about red lights and no lights when developing a film, about printing - and about bicycles, of course.

Although I had seen films like 'A Taste of Honey' and 'Saturday Night and Sunday Morning' that portrayed life in the north of England, I had no personal experience and little understanding of the north of the country, the attitudes of its people, the landscape and much of the history. I was invited to stay with Anthony and his parents in their council house in Mixenden on the outskirts of Halifax. Anthony and I hitchhiked north from Canterbury.

His mother welcomed us warmly and offered me the spare room – although it might not have been a spare; perhaps Anthony's brother vacated his room for me and moved in with Anthony for a few days. His younger brother, who suffered from acne and whose name I have forgotten, had a girl-friend named 'Dell' or 'Dellie'. She had left school aged fifteen and worked in a factory, doing something that made her hands look red, sore and raw. I had no knowledge of factory work. Coming over the hill in a car and seeing Halifax in the valley below, I was struck by the degree of smoke belching from the chimneys across the town.

We caught a bus from the centre of Halifax to Mixenden, which I remember as being on a slight hill, and walked to the house from where the bus dropped us. I washed my hair in the bathroom of that house. I stuck my head under the hot tap and turned it on.

There was a persistent searing pain in my scalp. I jerked my head up again, banged it on the tap, quickly turned the tap off and groped for a towel. I remember that sharp pain on my scalp. The water had been scalding hot, something I had never encountered anywhere before. Our water at home was heated by a Rayburn and did not reached that sort of temperature.

Once my scalp cooled down and stopped being so painful, I had a second attempt at washing my hair. What I noticed then, more than anything else, was how the shampoo lathered and how soft the water felt on my fingers. I had heard about water being 'hard' or 'soft' but this was the first time I knew what that really meant.

One day, Anthony and I caught the bus to Haworth, the Pennine village where the Bronte sisters, Charlotte, Emily and

Anne, had grown up and where they had written their novels. We visited the Parsonage Museum. I saw some of the floral-patterned frocks on display that the sisters would have worn and was amazed at how small their waists must have been.

But although the Parsonage was a worthwhile place to visit, I would have liked to have seen the houses or inns that were the original bases for Wuthering Heights and Thrushcross Grange. Anthony told me that 'Top Withens', a ruined farmhouse near Haworth, was said to have been the inspiration for the location of the Earnshaw family house 'Wuthering Heights'. I would have liked to have made our way to it to experience the atmosphere but Anthony told me there was nothing to see, just a ruin.

Mrs R., Anthony's mother, appeared to assume that Anthony (whose name she pronounced as it was written, with the 'th' with her tongue between her teeth, as in Bournemouth) and I would become engaged, very soon. She didn't actually voice this but this assumption lay behind much of what she said.

I gained the impression that she considered I would be a good daughter-in-law; not me personally, because she had only just met me, but that she considered I came from a 'good' and 'acceptable' family, with money and property.

I suspected Anthony as the source of this rather doubtful information and that his mother had looked on it very favourably indeed, with a degree of pride despite her sending a few sidelong verbal shots towards 'Dellie' about girls not getting pregnant too soon or rushing into making any life decisions.

She needn't have worried. Anthony was a good friend but with limitations, as far as I was concerned. He took himself very seriously, he could be melodramatic and he didn't appear to value other people's property.

When Mrs Stevens had asked both of us to go into the loft of her house and sort out some of her books, I was aghast to find Anthony ripping the dust covers of each of the hard-backs. When I had asked him why he was doing that, he said it was because he didn't like dust covers, found them a nuisance.

He had slightly different principles from any I had encountered before and he seemed more enthusiastic than I to endorse the views of Enoch Powell, which one of our hitchhiking lifts had repeated while taking us through a northern factory area, about the impact on the immigration debate in Great Britain and referring to 'rivers of blood'[viii].

The following year in his single room in college, Anthony and I engaged in some foreplay but neither of us was prepared to assume that his room was soundproof, nor to take the risk of my becoming pregnant. Anthony was too ashamed to be caught buying condoms from the chemist or from the newsagent in Longport; he didn't see the point either of spending on a deodorant for himself and anyway, as I had discovered, he had a spotty back.

Towards the end of our first year at Christ Church, we were told by the National Union of Students that our current Executive was obliged to resign, that we needed to appoint new officers. Having only seventy-five people at the college, there wasn't a huge range of choice, especially when we took out of the equation those who weren't interested. But by far the most obvious people for these posts were Peter J. and Hilary, both of whom seemed quite naturally to command authority. They were both duly appointed, with Ray C. and Wendy T. acting as treasurer and secretary respectively.

Peter seemed to get on particularly well with the authorities at the cathedral, without any dissemblance or sycophancy on his part. Hilary had the backing of the 'House of Women', the name we gave to the digs in which she and seven other female students were lodging. They both did an excellent job while not neglecting their academic studies in any way, and both were highly respected by Dr Fred Mason, the Principal and his Vice-Principal Miss Young.

September 1963 brought a second intake of students to Christ Church, with an increase in main subjects that were offered for study. A bursar, Mr Knight, was appointed by the college authorities to deal with the increased financial demands, and the Reverend Neville, who worn a shiny black leather jacket and drove a Citroen Safari car, was appointed as college chaplain.

'Art' was added to the list of possible main courses with Colin Dudley, whom we students called 'Cuddly Dudley' as the new tutor. Tony Edwards was the college librarian who took care of the increased number of books, and loans and unreturned or 'missing' books. And music was also becoming increasingly important.

During this year at the college, two students were sent down for behaviour that the Principal and Vice-Principal decided was unacceptable, particular in a Church of England college and amongst adults training to be teachers to lead young people.

Arriving in the year after mine, Linda was fairly buxom and had long blond hair. When she first took up position in the lower common room, leaning backwards against a radiator and thrusting her bust forward, she announced, flicking back her long hair and with a cheeky grin to anyone who was in the room, 'Now that I'm here, I'm going to be a good girl.' But within a term or two, Ian, one of the first-year cohort, had been found in Linda's room engaging in intimate behaviour, so rumour had it, and despite each being over eighteen, that was sufficient for Dr Mason to send them both down, to require each of them to leave the college. For good.

A year on and he was telling two students, one male, the other female and attracted to each other, that they must keep away from each other while in college. They were both over twenty-one years of age. As far as I know, neither of them argued with this decree or considered it beyond the Principal's remit. Most of us just did as we were told, we considered it to be the norm.

We students decided that Christ Church College students needed a student newspaper. As a way of getting things started, Neale, who appeared a year or two older than the rest of our year, called together a group of people who might be interested.

We compiled this production by writing individual short pieces, typing them on a typewriter, cutting the relevant passage from the paper on which it had been typed, positioning it and pasting it onto larger sheets. When we were satisfied with it, Neale would take these sheets to somewhere in the city and have them copied double-sided onto A3 sheets of paper.

These were then folded by members of a working group and put together to form a newspaper. We called this publication

'Insight' and charged 1d or one old penny for it. We also published a termly magazine, called 'Bestiary', to which students could subscribe articles, poems or short stories. We adopted the name from the illustrated natural history bestiaries of the Middle Ages.

By Easter that year, I had researched and put together an itinerary for an accompanied trip to Switzerland for up to fifteen students, staying at Engelberg Youth Hostel. I can't remember the exact cost but I planned that we would cross the English Channel and travel by train together as far as Lucerne, cross the lake at Lucerne by ferry and catch the little funicular train with wooden slatted seats that ran from Stans up the valley to Engelberg. I typed out the details and posted these on the Students Union notice board in the junior common room, inviting people to sign up if they were interested. People began adding their names.

In the summer term of 1964, the serving Executive was required to resign and new prospective candidates for the various posts were invited to put themselves forward.

Almost at the same time as I advertised this trip to Switzerland, I decided to stand for election as Vice-President in my final year at Christ Church. Anthony thought he might also stand for President. I didn't think he would make a very good President, especially coming after Peter J. who had done such a good job in promoting the college and working with city and cathedral representatives.

But I didn't like to say so to Anthony, it wouldn't have been very supportive of me. Neither did I want him to think that everything I did, he was destined to follow or copy.

As it happened, two other people put their names forward. Someone called Barbara from the second intake of students and who was therefore at the end of her first year at Christ Church, found a proposer and a seconder for her to stand as Vice-President. A man called Richard, a mature art student also in his first year at the college, stood for the Presidency.

I knew Richard only by sight. I had seen him around the art department of the college, wearing ill-fitting corduroy trousers and holding the hand of a little girl who looked about three years old. Following the hustings, Richard compiled details of what he had done in his life so far, including being a divinity student at King's College, London for a year until he had got married and had children.

He wrote out his 'manifesto' with a socialist bias, giving reasons as to why he thought he should be elected. I suspect that this clashed with current President Peter's principles.

Peter wrote out his own view of how things should continue and gave this to Richard. Richard reacted by making no comment but posting Peter's writing on the Students Union Notice board, a response which Peter conceded was quite a smart move on Richard's part.

We were both elected, Richard as President and I as Vice-President with considerable majorities. Natasha, or 'Tasha' as she was known, was elected as Secretary but I don't remember the name of our Students Union Treasurer.

Richard and I agreed to allow the summer term to finish properly but to get in touch with each other before the start of the following academic year, so we might begin to plan in detail before the third wave of students was due to start at the college in September 1964.

At the end of the 1963-64 academic year, I led the small group of Christ Church students to Switzerland and back quite successfully. It was possible to arranged several additional day-trips during our stay at Engelberg as well as celebrating Wendy's birthday with a party and Swiss fondue organised through the Hostel.

My parents were still living in Elm Hollow, the house that Dad had designed and had built in Letchworth. But Dad would be sixty on 3rd September 1995 so he was due to retire, which meant he and Moo had to think whether they still needed a five-bedroom house with an acre of garden to manage – or, if they thought it sensible to sell Elm Hollow and buy something smaller, where they might wish to go.

There was still TCP Grandma to consider. Grandpa had died a couple of years earlier, not long after Christmas while staying at our house.

TCP Grandma and Grandpa had become accustomed to coming to stay with us in Letchworth for what TCP Grandma called 'the worst of the winter', which in real terms meant that they would arrive, plus suitcases, sometime in October and be taken by car back to Sandgate by late March or early April the following Spring.

They would sleep in the spare room but spend most of their days downstairs in armchairs stationed by the dining room fireplace.

Neither of Dad's parents was very active by then. Grandpa would still puff on his pipe and TCP Grandma would get on Moo's nerves by telling her what to do, such that Moo would frequently retreat to the kitchen and mutter under her breath. It wasn't in her nature, nor permitted by her upbringing, to say 'Oh, for goodness's sake, do shut up, Woman.' More suppressed tension in the home.

In previous years, TCP Grandma had shown an interest in the Spiritualist Church in Letchworth, the one that Dad disrespectfully referred to as 'the boogie-woogie place' in Gernon Walk. More recently, and being dependent on Dad to take her anywhere, she had been content to sit in her favourite armchair in the dining room, and knit.

She had a penchant for Woolworth's Devon Toffees so whenever Moo had to go into the centre of the town to place her grocery order with Moss Bros the Grocers (we didn't have a telephone by then, that came only later and only as a party line shared with Mrs Coverley who lived next door), Moo would be required to buy a quarter of a pound of Devon Toffees from Woolworth's that would be tipped into TCP Grandma's oblong toffee tin that she kept on the bottom shelf of the tea-trolley. If I were home from college, this trip to Woolworth's would fall on my shoulders too.

TCP Grandma would give me the money first, and in the exact coins. And she would know, to the very one, exactly how many toffees she should receive in that little white paper bag with its top corners screwed and twisted to resemble tiny ears. And she would count. Trust didn't come easily to TCP Grandma.

A week or so before Christmas each year that she was staying with us, TCP Grandma would want to have her hair permed, using a Richard Hudnut home perm - TCP Grandma always misread and mispronounced this, asking for a Richard WhoDunt, as if the process were akin to a detective novel.

She would ask Val to administer the perm if Val were around, Moo if there were no Val. Then me. Moo might correct her because that misreading would irritate Moo, she would talk about and stress Richard H-u-d-n-u-t, all quite pointless because TCP Grandma was a slightly deaf and especially towards any correction or guidance from Moo.

Then we had to locate the curved metal clasps that would create the waves that TCP Grandma liked in her hair. She didn't like anyone using rollers and hairpins, 'They hurt my head' she complained. They also caught on her so-called 'invisible' hairnet.

During the first week of September in what was to be my final year at college, I phoned Richard to ask 'Have you been able yet to all the things we had agreed you would do before the start of term?'

After the initial pleasantries, it transpired that he had done none of them.

'I've been busy buying new Ercol furniture with my mature student grant cheque. I've also spent other days by the sea with my wife Doreen and then visiting my in-laws near Maidstone. So no, I haven't done anything yet, I haven't had time.'

I sighed. I supposed it was understandable. But it meant that all those jobs in preparation for a new intake of students would need to be compressed into one or two days before the official start of term and the new students' arrival.

'In that case,' I responded, 'I will need to arrive two days early at the college - which in turn means that I will need to arrange with the college matron to have my new room in Fisher Tower ready for me. Then we really ought to meet and get things done.'

As I came off the phone after talking to Richard, I swore. 'He is so lazy and unreliable,' I told Moo, who had heard and raised an eyebrow at my language 'that I think a year working with him may prove tricky. He's done nothing that we agreed he'd do.'

That year of running the Students Union was eventful. Some of the new students, keen to shed the shackles of school, found it hard to realise that their learning was their own responsibility and that, even though they were away from the constraints of home, there were rules about locking-up time in the hostels and the requirement to request a pass for a weekend away from college.

Men had to be out of the women's hostels by 9.45pm in the evening and were not permitted there again until after 10am. Similar rules applied to women in the men's hostel.

Having grown used to living at home in a house with animals, I decided that a hamster would provide good company. I kept it in a cage, with its own trundle wheel and a ladder, in the curtained-off space underneath the wash basin in my room. My room, a single as many rooms were, had an adjoining door through to Tasha's room on the other side of Fisher Tower's lift. This was very convenient for working together and it further strengthened our friendship.

We used to compare our body measurements, wrapping a cloth tape-measure not only around our waists and busts but also around our thighs, then calves and wrists to see whether we were growing slimmer – we never did – or even (shock horror) gaining inches.

Tasha was a year younger than I but far more what my mother would have called 'ladylike'. Tasha didn't run anywhere, even if she were late. She had a natural sense of decorum, which I lacked. She got on quite well with Richard, who thought she was wonderful, even though he annoyed her tremendously on occasions.

I would see her grinding her teeth sometimes at something he had done, or not done, while maintaining a diplomatic smile.

He could, and would, do something deliberately to irritate her. And she would refuse to lose her temper or respond in any way that might be considered immodest or unprofessional.

Then Richard told us that his wife Doreen was pregnant, that the baby was due the following Easter. So, there was no chance of her becoming involved, or even interested, in the life of the college. She had other things on her mind by then.

This left Richard with a choice between non-participation or apparent disinterest in the college social life. He could either avoid the monthly college dances, go on his own and hope to find a female partner, or invite someone else, probably a woman from his art course.

Neither Tasha nor I offered to partner him, we didn't feel it was our responsibility. And by this time, Anthony was being insistent about coming to my room every evening for coffee before chucking-out time at 9.45pm.

I didn't invite him, he just turned up each evening without exception, unless there were a dance on in the new hall, in which case, he insisted on dancing every dance with me. Not that anyone else ever offered to dance with me, possibly because Anthony was always there at my side. And he was a good dancer, or at least and according to my memory, we danced well together.

Nor did Anthony ever suggest he might have a different partner for a dance or two. Where I was concerned, he was adherent. Velcroed to my elbow. I found it both annoying and reassuring, useful but constraining. It was not my choice but, like so much else during my childhood and adolescence, I accepted it.

On one occasion in early February that year, Richard made some wry comment about being so sorry for his poor postman, having to struggle to his front door with such a heavy sack on Valentine's Day, that Tasha and I decided to call Richard's bluff.

We each made several really soppy Valentine cards, complete with red satin-material hearts, popped them unsigned into envelopes and posted them into Richard's designated pigeon hole by the door through to the tutors' office block.

We waited to see the reaction.

But Richard took them seriously, didn't realise the cards were a joke, perhaps didn't even remember the remarks he had made to us about his 'poor postman'. Instead, he assumed he had several admirers. We decided not to own up, that it would be unkind to do so, he looked so pleased with himself.

In 1965, Her Majesty the Queen was due to distribute the Maundy Money to the elderly citizens of Canterbury that Easter. At the same time, while visiting the city and as head of the Church of England, it was considered fitting for her to visit Christ Church College as the first new Church of England College for many years, to see the chapel and to open it officially. It would take place during the college's Easter holiday but Richard and I were asked to attend.

It was also proposed for Dr Mason as Principal and Richard as President to show the Queen around the building and for me to accompany the Duke of Edinburgh. I had a black and white photograph somewhere of the pair of us, Richard and me, standing in the entrance hall and shaking hands with the Queen.

As I watched the maroon royal cars coming down the college driveway, I felt incredibly nervous. But once the Queen was inside the building and meeting Dr Mason, my shyness fell away, because I had a job to do. Dr Mason may also have been nervous, because he muddled up the arrangements and instead of Richard accompanying the Queen and the Duke of Edinburgh being with me, I found I was accompanying the Queen.

Although I had thought about what to say to the Duke, I was overcome with the idea that, if I initiated any introduction to the Queen or spoke before she did, that she might suddenly say 'Off with her head' and have me hauled away and decapitated on the spot. Ridiculous, of course.

But the 'Alice in Wonderland' thought was there and no matter how much Dr Mason hissed his 'introduce so-and-so' instruction in my ear, the thought persisted and I couldn't and I didn't. And anyway, it had been his error in the first place.

Much of the rest of that day is now a haze. I do remember how the Queen seemed to take real pleasure from her visit to the college library and having the time to look at some of the children's picture books that we had there.

Anthony was standing in one of the science rooms, explaining some experiment. He wouldn't have wanted to have been left out in any way so he had returned to college early from Halifax.

We were asked to gather in the hall, where Peter, looking almost cherubic, read the address to welcome the esteemed visitors. I wondered much later why it wasn't Richard, as the serving president, who was asked to address the visitors. Whoever decided that it should be Peter, was very wise; Peter made an excellent job of it. Richard had a slight speech impediment, causing him to pronounce the letter 'R' as a 'W' – but I don't think that would have been the main reason for Fred to choose Peter.

I remember, with a smile, how we were seated on rows of chairs in that hall, the Queen and the Duke in the front row with the Archbishop of Canterbury in the row behind, and me either in the same row or the next one behind. While the Archbishop, Dr Michael Ramsey, waited for the Queen to be seated, he placed his hand on the vacant seat of the chair in front to steady himself, only for find the Duke lowering himself onto that chair.

He whipped his hand away very quickly, but not so quickly that the Duke didn't see his hand there with its ceremonial amethyst ring on the middle finger of his right hand.

Very quietly, Dr Ramsey bent his head forward and whispered to the Duke 'You're supposed to kiss it, not sit on it.' The Duke of Edinburgh just grinned.

Richard was not around in the college for the rest of that holiday, his wife was due to give birth to their third child.

Having returned to Canterbury early for the Queen's visit, I spent much of the time sitting in 'The Leopard's Head' public house just past St Gregory's Church, writing my dissertation. I gave it the title 'The Devil in Literature in the late Medieval and Tudor Periods' and typed it up on Moo's 'Brother' type writer.

The dissertation seemed to bring together some of what I had read during my 'A' level German studies, aspects of my English course at the college including the Mystery Plays and Marlowe's 'Dr Faustus' - and a fair-sized dose of Christianity.

Chapter 6

Naked Swimming

1965 brought a huge amount of change for me. Quite apart from the reading required for my English course, the essays on various literary works that I had read, the knowledge and skill that I needed to acquire on how to encourage young children to read, write, become aware of numbers and their relationship one with another while also developing an understanding of the world and how it works, I needed to understand my function and responsibilities as Vice-President of the Students Union - and this before the start of the Autumn Term.

To fulfil my new role properly, I felt that I needed to know more about Richard, to understand how his mind worked, what things in life he considered important. And how he, and I, intended to take the college forward.

That, I guessed, was going to take more than a cup of coffee. Or, if he could spare the time and were able to meet me there one evening, a half of lager at 'The Leopard's Head'.

According to what Richard told me, he had been living in central London with his mother during the Second World War. As far as he knew, he was an only child. His father had volunteered to join the army before call-up and had served in North Africa. Richard, who had been born in 1938, had been given the names Alfred Richard Vernon.

I asked him 'But why are you known in college as Richard rather than by your first name?' He shook his head, said 'I don't like my first name, I never use it. The 'Alfred' part of my name came from my mother's father. My paternal grandfather was 'Richard William' and I suppose the name 'Vernon' was the name of a family friend.'

The school in London that Richard had been attending was evacuated to Weymouth during the Second World War. I understood how this could happen. The school that my brother Colin and sister Val had been attending was evacuated to North Wales and fortunately for them, Moo was asked to go with the school and act as the school's cook. Moo's cooking that I experienced growing up as a child was far from 'cordon bleu' but it would have passed as adequate during wartime, even if her custard was, as I had found years later, often lumpy. And I knew she could create a nourishing meal out of very little.

Richard went on to say 'I completely lost touch with my mother but my father was able to track the school down and eventually found me again in Weymouth, being looked after by nuns. I started school as a boarder at Town Close Preparatory School in Norwich while my father was working in a bank in Ipswich. But at the end of one summer term, I was quite shocked to hear the Headmaster of Town Close announce that 'the school will be saying goodbye to several pupils including Richard, who will be leaving us to go to the Royal Masonic Boys School in Hertfordshire.' It came as a complete surprise.'

'Hadn't anyone told you this? Or discussed it with you? Shown you around your new school?'

'No. The odd thing is that I remember my mother had sent a present to the school for me, a doll.'

'Didn't it occur to you that that was an unusual present for a lad at a boys' boarding school?'

'I suppose so, I don't remember much about it. But as far as I can remember, that was the last time I heard from my mother. I was told years later that she had fallen in love with an American soldier, she had left my father and went to America. According to my Aunt Jan, my father's sister, my father was very hurt by his wife leaving him. He could forgive her for leaving him but he couldn't forgive her for abandoning her son.'

'But why did your father volunteer for the army before war had been declared, especially at a time when he knew that his wife was expecting a baby?' I asked Richard. 'I assume your father knew that his wife was pregnant?'

'I don't know the reason, nor the year my father enlisted. Perhaps he could sense trouble ahead with Germany. Nor do I know my father's regiment, nor what his role and rank in the army was, only that he apparently served in North Africa.'

Because I knew he was living near the college, I asked Richard more than once 'Can you tell me more about your current family situation?'

'My father is a Freemason. I assume that was why he chose to send me to the Royal Masonic School as a boarder.'

'That's interesting, my father is a Mason too - and while I was at school in Letchworth, our teams sometimes played against Royal Masonic Schools, either in rugby for the boys or hockey for the girls.'

'Well, I certainly wouldn't have been included in either the rugby team or as a spectator,' Richard assured me. 'I hated sport at school, especially cross-country. I suffered from asthma as a child and that held me back,' he said, adding 'The school's games masters were totally unsympathetic towards the difficulties I experienced in breathing during any physical activity. But I enjoyed swimming and had taken part in that, and occasionally in cricket.'

When Richard was telling me all this, pausing in between to see whether I was taking it in, I had no doubt he was telling me what he understood to be true. And I detected no sign in him that he was asking for sympathy, nor expecting it, nor holding anything back.

He was just letting me know what had happened to him so far in his life and some of the reasons for it. I felt that I was beginning to trust him, despite a certain laziness on his part that I had already discovered, and by his own admission.

'I didn't flourish academically, socially nor in physical activity at Royal Masonic. My nickname was 'sloth' while I was there. My father was sufficiently concerned that he referred me to an educational psychologist who suggested that my troubled family circumstances was stopping me from learning sufficiently.'

Richard didn't mention his behaviour or social interaction at the school to me, so I didn't ask. 'As a result,' he continued, 'I was sent to Red Hill School, described as a 'Progressive Boarding School for Delinquent Children and Adolescents' or in other words, for maladjusted boys who had either gone off the rails or who weren't doing as well as they could be, near Sutton Valence in Kent. It was run by Otto Shaw. I had the greatest respect for him.'

I didn't deduce whether there was any connection but Richard said 'And I told Otto Shaw, that I wanted to become a bishop. Otto Shaw, on hearing this, told me that he thought I was 'an immaculate virgin'.

I must have looked puzzled when Richard said this and I asked him what the headmaster had meant.

'It meant I was a 'perfect cunt.'

'That's a word I haven't heard before – and I still don't understand what you or Otto Shaw meant, but it clearly wasn't intended as a complementary remark.'

'Whatever the reason or whatever Otto Shaw thought of religion in general, of me becoming a bishop or my chances of doing so, I started attending the local parish church in Sutton Valence. I joined the choir and met Doreen as another member of the choir and daughter of the choir master and church organist.

Although I was nineteen, I stayed on at Red Hill for a further year, acting as a teacher for the younger pupils.'

Richard didn't say much about the relationship with Doreen, only that 'I made her pregnant during my time at Red Hill, so I was told by Doreen's family to marry her as soon as possible.'

'Where you in love with Doreen at the time?'

'I don't think so, but I thought I ought to do what I and Doreen's family called 'the right thing' – and soon we were married, in the parish church. Then I realised I needed to earn a living and I had only minimal qualifications.

I was able to use my own experience as an ex-pupil at Red Hill and then as an auxiliary teacher, and I was appointed as a temporary teacher at another special school in Surrey, not far from Crawley and East Grinstead. The baby was due the following Spring.'

He also told me 'I spent a year at King's College, London training for ministry in the Church of England. While I was there, I studied Greek and some Hebrew but found Hebrew difficult. I lived in University accommodation in London.'

From what Richard was saying, I couldn't make out where that time at King's fitted into his timescale of things, whether this had been before or after he had been teaching unqualified at a special school. But I didn't like to interrupt his flow about his life.

'I found some accommodation for us both in Ashurstwood, near East Grinstead. It was quite isolated and I had to trudge through deep snow that winter to get to and from the school where I worked. In time our first child, our daughter named Ruth, was born.

After a year of teaching at the school, the Head of that school told me that as I was unqualified, if I wanted to retain my post in the school, I would need to gain a teaching qualification as soon as possible.

So that was why I applied to Christ Church College for a place.'

He had not opted for the Divinity main course at Christ Church, instead he had chosen to study Art. I did wonder whether this had been at the Principal's suggestion - because we first year students all knew that Dr Mason, before being appointed Principal at Christ Church, had been a Methodist working in Kuala Lumpur in Malaya. He had been Professor of Education at the University of Malaya in Singapore where he organised the training of local graduates wishing to enter the teaching profession.

Although we were told that he had studied at Cambridge University and wished the college scarf to be in red and light blue to reflect his time at Cambridge, Dr Mason's honorary doctorate, awarded while he was in Malaya, had been in law. As I understood it, only after returning to England had he studied for holy orders at St Augustine's College, Canterbury.

I knew that Richard had recently been granted a mortgage and had bought house in College Road, Canterbury so he could live locally. He now had two daughters, a dark-haired smiley one aged three-and-a-half called Ruth, the other named Elizabeth or 'Lizzie' with fairer hair was approaching her second birthday. I saw, when I met Liz out with both her parents in the city, that she had a squint in one eye.

A week or so later, Richard asked me 'Would you come round to our house for a coffee during the daytime, to meet Liz again? Because the optician has prescribed spectacles for Liz to try to correct her squint and you are the only person we know who wears glasses. Then perhaps Lizzie will see you wearing them for reading – perhaps you could even read her a story - and she would see you putting them on and taking them off - and you could explain why you need them.'

I did just that. I walked to their house at the far end of College Road, knocked on the door, went in and was invited to sit down on the new sofa.

I was able to talk a little more to Doreen, whose main topic of conversation seemed to be her children and her experiences of childbirth, as well as her current pregnancy and, for some strange reason since I didn't know her that well, Richard's sperm count.

'The doctor told me he's absolutely teeming with sperm,' she told me as if this was something I wanted or needed to know.

I got the impression that Doreen hadn't much else that she could talk about, no interests or experiences other than the netball she had played at school. I was left feeling that she could have made more effort, been more involved in college life, there were plenty of students who would have been more than willing to babysit during the evening in exchange for a couple of quid, a coffee and comfortable sofa where they could sit and read or watch television. But Doreen seemed to show no interest in the college, its activities or in the role her husband played there.

Within a few more weeks, Lizzie had her own pair of pink-framed National Health spectacles. She realised how much better she could see things when she was wearing them. But she still appeared, to me at least, a slightly unhappy child.

Doreen too struck me as being slightly resentful, trapped by circumstances. I did my best to encourage her to take up music again, go to church, even join a netball team, but she didn't seem interested. I felt it was a hopeless case of 'taking a horse to water but . . '.

Miss Gaye, the college's tutor for primary maths, visited Twydall Primary School near Rainham, the school at which I was undertaking my final teaching practice. She spent half a morning observing me and looking at my lesson plans and observations.

Within the term, I was awarded a merit for my final teaching practice, despite one of my class, a six-year-old lad called Clive having flushed Miss Gaye's vivid green felt hat that she had taken off and unwisely placed on a chair, down the school toilets. She didn't hold it against me but I concluded that she hadn't had much experience of the mysterious ways of younger children. Or perhaps she didn't realise that Clive was in the class I had been teaching.

Nevertheless, I passed my final exams at college as well as the teaching practice.

Dad was due to retire from his job. With Colin and Val now married to their respective partners and living elsewhere, and Dad's father dead, was there still a need for a five-bedroom house? If not, where would Moo and Dad want to live? Would they want to stay in Letchworth? They decided not. But there was still TCP Grandma, by then well into her nineties, to be cared for.

Dad said 'I would really like to live in Kent again. I'm a man of Kent and I wish to return to my home county. When we were first married, Moo and I had a house in Bexley Heath where Colin was born. Perhaps we could find somewhere with a smaller garden, and not far from shops because Moo can't drive. Somewhere near Canterbury, maybe?'

A plot and half-a-house was for sale in Wootton, a hamlet among hills wooded with sweet chestnut trees, midway point in a triangle between Dover, Folkestone and Canterbury.

'I've been told that the builder has gone bust' Dad said, 'and hasn't been able to finish the house. Someone knowledgeable and able to supervise the building needs to buy it. I think I could do that. I'm told it had been planned as a chalet bungalow.'

The rooms in 'Elm Hollow' were being repainted by both my parents and prepared for sale. Dad and Moo bought the place in Wootton that they would call 'Owl Cottage', with funds they had inherited from Grandpa. They would not move there until September 1965 when Dad would be sixty. Until then, 'We need someone nearby to keep an eye on the property. Your mother and I would visit from time to time, of course, decide what to do with the garden and so on. Until we sell 'Elm Hollow' and can move in. For good.'

Once or twice a month during my final year at the college, I would catch the bus from Canterbury to Folkestone and get off at Denton by the Jackdaw public house and the old bakery. It would take me about ten minutes to walk up the steep road to Wootton, where there was a very small village shop. If I turned left at the junction by the shop, I came to a group of four houses, each newly built or in the process of being roofed. Owl Cottage stood in the middle of the row, well before coming to the little parish church. I had a key to the front door and could let myself in, check that no one else had entered uninvited and that everything was as it should be.

Sometimes I would go there with Anthony, only because it was somewhere away from college to visit and walk in the countryside. We could even walk from the house down the road past the church and past the wooded area on the left where purple and white wood anemones grew profusely every springtime among dogs' mercury in the undergrowth and the more occasional primroses.

Anthony didn't find this sight as amazing as I did, he wasn't really into wild flowers; or wild life at all. Maybe because he was brought up among industry, factory chimneys and brick dust.

After leaving 'Owl Cottage' and passing the churchyard in that direction, we would come to some farm outbuildings on the right at a dip in the road, next to what was later to be known as Lydden race track. Then, if we carried on walking, we would hit the main Canterbury to Dover road. With luck and an up-to-date bus timetable, we could stand beside the request stop and hold an arm out to halt the double-decker bus from Dover that would take us back to Canterbury bus station.

I was quite happy to make this journey on my own down the lane because it was peaceful, although, if it were dark, walking past that wooded area, there were often odd cracking noises which could make me feel slightly anxious. But I assumed there was no one else near, no other houses or signs of friendly life. And I wasn't normally easily unsettled.

Once or twice, I invited college friends to join me there for the weekend. We would put together whatever food we had or had brought with us, and share it. I remember trying to create a meal from a tin of tongue, which was all the meat that the village shop had in stock, and porridge oats. It wasn't nice and some of my colleagues said they couldn't eat it. Neither could I, although I hated to see food wasted.

The house had electricity and a new telephone had been connected so if we brought sleeping bags and were content to sleep on inflatable mattresses on the Marley-tiled floors, it could be quite fun. But on more than one occasion, I was surprised and perhaps even slightly shocked to realise that some of my friends, the ones with established opposite-gender partners, were not only sharing the same mattress but actually having sex, even the ones who regularly went to chapel. Of course, they were being discreet. But a night at my parents' house had given them an opportunity that being in hostels in college without discovery made more difficult. Such goings-on weren't for me, I felt. Too much guilt and not enough pleasure - not with Anthony, certainly. Nor among college friends: that would be far too indiscreet.

Now there was just the separation from College for me to handle. Three years was a long time, college life and my fellow students had made a deep impact on me. All that conviviality. And recognition. Suddenly, too suddenly, it would be gone, to be enjoyed and celebrated by other year groups younger than mine. I could feel I was going to miss it a great deal.

Perhaps because we were the first year of students, the college had no exit strategies to help us handle the transition. Or perhaps they expected we were all looking forward to a glorious future in classrooms and staffrooms, making new friends with other staff members and parents. Quite an unrealistic perception but in its naïve way, almost endearing.

It was the last two weeks of the summer term. The students in the two years below mine were throwing a 'bon voyage' party for us. The following week, Richard and I should have been holding some sort of sherry do to say 'thank you' and 'goodbye' to the Cathedral, City and College dignitaries.

We had sent out the invitations. Except it wouldn't be goodbye from Richard because, being from the intake below mine, he was going to remain there another year, even though he would no longer be President. Nor 'goodbye' from Tasha. I felt I was about to lose my best friends, certainly Tasha because she and I had shared a lot of thoughts and confidences as well as a set of single rooms with an adjoining door.

Richard, Tasha and I travelled to London in Richard's white van to a National Union of Students event, the final one that we would all attend together. We came back quite late in the evening; it had been a sunny day although we had been shut indoors in discussion for much of the time, and the fresh Kent country air was warm and welcoming.

I was in the front passenger seat beside Richard, with Tasha squatting on a cushion or something similar just behind our seats. There was a full moon and a clear sky, the main road back to Canterbury became a silver ribbon.

'I'd love a swim' I declared, *a propos* of nothing. 'Do we have to go back so soon?'

'Well,' Richard responded, 'it is a beautiful night so why don't we go on towards Broadstairs and look at the chalk cliffs from there?'

Richard apparently knew a spot where we could drive almost as far as the cliff edge, then find a white chalky path that led from the cliff onto the sands of Kingsgate Bay. I had never been there before; the Isle of Thanet wasn't an area that Anthony and I had ever explored. But I didn't give Anthony a thought that night, the night was too magical.

The three of us stripped off all our clothes, even Tasha although doing so seemed so unlike her, not at all modest or 'ladylike', and we danced about on the sand in the moonlight, tiptoed at the waves' edge and then plunged into the water and splashed about until the novelty of what we were doing, the intense freedom of it all, wore off. We climbed back up the cliff path.

'I think I've got some cloths or blankets at the back of the van,' Richard offered 'so we can use those to dry ourselves.'

We did so as best we could, then still rather damp, we wriggled back into our clothes. I don't remember how Tasha and I managed to get back into the hostel that night, how we either dodged the night-porter or waited until early morning for someone to let us in. Perhaps, since we knew we were going to London, we had signed ourselves out for the weekend, because we were supposed to set a good example.

Richard managed to get home without any repercussions from Doreen, because there had been nothing to be 'repercussed' about. Except, perhaps, after a hard day, going swimming in the sea at night with two naked women and getting back home later than expected.

But the experience brought the three of us even closer together, although I had already realised, from the way in which he would tease her, that Richard was quite keen on Tasha which, in the years to come, was to prove very distressing and extremely emotionally painful, for me.

All the invitations to the Cathedral hierarchy and local dignitaries to a final sherry-and-nibbles party had been written and sent out in Richard's name. It was time to recognise the first successful three years of a Church of England Teacher Training College, to be celebrated, not by the Principal,

Vice-Principal and staff although I'm sure they held their own event, but by us, the very first intake of students.

Richard had to be away from Canterbury for a couple of days again, for another conference, at Ormskirk, I believe. But for catering purposes, I needed to know that day how many acceptances there were, whom we might expect to attend our farewell sherry party and to make any necessary arrangements for them.

With that in mind, Richard had asked me and Tasha to open any envelopes addressed to him that were placed in his designated pigeon hole among the open mail block in the hallway that all students used.

It felt an uncomfortable thing to be doing, opening someone else's mail, but Richard had asked us to do so, so we started, putting them into 'acceptance' and 'unable to accept' piles. One from the Archdeacon, another from someone whose name we didn't recognised, one from the Dean and one that . . . .

'Oh, my goodness! The idiot.' Tasha, hearing my intake of breath, looked over my shoulder so that she could also read the hand-written letter. It said something like this.

Darling Richard,

I am sorry to have to tell you that I think I might be pregnant. I thought you should know.

I don't want you to do anything about this because I don't want you to break up your happy family, I would feel very guilty if you did that. And I still love *you very much. I haven't told anyone else about this and I won't.*

With still more love,

Anne. XXXX

'What are we going to do?' Tasha asked.

'Nothing,' I told her. 'Well, nothing yet. I suggest we put the letter carefully back into its envelope and put the whole thing back into Richard's pigeon hole. And if you and I need to talk about it, that we do so somewhere else that's more private. Richard will probably go to his pigeon hole when he comes back into college. Until then, we just wait'.

Chapter 7

The White Van

It didn't take long, in late June 1965, for Richard to seek me out. He started the conversation by asking me about his incoming mail, the number of invitation acceptances . . . and then, waving in front of me the opened envelope that had contained Anne's letter, 'I suppose you saw this. And read it?'

I told him I had, that Tasha and I had been opening and sorting the mail together and yes, we both knew what that letter contained. And had put it back where we found it, hoping no one else had cause to see it. And considered what the possible consequences might be, for Anne and for him. And were we right in assuming this was Anne Y?

Anne was from the third intake of students so in her first year at Christ Church. Richard was in the year below mine. Richard would have known about Ian and Linda having been sent down the previous year because when I mentioned the incident and the outcome, he described how he had seen Linda, her buxom appearance and long fair hair, leaning back against a radiator or windowsill in the Union building - and how that image had stuck in his mind.

But it obviously hadn't occurred to him that he might encounter not only a marital showdown with Doreen but also, if Dr Mason and Miss Young treated him as they had Ian and

Linda, that he might be told to leave, might never qualify as a teacher, which was his reason for being at the college in the first place.

I could understand why Anne might find Richard attractive. She was, I assumed, eighteen or nineteen, straight out of school, short, fair haired and quite chubby, whereas Richard was tall, good-looking, dark and in his mid-twenties - and the President of the Union, so seen among his colleagues as having a measure of power and authority; and obviously, since the recent birth of his third child, also virile.

I asked him how this had happened; and then rephrased my question because I obviously knew <u>how</u> it had happened, if she were indeed to discover herself to be pregnant.

'She told me she found me attractive and invited me for coffee,' Richard explained. 'So, I went to her room in the ground floor block of single rooms that led from the base of Fisher Tower to the science block and library. And she told me she loved me so we had sexual intercourse. In fact, she vacuumed me up, I felt almost helpless, sucked in like a bit of fluff in front of a hoover.'

Richard was not being flippant; he was frowning at the memory.

I raised eyebrow and as I tried to dismiss my mental picture of Anne's private parts as vacuum cleaner hose, I had to suppress a private smirk. 'And now, how do you feel about her?' I asked, trying to be serious and fulfil my 'Vice-President' role of being supportive towards my fellow students and especially towards my co-Executive member, however much I thought he had been a twerp.

This was no time for me to remind him that he was married and a father of three, because he knew that already. Or that he had wanted to be a bishop, or even a vicar, and that should have guided his behaviour.

I felt a huge loyalty and a responsibility to help him, and Anne too, if necessary, out of a tricky and possibly life-changing situation into which they had both got themselves.

'Would you like me to have a word with Anne?' I asked, not sure what good that would do nor what I would say.

'Yes please', he said almost gratefully.

'How high are the chances that she might be pregnant?' I asked. 'Did you use . . .?'

'No', he said, 'there wasn't time, I didn't have a condom on me and it all happened so quickly.'

'Not a boy scout, then,' I muttered under my breath and paused before saying 'I'll see what I can do,' while having no idea what I could do, even if I wanted. But I was genuinely concerned for him because President or not, he had no idea what his next move should be. He looked bewildered.

'It might be an idea if you gave Anne a wide berth for the time being,' I advised.

And then 'I suppose, if she is pregnant, that any baby is likely to be yours?' He said he was in no doubt.

Only years later did it cross my mind that Anne might not have been the first female student with whom Richard had had intimate relations. If there had been others, then he never said. Not to me, anyway.

I knew, because he told me, that he admired women who were physically tough 'like my cousin Judith' he had once confided although I hadn't at the time heard him mention any cousins except, once, 'cousin Jill'.

Richard also confessed a penchant for fair hair, intelligence and strong eyebrows. I lacked well-defined eyebrows because mine were so fair they were hardly visible but Tasha had beautiful ones, quite dark.

As far as I could tell, Richard had no gender-related prejudices or stereotypes, he admired people who could use their hands, solve practical problems and had imagination. And like so many other men I've encountered, women with long fair hair.

One of the other female students came to speak to me, expressing some concern.

'I think you ought to know, Anne is saying she is in love and because the object of her affections has not responding as she would have wished, she feels rejected and is threatening to throw herself out of her bedroom window,' this fellow student confided.

I told the student who was telling me this 'I don't think you should worry too much. I am aware that Anne's room is on the ground floor beside Fisher Tower, so if she does as she is apparently threatening, she is unlikely to hurt herself too much. I already know a little about this and I already have the matter in hand. I think that with care, it should be possible to avoid anyone being sent down by the Principal, escape any scandal and sidestep long-term emotional damage or upset relationships.'

I spoke with Anne a day or so later. She confirmed that she and Richard had 'made love' and that she thought as a result, that she was pregnant.

'How many periods have you missed?' I asked, trying to sound matter-of-fact, 'and how late are you this month?'

She said this was the first she had missed, that the encounter with Richard had occurred only a few weeks previously.

I deduced that she might well not be pregnant at all, that any menstrual delay was probably the result of anxiety. And guilt? I didn't know the extent of any guilt, Anne hadn't appeared at Matins in the chapel on a regular basis, as far as I could remember. But she had, in her letter expressed a concern about causing a split in Richard's family. So perhaps any guilt was based more on social factors rather than religious ethics - and on the Church of England Christian behavioural aura that ran through the foundations and daily life of the college.

The fact remained that if Dr Mason and Miss Young picked up on this, even as a rumour, then it was probable that Anne would also be sent down.

It was my guess that Anne was not using the suggestion of pregnancy, or the mention of causing a rift within Richard's marriage, as any threat or form of pressure on him. It seemed more likely that she was communicating her own anxiety - and because perhaps there was no one else at the college in whom she could fully confide. So, was she lonely and perhaps homesick, missing the love and care from her family, I wondered?

It was my responsibility towards her and Richard, as Vice-President and as Richard's 'Vice', to be supportive and help her find a way forward. Calling her 'an idiot' wasn't going to help. Nor would it be helpful, at this stage, to shatter any delusions she had about being in love. The situation needed a practical answer.

It was also time for the students who would remain at Christ Church for at least one more year to elect a new Executive. I did wonder whether Richard would stand for re-election but either the idea didn't appeal to him or perhaps he was too intent on avoiding any further trouble either at home or within the college.

I can't remember who became President; in those days it was most likely to have been one of the men because such were the subconscious expectations. Tasha was elected Vice-President. That made absolute sense to me, she understood how things were done, she knew the students and the staff, she knew the history of the college, such as it was.

I don't remember the names of the other Executive members but I felt that with Tasha in position, the college was in good hands, and that she had the academic ability to cope with the work level. She was bright and her main subject was Maths.

During a Students' Union Meeting, the names of the serving Executive came up. Someone in the third cohort, a married day-student maybe who rarely attended Students' Union Meetings, said 'I'm not sure who the current President is. Would someone please tell me?'

Someone explained 'Richard is the President and for the past year, Lorna has been his Vice.' This led to raucous laughter, which surprised me. The term 'Vice' was nothing new but perhaps it had always been in full as 'Vice-President'. I suspect I may have blushed at the very thought. Or maybe there was a hint of a rumour that Richard's marriage was not as solid as some people had imagined. Or perhaps he had had other dalliances with other female students in his year and the year below his. Or perhaps someone had seen him appearing from Anne's room, or spotted me emerging from Richard's house when I had visited Doreen about her daughter Liz's spectacles and wondered.

Whatever the reason, I ignored it and let it run when someone else referred to me again as being 'Richard's vice'. After all, it was, as a religious institution, as much focussed on good and evil, sin and vice as upon the teaching profession. And referring to me as someone's vice struck me as almost amusing, because I couldn't think of anything or anyone less likely to be described in this way.

But it did take the focus off Anne, had anyone suspected her of having had some sort of intimate engagement with Richard. I brushed it aside to concentrate instead on helping Anne to prove to herself that she was not pregnant.

I talked to her privately again the following day. I told her, as politely and as honestly as I could, 'I know, although he is married, that Richard fancies quite a number of the female students in your year and the one above. Perhaps' I suggested 'it might help you to become more actively involved in the college physical activities, take up some sport perhaps to put some colour in your cheeks? Or even horse-riding?

None of the other students goes riding at college, as far as I know, so it might give you an advantage over the others in your year. Riding could be something that sets you apart from everyone else, you could be a latter-day Lady Godiva at the next Rag Week perhaps, and it might give you something to offer in general conversation?'

Seeing her show a tiny spark of interest, I offered 'If it would help, I wouldn't mind going with you just for the fun of it. I'm sure there must be a riding stables in Harbledown or Bekesbourne that would take us both out on a leading rein and perhaps encourage the pony or horse into a gentle trot?'

I thought a little bumping up and down in the saddle over chalk bridleways would be likely to get any period started, if it was, as I suspected, just a delayed onset.

As things turned out, all this equestrian nonsense proved unnecessary. Within forty-eight hours, Anne was able to tell me that her period had started. I didn't ask her whether she would be continuing her relationship with Richard. I assured her 'Apart from Richard and me, Tasha is the only other person at the college who knows about the situation and about your letter. I'm sure that Tasha will be able to deflect any rumour, should the situation demand it - because it would be, I hope, only a rumour.'

Anne might be feeling hurt, used, even rejected but in time, I was sure she would find someone else to be 'in love' with.

Situation sorted, I assumed. Except that I was still being considered by some people as Richard's vice. And that that, or something similar, even a remark from Richard possibly, had caused a severe row between Richard and Doreen - in which, a month or so later, they appeared to have come to blows.

Many of my fellow students, the ones in my year and in Richard's, even some of those I had regarded as my friends, began avoiding me, not including me in events, shunning me as if I had some contagious disease. It was as if, by mixing with me, they might be tainted, become associated with immorality, or be thought to have condoned whatever it was they thought I had done.

They felt they should show their disapproval. But I was being shunned and that hurt, it really did. And I tried not to think thoughts about my 'friends' and their deeply professed 'Christian values'.

Only a woman named Diana from the third intake of students, or perhaps from Richard's year, went out of her way to strike up a conversation with me - and she was a devout member of the Christian Union. I was grateful to her for that, not only for not pre-judging a situation that was not a situation at all, but for taking such a positive stance. She was the only one.

I didn't feel welcome in college any more. I felt I was regarded as some current Jezebel. Nothing physical had occurred between Richard and me at that stage, except that swim at Kingsgate Bay with Tasha there too. I had just been called, at an open meeting, his 'vice'. I thought afterwards, perhaps they were jealous, because he was quite good looking.

But he was also rather immature, not unlike a teenager; he got enjoyment from being deliberately annoying, as I had witnessed too many times. I attributed this to what he had told me about his childhood, his time in a school for 'maladjusted' boys.

His behaviour reminded me of Val's, the way in which they both could get other people's attention by being irritating. So,

I rationalised, I could deal with it in the same way as I did Val's. I would ignore it, or go along with any suggestion in the hope that whatever had been suggested would be dropped - because if I openly opposed it, I was sure he would cling to it and pursue it all the more in order to prove a point.

Somewhat half-heartedly, I tried to be supportive to Doreen, while remaining loyal to Richard, because he was a fellow-student, even though he was a year below me and we had been working together on student-related issues for a whole year. In that time, I had grown accustomed to his strengths, his habits, mannerisms and faults, such as his apparent laziness and procrastination, to how irritating and almost juvenile he could be. And to recognise that fundamentally he wasn't particularly happy at home, that his main companion in the family was Ruth, his four-year-old daughter.

Dressed in baggy corduroy trousers and a hand-knitted rust-coloured jumper with sleeves several inches too long, Richard would wander from his house at the end of College Road through a gap in the ancient abbey walls and into the art block, holding Ruth's hand.

Doreen had gone into the city with the younger daughter, leaving Richard in charge of Ruth. And he had told us, his fellow students, that there was another baby on the way, due that Easter not long before my final exams. That would occupy much of Richard's time and it would leave me to deal with Executive matters that were really his responsibility.

I'm not sure how our relationship developed into one that was physical as well as emotional. I kept up a friendship with Richard and I tried to maintain a reasonable relationship with Doreen. I had even been invited to the christening in St Gregory's Church of their third child, Matthew.

I assume that Richard and I must have behaved, on occasions towards the end of my three years in Canterbury, in a conspiratorial way not only to confer over Union business but even more to discuss the situation over Anne and a slightly different one over Doreen. Richard told me he regarded me as emotionally strong, the one who could hold things together, who didn't panic but who was confident that things would sort themselves out - and who was unlikely to tell him what to do unless he specifically asked. And who, later especially, would do as she was asked.

After those semi-compliments, I was beginning to like him.

One of my visual memories is of the pair of us standing in the kitchen of Owl Cottage. Moo and Dad had brought some of their kitchen equipment to the cottage in advance of any major house move and were storing them in the lower kitchen cupboards. Richard wants to pour some gravy from a saucepan into a jug (why gravy? Are he and I preparing dinner together?) and is ferreting about in a lower cupboard to find something suitable. He pulls out a blue transparent plastic measuring jug, a jug that I have never seen Moo use, and says something to the effect that 'this will do'. He pours the gravy into the measuring jug while I stand back, I watch him do it but say nothing, because I can see that the jug has a split that runs lengthwise across its base. The gravy slowly drips through the split at the bottom and onto the work surface.

Richard looks at my face, at the way I am watching the drip, drip of gravy and handing him a dish cloth so he can mop up the mess.

'You knew it was cracked, didn't you?' he says. I nod.

'So why didn't you say something? You just watched me do that and you didn't say a word. Most people would have told me not to do that, not to use that jug. You wanted to see what I would do.' And then 'If I was not already married, I'd marry you for that, for not saying anything, for not telling not to do it but letting me go ahead, while all the time knowing it wouldn't work.'

That visual snapshot sticks in my mind because it seems such an extraordinary thing for him as a married man to say, and such a strange reaction. And I note it because it tells me something of how Richard's mind worked. I am recording these images in what I think, retrospectively, must be sequential order but I may be wrong about that.

But one of the important things, or omissions, is that I have no memory, visual or verbal, of any declaration of love from, or by, either Richard or myself. Things just 'happened', perhaps out of familiarity or loyalty - or because I was missing the convivial surroundings of college life and Richard was wanting something, or someone, more than his life with Doreen. But they did not happen, certainly not on my part anyway, intentionally.

This next image is of a dance or a party somewhere. I don't know where but it is not in college. It seems to be in a large hall with a hard floor and there are no lights on except perhaps a glimmer from a nearby room. I suspect, with hindsight, that it is somewhere away from college but near Canterbury because I think Richard and I arrived at where-ever-it-was, by travelling there in his white van.

There is music playing, a record somewhere in the room which adds to my image of the event having been a party. Several of our college companions are here, not the 'churchy' ones from the first cohort but from the second- and third-year intake.

Sue Pusher is here, she uses hairpins which she often takes out at a party and leaves behind, only to have to return to collect them the following day. There are mattresses, single ones mostly, on the floor.

We are quite tired and we are told by the party-giver that we may use the mattresses and sleep there until morning, if we want to.

I have no memory of any alcohol or water being available and my throat is quite dry. I don't know what we are wearing but we are certainly wearing some sort of party-gear. Richard and I have been dancing and are now lying side by side on a single mattress, resting with our arms around each other. It is neither hot nor cold but I would like some sort of cover, even a towel or a blanket. Not for privacy but because my arms, which may be bare, feel chilly. A Beatles recording of 'Yesterday' is playing.

I whisper to Richard 'I don't know about you but I find the words of the Beatles' song are quite apt. Because, although I am not longing for yesterday, life was simpler in my first couple of years at college when I was with Anthony.'

Then I realise, with a degree of horror, 'And judging by the odd noises, I think other couples are making love to each other. This isn't what I want, certainly not here or in this way on someone else's mattress. Richard, I think it's time we went, or time I went. You stay if you want to, this isn't for me. The whole occasion has suddenly turned quite sordid. It's not what I am about.'

We rise to our feet and walk back to his van, to wherever home is. The memory and appropriateness of the song 'Yesterday' stays in my mind for years to come.

This next memory is quite hazy. Now that college has finished, to earn some extra money I have a weekend job, working as a waitress and part-time cook at the 'Jackdaw Inn' in Denton. Richard also has a temporary job, he works in 24hour shifts as a steward on the Cross-Channel ferries; he is normally working on the 'Lord Warden' passenger vessel.

For some reason that I don't remember, perhaps I have held an end-of-term cheese and wine party in my parents' empty house in Wootton but unusually, Doreen has come along too with Richard. Doreen and Richard spend the night, or part of it, at my parents' house. Doreen encourages Richard to tell lies about his shifts. 'If there's money in it, then go for it,' I am shocked to hear her say. Richard and Doreen sleep on an inflatable mattress on the floor while I and any others are at the other end of the room.

Quite suddenly Doreen peels off her nighty to reveal her breasts and encourages Richard to make love to her, regardless of anyone else who is awake. Richard tells me afterwards 'I rejected this invitation, I felt sick at the thought.'

Fortunately, I have no clear image of this, only a hazy picture of where, in the sitting room, people were bedding down. And of the Lilo inflatable beds. And the unzipped outspread sleeping bags.

My next memory snapshot is of the front room of 'Owl Cottage', the room that will become Moo and Dad's bedroom.

It's a hazy image, a scene taken after I have come down from college and before Moo and Dad move into the cottage. There is a bed standing under the window in the room so perhaps my parents visit sometimes and stay overnight before heading back to Letchworth in Dad's car. Richard has taken his trousers off and for only the second time, I see his bare legs. I am struck by how long and slim they are, I think they are almost wasted on a man - and how they are unlike mine, which are thick, with no sign of ever having been slender or attractive. Mine are just, as legs go, 'useful'.

My knees are double-chinned: that too runs in the family. I have no visual image but a memory nevertheless of Richard's lower half being uncovered. Did we have sex? I don't think so, but I recall only his legs. But I remember thinking, at some stage but not necessarily at this point, that if that is the best love-making performance that Richard can offer as an accomplished married man accustomed to having sex on a regular basis, then I have some sympathy for Doreen.

I decided at about this point, that Richard was becoming too attached to me, too dependent. I thought that perhaps what he and Doreen needed was to spend a quiet evening together away from home and all his other responsibilities, having a relaxed meal without worrying about how he was going to manage to pay the bill. This may also have been, on my part, a way of lessening any feeling of guilt I was having about my perhaps being a factor in causing a marital break-up because I could see and as far as anyone could tell, that the marriage was, at best, tenuous.

With the help and agreement of Anita, the 'Jackdaw' public house landlady, I decided to have 'won' a three-course evening meal for two at the Jackdaw, which I would pay for in advance. Anita and I designed the 'winning ticket'. I presented this to Richard, saying 'I won't be unable to use this because it's for a night when I will be working. But if you and Doreen can find a babysitter..' - and I even suggested a couple of names - 'then you are welcome to use my ticket'.

They arrived at the pub for the meal and ate well. 'But they didn't' Anita reported back to me, 'talk to each other much, there didn't appear to be much connection between them. They left early, before any coffee'.

In my next mental image, Richard and I are going towards London in Richard's white van. The van's registration plate is WFN 767. Referring to it, Richard says wistfully 'I wish it was 007'. I am amused that he sees any resemblance at all between himself and James Bond except, perhaps, in height and hair colour.

Somewhere, probably not in the van because in those days, it was not usual for a car to have an audio-player or a radio, I can hear the song 'Help'. Perhaps we are on our way to see the Beatles' film 'Help' which was released that year. But in my mind, I can hear 'Help' being sung and thinking how apt the words are, yet again to our current situation, Richard's and mine.

Richard says, *a propos* of nothing 'I need to stop and find a chemist'. I ask him why. 'Because I need to buy some razor blades, I haven't shaved properly.' His chin looks well-shaven to me and I say so. Much later the same day or perhaps the next, he confesses 'What I needed to buy was not a packet of razor blades at all, but a packet of condoms.' I have no memory, visual or otherwise, of the rest of that day, not whether he needed the condoms, nor where we spent the night or that evening.

The absence of any detailed memory makes me now question other things, such as what he might have said to Doreen, how he explained his absence from home, how she was managing to look after three young children, one of whom was still, presumably, a breast-fed baby. And Richard had their only means of private transport. How thoughtless, I now realise that we both were. And selfish. Perhaps Richard had made provision for all of these, although that seems unlikely to me, knowing him better as I now do - or did.

Do I have regrets? Not exactly, as things turned out; I gained as well as lost a great deal from my time with Richard. But a sense of shame certainly, about how thoughtless I was. And how unaware, how naïve. But flattered too, and I needed that at the time, it raised my rather low self-confidence.

Any time with Richard was also a way of my cutting back on contact with Anthony, it gave me a reason to block him wherever I possibly could.

Having left college, I had to decide where to apply for a teaching job. I don't remember Christ Church offering us any help with this but maybe they did. Many of my colleagues decided to remain in Kent. Sue was going to teach in Bristol which, along with Norwich, was known at the time as an excellent authority. There was a possibility of my also applying to Bristol – but I wanted to have a room on my own, to prove to myself that I could be on my own, that I wouldn't feel lonely. I had nominally agreed to share a room with another student but I was finding her extremely dull and lacking in imagination or initiative. I decided to apply to the Education Authority in Kent, which would be sufficiently near to where my parents would be moving and sufficiently near London for the theatre – and probably away from wherever Anthony was going.

I was offered a teaching post at Edenbridge County Primary School, with headteacher Miss Lilian Cattaway and the caretaker aptly called Mr Startup. Next, I needed to find somewhere in the vicinity to live.

By early September in 1965, I had been offered a downstairs living room, an upstairs bedroom and the use of the kitchen in a house in Edenbridge. It wasn't ideal, the house belonged to a Miss Styles, one of the school cleaners so I had doubts about the privacy of the contents of my waste paper basket as well as concerns regarding sharing a kitchen. But in its favour, it was very near the school in which I would be teaching.

The class I was given was the first-year juniors, the seven-to-eight-year-olds, an age group that I really enjoyed teaching. I had found, even in my teaching practices, that their minds were like blotting paper, they would soak up and usually apply whatever they were taught. They could therefore be hugely rewarding, especially for a probationary teacher.

My next hazy memory snapshot or video involving Richard is from that time.

Miss Styles, my landlady, tells me there is someone waiting at the front door to see me. She lets him in - except, in this case, the 'him' is 'them'. Richard and Doreen are shown into my front room and they greet me. Miss Styles hovers, she looks unsure. She knows that some new families, people not from the village, have been settled on a site on the outskirts of the town. She tells me afterwards that she thought that perhaps these two, the man and the woman, were 'some of them', because the man has a black eye and a bruised face, both of them look as though they have been in a fight. She is worried for my safety, she assures me, and possibly for her house and possessions as well. I tell her 'I know both of them, the man is a friend of mine from college and the woman is his wife.' Richard and Doreen stand there, appearing uncertain what to do or say next.

Miss Styles disappears into her kitchen. She leaves the kitchen door open, in case . . . But there is no need for 'in case'. And I do not know why Richard and Doreen have arrived. I assume they have the children in the back of the van parked outside. They seem to have something they want to discuss with me but I don't remember what. I do remember that Richard seems apologetic and Doreen more militant, towards him rather than towards me.

Richard is wearing his usual rather baggy brown corduroy trousers and the equally badly-fitting rust-coloured hand-knitted jumper. I don't recall offering them a cup of tea or coffee and after what seems ten minutes or so, they leave together. Miss Styles reappears and tells me 'I thought they were Gypsies, because we have Gypsy children at the school and they might have been parents.'

I do not know how Richard knew where I was living but I suppose that at some point I must have told him, given him the name of the school and my address. Given them by letter or in person because neither he nor I had access to a telephone, other than by using a public telephone box.

My other memory of lodging at that same house involves Anthony.

I am upstairs in the room I use as my bedroom near Edenbridge Primary School. It is the weekend and I am peeping out of my bedroom window at the front of the house. From there, I can see to the left as far as where the lane in which my house stands meets the road, and where there is a metal bench seat.

There is a man sitting on it. He has his legs crossed and he is gazing towards my house; then he looks away, then back again towards the house. It looks to me like Anthony. I think the man is Anthony and he is waiting for me to come out, to see me and to persuade me to . . I don't know what. But he is stalking me, he won't leave me alone, just as he wouldn't leave me alone when we were students in college and he kept turning up, every night, uninvited but as if by right as if I belonged to him, with him, like a possession.

I am almost frightened but scared of what, I can't make out. But there are things I want to buy from the shops, I don't have any milk or anything for this evening's meal. But if I open the front door, I can't escape him. I don't want to have a row, a showdown because I am slightly scared of his melodramatic responses and so close to where I teach as well.

It's not that I fear violence from him because I don't know what he would be violent about, but I am nervous. I stay indoors. Until I realise two things at the same time and it takes me over an hour, - that I am being silly and anyway, it isn't Anthony at all, it is someone quite different and Anthony doesn't wear a hat like that.

I realise how difficult I find it to say 'please go away and leave me alone' – or 'no,' to anyone. I am scared by loud confrontation, particularly involving someone I know well.

By now, in my mental snapshot album, there is a series of linked photographs. I have moved from Edenbridge to a flat in Tunbridge Wells. This is partly because I can see trouble brewing if I am to stay living with Miss Styles. Sharing a kitchen presents less of a problem than the difference in our waking and working hours.

Miss Styles wakes at dawn so that she can clean the school before the staff and children arrive. To wake so early means that by 9pm or just after, she is in bed and needs the house to be quiet so that she can sleep. On one occasion at about 11pm, I drop the saucepan in which I am about to boil milk for a late-night drink. It clatters on the tiled kitchen floor and wakes her. I hear her sigh very deeply and manufacture a cough. I know the next day that I am in trouble.

I look for a flat away from Edenbridge at the same time that Jenny, who teaches at Edenbridge Primary and is also straight out of college where she trained to teach juniors, tells me she is finding difficulty in handling her upper-infant class. Jenny and I talk with the headmistress Miss Cattaway, and I suggest we might swop classes. Jenny lives with her parents in Tunbridge Wells. She has her own car and drives to and from Tunbridge Wells each day. I find a ground floor flat to rent in Molyneux Park Road in Tunbridge Wells, in a large Edwardian house that has been converted into a block of flats.

My flat has a private side-entrance door, a bathroom with a hot water tank over the bath, a small kitchen area and a living room with a convertible couch with a back that can fold down to become a four-foot-wide 'almost double' bed. There are tall cupboards either side of the blocked-up living room fireplace, for storing clothes and bed linen. The room is always dark because the living room windows, which look out over a back garden that someone seems occasionally to tend, face north. I buy or have borrowed an electric fan heater, which keeps away most of the chill.

Jenny is finding it expensive to run her car so we agree that she will give me a lift to and from school, while I will contribute a reasonable amount towards her petrol each week.

On the way back from Edenbridge, we usually stop at a shop in the town and buy four ounces of American hard gums, which we chew all the way home while discussing our separate lives. It proves a very therapeutic arrangement.

My first salary as a teacher, before National Insurance and Income Tax deductions, is pitifully little. I decide to augment it by getting a part-time job, working at weekends and in the evenings at the old people's missionary home also in Tunbridge Wells, for some extra cash. My job, I am told by the Care Home owners, is to do the evening washing up, and in the mornings to make the toast for breakfast. Nobody apart from the owners talks to me and I don't meet any of the residents.

I am bemused by an embroidered sampler sign, framed and suspended over the toaster, which reads 'Watch and Pray' - which seems counter-instructive to what I am employed there to do. The toast has to have the crusts cut off and each slice, from the sliced loaf, is to be cut diagonally and divided into two triangles. Then buttered. Because 'the residents prefer it that way.' I comply because I am paid, at the end of each week, in cash. But I am tempted, just occasionally, to rebel and cut the toast quite differently.

My relationship with Richard was progressing. He would appear quite suddenly at the weekend and stay for several hours, parking the white van on the road outside the flat. On one occasion, he arrived unexpectedly, carrying a battered leather suitcase which he unpacked as I watched. It contained two bath towels, one yellow, the other orange, some toiletries, a second jumper yet again hand-knitted, two shirts and a pair of corduroy trousers.

These items he stowed into one of the living room cupboards on an almost-empty shelf. He said 'Doreen told me which towels I could take.'

'I'm sorry that I couldn't bring my favourite coffee set, one that was made,' he said, as if I should have known the potter's name, 'by Bernard Leach himself, but it's also Doreen's favourite and our only drinking mugs at home so I left it there with her.'

I already had several Denby 'greenwheat' mugs and two 'chevron' Denby egg cups but Richard was quite dismissive about Denby and mass-production methods. I decided nevertheless to continue to collect them when I could afford it.

Richard was enjoying the pottery that he was studying at college as part of his art course. Whenever we could, on a Saturday we would walk or drive down to the Pantiles in Tunbridge Wells and order coffee and cake from a small Middle-Eastern restaurant. The restaurant owner served our black coffee with cream in hand-thrown stoneware mugs and, once I had made a mess of trying to float the cream on top of the coffee, he showed us both just how to use a teaspoon to do this properly.

'I like that,' Richard said, as with two fingers he stroked the side of his warm mug and lifted it up by its sides to gaze at its handle. 'Coffee always tastes better in a proper stoneware mug with a well-sprung handle.'

'What do you class as a 'proper mug'?' I asked, thinking again about my Denby ware.

'I much prefer drinking from stoneware,' he responded 'and especially if it's been made by a studio potter. Do you know the difference between stoneware and earthenware?' he asked.

I shook my head. 'Please tell me.'

'Well, for a start they are made from different clays and are fired at different temperatures.'

'Go on,' I encouraged 'because you know things I don't know, things I've never thought about before.'

'Stoneware, which is what these mugs we are using are, is made from a particular clay which is fired at a temperature of 1,200°C. This results in a more durable product, with a denser quality that makes it feel more like stone. It's good to use for mugs because when it's finished, it will be waterproof. And it doesn't need to be glazed. Earthenware, on the other hand, is made from a different clay and has a surface that is much more porous than stoneware. Earthenware is fired at a lower temperature and must be glazed or painted before use. It's often a more economical choice of dinnerware, but it tends to chip and break more easily than stoneware. And stoneware pottery doesn't normally absorb flavours, such as fish or spices.'

'But what's wrong with my Denby ware? Because my mother always uses that rather than Pyrex dishes when she is cooking. And all our dinner plates at home are green Denby. We have 'Frostpine' china cups and saucers but we use them only for special visitors. And Aunty Dorothy has a special Minton dinner set that she never uses and keeps in a glass-fronted cupboard.'

'Denby is stoneware, glazed. But' he added dismissively 'it's mass-produced.'

I enjoyed learning from Richard, he seemed to know things that were totally new to me, far outside my experience. Despite being hard up, we went almost every weekend to this restaurant for mid-morning coffee and often ordered baklava as well. On one or two special occasions, the end of the month perhaps after my salary had reached my bank account, we had dinner at this same restaurant.

Our favourite meal was the restaurant's speciality, 'roast pork tiki-tiki' a Hawaiian dish served on a bed of rice, involving pork cooked with honey, soy sauce and aniseed. This helped us to deal with parting each Sunday evening, when Richard had to return to Canterbury and to his course at the college.

On one occasion, when we had just come from a concert of Nielsen's 4th Symphony held in the concert hall in Tunbridge Wells, we walked past a very small craft shop and Richard stopped. He had seen a rotund Briglin studio pot displayed in the small window next to the shop doorway. The design appeared to have been scratched on with a sharp pointed tool. He admired it. I saw the price.

Without thinking, I went in and bought it for him and gave it to him as a present. He seemed genuinely touched by that even though, he told me, 'Briglin Pottery is studio pottery, founded about twenty years ago that started in the basement of premises in Baker Street, London. Its object was to produce well designed, attractive pots that could be used in the home and to sell them at affordable prices. Briglin are beginning to produce in larger quantities now, it's not quite 'mass-produced' but their products have become quite popular.' But he thanked me for it anyway. 'I will always look after it well,' he said.

Apart from Jenny, of whom I began to see less and less as she picked up again on her pre-training-college friendships, I knew no one else of my age in Tunbridge Wells, or Edenbridge, apart from Richard. I was still missing the active social life of college in Canterbury, especially the dances that Anthony and I used to enjoy. At Jenny's suggestion, I sought out the local 18 Plus Group and joined them for a while. I don't recall talking to anyone or being introduced as a new member; but I did travel by coach with the others on a visit to Hastings to their local 18Plus group.

I was taken to a dance, with pale mauve lighting or perhaps that was the paint on the walls. The dance was a lot of jigging up and down, nothing like the dances we had had at Christ Church which were mainly ballroom, and no one spoke to me on that occasion either. That was the last time I went.

I joined three evening classes during that year. One was in Tunbridge Wells, looking at English Literature. I enjoyed the set reading and discussions even more than I had at college, perhaps because this class was a choice and I felt I knew what I was talking about. Not like at Christ Church, where the number of people – and we had been nearly all women – was so high that we had to be divided into two groups, those who had studied English at 'A' Level formed one group. The group I was in was made up of those who had not studied or taken 'A' level English, plus a few waifs and strays.

The other two evening classes were held in Tonbridge, a short journey away by either bus or train. One of these was bricklaying. I don't know why I had chosen this course, except that I thought it might prove a useful skill to have. I knew a little about it, having watched the builders working on 'Elm Hollow', the house that Dad designed in Letchworth near the golf course.

This was fine for a couple of weeks, although it didn't take long for me to realise that all the others, who were men or lads who had already left school, had had far more practice than I had.

After working in a group of three or four to build a wall along the workshop floor, our next set task was to construct a fireplace. Not just a chimney but a fireplace with a space for a fire with a brick surround. By this time, I knew I was out of my depth and apart from that, getting to Tonbridge not once but twice a week in the evenings after a day of teaching was costing me in time as well as money, and energy.

My other Tonbridge adult evening class was Law. I had chosen this because Richard said he had studied some Law at King's and he already had a number of books on English Law. I thought this might be interesting, and also useful.

I can't remember whether we were looking at criminal law, civil law or both but I suspect it was civil law because I do remember something, just a little, about the signs saying 'Trespassers will be prosecuted' and that, for the sake of accuracy, they should say 'Trespassers may be prosecuted'.

I learned that trespassing may be considered a crime, a civil wrong (or a 'tort', we were told), or both, that it depended on the circumstances and whether any damage had been caused. This was interesting, and I enjoyed going until, having missed a couple of weeks because I had a heavy cold, I entered the classroom only to find that the others were sitting an exam, about which I knew absolutely nothing.

I left, went home early and didn't go back again.

On one occasion, Doreen appeared outside my flat at the weekend. She banged on the door, shouting 'Come on out, Dick, I know you're in there.' As it happened, Richard was elsewhere that weekend, having left the van with Doreen. She seemed to have the children in the back of the car, including the baby of course, so I assumed she was on her way either to or from visiting her parents in Sutton Valence.

I called out through the door to her 'He's not here, Doreen, I don't know where he is but he certainly isn't here.' I heard her say, very loudly, 'No, Daddy's not there, he doesn't love you any more', slam the van door shut, rev the engine and drive off again quite quickly.

The following weekend, Richard travelled to Tunbridge Wells by public transport. It was early springtime and sunny, we went out for a walk along the road past my flat. I was remarking to Richard 'Aren't celandines early this year?' when I looked up and 'Oh my goodness. Quick, this way,' as I saw the white van coming from the top of Molyneux Park Road. 'Let's disappear into this beech hedge and hide,' Richard advised, 'it might avoid a major confrontation.'

I don't know whether Doreen saw us or recognised us because we were both wearing anoraks and the sun was shining on the van's windscreen. But not long after that, Richard said, with resignation 'Hiding from an angry violent woman is no way to live. If we are ever to have a settled life together, we need, at some time in the near future, to escape to where she can't find us.' I remember that 'escape' was the word he used.

Chapter 8

A Kiln and Rush Matting

In Spring 1966, Richard arrived unexpectedly at my flat one evening. As he put his bag down onto the kitchen floor, I asked him whether Doreen knew he had come to see me.

'No,' he said, shaking his head, 'and I don't think she cares much. We were having an argument. She was frying eggs and sausages for the kids' tea and she told me to go off and buy another loaf of bread. But instead of that, I drove straight to you.'

I asked him 'So, did you buy the bread and return home with it before setting off to see me?' He told me he hadn't, he had ignored Doreen's instruction and had taken himself as far away from her as he could. 'She had a frying pan in her hand,' he said and, by way of explanation, 'with hot fat.'

'It's lovely to see you' I told him 'but you have their only form of family transport and as far as Doreen knows, you are still out searching the Canterbury bakeries or food shops for bread, and she will be waiting for it, wanting to feed the children, worried.'

'She won't be the slightest bit worried,' Richard responded, pulling a face.

'Nevertheless, I suggest, much as you don't want to, that you should go back home either this evening or very early tomorrow morning, and with a loaf of bread for the children's breakfast'.

That was what he very reluctantly did. I have no idea what he told Doreen, where he said he had been. Or with whom.

Since we had no easy way of getting in touch with each other, it was a complete surprise for me to find Richard hovering by my door a week or two later when I returned from teaching. He was holding a suitcase but this time it was large and obviously, from the sound he uttered when he lifted it, very heavy. His white van was nowhere to be seen and he looked shattered. I unlocked the main door and we went indoors together, me with my school bag and Richard heaving his case.

I turned on the cold tap, filled the kettle and switched it on. 'Tea or coffee?' I asked, sensing that any further conversation or questions from me needed to wait. I made a drink for us both, in silence.

'She came at me with a knife', he blurted. 'I hid in a cupboard but she found me. I was frightened for the children. I thought that if I left, got out of the house, she would leave the children alone, not hurt them . .' he paused '. . because she wasn't angry with them. Just with me.'

I established quite quickly that Richard hadn't been physically hurt or cut. But he was still shaken and seemed very scared. I couldn't make out, and it didn't matter either way, whether it was Doreen who had bundled Richard's clothes in the suitcase or whether he had done that himself. As he unpacked his belongings in my living room, I saw that there were several books among his possessions, books on law, religion and a couple on art, so I assumed he had thrown them into the case himself.

'I came by train, then caught a bus from the station to here' he explained, 'so I could leave her the van. She said she'd need that,' he paused again 'for shopping - or anything. Because she can take the children in the van with her, they can even sleep in it on a long journey if they need to.'

I knew they had both let the children sleep in the van if they were going anywhere that the children might find tiring, or not interesting. The van had no side windows, only ones in the driver and front passenger doors and on the rear double doors. It was a Ford van, only the size of a private car but designed for commercial use, so whatever was in the rear compartment was hidden from view from outside, unless anyone put a face right against the rear windows and peered in. Even then, it was too dark to see in properly.

On one occasion I had been quite amazed when Richard went to see a film that interested him at the cinema. He parked the van on a car park behind the cinema, left both the girls in the back of the van and locked the doors. At least, I assumed he locked them. 'They'll be fine,' he had reassured me. 'It's warm and dry, it'll be like camping for them.'

Now I was wondering about several things. Nothing life-threatening as such, but practical things such as whether I had sufficient food for both of us to eat that evening? And enough milk for breakfast? Whether we would have sufficient room on the fold-down settee for both of us to be able to sleep comfortably or whether I needed to sleep on a rug on the floor? I had two sleeping bags that would unzip and open out to form lightweight duvets, and there were two cushions that

I could put with the one pillow I owned. So I knew we would manage. But I was still worried and not only about the practicalities.

Was Richard living and taking up room in my flat with all his possessions what I really wanted? He seemed to have attached himself to me and although I felt quite flattered by his affection, was any of this my choice? I had been supportive towards his past and current situations but had he, and had I, misread and misunderstood my responses? Did I want him to leave his wife and move in with me? What did I really feel about him, and about the current situation? I was not accustomed to making choices for myself. Was I just used to having him around, had enjoyed his company and had mistaken that for love? Did I know the difference?

More important but less pressing that evening was the question of college and Richard's art course. We needed to talk about that, and almost immediately.

'If you are going to continue at College as a student, you will need to be able to travel to Canterbury on a daily basis,' I told him.

'And I'll also have to produce whatever works of art, paintings, sculpture or pottery are needed for assessment by Mr Dudley as my art tutor, and possibly by an external assessor from Canterbury Art College or even London University, as well as look at a range of art works in galleries in the South East of the country,' he responded.

'All these will need time and money as well as a base, a place where you can study, create and sleep without being disturbed. And since you are in your final year, there could also be a final teaching practice, which would probably require lesson planning and resources. Even if Doreen says nothing to anyone, it might very soon become apparent that you are travelling to and from Canterbury by train each day rather than living in your own house in College Road, only a hundred yards from the college'.

Richard nodded.

'So', I went on 'you might not wish to do so, but it would make more sense for you to return to Canterbury, return to Doreen, and continue at home as normally as possible, for the next nine months or so.' I paused to see if he were still listening and taking this in.

'Then, having been awarded your Certificate of Education, you would be a qualified teacher and in a far stronger position to apply for jobs.'

I went through all this with him, pointing out the advantages of his returning to his house because he would still need to be paying the mortgage on it each month. Would he, I asked him, be able to afford not to live at home?

All my rational arguments, my pointing out that the children would miss him and he would miss them, made no difference. He mistook my comments for personal rejection and started to pout.

'To be honest, I'm too afraid of Doreen to go back home. I don't feel safe there any more.'

Although I had decided, almost at the last minute before leaving college the previous summer, not to share a flat with anyone but to live on my own, I had to admit to myself that it could be lonely sometimes, that having someone else living in the same flat or apartment would probably be better, after a long day at work, than coming home to a cold, empty house.

And we had worked together for a year on the Students Union Executive; I did owe him some loyalty, at least a duty of care from one human being to another.

He was familiar; over the past year I had grown used to having him around, seeing him every day, doing what he said or what we agreed. And would it be such a huge step to go from joining each other for coffee in The Pantiles to sharing a kitchen and what little cutlery I had? And we had had sex, even if only just the once, so perhaps we ought to be living together? Because it meant something, wasn't that what it was all about, this love and sex? Didn't one thing equate to the other?

Rev. Smart had said it did, and so had the Baptist Elders; or they had hinted as much, because they wouldn't refer to sex or intercourse outright, it would be far too shocking in a Sunday sermon. Wasn't I now obliged to . . I wasn't sure what? It all seemed such a muddle, I didn't know what I felt; or thought; or believed; or wanted . . except that doing what I wanted was classed as selfish - and being selfish was wrong. Wrong with a capital 'W'. Or an upper case 'R'.

As things turned out, it was Doreen who made the decision for me. Things might have blown over but for Doreen and the cello. Moo telephoned me at Edenbridge Primary School and asked the school secretary to give me a message; would I please phone home that evening.

So, there I was, in a public phone box at the top of a hill in Royal Tunbridge Wells, jingling what few coins I had, dialling my parents' number and getting through to my mother.

'Well, that was a bit of a bomb-shell, Dear,' Moo said, rather too loudly over the phone. 'Now, how are you off for money?'

Ever the thoughtful woman, my mother. Even when she had just been given some news about me that she found astonishing, even shocking.

She told me that she had just had a visitor. A woman had come to the front door of their cottage in Wootton. No, not a friend; someone she had known about but not met before. Carrying something big. In a fabric case.

'Came in a white van,' my mother explained. 'It was that wife of the chap you do things with at the college,' she continued, quite forgetting her normal strict adherence to English grammar and not saying 'with whom you do things' . . so, I deduced from that that she really was quite upset. 'His wife, Doreen – or Pauline, I forget which. She brought back the family cello we lent him, you know, your friend Richard. Said Richard wouldn't need it any more, wouldn't be playing it. I asked if he'd lost interest, because I told her I thought that it was a pity if so, because the cello is a lovely instrument although it isn't easy at the beginning. But she said, 'no it wasn't that, it was because Richard had left her. Left her and their three children. Left her for another woman'.

My mother paused for breath and I felt something at the back of my neck begin to tense. Then it came.

'I said I was so sorry to hear that and then I asked her, Pauline or Doreen, whether it was anyone she knew. And she said, 'Yes, it's your daughter Lorna, they're having an affair'. I think I then said 'are you sure', or something like that and she said I had better ask you. So, what's been happening? What's the situation? Because I need to know, and what to say to your father.'

'Oh, well played, Doreen!' I thought as my mother recounted this. And the initial reaction at home, my home, had been as I might have expected. Or perhaps not. My parents were brought up, as I had been, with strong non-conformist Christian values regarding truth, trust, responsibility, morality in general and sexual in particular. But also with compassion, understanding, compromise and a practical approach to problem-solving. Hence my application to a Church of England training college when a 'non-conformist' one hadn't been a possibility.

I realised Moo felt that I had let her down, been a disappointment. Again, but in a different way this time. That I had let both my parents down. Although I'd not let myself down, I didn't think, not exactly. Although I found myself in a tricky position, I had acted according to my conscience, social responsibilities and, despite a few wobbles and misgivings, I'd stayed within my code of moral integrity. But this wasn't the time to explain all that either to her, or to anyone really. Not at this point.

I was glad this was a phone call, though. I am not very good at handling disapproval, especially from family members or people I care about, it makes me shrink. And a hurt look from my mother, with those thick pink-framed National Health glasses that she wore and her penetrating hazel eyes, could cause me to wither.

From my mother's tone, I realised that I had disappointed both my parents yet again. And this latest news was a total shock to my mother, to both my parents.

I needed fresh air.

Royal Tunbridge Wells and the surrounding area had struck me as a geological oddity. It was quite different from the terrain in East Kent that I knew so well. Most of the soil seemed to be either sand or clay, but around the town, which was built on a series of hills or 'mounts', there were several outcrops of grey rock. Some of these rocks were used by people training for rock climbing but one outcrop near the part of the town in which I lived, became a favourite place for Richard and me to bring a picnic.

I don't remember our ever having a conversation or discussion that suggested or confirmed that Richard loved me, or that I loved him and that we intended to be with each other for all time, but somehow it was there. I think it was, anyway, unvoiced or not remembered. Nevertheless, it was a commitment. Or perhaps it became one, by default simply through being accustomed to each other.

On one occasion, we had walked into the town for a coffee at our favourite coffee-shop-cum-restaurant in The Pantiles and instead of going straight back to the flat, we went towards the rocks on our way home. It felt the weather for a mini-adventure.

There were not many people there so we thought it safe to clamber on to the lower rocks and from there to scramble on to the taller ones. Richard took his shoes off, he was always keen to get as far back to nature as he could, and I followed his example, leaving my shoes at the base of a rock against the curled green fronds of emergent bracken. The rock felt surprisingly warm against the soles of my feet, the sun had been shining since early that morning.

We sat there, gazing into the distance and appreciating the lack of noise. One of the roads crossing the area ran not many yards behind where we were sitting but while we were there, there was no traffic, there were no people walking near, no planes in the sky.

The air was still and peaceful, I felt light, and at that moment, carefree.

Richard reached into his back pocket and took out a penknife. Still sitting, he bent forward toward the facing rock and began to drag his knife vertically down the grey sandstone. While I watched, assuming he was trying to sharpen his penknife, he carved a capital 'R' and a capital 'L' on the face of the rock. I was puzzled as well as shocked. Shocked because these weren't our rocks, they belonged to the public and what Richard was doing looked to me like vandalism.

'Rocks aren't roads, they don't normally have a left or a right-hand side,' I said, 'so what . .?'

'That's for us', he replied, 'you and me, our initials'.

Looking up at me, then down at the initials, he said something such as 'I hope it proves as permanent as we will be together.'

'That's all very lovely but I don't think you are allowed to do that,' I said, warily 'I hope no one saw you and it gets you into trouble'.

'I don't really care, and anyway, there was nobody watching.'

It didn't take long for the news that Richard had left Doreen to reach Dr Frederick Mason and the college authorities.

Richard told me how he had been asked to go to the Principal's office, how Dr Mason had asked him where he was now living because, he had explained, the college needed to have an up-to-date address. Richard even wondered whether Doreen had tipped the college off; but he decided that she would have known the likely outcome, that he would be told to leave if it was known that he had left his wife. And that might have had a negative financial effect on her and the children.

Richard told me that he had told Dr Mason that he and his wife were going through a difficult patch, after the birth of their third child - a little time living apart from each other seemed a good idea. Dr Mason had then asked him where he was living.

'Ashford', Richard told me he had said, 'because it was the first place on the main train line that came into my head.'

Dr Fred Mason had asked him whereabouts in Ashford.

'He was looking at the telephone on his desk when he spoke,' Richard explained 'so I knew that he was going to check wherever I told him.'

'So, what did you say?' I asked.

'I told him I was staying at a pub that offered rooms. I thought that was a safe bet. But then he asked for the name of the pub.' Richard paused. 'I knew I was on a cliff edge, so to speak. So, I made a wild guess. 'The White Horse', I told him.'

I must have frowned, I was confused - and I was also concerned that Richard had lied.

'And luckily, there is no 'White Horse' pub in Ashford, it doesn't exist,' he explained. 'Fred picked up the telephone directory, looked up the name but he said it wasn't listed in the book. Thank goodness I had picked that name and not any other. I told him I knew it was under new management so perhaps it wasn't listed in the directory he was looking at. And that I wasn't sure of the address but it was on a street corner. I think I got away with that.'

Richard was quite pleased with himself when he told me this. But he also suggested that, once he had finished his course at college, it would be sensible for us both to look for jobs away from Kent. Because, he suggested, if the National Union of Teachers knew we were living together and not married, they might refuse to allow either of us a job.

Much later, I wrote to N.U.T., explained the situation and asked whether this were true. In reply, the Union advised me to use my discretion at any interview regarding my domestic situation. Teachers, they replied, were supposed to set an example and uphold morality.

When I had first applied to Kent County Council for a teaching job, I had also applied to Norwich City, which had an excellent reputation and was an authority run quite separately from the county of Norfolk. Then, on reflection, I had decided that it made sense for me to stay in Kent at least for the first two years, it was an area I knew, where I had family connections. But when both Richard and I needed to earn a living away from Kent, this time Norwich and Norfolk seemed the obvious authorities to which we should apply.

Richard had been awarded his Certificate of Education and with his background, he thought he should offer either art or religious education as his main subjects. He would be teaching in a secondary school, of course, whereas I looked for a primary, and if possible, an infant school, because I had enjoyed teaching those six-year-olds in Edenbridge, they had surprised me.

They had shown me that some of what I had learned at college didn't apply to them. They didn't all want to sit on the floor to listen for a story. In fact, one girl called Lily Smith refused to sit on the floor at all, she came from the newly-built site on which the Gypsies, who used to park alongside the A2 main road, had been resettled.

I found both her and her mother to be delightful, kind and generous. Lily had an elder sister Minty, also starting at the school.

I was shocked to be told by the headmistress and her spinster-teacher friend, that Minty, who was so-called because she had been born in a mint field, was not allowed to bring her doll on her first day at the school, because 'dolls aren't allowed'.

Poor kid, of course she wanted something from home, something familiar with her, among all those strange faces. I learned a lot at that school about children and how they might behave, and about teachers without experience of children of their own.

Richard was offered a post in one of the Thetford Secondary Schools, teaching religious education and a small amount of English to the 'less-able class', as he told me. It was many years and one marriage later that I found out that Richard and my former best friend John B. from Baldock, had both been teaching side by side at the same Thetford secondary school.

The once market town of Thetford had received a large number of London overspill families, a large number of council houses were built, the schools had to expand and take on many more teachers for all those extra children.

I was offered a teaching post in Earlham Infant School, in an estate on the outskirts of the city of Norwich. In that case, Richard and I both needed to live somewhere between central Norwich and Thetford so that we could travel to our different schools. During this time, Richard was finishing his art course in Canterbury so it was up to me to find us both somewhere to live.

After a great many enquiries, I found a vacant flat on the first floor of a large converted house at one end of St Giles Street, where the traffic lights allowed cars and buses to cross over the ring road from St Giles Street and continue along Earlham Road, past the Catholic Church and away from the city. There was a parking space between the flats and the next-door butcher's shop.

Our new-found flat had a galley kitchen, three rooms large enough to be bed- or sitting rooms and a small bathroom. In one direction it overlooked the butcher's shop and in the other, it looked out across an enclosed communal courtyard, over the different iron staircases that led to our front door and to the other upstairs flats.

A group of university students lived in one of these, an antique dealer and his girl-friend Josie in another. On the other side of the road lay a chemist with wonderful old-fashioned bottles on display, and wooden drawers with brass handles with the word 'tinctures' printed on one of the drawer fronts. There was also a sweet shop with a red post-box mounted on a wall outside, a gallery selling antique books and maps, and on the corner of Cow Hill, a draper's shop with bolts of tweed displayed in the window and a sign saying that they were able to offer 'hand-made suits, made-to-measure'.

We had minimal furniture in our flat. Richard brought a wooden workbench with him which served as a general table. We bought a second-hand mattress and put that on the wooden floorboards of one of the rooms. Some rush matting had been standing by a dustbin outside one of the pre-fab properties along Grapes Hill. Richard helped himself, carried the matting home and it went onto the kitchen floor. I had a Baby Belling cooker that my mother had used as a camping stove, it ran off a gas bottle.

From an antique shop at the bottom of Grapes Hill, we bought an oak dining table. The dealer wanted twelve shillings and six pence for it but we offered him all the change we had, which amounted to just over eleven shillings, and he appeared glad to accept that. With considerable pride we carried the table home up Grapes Hill and up the iron staircase to our flat.

On most Sundays, we would get up quite late and attend Matins at St Peter Mancroft Church before returning home for something for lunch. It was in that flat that I realised the benefits of having a fridge. I had bought bacon for breakfast and put the rashers that we didn't need on a shelf in a build-in cupboard in the kitchen.

Several days later, I went to the cupboard to prepare a cooked breakfast, only to let out a horrified shriek. 'There are white things crawling all over our bacon. Can I just brush them off, do you think? We can't afford to waste all that food.'

'They're maggots,' Richard told me. 'You had better throw the lot in the bin. And next time, we'd better stick to having just eggs.'

It cost £30 per week for Richard to drive to Thetford and back, not far off what he was receiving in salary. There were also maintenance payments to be made to Doreen for the children, and the mortgage to be paid on their house in Canterbury.

To help supplement his income, Richard took a job as tutor for an adult evening class in pottery at Earlham High School. I was working at Earlham Infant School, teaching during the daytime and Richard would be in the High School one evening a week, teaching pottery. But what Richard really wanted was to be a potter, working from home, every day if possible. Our upstairs flat in St Giles Street wasn't sufficiently large, nor was it appropriate to accommodate a potter's wheel and a kiln. Nor did we have the correct electricity supply. We needed to rethink.

By chance, we drove to Blakeney one summer weekend. Richard was always attracted to estuaries and the sea, because he had lived with his father and his step-mother Margaret, at Felixstowe as a teenager where he had learned to sail, he told me. He looked longingly at the boats pulled up onto the Blakeney foreshore shingle or moored at the quay. To take his mind off boats for a while, he suggested we might look at whatever was going on in the small wooden building, just on the far side of the road from the car park.

Inside the wooden hall and spilling out over the steps was a crowd of people. We had difficulty pushing our way through to see why they were all there - and then we realised it was an art exhibition and that most of the men, the younger ones certainly, were talking to Frankie, a very attractive-looking blonde who, we learned, was the artist.

Richard saw a painting of olive trees standing among iron-red earth that he liked. He talked to Frankie about it, saw why she was pleased with it, and bought it. He asked for her contact details as well. I don't remember being asked for my opinion. If I had been, I would probably have gone along with whatever was suggested or proposed, because that was how I remember so often behaving. It caused less of a problem that way. And I was being what Moo would have termed 'reasonable'. And polite, by not disagreeing. Anyway, what did I know about art.

Frankie, we learned, lived in Cambridge. She had formed a liaison with a married man, an art dealer and restorer, who lived in Walsingham, and she needed somewhere in Norfolk to live at weekends. We offered her an unfurnished room in our flat where she could meet her art dealer friend and occasionally paint as well. I suspect we felt some empathy for her relationship situation.

By October, our joint lives were moving on extremely quickly. Frankie had agreed to visit us in Norwich. She was coming to discuss the possibility of exhibiting her paintings with us, in a gallery we were just creating, in a house on a corner of Bethel Street that we had decided to rent, not as a place where we would live but because that house had a rear kitchen in which Richard could have a small kiln. It also had an upstairs.

We thought we could cover the monthly rent by letting the upstairs rooms to students at the new university, while the front room on the ground floor could act as a gallery for painting, pottery or general arts and crafts. By this time Richard had begun making jewellery out of sheet copper in one of the rooms in our St Giles Street flat, mostly brooches but a few pendants too. He would use his wooden workbench as a place on which to cut the metal sheets into smaller pieces with tin snips, to plannish the copper with a tiny hammer to encourage it into the required shape and to give it a beaten finish.

He thought of enamelling. He knew it was possible to enamel onto copper but that ideally the process needed a small kiln rather than a blow torch. So, there was his kiln idea, the kiln that he especially wanted.

In the back kitchen of the house we rented in Bethel Street, he would cut the copper into a shape as before, support the shape on a trivet, coat the copper with guar gum, sprinkle it with enamel power, and place it in the hot kiln. In a surprisingly short amount of time, the enamel fused into glass. I can't now remember how we were able to introduce a coloured swirl into the background colour but we did. I quickly learned how to do this as well. Richard would attach either an earring clip or a drop earring fastening, (parts that were known as 'findings'), a thin leather thong for a pendant or glue a pin on the reverse side to form a brooch. We also found that unless we enamelled both sides of the copper, the copper would warp, it would distort and crack the enamel.

In his previous life with Doreen, Richard told me, he had sold copies of Encyclopaedia Britannica as one of the ways by which he had earned a living, as well as persuading the owners to let him clean the windows of the gateway block of flats in Dover, and being a driving instructor. 'I'm quite a good salesman,' he claimed, 'people seem to trust that I know what I'm talking about, so they are quite willing to look at what I have to sell or can provide.'

This proved to be both necessary and correct. He was able to convince local craft shops to place a small order for earrings or pendants; we would make up a small package and send it to the shop. This was done on a sale-or-return basis for the first one or two orders. Then, if the enamelled items sold well, the shopkeeper would sometimes buy outright and send us a cheque.

We had stiff commercial competition, however. Foye Forge, a company based in Cornwall, was producing not only goods in the same metal but also copper brooches in the shape of leaves, which Richard couldn't do by hand. Theirs were cast.

Purely by chance, I had been given some 'Conran' cotton fabric samples. They were not sufficiently large for me to make them into anything useful for myself but they did give me an idea. I had, along with the rest of my possessions, brought my hand-operated Singer sewing machine with me to Edenbridge, Tunbridge Wells and then Norwich. I would, if I had sufficient fabric, make girls' dresses or smocks out of the samples, and sell them, if I could find a willing buyer, a shop even, who might take them on 'sale-or-return'? With this in mind and the need for extra cash, in my spare moments I began planning, cutting and sewing.

A craft shop in the High Street of Tunbridge Wells had taken a couple of the garments and displayed them in their shop window. And they had sold. Now that we had some form of introduction into craft shops, I was able to offer them children's smocks, lined with synthetic material and fastening at the back, to go over a tee-shirt or a blouse. We often spent the extra income on a visit to the Nouverre Cinema or a concert in Norwich's Assembly House.

If ever we had any extra money coming in, Richard couldn't resist spending it almost immediately. Money for him fulfilled the cliché about burning a hole in his pocket. He didn't save or hoard it; he could never have done that. Instead, he would spend it as quickly as possible on things he wanted. Because, I imagined, it meant power, it could make his wishes come true. Money was his magic wand.

It was after such a concert of Mozart's Clarinet Concerto in The Assembly House, that I realised how much at that moment Richard was missing his three young children. He had sat in that Music Room, listening and thinking about them. As we emerged from the Georgian building and started to walk the short distance along the pavement back to St Giles Street, he talked about going back to see them that very weekend, how much he wished he was still living with them, how much . . . I remember his voice tailed off. And I felt, quite suddenly, very insecure. Because it dawned on me then that he could, at any moment, leave me and return to Doreen. Their house in College Road was in his name as was most of the furniture, the van too. His children bore his name. All I had was a rented flat, a job, a table, an ancient sewing machine and some matting that no one else thought worth keeping.

I suggested 'Perhaps we could invite the children to stay for a few days. We could show them around Norwich, visit the castle, take them somewhere, to a park perhaps. They could sleep in the room that Frankie used, or the room we call the 'sitting room' but has no arm chairs, or if they really want to be together, on inflatable mattresses or foam plastic at the end of our bed.'

Richard did not jump at the idea straight away but an hour later he suggested 'If Doreen were prepared to hire a car and drive the kids on a Friday night or Saturday morning as far as Chelmsford, which seems about half-way, then we could meet them there with any luggage items and bring them back to

Norwich. We could do something very similar after lunch on Sunday so that the girls would be back in time for school on Monday morning'.

Meeting Doreen wasn't too pleasant but we each managed to stay polite even if the atmosphere was a trifle frosty. Inevitably the conversation during this meeting would turn to money, to Doreen not having sufficient and Richard not having any either. The children seemed to enjoy coming to see us although rather too frequently, I was left to look after the three of them while Richard nipped out somewhere.

I remember Matt, aged between two and three years, picking up a carpet sweeper that Moo had given me, pushing it around the limited space on the kitchen floor and the sitting room, then saying to Frankie 'I've done your room.'

He hadn't, of course, the door to Frankie's room had remained shut the whole time. Frankie smiled, thanked him and said how like Richard Matt was, by saying he had done something even though he hadn't, only wishing that he had. I remembered this because it was such a good observation.

I don't know whether we approached the bank for a loan to buy the enamelling kiln but we certainly didn't already have the money ourselves. The Norwich bank manager suggested, since we were not married or in any way related, that we should sign some sort of legal partnership agreement. We asked to open a joint account, because we needed a separate bank account, one that was not already belonging to either one of us. We signed it and held to whatever it said. At some point in our lives, we also joined COSIRA, the Council for Small Industries in Rural Areas.

But our main financial problem was the purchase tax, the additional amount that traders of 'luxury goods' - and our goods were classed as jewellery and therefore luxury - were obliged to add to the wholesale purchase price. Adding this was not a problem as such, but the tax was due to be paid back to the Inland Revenue at the point of sale rather than when we received payment for the goods. Partly because of this, we were constantly moving in and out of debt for most of our lives together.

Through Frankie, we got to know her art dealer friend and his younger brother David who was a property dealer. David was making money by buying up derelict property in Norfolk and employing part-time labourers to make essential renovations. Then he would sell the houses to outsiders and make a handsome profit.

Our flat in St Giles Street had been let to us on a six-monthly basis. I wondered if it would make more sense for us to buy a property somewhere in the country and to continue making jewellery from there, even pottery for Richard.

When we had first come to Norfolk, we had looked at an empty cottage with a barn in Tasburg, just off the main Norwich to Ipswich Road. It appeared ideal for Richard's purposes but we had no money to buy any property at that time, nor had we held our jobs for very long. We abandoned that idea. Richard had the house in Canterbury and was already paying the mortgage on it each month so the idea of him being allowed to buy a second property was out of the question, even if we could have afforded it.

But by now I had been teaching at Earlham for over a year and as a teacher in a country with a shortage of teachers and a rising birth rate after the last war, I thought I was more or less guaranteed a job somewhere in the county. Frankie told us about several small houses in the countryside north of Norwich that the art dealer's brother was hoping to sell and through Frankie, we came to hear of a house that looked as if it might prove ideal for us. It had, as an option, five acres of land - and a flint barn.

We looked at it on a particularly windy day in February. The house had once been two cottages. The pantiles on the roof were half-off, one of the chimneys looked unstable, the stairs ran steeply from a living room to two small bedrooms, the kitchen had been a slightly later addition with a concrete floor and bare walls, and the wind whistled through the whole property. But it looked fundamentally sound, despite being so draughty on that first visit. It had been one of a group of farm labourers' cottages; we were told that it had belonged to Tommy Dack, the local shepherd who was now living elsewhere in the village. It lay on the very edge of Billingford, a small hamlet between Dereham and Fakenham.

There were fields on all sides of the property and a dense pine wood half a mile away that was managed by the Forestry Commission. There was no drive or path to the cottage apart from a farm track that led from a country lane to the farm. But just outside, on the verge of the farm track by the entrance to the cottage, grew a patch of white violets - and that clinched it, for me.

I established the asking price, and contacted the Woolwich Building Society. The manager laughed unkindly. 'Where is your husband' he asked, 'because as a single woman, you can't buy a house without a husband. And why on earth would you want to buy a house on your own? What about your father, couldn't he buy the house for you? Wouldn't he be prepared to act as male guarantor?'

'I am not prepared even to ask my father,' I told the manager. 'This is to be my house and I am going to stand on my own two feet.'

It was a battle. I told the manager 'My grandmother has shares in the Woolwich Building Society.' I was not sure whether it was completely true or whether that made any difference but I did know that TCP Grandma had sometimes mentioned her having money with 'The Woolwich'.

Dad drove to Norfolk and looked at the house, gave his opinion. He was very good like that and he knew his stuff where buildings were concerned, what to look for, any weak points. At that time the only water was from a well just outside the back door. There was no mains drainage in the village, there had been only a privy in the back garden somewhere. The asking price was just over three thousand pounds for the cottage plus its five acres once the renovations were completed, with the option to buy the barn for a further thousand.

Dad lent me several hundred pounds towards the deposit, on the understanding that I would repay it 'when I was able'. Aunty Marian gave me some money as well, such that I had sufficient for the deposit. And after a great deal of discussion and insistence on my part that I wanted to be independent of any male guarantor, I was granted a mortgage.

I did not realise until many years afterwards how few single women in 1966 would have been so fortunate.

Chapter 9

Barn Renovation and Lizzie

The next time we visited the cottage in Billingford, the bathroom was being installed. The only space into which a bathroom and all necessary plumbing could easily fit was downstairs, in a small area between the two main rooms. The space was so limited that the bath could not be the standard length, instead it had to be extra small and crammed against a side wall to allow access to the washbasin, toilet and metal-framed window.

The sanitary ware was new, albeit a pale blue which would not have been my choice. And when Richard's children came to stay, the bath was quite big enough for each of them, it was only for an adult that it proved tight in length and width. Economical though, since with someone sitting in it, it needed very little extra water to cover one's bottom or legs. There was no hope of a shower being installed. In the 1960s, showers in private homes were the exception.

In the room we called the dining room, there was a solid brick chimney and, in the fireplace, a cast-iron range bearing the crest of the Earl of Leicester; all the cottages stood on what had once been the land belonging to the Earl of Leicester and were probably tied cottages for his farm hands. The crest looked as if an ostrich were holding a snake in its beak but

I was informed that the reptilian-looking object was actually a horseshoe.

When the cottage had been two separate semi-detached dwellings, this range had been the main means of cooking and heating for one of the dwellings. I used it once or twice. With a fire sufficiently banked up, it was adequate for heating a kettle but unreliable for cooking anything that needed more time and a consistent temperature. Consequently, the house was cold and the upstairs felt damp with grey clouds of mould growing on the walls in our bedroom. The solution to this was applicable only in summer when the weather was warmer. If we slept with one of the bedroom windows wide open, there was less condensation from our breath and fresh air could circulate.

There was no roof insulation that I could detect, nor a damp course, whether injected or inbuilt, because the main walls were flint and had been constructed some one hundred and fifty years previously when such things were not considered necessary in farm-workers' cottages.

The ceilings and all walls except the chimney had been plastered, the chimney breast had been chiselled and chipped so that plaster would adhere but no plaster had been applied. The brick chimney was painted in a mid-blue coloured gloss – I painted it myself because Richard didn't normally involve himself in decorating - and it was possible for anyone to pick out the underlying outline shape of the bricks.

The dining room had a half-glazed door that led straight into the garden. Should anyone slam or close the door too suddenly, the glass might well fall out, as did happen once. The only window in that room had a metal frame and was subdivided into smaller oblong panes. Metal frames, as I knew from the house in Letchworth that Dad had had built, provided strength and security that timber frames couldn't. And if not regularly painted, they would also rust, as I was to discover.

For an extra thousand pounds, I had been able to purchase the barn and the land on which it stood, as well as the cottage. The barn, we thought, could be somewhere where Richard could establish his pottery.

The building attracted me because of its shape; three sides of a rectangle. I even wondered if it had been built on the much earlier foundations of a Roman villa. This was fanciful, but not completely impossible, because I learned that a Roman helmet had been found some fifty years previously, in mud dredged from the nearby River Wensum.

I also had a suspicion that an earlier ancient track would have preceded the one that went past the cottage entrance, leading on beyond the farm drive and then past the woods to a possible river crossing place, before arriving at North Elmham Saxon Cathedral.

The barn had three sides, the one facing the footpath across the fields and towards the road being taller and consisting of three compartments. The roof on the taller side of the barn was higher and appeared older. The roof trusses, rafters and king posts were made mainly of oak, but the purlins were of a softwood, possibly pine. This earlier section had been subdivided by clay lump walls into three areas, plus an adjoining outhouse; it was enclosed with walls on all sides except for the main entrance and in the central compartment that appeared to have contained straw in the past and had compressed dung in the floor. This central part had a wooden door that opened onto the courtyard.

To allow access to the end section without needing to go out of the barn, across the courtyard, and back in again through where the wooden double doors had been, we needed to knock a way through the clay lump and into the next room that was to become the main workshop. We did not fit a door to this more direct route but we did create a doorway and an arch. To do this, we needed to design and construct a proforma, and required some technical help with the central brickwork.

I remember how resilient I found clay lump to be. It wasn't at all flimsy or crumbly as I had expected. Even when I hit it really hard with a lump hammer and chisel, it absorbed the shock waves and wouldn't easily give way. No wonder, I thought, that local Norfolk people used clay lump as wall-building material; it was extremely robust.

Nearest our drive, the drive we created from the farm track that had run past the cottage and as far as the barn, there were large old wooden double doors across two wide openings to the barn. These doors were tall enough and opened wide enough to allow access for a cart, or tractor.

We made more than one attempt to lift those doors off their hinges to give us better access to the barn. The vertical lengths of wood that made up each door were grey and splintered, such that it was better to use gloves when handling them - and sturdy boots too, because each door was very heavy, broad and cumbersome to negotiate. With our arms outstretched and chests pressed against the wood, we had to carry each of the doors to somewhere else to store them.

The other two lengths of the barn were open to the air on one side, with the roof supported at regular intervals on metal stanchions to allow cattle to wander in or out for shelter or access to an enclosed courtyard.

The courtyard had the remnants of wooden gate posts attached to stubby brick walls at the south-facing entrance, so that any livestock could be completely protected. But these gates were off their hinges, had fallen to the ground and nettles were growing vigorously through and around them. We made a bonfire and burned them.

The courtyard itself, which could have been lovely had we done anything creative with it, was full of builders' rubbish, old rusted tools, weeds and stagnant water; stagnant because there was no guttering to any of the roofs, no downpipes and no drains.

Inside the barn there was no sign of cattle, apart from the compound layers of dried dung, nor of the sheep apparently kept and tended by Tommy Dack, the shepherd who had previously lived in the cottage.

The floor surface of the first compartment in the older part of the barn, the part that we assumed had been a tractor shed with the huge double doors, was covered with grey granite sets placed onto a sand-and-clay mix, the same granite blocks that I had seen used for roadways because they were hard-wearing. We needed to remove these and to lay concrete.

The blocks were heavy, each one was heavy. Heavy to lift, heavy to carry and dangerously heavy to put down because our fingers were holding the underside and it was tempting to deposit each hefty block somewhere beside the gravel drive very quickly, too quickly, which could crush our fingers or scrape the skin off our knuckles.

After we had moved what little furniture we possessed into the cottage, we set about tackling the barn more methodically during one school summer holiday. After we lifted the existing granite flooring from the floor, we had to find a source of hardcore. I knew what we needed to do only because Richard told me.

His previous experience of working on Dungeness Power Station and with his father on a house in Suffolk proved useful. He was also good at finding and employing suitable labourers, but poor at paying them on time, whether in cash or by cheque.

Some of the hardcore material came from the spoil dumps from the other cottages that had been renovated on the site. We pick-axed into it, shovelled it, wheelbarrowed it and dumped it in the entrance room onto the sand-and-clay mix that had held the granite blocks.

I asked 'Why did we bother to move those blocks in the first place, couldn't they have acted as hard core?' Apparently not; and 'they are cuboid,' Richard pointed out, 'they would have made the final floor too high - and we also need to incorporate a damp-proof polythene membrane.'

Richard and I worked as equal partners as we had done in the past. There was never any suggestion from either of us that there might be jobs that I could not do, was not strong enough to tackle.

I was physically tough, Richard expected me to be just that, and he said at one point in our lives together 'what I like about you, Lorna, is that you have the strength and constitution of a Saxon ox. You're a good person to have at the other end of anything heavy.'

Not exactly a standard compliment but Richard didn't pay compliments. After we had had our three children, his favourite nicknames for me were either 'Bagpuss' or 'Porridge'.

I was even pleased that I was regarded as an equal with no allowances made for gender or differences in strength. I enjoyed his confidence in me, the fact that he thought I could manage the task, any task. The only person who had ever been protective towards me was Colin - and Richard was so very different from my brother.

I would thump down with a sledge hammer on the broken bricks to produce hardcore and shield my eyes from any sharp flying fragments of brick. As soon as the floor consisted only of orange-and-red brick dust and shards, we spread sand on the top.

We had ordered a huge pile of this from a local builders' merchant, and we were able to shovel the deep yellow sand from the heap and into a metal wheelbarrow, trundle the barrow along a scaffolding plank laid on top of the hardcore and gently, very gently, tip it out on one side of the plank, then the other, carefully raking or brushing it with a soft broom so that it filled all the spaces between the brick fragments in the hardcore. Once that surface was ready, 'We now need to lay a double sheet of heavy-duty polythene on top, to act as a damp course,' Richard advised.

The polythene had come in a long roll six feet wide, densely wrapped around a cardboard tube. To put it temporarily out of the way, Richard stood the roll up on end and leaned it against a wall in another area. At that very moment, we heard the ready-mix lorry arriving with the drum turning to keep the concrete moving.

Somehow, in our excitement and just as we needed to unroll the polythene and cut it to the right size, Richard managed to place his foot on one projecting end of the cardboard tube and without warning, the whole roll fell against the side of his head.

'Damn, that was heavy,' he said, 'it really hurt.' Within a minute, he complained that his head ached, he felt sick, and was going to vomit.

'In that case, I suggest you go outside rather than being sick onto the sand and hardcore, and just where we are going to tip and spread our new concrete.' I felt weary and not very sympathetic, I decided at that moment that no one got concussion from a bit of polythene.

'But if I do,' he responded, rather too willingly, I thought, to get out of doing the job in hand 'you will have to manage the polythene by yourself. Unroll it, cut it and lay it in place straight away, because the ready-mix lorry with the concrete churning can't wait.'

There was no time to argue and anyway, we rarely argued. I did as I was told.

I lifted the scaffolding plank, laid it somewhere within reach but out of the main room in which we were working, and I cut the polythene to what I hoped, and had measured, was the correct length. Then I replaced the plank so that I could walk on it across the polythene without disturbing anything.

I asked Richard if he felt any better and he said he did, that he had vomited into the drainage ditch that ran between our barn and the houses on the road, although I could see no sign of vomit among the lengths of long grass.

'I think,' he said rather pathetically 'I feel able to supervise the ready-mix lorry so that the driver can tip small loads, bit by bit onto a heavy-duty board to allow us . .' (and in this case 'us' meant me) . . to shovel the runny concrete into the wheelbarrow, up the outside step, onto the plank and tip it very slowly and gently in measured amounts onto the polythene membrane.'

Once all the runny concrete was in place, we needed to stand on different planks either side of the area and with a third length of wood, tamp it down to get the concrete to settle, to consolidate and form an even and level surface.

Out came the spirit level to check this. The tamping produced a slight texture with ridges in the concrete but Richard said it would be fine. We laid the concrete floor in the rest of the barn in the same way but in two separate loads.

Once the concrete floor was completely dry throughout the barn, we ordered made-to-measure window frames to form large windows between the metal stanchions. Richard got in touch with a local bricklayer, a very nice chap called Tom, an ex-Merchant Navy man who came from Melton Constable, to help us at the weekends.

Tom bricked around the metal stanchions to form brick pillars from floor to roof level to which the window frames could be attached after they were delivered. He also told us how to cure a fresh fleece which, though interesting, was information that we never had the opportunity nor the desire to use.

At some point during one winter, I saw snow creeping in underneath the tiles and falling on to some studio pottery that we were displaying. That must have been before the fibreglass was installed, when it was possible to stand inside the barn, look up and see daylight through the gaps in the tiles.

A few years later, when necessity required it, we tackled the roof and the roof tiles. That time though, we employed help.

It was not deemed necessary to have the roof trusses or the tiling battens replaced but we did employ two local chaps called John and Harry to work on the barn roof. It was John and Harry who lifted the tiles, unrolled and placed the rolls of fibreglass in position to act as insulation, then replaced the tiles. Too frequently, in a high wind, tiny shreds of orange fibreglass would drift gently onto the floor.

I used a wide brush to treat the flint-and-brick interior walls of the main barn with some sort of stabiliser. Once it was dry, I covered the inside flint walls with my own mix of white masonry paint plus a small amount of sand. The sand gave an interesting finish and filled in any gaps between the flint and the mortar.

We bought lengths of rush matting to place on the floor of the gallery, to absorb echo and soften the tread. Once the large windows were glazed by either me or Richard who was the one who measured and ordered the glass, the gallery was almost ready.

We had the idea of hanging lengths of butter-muslin on the inside of the windows to cut any glare and hide the mess in the courtyard, but that was never done.

Our first plan was to use the entrance and the middle section of the three sides of the barn as an art gallery, leaving the older taller section that faced the drive as a workshop area. Richard placed wooden work benches against the interior clay lump walls and the small enamelling kiln stood on one of these, with metal shelves above for holding jars of enamel powder.

The central one of these three rooms was used as an office where we could keep track of materials coming in and going out, and maintain paperwork, using the Kalamazoo index filing system for materials, and an accounts book.

At one point, Richard decided we would print our own gallery catalogues to show members of the public which paintings or art works were being displayed that month. He found a printing press advertised for sale, bought it and had it brought on rollers into the barn where it stood on the concrete floor. I don't remember the name of the press but it had a large wheel at one side and no platen that I can recall. We didn't keep it for long, I think Richard was being nostalgic about his days of helping to produce 'Insight', the college newspaper, but he had not the skills, the time nor the resources to design and produce art catalogues.

Instead, we asked Daedalus Press, based in Stoke Ferry, to design and produce them for us. Casper and Juliet, the husband-and-wife owners of Daedalus Press, had got to know us partly by chance but also intentionally. They had been driving past, seen the 'Craft Shop' sign at the end of the drive and had come to look. Like us, they had realised that there was a limited number of like-minded people living in any rural area with whom one might get on well and have sufficient things in common.

Having talked with Richard, they thought we might get to know each other better and invited us to their house for an evening meal. From then on, we saw them on an almost fortnightly basis and became good friends for many years until they moved away.

Sometimes we invited one or two of my former college friends to stay for a weekend. Sue was one of these, she had only recently married a man who was studying in Cambridge for his Ph.D and he would spend every day he could, she told us, trying to determine the angle at which a drop of paint separated and fell from the brush, or something like that.

That left Sue on her own in their rented flat so she would come to stay with us for a couple of days in the cottage.

Tasha came once. She had been brought up in North London, not far from Barnet. I think she found the countryside rather dull. As she left, she asked me 'But what are you going to do all day, stuck out here on your own?'

We also invited Katy to stay. Katy had been two years below me in the intake at college, she came sometimes on her own and on other occasions with her boyfriend. Both Katy and Tasha, Sue too, sometimes bought a painting, some jewellery from the workshop or even a tie that I had made but I think they did so only out of gratitude for having received our hospitality. Richard had very few friends of his own and none from college so it was always my female friends who came to stay.

One year, Richard invited his two daughters, Ruth and Lizzie, to come for a week during their school holidays. They behaved well and I applauded how they switched from behaving as they might have behaved at home, to adopting our ways and rules while with us.

They washed themselves regularly, would change their clothes when I suggested it by not wearing the same vest at night as during the following day - Moo would have been horrified at the very idea - and although bemused by table napkins and cutlery place settings, they followed the table manners and routines that they saw us maintaining at meal times.

Richard would drive the van to Chelmsford, the half-way point between our two houses, where we would wait in a pub car park just off the main road, for Doreen to arrive from Canterbury with the girls. There was no discussion regarding Matt staying at our house at the same time too - and there probably wouldn't have been room, or that's the excuse that Richard would have given to Doreen. He didn't appear to have created the same bond with Matt as he had with the two girls and especially with Ruth, who seemed to have acted as Richard's main buddy and go-between at times when he had been living with Doreen.

He got on reasonably well with Lizzie, but she had been the surviving one of twins undiagnosed as such before they were born. He told me that he had had to deal with the burial of the stillborn one and had paid for that.

He always seemed a little uncertain of interacting with Lizzie, although that may have been on account of her squint, of him not knowing whether she saw him or how she saw him. Doreen told us that Liz could be naughty and run off sometimes if they were out in the town together.

When Liz was staying with us, she would wet her bed every night. That didn't matter to me, it was something I was used to but I am not sure how Richard handled that, if he handled it at all. When I mentioned it, he attributed it to Liz being unsettled either at home or with us and he left me to deal with it. He told me that he used to do the same thing when he was at boarding school.

I reassured Lizzie that it really didn't matter to us, except that having a wet bed and wet pyjamas must be uncomfortable for her.

We had no modern washing machine at that stage, only the one that had belonged to Moo and that she had passed on to me. I had to fill the tub with buckets of hot water from the tap or from the kettle but it was easier than washing bed linen by hand. After a year or too, I bought a new washing machine from my salary. Moo handed her electric tumble drier on to me, which was also a great help.

By the time Lizzie was seven, I discovered that despite her having been in school in Kent from the age of four onwards, she could write her name only as Eli B. She could not read, neither did she appear to know how to do so, nor to understand what reading was all about. I started to tackle this by reading a story to her every night when she was in bed.

She could look at the pictures – I made sure there were plenty of pictures – and they helped her to maintain her interest. Ruth could read quite well for her age but Doreen told us that Ruth had a hearing problem and might need a hearing aid. The message I received from Doreen about two of her children was not one of particular care, love and concern, more that they were in some way 'defective' - but that might just have been the way I interpreted it or the way she gave Richard the information in front of me.

But I didn't pick up on any deep love for them from her, I got the impression that they were a nuisance, that their very existence was holding her back.

We learned from Doreen that Liz was in the class at school for the 'backward' children, that her teacher had said that she would learn to read and write in due course and that the school was not worried. Nor did Doreen voice any concern.

I didn't take very long for me to determine that Liz could and would be able to write her name if someone were willing to spend sufficient time with her on a one-to-one basis; and this was something that Doreen wasn't in a position to do, having Matt to look after as well.

I used what infant-teacher skills and knowledge I had and they paid off. After the first week of the school holidays and the girls' stay with us, Liz was able to pick out some words that she recognised written on a card or on the page. She was delighted to find, if the same font and case were used, that a word, any word, had the same outline shape, whether printed on a page or written in felt-tipped pen by me on a piece of card. She seemed to enjoy matching words and their shapes.

We also played 'road pairs', a game depicting road signs, almost every day and she was able to hold the shapes in her mind and remember where she had last seen a card turned over. It didn't matter if she didn't know what the road sign or the word meant, the important thing was that she could recognise identical shapes and, over time, see minor differences between the road signs for different T junctions, and between short words such as 'bed' and 'dog'.

Richard contacted Doreen to ask whether Liz could stay for longer because, he told her, she was beginning to learn to recognise simple words, and to copy underneath my writing.

Doreen agreed. Richard told me that she seemed almost relieved at being without the girls for some time.

In general conversation as well as in their behaviour, it seemed that Doreen and Liz didn't like each other very much; neither of them had much respect for the other and although Liz enjoyed the protection and company that Ruth offered, Liz would be happier away from her mother. Lizzie even said as much.

After considerable thought, I suggested to Richard that Liz might stay living with us for the coming school year, we could enrol her at a local school and during the holidays she could either return home, or Ruth and Matt could come to stay with us too for week or so.

Doreen and Liz both thought this was a good idea. Our local primary school at North Elmham didn't seem to have room for Liz but we managed to find her a place in the infant class at Guist Primary School. Then came the problem of how to get Lizzie to that school.

Long before we moved from the flat in St Giles Street, Richard had given up his post as a teacher in Thetford. In fact, he may have been asked to resign, either because his class control was poor or he didn't arrive at the school on time. I hadn't learned to drive by the time we moved to the cottage, the school bus picked up children from our village only for North Elmham primary school and there was no regular bus going towards Guist at the right times of day.

Richard wasn't willing to commit himself to driving Lizzie there and back twice a day, the petrol would be too expensive and apart from that, he didn't have the time, he said. He also managed to fall out with the Guist infant class teacher quite soon by suggesting, as he recounted to me, that the class might enjoy having a sand-tray or water play because as he tried to tell her, 'Different forms of play are a way of discovering how the world works'.

The teacher at the time apparently told Richard that she didn't agree with his new-fangled modern ideas and that she was much more in favour of rote learning. But she mentioned that there was a girl called Lynne of about Lizzie's age who lived in between us and the next village whose father brought her to school in his car each day.

'She suggested,' Richard told me, with some pleasure, 'that it might be possible for both fathers to share the responsibility!'

Richard met with Lynne's father and it was agreed that they would share the transport, taking and collecting both girls to and from Guist. Lynne's father indicated that he was pleased that Liz would provide company for Lynne during the journey. I guessed that Lynne was an only child but we didn't know much about her family except that her father was learning Italian at an evening class because he wanted to read Italian literature in the original language and because they went to Italy on holiday most years.

I don't remember whether Richard ever took his turn in the driving, nor whether there was any financial arrangement whereby he paid his half of the petrol costs.

Through Frankie, the female artist who had stayed with us when we lived in Norwich, we got to know her art dealer friend. Through the art dealer and from Frankie herself, we also heard about several artists who, they thought, might appreciate having somewhere local where they could display their work.

In the years in which we had the art gallery, we held monthly exhibitions to display the work of John Harris, who had been one of Frankie's Cambridge Art School friends, Jonathan Bowden, who also knew Frankie from his days in Cambridge, Julia Ball who lived and worked in Cambridge and was a friend of Juliet's, and John Ashby, whose watercolours of Scotland we admired.

We were introduced to Barry Newis, whose large oil paintings of landscape structure and building sites were almost three-dimensional and, as I was to learn, reminiscent of the works of Auerbach and Bomberg.

We also displayed the unusual work of Barry Kirk, who had developed an individual method of using modern synthetic media mounted on canvas to produced three-dimensional female figures clad in silver mackintoshes.

The local sculptor Edward Barker displayed his small abstract bronze sculptures that were based on the form of natural objects, such as seed heads or winged seeds. We occasionally displayed hand-thrown studio pottery that Richard particularly liked, such as the domestic ware made by Terry Godby of Pelican pottery in Lincolnshire but there seemed no point in showing work of local potters, because people could already visit their potteries.

Our criterion for selecting artists was not whether we thought that their work would sell, because too often it didn't, but whether we liked the work and thought it worthy of bringing to the attention of the general art-appreciating public. With this in mind, and giving due consideration to the financial position of many unrecognised artists, we made no charge for displaying their work but we would ask a small percentage commission on any work sold.

Quite often Richard would offer to frame the paintings very simply, leaving the artist to produce only the art work. The art work was usually delivered to us on the Friday before the weekend Private View. Richard and I would spend the evening deciding where to hang or display each piece, at what height and which pieces should be next to each other. Then might come the simple framing, attaching wires to the reverse, placing the work around the walls to see how the whole exhibition would hang together.

We would be lucky if we were able to get more than a couple of hours sleep that night.

We would hold a Private View at the beginning of each exhibition, inviting patrons to come and enjoy a glass of sherry while looking at the work on the walls or on display stands. I cannot now think how we managed not to lose more money at this. But I do recall how embarrassing I found it when patrons had bought their chosen work, paid for it, collected it after the end of the exhibition and the artist called to collect any unsold paintings and his money, only to find that Richard was reluctant to hand the money over.

Richard had a problem with money, especially when it wasn't his. He wasn't a thief, not intentionally, but he found it hard to have cash in his hand or bank account, only for it to disappear again. So, he would procrastinate, pretend to be out, not at home, not answer phone calls, lie about having sent a cheque when he had done no such thing.

I felt totally compromised, it was partly my business too although I couldn't access that dedicated bank account on my own, but I felt a huge conflict between honesty and loyalty, between telling the customer or artist the truth and being loyal to Richard and backing him up.

On one occasion when Richard knew he owed someone rather too much money, from our upstairs bedroom window we saw two tall men park their car by the track and walk towards the cottage, carrying something heavy. They looked grim, determined.

Richard immediately thought they were someone's strongmen, bouncers or 'heavies', that they had come to get their money - and by force if necessary. He sent me out to meet them while he hid upstairs behind the bedroom door.

I met them halfway down the drive. They were bailiffs, they had come to deliver some sort of final demand; they hadn't come to beat Richard up at all. Richard said afterwards that he had thought they might be Ronnie and Reginald, the Kray twins.

While helping to establish an art gallery in the middle of the Norfolk countryside, I was also teaching full time in Norwich to provide an income, and each evening and at weekends, helping to make jewellery. Initially this was enamel onto copper, resulting in costume jewellery, until we thought of enamelling on silver while being careful about the proximity of the melting temperatures of fused powdered glass and silver.

Our kiln had no temperature gauge so Richard did this using a blowtorch. We also considered cloisonné work, and the feasibility and relative cost of using gold. We abandoned the idea of enamel and cloisonné and instead we would set semi-precious cabochon stones into gold or silver, using wire and a drawplate. Richard had been granted a gold licence which allowed him to buy gold and have it delivered to our premises by Johnson Matthey, Betts and other recognised U.K. bullion suppliers.

My job was to attach the appropriate fittings or findings, pack up the items with a despatch note, label and take them with the invoice, which I also hand-wrote, to the local post office. I kept a record of late payment by shops but it was Richard's job to phone them, talk to the manager or buyer and remind them that settlement was overdue.

I enjoyed my teaching. The other teachers at the school were much older than I and most were married. To be at the school well before the start of the school day, I needed to wake by 6am, dress, eat breakfast and walk the mile and a half to the bus stop at Bawdeswell, to catch the bus to Norwich not long after 7am. Although our village was very much from the farming community, I was surprised to notice how few houses had their lights on by half past six on a dark morning. I got off the bus at the Drayton roundabout and either caught another bus or walked towards Earlham.

Travelling home after school was easy. The school secretary would normally give two of us on the staff a lift into Norwich, drop me near the bus station where I could do some food shopping at Iceland before catching the bus back to Bawdeswell. Richard would meet me from the bus stop and drive me, with our food shopping, back to the cottage.

Richard would often request a loan from the bank, to cover wages or the expenses of mailing, or of holding a private view every month. He would too frequently write a cheque to a supplier, only for the cheque to be returned.

Because Richard kept the accounts and I was not involved in that side of the business, I have no way now of ascertaining whether he knew in advance that there was insufficient money in the account or whether the bounced cheque reflected a lack of financial diligence on his part.

The bank would call in the loan which we were not in a position to repay within the bank's time frame or, more often, they would close the account. In this way Richard worked his way through Norwich branches of Barclays, Lloyds, Midland, Royal Bank of Scotland until it became almost impossible for him to get a fresh bank account.

Fortunately, this moving of business bank accounts didn't have an impact on my personal account, which received my Norfolk County Council salary each month so we still had money to pay the household bills – until Richard wanted, or needed, to borrow some money from my personal account. Then I would find there was insufficient money to pay the mortgage, and the grocery bill from the local village store.

Mr James, who ran the shop, was kind and sometimes let us defer payment. But the other villagers shopped there too and it didn't take long for word to get about.

By then we were employing several women from the village to help make the jewellery. Richard and I would tour different parts of the country, Richard trying to persuade shop keepers to look at our rings and earrings and place an order while I would wait in the white van, planning which should be the next town we might visit and providing Richard with a sandwich which I would make on my lap, a bowl of home-made muesli or half a grapefruit.

We made no appointment in advance because were we to do so, to ring up in advance, it was far too easy for the shopkeeper to say no.

To save money during school holidays and while we were touring the country for several days at a time, unless we had friends who lived in the area and who could offer us a bed for the night, we nearly always spent the night in a tent or asleep in the back of the van.

While visiting Kent and driving one autumn evening in fog, we found what looked like an ideal spot on which to pitch our small two-person ridge tent. It was a stretch of short grass, quiet and sufficiently off the road and sheltered by a thick hedge. Only in the early morning, as we were rolling up the sleeping bags and unpegging the guy ropes, did I discover from a notice board beside a gravel path and a gate, that we pitched the tent on the front grass of Ellen Terry's early 16th-century house and cottage at the National Trust's Smallhythe Place in Kent.

We packed up and moved off before anyone from the National Trust noticed.

On one occasion, just outside Brighton where we thought we might call the following day on suitable shops in The Lanes, we pulled the van off the carriageway and onto a small patch of grass just beside the main Brighton to London road, and pitched the tent right beside the van. There was little space to do anything more.

There was a hard frost that night and it was extremely cold. In the morning, sufficiently early to allow us time to drive into Brighton and park before shops opened, Richard perched himself on a wooden fence, held up a small mirror and shaved himself in the old-fashioned way while I cooked breakfast over our small primus stove.

Several motorists hooted or waved so I suppose this was an unusual sight for them on their daily commute. Or perhaps they thought it was a really silly and potentially dangerous place to pitch a tent, and in the winter too, for two young people to sleep under canvas in the frost with no protection at all from any possible road accident. In those days we paid little heed to our personal safety, we had total confidence that we would be all right. And I didn't drive, not by then, so my general level of awareness was not attuned to road safety.

More frequently when we were on the road and camping like this, we would be disturbed by some local official or policeman. With the tent pitched on the outskirts of Ely and on a grass verge in the rain, from my prone position inside the tent, I saw a light outside shining onto the canvas.

I heard a deep male voice speaking and encountered the toes of a large pair of black shoes, shiny in the wet, shoving themselves under the door flap, onto the groundsheet and against the foot of my green sleeping bag, which was slowly getting wetter and wetter from the water dripping from the damp canvas and forming a small puddle on the groundsheet near the tent entrance. A policeman again, checking who we were.

Richard wasn't really an 'outdoors' or physically active guy, although he thought he was; camping was simply his way of saving money when he needed somewhere to sleep. On one occasion when we were on holiday in Devon and met my parents there, he said he couldn't see the purpose of going for a walk just for the sake of the exercise or the journey 'because' he would ask, 'what is the point, if it isn't somewhere you need to get to in the first place?'

Telling him about the benefits of exercise and that 'you never know what you might see' didn't convince him. He had no interest in flora or fauna and little interest in history, geology or physical exertion. But he was creative and inventive, his approach to problems was in no way constrained by conventional thinking or accepted solutions.

On one occasion, I saw huge thistles with brown spiky heads growing among tall grasses in a field just outside the gates of Bylaugh Hall. I mentioned, as we parked near the neglected and derelict Hall to gain a better view of the architecture, how I would love a few thistle heads to spray with gold spray paint and to use them as a Christmas decoration.

Without a word, Richard got out of the van and opened the rear doors. Clutching his toolbox and a tow rope and wearing only sandals on his feet - he rarely wore ordinary shoes, in fact, I'm not sure that he even had a pair - he made his way carefully toward the thistles. He had no knife or gloves.

He walked around one of the thistles, looking at it all the time as if willing it to give itself up, snap its own stem and hand itself over. Then he carefully lay stomach down on the field, avoiding the nettles and other thistles, wrapped the tow rope around base of the thistle stem and pulled hard with a jerk. The thistle refused to yield.

He reached into his toolbox and pulled out . . . a spanner. With the rope still round the thistle stem, he slid the spanner head round the stem just above the tow rope. Then, pushing the rope down hard onto the thistle leaves and holding it there with the spanner, he jerked the rope and twisted the spanner at the same time. The thistle stem gave way, its fibres tore rather than snapped and it lay on the ground.

With his fingers in an arabesque, Richard picked up the thistle, then his tools and the rope. 'I hope you don't want any more', he said, grinning at me, pleased with his own success and placing the thistle into the boot on top of the tool box. 'Thank you but one will be quite enough,' I replied.

Another of Richard's bright ideas was the swimming pool. Not the swimming pool for which he, along with John and Harry, had started to dig the pit just outside the cottage's sitting room - which, in the end, became an excellent sand pit for the children. This time, the idea was not only to have a swimming pool but for it to be constructed and positioned in the barn courtyard, the courtyard that had yet to be emptied of rubbish, drained, dug out, pipes laid, paved and made into this sheltered open-air pool.

This was another of Richard's ideas that started well but grew in his mind and became completely impractical. It was no use my saying anything against it. Experience had shown me that if Richard set his mind on doing something, then he would go ahead, regardless of objection or opposition; in fact, opposition only seemed to add to his determination to pull the whole scheme off, whatever it was, to show that it would work, prove that he was right.

The good start to this latest scheme was the idea of installing ceilings to the entrance room of the barn and to the room next to it that we used as an office. The horizontal sections of the old roof trusses provided the wood onto which we could affix the chipboard panels that acted as high ceilings; and once Richard had built a second half-wall of concrete blocks in the entrance room, he was able to incorporate the ends of wooden beams into the concrete blocks and tie the other ends into the adjoining clay-lump wall to form stairs; stairs for which we needed always to be wearing shoes because the wood used for steps was sawn pine and splintered very easily.

But it gave us one and a half upstairs rooms, one in the centre of which it was possible to stand at full height if we were careful to avoid tripping over the main oak beam running the length from the outside wall of the barn to the inside one. The other 'room' over the entrance provided us with more storage but it was more like a loft or an upstairs cave. There was no height to stand, not even if we bent double. Anyone wishing to get into that space had to crawl over the beams to gain access and to slither across the panels of the chipboard floor.

Richard and our builder workmen were able to put a window into the main upstairs room that looked out over the courtyard. That gave room for Richard's big idea to develop further.

'Why don't we install a slide', he said, 'from the upstairs room down into the swimming pool?'

I tried to point out that it was a lovely idea but as things stood, it was completely impractical, that it was a dream, nothing more. We had no swimming pool. It would take months, years even, to create a swimming pool in the courtyard and more money than we were ever likely to have.

Even so, the idea of clambering out of the upstairs window, climbing onto a slide and sliding down into a pool would be only the start. We would then need to climb out of the pool, come back while dripping wet through a doorway yet to be established into the longer 'art gallery' part of the barn, grab a towel from somewhere, walk back through the length of barn as far as the entrance, find some shoes, dry our feet and climb up the splintery wooden steps with no handrail to get back into the upstairs room. Then repeat the whole operation over again, for it to be any fun.

Fortunately, domestic circumstances prevented Richard from embarking on his scheme, otherwise he might well have ignored any building regulations or the need to ask for planning permissions. He would probably have requested a loan to pay for this latest scheme that I thought and said, was 'very imaginative' but also 'downright daft'. Richard, I thought, was a harmless dreamer.

During this period when we were running an art gallery and manufacturing jewellery at the same time, I was often on my own with the three women helping to make jewellery.

Richard was frequently away touring the southern counties in the van, trying to get orders for our jewellery, leaving me to look after Lizzie on my own, changing her wet sheets, giving her meals, helping her get ready for school and meet Lynne's father at the end of the drive. Then at the end of the day, helping her with any homework, reading her bedtime stories, helping her to read whatever books she had brought home from school. We had no television, only a Bush radio that Dad had lent to us.

I realised that if anything should happen to Lizzie whereby she might require hospital treatment, I had no easy way of getting hold of either Richard or Doreen as her legal next-of-kin.

Neither had I any right in law to make any decision concerning Liz's health, education or general welfare.

In time, Richard bought a fly press and a sheet metal guillotine; he installed both items in the long end of the barn, at the same time moving the manufacturing operations from the one taller room to the longer arm of the barn, where it was cold and with no heating except for an electric heater over the main visitors' entrance, which was switched on only when we heard any visitors coming.

Many of our weekend visitors were not seeking to buy anything. Quite a number of them came to the Norfolk coast from Cambridge for a few days' relaxation and the gallery gave them an inland destination or midway stopping point. Very occasionally one might buy something, a watercolour perhaps, a pot or a pair of earrings but really, they had come just to look and pass the time before moving on to a country pub for lunch.

More regular visitors were men from the RAF station at Swanton Morley. Two called Derek and Charles came, usually together, to almost every exhibition. On one occasion, Derek had said he thought that Richard was the hub of the business but that I was the spokes. I was pleased that someone had recognised that I played an important part. They and others from the RAF camp came so regularly that we were invited one year to the Summer Ball at Swanton Morley.

I was very excited to be invited, I hadn't been to anything similar since leaving college and this was to be a Formal Ball with seafood, we were told, especially flown across from Normandy. But I also realised I had nothing suitable to wear;

no money with which to buy anything either. And Richard had already accepted the invitation.

I felt embarrassed and compromised. I had the ability to make an evening dress, I thought, I had done so at college - but we had no money with which to purchase material and even if we had, it would mean a daytime trip into Norwich to look at material, choose it and then select a pattern; then buying the necessary haberdashery accessories such as bias binding, a zip or buttons, thread, lace and other trimmings.

In the end, I settled for wearing a cheesecloth Gypsy-type short-sleeved blouse that I had had for over a year, under a sleeveless red taffeta frock that I had made myself for some formal event at college. It would, I thought, just about do without being totally out of place or uncomfortable, because the weather was not warm in the evenings and we would be outside for some of the time; and I had no shawl or stole or wrap. We stayed in touch with Derek and his wife and exchanged Christmas cards after they had moved from RAF Swanton Morley to Henlow.

Richard had little idea about what was appropriate, he appeared to me to be quite insensitive. He wasn't able or willing to sense when he needed to leave someone's house or not be there in the first place and when I could see our host and hostess getting tired, or when I was feeling tired and I might hint at him that it was 'time for us to go home'. Richard would be almost insistent about staying longer because he wanted to, such that we began to get a name for being the last to leave someone's house or party. I felt I was becoming the nagging one when I might tell him, yet again, that we needed to leave. I remember two incidents like this, when I would have preferred the ground to have swallowed me up.

For no particular reason, Richard had decided that we would drive to Henlow and call on Derek and his wife, completely unannounced and uninvited one Sunday afternoon. We did just that. He found the correct house on the campus, parked, and told me to get out of the car. He knocked or rang the doorbell while I hoped fervently that they would be out or busy in the garden and not hear the bell. But someone came to the door and politely invited us inside.

We were offered a cup of tea and a Club biscuit. I think we may have had Lizzie with us at the time because I remember that she, or another child, appeared bored and was invited to go upstairs to Derek's daughter's bedroom so that she could play with the daughter's toys.

I thought, once I could persuade Richard that it was 'time we left, Dear' and I had thanked our host and hostess, that they had dealt with the occasion extremely well. But I was embarrassed and vowed not ever to call on anyone again without either being invited or giving them prior warning. I would like to remember this as an isolated incident. Embarrassing, yes, but as a one-off. But it wasn't.

Richard couldn't comprehend that other people might have other plans; he had the impression that he was welcome anywhere and at any time and for as long as he liked. I wasn't able to shake him out of believing that. Somehow, perhaps during his time in the school for maladjusted children, someone appeared to have convinced him that he was always welcome, had boosted his self-confidence, indicated to him that it was perfectly acceptable for him to thrust his company upon other people and he hadn't the sensitivity or desire to realise anything different. That manifested itself in different ways, a year or so later and again, physically, many years later.

Had it been even later that that, he might have got himself into all sorts of legislative trouble. But I'll come to that in a while.

For the first Christmas that we spent living in the cottage, I had bought a new gas oven to replace the Baby Belling hob that we had stood on an upturned tea-chest in the kitchen. I had bought a chicken from Iceland and I put it in our new oven, setting the timer to come on and switch itself off again in time to give us a well-roasted bird for our Christmas dinner.

At 11 o'clock or thereabouts, when we came downstairs and into the kitchen to start to prepare the vegetables, the oven was cold. The automatic switch hadn't turned the oven on. I turned it on manually. But it meant that the meat wouldn't be ready for several hours yet. While we were waiting, we decided to drive up to Holkham, to walk in the woods and on the beach and have our Christmas dinner when we got back.

On the way there, we went past the turning to Walsingham, where Frankie's art dealer friend lived with his wife. Without discussion, Richard turned the van towards Walsingham, drove into a small square enclosed by Georgian houses, parked the vehicle outside one of them and rang the bell. It was the art dealer's house and by then, approaching midday.

Through one of the downstairs front windows, I could see the wife with a vacuum cleaner in her hand, cleaning the carpet. Richard saw her too, saw what she was doing and rather than wishing her and her husband a Happy Christmas and quickly backing away, he just stood there until she opened the door and felt obliged to ask us inside.

It didn't occur to him that the wife might be trying to clean up before guests arrived or before the whole family came downstairs for Christmas dinner.

I explained to the couple that we were 'just passing' and had our meat already waiting in the oven at home. But Richard told them it wasn't. And Richard, had I not intervened, would have gone indoors, accepted any drink or hospitality quite oblivious that this was extremely bad timing on his part. But it was typical of Richard and his complete unawareness of how other people might be feeling. I could cope with my embarrassment, but I wished Richard could feel embarrassed as well. He remained in denial, socially unaware that his company might not be wanted at that particular time.

If this sounds very negative, I have to remember that he had a kind side too. There was nothing intentionally unkind about Richard. He was simply focussed on himself and on what he wanted. He could be and often was very thoughtless, unaware and, as Moo would say quite often quietly to me, 'pig-headed'. To put it bluntly, Richard was insensitive, arrogant, often socially inept. But he could be kind and he meant no harm.

Remembering the RAF Ball and my lack of a suitable dress, some months or perhaps a year later, Richard was in London on his own, buying semi-precious stones. He returned home carrying a large cardboard box. He explained that he had been walking around Knightsbridge, had found himself in Beauchamp Place, looking in fashion designers' windows.

On the spur of the moment, he had gone into a shop, looked through several long dresses and had bought me an evening dress so that, as he explained with pride at his own initiative and generosity, when we are next invited to a posh event, I would have something nice to wear.

It was lovely, and it fitted well, he had got the size completely right. But I was never able to wear it to any suitable occasion. The RAF Swanton Morley station closed in September 1995, by which time Richard was living elsewhere and my gorgeous frock would have no longer fitted.

It stayed on a top shelf in my wardrobe for years until someone pointed out that it was no longer fashionable. In the end and persuaded by my younger daughter, I gave it to a charity shop.

Doreen had said more than once, and had written in a letter to Richard, in several letters, that she was not willing to seek a divorce from Richard on the grounds of his adultery. She said that she had married him 'for better and for worse' and if things had got worse, then it was up to her 'to make things better'. Neither Richard nor I could see how 'making things better' was possible for Doreen if Richard were living elsewhere and with someone else.

I suggested to Richard that we might consider formally adopting Lizzie, so that if Richard were away again and there were to be some sort of accident, I could make legal decisions about Lizzie's health and any treatment. I would, I said, of course undertake to keep Doreen informed of any significant events or changes.

Richard must have put this suggestion to Doreen because, I was told, Doreen could see the common sense in my idea. She quite liked the thought of not having to worry about Liz who had been born, as I learned later from Richard, with a hole in her heart; but Doreen's concern was that by losing Liz, it would break up the family, her family of three children.

I thought very hard about the adoption idea. I had seen how protective Ruth could be towards Liz, even when Lizzie was misbehaving. Doreen must have mentioned to Lizzie's school the suggestion that Liz might live more permanently with her father and his partner, because the next time we visited Canterbury, there was an appointment that had been set up by the school or local authority, for Richard, me and Liz with the Educational Psychologist.

I don't recall whether Doreen attended as well; she may have been waiting in an outer room. Richard had a brief conversation with the Education Psychologist, the Ed. Psych didn't talk to me at all, then Liz was brought into the room and confronted with a dolls' house. I'm sure there must have been more to the interview and what I later assumed to have been 'an assessment'.

There were three dolls in the dolls' house and very little furniture. I don't know how each of the dolls was dressed, whether any appeared recognisable as children or mother or father figures but I would have remembered if one or all of them had been anything other than white. Liz was observed by the Ed. Psych. in how she played with the dolls, the number she chose with which to play, whether she chose the three or just one. This, I gathered, was to form the basis of any decision about Lizzie's future.

I don't know whether Liz was asked what she would prefer to do as a living arrangement, for real.

Three things happened almost concurrently. I suggested to both Richard and Doreen that if Doreen were concerned about 'breaking up the family', as she put it, then I was willing to adopt all three children, if that would help. It was not at all what I wanted, I didn't think we had enough room for all three children but I was sure we would manage somehow.

Doreen appeared to toy with the idea and told us she had discussed it with her parents.

According to Doreen, her mother whom Liz called 'Nanna' was the one who was totally against the idea of us adopting all three children, on the 'whatever will people say?' basis. I did wonder whether Doreen thought I might not be able to cope with Matt, because on one occasion when Richard had told her he was going camping somewhere with me and Doreen was taking the girls to visit their grandmother, she handed Matt, still a baby at the time, to Richard and told him to 'deal with him', until she was back.

We had pitched the tent on a grassy bank beside a small stream and Matt was beginning to cry. Richard passed Matt to me to hold. One of us, either Richard or me, decided as Matt had only just been fed by his dad from a bottle, that he probably needed to have his nappy changed. Doreen had provided Richard with a bundle of towelling nappies as well as a bottle. I unpinned Matt's soiled nappy and washed the contents out into the stream, dried his bottom on a soft dry nappy, and handed him back to Richard.

I had no idea how to fold and put on a nappy, I had never done it before on any baby and I didn't want to put it wrongly. I suppose Richard and I passed whatever test that was meant to be.

The only public telephone box in the village stood outside the post office. I pressed Richard to have a phone installed in the cottage, now that Doreen had stopped sending us nasty messages about money, so that even if I couldn't get in touch with Richard, he could get in touch with me every day or two if he were away.

Although I had warned him as to its whereabouts before he even began digging, Richard managed to put a spade right through the newly-laid telephone cable while he was clearing the ground near the base of the cottage for something else, perhaps making the pit that was to have become the first of his swimming pool ideas.

He came indoors looking sheepish, saying 'guess what I've just done.' He didn't like to inform the telephone company who had only just laid the cable and I'm not sure now whether it was only the outer rubber that the spade cut through, but he wrapped Sellotape or insulation tape thickly around the section of cable and buried it again. The telephone seemed to work quite well afterwards, so no harm done.

Doreen had been unwilling to petition for a divorce on the grounds of either desertion or adultery. But in 1969, the divorce laws changed when the Divorce Reform Act was passed. A marriage could be ended if it had irretrievably broken down, and neither partner any longer had to prove guilt or fault.

With all the publicity that caused, Doreen realised that Richard could request a divorce on his own behalf and as far as I can remember, Doreen was the one who sought a legal split of joint assets and finances.

The divorce, the decree nisi and decree absolute that Richard had wanted came through quite quickly. After he had been living separately from Doreen for over ten years, there could be little doubt that the marriage had irretrievable broken down. As soon as he had the decree absolute, Richard applied for a marriage licence.

Chapter 10

Squirrelling

Years after I married Richard, I wrote in a diary 'I married Richard because it seemed the right thing to do, after all the upset and trouble I'd caused'.

This was not a time for a major family celebration. I don't remember Richard ever having proposed marriage apart from that off-hand remark he made to me, years before, in Owl Cottage. He took for granted that we would, when it became legally possible, get married. I had no engagement ring and when the day came, no wedding ring.

At some time during our period of co-habitation before Richard's divorce, Val had said to me, in front of Moo, 'you know you'll always have to work to support him and his kids?' She didn't mean it unkindly and I don't think she had second sight or any detailed understanding of Richard and his character. She was simply aware that marrying a man who had been married before and who had children to support, meant that I couldn't expect a life of luxury, even if that were what I might have wanted.

Not long after Val's observation, Moo mentioned, by way of caution, that her cousin Jocelyn, whom she apparently told about my domestic situation, had advised her that 'once he

(Richard) has left one wife, it will be far easier for him to leave a second one.'

When Moo told me this, I repeated it to Richard, whose response to me was 'On the contrary, if I've left one wife and I know what that involves, it's definitely something I wouldn't want to do again.'

I loved him but I had also grown used to him, to working with him and having him around, I couldn't easily imagine life without him. I remember thinking how irritating he could be, usually deliberately in order to gain attention, and that if I could deal with Val behaving like that, then I could deal with Richard because it was familiar, behaviour that I knew how to handle – and I reflected on the derivation and meaning of the word 'familiar'. I don't remember either considering or being able to distinguish between love and familiarity, between making a considered choice, or drifting from what had become a friendly working relationship into a domestic norm.

I wasn't starry eyed or on a Disneyesque pink cloud. Marrying Richard just seemed to me to be the obvious thing to do, we got along quite well, marriage was a ratification that would settle a number of issues that seemed to bother other people.

I don't think Moo told anyone else in the family apart from her sister Dorothy and my brother and sister. My father's parents had both died several years before. I don't remember my father making any comment on my intended marriage. When Val was getting married to Don after she realised she was pregnant, Dad referred to his relief that she was marrying the baby's father because 'she's become second-hand goods', an expression which shocked me both at the time and even now, especially having come from my father, with all those implications about women being tradeable items, akin to possessions. I might have wanted to challenge him on that, but I had neither the appropriate language nor the courage to do so then.

I would have preferred to have married in church, because I felt that that would make it seem special, give it authority - and because Richard's first marriage had been in a church and I wanted the same thing for me. But it wasn't possible then for a divorced person to re-marry in a church, our wedding had to be a Registry Office affair. So, there were no wedding invitations, no flowers, no gifts apart from a small fridge from my parents and a double duvet which they told me was from TCP Grandma.

My parents did come to the Registry Office in Dereham for the ceremony, such as it was. I wondered whether they had come to check that we really were getting married. And I was partly right, they did have an ulterior motive. They had come to look at houses in the area that they might buy, now that they had decided to sell 'Owl Cottage', the chalet bungalow in Wootton, a village where there was no street light, no bus service for Moo and no shop, because it had closed.

I wanted to wear something special for my wedding, I wanted to feel special to someone, to Richard. Not the full-length white bridal gown because I thought that would seem silly under the circumstances. I made myself a knee-length short-sleeved dress in white broderie anglaise. And from my teacher's salary, I was able to buy a coat from 'Bonds' in Norwich, a summer coat with a grey background and a gentle red-and-blue check pattern, a coat that I considered was a bit short because the hem fell just above my knees but Richard said that the length quite suited me. I wore a hat that I had bought new, again from 'Bonds', navy straw with a wide brim. There were no photos as far as I can remember.

I'm also not sure whether Moo and Dad took us for lunch afterwards at The George Hotel on a corner of the road opposite Dereham Registry Office, or whether we had a cold lunch sitting round a table in my parents' Volkswagen Dormobile in which they had driven to Norfolk for their house-hunting episode. Conversation between the four of us seemed to be rather stilted and brittle, I got the impression that my parents felt either ashamed or embarrassed about the whole situation.

Several weeks afterwards, I bought Richard a wedding ring. Not a standard wedding ring exactly because I couldn't afford gold, but a ring in silver that he wore. A year or so later, I bought myself a silver ring and wore that on my wedding-ring finger, I hoped that anyone who knew I was married assumed that the silver was white gold. Richard didn't appreciate why I wanted a wedding ring at all, he assured me that it was enough for him that we were living together.

Teachers from the school where I was teaching gave us a couple of striped hand towels as a wedding present, which was kind and very useful because we had hardly anything in terms of bed linen, towels or kitchen utensils. Generally, we made do with what we had, most of which was either damaged or second-hand.

By the time Doreen and Richard were divorced, Lizzie had gone back to live with her mother and she seemed far better able to cope with that. I had resolved not to have children of my own until I was married. It wasn't because I didn't want children. On the contrary, after having been a surrogate mum to Liz, I wanted children of my own, four if possible. But I didn't want any child of mine to be illegitimate because I could not predict what society's attitude might be in the future towards a child, any child, born 'out of wedlock', as Moo would say.

After Doreen realised that Richard had left her and was not likely to return, she decided that she did not want maintenance payments from him for herself, only for the children. He sent her a cheque once or twice but it was like the other cheques he sent or said that he had sent to suppliers, it would fail to arrive. Doreen wrote to him about going to court to force him to make regular payments but in the end either she or the court gave up. It was not possible to force someone to make a payment from money that the person does not have and is not earning.

Richard would do his best to ensure that nothing he owned - and he owned very little - was in his name and so could not be sold to raise money. His openly-professed lack of money to other people sounded to me like a poverty competition, almost an expression of one-'down'manship.

He would do what he called 'squirrelling'. He would hide funds or goods, or pretend that anything he owned belonged to someone else. Not having any money became an aim for him; avoidance was his way of being free from obligation and in this case, the obligation to pay. He didn't like to feel that he <u>had</u> to do something. Years later when I was research Richard's family tree, I discovered that the surname of one of his Suffolk ancestors had been 'Squirrel'. I don't think Richard ever knew that.

There was one particularly silly conversation in which he argued 'I don't see why I have to drive on the left-hand side of the road or below a certain speed. It isn't something I've been consulted about and certainly not something I have agreed to. I prefer to judge for myself rather than have someone who isn't even there make a decision for me.'

There seemed no point in my contesting this, he wouldn't have listened anyway because he knew he was right.

One of the artists whom we met through Frankie and her Cambridge Art School associates was called Jonathan, better known as Jay. I don't remember whether we showed any of his paintings in the gallery, only that later on he became more interested in pyrotechnics and that his mother owned a large house in Cambridge called Fenella, on the far side on the Backs. Richard and I went there once.

The family kept the grass on their lawns at a reasonable length, not by using a lawnmower or having a gardener but by letting their pet guinea pigs graze on the grass in small moveable enclosures. 'The advantage of that,' Jay told us 'is not only that it's cheaper, but also that they don't need to stop work for lunch.'

For some reason, Jay was kind enough to suggest, when he and his mother were spending time overseeing the renovations of the house they had recently bought in France, that Richard and I might like to drive down to the Dordogne area and stay with them for a couple of weeks. This must have been one Easter, before we had either Lizzie or our other children. I remember seeing the stitchwort growing on the grass verges and the blackthorn coming into bud.

We were not the only people staying with Jay and his mother that year. Someone called Paveen was also there, she may have been Jay's girlfriend. I remember her, not because I can picture us all together sitting around the dining room table that was lit only by a central candle each evening, but because it was Parveen who informed us that she had encountered a snake lying across the road when she had been out for a walk that day; and that she had been very wary because, with her Indian background, she had learned to be extra cautious where snakes were concerned, to look at wherever she was putting her feet.

Apart from a brief visit to Riberac market, where I bought a fancy quiche tin that quickly rusted once I got it home and into our damp kitchen in the cottage, and going out to a restaurant one evening where we dined on a thin soup with pasta, followed by Lapin à la moutarde and some sort of rum baba dessert, my main recollection of this visit was of a flicking candle at the evening meal and of sitting stark naked and cold, for hours on end, in a small chalk quarry.

Richard had decided, on noticing the chalk pit set back from the road and within a five-minute drive of Jay's house, that this Easter holiday would be the ideal occasion on which he could try his hand at sculpting. Finding a large lump of chalk lying on the ground, 'This might do well,' he assured me or with words very much like that, 'and if I can borrow some tools, I could start working on this this afternoon.'

There wasn't any discussion with me but I was very biddable in those days. We returned by car to the chalk pit, Richard parking the car so that it half-blocked and hid the entrance from the road from any passing traffic. Richard positioned his lump of chalk on something near the quarry entrance, sat me in the centre of the open space on either a stool he had borrowed from Jay's mother's house, something from our car or a stack of flatter lumps of chalk.

'I need you to be naked,' he instructed 'because I'm not just doing your head. This is going to be your whole body. And you need to be comfortable because I can't do this if you move at all.'

I can testify that the weather in March or April in the Dordogne, even if the sun is shining or unless it is an exceptional year, cannot be described as warm. That year was not exceptional, the sun was weak and although sides of the chalk pit, which was no wider than a bomb crater, gave a measure of shelter, I was naked while Richard was wearing his corduroy trousers, a shirt and a woollen jumper. I don't remember what I had on my feet, if anything. But I do remember saying 'if you are thinking of doing this again tomorrow, couldn't I even bring a book to read – because sitting still for several hours is quite boring really?'

'No, you can't have a book. First, it will alter the contours of what I am sculpting. And secondly, because you will need to turn over the pages and that will change the position of your arms as well as cause you to move the position of your head. This is my one chance to see whether I'd be any good at sculpture.'

'But could we spend just part of one morning or afternoon exploring the area, going for a walk up the road as far as the next village?'

Apparently not – although a brief visit into Riberac was something to which Richard would agree, because he was also interested to see what there was in the street market, so long as we didn't spend any money. Although I did, but only on one item of cooking equipment, which Richard thought was probably worth the expenditure because it was connected with food and in this way, would pay off, he thought. And it was French, so he could proudly tell any visitors where we had bought it, should they ever get to see the actual crinkly-edged quiche tin.

I had assumed that Richard would grow tired of sculpting after a day or two, but he didn't. The most disappointing part of this, for me, was that at the end of our stay, Richard didn't load the half-sculpted lump of chalk into our car with the rest of our luggage. No, he left it on the ground in the chalk pit, saying 'It isn't good enough but next time, I'll do better.'

I could have taken this as a prophetic gesture or remark but I didn't. I just remember the cold, the green and white colours of the young stitchwort and blackthorn blossom around me and the waste of an opportunity for me to enjoy my Easter holiday. I didn't even get an Easter egg.

Richard had so assured himself that he was an artist who had not yet found his ideal material, that he left that half-carved lump of chalk behind. 'It's not worth carrying on with it,' he told me. I don't know why but for some reason, I felt it was my fault that the chalk sculpture hadn't turned out to look like me at all, that I'd let him down in some way. It looked only like a large lump of distressed chalk.

Almost as compensation to himself as much as to me, on the way home we stopped in a small town and went into Prisunic for some French-ruled stationery. While there in the supermarket, Richard saw a cotton dress that he thought would suit me, and persuaded me to buy it. It was pretty but there was no design to it. It was simply a doubled length of material, cut to size and had an inch-wide section of black elastic attached inside to denote the waist. I might have liked to have worn it in warm weather but I never did. It ended up with the sections of material being remade by me into a different dress for one of Richard's girls, and as part of a patchwork duvet cover.

When Richard was told, in conversation, that an artist acquaintance needed to get to the post-box because his ex-wife was expecting him to have sent some money towards the upkeep of their daughter, Richard queried 'But why are you sending money at all because,' Richard told him, 'you don't have to.'

Geoffrey, the artist looked puzzled and asked Richard 'But don't you want to be supporting your children?'

Richard looked equally puzzled that such a question should have been posed, because to Richard, the answer was obvious. No, he did not want to have to do anything, he did not want to support his children financially, wasn't it enough that he was their biological father?

He was willing to have them, two of them at any rate, to stay for a week but he didn't see why they should be a financial drain on him, especially when they were living with their mother. He preferred to shrug off any constraints or restraints.

Part of that was demonstrated by his strong preference for wearing sandals rather than shoes. Sandals without socks and quite frequently, when the terrain allowed it, bare feet. He refused to wear a conventional shirt and tie, even for an appointment with the bank manager and asked me, since he knew I could sew, to make him a soft shirt out of corduroy, one with buttons and if possible, with some sort of tying method at the neck. I did that because he asked and it was something I could do – Moo had told me that a wife should always support her husband - and because by making it and seeing him wearing it, I could feel my skills were appreciated.

Not long afterwards, Richard asked me to make him a purple velvet shirt with similar tying strips at the neck, for him to wear at Private Views. I had not often cut out and sewn velvet but I knew it could prove difficult. Velvet material has a nap and I knew it was important to respect the nap by laying and cutting all the pieces of the pattern in the same direction, otherwise the material would reflect different levels of light and the colour of different parts would appear lighter or darker. It would also be possible to see from the raised pile, as I discovered, where it had been pinned or tacked, long after the pins and tacking stitches had been removed. Corduroy also had a nap and would behave in a similar way.

But Richard's terracotta-coloured corduroy shirt was to be an everyday shirt, the nap would be rubbed one way or another in the course of his daily activity so a little differentiation might matter less; nevertheless, I had respected the nap on that too when cutting out the material.

Texture and colour in the clothes he wore mattered to Richard far more than any current fashion or convention.

Following discussion with Richard, I stopped taking the daily contraceptive pills that I had been taking ever since they first became available. I had been pressured by Richard, years before, to travel by train from Edenbridge to London to find the address of a private doctor in Harley Street who was prepared to supply me, although an unmarried woman at the time, with a month's supply and a prescription.

Now that I was married, I was happy to consider the idea of having a baby of my own.

It didn't take long for me to know that I was pregnant. I don't remember there being any pregnancy testing kits for sale in a chemist's but if there were, I didn't use one, I didn't need to.

After the first missed period, I was hopeful. After the second and a visit to the doctor's surgery in North Elmham, I was sure. As I was told and had already worked out, my baby was due in late March or early April 1972. I gave the baby the nickname of 'Ichabod'. There were no scans possible then so I had no idea of the gender, but I secretly wanted a girl.

I don't remember much about that first pregnancy except that, as the time grew closer, I attended antenatal classes held in a hut on the campus of RAF Swanton Morley. Richard would drive me there in the van, drop me near the hut and after an hour or however-long-the-classes-lasted, would leave home to pick me up again as I started out along the main road to walk back home. I rarely got as far as the bridge before Richard would meet me.

The classes were for anyone pregnant and living on the RAF station or in the surrounding area. Nurse Morton, the community nurse in charge of the classes, told us that she had been asked by the RAF officers' wives whether they could have their classes separate from us locals, and she had said 'no'. Because, she told us she had replied, 'your baby got inside you in the same way as anyone else's and it will come out the same way too, so why do you think you should be treated any different?' A fair point, I thought, and none of us looked very glamorous, lying on our backs or on one side on the wooden hall floor.

We were shown how to breathe, taught how to relax and I rarely lasted for more than a few minutes before I fell asleep. As floors go, it wasn't comfortable but it was away from any other concerns or preoccupations, so I could relax. I didn't know any of the other pregnant women but we were there to know how best to give birth, not to make friends necessarily so there was, for me anyway, no camaraderie.

But I did find some of the exercises funny so I would giggle, and often be the only one to find the situation amusing. I could see the ridiculous in many situations that other people found quite serious, it's just the way I was, I had a positive disposition that found amusement in things that other people seemed to regard as quite ordinary and mundane. And I had to be quite careful because, as Moo had told me more than once, I could often appear quite flippant.

On one occasion while Richard was away and the baby wasn't due for over a month, I decided that the corner field was choked with long dry grass and that the best way of getting rid of the dead stuff would be to burn it off, so that the fresh new grass could come through later in the Spring. I set fire to it against the hedge that lay between the corner field and the farm track. I watched with some pleasure as the flames, slowly at first, spread to another patch of dead grass, then another and another towards the centre of the field.

After about half of the grass was alight and slowly burning with grey smoke, I heard Mrs Ashton calling my name. Mrs

Ashton lived in one of the houses that had been renovated next to the road. She walked up the farm track and onto our shingle drive towards me. Richard had phoned her, she told me, because he had tried to contact me and was concerned that our phone had rung and rung but I hadn't answered, so was I all right? I told her I was fine so she said she would ring Richard back to assure him that I was OK, that I had just been outside and not heard the phone.

I was surprised that Richard had been sufficiently concerned about my welfare to have rung a neighbour; but I supposed that there could have been a chance that I could have been lying somewhere with a broken bone, or eight months pregnant and fallen over and set myself alight in the field along with the dead grass, if Richard had known that was what I was doing. I hadn't had anyone show any particular concern before about my general safety, so I was puzzled that Richard had been anxious. But it was his baby I was carrying, so it made sense.

Only a week or so after Richard returned home after a sales trip, he and I went to London for the day in late February. I had always wanted to go to the Royal Opera House in Covent Garden to see a ballet. I had managed to obtain tickets and good seats near the front row of the stalls for an evening performance of 'Romeo and Juliet' with music by Sergey Prokofiev.

Moo told me 'I think you're unwise to go. You're taking a chance, being so pregnant. Is Richard happy for you both to be going? '

I explained 'But this is a chance in a lifetime and something I really want to do - and it will be easier this month than once I have a baby to look after. If anything unexpected happens, if I go into labour early, then we will deal with it. But right now, I'm fine and I expect I will be fine too when I'm sitting in the Royal Opera House.'

I remember how excited I was, totally enwrapped by the music, the dance, the movement, the colour. I smiled at how the unborn baby was enjoying the music as well. I could feel it moving about inside me when the orchestra played loudly, less if the music was quiet, and during the interval.

At the end, members of the audience in the circle threw daffodils and other flowers down onto the stage, something I had never seen before. After we returned home, I reassured Moo that I had been fine, that the baby and I had both enjoyed ourselves tremendously. Moo said 'I wonder if the baby will prove to be musical after it's born?' I said I thought it quite likely, which pleased her. At least perhaps I could produce a child who was musical.

I took my driving test when I was eight months pregnant. The examiner, a kind man called Arnold, may have been keen for me to pass and not return the month later, in case, by executing the required emergency stop, the shock might startle me into labour.

After minimal discussion, I decided I would prefer to give birth at home. I had never been in hospital except as an out-patient. 'I'm pregnant, I'm not ill,' I reasoned, 'so why would I need to be admitted onto a hospital ward?'

To my surprise, the community nurse who was also to be my midwife said she agreed with me. She agreed on the grounds that if anything went wrong with the birth, it could take any ambulance so long to locate the cottage, collect me and take me down the bumpy track and on to the minor road, then the fifteen miles along the main road into Norwich, that my baby might have arrived in the ambulance by then anyway.

Moo and Dad sold 'Owl Cottage' in Wootton and bought a house in East Dereham. They said they had been looking for a property somewhere between the outskirts of Cambridge, where Val and her husband Don were living with their five children, and me in rural Norfolk.

My parents' new house in Quebec Road in Dereham was late Victorian. It stood discretely back from the road behind a thick hedge and double gates. It had a sizeable garage - Dad hated having to have his car standing outside in the rain and frost - and a small and easily manageable garden. It would take either of them no more than ten minutes to walk to the shops and back, so that suited them well. And there were daily buses to Norwich.

It was the largest house they had had since Moo was a child, which didn't sound much like 'down-sizing' to me, but Moo, like me, enjoyed having ample space and rooms in which to move about, and visitors to stay if necessary.

Perhaps the house in Dereham was not so very different in size from the ones in which she had been brought up and lived in St Mary's and St John's, in Bedford. Moo enjoyed having people around her, she and Dad could be very welcoming and hospitable.

My first photograph of my daughter was taken when she was being held in Moo's arms. We called her 'Nell' after a female member of Moo's family, with 'Sarah' as her middle name. I was much in favour of a child having a middle name, of giving him or her a choice of which to use in later life - and a name not so obscure that people had to ask how to spell it. Perhaps that was a reflection of my childhood wish not to be called 'Lorna', but 'Susan' or even 'Mary' instead.

It had been, according to those who knew about these things, an easy birth. Richard must have telephone the district nurse to say how frequent my contractions were, that he thought the baby would be on its way quite soon.

I sat on the padded bench seat at the dining room table and was told by Richard to keep folding the leaflets for our forthcoming art exhibition, and wondered how many more I would need to do before I felt a need to push and could stop folding. I asked between the regular contractions 'Am I nearly there yet?' and was told by the nurse 'If giving birth is like climbing Mount Everest, then you've only just reached the foothills of the Chilterns. Keep folding and be patient, the baby will come soon enough.'

In time, I retreated upstairs to where we had placed a single bed beside the double bed in our bedroom. I felt relieved that Richard had been through this sort of thing before. He had been present at the birth of his other children; he knew what to do even if I didn't. I refused the offer of gas and air; I was determined to give birth unaided by such modern accoutrements. Nurse Morton, whom I had usually been seeing, was off duty so I had a younger midwife with me who was less dictatorial than Nurse Morton.

Nurse Williams was gentle and regarded Richard with respect whereas Nurse Morton had addressed him with what seemed to me like contempt. I gathered from Nurse Morton that she hadn't much time for men and their sexual desires, despite the fact that such desires were keeping her, as a midwife, in a job.

Once Nell was born and had been weighed and measured, Nurse Morton came back on duty. She showed me how to hold a small baby, how to support her head by cradling it with my hand, how to put her to my breast so that she could enjoy her first feed of the essential colostrum. With a little help, Nell was able to find my nipple, to put her mouth around it, but she did not seem able to suck.

With the intention, I am sure, of helping her, Nurse Morton poked her cheek with the nail of her index finger, not once but several times until I persuaded her to stop. 'That's my baby,' I protested, 'and I don't really like you doing that, in case you hurt her.'

Nurse Morton looked surprised, even wounded. She assured me that she knew what she was doing but that wasn't really my point. I wanted her to ask me before jabbing her sharp nail into Nell. Nell wasn't her baby and I felt she was taking advantage of my ignorance and apparent helplessness. And I also felt she was being rude, disrespectful toward my baby. Within a few tries. Nell began to suck, first tentatively with gaps in between so that she could get her breath, then eagerly.

'You shouldn't stop what you are doing and pick Nell up the moment she cries, because she is manipulating you', Richard would say, knowingly. I didn't say that if Nell wanted me, I was going to see to her because, at only a few days old, she was telling me something and might not be able to wait. Or, that if anyone were manipulating me and telling me what to do and when, it was Richard.

Again, I found I was fighting between my inner feelings of maternal love and care for my baby, and a sense of loyalty to my husband who had fathered babies before - and arguing to him that a few-days-old baby might not have the nouse as yet to 'manipulate'.

I was amused when Nurse Morton told me, on her final visit to sign off as my midwife 'And don't let your husband get at you for a few more weeks, because your uterus and vagina need to repair themselves.'

'Get at me?' I thought, 'as if I were some farmyard animal?' and once again, I decided that for Nurse Morton and her husband, life either contained little sex or little pleasure on her part. No wonder she rode a horse.

It was time to get rid of the mini that we had bought in exchange for the white van. It needed too much done to it and as Richard said, with a car there is always likely to be one bill that you wish you hadn't had to pay. It seemed wise to get shot of it before it failed its MOT test and now that we had Nell, to buy something newer that was better suited to our needs.

Richard found somewhere that was selling a Hillman Minx estate car that appeared to be in good condition, with undamaged red paintwork and an engine more powerful than either the Ford van or the mini. It would, he thought, be ideal if we were to have any more children and it was also sufficiently spacious to accommodate his other three children as well.

He took delivery of the Hillman on the same day on which I gave birth. After I had been cleaned up and the placenta had been disposed of, I came downstairs to see, through the kitchen window, Richard sitting outside the back door of the cottage in the driver's seat of his car, grinning with pleasure, rocking backwards and forwards and patting the steering wheel. I thought at the time how we had both had a present that day as if we were small children; I had the equivalent of a brand-new dolly and Richard had a new red 'brum-brum'.

It wasn't long after Nell was born that we were due to mount the next exhibition in the gallery. At the next Private View, I wore a camel-coloured overcoat on top of my other clothes to walk back and forth from the house to the barn - and saw in horror, first a wet patch spreading across my blouse, then a steady drip, drip of milk onto and down the coat lining. It was clear that I had no problem in making sufficient milk for my baby, only that I needed to be somewhere other than in the gallery part of the barn, handing out glasses of sherry and bowls of peanuts.

I left Nell in her blue flower-patterned carrycot, resting on the carrycot stand and wheels, in the main workshop area, but I was needed to talk to our guests and visitors, in case they were interested in buying something. Yet again, I felt I should be in two places at once, attending to two different people or sets of people. I realised why some other young mothers looked tired and worn out.

As Nell grew, people would tell me what a lovely baby she was, how lucky I was. Dad took to her straight away although he had always seemed to me to be very wary of babies and of small children in general. As well as the carrycot and wheels for which my parents had paid, I had bought a red padded sleeping bag from 'Mothercare', with two handles and a zip along one side. With Nell snug inside this, I was able to move her in and out of the carrycot or onto our bed without waking or disturbing her.

After using it quite frequently, I thought the stitching on one of the carrycot handles was coming slightly loose so I took it to a local shoe-mender in Dereham and asked him to re-stitch the handle. The following day, I was taking Nell to visit Moo in Quebec Road. Dad was going into the town for some shopping and he offered to collect the mended carrycot for me. He came back into his house swinging the carrycot by both handles and grinning to himself. Moo asked him what was so funny.

'Well,' he said, 'I was coming back along the High Street, gently swinging the carrycot, when an elderly lady stopped me and asked if she could have a look at the baby. When she saw that the carrycot was empty, she said, 'but where's the baby?'

I looked at her, and the carrycot, in assumed surprise, and said 'Oh my goodness, I must have dropped it. Can you see it anywhere?' And then, because the lady looked so concerned, I pretended to reassure her by saying 'never mind, I live quite close so it will probably find its own way home'. I left her looking up and down the High Street, then back at me with a puzzled look on her face.'

That was so like Dad, he would tease, would see the ridiculous side of life and would exploit it if it did no harm. Moo was more prosaic. She was honest and straight but lacked his wicked sense of humour; whenever Dad was being his silly self and he and I were giggling, Moo would take it almost seriously and respond with 'Oh dear, Leslie, I do hope you haven't upset anybody.'

Before Nell was born, a woman called Trudi Robitschek had been in touch with Richard. I don't think she had ever been to our mid-Norfolk country gallery but she got to hear of it somehow, probably through the Norwich Twenty Group of artists.

Mrs Robitschek lived in the row of terraced houses known as 'Gildencroft' in Norwich. Gildencroft lies in the St Augustine's area of the city and Gildencroft, run by Norwich City Council, provided supported or retirement housing for older people. Trudi Robitschek, according to what Richard told me, was in touch with an artist, Vlastimil Beneš, who lived in Prague and who was well-recognised within his native country of Czechoslovakia.

Beneš had hoped to have an exhibition of his work in Western Europe but in 1972, any permission for him to send his paintings out of Czechoslovakia was restricted by the ruling Communist Party. The Czech authorities had previously stated that they were also unwilling give permission for Beneš to leave the country, even to attend an exhibition of his own work in Western Europe.

I already knew and had seen on television and in the newspapers, of the Soviet invasion of Prague in August, 1968. A visit into a communist country, still overruled by Russia, that Trudi was proposing in order for us to meet Beneš, didn't seem to be easy to organise; nor to negotiate and ensure a successful outcome.

Richard and I visited the Czech Embassy that was located at the junction of Kensington Palace Gardens and Bayswater Road. I assume that we travelled to London by train, but I remember only a few details of that visit now. We must have made an appointment, I imagine by telephone, so maybe Trudi made those arrangements on our behalf.

When we began the planning, I was heavily pregnant with our first child, due in late March. We may even have begun planning the visit the winter before. I know we had someone with us at the start of the interview at the Embassy, a man who introduced us to whomsoever we were meeting and who then went away, leaving us to talk alone with the Czech authorities. That might have been Norbert Fryd who was a Czech writer, journalist and diplomat. Until the early 1970s, Fryd had served as a delegate to UNESCO so it may have been he.

We were told in advance by that man who first accompanied us and whom I think we had met outside the embassy building before the time for our appointment, 'The conversation might be recorded and will certainly be being bugged and listened to in another part of the building.

So please would you be very careful what you say and to whom. Even if you imagine you are alone,' he said 'because the communist regime could very easily become suspicious and suspect that your proposed visit and exhibition is a cover, a front for something else.'

The unknown man came in with us in order to introduce himself, Richard and me. Before any Czech official entered the room, our helpful man put his finger to his lips, pointed to the lights hanging on chains from the ceiling, cupped one ear with his hand and raised an eyebrow. I nodded. Yes, I had understood that we had to be cautious about what we said, because the Czech authorities could be quite sensitive about the current regime and how democratic Britain regarded it. And yes, I had also understood that the conversation between Richard and myself, any off-hand negative remark, could be overheard and might well count against us.

After a very quiet two or three minutes, a Czech official entered the room, carrying a leather briefcase. The unknown man who had accompanied us made a few introductory remarks about his purpose in being there with Richard and me, then withdrew. It was now up to us to convince the Czech Embassy official that the gallery, our art gallery that was not in Bond Street or any other major city, nevertheless had a good reputation, had ample wall space, was well-lit, had a mailing list of regular clients and was well-able to cope with the number of visitors and possible art purchasers that we might expect. And that being in the country, standing on its own but with a cottage nearby with the only vehicular access being past the cottage, we had paid due regard to the potential safety and security issues.

The barn and art gallery had no intruder alarm system, which had occasionally concerned me because we were also handling silver and gold, but Richard managed to assure the Czech authorities that it would be difficult for anyone to break in, to steal any of the major art works and make off with them in a vehicle, without being heard.

Richard was also able to assure our interviewer that the doors had five-lever mortice deadlocks and that we lived almost on the premises.

The Czech official asked 'Are you in a position to travel to Prague to meet with Beneš, to help Beneš and Art Centrum to select which of the many paintings we considered might interest the British art buyer market?' We said we were quite willing to visit Prague if the necessary permission were to be given and hospitality or suitable accommodation could be found. The Czech official then excused himself for a few minutes and left the room, leaving his briefcase on the floor beside his chair.

Raising an eyebrow at me, Richard pointed to the briefcase and put his finger to his lips. There was no need, I was well-aware that inside that briefcase might be a small tape-recorder left running. I had done something similar when, as a student in Canterbury and wanting to tape Evensong in the Cathedral, purely for my own enjoyment, I had taken my small cassette recorder, concealed in Anthony's briefcase, into the building, placed it down beside our feet in the choir stalls and switched it on.

Mrs Robitschek's idea was for Richard to travel to Prague, to talk with the Czech authorities and to try to get their permission for Beneš' artworks to be sent to England for an exhibition; and, if possible, for Beneš himself to be at the exhibition's Private View and formal opening. Richard warmed to the idea. He thought it could bring the gallery increased recognition. He and I discussed it.

Trudi Robitschek suggested that Richard ought to travel by car in case the authorities at Art Centrum, the Czechoslovak Center of Fine Arts in Prague, would allow him to bring some of the paintings back with him to Britain. But Richard was unwilling to drive alone there and back across Germany to Prague, or to leave me on my own in a village with no regular bus service, no car to drive and a baby not yet six months old.

Mrs Robitschek did most of the initial negotiation with both Beneš and Art Centrum because she too was Czech. She knew Beneš personally, she could speak the language and seemed well-able to negotiate with the communist authorities.

The communist authorities' main fear, she told us, appeared to be that Beneš, once in Britain, would defect. Richard and I decided that we should go together to Prague and that we should take Nell with us.

My presence was considered to be an advantage because I could speak German, not fluently but enough to help Richard ask his way or to buy goods in a shop. And I could not leave Nell behind.

Besides, having a baby with us would, Richard hoped, emphasise that we were not trying to smuggle anyone in or out of Czechoslovakia or have a negative political influence on the local people; we were there simply to arrange something as innocent as an exhibition of paintings by a well-recognised Czech artist.

I did not particularly enjoy that visit to Czechoslovakia. I cannot remember how the whole thing was funded but I know we didn't pay for much ourselves; we were not in a position to do so. On our way across Germany, we camped. We took our own small tent and it turned out to be a hot August in central Europe.

One camp site had a white hill just beyond it, a hill that looked as if it had only recently been made. It shone slightly and had no visible vegetation; it seemed to be made of chalk or china clay. There was a chair lift to the top and people appeared to be skiing down it. But it was the heat that I remembered most and trying to keep myself and Nell cool.

When we woke at 7am, the air was pleasantly warm. By 9am, it was oppressive.

Nell was still breast feeding but I had been advised to start her on solids as soon as possible. My way of dealing with that was to have packets of dried food, bacon-and-peas, or beef-and-carrots, to which I could add boiled water that I carried in a flask, and to mix up a meal in a plastic bowl whenever it seemed to be meal-time. It was possible to buy mashed baby fruit in tins and later in glass jars, but these were too expensive for us.

Richard was quite strict about Nell's meal times, although he was less rigid when it came to his own hunger or his need for something sweet to suck or chew. It became easy to change Nell's nappy by lying her on the changing mat on the ground and folding the nappy into a trapezium shape, pinning it into position after sliding my fingers between the nappy and her tummy to protect her from the sharp point of the nappy pin.

Each nappy had a disposable liner as well as the softer muslin liner and terry-towelling nappy, so that somehow made the bottom-washing-and-cleaning process easier.

When we crossed the border near Cheb between Germany and Czechoslovakia, I felt unsettled. Men were patrolling the barbed wire fence, carrying what I took to be rifles or machine guns, with some guns trained on the incoming and outgoing vehicles. And on us.

At the main check point, Richard stopped the car. We got out, leaving Nell asleep in the carrycot on the rear seat. The authorities on each side of the border checked our passports and papers and with minimal conversation, gestured that we could return to the car and they waved us through. We took long deep breaths of relief.

But somewhere still very close to the border on the Czech side, I realised that it was time for me to change Nell's nappy and give her a feed. It was a wooded area, the straight main road leading through a thick dark forest of pine trees had no lay-bys or no easy stopping places – except that away in front of us, I saw a lone truck turn off to the right, along a side track that proved, when we also reached it, to be covered with soil, grass and pine-needles. It led into the forest.

I asked Richard to follow the track, to see where the truck had gone because that might be a good place in which to see to Nell and her needs.

I had just lifted Nell out of the car, knelt down on the ground and placed her and the changing mat onto the dry pine-needles, when another truck arrived. It pulled up behind us. Two men jumped out and walked purposefully over to us, carrying guns.

Their hand and arm movements made it clear that we shouldn't be there, that we should go back to the road immediately. Still kneeling, I gestured towards Nell, to the changing mat and asked, with what I hoped was a smile, 'Warum?'

They told me quite clearly in either German or Czech, it was such a torrent of language that I couldn't make out which, only the gist of it that was that whatever objection I had, it was over-ruled with the word 'verboten'. Their faces clearly showed that an immediate response from us and departure were essential.

As Richard reversed the car back to the main road, we saw at the rear of the second truck, the one that had then pulled in front of us, a black-and-yellow triangular 'nuclear' or 'radiation' sign. Whether the truck was carrying toxic waste material or whether there was a nuclear processing plant or dump in that forest, we didn't wait to find out. It seemed much wiser to obey instructions, get out of the area and move swiftly on.

With me map-reading and Nell later made content at the rear of the vehicle, we headed towards Plzeň or Pilsen. I saw a tall chimney protruding from among other buildings, with the name Pilsen written on it. I asked Richard what it meant and he explained the manufacturing process of lager to me. From there we headed along the main road for Prague.

The Hillman had a GB sticker of course, and a British number plate. I was not surprised when our red estate car began to attract some attention from pedestrians on the roadside pavement. But I was surprised when a heavy black car hooted at us from behind, pulled round and in front of us and gestured that we should pull over to the right onto a tarmacked area outside a group of shops. Richard wound down the car window as the chap accompanying the driver of the black car walked up to us.

The driver's passenger asked us, in good English, where we wanted to go. Richard gave the man the address, Beneš' address, because we had been invited to stay with him and his wife for a week or so. The man from the black car nodded and gave us directions, not only to the street in which Beneš had his apartment, but also to the actual block - and told us on which floor of the block we would find Beneš' apartment.

I found the man's detailed knowledge of the exact location of the flat to be quite unnerving. Of course, I reasoned, we were expected and our car was very easy to pick out from the other minimal traffic that was circulating.

For several years afterwards, Richard maintained that we were followed right as far as Beneš' apartment block, but I don't remember that happening - although, of course, I was not the one who was looking regularly into the rear mirror of the car. But I suspect Richard was just being fanciful and imagining himself as an artistic James Bond.

I don't recall how Trudi Robitschek travelled to Prague and then to Beneš' flat. There had been no suggestion that she might travel by car with us, the idea of camping might not have appealed to her, nor the likelihood of being woken each night by a crying baby. She arrived shortly after Richard and me, which was just as well because Beneš and his wife spoke and understood very little English.

Before we left England, I had asked Trudi how I could reimburse Beneš, what kind of gifts I should take for him and his wife since they were offering us hospitality and I was conscious that our stay in their apartment might cost them domestic disruption and financial loss.

Trudi assured me that holding the exhibition and having British people see and admire his work was all that Beneš would want; but that if we were insistent, then the things that would be most welcome were items that were not easily obtainable at that time in Czechoslovakia or were too expensive.

And she said, to my amazement, 'Cotton is proving hard to come by so I will be taking a Marks and Spencer cardigan for Beneš' wife and some cotton dishmops.'

We couldn't afford anything from Marks and Spencer but I found a soft green woollen jumper in British Home Stores in the size that Trudi had suggested. I realised then how difficult it could be to buy a present for someone one has never seen, never spoken to or ever met.

I know how embarrassed I felt because our gifts, compared with Trudi's, seemed to me to be totally inadequate.

I remember the trams and trolley buses in Prague and wondering, from the words written on the bus doors, which word meant 'entrance' and which 'exit'; or whether they meant 'men' and 'women' and deciding that the best way to find out would be to stand and watch what other people did. I didn't try to learn the language, not even the words for 'please' and 'thank you' in case I got them muddled.

When I had been about twelve, we had had two young Danish lads to stay with our family as part of some Rotarian exchange scheme, and one of those lads, whenever Moo spoke to him or offered or asked him something, would respond with 'no, thank you', because that appeared to be the only English that he knew. I did pick up the Czech word for chicory, the soft blue flower that grew in abundance by the roadside, but it was of little use in general conversation.

It didn't take long for me to realise that Beneš was keen not to be caught criticising the communist government. He took steps to avoid having searching conversations with us indoors; instead he took us into the city and talked with us as we walked across Charles Bridge, the Gothic stone bridge over the River Vltava that connects the Old Town and Lesser Town. From time to time, he would look over his shoulder to see if anyone were listening or following too closely behind him.

Once or twice, when the weather was sufficiently warm, Richard, Trudi and I would walk together around the cobbled streets of Prague, with me curling my right arm around Nell's little body, dressed in a pink and white nylon frock and with her feet bare.

If they saw us and heard us speaking English, middle-aged and elderly women would come up to us and without saying anything that we could comprehend, would look at us, smile benignly at five-month-old Nell and lightly touch her feet. It seemed to me to be almost biblical.

There weren't many women at all, walking about in the streets or shopping. I didn't see any other babies or young children out with their parents; it appeared that Nell being carried around by her mother was a sight sufficiently unusual for the local women that they felt the need to come closer and have a better look. And often, almost too often, one by one they would pat the fair hair on her head, feel her fingers, then her toes. I, as a new young mother, wondered if the women considered she was under-dressed, cold or that I was neglecting her in some way, or that the sight of her, with me carrying her, was quite unusual in the city during daytime. I was not so very wrong.

I asked Trudi why the few women that we saw had behaved like this. According to Trudi, the aftermath of the war had brought such economic hardships that it was essential to have the labour of all healthy adults, so day-care for young children was seen as a necessity when most of the women went out to work in a factory each day.

If they were married and had children, the children would be looked after in a creche from the time they were babies until they started school.

One afternoon as we strolled with Trudi through the city, we came to a Jewish cemetery. Grass grew among the stones, most of which were upright although some had assumed a strange angle. The inscriptions were in Hebrew. I passed Nell over to Richard while I stooped to look in more detail at the writing, because it was a script I hadn't previously seen.

As I stood upright again, I realised that all was not well with Trudi. There were tears creeping down her cheeks. I asked her what was wrong. Between sniffs, she said 'I feel guilty that so many Czech citizens, so many of the people whom I knew have been killed, while I remain alive.'

For some reason, Beneš decided that he would like to take us somewhere in the Czech countryside and I heard him discuss with Trudi whether we might all go to visit Karlovy Vary[ix] (which I misunderstood to refer to a person called Karl, from a place called Vivary) or Kutná Hora where Beneš had a dacha. I assume Beneš, his wife and Trudi must have travelled in Beneš's car because there would not have been room in our Hillman for everybody, plus the luggage.

I was fascinated to see, on either side of a main road in the countryside, fruit trees growing, and laden with fruit. I asked Beneš about them, to whom the trees belonged, who was responsible for picking the fruit and whether we would get into trouble if we stopped and picked some.

Apparently before World War II, Czechoslovak agriculture had consisted primarily of small to mid-size family farms. But even before the last World War, Czechoslovakia had seen a need to increase the importance of its industrialisation and reduce the relative value of agriculture in the economy. Large numbers of farmers, especially the young, had left agriculture and the countryside for more attractive industrial jobs. After the end of the War and under communist rule, a policy of collectivisation was initiated and by 1960, collectivisation was complete. By the time Richard and I were in the countryside, there were simply not enough people to pick the fruit; the active farm population consisted largely of women and older men.

I don't remember receiving a straight response as to whether we would be allowed to pick the fruit. I was given a rather vague answer to the effect that we could pick the fruit if no one were watching but that we might get into trouble if we did because the trees and the fruit belonged not to us but to the Czech people. All of which seemed fair enough to me, but I remained concerned about the amount of waste.

The dacha, just outside Kutná Hora, looked like a farm building in one of Beneš' paintings. It was quite small, standing on its own on a patch of grassy ground with the whole plot being surrounded by a fence or a wall with a single gate to allow passage through. Standing on the ground just outside the dacha was a slatted wooden table that I thought served as a picnic table. I saw no sign of a barbecue.

Either Beneš or Trudi told me 'The family doesn't often eat outside because wild boar might be attracted by the smell of food and come out of the forest and crash in. Hence the need to have a strong gate in the perimeter fence, and to keep it shut and often locked.'

The sleeping arrangements in the dacha were dictated by Beneš and Trudi, until I objected. The initial idea had been for all the men to sleep in one room and the women in another. We tried this for one night. After that, I said that I wanted to have Richard beside me and Nell, so the three of us ended up sleeping in a general area.

I don't recall there being any actual beds so perhaps everyone slept on the floors. Or more likely, Richard and I used whatever mattresses we had carried with us in the car for our transit nights in the tent. And there was a general feeling that everyone helped with the cooking.

On one occasion, Beneš suggested 'I thought we might walk through part of the forest to see the outside of a building, it has some interesting architecture. The terrain underfoot will not be suitable for pushing the carrycot on its wheels so I am thinking that Nell will remain asleep in her carrycot. While we are all out, you can place it outside on the picnic table.'

We had left the dacha and the grounds for only one minute until I ran back. No, I was not happy to leave Nell there, even though Richard said I was fussing unnecessarily. I had remembered about the wild boar and although I was told that of course one wouldn't get into the grounds and push Nell's cot off the picnic table, I still had visions of my baby being gored by a ferocious wild animal.

Instead, I left the carrycot standing on the picnic table, I picked Nell up and carried her with me in my arms all the way, there and back.

Something not dissimilar happened when we travelled by car to the centre of Kutná Hora. There was a general lack of communication about our destination, probably not deliberate but partly because there was a language barrier and also because we, as guests, didn't like to ask too much in terms of what, why and when.

When we arrived in the town centre, Richard parked the car with its nose pointing towards a religious building and the back of the estate car facing outwards, to be viewed by any passers-by. Trudi told us 'Kutná Hora is known especially for its medieval silver mine. The mine was discovered in 1967 when a hydro-geological exploration of the centre of the town was carried out. In 1300, King Wenceslas ll established a new mining law called 'Prague groschen', a currency with a fixed content of silver. Despite the new law, its amount at 90% silver and 10% copper varied over the years, depending on the town's economic fortunes.'

She went on to tell us that a century or so later, a fortified castle known as Vlašský Dvůr, which meant 'Italian Courtyard' was established, which would become the site of the Royal Mint and Treasury, along with smithies and a coin-striking works. A royal residence was also established for use by Czech kings.

Armed with this information and leaving Nell asleep in her carrycot at the back of the car, everyone set off to walk to see the sites. Richard locked the car and put the keys into his pocket. I went with everyone else to see what it was that they were visiting but I felt unhappy about leaving Nell. I told Richard I would walk back to the car just to check on Nell.

He wasn't pleased that I was leaving the group and I didn't have the sense to ask him for the car keys. That was unfortunate, because when I returned to the car, I could see through the rear window that the August sun was shining in, straight onto Nell in her cot and her forehead was damp and sweaty. She looked distressed.

After cursing myself for not having thought about the keys, I walked as fast as I could to where the rest of the party was, found Richard, asked for the keys, ignored his protests about my leaving the group again, and started back to the car once more, realising how hot the air was becoming, how little air movement there was and how much Nell needed me right then.

I felt very guilty for having left her in the car. I don't remember whether I picked Nell up and rejoined the group or whether Richard followed me back to the car, because it wasn't important. What was important was that I was able to rescue my baby out of that hot car before she became overheated and something more terrible happened. But I knew at that moment that I couldn't necessarily depend on anyone else to keep my baby safe, certainly not on Richard despite his previous experience of fatherhood. He did not want our daughter, or any children, come to that, to become a hindrance.

It was now up to me to make sure that my baby, any baby of mine, was safe and felt secure, was well-fed, comfortable and provided for.

I went with Richard to the Art Centrum warehouse which stored the paintings that Beneš was not able to keep in his flat. Together we chose several works showing deserted farmsteads, old farm machinery and mine workings that we thought might appeal to the British public and with subject matter to which the Czech communist government would not object. We turned down the offer of paintings of elderly women, or women that seemed to me to be elderly, with their stocking tops and plump bottoms on display.

Art Centrum wasn't willing for us to transport any paintings back with us. Instead, they said they would rather wrap them up in their own special way and complete the paperwork once they were ready for dispatch.

On our final evening and after Trudi had left to return to Britain, Benes took us out to a restaurant in Prague to give us what he described as a typical Czech meal. We were served with a soup, thick with chunks of meat almost like a runny stew. And borsch, beetroot soup with a dollop of sour cream on top which we were told to stir into a swirl and then into the soup. I have a feeling that the dessert might have been some sort of rum baba or plum dumplings. And vodka, of course. Or Slivovitz. I imagine that we either took Nell with us into the restaurant, or that Mrs. Beneš kept an eye on her, back at their Prague flat.

As we packed our belongings into the car, ready to drive back to Cheb, then across the border into Germany, the Netherlands and onto the ferry back to Dover or Folkestone, Beneš was almost tearful. I think he was very sad that he would not be coming with us.

Just as we were about to leave, he handed me a piece of hardboard not much larger than a sheet of foolscap paper. 'Please take this with you,' he said with mixture of hand-gestures and more English than I had heard him use before, 'it is only a rough thing and something that I will never be able to sell at an exhibition so I wish that you have it. Put it somewhere safe to remind you both of me and the dacha.'

I glanced at what he was passing to me. On one side, it was a rough painting of a privy not unlike the one we had used outside the dacha, with a crude sketch on the privy rear wall of a naked woman with typical buttocks and oddly shaped legs. We had already packed our clothes and camping gear so to keep it from any damage, I slipped the piece of painted board between the base of the carrycot and Nell's bottom sheet.

It would be safe there, I thought, away from any possible damage or getting lost as we unpacked and repacked our camping gear each night on the journey home.

As we slowly approached the border crossing from communist Czechoslovakia into Germany, we were unexpectedly stopped by the rear red lights of a vehicle in front. Then the rear lights went off and everything went black. A vague shape appeared at Richard's driver window. There was a tap on the glass. Richard wound down the window. 'No lights now' said the voice. 'No talking. Switch engine off and passports ready.'

Once he had been given the signal to start the engine again, Richard very gradually inched the car forward, being extra careful not to hit the rear bumper of the car in front. Everything was still black. Further forward. No sound except the car engine. I was pleased that Nell was asleep, didn't cry, in case there were guns trained on us, as before; in case the border guards were jumpy, nervous.

Then suddenly, floodlights switched on. The red-and-white striped barrier at the crossing was down across the road. We had reached the border office.

Without getting out of the car this time, we handed our passports to the official, gave a brief account of where we had been, whom we had visited and why. A telephone in the border control hut rang. An official answered it. We waited. A tap on the window again, our passports were handed back . . . The barrier was raised and we were waved across and into Germany.

We had to go through the whole procedure again at the German border post but this time under the search lights and without the same degree of tension.

Once we had our passports back in our hands again, we sped off into the night, towards the site where we had stopped on the way coming. We left Nell asleep where she was in the car. Hardly bothering to pitch the tent correctly, we clambered under the canvas, unrolled our sleeping bags and slept deeply until the morning sunlight woke us.

The exhibition, from 8 October until 14 November 1972 proved to be a huge success. Daedalus Press produced an excellent twelve-page black-and-white catalogue showing Beneš' painting of 'Lustgarten' on the front cover and text by Norbert Fryd, translated from the original Czech.

Although, as we had expected, Beneš was not given permission to attend the Private View of his own exhibition, the Czech government did send a Czech minor diplomat called Pavel to represent the country and to say a few opening words to the assembled art-lovers. Many of the paintings were sold, including the larger ones and some, we were informed, were destined for the boardrooms of large companies.

One month later and quite by chance, we heard through the media that Pavel had defected. I wondered then whether the Czech authorities wished they had granted Beneš' original request for him to come to Britain for the opening of his own exhibition. He had, at least, a wife and home to which he would have wished to return. And we wondered whether Beneš ever knew that his diplomat replacement had indeed defected, as if in his place.

I had the small painting of the privy framed. It is unsigned but for anyone familiar with his semi-naïve style and brushwork, it is clearly recognisable as having been painted by Vlastimil Beneš. It now hangs on a wall in my bathroom, facing the bidet. That seems to me to be a fitting place.

Chapter 11

Betrayal

Following the success of the exhibition of paintings by Beneš, Richard was looking for another artist or group of artists who might welcome having an exhibition in a rural gallery.

Just as Nell was learning to walk, I was pregnant again. I had felt that once I was into having babies, I had better keep at it if I were ever to manage having the four that I wanted. Moo was very pleased to learn the news but warned me that, just because Nell had been such an easy baby and a contented toddler, I should not expect the next one to be the same. I queried that, told her that I thought Nell's good behaviour was 'just a question of upbringing' and that I expected the next baby, whether boy or girl, would be very similar.

I remember Moo raising an eyebrow. Only that, just raising her eyebrow.

Richard was still going to trade fairs to promote and sell our jewellery. Most of these were in Britain but one was held in Belgium. I don't remember what we did with Nell when I was with Richard in Belgium, when some other visitor managed to hold her cigarette against my dress, a lilac cocktail dress that I had bought purely for the occasion, which caused a noticeable cigarette burn hole on the fabric.

If I were not in a position to go with Richard to a trade fair, he would often return home afterwards with a present for me, with something he had bought or more usually something he had acquired by exchanging jewellery for it.

One summer when I was heavily pregnant with my next child, he came home with a brown corduroy pinafore dress with thin shoulder straps that he thought I would wear during that summer until the baby was born. It was a kind thought. But totally impractical too. Corduroy, as I hinted to him, is not an ideal fabric for a sundress. Instead, I used it after the baby was born, with a blouse or thin jumper underneath; it hid my non-diminishing bump very well.

I nicknamed our unborn child, whom I assumed would be a boy, 'Boris'.

Before he was born, Richard and I discussed an endless number of names that would seem to fit with the baby's surname. None seemed right. No, not Nathan, we decided. Nor Benjamin. Not any of the names that were floating about as being popular. We wanted our child to have a name that was distinctive and carried no class-related stereotype. So definitely not Gareth, nor Tobias, nor Dominic, nor Wayne. We quite liked Madoc but it didn't go well with the baby's surname.

In the end, after he was born and we had established his gender - and possibly in deference to Richard's political leanings - we settled on 'Keir' followed by 'Timothy' in case he wanted to use a different name when he grew older.

At the same time, the Norfolk and Norwich Triennial Festival Committee was looking to mount a large open-air sculpture exhibition somewhere in the city or in the county. The

Sainsbury Centre had not been built on the campus of the University in Norwich by then.[x] The Beneš exhibition had shown that we had the capacity to hold a large well-publicised exhibition. We offered the Committee the use of the garden and the mown field behind our house, with all publicity and associated costs to be covered by the Festival Committee.

All we needed to do was to indicate where our boundary was, and the position of any fruit trees that we wanted not to be damaged or disturbed.

At the beginning of October 1973, large sculptures arrived on a low loader and were positioned. In due course, people would arrive during the days of the exhibition, and stroll around the land with a catalogue in their hands. Neither the gallery nor the workshop part had toilet facilities – our staff had been accustomed to walking up to the cottage if they wanted to use the loo - so very occasionally, we thought, someone might knock at the cottage door and ask about a toilet. It wouldn't, I assumed, present me with a major problem so long as I remembered to move the bucket in which dirty nappies were soaking.

By now I was attending to Nell and her needs in the morning until it was time for me to make a drink for the three local women who helped us make the jewellery. After the kettle in our kitchen had boiled and I had walked down the drive to the workshop, carrying a tray of drinks, Richard would expect me to stay in the workshop and assist him there, sorting and packing orders or dealing with telephone customers until lunchtime.

We had abandoned any idea of enamelling by then and were setting semi-precious cabochon stones into mounts in silver or gold to form rings, pendants or earrings.

The Norfolk Triennial Exhibition was due to open in early October with a private view. My next baby 'Boris' was due at the same time. I was concerned that the two events might happen on the same day. Since I needed to be present at each of these events, I could see a potential problem. I discussed this with Richard and Nurse Morton, who would once again be my midwife.

We could not alter the opening date of the Triennial Exhibition but I could do my best to ensure that the baby was born on time, because if it came only a few days late, it would clash with the opening of the exhibition.

On the day we had calculated that the baby was due, nothing happened. No baby, no contractions, no waters breaking. The following day I contacted Nurse Morton. Richard was becoming concerned, wondering how he might manage to greet visitors to the exhibition without my help, or how he could help with the birth as well as welcome visitors to the Triennial Exhibition.

When 'Boris' was three days late, Nurse Morton and I thought we should 'begin to hurry things up a little', as she put it. As far as she could tell, the baby seemed to be a correct size and weight to cope with the birth, it just wasn't coming. It was, we both believed, time to move to 'plan B' to jump-start that baby.

Feeling rather like Dennis the Menace out of the Beano comic, I had acquired a bottle of castor oil and under the direction of Nurse Morton, I tried to drink it from a teaspoon. It was disgusting, almost impossible to swallow, it stuck in my throat. It was like trying to swallow thick cold phlegm from a spittoon. By mixing in a small amount of Ribena, I tried to change the flavour. Pointless, the blackcurrant flavour didn't help at all; the oil still became stuck. In desperation, I tried spreading marmite onto slices of white bread, making it into sandwiches and attempting to swallow a mouthful of that between doses of castor-oil-and-Ribena mix - until Nurse Morton said that was enough.

Thinking it was all over and that I could rest for a while, she instructed me to find her a bucket, to lie on my side on the Chesterfield sofa on a plastic sheet and the towel that she produced. This was to be my first understanding and experience of having an enema in addition to the castor oil. The two together were not unlike using a combination of Dyno rod and a sink plunger.

It was not fun but within a few hours, I went into labour. While Jean, one of the women who helped with the jewellery-making was in our kitchen looking after Nell who, she told me later, had been happily sitting on the draining board with her feet in the sink, upstairs on 9th October I produced a boy, a little over the average weight but from what Nurse Morton and I could tell, perfectly healthy.

Nurse Morton was concerned that with my lack of sleep and so much else to do with the gallery, I would not have sufficient breast milk for such a large healthy boy. In case I had a problem, she told me to me to stock up with a tin or two of evaporated milk. I was soon able to prove that there was absolutely no need for that, any problem I might have involved stopping a surfeit from being produced and flowing freely when it was less than convenient.

Although it was deemed to have been a success, I disliked the intrusion that I felt the sculpture exhibition caused. I did not want people wandering past the back of my garden, gawping at whatever was hanging on the washing line, at any of Nell's toys that was left outside or noticing and commenting to each other on whether the windows were sufficiently clean and the curtains drawn back. I felt that it was my cottage where I and my family lived and I wanted the peace and quiet that should have gone with all that.

I didn't want our weekends to be interrupted by people coming to the art gallery for their own amusement and not buying anything; or if they did, not buying anything much, other than a twisted silver ring that would cost them less than the price of a bag of potatoes.

The price of gold and silver had risen dramatically on the stock market but there was a limit to what we could charge for a handmade item of jewellery while we still had to compete against machine-manufactured items, where the basic shapes and mounts had been cast. I felt that life had become out of balance somehow and I wasn't sure how to get the balance right again. It had become all work and, despite the fun of having the children and the enjoyment they gave, no play or very little. I did not know whether Richard felt this as well. There was little time in the evenings for discussion.

After I had fed Nell her tea in the late afternoon or early evening, put her to bed, given Keir his night-time feed, switched on the baby monitor in the house and returned to the barn to prepare more items to be sent by post in the morning, I would either cook an evening meal or we might decide not to bother with food and tumble exhausted into bed. Occasionally, I would ask Moo and Dad to have the children for an evening so Richard and I could go out somewhere together even if we could not really afford it.

I was happy for Moo and Dad to look after the children, once I had checked that the bleach was out of Nell's reach and the kettle and its flex had been pushed to the rear of Moo's kitchen work surface. I had tried to find a babysitter from the village but no one whom I would trust was willing and available. And even if I had been able to get someone local, she would have required payment from money which we did not have. It was hard enough to find sufficient money for the women's wages each week.

I did consider whether to return to teaching for a term or so, just until we could get ourselves back on our financial feet. But Richard was against it. It would mean that he would have to be responsible for all the childcare and he certainly didn't want to do that.

I dropped the children off at my parents' house early in the evening and once, only once, Richard and I went to an Indian restaurant in Norwich for a meal to celebrate a birthday. We ordered our starters and main dishes. Richard liked Indian food, he said he thought that it was because his mother had Indian relatives. He didn't know much about his mother; he had a few photographs of her but nothing that had belonged to her except some sort of thick pyjama cord made from twisted silver threads.

Richard and I sat down in that restaurant, no one else was in that part of the room and we sat in silence. Because I felt I should say something, I said 'hello' as I looked straight at him and smiled. 'Hello' he said back, flatly. Silence again.

I thought at the time that because we spent every day and every night together, there was really little we could add to our day-to-day business or domestic talk. We had nothing new to say to each other, we had milked each other conversationally dry until something or some event could inject some excitement.

The positive interpretation of that minimal exchange might be that we knew each other so well that there was no need for conversation. But I needed to learn something new or do something new. I needed stimulus, personal success, adventure.

Neither of us seriously considered the idea of Richard returning to teaching. I was not sure what references he might be able to get from his previous school in Thetford but teaching certainly was not what he wanted to do, for five days a week. Since he couldn't be a potter and the art gallery was becoming a burden, he wanted to make jewellery and to sell it to as many shops as he possibly could.

To avoid the staff having to walk up to the cottage to use the loo in our bathroom in which I might also be bathing Nell or Keir, Richard decided to approach the bank for a loan so that we could convert the barn outhouse that butted onto the main workshop, into a toilet with a washbasin. If, at some time in the future, the barn could ever be made into a house, then to add a shower made sense, so that the outhouse could become a bathroom.

To help a little to fund this, Richard advertised the fly press for sale and the sheet metal guillotine that we had used when our jewellery was made from copper sheet. But we would still need a sizeable loan. And whenever Richard had any money, either in the bank account or in cash, he would demonstrate an urgent need to spend it almost immediately and on something that he wanted, as if doing nothing with the money, having nothing other than a black bank balance to show for it, were a waste.

One of his frequent expressions, when I suggested financial restraint regarding a proposed purchase, would be 'but can we afford <u>not</u> to buy it?'

The car repair garage fitted a safety belt that I had bought as a present for Richard for his driver's seat: I was concerned that he might have an accident when away, driving from town to town and shop to shop. During the process of installing the safety belt, the main mechanic discovered that the grey mini, with which Richard had replaced the Hillman that had failed its MOT, had been fabricated from two quite separate Austin Mini carcasses.

'The two chassis' the mechanic told us afterwards, 'appear to have been damaged in an accident or accidents at some time in the past, then soldered and welded together to form one carcase. If the Mini were in an accident again,' Richard was advised, 'the two sections of bodywork might split under the impact and,' warned the mechanic, 'divide into separate parts and travel in different directions just as, at the same time, your own bodies might.'

That presented an unpleasant picture in my mind, even before I considered what might happen to any children we might be carrying with us in the car. While it was in the garage, the grey Mini was re-sprayed in yellow and turquoise, which were the only colours that the garage had available. It looked unusual but the paint covered up work done to hide the joins. It was also easy to pick it out in a crowded car park. But Richard thought we should get rid of it any way, as soon as we could afford to do so.

When it was sold, I asked Richard whether he had told the new buyer what we had discovered about the Mini and its history but he said no, it was a case of 'caveat emptor' or 'let the buyer beware'. I hoped that in future, we would ensure that any other car we bought or sold was first inspected by the AA or RAC and declared to be sound and fully roadworthy.

Richard had always wanted a Citroen Safari like the one he remembered the Rev. Neville having driven when he joined the college in Canterbury. Richard's rationale for suggesting this purchase was that the Safari estate, known as the DS had, he said, 'a novel hydro-pneumatic suspension system including an automatic levelling and variable ground clearance' which, he thought, would deal with any difficulty that we might encounter when driving over the sandy pot-holed farm track as far as our drive.

When needed, he explained, the car could go up and down several inches in the air at the pull or push of a lever. It also had two additional seats at the rear which would fold down or be put up as necessary so, Richard assured me, a car like that could easily carry not only our children but his other three as well.

I was not completely fooled by this justification of his choice of vehicle, I was far more concerned about the financial side. But, Richard told me, the bank wouldn't lend us the money if they didn't think it safe to do so. I was always subconsciously aware of the rather difficult childhood which Richard had told me about many times; I was keen that he should have a better time when living with me, have the things that he wanted, even though he hadn't been able to buy or install a pottery kiln.

I did not attempt to restrain him although I could suggest and advise extreme caution. I knew that had I tried to put the brakes on, told him I was against an idea, he would go ahead with his plan regardless of whether or not I approved. And most likely sulk. It was just the way he was. It took me several years to realise that that was what the word 'sulk' meant. I hadn't met such behaviour prior to living with Richard. With Val, it had always been the bad temper and spiteful behaviour that the rest of us found so unpleasant.

Although Nell was still in nappies during the day, I was able to have her admitted into North Elmham playgroup for half a day a week. I could drive her there, take her in and stay for as long as she seemed to need that reassurance; then go back home, see to Keir, settle him in the carrycot parked just outside the barn with lengths of coloured ribbon attached by a nappy pin to the carrycot hood, that he could watch while they fluttered in the breeze.

He would lie there quite happily, watching the ribbons or the leaves in the trees above, or any birds flying past. He wouldn't cry or be startled, even if a plane flew noisily overhead. He just lay there and occasionally gurgled if he were not asleep.

With Keir lying safely just outside, within view and in earshot, and Nell at the local playgroup, I was able to work in the workshop with Richard, helping to order, unpack, sort, polish, package, label the jewellery while also being available to make tea for the staff, lunch for Richard, collect Nell, shop for essential groceries and from the post office on the way home, post packages of jewellery to craft shops.

From time to time, where we were already selling to a shop, we needed to stimulate the shop manager into not forgetting about us, into reordering. To do that, we needed a reason to contact the shop again, to make a courtesy call perhaps, or we had to produce something new, a new design or a different range every so often. Two or three times a year, Richard would travel on his own across the country to visit craft shops, leaving me at home with the workforce and the children.

I wasn't keen on him camping on his own, it seemed more sensible to me that he should ask any friends or relatives that we had in that area whether they could give him a bed for the night.

We had one craft shop in Bath that we supplied but I thought it would be good if we could find a couple more shops in the Bristol area that might place an order. With that in mind, I contacted our friend Natasha, who had been to stay with us in Norfolk before we had the children, to ask whether she could put Richard up for a night or two. Tasha lived on the outskirts of Bristol. She had good taste so I thought she could also recommend suitable shops in Clifton or Bristol that Richard might visit for a possible order.

Three or four days later, Richard was back with a full order pad and a half-empty display case. He was pleased with himself. He had sold half of his samples on the spot in Bristol and gained orders in new shops on his way across the country back to East Anglia.

He had also had time to visit the Arnolfini Gallery and had felt pleased that we were no longer reliant on the celebrity art market to sell insipid watercolours of boats at Blakeney, that we had left that life far behind.

Remembering the conversation that Richard and I had had in the Indian restaurant in Norwich, and had not managed to have because we had nothing new to say to each, I suggested that we might do something together, something completely new and possibly active, one evening a week on a regular basis. 'What about badminton?' I asked. There was an adult beginner's class starting in Fakenham High School at the start of the next term. Could we both sign up for badminton once a week? And what about a babysitter?

We tried leaving the two children with Moo on a couple of occasions. But badminton lessons started at 7.30pm and went on for two hours so that by the time Richard had driven us both back from Fakenham to Dereham at the end of a session to collect the children, it was getting late and if Moo were tired that day, she wanted to go to bed. And so did we, we would still have the drive from Dereham back to the village, then the rigmarole of a late-night top-up for Keir, a quick bedtime story and a song for Nell and a snack for each of us.

We did try bedding Nell down on the stage in the school's hall with Keir in the carrycot but it was not successful; the opportunities for Nell to have fun were too great, such that the whole idea of Richard and me having time together became loaded with tension and parental responsibility.

It is not possible to concentrate on strategically placing a shuttlecock, while also trying to keep a child from playing with the long stage curtains or laughing too loudly.

And then we had to decide which of us, whose turn it was, to leave the badminton court and the game to see to the children.

It seemed simpler for us to stay at home and watch programmes on the second-hand television that someone had given us, although an aerial as well would have been helpful. But watching a screen together, despite the interference, gave us each a feeling of resignation, endurance even, more than involvement and excitement. The fall-back position was to discuss our finances and how to get ourselves out of permanent debt.

I was several feet up a ladder, repainting the rendering on the outside of the cottage in a gentle grey, when I realised that I was pregnant again. I came down the ladder quickly, put the paint pot and the brush down on the ground, leaned backwards against the cottage's rear wall to get my breath, to keep my head from spinning, focus my eyes. Struggling out of my overalls, I heated some soup for lunch, found some sliced bread and prepared myself to give the news to Richard.

I had felt no fluttering but I was almost sure; I knew my body and I decided that this time it was twins, identical girl twins whom I temporarily nicknamed 'Aniseed and Coriander'. And although this was an intentional pregnancy, I was only too aware that the cottage lacked space. It had two upstairs bedrooms with a further small area, not really a room at all but just large enough for a cot, outside where the airing cupboard stood.

After lunch, I finished painting the apex and the outside walls. Richard returned to the barn.

Richard had plans, he told me. He would order some concrete blocks, 'will they be expensive?' I asked, 'because we have the invoice to Betts to pay and . . '

'I'll build a play area on the back of the dining room. That would give us more downstairs space. But first we would need to clear the area so that we could put down a concrete base.' He ordered the necessary number of blocks, which were delivered. And which stood untouched in a stack for several months.

Richard was never short of ideas. He was someone who started things off, a 'Shaper' who enjoyed the beginning but who rarely completed anything because that was the boring part; whereas I was, when necessary, an Implementer (and with Richard, it so often became necessary) and also, as I was to discover years later through a Belbin analysis during my teaching years, I was a 'Completer Finisher'. I had always thought my natural role was as a second-in-command, someone who lacks ideas but does what she is told, who finishes things off. Living and working with Richard, that was how my life was panning out.

We were lying in bed one Saturday or Sunday morning. Nell and Keir were still asleep. I was snuggled up close to Richard, my head on his chest and his left arm around my shoulders. I felt very happy and said 'If I were to die right now, then this is how I would want my last moments to be.'

Richard did not respond immediately. I do not know how the subject moved so rapidly but within a few minutes he told me, and I don't remember exactly how nor why but it was 'You remember when I went to Bristol, you suggested that I should stay with Tasha? Well, I did, she was well and it was fine.

After we had had dinner that evening, I made love to her. We had sex that night, not just once but at least twice.'

I don't remember exactly what I said next. Or quite how I reacted. But I was completely stunned. Nor only by Richard's behaviour but by the disloyalty from one of my closest friends as well as from my husband. I was bewildered as to why it had happened. I knew, of course I knew, that Richard had always fancied Tasha.

When she was acting as Students' Union secretary, he had made it clear that he thought she was marvellous, that he thought she had lovely eyebrows, liked the way she did her hair and so on, she appeared so poised and at the top of her game, although he would never have put it in those terms.

But I also knew, because Tash and I had adjoining rooms and she had said so, that she didn't fancy him one bit, considered he was a bit of an idiot at times and quite annoying. But she had been patient when having to put up with him. So, from what Richard had told me and I assumed it to be true, it was Tasha's behaviour that surprised me most. I didn't understand it at all. It didn't sound a bit like the sort of thing she would do. She had always appeared so 'proper'.

I needed an explanation. Not from Richard, who seemed unpleasantly keen to tell me exactly what he and Tasha had done and in detail that I found quite unnecessary, almost boastful as if I were his best mate at the rugby club. He seemed unaware that I might have an emotional response to being given this level of description. More than that, he appeared blind to the fact that I might entertain any emotional response at all.

For him, it seemed to be something that he considered had happened in the past, something that should not be affecting today and certainly not the future. So, I think he said, please would I not mention it or 'go on about it'. He might have added 'and dry your eyes'. But that was unlikely because, although I knew from something Richard had said in the past that he did not react empathetically to seeing a woman cry, it was even more unlikely that he would have noticed that I was in any way upset.

For him, what was then important was that we should get on with the day, focus on what we needed to do and to get done.

Still wanting some sort of explanation, perhaps a signpost to the way ahead and even closure, I stopped staring blankly at the mahogany chest of drawers in our bedroom which was where I had been standing after I had got out of bed and where the impact of this had really hit me.

I sat down and on airmail notepaper, wrote a letter to Tasha who had, by then, moved to the other side of the world. It simply stated the bare facts that Richard had told me and I wanted to know why they or she had done what had been done. All my letter asked was 'Why?'

I was like a dog wrestling with a bone. If I shook it this way and that in my mind, thought about it for long enough, it would all become clear, the answer would fall neatly into place. Only we didn't have a dog, although I would have liked one and we had plenty of outside space; because Richard had said it would cost too much to feed, that we couldn't afford it.

I told Richard I had written to Tasha. He couldn't understand why I had done that, why I had felt the need to do that.

In time, an airmail envelope addressed to me arrived, from Tasha. The gist of her letter was that the sex with Richard wasn't important, that it meant nothing at all.

In a fleeting moment of loyalty before any other emotion or reaction could cut in, I felt defensive towards my husband, his genitalia and his sexual performance. 'Was it really nothing at all?' I thought, 'I know his penis is rather small but there's no need to be disparaging or sell him short.' And I remember then giggling ruefully at the wording of my own thoughts, at how my subconscious could decide on which words came uninvited and unselected into my mind, at my visual picture, at my need to defend my husband's physique and performance, despite his cheating, his unfaithfulness.

I pulled myself together to focus again.

I thought, 'Perhaps he feels threatened by my having had a son, another man in my life albeit still a baby. Maybe I need to boost Richard's self-confidence, encourage him to do so himself. So that he has confidence in his abilities, in his looks. Or not knock it. Or be seen to compete. He needs to be Mr Big. And for me to see him as Mr Big. Which is tricky when I am the one who has provided the home, the initial income, the financial credibility, the furnishings, the background family ties.

Perhaps we need a party. Which, sadly enough, will also be up to me to organise.'

Choosing the time and place, I read Tasha's letter aloud to Richard.

After I had done so, read the letter to him and put him remotely more in touch with Tasha, with that particular part of the past, he told me how his closeness with Tash had started. 'I couldn't call it an affair,' he said, 'because it wasn't as affair as such, it was a one-night stand with someone I already knew quite well.'

Apparently and according to Richard, over an evening meal Tasha had been telling him about the time she had spent teaching in Canada; about finding herself pregnant by a man she did not love, could never imagine herself marrying, about bringing disgrace onto her family, wondering what she should do for the best, and finally deciding to return to

Britain, tell her mother and have the baby adopted. She had, Richard told me, looked quite sad and since it was a situation not totally different from the one in which he had found himself with Doreen, he had sympathised, comforted her, given her a big hug. 'It brought us together', he told me. 'we had shared experiences, talked about regrets, lost opportunities and changes of circumstances. So, at the time, our going to bed together seemed obvious.'

Part of me was pleased that he had been so kind towards my close friend. 'But why,' I wondered, 'had he told me? Might he have been dealing with his own feelings of guilt at keeping it secret; but why tell me, why burden me with that? What was the purpose of telling me, other than to make himself feel better? Did it bring us any closer together? No, it didn't. Did it increase my sense of trust, of self-confidence? No, it didn't. Did it make me admire or respect him more? Again, no. So why tell me?

He had told me because . . . he wasn't sure why he had told me. Because he didn't like secrets, didn't like having a secret from me, wanted my approval for his having told me, having 'confessed'. Or because he wanted me to know that Tasha approved of him, fancied him? Was he wanting to make me jealous? Or imply that I wasn't attractive enough for Richard, needed to make more personal effort about my behaviour and my looks?

I was seven months pregnant, for goodness's sake, and clearly not slim and agile. But whose fault was that? Who needed me to be working all hours of the day, who needed me as a work buddy as well as a wife?'

My mind in turmoil. I needed a friend to help me out, to help sort me out. But I had already told my closest friend, had told

Tasha and she hadn't helped at all, she had made it worse, had caused much of the turmoil. I had no other close friends. Perhaps that was part of the problem. Or the solution. Perhaps we needed to socialise more, mix with more people, meet more people. Perhaps we did need that party.

At one of the antenatal classes at the RAF base, Nurse Morton had told me that in order to avoid the various veins in my legs that were beginning to look like navy drainpipes, I ought to rest for several hours every afternoon. 'Lie on the bed or on a settee for just a couple of hours,' she had advised 'and if possible, use a pillow or a cushion to raise your feet higher than your head.'

I wondered how on earth Nurse Morton thought that could be possible, not with a daughter still a toddler and an energetic Keir who had started to climb rather than crawl or walk and who had already managed to reach the top of the bookcase; until he fell back onto the sitting-room carpet.

As he fell, he had bitten into his lower lip with one of his new top teeth, which had left a scar. How did a community nurse and a midwife imagine, I wondered, that I could safely rest for several hours and in doing so, take my eyes off my energetic son and my daughter?

One afternoon when I was still heavily pregnant with my third child, Richard had what he termed 'a bright idea'. The stairs ran from behind a door in the cottage sitting-room quite steeply up to the landing and the spare bedroom. I can't remember whether we had carpeted them but I suspect not. Richard's idea was that at some time he could change the bottom three or four steps so that instead of continuing straight and ending behind the door in the sitting room, they should be turn at a ninety-degree angle so that they would end in the passageway almost opposite and near the bathroom door.

It sounded a sensible plan to me in outline and I said that I thought it would be much more convenient. Then I forgot about it, there were more important things to be done that were more immediate. For a start, I reminded him, there was still a stack of concrete blocks by the back door that were waiting for him to do something about them.

After dropping Nell off at the playgroup in North Elmham, Richard would take me on to Swanton Morley for the antenatal class again, arranging that afterwards I would walk down the road and he would drive to meet me somewhere between the entrance to the Base and the bridge over the River Wensum. He was slightly late on one occasion so I stood by the bridge, using my arms to take some of my weight so that I could rest one tired leg, then the other. The water under the bridge looked deep, the colour of instant coffee before milk had been added and I stood wondering whether it would be safe for swimming, whether there was weed at the bottom of the river that I couldn't see, and whether the water was contaminated by a run-off from the field where the cows grazed.

Finally, Richard appeared. He apologised for being late but he'd been busy and he was here now, wasn't he? I climbed into the car and he drove us both home, stopping only for a minute or two at the village shop to pick up some breakfast cereal.

As he pulled the car into the drive, I said I was desperate for the loo so please would he bring the shopping into the kitchen while I headed indoors and made straight for the bathroom. That done and feeling much better and emptier, I walked back into the kitchen, looking down and concentrating on pulling my top over the waistband of whatever I was wearing, to fill the kettle with water and switch it on. 'After the afternoon's exertions and lying on the hall floor at the Base, what I need now,' I told him, 'is a cup of tea.' I got out two mugs, tea bags and the milk from the fridge, then saw Richard was grinning, looking smug.

'You didn't notice, did you?' he stated rather than asked. I was puzzled, I had no idea what he meant so I went back into the dining room to look out of the window. No, there was nothing unusual there, the platform of concrete outside the garden door was just as I had left it. And I had seen, when we had driven in, that the concrete blocks were in the same place.

As I turned to return to the kitchen, I noticed that there was more light than normal coming from the hallway. I walked back towards the bathroom and . . . there was a huge gap in an interior wall, the door through from the stairs to the sitting room was shut so the stairs were as dark as they normally were . . except that there was more light coming from upstairs and the three bottom stairs were completely missing. The bottom of the staircase was completely missing, the lowest part of the wooden stairs, now without any carpet or covering, ended several feet up in the air. I gasped with incredulity. 'But how do we . .?' I began to ask.

'I didn't have time to completely finish the work,' Richard explained, as if I could not have already seen that. 'I just need a couple more hours and by tomorrow afternoon, it will be done.' I thought quickly about how to be tactful, encouraging and grateful while feeling exasperated, all at the same time. I had to admire Richard's skill at practical work. 'But how' I queried again, as gently as I could 'do we get ourselves and the children upstairs to bed this evening?'

Richard thought for a moment. I realised that this was something that he really had not had time or the forethought to consider, he had been carried away by his own idea and progress.

'Easy' he said, grabbing an old chair from the dining room and placing it in the passageway. 'We hold the back of this chair, climb onto the seat, stretch across, reach the nearest stairs and climb up just as we normally do.'

I bit back the words, not saying 'but Richard, I am seven and a half months pregnant, I weigh a ton and I can't judge the width of my own vehicle. How on earth do you think I am going to manage to climb up and step onto the seat of that rickety old chair, grab on to the back of it while also holding one or both of the children, not falling or losing my balance, reach the stairs we still have left without having a handrail to hold, avoid falling down the gap, reach the top, and in safety?

And how, when I need the loo in the middle of the night and in the complete darkness, how am I going to get downstairs and back up again without hurting myself or the baby in my tummy while you are snug upstairs, fast asleep and snoring?'

No, I didn't say any of that, or not much of it. But I thought it. I amended what I did say because changing the stairs, turning them round was, in essence, a good idea and in the long run it would be very helpful. It would also mean we would not have the walk through the hall passage and into sitting-room every time we wanted to go upstairs.

We could also dispense with the door from the sitting room to the staircase, all in all it would seem a more integrated, more convenient layout.

But it needed to be finished before I gave birth, before asking Nurse Morton to attempt an assault course, or encountering her comments if she saw what I was needing to do several times every day, before I became really concerned about whether Nell or Keir would manage, or hurt themselves while trying.

It needed to be an absolute priority, and if possible, if we could afford it, we needed to carpet the stairs too, because as simple wooden stairs they were harsh, noisy and uncomfortable for any small child going down them on his or her hands-and-knees, or bottom.

A couple in the village with four children were throwing a party to celebrate the husband's birthday. I didn't know either of them well, our only contact had been through meeting Pat in the village shop when she had had her youngest child Sophie with her. Sophie was nine months younger than Nell but I remember the first words that Pat spoke in my hearing in the shop. She was talking to Sophie and warning her, with one eye on me, a glance at Nell and a grin on her face, to be careful with the bag of sweets that she had just bought and handed to Sophie, 'in case that little girl nicks one.'

I bristled slightly at this and said, probably rather sanctimoniously, 'My child doesn't steal; nor does she know what sweets are because I've never bought them for her.' What a self-righteous prig I must have sounded.

Despite that, Pat invited me and Richard, whom she had hardly met, to a party at her house that she and her husband Chris were having for Chris's birthday. We went, clutching a heavy glass ashtray as a present for Chris whom we knew smoked a pipe, and leaving the children with Moo. I was still pregnant but 'Aniseed and Coriander', as I called the unborn 'twins', were due in the coming May.

At the party Richard was introduced to Catriona, who was short, dark, petite almost doll-like with twin boys who were about the same age as Nell. Her twins, we were told, went to a playgroup at Lyng, a village ten minutes' drive away.

Richard seemed to get on well with Catriona. She had seemed, he told me, quite bright and refreshingly uninhibited, something I felt I was never likely to be. I found her husband Jack unattractive. He was tall and slim, with a pronounced Adam's apple and a squeaky voice, plus an almost childish sense of humour. Together they ran some sort of smallholding just outside Bawdeswell.

That Spring and before my baby was due, we held a small party in the cottage. It had to be small because we did not know enough people to make it any larger. I didn't know how to throw a party, what to do to make it work but I made a large pot of chilli-con-carne and offered that to everybody, along with the one bottle of wine that I had been given by Moo and the other bottles that people brought with them as offerings.

I dimmed the main lights and lit the downstairs rooms with candles. We possessed few records but I had an L.P. by the Electric Light Orchestra playing on the borrowed record player.

By late evening, several people had left to go home but a handful remained, curled up on the settee in the sitting room or chatting quietly on rugs or the cushions on the floor. The music was playing.

Catriona was sitting in a basket chair. The lower half of her body was covered with one of the sheepskin rugs I had had since I was a student. The lights were dim, most of the candles had burnt out. Richard was half in, half out of the basket chair with Catriona, his feet were still on the ground but the rest of him seemed almost slumped over her. Only afterwards, when the party was over and everyone else had gone home, did I realise what had been going on. I realised only because Richard told me.

He had been walking his fingers up her slim legs, through the leg of her pants then touching her lower regions, stroking her pubic hair. He had asked her if she objected or liked what he was doing.

She had apparently said she liked it but there was something she would enjoy more. He had asked her what that was, to which she had answered, he told me, 'Penetration'.

So, with that much encouragement, covered by the sheepskin rug, and with a room still half-full of people, he had continued with this foreplay and possibly more, while I was within eight feet of them, seeing to the record player and making sure our guests were comfortable and happy.

When he told me this, what was I supposed to do or to say?

With Richard's and Nurse Morton's help, I gave birth to my third child on 20th May. I had ordered two dozen small chrysanthemum plants in red and yellow and they were delivered on that Tuesday, just as the washing machine was finishing its cycle. I went out of the dining room door to hang the damp washing on the line in the garden, then started to plant the red chrysanthemums. Feeling that I wouldn't have time to plant them all before giving birth, I put the rest of the plants into a cardboard box, went indoors and climbed the stairs.

My baby, a girl and not twins, arrived within twenty-four hours of the very date on she was due.

Someone looked after Keir but Nell was in the room with me, stroking my back in her three-year-old way and being generally interested and caring. I wanted this to be, as much as was possible, a happy family occasion. I did not want Nell to learn that childbirth was likely to be painful, nor to see me in anything other than minor discomfort, so although I had rejected the gas and air initially, I accepted the help rather than suffer pain and have Nell becoming concerned. Nell peered at where she was told the baby would appear. The top of its head became visible and Nell excitedly said 'I can see it!'

She told me afterward that she had thought it was a big poo, which suggested to me that once the baby had arrived, I would need to do some more work with Nell on basic human biology and on the nature and purposes of fundamental orifices.

Nell referred to her baby sister, who had fair hair and skin the colour of honey, as 'Lallo', a childlike abbreviation of the name we had decided to give her. I placed Lallo in the cane washing basket that I had bought especially for the purpose, and laid the woven basket, with its mattress and covers, on the dressing table shelf beside the bed.

With her that close, I could rest and be with her, put my finger into her tiny hand and relax for a while.

But not for long. Nurse Morton told me to lie there for only an hour, then to go downstairs, have a warm bath and get dressed in something warm and loose. Having done that and because there were drops of rain forming on the window, I knew I ought to collect the washing from the line before it got wet all over again; and there were a dozen yellow chrysanthemum plants that I needed to get into the ground, otherwise they might die.

I planted them, not enthusiastically because as flowers, I do not much like chrysanthemums; but I had bought them and I didn't want them to be wasted. I thought they might look cheerful in the garden.

Chapter 12

Totally Natural

I tracked back in my mind to remember how and when Richard's desire for nakedness started. It must have been when, with the encouragement and infectious enthusiasm for that geographical area from our friends Pat and Chris, we decided to go for a holiday to the south of France for a couple of weeks. There was a flat in La Ciotat that they were in the habit of renting each summer, justified by Chris's professional need to keep his French vernacular language up to date and Pat's wish for a relaxing family holiday near the sea.

'Why don't you come to the same place', they asked, 'if you can find somewhere at a reasonable price that you could rent for a couple of weeks? It's not worth going all that way for any less. We take our flat for a month.'

I don't remember how we contacted the owner of the flat we used, I only know that the owner told us on the day we arrived, that she had pricked herself in the eye with a thistle or some such plant and that was why her eye was weeping. Richard sympathised with her. It was a two-bedroomed first floor flat, situated a few roads behind the port and the main sea front, and a five-minute drive from where Pat and Chris, with their four daughters, were staying.

'There is nothing wrong with the main town beach', the owner of our flat told us, 'but because it's very close to the port and the yachting harbour, occasionally the sea does have a thin film of oil and the beach can have various items of rubbish brought in by the waves. But it's fine usually, and around the harbour is interesting, especially at night. There's plenty going on there. Everything stays open until late.'

However, either Pat or Chris told us that they would usually drive a few kilometres further east along the coast to another place where they would park their car, if only they could find a space, scramble down a steep unsurfaced cliff path carrying all the belongings that they would need for a morning's sunbathing, find a vacant spot on the sand and establish a base for themselves.

I don't know how Richard and I managed our finances to be able to afford the cross-channel ferry fare, the petrol and the motorway tolls but we did. It was amazing to me how Richard would sanction expenditure if it were something he wanted to buy or to do.

'I think,' Richard said with self-assurance, 'that being away from Norfolk and the spores on whatever grain is growing in the fields surrounding our cottage is extremely beneficial for my health. It prevents my asthma from getting any worse.'

In all the years I had known Richard, I had never seen or heard any sign of this asthma, it was something he talked about quite often but which had never manifested itself; not to me, certainly, nor when I was in the vicinity.

It did, or the fear of it did, become apparent whenever it was suggested to him that Matt might come to stay for a week or two. Then he would become very slightly short of breath at the very thought but there was no sign of the asthma when Ruth and Lizzie stayed with us.

In case I might point this out, Richard pre-empted that observation of mine by saying 'When the girls are with us, we often go for the day to Blakeney, Burnham Overy Staithe or Holkham, where there are no wheat or barley fields, just sea and sand and marram grass. And although Matt stayed for a shorter amount of time than the girls last year, fewer than ten days, that was the very time when the spores had developed and were spreading in the air. Or perhaps it was a different time of year when the girls came, so the wheat was at a different stage, or the weather was not as wet or as dry.'

I found his explanation plausible but unconvincing. He assumed medical knowledge but didn't ever visit a doctor about his asthma nor in all the years I was with him, did he possess an inhaler.

Whatever, we drove to the South of France for a holiday.

Our friends said they would show us the beach they preferred and they drove out of La Ciotat ahead of us so Richard would know where to turn off the main coastal road into a minor road, and where to park. Once we reached the beach and the sand, we found an empty stretch near to where Pat and Chris were placing their belongings.

We planned to stay there for most of the day, our reading and swimming pausing only while we had a picnic lunch that I had thrown together. Several of the local women were sunbathing topless, lying without wearing their bikini tops or with the upper part of their swimming costume rolled down.

Richard was not an avid reader, not like Pat or me, so having gazed at the topless women for some time, he said 'I'm going to explore further along the beach, past the place where the rocks from the cliff have fallen into the water, because from where I am at the moment, it's impossible to see what lies beyond them.'

With that, he left, striding off across the sand. I told our three children who were looking towards where their father had gone, 'Stay with me, please. No, I don't know exactly where Daddy has gone but I'm sure he will be all right. He'll come back in a little while and tell us all about it.'

And he soon did. He looked pleased with himself and with what he had discovered.

'Around that corner', he said, 'is another cove, sheltered by the cliffs at the back and with a stony beach, with large stones for sitting or lying on. And very few people. But the one or two people that were there were completely naked, not just topless. Shall we', he asked me, 'all go round there, and you can see for yourself how clean it is?'

Leaving Pat and Chris under their beach umbrella and indicating that, if we did not see them before, we would join them and their girls again for a meal that evening, I followed Richard, keeping the three children close.

Getting around the headland and across a rockfall wasn't easy. The rocks, large ones, boulders almost, had rolled down from the cliff and come to rest where the sea met the land.

Smaller rocks the size of large bags of flour had been brought to the base of the cliff during the last storm and tumble-washed pebbles in a variety of muted shades had filled in the gaps, such that the surface under our feet kept slipping and it was hard to get a firm foothold without getting our feet wet from the seawater that had seeped or flowed towards the headland. In many places I had to pass the towels and the cool-box to Richard, lift the children, child by child, and hand each one either up or down to their father.

Once we had negotiated our way there and seeing the height and gradient of the cliffs at the back of the cove, I paused to think, to assure myself that we couldn't be cut off by the tide. That of course we wouldn't, because this was the Mediterranean.

After the last of the screes of stones and clutching our belongings, we arrived at the spot that Richard had talked about. Yes, it was almost deserted, which I found slightly unsettling at first and then, as Richard removed all his clothes, rather reassuring and almost private.

'We can stay there undisturbed for several hours', he said, excited at the prospect of having a beach almost to ourselves. 'There are smooth rounded boulders we could perch on, sit or stretch out. I can't see any weed in the sea and there seems to be a gentle slope from the shallow water into where I suppose it gets deeper.'

The water was tepid, the sun shining on the sand in the main bay and on the stones had kept the water at a cool but not-too-bracing temperature. The cove appeared safe for the children and provided ample number of things in that natural but unfamiliar environment with which our imaginative and inventive three could engage themselves and become engrossed.

The first item was a short stick that Keir threw a couple of yards into the water. He watched it move from side to side with the breeze but neither towards him nor away. 'Look at my stick bobbing about, I'm going to call it Bobby', he announced and Lallo copied him saying 'Bobby, Bobby' as she too watched it.

Asking first 'Will it be all right if I go in?' Nell peeled off her tee shirt, shorts and plimsoles, waded into the water, grabbed Bobby and brought the stick back to land.

The children spent almost an hour with that stick, the water and the stones, throwing the stick back into the water, tossing pebbles at it to try to sink it or move it one way or another, Nell going back into the water, grabbing hold of the piece of wood again, passing it to one of the others for either of them to fling again into the sea.

Once I had checked the depth and for any current, Nell was the first to wade further in where the water was deeper, then to swim in and grab hold of 'Bobby' again. By this time everyone was naked. Richard, whose darker skin allowed him to be exposed to the sun for far longer than I could bear, was lying on his back, stretched out across a boulder with his eyes closed.

I didn't like to do that, the surface of the rocks was too hot and I needed to keep watch over the children, and apply sun-cream to myself and regularly to each of them.

'You need to drink plenty of water, or Orangina if there's any left,' I told them. 'And no, it won't be lunchtime yet, so it's no use your telling me that you're 'starving hungry'. There's only our lunch in the cool-box, nothing else. Except there might be a boiled sweet or two. But only if you promise not to ask again or fuss if there is only a green one left. And remembered to pass any sticky wrapper back to me.'

By five o'clock in the late afternoon, the sun would still be shining, beating down heavily on the south-facing cliff behind us, reflecting off the cliff and down on to the beach below. There was no shade at all, not even behind a boulder. I had been feeling too hot for several hours despite having taken myself in and out of the water several times in an attempt to cool down - and realising that swimming on my front didn't help one bit in keeping the sun off my shoulders.

If I swam or sculled on my back, it was harder to me to keep an eye on each of the children.

We had all enjoyed a picnic lunch of baguette, local cream cheese with peppercorns or garlic, fresh rolls and tomatoes. Richard might be asleep by mid-afternoon, it was hard to tell if he weren't moving at all.

'Soon we will run out of water or anything to drink.' I advised his recumbent body, hoping he was listening. 'My back is burning. Are you willing to rub cream or sun lotion over it? Otherwise, it will turn red and sore. I could ask one of the children to do it but it's hard for them to do it properly. And there's likely to be a fuss because the lotion feels 'all sticky',' and I mimicked a child's voice in saying those last words.

'I think you are being rather extreme by insisting on smothering yourself and the children with that stuff,' Richard told me.

'I know you don't think you need it,' I responded 'but the kids are younger than you and their skin isn't as tough as yours. It's especially important for Keir with his freckled skin, he will burn otherwise. And I already am, I can see my arms are already quite red.'

An hour or so later and still under the burning sun, my back, arms and legs were very sore. I reminded Richard 'If we are to meet Pat and Chris for a meal this evening, we need to get going soon. It won't be fun climbing back into a hot car but we can wind down all the windows. Then we can drive to Carrefour to replenish our supplies for tomorrow and pick up a bottle or two of wine for this evening.'

The evenings in La Ciotat were fun, despite the need to slap on the insect repellent in case we ate outdoors on the balcony as the sun went down. Richard would then drive us all from our friends' flat to where we were staying, and I would settle the children into their beds.

The flat we had rented was not available the following year; we couldn't have afforded it again anyway. But Richard's new delight that he had found in nudity in the South of France led him to research areas in Norfolk where he could swim and sunbathe while wearing no clothes.

We already knew that people swam off the beach at Holkham without wearing swimming costumes, and that they might even sunbathe naked there, lying undisturbed among the dunes, marram grass and a dry scattering of rabbit droppings. Richard discovered something else from a 'Health' magazine he was reading that he had not known before.

'Just look at this,' he said, very excited. 'British Naturism is an organisation which provides private venues where club members can go, strip off as soon as they arrive, and socialise with each other unclothed. I'm very interested. Aren't you?'

I wasn't, not particularly. But suddenly the need to drive to the coast became less important, especially if there were somewhere else where Richard could visit when the weather was not so pleasant, while still enjoying shedding his clothes.

'This being naked is totally natural. Shall we find out more about it?' he asked, not expecting a negative answer. He found an address and the opening times; together we went to investigate, leaving the children for a few hours in Moo's care.

As Richard drove the car through the entrance, along the unmade-up muddy track that served as a drive and through the woodland, I wondered aloud 'At what point do you think we will need to take off our clothes? And where will we put them, if not back in the car and on our seats? And how, if I need my spectacles to read or sign anything, shall I carry them if not in their case in my pocket? And what about money? I don't feel safe leaving my handbag in the car, I don't know these people. Does carrying a handbag count as clothing, do you think?'

I was keen not to be thought difficult or non-compliant but as yet, we didn't know what it was to which we might choose to agree, to sign up. 'And car keys? Where do people put those so that they are safe?

And before you make any silly suggestion, they need to be still hygienic. And we need to feel comfortable.' And then 'But what about shoes, footwear? The ground vegetation might sting or prickle, and not only near our feet.' It wasn't the nakedness that was troubling me, it was the practicalities.

We walked towards a sign saying 'Reception'. Now all, I thought, with a wry smile to myself, will be revealed.

After signing some sort of agreement about our behaviour ('Whatever do they think we are going to do' I whispered to Richard, 'in broad daylight and among all those nettles?'), behaviour which included the taking and, in this case, the not-taking of photographs of other people, we were shown the way to the clubhouse, the toilets and the leisure facilities.

I don't remember where or when we took off most of our clothes but I'm sure we kept our shoes on. In fact, I know we did because I remember seeing people playing tennis on the line-marked tennis courts and wearing their tennis shoes, and considering whether naked men, or women come to that, playing tennis, running from this side and that side with their bits bobbing up and down, was a pretty sight or just plain ridiculous.

With other people brandishing their rackets and aiming towards a flying ball, I thought that the game was prone to accidents or ridicule. Or was it only I who could see the funny side and the potential for lasting physical damage?

And I blithely wondered whether any ambulance personnel who might arrive to access any physical injury, to cart a player off to hospital, would also need to undress completely. I came out of my mental musing and tried to pull myself together and take the whole thing seriously, as Richard appeared to be doing.

Was this, I wondered, somewhere where we could bring the children? Would they be physically and emotionally safe? If Nell and Lallo didn't already know, it would save either of them from having to do what I had done as a teenager with my friend John, to discover what his male private parts looked like.

To go with her long-haired 'Sasha' doll, we had given Nell a 'Baby Gregor' just after Keir was born so that she knew what a baby boy would look like unclothed. I thought she would take the nakedness here in her stride.

What began to surprise and almost concern me during the times that Richard and I went to the naturist site, was the air of moral purity about the whole place. I felt it was almost as if there were a sign at the entrance, saying not only 'Reception' but 'Abandon lascivious thoughts, all ye who enter here.' To me, the atmosphere felt unnatural, so free of lustful or amorous desires that it almost reached the point of sterility.

I wondered again about the Biblical portrayal of the Garden of Eden, about a naked Adam, and Eve becoming pregnant, about a Hebrew view of righteousness, of holiness and sin, about what in those days it might have been appropriate to record in religious writing.

After a little investigation later that year, Richard discovered that there was a 'liste de plages naturistes françaises' and a naturist camp and caravan site called 'La Bédoule', not all that far from the beaches at La Ciotat and Cassis. He suggested to me 'You know, if we joined the International Naturist Federation as a family and if you were to include the three children on your passport, we might again have a holiday in the South of France at a reasonable price.'

That spring, the Norfolk and Suffolk Guild of Craftsmen made contact with Richard. The Guild had been asked to mount a British Craft Fair for the benefit of American tourists. It was to take place in the moat of the Tower of London. Would we like to join with other local crafts people and take our silver and gold jewellery to sell there? 'Yes, we certainly would', Richard had responded.

So early one Saturday morning, with other craftsmen we gathered at someone's house near Needham on the Norfolk/ Suffolk border and with minimal display equipment and a case of handmade jewellery, we boarded a coach that had been hired to take us to London and the Tower. I remember only isolated details about that trip. One was that Richard put pressure on me as to what I should wear.

'I think you should wear your cheesecloth Gypsy-style blouse with no bra underneath and a full skirt,' and as I raised an eyebrow at him, 'so that you look 'Olde Englande-ish'. I don't think he asked me to have bare feet as well, I would have remembered that. But I do know that he had his sandals on, the open-toed sandals that he always wore.

Once we had unloaded the goods and equipment we had brought into the moat and had found our pitch, I was so surprised when some official at the Tower told us 'You can plug in a display light if you want to illuminate your jewellery on the display table and display case. At various points within the moat there are electricity power points, they're concealed from general view but they are there if needed.'

I wondered how often and under what circumstances anyone really needed to plug in something electrical within the dry moat of the Tower and at what point in history these might have been installed.

A large number of American and Canadian tourists were wandering through the displays of crafts. I remember asking myself whether we had brought sufficient change for the float in our cashbox, making sales and wishing we had bought better quality little boxes to put the earrings, rings or pendants in, and taking a great deal of cash, more than we had dreamed possible.

Towards the end of the afternoon, I spotted, lying on the grassy ground near our display table, a brown leather wallet.

I picked it up and opened it. Inside was a fat wad of dollar notes. No name or address, just American notes.

I wondered what best to do, to which official to hand the wallet, how to make it known that it had been found without the owner having any means by which to identify it as being his or hers, whether to broadcast the information or whether to wait and see if anyone came to ask about a lost wallet.

I told no one except Richard about what I had picked up from the ground and I hesitated for several seconds before mentioning to him, nervous of what he might suggest we do. We waited and concentrated on talking to visitors, answering questions about hallmarking, the carat of the gold, the name and colour range of each gem and British daily life; and selling our jewellery.

Towards the end of the afternoon, an American gentleman to whom we had sold some items earlier in the day approached our stall. 'Excuse me,' he said with some embarrassment 'but I've mislaid my wallet. I don't suppose you have seen it? I know I bought something for my daughters from your stall.'

I handed the wallet over to him. He looked so relieved, he flicked through the notes and thanked me profusely. I was pleased. I felt that I had done something to help him enjoy his stay in Britain and to see that we British could be an honest lot.

I don't know what Richard thought or felt about that, he didn't say, he just looked wistful.

Sometime in the past, Richard had told me 'When I was a teenager and living with my father and step mother in

Felixstowe, a friend and I went sailing. We went far out to the sea, probably too far because someone had seen where we were and he thought we were in some danger.'

'And were you?' I had asked.

'I didn't think so,' Richard replied, 'but someone sent someone to bring us and our sailing dinghy back to shore.'

I had my doubts about this story, about certain elements of it, but I gathered from that, that Richard wanted to sail again, to have his own boat and sail it along the North Norfolk coast, probably with me, even though I had no idea how to sail.

It may have been the income from the craft fair at the Tower of London moat that provided much of the money for the boat. I don't remember who sold it to us but I suspect it might have been the father of someone I knew through Lyng Playgroup. It was known as a sharpie[xi], a fibreglass sailing boat of the sort that were quite common on the North Norfolk coast, at Wells-next-the-Sea and Blakeney in particular. It arrived on its own trailer which we had also purchased and the one rested on the other on the drive between the cottage and the barn.

When we had had the flat at the top of St Giles Street in Norwich, we had had an unclassed wooden dinghy that we named 'Piggy' because it had a ring at the end of its nose. I don't remember where we bought that but I know it was sufficiently light to go on the roof-rack of the van we were driving at the time. We used to keep it upside down at the foot of the iron staircase that led to our flat.

One day Piggy was missing. No sign of it anywhere. According to the police when we reported the loss, it had been found abandoned beside the traffic lights between St Giles Street and Earlham Road. Richard and I had to drive to the Bethel Street police station to collect it from where it was being stored in the police compound. Whoever had taken it from our block of flats had had the sense to leave its oars behind. I don't remember us ever actually sailing Piggy, only rowing it; I don't remember it even having a mast.

After we had regained possession of Piggy, we put it on the roof of the van and drove to Thorpe beside the river. We lifted the boat from the van roof, carried it across the main road and slid it into the water, where we got in and paddled ourselves about until we wanted more action, more excitement.

It was there at Thorpe, not far from the church, where Richard had once reversed the van into me. I had got out of the van, been doing something at the back of the vehicle or opening the rear doors for something, and Richard hadn't noticed that I was missing from the front seat. He said afterwards that he had no idea where I was. He put the van into reverse, I don't know why, and bang! The van hit me hard enough to make a noise, knock me off my feet and startle Richard into an abrupt stop.

I was so shocked that I burst into tears. I wasn't hurt or anything, just shocked because, as I explained to him between gasps, 'You backed into me.' And instead of him being apologetic or concerned, he was almost cross and ask me accusatorially 'Well, what on earth were you doing standing there?' I felt upset, emotionally not physically hurt. It was long before we were married but my best friend, my partner, had just driven into me, backwards, could have run me over.

There had been no routine from him of 'mirror first, then indicate'. I explained, once I had calmed down and dried my tears, that I was upset because he hadn't looked, it was lucky it was me he had hit, because it could have been a perfect stranger who might have called the police - or even been a child.

'Don't be so daft or so melodramatic' he said impatiently. 'You weren't hurt, were you. So why all the fuss?' which was not a question at all, just a put-down. 'Come on, let do what we came here to do.'

No reassurance, no arm round my shoulders. He wasn't able to see this from my side, he didn't empathise or offer any comfort, he just wanted to get on with putting the boat into the water. But I remember the bang, my tears and Richard's lack of appreciation of things from my point of view, his lack of emotional response other than irritation at me. I wanted him to care about me, to think, had I been bending down at the time, what might have happened. But he didn't.

Several years after Piggy, which must have become unusable as a boat, Richard bought a Mirror dinghy. By then, we had the children and Richard had thought it would be good for them to learn to sail.

On one occasion, Richard drove our vehicle to the bank of Ranworth Broad where we had seen on a map that there appeared to be a public landing stage. After we had been for a short sail on the Broad – I hope the children were dressed in life jackets or buoyancy aids but I don't remember – Richard brought the Mirror back to the bank. I and the children climbed out and stood on the bank. Richard stayed in the boat and began to pass us things – the mast, with the sails – for me to lay them on the grass before we loaded them into the car.

He passed an oar to Keir who passed it to me. Then another oar to Keir and I took it from him. Richard was fiddling with the centreboard, trying to lift it but he needed to use both hands. 'Here', he said to Keir, passing him the painter, 'hang on to this and don't let go.'

Keir couldn't have been more than four or five and we already knew that he had a hearing loss. But whether or not he heard or became distracted by something much more interesting on the bank, I don't know. But he dropped the rope.

The next thing I heard was Richard shouting 'Oy!' at Keir, at me, at anyone else on the bank of the Broad and seeing an angry Richard, sitting in the Mirror as it slowly drifted with the wind from the bank and towards the centre of the Broad.

A man on the bank, a total stranger who had been watching this, moved towards Keir and said quietly, 'If I were you, Laddie, I wouldn't be too sure of getting any pocket money this week. Or your father back any too soon, either.'

By this time, I was clutching my stomach with laughter that I was trying to control, from the sheer ridiculousness of the situation. But Richard couldn't see the humour at all. There was Richard, the keen sailor, oar-less, sail-less, and helpless. But he was in no danger so I chuckled rather than worried or fretted. The children and I waited on the bank, watching Richard and the Mirror drifting slowly and almost gracefully away from us and toward the far end of the Broad.

After an hour or more, a dispirited Richard reappeared, walking along the edge of the bank and towing the Mirror on a rope behind him. He told us 'I used the centreboard as a paddle, I paddled myself with the wind towards the main sailing clubhouse. Once I got there, I pleaded for a small length of rope, any rope, so that I could attach it to the bow of the Mirror and walk my way back to where you all were. And no, I didn't think it was at all funny and I still don't.'

I rather lost confidence in Richard's sailing abilities after that, and in his sense of humour. But I had to hand it to him for resourcefulness and tenacity in getting himself out of a tricky situation.

Apart from where the River Wensum flowed under a bridge on the road from Swanton Morley, I knew of nowhere close by where we could swim. On one occasion when Ruth and Lizzie had come to stay, I suggested to Ruth 'If you are as hot as I am, let's take our swimming gear, just in case we find somewhere suitable nearby where we can at least dip ourselves into the water. We could ask your dad to keep an eye on Lizzie, because I know she's scared of the whole idea of going into water.'

I took the car and Ruth and I swam in a pool near that bridge, keeping our mouths firmly shut because the field by the bank contained cows and cow pats. Lizzie stayed at the cottage with her father; it was at least a year later that I taught Liz to swim and bought her a two-piece swimming costume that she liked.

During the scorching late June and July of Queen Elizabeth's silver jubilee that we experienced in rural Norfolk and while Doreen had her three children with her in Canterbury, we lifted our pine table from the dining room and stood it on the dry grass in our back garden. There it stayed for over a month. We moved our daytime living from indoors to outdoors. We all ate outdoors.

Because the weather was so warm, Richard found the money to buy a large red-and-blue plastic paddling pool. It was not the inflatable sort, it had plastic sides made rigid by inserting a frame of metal poles, with triangular blue hard plastic seats that clipped into position at each corner. It was two metres long and after being filled with water from the hose pipe, it was possible to lie stretched fully out in it and almost covered by the water. That paddling pool remained in our back garden all summer, just a few metres from the pine dining table.

The first time a visitor drove audibly along the gravel drive towards the cottage as far as the concrete slab by the kitchen door, I wondered how Richard would react. I was in the kitchen while he was in the paddling pool, naked, with one or two of our children in the water with him. I could see who our visitor was. I waited. Would Richard shout 'wait a minute' towards the visitor's car and grab a towel? Or keep very quiet and hope I would deflect or divert whoever it was? Nakedness on some beaches in the South of France might be normal, but in rural Norfolk, it was certainly less common. I waited.

I saw a married couple get out of the car, a couple I recognised, whose children went to Lyng playgroup and whose children were friendly with Nell. How would they react to this? Would they even notice people lying in the paddl . ? But at that point, Richard stood up, and quite unabashed, waved a naked greeting at them from the pool.

'Hi', he said or something very similar, 'how nice to see you. We are in the back garden, so do come around and join us.'

I wasn't sure what the rules or conventions were for entertaining one's children's friends' parents in the garden while stark naked. Does one offer them tea or a stiff drink? A towel perhaps and a chair? Richard appeared quite unembarrassed, unaware perhaps that this was not a normal Sunday afternoon event. Not for anyone. I filled the kettle and emerged from the kitchen, suggesting to Richard in an almost parental way, 'You might like to find yourself a large towel – in case you get cold, standing there dripping wet and with your feet still in the water. Here.' And I threw him one I had grabbed from the bathroom.

Richard appeared blind to the fact that this was not a scene with which our visitors were familiar, that they had had no previous guidance on how to behave or react in this situation; whether to run for the hills or take a deep breath and play along as if everything were perfectly normal. I became aware how filmic it was, the garden scene, the colour, the wide eyes and open mouths.

For just a moment I stood wondering what movie rating it might command, whether this was a 'U' as suitable for all ages, or an 'A' for adults only. And the dialogue. Would 'How lovely to see you?' be considered crass or appropriate. Or something more forthright along the lines of 'Get your kit off and let's have a party'. Or even, with the camera providing a close-up on Richard's scrotum and flaccid damp member, 'Good gracious, is that it?'.

But one way or another, it was up to me to bring it down a notch, to change the amazing and incredulous into perfectly normal Sunday afternoon viewing. And to avoid anything as hackneyed as 'Tea, Vicar?' But this was far from 'Le Déjeuner sur l'herbe'. For a start, I was fully clothed. It was becoming less Édouard Manet and more comedy, almost a clip from a Monty Python sketch.

'Would anyone like some tea and a slice of cake?'

How like my mother I was becoming, regardless of the external situation. And how useful a model my mother had been, demonstrating how not to let a situation unsettle me but to take charge of it where possible and steer it out of danger. I was pleased that Jeannette and Nigel had not brought their children with them, to witness this. Because had they done so, this scene might have been embroidered, retold all around Lyng Playgroup and might have driven Nell to a state of embarrassment about her parent's unorthodox behaviour. But it did do the rounds of Playgroup leaders and helpers.

I was aware that any behaviour attributed to Richard would also become attached to his wife and assumed to be endorsed and emulated by me. I found it difficult to maintain tacit loyalty, to uphold Richard's right to do what he liked in his own garden, my garden, as long as it was legal and hurt no one, while also making it clear to anyone within range that Richard and I were not joined at the hip, that we were separate people with separate thoughts and individual . . . and then I would be stuck for a word . . individual needs? Was Richard's nakedness a need or a preference? Was it something very basic within man's development, something primaeval? Was it a manifestation of freedom or exhibitionism? Then came the big question, how well did I know my husband? How did he behave when I was not with him?

We had quite a lot of land to maintain. The patch in front of the cottage consisted of meadow or couch grass, it needed to be cut in order to keep the place tidy, as also did the stretch of grassy land between the barn and the cottage. To do this, Richard bought himself a ride-on mower.

It was another example of expenditure which was not discussed and over which I had no say or control. It just arrived one day, a red Mountfield mower with a black seat. Richard was handed the keys, shown how to work it and he was off across the front field, happy as could be: he had a new toy.

From then on, he would willingly mow the grass, riding up and down in lines beside the drive but completely naked. I suggested that riding a mower while wearing no clothes could be dangerous but 'I don't see why you think there's a problem. I'm on the seat, aren't I, not under the machine or lying on the grass. Where's the danger in that?' he countered.

His behaviour did become noticed by anyone from the village who called, by Willy the Baker or anyone delivering the newspaper. And by the local farmer, the men who drove the carrot and potato lorries up and down the track. By my parents, who said nothing but probably thought plenty. I didn't see the reason for it but Richard became referred to by the villagers as 'the Marxist Artist' after he had stood as a candidate for the local Labour party, or 'the Mad Artist' which was even odder. An artist he was not, he had simply owned and run an art gallery; and he certainly wasn't mad. I didn't think so, anyway. Just a trifle unusual.

I wondered why wearing no clothes was linked in people's minds to madness, to mental instability. Richard was only exercising his right to wear and do as he wished on his own property, on my property, as long as it upset or offended no one. Seated on the ride-on mower, his lower half and private parts were completely hidden from view; and from a side view, people could see only that his legs and trunk were bare. Surely no one could feel offended or threatened in any way? So why did anyone see this as a problem, I wondered. It might be a bit unusual, a bit odd from the local village point of view, but perhaps they had a 'thing' about their own bodies, about accepting their own nakedness as well as other people's. And I wondered more about how Norfolk people, the local village people, saw 'difference'.

With three children, we were running out of indoor space. With my encouragement and without planning permission, which he assured me we did not need, - 'We don't need it,' Richard told me 'and even if we did, who's going to know if we add anything on to the back of the house? It isn't visible from the road or the track and the local guys on the farm lorries couldn't care less' - from the pile of grey concrete blocks that he ordered and that had been delivered, Richard began constructing a concrete block single storey 'conservatory-type' edifice adjoining the dining room but not extending the length of the house.

'When it's the right height, I can give it a corrugated plastic roof to keep the area dry,' he suggested. We didn't discuss what the 'right height' might be. 'In the past, builders used to build by eye,' Richard said, 'so when the height looks about right or I run out of blocks, I'll stop.'

On one occasion, Richard received a phone call and almost immediately afterwards, he disappeared somewhere in his car, saying as he drove off 'I'm just going to investigate buying a cement mixer.' Something inside me made me doubtful, it didn't seem likely halfway through a job. Before this, he had been mixing cement on a wooden board, one of the old barn doors placed on the ground in the garden.

I tried hard to think, to try to connect with wherever he was, to try to see whether I could use the powers of my mind to locate him. I couldn't. I hadn't really believed in extra-sensory perception, in telepathy but here was proof that it didn't work. Not in this case, anyway. But I later recognised that suspicion is often based on accumulated prior knowledge and experience.

Much later, long after the concrete block building episode and after no cement mixer had appeared, I asked him where he had disappeared off to so suddenly. He confessed, 'I went to see Catriona. She said she needed to see me.'

'But you were gone for over an hour,' I said, 'so I was beginning to get concerned. Was it anything important she wanted?'

'Not important now,' he told me, 'so let's see what the children are up to.'

During the building process, Richard inserted a prefabricated window frame into the rear wall of the blocks that would look onto the back garden. The concrete floor had no damp-proof membrane so it would have limited use as a room. But it did offer us the essential additional space.

Then one of us, I don't remember who, had a bright idea. 'I've been thinking,' the one of us said 'Why don't we sell the cottage and make the barn into a house?'

We discussed it. But there was an obvious drawback to the plan. If we had permission, the skills and the finance to convert the barn into living accommodation, we would lose the current workshop space. If we were to lose the workshop, then how and where would we continue to make and sell our jewellery? We did not consider using any other local premises as a workshop because there were no other alternative premises within the village that might have proved suitable. And other premises away from the cottage would have involved the inconvenience of working away from where we lived, as well as rent and upkeep of those unfound premises.

But I had, before the need for more living space ever arose, used the corner field which was then lying fallow, as an additional recreation area for the children. And in case in the future it might have been served as land on which to build a number of new houses, I had expressed a wish to buy it.

To buy it, not because we wanted or needed the land but because if I owned it, it would prevent anyone else from turning it into a gravel pit and the heavy traffic that that might have caused, or into a mini-estate which might crowd us or lower the value of the cottage and the land we already had.

I enquired what the purchase price might be; and made an offer for it, subject to my being able to find the asking price of £300. There would be further restrictions on any sale, the vendor would impose a covenant regarding future land usage. But first, I needed to plan how we might raise the money.

Planning how we might raise it involved my presenting a case to any potential lender. Dad had already lent me some money for the deposit on the cottage before I could even convince a building society to give me a mortgage, so asking Dad again seemed to me to be unethical. To reinforce that feeling of mine, I knew that that loan from Dad of £400 still had to be repaid, so even approaching him for finance appeared to me to be wrong. And he was now retired so his own finances were also limited.

I thought he would back me if I could present a reasoned case for making the purchase but that would be as far as my father could go.

Having discussed the situation with Moo, she suggested that I might approach Aunty Dorothy, not for a loan, but to see if she might give me a hundred pounds as a starting sum. Moo said she would explain to Aunty Dorothy that if I owned the land instead of anyone else, it would maintain the value of the cottage and surrounding plot.

Aunty Dorothy quite reasonably asked how I would use the additional land which was just under an acre and I explained that Richard and I considered several uses that would enhance the value of the plot and could increase the range of wildlife that could make use of it. Aunty Dorothy was very keen on the countryside, wildlife and nature.

I explained to Moo, and thereby to Aunty Dorothy, that one idea I had considered was to plant saplings of bat willow, Salix Alba Caerulea, and to grow and then sell bat willow, the wood that was world-famous as being the best willow for making cricket bats. Aunty Dorothy's husband and my Uncle David, was a keen cricket player and I had already made enquiries to check the viability of this scheme.

Moo also suggested I could approach Aunty Marian to ask whether she would help me. I explained to Aunty Marian what I had in mind and as a result, Aunty Marian gave me a further hundred pounds. Both these women were childless and appeared to have surplus money. Moo was firmly of the opinion that money, in itself, was useless; that if one had extra money that was not needed for regular daily living, the person with money had a responsibility to make that money work for the benefit of other people.

Moo held firmly to her principles, principles that she never had personally the opportunity to put into practice, not these particular principles anyway about having surplus money. She implied that Aunty Dorothy and Aunty Marian would be of the same opinion. Fortunately for me, Moo was right.

There seemed no possibility of Richard managing to raise extra money for land purchase and certainly not from any of his relatives. He had, he told me, almost completely lost touch with his father, who by now was living, he thought, with Margaret, his second wife, on the Island of Jersey. According to Richard, his father Horace had lost touch with his brothers and sisters, had moved to Jersey to take up a job working in one of the banks.

Consequently, Richard knew the whereabouts only of his cousin Margaret who lived in Dersingham, not far from Sandringham; and that his aunt Kathleen lived in a moated farmhouse in Old Newton, just outside Stowmarket in Suffolk. Richard said that he had last seen his father several years previously, after Ruth and Liz were born.

His father had, Richard told me, come to visit their Canterbury house at the far end of College Road, arriving in a shiny well-polished car. Richard remembered that Horace had said 'hello' to his son and to Doreen but was anxious that the children should be deterred from touching his car in case they left dirty fingerprints on it. The visit of father to his son had ended more or less at that point, Richard said.

I had asked Richard whether his father knew that his son had left his wife and three children, that he had remarried and had moved to Norfolk. Richard said he had either telephoned or written to his father to tell him this, and that Richard and I now had three children of our own.

Horace had, Richard said, written back indicating some displeasure at Richard's actions. He showed me the letter, the letter in which his father appeared to be disowning him because Richard had apparently abandoned Doreen and their children. In that letter to his son, Horace appeared, if

I correctly quote what he wrote, to doubt or deny their 'consanguinity', despite his signing off as 'your affectionate sire'.

I bought the corner field. Although I had had the idea of using it to cultivate bat willow, I also investigated the idea of having a small flock of sheep to graze it. Aunty Dorothy was a keen spinner and weaver and she would collect any sheep's wool that had been caught on barbed wire. She would then spin it and use it within any rug she might be weaving. But one look at the book I had borrowed from the library put me right.

Although Tommy Dack had been the shepherd and it was in his former cottage that we were living, it was the chapter on 'Sheep Diseases' and the illustration of blowfly maggots that put me right off. I thought I could deal with maggots *per se*, but it was the vet bills that would worry me most, and the responsibility of knowing when to call a vet and when it wasn't necessary.

In the end, it was Nurse Morton who solved the question of what to do initially with the corner field. She wanted somewhere safe in the North Elmham area where she could graze and keep her horse called Duke. We came to an agreement by which she might use the field for the horse but that any shed or shelter had to be temporary and moveable. I had bought the field subject to accepting a covenant, stating that if the land were used for building houses, then I would pay the vendor an additional sum because land for housing was worth far more than agricultural or pasture land.

It was agreed that Nurse Morton could use the field as grazing land for less than 365 days in any one year, such that she did not build up usage rights, and that any additional fencing was her responsibility but it was my duty to maintain the hedging and any trees on the field border.

The horse took up residence. We rarely heard it and saw Nurse Morton's purple Ford car only occasionally when she drove onto the field and saddled up the horse, ready for a ride into the local Forestry Commission wood. During these times, with the horse out of the way, one of the children might wander into the field or wave to the nurse to say 'hello'. It was on one of those occasions that a very nasty accident to Keir was avoided, only by chance.

Despite my brave words to Moo about children's behaviour being dependent on upbringing, it was not long before it became apparent that Keir's needs and much of his behaviour were the result not only of nurture but also of his innate human nature. Whereas Nell had been content, happy even, to sit and draw, to play with fuzzy felt or her cardboard-box dolls house, toy farm machines and a Tonka Toys concrete mixer, Keir needed far more to develop his gross motor skills, to use his arm and leg muscles, to climb and swing, to lift, pull and push heavy objects.

That may have been the first time that it really dawned on me that boys and girls, and presumably men and women, had different physical needs and that there might be different expectations from the one upon the other. I had been brought up in a household where there had been no gender distinction made, certainly none that I as a child or a teenager noticed.

Through Moo, Val had passed on the heavy tricycle that most of her children had had when they were young. Keir found that he could sit on it and just reach the pedals. He could also load the small saddlebag with precious items and transport them and himself all around the outside of the buildings and the land. He would pedal up and down the drive, over the gravel even into those areas or edges where the gravel was loose and mobile. Standing on the pedals and gripping hard onto the handlebars, he could pull himself and the tricycle over bumps in the turf, across tree roots and even down and up shallow ditches.

Keir had decided to ride the tricycle across the corner field while Nurse Morton and Duke the horse were out of the way. It was fun for him and quite a challenge, especially where the field was uneven, where Duke had left hoofprints in the grass that had created ruts when the soil dried and where Nurse Morton's car tyres had done something similar.

Where the grass was long, all Keir's strength was needed to push hard on the pedals to avoid the wheels getting entangled or coming to a standstill.

He was so engrossed in his private world, steering the 'tank' or 'heavy lorry' that the tricycle had become, that he did not hear the thunderous clip clop of Duke as he trotted, with Nurse Morton on his back, down the track and into the field.

Out of the corner of his eye Keir must have seen something move against the hedge and quickly, so as not to be discovered in the field where he was forbidden to go whenever Duke was there, he told me afterwards that he jumped off his tricycle, ducked under the fencing and ran down the gravel track towards the barn.

Half an hour later, Nurse Morton was knocking at our kitchen door. Fortunately, I was in the cottage and heard her knock. She looked mildly apologetic rather than cross. 'I'm sorry' she said, 'I didn't know it was there. I didn't see it at all when I backed the car, all ready to drive out of the gate.' I was not sure what she meant and I waited for her to explain.

She told me that as she was reversing, she had heard a clunking sound, a rattle and then everything had gone quiet as her car came to a stop. She said she had got out, looked towards the back of her Ford and there, twisted and misshapen under the rear wheels, was Keir's tricycle. 'I just didn't know it was there', she explained.

I was so relieved that it was only the tricycle she had run over and not my son. We knew that both she and Keir were at fault; he should not have been riding his tricycle there and she had not looked in her rear mirror before backing. I think both she and I were relieved, it could have been so much worse had Keir been sitting on that tricycle, had she not looked and had . . . . It was too horrible to think about.

She did not offer to pay for a replacement, instead we used it as reinforcement within some footings and foundations of a new building. I image it is still there somewhere.

Chapter 13

Open Marriage

It is 1977-78. Richard and I are still living in the renovated flint cottage on the outskirts of a small hamlet between Dereham and Fakenham. We are standing in the dining room, beside the brick chimney and the black cast iron range which I rarely light because it doesn't keep us warm at all and neither the oven nor the top plate gets sufficiently hot to cook anything. It has been in the cottage for years, ever since I bought the place: in time we ought to rip it out and replace it with something efficient but at the moment we can't afford anything else.

It has been a week since Richard went into the nearest town and came back with a paperback book he had either bought or been given, entitled 'Open Marriage'. Richard had pressed the book into my hands. 'I got this especially for you and I would like you to read it. Because I would like us to try this, to have an open marriage.'

'I don't understand what that means' I responded, not looking yet at this unexpected gift. We have been married for only five or six years and Richard doesn't give me presents, especially if they cost him anything. 'What is an open marriage? What's open about it? Open in what way?'

'Just read the book and you'll find out.' I look at the front cover, then inside. Written in 1971, it was published in 1973 in America. It appears to be second-hand.

'And if you don't agree, if we don't do as this suggests, even recommends, then I think it could have quite a negative impact on our marriage. Doing as it says will keep our marriage fresh - which is what I'm sure we would both want. Because I'd like to stay married to you.'

With three young children to care about, a house and garden to organise and a jewellery manufacturing business to run, I have little spare time to read books and certainly not this one. I already belong to a book club and I prefer novels, or my choice of historical non-fiction that arrives each month by post, unless I cancel.

I would be surprised if Richard has read it too, he isn't much of a reader; I suppose someone has recommended it or he's heard about it on the radio. And it is very unlike him to buy me a present, to buy me anything at all. He doesn't willingly spend money. I have the general impression that he doesn't think I am worth spending money on or perhaps does not know what to buy.

On the rare occasions when he does part with money and purchases a tool, some equipment or on one occasion a very tall peppermill, he will justify the expenditure by saying 'It's an investment; and can we afford <u>not</u> to buy it?' I suppose that, perhaps, he has heard about this particular book from John White, who occasionally visits our art gallery, not in order to buy anything but just to look at the paintings and to see what exhibition we have running that month.

Or from Catriona Day, whose company he sometimes seeks and whose husband runs a small holding in the next village. He has become particularly friendly with Catriona after our last party, although neither of us has much time for Jack, her husband.

We learn that John and Rosalind White were married quite recently and are new to the area. Since there are very few people living in our hamlet with whom we have anything much in common, we know very few whom we can actually call friends. There are the people who come fairly regularly to the gallery, other people who, seeing the 'Craft Shop' sign where our gravel drive meets the lane, may drop in on the off-chance of finding something interesting among the studio pottery that we buy in or the jewellery that we make and sell.

John and Rosalind told us almost in conversation when they came to our house for dinner a week ago, 'We've taken a new lover between us, a woman. We share her.'

Richard and I had raised an eyebrow at this and at each other, made no reaction in front of them, then on some pretext had scuttled into kitchen to collect the dessert and whisper in consternation 'Did I hear that correctly? And did you?'

It has been a week since Richard gave me that book and we have been invited back to John and Rosalind's house for a meal. We are apprehensive about this visit, about whom we might meet but are anxious not to appear biased or judgemental. Richard has already shown me that his attitude to marriage is not as orthodox as mine. But I am not keen on this 'open marriage' idea of his. Not keen at all. 'It's not what I signed up to,' I tell him. 'Not at all. And I hate the idea of sex not being exclusive.'

'But if we don't try it, if we just dismiss it out of hand,' he argues, 'we will never know if it's right for us.'

Now here we are, enjoying a convivial meal among friends. John and Rosalind's house has a log burner, a large downstairs room that was once the school room, a mezzanine floor and stairs which, John tells us, once led to the upstairs part of the headteacher's house. As we are unable to get reliable babysitter in our village, our three young children are bedded down in the back of our Citroen Safari, parked safely away from the road and in the schoolhouse driveway, right beside the house. They are on mattresses and in soft sleeping bags with their favourite soft toys. 'Car camping' they call it. We trust they will soon fall asleep; they usually do.

Although Richard has locked the car and assures me that the children will be safe, they can get out if they need to, they can unlock it from the inside, and one of us comes out to the car every hour or so to check that they are all right and asleep and not arguing - and to reassure ourselves and them, that we are nearby and on hand if needed.

We enjoy a very pleasant meal, a beef casserole, with the bottle of wine we have brought. As we all agree, Rosalind is an excellent cook. She is hardly dressed for cooking now though; her rich brown hair is loose around her shoulders and she wears a white silk blouse over a shiny black calf-length skirt that swings gentle as she moves. I help clear the dirty dishes into their kitchen while John come in too, fills the kettle.

Quite suddenly, 'Rosalind and I would like to have sex,' Richard announces to me and to John. 'Her leather skirt is having a huge effect on me . . . . on both of us, so we are going upstairs to the bedroom. If you and John want to do the same . . .' He doesn't finish his sentence, perhaps because he sees my face.

Or because his mind is made up, regardless.

They disappear while I, stunned by what Richard has just said, remain downstairs and speechless with Rosalind's husband John. John appears keen that he and I should follow suit, go up to the mezzanine floor together but I ask for another cup of coffee. 'Please?'

This proposed intimacy isn't what I want. Not at all. I hardly know John. As he deliberately places his hand on mine as he passes me a coffee, I hope he may be beginning to realise that this simply isn't going to happen. Not with me, not with him. Because he isn't Richard, he's not what I signed up for. And as he moves closer, he doesn't smell right, not unpleasant but not familiar, he doesn't smell like Richard.

I suggest to John, since he appears quite content with what his wife is doing and with whom, that we just pass the time and talk as best we can while Richard and Rosalind are upstairs and . . .

But I can't talk sensibly to him while my mind is on them, on what they are doing, I want to stop it, to stop us, to stop them. I don't understand, I want to go home. Take the children and drive home. Right now. I feel confused and very hurt, it's painful, almost too painful to breathe. But Richard has the car keys in his trouser pocket and his trousers are now probably in a crumpled heap on their bedroom floor.

I don't want to climb those stairs, fumble with his corduroy trousers to find the keys while he is . . . because I might see . . . . And I don't wish to carry that image in my head, his bare bottom, Rosalind's spread legs . . .

In the end I decide, quite coldly and deliberately, that the only thing I can do is to put all my emotions on hold, mentally place them in the chest freezer that we have at home; and slam the freezer lid shut. Firmly. Because if I don't bury my feelings, put them on ice, my reaction might be to kill him. Certainly, to wound him as he is wounding me. To hit him. Hard. Over the head with the wine bottle. Or with whatever bedside light John and Rosalind might have in their bedroom. Anything. Hit. Punch. Hard. Because I hurt so much. And I am so angry with him for hurting me like this, for not considering my feelings, for doing what he is doing.

So, John and I just talk. Downstairs. I make no sense. I sip coffee. I shake. With suppressed violence. Anger too. With love for my children. With the need to protect them. With pain. From what is happening. Right now, with their father, from what he is doing. From what might be the outcome, from my own reaction, whatever that might be, with panic. With desire to run away, drive away, drive anywhere. With our children. <u>My</u> children. Thinking about them is what is keeping me grounded.

When Richard and Rosalind eventually come downstairs, they are looking smug, self-satisfied.

I am boiling. But I remember my manners, after all, we have been dinner guests. I must put my feelings on hold. Until it's safe to let them show. Carefully. 'Thank you for having us' is rather too apt. And not true because 'thank you' isn't what I feel, at all. Quite the opposite.

I say nothing to Richard as he drives the few miles home.

'Are you all right?' he asks, wanting some reassurance before we reach our cottage.

'Fine!' I snap, to put myself out of his emotional reach, out of my own emotional reach, for both of us. 'I'm fine because I'm in the car with my kids and they are fine too.'

Before long, Richard begins to tell his associates, people that he knows through his business dealings or through other colleagues, that we have 'an open marriage'. This is so like Richard. If he has an idea and isn't immediately and repeatedly challenged on it, he assumes that other people – and in this case, me – are in total agreement. And if I dare to disagree, he will sulk. And do so for several days, which creates an uncomfortable atmosphere and will rub off on the children and their behaviour.

So, Richard mentions to men, and occasionally to the few women whom he meets, that he and I have 'an open marriage'. I assume this is intended to indicate that Richard is a modern man, and that any men who are married are welcome to make overtures to me, should they wish to do so, as long as Richard can seduce their wives. In Richard's defence, I would have to point out that this is in the nineteen seventies, when new ideas from the sixties and the U.S.A. take their time to hit rural Norfolk. This is a time of the social movement of 'Free Love' which separates the state from religion, convention, and sexual matters such as marriage, adultery and birth control. Car key parties and partner-swopping are all the rage, following the easy availability of the contraceptive pill - and possibly, the decline of the impact of the established church.

Again, I feel like a bargaining chip, so that Richard can have what he wants. It makes me feel like a pawn, a tradable commodity, redundant, the wife out of Thomas Hardy's 'The Mayor of Casterbridge'.

I am not consulted, perhaps because he knows what my opinion will be. Instead, Richard will decide what I am to wear to that party and this party and will sometimes bring back clothes from the National Trade Fairs that he has visited. They aren't often the sort of clothes that I would choose for myself. They can be quite revealing. I feel as if I am 'on offer', being marketed.

I do wonder, just once or twice, if they are what he himself would like to be able to wear: because sometimes his gait when he is running makes me wonder about his sexuality, the gender that has been attributed to him. And the small size of his sexual organs does little to remove that thought from my mind. But the clothes are a present, so I feel obliged to wear them.

And I know better than to offer any dissent or criticism, it would be not only rude and ungrateful but also lead to further sulking and perhaps some biting comments from him.

On one occasion he returned home from Harrogate Trade Fair with a two-piece outfit made from sludge-green Tricel. He said that it would be lovely to see me wearing it in the summer. Tricel was, and possibly still is, a synthetic fibre made of more than 92% acetylated cellulose. At the time, it was advertised as having excellent elasticity and being resilient to wrinkles, mould, mildew, and insects. It was also non-absorbent so would cling to the body in hot weather and make the wearer sweat. Putting in on, I thought I looked like a fat frog. Not ideal summer wear. With or without a pond.

This two-piece comprised a bodice with short puffed-sleeves, a rounded neck and finished with stretchy elastic well above the waist to display a bare midriff. The trousers were elasticated at the waist and at the ankle. I wore it once, only because Richard was so insistent that I should, and even then, in the garden to protect my legs from stinging nettles.

As a child growing up during the years of rationing, most of my clothes were handed down from a distant cousin or from my sister. There had been one dress that I liked wearing, a rich brown velvet frock that had been passed on from Aunty Dorothy's niece Margaret. And another in a blue floral Liberty's material that was made for Valerie when she and Colin were invited to the Lord Mayor of London's party one year. She also had shiny saxe-blue shoes with a strap which, when I grew older, I sometimes wore although they didn't fit because Valerie's feet were two sizes smaller than mine.

Most of my clothes were hand-sewn by Aunty Dorothy who was good at such things. Moo, having minimal fine-motor abilities except when playing a musical instrument at which she proved proficient, attributed her lack of skill to her being left-handed, which as I grew older and started work as a qualified primary school teacher, I realised was ridiculous.

I would climb trees, dig holes, dam streams, clear the muck out the chicken house, build dens, saw logs, mend or change inner tubes and tyres on my bike and get filthy hands by doing it. Moo used to say, at the end of a non-school day, that my being dirty or my clothes being dirty was not a problem but 'a sign of a day well-spent'. She didn't once fret about my skirts being torn or needing to be mended, even though clothing was expensive and difficult to acquire. Her frocks or skirts, and most of mine and Val's that were not passed down from some other relative, usually one of Aunty Dorothy's nieces, were hand sown by Aunty Dorothy.

Aunty Dorothy let me choose the material from the very limited stock that she already had, and sewed according to Moo's suggestions and our needs, Val's and mine. She often produced identical frocks in two different sizes. I remember, when I was aged six, wearing a red gingham dress with a deep hem, smocking - so that it could stretch across the chest as I grew- and short puffed sleeves. That was fine, I felt, for me when I was five.

Regardless of the deep hem which was let down each summer, by the time I was ten or eleven, it was too small for me. But then there was still Val's red gingham dress, the larger edition, that she had outgrown or rejected years before; it was too good to be wasted. So I, aged about eleven and about to enter a secondary school, was dressed in a gingham frock with smocking and puffed sleeves. Had I had, at that age, any sense of self-worth and self-criticism, I would have realised that up-and-coming teenagers did not normally wear smocked dresses that made them look like a cross between 'Little Bo Peep' and Dorothy in 'The Wizard of Oz'. And no one in my family, not even Val, would have ever commented on the appropriateness or otherwise of my clothing. Except, perhaps, TCP Grandma.

I realise I am now resistant to being told what to wear - unless I ask my younger daughter for advice and her opinion. She can get it wrong, of course, but I trust her judgement. And her motivation.

Now, if friends or female colleagues from the children's playgroup come to our house for a meeting, quite often Richard will come up behind them, grab them around the waist, run his fingers up their chests and place his hands on their breasts. He will laugh, make it into a joke, as they may also do, to avoid any embarrassment. And I am embarrassed too. For them, about him, and for myself. Then the rumours about my husband begin to spread. I lose friends, lose the friends that they might have become without Richard's behaviour. And he doesn't see, can't see, what he has done wrong. Isn't it what they wanted?

'No, Richard, it really isn't.'

'But why not?'

'It just isn't, even if you imagine it is.'

'How do you know?'

'How do <u>you</u> know it's what they want? Do they say so?'

Fortunately for me, on one occasion someone did say something. Not to Richard, but to me.

I don't know how this fitted into the timescale of things but on one occasion we were hoping again to sell our jewellery to shops in the Bristol and Bath area. I had contacted my friend Katy and asked her whether it would be possible for us to spend a night with her in her flat. We could, I told her, sleep on the floor and we would bring our own towels and sleeping bags to avoid causing her any extra washing.

I don't know whether we had the children with us but after visiting the Bristol dock area, we spent the night as arranged with Katy in her flat. I must have slept soundly. In the morning and before breakfast, Katy came up to me and asked 'What was all that about, last night?'

I didn't know what she meant so I asked 'What are you talking about?'

'Well, after we had all said goodnight to each other and gone to bed, at some time during the night, Richard opened my bedroom door, came into my bedroom and tried to climb into bed with me.'

'So, what did you do?'

'I asked him what he thought he was doing – and I told him to go away, to go back to where you were sleeping.'

When Katy told me this, I related it to Richard and asked 'Well? Katy is my friend. What did you think you were doing, and with me, your wife, in the next room?'

He told me he did not remember anything about going into Katy's bedroom and trying to get into bed with her. 'But perhaps,' he said 'I had been to the loo and was trying to find my way in the dark back to you.'

I didn't believe a word of it. I believed it was another case of Richard trying it on, thinking that every woman, any woman, was either fair game or was actively wanting to have sex with him.

After letting the matter drop for a couple of days until we returned home, I tried to talk to him about personal space, but he didn't seem to understand, or didn't want to.

He told me that my attitude was 'prudish' and that 'jealousy is not an attractive feature, Lorna'. He did not appear to understand that people often want different things. Even that men and women might have different wants, needs, priorities. Exclusivity even. He could not understand, certainly not empathise. And then the sulking would start.

He could keep it up, the not talking, not looking at me, leaving the room if I walked in to it, for several days until I either apologised for being critical or said something, did something, to which he had to respond. This wasn't easy when we were trying to run a business together; and in front of our two or three employees from the village, I found it embarrassing as well as unproductive.

For a while, I wondered, but only briefly, whether we had worked together, been together, for so long that Richard didn't appreciate or even understand that we were two different people with different likes and dislikes. That women were not a carbon copy of men. That I had my own ideas, even if they did not agree with his. He seemed to want to control what I did, how I behaved, what I wore, how I reacted, what I thought or believed. Not unlike my upbringing, I later realised. And when he found I was not controllable in that way, then the criticism began as to how I treated the children.

Chapter 14
Feeling a Failure, 1978

It is not at this stage that I begin to feel a failure again, a disappointment as a wife, friend, lover and mother. This self-doubt begins much earlier: I suspect it starts as an implant.

I have a snap-shot memory of going into my two youngest children's bedroom: because I feel that I ought to, that I have to, leave them. Richard has intimated to me that as a wife and especially as a mother, I am inadequate, I do not do what I am told or what he wants; so, either I reasoned with myself or perhaps he has suggested it, they would be better off without me, if necessary, the children with him on his own.

I do not know what, if anything, I have planned to do, only to leave. But I know how little I value myself; how I have been told, more than once by the Baptist Minister and the Elders that I am unworthy, a miserable sinner, no good; how I know I am taking up unnecessary earth space and resources. That no one will miss me if I leave or die. That it may even be a good thing.

Nell, my eldest child and older daughter, is not in this room. She sleeps on a folding bed in a small area, so small - no more than 1 metre wide by 2 metres long - that we can hardly call it a room, that leads from the narrow landing in the cottage to the tiny airing cupboard.

Into that space in front of the airing cupboard we have been able to squeeze a fold-down bed, with its foot-end raised at right angles to the wall and against it. The space is not long enough to allow access through from the landing door while still accommodating a full-sized single bed. Nell is only five years old at this time so she can easily and comfortably fit on the two-thirds length of a normal single bed.

It is night. Richard is asleep on the right-hand side, his side, of the double bed in our room. But I am awake. And so sad, so very unhappy. Something has happened or been said to trigger my sadness. I have been told or shown in some way that my children will be better off without me. That I am useless. That I have changed from being the woman I was when he first knew me, Richard has said, to the person I am now. That I always put the children's needs first and never his, and that that is bad for everybody, the children especially - because I fuss around them too much. That Richard will be happier, have far more choice and freedom, if I leave him - and particularly them.

At this moment I believe it. At this point I do not question how they might manage financially and practically without me. Only years later I realise how close I come, or might have come, to leaving.

Thinking that this will be for the best, the best I could do for my three young children, I tiptoe out of our bedroom and along the landing. The door to Nell's room is open, it has to be, we cannot easily close it because there is not enough space. She is fast asleep. I kiss the top of her head, very very gently so as not to wake her, whisper 'Goodbye, I love you' and 'Look after them all, I know you will.' With tears in my eyes, I leave the room.

The other bedroom is at the top of the stairs. I lift the Norfolk latch, slowly and quietly because it tends to make a clicking sound, cross the red-and-black mottled carpet that we have begged from my parents' house, and walk across to the bunk bed. My three-year-old son Keir is asleep on the top bunk under a seersucker-covered duvet. He wears a nappy at night with elasticated plastic pants over the top. He is sleeping soundly, he is a deep sleeper, rarely waking until morning. And by then, I'll be gone.

I bend to kiss Lallo in the same way that I've kissed Nell. But I want to hug her, she is my youngest, the littlest one, so small and fragile, the easiest birth, the one whose skin was the colour of honey when she was born at home, in a bed in the next room.

On my knees by the bed, ducking and stretching so I can reach her under the top bunk, I slip my arms under the blue-and-white cover and gently, so gently around her body. I sniff her head, her forehead, kiss her fair hair but then . . . although still asleep, her little arms come up and she hugs me, holds me with the warmth almost of an adult, her arms clasping but not meeting around my back. She is giving me exactly what I need at this moment, what I am lacking from her father. Her hug feels personal, not her dream, not automatic. It is for me, her mother. It is a huge gift.

And immediately I know I cannot leave, not after this, I just cannot. I shake my head from side to side, eyes brimming with hot tears and I need to stand up in case my tears and snot drip onto her. I do not remember returning to our bed, climbing in beside Richard but that is what I must have done. And in the morning, in the light, life is lighter, not much but light enough. We are still here together and alive. I feel as if Lallo has handed me back my life, that I owe it to her, to the warmth and spontaneity of that hug, to the realisation that she thinks I am important to her, that she loves me, unconditionally.

I am not sure what I believe in any more, I am not even sure who I am. But I know I believe in my children, in how important they are, to me.

Chapter 15

Sanctuaries, Success and Selling

Realising and visualising how close I had come to rock bottom, I determined that the only way to move from the bottom was 'up'; and that doing that was completely up to me. I even smiled to myself at the aptness of the preposition. I reflected on the things that I had said or done to which Richard had objected. He had told me that I was always saying 'no' to things he suggested or did, that I curtailed him too much, that I made a fuss when I asked him to be more gentle with Keir, not to shout at him so much because he probably wasn't being deliberately disobedient, despite Richard telling me 'You let that boy get away with things, he doesn't do as he's told and he needs to learn', even though I suggested that perhaps Keir hadn't heard properly because of his deafness.

I remembered how I had been the one to notice when Keir, lying in his carrycot on its wheels outside the barn, had not even stirred when a jet plane had flown low overhead. How I had been the one to remind Richard that Ruth had had a hearing problem when she was small. How, in the end, I had taken Keir to see Dr Pearson at the North Elmham surgery and had told the doctor what I had noticed, what I thought, what I feared. 'I think he might have a hearing problem. His half-sister had one and she needed to wear hearing aids.'

How Doctor Pearson had taken me seriously, how he had put his hand in front of his mouth and asked 'Keir, would you like some Smarties?'. And how Keir had not responded, had looked around the room - and how the doctor told me 'I think he may have a problem. He's probably been lip-reading for most of the last three years. We've leave it for the time being in case it's something developmental and he grows out of it. But we may need to make further tests once he starts school.' But, as I wanted to say to Richard when Richard got cross, I hadn't made Keir deaf, had I? I had just found out why he didn't always do as he was asked. It was because he couldn't hear properly.

I hadn't encouraged him not to do as Richard told him, I had been sticking up for my son, our son, because I felt his father was misjudging him and punishing him for the behaviour that his father considered 'naughty' and 'disobedient'. 'That poor boy was told off so often, he's probably become quite bewildered,' I countered.

On a separate occasion when we had been in the sea at Holkham, I hadn't been making what Richard termed as 'an unnecessary fuss' or being 'unfriendly' towards a stranger. The stranger, naked in the sea, was pretending to be nervous of the water. He had called to Nell, also naked, to come close to hold his hands because he was still afraid. 'There's nothing to be afraid of,' Nell had called back to the man, avoiding my habit of correcting her grammar by continuing with 'Look, I'm much younger than you and I'm not afraid.'

'But you are a brave girl, much braver that I am,' the stranger responded 'so would you be really kind and come and hold my hands?' Then I saw my beloved elder daughter jumping up and down, holding a stranger's hands and coming so close to him that her nubile body was rubbing against his torso, against his genitals.

'Nell, would you please be very kind and swim over towards me for a moment?' I asked. I wasn't making a fuss or being impolite to someone we didn't know; I was safeguarding my lovely daughter. I wasn't being nasty and suspicious and thinking every naked man was a pervert. I was just being cautious. I tried to explain my concerns later to Richard but his response was 'You're becoming far too suspicious. Nell was enjoying helping him and now you've spoiled her moment of kindness.' I really didn't think I had spoiled the family day out by being over-cautious or a prude.

Richard told me that I was becoming depressed. He said that when I objected to him fooling around physically with the mothers of the children's playgroup friends, it rebounded on him and on the children and made them all grumpy. 'And that shows', he said, 'that you've lost your sense of fun and proportion.'

From want of anyone better to talk to, I went to see Dr Pearson and told him that I had a problem, but one that he might not be able to solve. He was kind and understanding, he asked whether I wanted a course of antidepressants. 'No, thank you,' I responded, 'I'm not depressed, so you can keep your antidepressants. I'm just fed up.'

I felt I needed a sanctuary, somewhere private where I could be alone and not be verbally attacked, criticised or 'got at' by anyone, least of all by Richard. The first place I found was not surprising, it was the local church on a Sunday morning. I thought that, if I went to church and took Nell with me, there was a good chance that Richard, with his background of wanting to be a minister or a bishop, would respect my sudden 'church-going' and not pursue me there nor raise any real objection.

It was blissfully peaceful. Nell and I would walk up the hill together to the churchyard and in through the porch. Rhiannon, one of Nell's friends, also went each Sunday. Rhiannon had moved into our village fairly recently from a village near Cambridge, her father was a writer and an editor. The parents had quite a large house with land and Rhiannon's mother had the idea of becoming self-sufficient. Rhiannon did not go to school locally, instead she was taught by other people in her family.

On Sunday mornings, Nell, Rhiannon and Rhiannon's mother became the choir. There was only the vicar, a server and no more than three people in the congregation. The music was dire, played at funeral speed by Mrs Woods on an ancient harmonium. It would have helped had I been able to have a good sing but I held back on that in case someone thought I was being too loud, or singing out of tune. I felt I was rather using the church, being slightly hypocritical in saying the creed while not having attended regularly before but I hoped that God, should He or She be there, would understand.

My second sanctuary was in Ber Street in Norwich. There was a tanning shop there where, for a minor sum of money and taking a magazine, I could go into a booth, strip off and stand or lie under a sunlamp for a set number of minutes, feel the warmth and comfort that I felt my life was lacking.

By chance, I found a third place, another refuge in which I felt I might begin to flourish. A local couple, George and Cecilia Scourfield, who owned a second-hand bookshop in Fakenham, were running a sort of literary drop-in centre. Every two weeks or so, they would have an open evening to which any prospective writer could come and share his or her work by reading it. People could also talk about a book or a poem that particularly interested them or that they could recommend. Rhiannon's parents told me about it and on a couple of occasions, offered to give me a lift there and back.

I enjoyed going there, it was like having a much-needed drink of clear fresh water. I came home uplifted and inspired, but back to a husband who would accuse me of all sorts of things, including being in love with another person there, an accusation that it was hard to refute, not because whatever he said was true but because I couldn't prove that it wasn't. 'You come back after you've been there, glowing with pleasure' he would say, 'so you've been up to something.'

It was hard to explain to someone who didn't understand the pleasure that can be gained from a good book or a meaningful conversation, just what I enjoyed and would continue to enjoy. I had found another group of people to whom words were important, words rather than pictures, paintings or semi-precious stones, words that could bring pleasure, excitement, questions, even a different world.

I mentioned to Richard that I would like to write. 'Write what?' he asked me.

'I don't know, not yet.' I replied. 'I just want to write. Writing and using words is my way of thinking. It's how I feel I can say the things that are important to me.'

He said he didn't understand. But sometime later he did ask 'What do you need in order to be able to write whatever it is you want to write?'

'I need space, and uninterrupted time,' I explained. 'And where possible, an upstairs room or a room with a view. Then I can gaze into the distance while I'm thinking.'

To Richard's credit, he tried to make part of this possible. He was willing to look after the children, once they were in bed and asleep, while I took myself off to the Assembly House in Norwich where I joined the Writers' Circle. After going for a few weeks, I submitted for comment a short story that I had written, based on a real-life experience.

I found the comments that I received a week or two later, unhelpful. One man, a Methodist minister whose work was also being scrutinised at the same meeting, was scathing about the subject I had chosen, adult baptism, because he thought I had been critical of the non-conformist church and the power of prayer. I set that story aside for a while and focused on articles for the local press, one commenting on what I thought were incongruous regulations regarding the change of use of a former primary-school building. Another article was about the use of popular scents such as lemon in household and cosmetic products. I was sent a small but not insignificant sum for each article.

I told Richard that I thought my short story about prayer and adult baptism might have some merit if I were to turn it into a radio play because, as I told him and the few other people who showed interest, 'I can hear it happening in my head, it's like a series of voices talking.'

Richard was willing to allow me not to start work in the jewellery workshop at 11 o'clock each morning but on two mornings a week, to have the time between taking the children to playgroup and collecting them again, for me to sit and write.

To be able to concentrate and not have my thoughts interrupted, I would drive from Lyng Playgroup to a layby on the main road, sit there and write until it was time to pick the children up again and resume being a wife and mother. I typed my play, which I called 'Gloria's Baptism', on Richard's typewriter and taking a big chance, sent it with a covering letter to BBC Radio 4.

To my surprise and huge delight, a letter of acceptance came back. My play was rehearsed and recorded at BBC Birmingham's Pebble Mill Centre that August and broadcast in the 'Afternoon Theatre' slot on 30 January 1980. At the time, I had a small cassette recorder and I recorded the broadcast, remembering how difficult it would be to turn the tape over quickly midway through the programme. I put the tape somewhere safe because it was important to me, it was evidence that my voice had been heard.

I told another local writer, one who had been trying without success to have his collection of poems published, that I thought my success had been a case of 'beginner's luck'. Nevertheless, it was luck that I was pleased to enjoy. The proceeds went into the house-keeping money.

With the encouragement of the editor friend who lived in the village and who also wrote plays and poems, I went to see what was happening at N.E.T., Norwich Experimental Theatre, which was organised and run by a group of enthusiasts who had negotiated the use of a theatre at the very top of Wensum Lodge in King's Street, Norwich. I watched a couple of rehearsals and several plays written by local playwriters. As an organisation, I didn't feel it was for me. I felt I had little in common with anyone else there, I didn't feel I had anything to contribute and my being there struck me as pretentious.

At the end of the N.E.T. evenings, members who were able to do so would walk along the street to the Ferry Boat public house and order half a pint or more. I was in two minds about all this, the conversations could be stimulating but often they went right over my head. While really wanting to go home, I would often stay there in case I might pick up some pearl of wisdom and continue to drink my lager.

On one occasion, after I had been working all day and then spending the evening with N.E.T., I was driving back along the main Norwich to Fakenham road towards the village when I realised I was falling asleep at the wheel of the car, for only a moment but that was enough. The change of rumbling note under the wheels, leaving the road and crossing the rough grass verge, the bumping jerked my eyelids open . . . and I saw a thick hawthorn hedge coming fast towards me. I came to my senses at that point and decided that Norwich Experimental Theatre and The Ferry Boat were places that I wouldn't visit again. I didn't belong.

Nell was experiencing some difficulty at her primary school. When I met her in the village as she got off the school bus just after 3 o'clock in the afternoon, she would often burst into tears. It wasn't, she said, because she was tired or hungry which had been my suggestion or assumptions. At first, I thought it was because she wasn't pleased to see me, that she didn't like me, rather as Lizzie had responded when faced with Doreen. But it was, Nell finally admitted, because no one had played with her. We discussed this, as she slowly cheered up on our way back to the cottage. But the tears after school happened too frequently, although there seemed no problem as I was putting her onto the school bus. So, I concluded, something was happening at school to make her so unhappy.

I went to see the class teacher and the headmaster. Nell's school report told me that Nell 'is sometimes slow to settle quietly and at other times appears to be dreaming but her comprehension of lessons and stories is good. Her art and craft work show painstaking detail and great mental absorption.' There was nothing written about her social skills and involvements. Miss Scott, Nell's class teacher with a long thick plait of fair hair, said that as far as she was concerned, nothing particular had happened at school that would cause Nell to be unhappy but, she said, 'Nell doesn't seem to have much in common with the others in her class, she doesn't seem to have a 'best friend'. She can manage the work without any problem. Perhaps' she suggested 'Nell is just a natural loner?'

I thought this unlikely. Nell had had several friends when she had been in Lyng playgroup and in the Elmham Brownie pack, so I couldn't see why she would suddenly shun the company of other girls of her own age. It seemed time for me to talk to Mr Welsh, the Head.

Mr Welsh said 'I don't know what Nell is doing in that class, I don't know what the class is doing either.' I suggested, as tactfully as I could while remaining assertive, as Headmaster he might like to find out? Mr Welsh came back with some information which proved unhelpful. He had talked, he said, to Nell's class teacher and they were both of the opinion that there was nothing wrong at school. But I wasn't content with that.

Keir was in a separate class; he was still in the Reception class and his teacher was Mrs Jones. I had heard a number of stories about Mrs Jones, most of which I took to be village tittle tattle. But when Nell came home from school one day and told me 'Keir was in trouble at school today during lunch time. Mrs Jones was cross with him and Keir hid under the mobile classroom. Mrs Jones tried to reach him with a broom but her arms weren't long enough.'

'So, what happened?' I asked her, while also realising that I was encouraging her to tell tales on her brother.

'He stayed there,' Nell said 'he said he wasn't going to come out so he stayed there until home time and the school bus came.'

While I recognised that Keir could be a handful, I was concerned about care and control, safety and Keir's general well-being as well as his learning, much of which appeared to have been, on that particular occasion, about the structure of the undercarriage of a mobile classroom. It was, I thought, perhaps time to reconsider whether Nell and Keir were thriving in the local school. And it would be to the same school that Lallo was soon due to be assigned. Perhaps a change of school might help.

I approached Mr Dodds, the school's previous headmaster who had moved to head up a Middle School in Dereham. I had always liked and respected him. But he told me 'At present we are completely full in the class that your daughter would join. I'm simply not allowed to enrol any more children until some of the current pupils leave and go elsewhere.'

'So, when might you have space?' I persisted. 'If I could find an Infant School in the town that would take my son, then I could ferry both children to school each morning and pick them up in the afternoon.'

'I might have a few spaces in September,' Mr Dodds told me, 'but I couldn't guarantee that. So, in the meantime, it seems as though your son and daughter will have to stay at their current school.'

This conversation took place at the beginning of the Spring Term. I wasn't content to keep both children at their current school for a further two terms, not if they were unhappy. I felt that I needed to make a few other enquiries.

At the time, Norfolk Education Authority was divided into separate areas, each area having its own Education Officer. The Breckland Area which governed our local schools had its head office in Thetford. With an idea in mind, I made an appointment to go on my own to see the local Education Officer. On the basis that a pair of jeans didn't seem quite adequate for the occasion, I wore a skirt and either black tights or stockings.

Having introduced myself, I explained the current situation regarding the local school and the anticipated gap before I could enrol the children in separate schools in Dereham.

'So, would it,' I asked him 'be in order and acceptable for me to teach two of my children and possibly the third, at home? I am a qualified teacher and I have worked for both Norfolk and Norwich Education Authorities on and off since 1966, teaching in primary schools. Is there anything you need to know to allow me to do this? Would you want to see schemes of work and so on, and evidence that each of the children is learning as much as if he or she were at school?'

It seemed that I had made a reasonable case. No, there didn't appear to be a need for me to submit anything to anyone, presumably because this was to be a short-term arrangement. The only aspect that concerned me was the children's likely lack of social involvements with other children. Nell had Rhiannon as a friend, whereas Keir and Lallo only had each other and whereas I thought they might be academically matched, Keir's social and physical needs were clearly quite different from Lallo's.

I agreed with Richard that I would spend most of the morning teaching the children subjects that could reasonably come under the headings of Humanities and English, while Richard told me he would take on the teaching of maths every day between 11.00 in the morning and lunchtime. I had a few misgivings about that. Although I had no reason to doubt Richard's computational and mathematical abilities, his teacher training in Canterbury had been in art and at the secondary school level. His experience in the secondary school in Thetford had hardly been a success.

Would he, I wondered, teach maths as he himself had been taught, possibly quite formally, at a preparatory school in Norwich? Would he think that primary school maths was all about 'doing sums'? Would he appreciate the diversity of language used in subtraction – expressions such as 'what is the difference between X and Y', 'how much less is X than Y 'or 'what do you need to add to X to make Y?' or would he resort to teaching the mechanics of subtraction by introducing 'carrying figures', as I had been taught back in the 1950s?

As things turned out, I was never to know. Richard appeared in the kitchen once at the agreed time one day but told the children and me, 'I'm in the middle of something today so maths will have to wait until tomorrow.'

On another occasion, he took up the time by discussing some business arrangement with me, then winding up the children by tickling them and playing with them around the kitchen as if they were his school pals.

After that, I think he forgot all about the arrangement and I took on the maths teaching, possibly not well, but at least I was reliable and consistent.

I enjoyed teaching my children. As well as providing the day with a structure, there could be a spontaneity about it. When we were talking about the Ancient Britons or Romans and one of the children became particularly keen to know more, we packed anything essential - camera, wellington boots, note books - into the car and set off towards Warham circular hill fort near Wells-next-the-Sea or in the direction of Norwich, to Caistor St Edmund.

Here, when I explained what I was doing and what particularly interested the children, a really kind chap showed us around a private part of the gardens of Caistor Hall Hotel and explained exactly what had been found there, and that we could see those finds in Norwich's Castle Museum.

I found the experience of teaching three quite different children at home to be exciting, very worth-while and unexpectedly expensive. I had assumed, before I started, that I would have a class of three pupils whereas in fact, I had three classes with one pupil in each. It was expensive because, in the days before the internet, we needed a stock of reference books at home. Or to make unplanned and immediate visits to Dereham library in the hope of finding a suitable book written with language at a suitable level, to support whatever interest had suddenly emerged, before the desire to know more wore off.

We could adopt a topic-based approach and generally cover most essential knowledge and skills from that. I shall not forget our time visiting Lowestoft fish market one grey November, the crates of fish, the ice, the hose pipes and running water, the fisherman we spoke to - and the art, maths, science and history work that came out of it, as well as our meal for that night. And I took great comfort during that time from being with my three interested and interesting children for much of the day.

Once or twice a month, I would go with the children to a former department store and carpet warehouse in St Benedict's Street, Norwich known as 'Premises', almost next to St Swithin's Church. Premises had been a recently established 'alternative' centre for performing arts. The children seemed to enjoy going there, perhaps partly because they took pleasure in visiting a café as well as in meeting like-minded children with like-minded parents who didn't mind their children getting covered in paint or plaster, as long as the experience and outcome were developmental and productive.

It cost very little, perhaps less than a pound entrance for each child and I thought it well worthwhile.

Concerned that we weren't selling enough jewellery to shops across different areas of the country, Richard thought it might be worthwhile for us to open our own shop in a lucrative town. He knew of premises in Bull Street in Holt that would soon become available. Would it, Richard wondered, be suitable for us as a shop window? I don't remember either him or me, even if I had been consulted, ever having done any research into footfall in that part of Holt.

Bull Street runs behind the main shopping area and at the time, little seemed to be going on there, except a butcher's shop and one or two other private stores. But almost before I knew it, Richard had taken on the lease of a shop for a limited period. He had decided to employ a salesperson named

Anneke, someone who was a champion golfer. I have no idea how he met her but I am fairly sure that she wasn't one of his conquests; she was more interested in playing golf and keeping her body in good shape for that purpose.

I was witness to the latter and to her tact towards her employer when Richard came into the shop carrying a large paper bag. 'Here,' he said, proffering the bag, 'I've bought us each something to go with our coffee,' and he produced a couple of doughnuts and a rather revolting-looking sticky bun. 'Help yourself, Anneke. You choose.'

I had eaten my breakfast in the car while Richard was driving to Holt so he knew I was unlikely to need anything more until lunchtime.

'That's really kind,' said Anneke, looking slightly aghast, yet thoughtfully at the buns. I guessed she was mentally calculating the high calorific value of each and how long it might take her swinging her clubs on the course at Sheringham to work all that off.

'But would you mind if I saved that until after I've had the salad that I made myself for lunch? I didn't think to bring myself a dessert.'

I was not surprised when Richard consumed the other buns. He had a sweet tooth and found it hard to control his hunger and desire for food.

Richard had not thought or planned carefully enough as to staffing the shop in Holt, he admitted to himself after a time. Holt is a Georgian town, frequented by the discerning, well-heeled and sometimes titled shopper but it does not necessarily attract the young. Anyone making a purchase of jewellery in Holt was, I thought, more likely to opt for gold and precious stones from an established jewellery retailer.

'Any sales today?' I might ask, after Richard had finished his telephone call to Anneke.

'No, not today, not actual sales but there was plenty of interest, people looking in the window' he would reply, hopefully.

Another day would pass, with the same result, or lack of result. And all the time we were paying rent, utility bills for telephone, electricity and water to the shop as well as Anneke's wages.

Richard asked some of the jewellery workshop staff, one at a time, to drive to Holt and take turns in running the shop. His argument was that, as they helped to make the items, they would be able to sell them with knowledge and enthusiasm and we had to pay them already anyway. But that idea didn't work out at all.

We also paid them petrol money and while they were in the shop, they weren't producing anything we could sell. And it was lonely, there wasn't the female camaraderie that working in the workshop provided.

We did not renew the lease on the shop in Bull Street. Richard decided that there was an insufficient number of potential customers in Holt. 'We need a shop somewhere where there are plenty of people, young people mostly. Ideally, we need somewhere in Norwich, not where we had the art gallery in Bethel Street but somewhere in the centre where there are people walking past, people looking in shop windows and wanting to buy things,' he said.

One of Richard's associates knew of a man who wanted to lease out his three-storey shop in Norwich. Richard made contact with this man, a Mr Black and viewed the property in question in Lower Goat Lane, a pedestrianised lane between a row of shops on either side and running from the market place towards an Italian restaurant and a multi-storey car park.

'It would be ideal', Richard said 'but first we will need to redecorate at least the ground floor and the first floor. And we will need something other than just jewellery to attract people in, because individual items of jewellery are too small to attract the eye of a passer-by. During my visits to craft fairs and craft shops, I've seen a couple of people or concerns whose work I would be more than happy to buy in and sell in our shop. There's a studio potter called Terry Godby who lives in Lincolnshire whose work I admire. I'd like to see that in a shop alongside our jewellery. He said he worked as an apprentice at Leach pottery before setting up on his own.'

By this time, in his mind, Richard had taken full possession of the shop, had redecorated it, produced a new shop sign and had filled the shop windows with up-market goods.

'And I also saw, at Harrogate or the National Exhibition Centre in Birmingham, some glassware that I really admired. It was beautiful, the company is called Cumbria Crystal. Lead crystal, hand-blown and hand-cut and lovely designs.'

'How' I asked quite genuinely, 'can glass be hand-blown? How do you blow with your hands?'. Richard explained that this was' just an expression' and so on, until he could see that

I had understood and that I wasn't trying to be pedantic or annoying by raising questions. At least I wasn't raising any objections: I did question the finances behind all this, only to receive huge assurances that 'everything will be all right because I've worked it out.'

Richard's 'working it out' involved another bank loan. It may also have involved offering the cottage and the land as security but I'm not sure about that because I don't think I would have agreed to it, had I known, had I been told – or been asked.

By this time, Nell started school at Dereham Church Middle. Keir transferred to the same school and Lallo began at King's Park First School in Dereham. It seemed to me that being taught at home had done them no harm and, in many ways, they were academically ahead of their classmates.

Richard and I joined in the activities organised by King's Park Parent Teacher Association. With the children, we attended the P.T.A. bonfire night and fireworks celebrations and met a small number of other parents who had children in Lallo's class. At the end of the school day, I would stand outside the school ready for Lallo to emerge, then drive quickly to the entrance of the Middle School to collect Nell and Keir. The end times of the school day at the two separate schools and the distance between them made it difficult for me to collect Lallo, settle her in the car and drive a mile or so across the town, park and still arrive in time to collect Nell and Keir just outside the school gate.

A sensible solution seemed to me to arrange for Nell and Keir to walk to where Moo and Dad lived at the town end of Quebec Road. There was only one major road for them to cross, at a corner just outside The George Hotel.

Walking the route through with them, we decided on the safest place to cross that gave them and any oncoming traffic the maximum visibility of each other. Moo and Dad were very pleased to do this for us, it gave them daily contact and care of two of their grandchildren for five days in the week. I would arrive after picking up Lallo almost at the same time as Nell and Keir reached Moo's house, just in time to be offered a cup of tea.

One of the parents' events at King's Park was a fancy-dress competition. I don't remember what I wore because much of my energy went into arranging and agreeing a suitable costume for Richard. Richard was over 6ft tall so the costume I had once designed for him, with doublet and hose when we had been at an Elizabethan event in Rainthorpe Hall, was going to look quite incongruous at a First School event. I remembered the sludge-green Tricel two-piece.

'How would you feel about going dressed as a frog?' I asked.

'Fine', he said, 'I'll go as almost anything so long as you can get it together in time and it doesn't cost us anything.'

By chance, I had a pair of googly frog-eye inserts that might have been intended for some stuffed toy but I thought they would do well, either sewn into a headdress or attached to the toes of a pair of green wellington boots. I rejected the boots idea because I had only two frog eyes and to look right, boots would have required four – and we had only two green boots anyway. Instead of having the eyes on his wellingtons, I made him a head dress from cardboard and green felt, with the swivelling frog-eyes attached.

I was pleased when Richard won a prize as a frog. It had been an excellent use of the green Tricel clothing he had bought for me, without hurting his feelings by my not wearing it any further. An even better outcome, I thought, was that he had split the trouser part, making it impossible to wear again. I put it in the children's dressing up box, complete with the green felt hat and googly frog eyes.

One of the other results of the competition was that Richard became known in an environment in which fathers quite often figure rather less. If he ever went to pick up Lallo from the school gate, one or two of the other mothers would recognise him and talk to him about nothing in particular. They got to know that he was a manufacturing jeweller which seemed to impress some of the women. They were all about my age or younger and two or three had children in Lallo's class.

One mother in particular called Jayne told Richard, and me if I happened to have accompanied him, 'I used to be deeply involved with the playgroup here. But now Rebecca and James have both started school, I need to find something else to interest me and take up my time.'

How fortunate, I thought, to have spare time on one's hands that needed to be occupied in some acceptable way and I wished, for just one moment or two, that I had a husband who could earn his own living unaided by me, who would bring home a regular sum of money each month or week, where paying the bills would become routine rather than a monthly struggle and a lottery.

Jayne and I quite often dressed in a similar way. It was the 1980s when Indian clothes were both in fashion and cheap. There was one particular design of dress with tiny shoulder straps that we both had and frequently wore; mine was purple and Jayne's was pink. Richard remarked to me 'You and Jayne seem to have quite a bit in common. You are both the same build and you've both been involved in playgroups. Perhaps we could invite her to our house one morning, for coffee or something and a look around the workshop.'

We had sold the cottage and most of the adjoining land. With the money from the sale, we were in the process of converting the barn into becoming habitable accommodation. Richard had designed and helped to build a purpose-built workshop in the corner field, and with full planning permission. Was that financed by yet another bank loan? I don't remember. The new workshop needed to have square-shaped windows – 'so that it doesn't resemble a bungalow', the Breckland District Council Planning Officer had recommended – several small rooms that could serve as offices, a small reception area and a toilet with a washbasin. It also had a large workshop area with wooden benches set against the windows to give natural light for assembly work.

We even had an industrial heater installed that was powered by gas. Warm air could be ducted through grills set high in the internal concrete-block dividing walls. The building wasn't finished, there were still some internal fittings missing and the floor was bare concrete. But the building was dry and could be warm.

For the first time, Richard considered security, not for us but for the semi-precious stones and particularly the coils of gold and silver wire. A large safe was brought into the building and concreted into the floor with deep bolts. It was opened by a combination that only he and I knew and had sufficient space to store most of the precious metal wire and items half-made.

We started work on the part of the barn that was to become the kitchen. I selected the kitchen units that I wanted, a multi-fuel Rayburn was installed once we had constructed a chimney, and I chose some Italian floor tiles that I really liked. Things seemed to be, to use a Norfolk expression, 'comin' a-gether'. And within budget, I could make choices.

We hadn't planned the intended layout of the rest of the barn but Richard did order a corner bath with a jacuzzi in the avocado colour, only because it was on offer at the time if we paid for it straight away. Ordering that was the outcome of another of Richard's rhetorical 'but can we afford not to buy it at that price?' questions.

The bath was stored at the far end of the barn, ready for whenever we decided where the main bathroom would be. Until then, we would make good use of the shower room, wash basin and loo at the other end of the building.

Richard decided to sell the 'Sharpie' sailing dinghy. It wasn't as much a decision as a response to an offer from one of the parents we knew from Lyng playgroup. One of the fathers had been wanting a Sharpie and hadn't been able to find one in adequate condition and for sale.

'Would Richard', the man asked, 'like to exchange the boat for a touring caravan?'

We had had a few holidays before when we had had Lizzie with us but we had had to hire the caravan in blocks of a week, and return it on time on a Saturday.

I could see that a caravan might offer us spontaneity, opportunities for holidays or the occasional weekend away.

As a child I had enjoyed caravan holidays with my parents, the absolute luxury of hearing rain pattering on the caravan roof while I was warm and snug in my sleeping bag on one of the single beds, the excitement of not knowing where we might stay for the night and the fun of exploring that evening or in the following morning. The idea of having a caravan brought back all those memories of pleasure, safety and enjoyment within the family.

With the cottage almost sold and our other buildings at the skeletal stage of development, 'I'd like to have a party,' Richard decided 'to celebrate what we have done so far, and while there is plenty of space in the buildings, before any internal walls are built or any furnishings are put in.'

I doubted that we knew enough people to hold a party but I ran through my brain a list of the people who might come if we invited them. We lacked genuine friends.

There were a couple of people from the village, one or two of Richard's associates from the arts and crafts world, a woman with whom I had played badminton at an evening class in Dereham if only I could remember her name, a couple of parents from Lyng playgroup with whom I had remained in contact, and Jayne and her husband Jeff from Lallo's First School.

We had been invited to Jayne's house in Dereham the previous Christmas for drinks before moving on for Christmas dinner at Moo's.

At the time, Richard had told me 'I was picking up some interesting vibes from Jayne. From the way she was sitting on the floor with her legs stretched out and slightly apart, I think she quite fancies me.'

'That was probably the sherry talking,' I suggested. 'and sitting like that on the floor would have been more comfortable than being cross-legged.'

We had invited looks of disapproval from Moo by arriving late for the Christmas meal. Moo, Dad, my sister Val, her husband Don and their children, and Aunty Dorothy and Uncle David had started before we arrived, which I thought was rather impolite of them, even if Moo had instructed them, 'Just start before your food gets cold. Lorna and Richard are bound to be here in a moment'.

In conversation with Richard about a party, I told him 'I could make a huge pot of chilli-con-carne in the *le creuset* pot that I use with the children for making fudge. It will hold more than enough and if I put in plenty of red kidney beans and make a large quantity of rice, that should cover most people's needs. But we'll need to buy some wine. Because although most people will probably bring a bottle, we can't be sure of that. We can have the main party in the barn and use the empty workshop as a creche.'

While I was busy thinking of the catering and childcare, Richard had his mind on other matters. 'I think I might try to seduce Jayne if she and Jeff come to the party,' he confided as if I were one of his male pals rather than his wife. 'I thought I'd move the caravan so that it can stand just outside the entrance to the barn. That would give us somewhere private but within easy reach of the creche, where I hope she'll deposit her children.'

In a rare brave moment, I responded with 'No, not right outside the front entrance of the barn. If you must attempt to make love to Jayne, would you please do so elsewhere? You could at least move the caravan to the side or the back of the barn. Then it won't be so much in my view.'

I was getting fed up with Richard regarding every female contact of mine as if she were fair game and of his desire to tell me all the details. I found it sordid to the point of tacky, and unaware as much as disrespectful towards any feelings I might have.

As luck would have it, earlier in the day, Jayne's son James, who was about four or five, had hit his head at their home on a radiator. Jayne was anxious not to leave him for too long, although she came to the party. I don't remember if Jeff came with her as well. But I know, because Richard told me, 'She felt the need to keep nipping back to the workshop to make sure that James was all right. We couldn't settle to anything because she was up and down all the time.'

I resisted making a comment on his phraseology because sometimes I could be too flippant for my own good. But I bore it in mind. I was also sure that, although Richard's intentions had been thwarted by James' accident, my husband was behaving like a frustrated teenage lad and that his desire would still be there.

I didn't feel like meeting his sexual needs that evening, not after he had been drinking and lusting after Jayne. I didn't wish to be anyone's fall-back choice. I just asked him, 'Have you washed your hands?'

Chapter 16

Coming to a Head

Rather than fight openly against Richard and his desire to have 'an open marriage' and sex with a variety of women, I decided to take an alternative approach. Although I totally disagreed with him, I thought that if I started to lay down the law to Richard or talk about marriage vows and exclusivity, it would make no difference and probably alienate him from me and from our shared business.

It would also perhaps produce domestic tensions that could rub off onto the children. I didn't want Richard's behaviour that I regarded as being 'immature and teenage boyish', to have a negative impact on Nell, Keir or Lallo.

I thought about Dad and Colin. How, when Colin had talked about giving up his accountancy training and joining the D'Oyly Carte opera company with which Colin was almost obsessed, Dad had advised him against it. But when Colin had persisted, had talked on and on about the parts he would play, the 'lost' operettas he could get the company to perform, Dad, through his various contacts, managed to secure a short-term job for Colin, touring with the Company.

At the end of that short spell with the D'Oyly Carte singers, Colin had quite willingly returned to his original training. D'Oyly Carte had not been the glorious experience that he had imagined it would be. For all those famous singers and actors performing night after night across the country, it had been nothing special, Colin had told me and told Dad too 'It wasn't at all what I thought it would be. For many of the actors and singers, it was nothing more than a job and quite a hard one at that.' Much later, Colin gained most of his accountancy qualifications. He also continued acting and singing only as an amateur and one year had been awarded a best amateur actor accolade by the Marlow Theatre in Canterbury.

I thought about Moo, about how Moo had been willing and so tolerant for Dad's Gilbert and Sullivan friend Frances to come to stay at our house for a few days. Dad had made every effort to entertain Frances while she was with us and he had sighed with relief when he had taken her to the station to catch her train back to Romford.

'I get on well with Frances' he would say 'and we have shared a lot in the past. But sadly, she has no sense of humour; I find her quite hard work sometimes.'

Having a sense of humour was fundamental to Dad. But although Frances and Dad had been friends and amateur operatic colleagues for many years, I suspect that that was as far as the relationship went. Dad knew that two or three days of Frances was as much as he could tolerate, that anything longer-term would drive him nuts. And she wasn't very bright although she talked non-stop as a running commentary on life, both of which annoyed Dad after a time. Moo was pleased to see her leave too.

'I welcome her as a guest simply because your dad likes her coming,' she would say, 'but when Frances is here and talking with your father all about their times in Romford, I can't hear myself think. Frances is exactly the sort of person that your father's mother would like him to have married. But he chose me instead.'

I asked her more about this, about what exactly TCP Grandma would have liked about Frances.

'Well,' said Moo, 'for a start, she can sew. She cares about her appearance, she's shorter than your father and she has neat curly hair. Grandma admired curly hair, she often told me that mine ought to be more curly, that I should have a perm more often, as she has.'

Somehow, from a series of scattered remarks, looks and innuendos, I gathered that Moo didn't much care for Frances, but that she would treat her with respect and politeness purely because that was the way my father would wish her to regard Frances and by doing that, Moo maintained my father's love and even deeper respect.

That was how, I decided, I would maintain a relationship with Jayne. It had worked for Moo, although I assumed that the relationship my father had with Frances was not a physical one and certainly not as close as I guessed Frances might have wanted. I would maintain a reasonably polite relationship with Jayne because she was, for the moment at any rate, Richard's choice of . . . . bosom friend?

The comparison between Frances and Jayne began to take a step further. Through my contact with 'Premises', I learned that a man called Jon Oram, who had been a drama advisor in Norfolk, was interested in setting up a Theatre in Education Company, which later became known as TIE Break Theatre. Jayne got to hear of this too. Both of us were interested to find out more, so in the spirit of polite collaboration if not actual friendship, I suggested that Jayne and I should go to the first meeting together.

Jayne's husband Jeff had been heavily involved in drama in Dereham so perhaps that was also how she became interested. Jayne didn't drive so we went together in my car. I don't remember the first one or two meetings because at that point Jayne seemed to lose interest. Or perhaps, with me occupied in Norwich, that became an ideal time for her to meet Richard and for them to develop their relationship further.

The TIE Break meetings continued on a regular basis at Premises. A chap called Dave joined us, as did three other women; one called Sian who later became a voice coach, Rosie with very curly dark hair who was at U.E.A. and someone else whose name I've forgotten but I know I liked her. Her husband Roger worked for television; they lived in a lovely cottage with internal beams in the village of Wreningham, just outside Wymondham. She allowed us to rehearse there once or twice when the Premises building wasn't available.

By this time, our main car had become a Volvo estate. I remember that particularly because of one incident involving Richard that could have caused an accident. I had parked on a spare patch of ground not far from the Premises building and enjoyed the morning practising some sort of 'show' we were going to perform with a dance routine that I found hard to grasp, the moves being set to a Michael Jackson song.

My mind and my body don't easily collaborate so my left and right legs refused to behave as my mind told them to do, so it was a slightly frustrating morning.

I came out of the building and was walking to the car park, when I saw Richard doing something with our car windscreen. As I grew closer, opened the driver's door and sat behind the steering wheel, I saw, all across the glass of the windscreen, 'I love Jayne' written in lipstick. Without some sort of de-greasing agent, it is very difficult to get lipstick off glass, to remove it completely. Using the windscreen wipers would only smear it further, completely obliterating any visibility. I was due to collect the children from school within an hour. I couldn't leave it and I couldn't easily remove it. I don't remember how I cleaned it off or exactly how long it took me.

I supposed I had always known this, to an extent. Richard's behaviour, if not akin to that of a child, then certainly was close to that of a teenager, an immature adult. I had made excuses for him to myself. I had known at college that he could be very immature in some of his behaviour, he hadn't seen or foreseen the effect that his behaviour might have on others.

I reminded myself that, if what he had told me was to be believed, he had lost all contact with his mother; he and his school had been evacuated to Weymouth in the care of nuns who, he said, never looked straight at him, showed him no physical love. He had been sent to a boarding school away from any friends and family, had been moved without warning from that boarding school to the Royal Masonic. His father Horace had married again, his second wife and Richard's stepmother was Margaret Croydon from an established East Anglia jewellery retail company.

Horace and Margaret had lived in Felixstowe. Richard had said 'I didn't get on very well with her, I don't think she was accustomed to children and certainly not to teenage boys.' From Royal Masonic, he had been sent to a private school for maladjusted boys before spending a year at King's College in the University of London, reading theology as training for entering the ministry.

Then he had been told he had to marry Doreen, only to have his father reject him in a letter because he had left his first wife and first three children.

No wonder, I thought, he was in a bit of an emotional mess, felt he was now in love with Jayne. But where, if that were the case, did I think I now fitted in? And how did I now feel and behave towards him? He was the father of my children, I still loved him or thought I did, but was that enough? Because I certainly wasn't going to put up with being just 'another woman' in his life.

At about the time that Prince Charles got engaged to Diana Spencer and we had cardboard cut-out masks of their two faces peering and waving from the rear windows of the Volvo, I remarked to Richard, 'I suppose you now have everything a successful man might want – a Volvo, a caravan, a home, a wife and a mistress.' He raised both eyebrows, looked pleased with himself and gave a brief nod.

I tried to discuss the periphery of this with Richard. The discussion needed care, not only to avoid it becoming heated but also because we had a business to run together. There were finished articles of jewellery to be sold, there were items in the process of manufacture, there were stocks of wire in precious metals, there were gems, mostly cabochon but a few cut and facetted.

My part in the business was no longer to design and help make items of jewellery; most of that was done by our staff. My job was to pick, pack and dispatch goods, create an invoice and maintain a record of orders, outgoing goods and incoming payments. All this, as well as the staff to consider.

Richard kept the accounts, placed orders for raw materials and chased up debtors for payment. During this time, to aid our finances, I took a temporary part-time teaching job at a Middle School in Dereham. It was another escape but an enjoyable and lucrative one. On those days after school, Nell and Keir would walk from their school to Moo's house while Lallo waited for me outside the King's Park School gates or walked part-way to Moo's.

To boost jewellery sales a year or so earlier, Richard had ordered a small sample number of lovely ring boxes, covered in a fabric resembling suede leather with a silk interior printed with the words 'Richard and Lorna . . . . ', followed by our surname.

I showed them to my parents, especially to my father who wanted Richard to make a special ring that he was secretly planning to give to Moo on their ruby wedding anniversary.

Richard was on the point of re-ordering the boxes in a larger quantity but then stopped. 'I've been thinking,' he told me. 'That wording inside is too long. I've tried to shorten it by replacing the 'and' with an ampersand but it is still too dominant, it overpowers the earrings or ring inside.'

I waited, unsure of what was coming next. Then it came. 'So, I've ordered another gross of boxes and I've told the manufacturer to omit 'and Lorna' because I think that will look better.'

It was not long after that name-change incident that I had a reason to look for the cassette recording that I had made of my radio play. I couldn't find it anywhere. It wasn't wherever I had left it, it wasn't in the likely places, it wasn't even in the unlikely spots.

Richard said he certainly hadn't seen it, 'And I don't know what you are talking about.'

His response reminded me of my earlier teaching days, of a child denying all knowledge of something he had done, verbally distancing himself from it. I hoped Richard hadn't taken it, or destroyed it because it was the only recording I had made. Then it struck me, that he hadn't recorded it or heard it either. He had decided to be at work rather than to listen to the radio for forty-five minutes, <u>my</u> forty-five minutes.

Almost a year later, I mentioned the cassette to Dad and my disappointment that it had 'gone missing.'

'Never mind, Love,' he said 'I think I made a recording. I might still have it somewhere.' And he had. After a long search, he found it and handed it to me. Years later, I was able to hand the tape recording that Dad had made, to a Norfolk I.T. specialist who was able to transpose it onto a compact disc, a disc which I still have. And I treasure it, almost as if it were another child.

Richard used an accounts book and a double-entry system of accounts. On one occasion he was in quite a panic, he couldn't account for £2,000 that he said had gone missing - until he realised that he had turned over two pages at a time and had misread the figures. This may have been partly why he decided to employ a woman called Joan to maintain the accounts, and to buy himself a Commodore PET home computer. He set this up in the new workshop and would spend hours at it. Whether or not it would have helped him with the accounts, I do not know but he was as fascinated with it and by what it could do, as he had been with Jayne.

Late into the evenings he would sit at the PET, picking the dry skin off his feet until it made a noticeable grey pile on the workshop's brown carpet tiles. I would appear, tell him that I was tired and heading for bed – and he would say, 'Wait a minute, I'll be with you before too long but just come and have a look at this, see what it can do.' And I would stand there for a further half-hour, my eyelids drooping, waiting for him to close the thing down, lock the workshop and come to bed in our upstairs room in the barn.

We had planned another holiday in the South of France, at the 'La Bédoule' naturist campsite that Richard had discovered. We planned to tow the caravan there and back and to use it on the site as our temporary home. Richard and I got on quite well during those warm weeks, I thought that he had forgotten all about Jayne, until two of the children told me that, on his way back from collecting a fresh baguette from the boulangerie, Richard had stopped at the public phone box on the road.

He had, they said, phoned Jayne and told her how much he was missing her. At this point, the children did not know about Richard and Jayne's relationship, they only knew that Jayne was Rebecca's mother and Rebecca was in Lallo's class at school.

Lallo and Rebecca weren't natural friends, but they were at the same ability level although Rebecca was several months older than Lallo. Sometimes, after school if I or Richard hadn't arrived by car by then, Jayne might walk with Rebecca and Lallo as far as the end of the road in which Jayne's family lived, where Jayne would turn off with her two children. Then Lallo could make her way along the short distance to Quebec Road and Moo's house, or I might have arrived and caught up with her by then.

Now, at the phone box in France and from what they overheard, it became first a puzzle, then clearer to the children that their dad and Rebecca's mum were very close friends indeed. Within half a day, one or all of them reported this back to me in a conspiratorial way.

Once the children were asleep in their bunks, I could talk more freely to Richard.

'I might have to go back home quite soon' he told me 'because Jayne needs me.'

'But we need you too' I said 'and this is our family holiday.'

'I could catch a train' he responded 'and leave you the car and the caravan.'

'Who's holding the reins here, Richard? Who's jerking the strings?' I asked. 'Because it sounds to me as if Jayne is making all the decisions at the moment. I've never towed a caravan and only once driven on this side of the road and then, only for a short distance. And we might have a problem over passports and the children.'

I can't remember exactly what the problem was or what I made it out to be. At the time, children under a certain age could be included on a parent's passport. But I know that, unbeknown to Richard and purely on the grounds of safety and to cover all possibilities including illness, I had either included the children on my passport too, or had obtained temporary passports for each of them.

But I do remember either Keir or Nell saying, amid the family tensions, 'This isn't a holiday at all. It's like being at home but with hotter weather.'

We all got back to Norfolk safely. Richard travelled with us. He was slightly sulky and conversations were short but we each survived the discomforts of the journey.

At some time after the phone box incident, when Richard was out in the car with the three children, one of them told me that Richard had stopped the car, got out, reached into a back pocket and taken out a photo of Jayne in a red velvet frame. He had shown it to them and said to them, 'This is the woman I love.'

He told me, on our return from holiday, that he would try not to see Jayne for a while and see whether he could handle that. I asked him 'Promise you won't see her or meet up with her again, at least until the children go back to school?' He promised and I accepted that.

A week or so later, I was in Norwich for several hours with the children. When I returned home to the barn and went up to our bedroom, Richard was lying almost in the bed. I asked him how his day had been. He was non-committal but told me 'I've been in the workshop most of today, planning what machines can go where.'

Then I saw grains of sand, several silver grains, quite a small pile clustered on the bottom sheet. I asked him what sand was doing there.

'Oh, that's builder's sand' he said. 'I must have got it inside my trousers.'

'That's not builder's sand' I responded 'because builder's sand is quite a different colour. I think that's beach sand, Holkham sand.' And then, rather tiredly 'Have you been to Holkham today? With Jayne?'

He denied it. Totally. Said 'I haven't seen Jayne. Not at all. I told you I wouldn't, didn't I. I've been working. So why are you asking me that?'

I was tired of the whole situation, of not knowing what Richard was doing, not knowing where I was, where I stood, not knowing what I was doing. I contacted Jayne almost immediately and asked her 'Have you seen Richard today? He says he hasn't seen you. He swore he was going to be working all day, but I don't believe him, I think he's lying. He does sometimes.' I felt I was being somehow disloyal but I needed to know. And I thought she needed to know that Richard didn't always tell the truth.

'We've been to Holkham,' she said brightly. 'We took a picnic lunch and spent the afternoon there.'

I was more disappointed than cross. Disappointed that he had lied yet again. Disappointed that he couldn't keep to his word. And cross that he thought he could get away with it, that he thought I was such an idiot that I would believe him.

'Tell me, Richard,' I asked, 'what is it that Jayne says she sees in you?'

'She says she likes me because I'm not like Jeff, I am unpredictable,' he replied. 'She says she never knows what I'm going to do next.'

'Yes, I can understand that.'

Richard suggested we should go for marriage guidance counselling, later called 'Relate'. Travelling together and sharing the costs, Richard and I went to meet a counsellor who lived near Thetford and whom Richard had found. We told her, individually and together, what we felt, what we thought, what was happening. We saw her together several times; then I pulled out because it didn't seem to me that we were getting anywhere.

Richard continued seeing her on his own and paying her. He reported to me that the counsellor had suggested that he might enjoy the physical relationship with Jayne because it brought him closer to Jeff. I thought it wise to make no comment on that.

Richard told me that the counsellor had said he might find he would have a third marriage. He said 'I told her that I would be completely against doing that, because I considered it was getting married that had destroyed our relationship.'

During this period, Richard would occasionally talk with Rhiannon's mother, tell her that he hadn't decided whether to stay with me or leave.

'I told him,' she informed me, 'that very soon he would have to make a decision because he couldn't keep changing his mind. Neither of you seems to know whether you are coming or going and that it isn't fair on you.'

Our friend Pat, with whom we had spent time in the South of France asked him and in front of me, 'But if you leave, Richard, and go to be with Jayne, won't you miss your children?'

Richard's reply left me speechless. He told Pat 'I expect Jayne's children will be adequate compensation.'

After six months, he still hadn't made up his mind. Or perhaps Jayne was beginning to cool off and rethink about her potential losses as well as her gains. Richard's birthday was at the beginning of October. He had planned to meet Jayne, he told me afterwards, sometime during the day and take her somewhere picturesque that she hadn't visited before.

Into the car he put a sleeping bag, a bottle of 'Head and Shoulders' anti-dandruff shampoo which we didn't normally buy, and a large illustrated book on Celtic Art along with other essential things. I only found out about this hours later, when I unpacked the car. From what he said on his return and from what I could independently deduce, he had the idea of taking Jayne to Wales but without discussing this with her in advance.

'I collected Jayne after she had dropped her children off at school' he told me later. 'She had several presents with her that she intended to give me for my birthday. We reached Birmingham before she realised that she was a long way from Norfolk and she asked me to stop the car and let her out. Her main worry was that she needed to get back to Dereham in time to pick James and Rebecca up from school that afternoon. But I refused to stop the car even for petrol so she tried to get out while it was still moving.'

According to Richard's account, they finally stopped beside a canal near the Welsh border. By this time, Jayne was really cross with Richard. Rather than give him the presents that she had so carefully chosen and wrapped, she threw them all into the canal and insisted he drive her home immediately.

Richard returned to me when the children were in bed and almost asleep. I was doing something in the kitchen.

'Where on earth have you been?' I asked him. 'I was quite worried when I realised you'd disappeared off somewhere again.'

'I'm all right' he said, 'but I've had a difficult day' as he sank onto the cane settee we had beside the Rayburn in the kitchen, 'and I'm very tired.'

'Oh, good,' I said sarcastically, 'so you're all right. That's good to know. And what about me and the children?'

But his eyes were shut by then, shutting out, I supposed, the things he didn't want to tell me, or to think about.

I filled a cup with cold water and threw the water over him.

'Well, you can wake up again,' I began 'because you can't just opt out of . . .'

He sprang to his feet and hit me hard across the head with the back of his hand. Hit my head across the temples. I fell to the concrete floor. I remember his shouting and I recalled the time he had said he had had with Doreen, when either she or Richard had produced a knife.

I put my hand to the side of my head, to the temple but I already knew. It was bleeding, my fingers were all sticky, there was quite a lot of blood. Grabbing a tea-towel or something to staunch it, I went to where the children were asleep, woke them, told them 'Come with me. Quickly, right away.'

I bundled them into the car and drove. I wasn't sure where was safe but I ended up at Sue Lloyd's house. Sue Lloyd, the Head of King's Park Infant School, who had had some inkling of the situation between Richard and Jayne because it had been the talk of the staff and the PTA. Sue, who had once said to me, 'If ever you need to talk to someone, Lorna . .'

I knocked at her door, the children just behind me. Her partner let me in. Sue let us sleep in her bedroom while she moved herself and her partner into a room elsewhere. She made up something on the floor for the children to sleep in the same room with me.

I remember only two things about the rest of that night. I remember that Sue had a bottle of Dune perfume standing on her dressing table; and that one of Nell's wobbly teeth fell out so despite the drama of the day, I needed to find a 10p coin to put under Nell's pillow that Sue had provided, just beside the tooth. Because Nell would remember and ask about the tooth fairy. And right then, I reckoned that Nell needed her beliefs.

The rest of that night was, and still is, a calm blank. I think Sue offered us cereal for breakfast in the morning. But she had to leave quite early to get into school before the rest of the staff and the children arrived.

I vaguely remember driving us all home. It didn't seem a good idea for any of the children to go to school that day. And I needed them, I needed to be with them, to know that they were safe. I remember thinking that I wasn't wanted because I couldn't or wouldn't provide what Richard needed. Because I wasn't his mother and he wasn't a child any more. Because of that, I felt I was being thrown away like a broken toy.

I don't know whether I still loved him, I think I did but my overriding feeling, the one most to the fore in my mind, was one of insecurity. Insecurity and concern as to how best to make my three children be, and feel, secure and loved.

Around mid-morning, Richard appeared with a bunch of flowers to say sorry about hitting me and to ask whether I was all right. I don't know whether or how he knew what had happened for the rest of that night, where we had been. I put the flowers in water but knowing that that wasn't the end of the matter.

Later the same day, I had a call from Jayne. Richard had presented her with a similar bunch of flowers, she told me. She had heard that he had hit me and she said she was sorry about it. That he shouldn't have done it.

'Too true he shouldn't have done it,' was my response to her. 'He shouldn't have done any of it.'

That night was the catalyst. Richard didn't leave straight away but it was obvious to me that that was what was in his mind. It was a ragged end to a marriage. Ragged because there were plenty of things to be sorted, and sorted together.

For a start, I was concerned about Richard's state of mind. Because it didn't seem normal to me to kidnap one's lover, take her to Wales equipped with a bottle of shampoo that no one in the family uses, only one sleeping bag and a heavy art book. It was almost as if these were grave goods, chosen to aid a safe passage into the next world. I wondered about depression, whether he was suffering from depression.

I phoned Dr Pearson, our G.P., and asked his opinion.

'Given what you have described,' he said 'it doesn't sound like depression. I would say it is almost the opposite, it sounds to me more like a case of euphoria.' Then he asked 'Is Richard taking any medication?'

'No,' I replied.

I managed to find a phone number for Richard's father, the father with whom neither Richard nor I had had any contact for very many years. I was interested to hear what Horace sounded like, whether his voice was like his son's. Once I had introduced myself, told him who I was and that I was his daughter-in-law, I explained 'I want you to know, should Richard decide to get in touch with you for whatever reason, that Richard has been behaving oddly recently and I thought perhaps you should go easy on him.'

Instead, Horace seemed to assume that I wanted either his help or money.

'I'm not wanting either,' I told him, feeling almost affronted. 'I was just letting you know that I think your son might be having a mental breakdown, that he might try to contact you.'

Horace appeared devoid of emotion, totally disinterested. He inferred that he had always thought that his son was unreliable, couldn't be trusted. I felt I was beginning to get the measure of Horace, to understand more about his ways of dealing with Richard when Richard had been younger. I said goodbye politely and put down the phone.

The next time Richard came to the barn, it was to discuss money.

'The bank is calling in the loan' he said, sounding almost surprised, 'so I've got these papers for you to sign. They are to request a mortgage on the barn. That would give us enough to repay the bank, otherwise we may have to sell it.'

I don't remember the mortgage application details because I didn't look any further.

'You must consider me a real idiot,' I responded. 'Why, when you are on the point of leaving me, would I tie myself up further with you financially?' and I handed the papers back to him.

He left. It was the first time I had completely refused to go along with any of his mad-cap schemes.

There was a period of time of his coming and going, collecting some of his things and asking to 'borrow' something else of mine. He said he would not fight for custody of the children because 'I know it would only damage the children.'

I told him I was quite prepared to fight him for them, if necessary, but that I would win. To a small extent I was almost sad that he was so quick to give up on his children, it seemed to me almost as if he didn't care. But I thought he was right, it would cause them damage and I was right, that if it came to a battle, I would win.

I could prove that I had provided for them in terms of a house, an education, an income and stability. Could Richard do the same, I asked? No, I thought not.

I went to a solicitor in Fakenham that an artist friend had recommended. I asked for a legal separation order so that our finances could be separated, so that Richard could not claim on anything to which he was not legally entitled. I don't remember the date on which Richard officially left me; somewhere during the summer of 1982, I think. By the time he did, I was almost relieved. There had been so much indecision from him that at last I knew where I stood.

His parting shot to me as he went out of the door, was 'but you never made a home for me.'

I continued as best I could to make the barn into a home. I continued to lay concrete paving slabs outside the entrance and with outside help, to complete the tiling of the kitchen floor.

A man I recognised as a parent from Lyng Playgroup appeared one day at the door of the barn, asking for money for work he had done for Richard on creating the driveway. I told him 'I quite understand that you want your money for the work you have done but at the moment I can't help you. Richard has left me and the children and isn't providing me with any money for food, let alone for other bills.'

The man, the father of Russell, a red-headed boy in playgroup with whom Keir had often played, began to threaten me.

'And it's no use you standing there demanding money' I replied, blocking the doorway. 'If I say I haven't got any money, then I haven't. And that's an end to it. You will have to try to get your money another way. And I hope you do.' As he drove away, I shut the door.

I suggested all three children should sleep together in the same room. Before, Keir had occupied the space above the entrance that had a roof so low that it didn't allow him to stand upright, he had slept there on a mattress on the floor.

The girls had had bunk beds in a central room with my bedroom just above. Now, for security and so that Keir could more easily get to the loo at night and I could more easily change him and his sheets – Keir was a habitual bed-wetter and from the moment he was out of nappies, I had had to get up and change his pyjamas and his sheets at least once and often twice a night – I moved the beds into the central part of the barn that had been the gallery and then had become the workshop.

It wasn't ideal but they had each other for company. There were no curtains at the windows, but the windows still looked out onto the empty courtyard so it was almost private, although cold. The flooring was bare concrete which I tried to soften with a rug that Val had made by hand in hospital and that Moo no longer needed.

The wind blew under the tiles and wisps of fibreglass would occasionally drift down onto the sleeping children, but it was as safe and as comfortable as I could make it. There was space for their toys and books and an overhead electric light.

'Many families in the world' I told them while also trying to convince myself, to put things in perspective 'would be glad to have what you have.'

We still had the kitchen, with a cooker as well as a multifuel Rayburn, a fridge and in the lobby space outside the shower room and loo, a chest freezer.

I continued to drive the children to school in Dereham each day. I let each school know the very basics about the home situation, that it was a damaged marriage but certainly not a broken home. I was pleased to know that each class-teacher would show appropriate understanding. Nell's teacher Mrs Roberts assured me 'I understand the situation but I'll make it clear to Nell that it will not be taken as an excuse for her to allow her work to slacken off at all or for me to accept any underachievement.'

Late one afternoon, a man called at the kitchen door of the barn and told me he was a bailiff. He had come to levy on any goods that belonged to Richard so that they could be sold to pay off any of Richard's debts to the Inland Revenue. I was in the middle of making toast and dividing a soft-boiled egg between three children so I was not very welcoming or sympathetic. The bailiff was business-like but quite kind. He began by listing the fridge and telling me 'It might raise. . .' I stopped him there.

'That fridge is mine, it was a wedding present from my parents. As far as I am aware, Richard has already sold or taken everything of his that might be worth anything. I suggest you call at where he is living now and see what you can get from there. Let me give you the address.'

Several months later in 1982, I appeared before a magistrate to request legal custody of the children, with Richard being permitted access on agreed terms. The magistrate asked me about the children's home conditions. I answered as accurately and as truthfully as I could.

'Are you telling me' he asked 'that all three children are sharing the same bedroom?' I told him that they were, but that the room was not quite what other people might describe as a standard bedroom.

'And how old are Nell and Keir?' he asked again, despite having their ages written in front of him.

'Well,' he said, 'if they are ten and nearly nine, as you say, and still sharing a bedroom, then I want you to promise me, to give me your word, that as soon as possible, you will do your very best to ensure that at least Nell and Keir have separate rooms.'

I started to say something about their relationship being far from physical other than the occasional scrap but he dismissed all that.

'You would be surprised what happens sometimes and in situations not so very unlike yours. If you give me your word that you will do your very best as soon as possible to ensure that your son and your elder daughter have separate rooms, then and on those grounds, I will grant you full custody.'

I gave him my word and with a lighter heart, I left the court room. But how, I wondered, was I going to provide what I had promised? How could I provide separate bedrooms when I knew, sooner rather than later and in order to pay off all the debts, we would have to sell the barn that I had hoped would become our home. Where would we live?

Richard was renting premises in Wellington Road in Dereham. Sometime after Jayne had appeared on the scene but before Richard had declared that he was in love with her, he had set up a computer software company called 'Grassroots Computers', with me as a co-director.

I thought the idea of me as a computer company co-director was about as absurd as Richard becoming the conductor of the London Symphony Orchestra. What I knew about computers was less than minimal and I certainly wasn't interested in them or what they could do.

One year, as my 'birthday treat', he had taken me to Harlow where Apple Computers were offering some form of promotion for half a day. I had looked forward to the lunch.

In Wellington Road, Richard was running a computer business on the ground floor, while he used the upstairs premises as a flat where he could live. Richard had had, as far as I was aware, no training in computer programming but had been fascinated by what the PET could do. He had developed his interests in computers by attempting to teach himself different computer languages such as Basic, Fortran and Pascal.

I don't know how successful he was. Richard would tell me that his business was doing so well that he had to turn customers away but I suspected that the shortage of customers might have been because early in the conversation, any potential customers would work out for themselves that Richard didn't really know what he was talking about and had minimal financial backing.

Occasionally during this time, Lallo might walk to the Wellington Road premises after school and I would collect her from there. Once or twice, Richard suggested I might call in for coffee if I were coming into Dereham for shopping but only if he could be sure that Jayne wasn't in the building at the same time.

Richard told me that sometimes Jayne would spend the night at the bungalow that she shared with her husband Jeff and sometimes with Richard in Wellington Road. Very soon, any suggestion that I might drop in for coffee was hastily withdrawn.

On one occasion, Richard asked to meet me at a Little Chef café on the outskirts of Fakenham. I arrived ahead of the agreed time and parked in the Little Chef car park. Richard arrived slightly late at the café door. After exchanging a few basic and somewhat chilly pleasantries, I ask Richard where he had parked, because I couldn't see his car in the designated car park.

'Eer, no,' he said, looking rather embarrassed 'I'm parked at the back of the petrol station.' I asked why.

'Because if Jayne or any of her friends happened to come past, I didn't want them to see my car anywhere near yours. She wouldn't like it if she knew I had been meeting you.'

'I promise I won't tell,' I said, with a note of what I hoped he could tell was irony. 'I wouldn't want the woman who spends one night with you and the next with her husband to think you were two-timing.'

'Oh, if it doesn't work out with Jayne, I already have one of two other willing women up my sleeve,' he confided, to my amazement. I felt almost sorry for Jayne. I wondered, did she know that Richard had established reserves for himself?

It reminded me of Richard's inability to make a decision or a choice. If he and I had been at a restaurant, which didn't often happen, the waiter would ask him 'What would you like to eat, Sir?' Richard would um and er, order one thing, then change his mind, while the waiter waited for ages and I was ready to say what I would like.

I had once asked him, 'Why does it take you so long, Richard, to choose what you want to eat?' His response almost explained how his mind worked. 'It's not difficult to look at the menu and choose what I want to eat. My problem is looking at such a wide range,' he said. 'When I choose what

I want to eat, I am also making the choice not to have all the other things I would like as well. I'm having to turn down those other delicious options. That's the bit I find so difficult.'

From what I could tell from hearsay at the school and from anything Lallo might mention, Jayne was coming and going, spending some nights with Jeff and others with Richard until either Jeff or Jayne made a decision and Jayne moved in with Richard. I'm not sure that Rebecca and James moved in with her, not at that time. They may have remained in the family home with Jeff but I think not. Because at one time, Rebecca was crying in the school playground and Lallo went across to comfort her.

'My Daddy has left home and gone to live somewhere else,' Rebecca had told Lallo, between her tears. 'I don't see him at bedtime and I miss him very much.'

With no money coming in from Richard, I wondered how best to feed my three children. From my mother and being brought up during the Second World War food rationing, I knew I could pick young stinging nettles, steam them and make them into a vegetable that would taste not unlike spinach.

I had seen the heavy lorries coming from the farm, bumping down the track towards the lane and spilling some of their load onto the track. I knew that if we nipped out with a wheelbarrow and collected up any carrots or potatoes before the returning lorry could crush them, then we had the makings of a meal.

But I drew the line at Keir pushing through the hawthorn hedge into the farmer's field next door, twisting and snapping off cobs of ripening sweetcorn. I told him to take them straight back to the field. There was a principle that I thought important for me to uphold, despite Keir's reasonable protestations 'That's pointless, Mum. They're not going to grow again.'

But I really wasn't into snaring and skinning rabbits, nor making my own home-made rosehip cordial. It was money that I needed.

By asking Gladys at the local post office, I learned that the office for social security was in King's Lynn. As far as I knew, no one in my family had ever been unemployed or had had to depend on someone else for money. Feeling both brave and embarrassed at the same time, I checked the level of fuel in the tank, found the correct address and drove the Volvo the forty miles to King's Lynn to see whether I was eligible for any form of benefit.

I parked in the car park nearest to the Social Security office. I explained the situation to an officer there, told him that I needed money but that I hoped that my need would be only temporary, because I wanted to get a full-time teaching job. Then I signed on. I had to ask for a small amount of money immediately, to be able to pay for the car-parking charge.

That done and the parking paid, I returned home feeling slightly relieved. I parked the Volvo in the village pub's car park to avoid the extra bit of petrol that getting down the hill and down the drive would have taken. I felt even happier when, once a fortnight, I received a payment. For the first time in my life since leaving the school in Edenbridge in Kent, I knew exactly how much money I might expect each month, and how best to budget.

Just that was a huge relief.

One summer afternoon, there was a cloudburst. Rain fell more heavily than I had ever seen it and I and the children, who were not at school that day, watched as the courtyard of the barn filled with water gushing from the roof tiles and into that messy central space. The water slowly rose higher but fortunately not as high as the bottom of the large window frames. I went to the glazed front doors of the barn and watched the water pouring like a river from the lane, down the drive and towards the barn doors. It was coming faster than I thought could be caused by a shower of rain.

Wearing our waterproofs and carrying a large umbrella, Nell and I went out and paddled over the gravel as far as the junction with the lane. Water was gushing down the hill from Bintree. As it reached the bend in the road where our drive met the lane, the very point where the lane was at its lowest, the river of water changed direction. It left the tarmacked lane and was flowing down the drive and towards the barn.

Nell and I scuttled back indoors and stood at the entrance, dripping wet but fascinated with both alarm and curiosity. Water swirled either side of the barn doors and around the sides of the barn.

'I hope that doesn't rise any higher' I said, chewing my bottom lip, 'because the barn has no foundations and it might start to seep through the flint walls.'

I thought perhaps I ought to tell Richard what was happening since the barn was partly his responsibility too. I rang him at Wellington Road but he refused to come. Mrs Ashton who lived in a cottage on the road, also phoned Richard and told him he should come and help. By then the water was coming slowly against the main barn doors and beginning to trickle underneath, spreading lethargically across the concrete floor in dark ribbons and down the step into the part that we used as the children's bedroom.

'I think we had all better start moving stuff quite quickly,' I told the children who were looking in amazement at what was encroaching towards their beds, upon their possessions, on their toys. I piled as much as I could on to the children's beds, hoping that the water wouldn't reach as far as the mattresses, and looked in horror. Nell saw me.

'Don't worry, Mummy' she said, putting her arm around my waist. 'It's only things. We're all right.'

It was 'only things' and we were 'all right': we were quite safe and we had each other. But afterwards, when the water slowly receded, I realised that it had been flowing through the septic tank, through the drainage ditches in the fields that had not been cleared of weeds that year; that everything in that part of the barn that had been on the floor – and most things in the children's bedroom were on the floor – would need to be disinfected, scrubbed several times and placed somewhere, anywhere possible, to dry.

Holding and scrubbing tacky brown deposits off individual pieces of Lego took a very very long while, even after the Lego had been soaking in a bucket of diluted disinfectant.

The strip of carpet that had been beside two of the beds was ruined, as were any items of clothing, notebooks, pens, books or batteries. The oddest thing I found beside Keir's or Nell's beds was a small dark-brown blob of something tacky. I was glad to recognise it as an Oxo cube rather than something far more disgusting. It raised the question as to which of my children had been secretly consuming Oxo cubes in bed rather than sweets, but perhaps, if teeth had already been brushed, a stock cube was a better option - and this was no time to have made a retrospective fuss about it.

I was sad about the loss of the children's toys. The children had had some of them for a considerable amount of time, one or two had been handed down from older cousins or friends. We had brought the toys from the cottage to the barn and they carried memories of who had given them to each child as a present, and when and where they had been played with.

I contacted the insurance company and they sent a loss assessor quite quickly. Nell talked at school about 'our flooded house and bedroom' and wrote about it too, in her 'News'.

The insurance company loss assessor came back to me within a couple of weeks. He had calculated the replacement cost of everything we had lost and as he got into his car, he told me it might come to quite a sizeable cheque. He was correct in that.

'Unfortunately for you,' he said with genuine regret in his voice because he had seen the devastation in the barn, 'I can't make the cheque payable to you. The insurance was taken out by your husband so it is in his name. I'm so sorry, but I need to make the cheque, and it is quite a large sum, payable to him. Could you give me his current address, please?'

According to what Richard told me sometime later, he had paid the insurance cheque into the bank and used the money to buy stair carpet for himself and Jayne, for the shop and flat in Wellington Street.

If Richard's conscience had not already troubled him about that, there was nothing I could say.

When I told the insurance man where the money had gone and on what, he said 'If you ever want to insure anything in this property again, I will tell my manager to insist that it is done either in your name as the sole insurer, or in your joint names.'

On the recommendation and suggestion from the Head of Dereham Church Middle where Nell and Keir went to school, I was offered a temporary part-time job at Toftwood Middle, teaching the class while the class teacher withdrew a small number of pupils for some extra English tuition, following a special remedial programme. Following that six-week job, I was offered a summer-term post at the same middle school, teaching Year 7 pupils under a head teacher who highly valued the arts and wider curriculum development.

Nipping home from the school one lunchtime to collect some books, I paused in the lane by Mrs Ashton's house and saw a thin twist of light grey smoke curling from beneath the barn roof tiles up into the sky.

For a brief moment I was tempted to turn round and head straight back to Toftwood School, knowing that it might solve a number of problems were I to do so. But instead, I approached the barn with caution.

Looking first through the glass on the main door, I saw flames, not huge ones but flames nevertheless.

The kitchen was filling with black smoke. I opened the door, not wide but just enough to let me pass through. The log basket that had stood by the Rayburn was alight and something by the Rayburn was smouldering. I realised what it was, that the phone was still intact and working. I cautiously entered the building and dialled 999.

It wasn't until the fire brigade came that I worked out what had happened, that I had unwittingly caused the damage.

Keir had had a wet bed again that night. Although I had stripped the sheets from his bed, removed the duvet cover and stuffed that with his pyjamas and the sheets into the washing machine, the duvet itself had been only slightly damp.

Knowing I wouldn't have time to wash it and get it dry before he needed it again that evening, I had draped the duvet over the rail at the front of the Rayburn, for it to air.

The Rayburn was alight, gently burning anthracite, coal and wood so that the kitchen would be warm when we all arrived home. The firemen explained that the duvet had overheated, smouldered and burning bits had dropped into the log basket. Fortunately, I had decided to return home that lunchtime, before the curtains could catch fire and set the roof trusses alight.

Nell remarked to me a few days later, 'Do you know, Mummy, it's been a real eff year, hasn't it?' I was shocked at her language. The 'f' word was not one that either Richard nor I had ever used and I wasn't sure where she had heard it.

'What do you mean?' I asked her.

'Well,' she explained, 'we've had F for flood and then F for fire. So, do you think there'll another F?'

This time, the insurance covered the complete redecoration of the kitchen. The work was done just in time for me to offer the barn, our lovely new home, for sale.

Chapter 17
Heat but no Handles

Mr Dodds, the head of Dereham Church Middle School, contacted me one day to ask if he could see me. Wondering what Keir had done this time, I called into the school and enquired when Mr Dodds might be available because, I told Mrs Napthen, the school secretary, 'He requested that I make an appointment.'

'He's in his office right now,' the secretary said, 'so why don't you knock and see if he's busy?'

I entered his office.

'It's about Nell,' he said without any further preamble. 'I wanted to check with you whether what she has been telling people at school is accurate.'

'If it's about myself and Nell's father,' I started to say but he stopped me at that point by shaking his head.

'Nell says that your home has been badly flooded including the downstairs room that she and Keir sleep in. She tells me that you've narrowly avoided a house fire and that from time to time, little bits of fibreglass fall from the roof onto her bedding while she is asleep. Is that accurate? She also says that she sometimes has to take responsibility for looking after her brother and younger sister and keeping them safe and out of trouble.'

'Well, Nell takes as much care of her siblings as any eldest child reasonably might. What she says about the barn that we were trying to make into a house is also true. Why do you ask?'

I liked Mr Dodds, I had always found him to be fair, caring and reasonable, both in his current role and in his previous job at North Elmham.

'Bearing in mind your current living conditions and safety, and the fact you have no actual house to live in, that all three children are sharing a bedroom at the moment which was, I am told, completely flooded and unusable for a time, I wondered whether I should get our Education Welfare Officer involved. I'm not for one moment suggesting that Nell appears to be in any direct danger or emotional distress' he went on, 'but I did wonder whether there might be a case for looking at a place at Wymondham College for her for next year. An assisted place on the grounds of welfare and safeguarding.'

'You mean, she wouldn't transfer at the end of year 7 to either Northgate or the Neatherd Secondary Schools?'

'Yes, Wymondham College takes in pupils from middle and primary schools so transfer from them is at the end of Year 6 in the primary school.'

'And when you say 'an assisted place', what exactly does that mean?'

'It means that the County Council's Education Department would cover the costs, both for tuition as they do for any other local authority school, and for boarding, for accommodation, food, etcetera. Because they consider a place at the school to be in the child's best interests, based on the child's home living situation. Otherwise, parents of Norfolk children pay for accommodation there and the children of parents who are not British pay for both tuition and accommodation - or their countries do.'

'And Nell would have to board, to stay there right through the week? What about at the weekends?'

'She would be allowed home for one weekend in every three, for what's called an 'exeat' weekend. And return to the school on the Sunday evening, ready for school again the following day, the Monday. Perhaps you might like to talk to Nell about it, to see what she thinks. Meanwhile, I can make a few enquiries, if you would like that.'

I went with Nell to look around Wymondham College during term time, so that we could ask pupils currently at the school what they really thought about it, what their concerns and highlights were, as well as witness one or two of the lessons in progress. Nell was particularly keen to see the sports facilities and the block of music practice rooms and classrooms. Having begun to play the violin at school, she had been playing the euphonium under the direction of Mrs Roberts and was keen to continue this, or even to progress from the euphonium to the French Horn.

I mentioned the possible place at Wymondham College to Richard. He did not come with Nell and me to look around, he didn't seem very interested. His only comment was that he didn't think it was a good idea, even if Nell wanted to go there, because he hadn't enjoyed his time at any of his boarding schools.

'But Nell isn't you,' I responded, 'You started at Town Close when you were much younger than Nell is now, and even earlier at the Catholic school in London that was evacuated to Weymouth when you lost touch with your parents. You were born towards the end of 1938 so you couldn't have been more than four or five, possibly six when you were sent with the school to Weymouth, and you had lost touch with both your parents.

Nell is eleven, she lives with her mother even if her father has moved out. Nell is not you, she's quite different. So, your experiences, even at The Royal Masonic and then Redhill, are quite different. They have no bearing on the current situation, whereas' I continued, 'I need to find somewhere where Nell can have a bedroom separate from Keir. At her age and with puberty on the horizon, she deserves some personal privacy. But you, with your 'let's all go naked' attitude, might not understand that. Nell's friend Freya from Lyng playgroup already goes to Wymondham College, and so do a couple of other ex-playgroup pals. She's spoken to Freya about it and she seems quite keen. And if it doesn't work out, then we can rethink.'

I was quite enthusiastic about Nell going to Wymondham College because it would mean that I could keep my promise to the magistrate and that she could be a child again amid other friends of her own age, rather than being the second adult in the family. It would also guarantee that she, at least, was being properly fed each day; and we avoided any intervention by Social Services.

Moo was also keen, mainly because she saw anywhere with 'college' in its name as being the next best thing to a public school and for Moo, a public school had status, was almost a guarantee of future academic, social or sporting success. I also have to admit to having had a shred of envy and visions of high jinks after dark at Malory Towers.

At about this time, our friends Pat and Chris, rather than travelling again to the South of France, accepted the offer of a month's stay in a relative's holiday flat that was situated near Pula and the coast of Yugoslavia.

Would I, they asked, like to go to the same area because my children and theirs all got on well together and it might take away some of the sting of Richard having left, of the flood and the fire as well as very soon having to sell the barn. And of the need to find somewhere to live.

'You deserve' they suggested, 'a break before life all gets difficult again.'

I took with me all the housekeeping money that I had, plus some extra for some additional teaching that I had agreed to do for Theresa, a girl who had just come out of hospital who was not yet thought well enough to return to school.

Nell went fruit picking to earn some extra money, as did I. I sold a few things, mainly items of clothing and outgrown toys, and raised some more cash that way.

We looked on a camping site directory and identified a campsite not far from Pula, as well as one or two where we could stop on the way there.

Richard had sold the Volvo in exchange for two second-hand Citroens, a white saloon and a beige estate. I decided to take the beige Citroen because it was an estate car and had room for the large frame tent that I had bought in exchange for the redundant caravan awning.

We packed the four-sleeper tent onto the front passenger seat and I made the three children comfortable on the bench seat at the back. We had a gas-burning camping stove and various pots and pans as well as inflatable beds, a Lilo pump and several sleeping bags.

We crossed the Channel by boat with our car below, Keir wearing a green jersey material 'Clothkits' tracksuit and Lallo a similar one in blue.

The route toward Yugoslavia took us mainly on autobahns across Germany, where I remember telling Keir, whose reading development was slower than Nell's or indeed than Lallo's, not to giggle quite so much at the 'ausfahrt' signs indicating the autobahn exit lanes, while also congratulating him on his reading at speed.

The car journey across the Austrian Alps and into northern Yugoslavia was not without its problems. At one mountain crossing, our car was so heavily laden that I could not hold it in a queue on a hill with the handbrake; instead, at one place, I had to give up. Rather than delay or annoy all the cars in the line behind us, I managed to turn the car round and go back down the hill again, to try to find a different route that our heavily-laden vehicle could tackle.

Once over the border and on a steep minor road on the Yugoslav side, in one place the tarmacked road had completely caved away. Some local people, possibly loggers, had bridged the gap in the narrow road with a series of slender pine logs laid horizontally to form a precarious but hopefully navigable passage.

Through the windscreen I looked at it, at the steep drop on my right and the sheer cliff on my left beyond where the tent was placed on the passenger seat and said to myself as well as to the children, 'Well, we don't have a choice. We can't go back so we have to go forwards. Hold on to the sides, everyone, and if necessary, shut your eyes because this is going to be quite bumpy.'

We came through without any of the logs giving way or shifting position. I stopped the car at the bottom of the valley and took a long drink of fresh water.

Once properly into Yugoslavia and getting nearer to where we were heading for, I saw in huge capital letters the word TITO on a hillside, picked out in white paint or chalk. Keir saw it too. 'Why does it say 'tits' over there?' he asked me, quite seriously.

Nell began to respond but I told her it would be better if she were to congratulate her brother on his attempts to read, than even try to explain his error or to tell him to what and whom it actually referred.

'Because Keir would have a limited understanding of the local and national politics', I advised her.

We spent a brief night on a campsite beside Lake Bled, not very far from Ljubljana and from there, we pushed on towards the site near Pula that from the book I had earmarked.

I remember the Pula campsite as selling very expensive water, being devoid of shade and so hot that both Lallo and I spent much of each day in our nightdresses because they were loose and cool. I gave up my pitch on that site and moved to one just outside the town of Labin.

There seemed to be a shortage of food available in the Yugoslavian shops that year. I was told that the best food was being bought up by hotel chains so our diet consisted mainly of bread, fruit and some sort of rather disgusting meat paste which we could spread on slightly grey bread.

At the Labin camp site, the Spitting Image 'Chicken Song' was being broadcast on most evenings and we were encouraged by the site organisers to join in with the actions as well as the words. I declined. Even on holiday, I thought it essential to maintain some sort of decorum.

There was also another lone adult camping. I don't remember his nationality, only that he said to me in public 'I would like to have bed with you because I have not had sex with a English girl. Most nationalities I have had but British, no. And I also have toothache, which is disturbing my sleep.'

The children and Pat found this screamingly funny and Pat did her best to encourage him while I adopted the stance of 'I'm British, I don't know you, and we just don't do that sort of thing.'

It was on a drive into Labin in Pat and Chris's vehicle that we saw two or three cows walking one behind the other, right beside the road and being driven forward by a man holding a stick. Several cows had their front and back legs tied together so that they could not run away or escape. Consequently, they could take only tiny steps forward.

I recall Pat saying, 'Look, that really is a case of minced beef' and after laughing, my having to explain the different meanings of the word 'mince' to my children.

Despite Pat assuring me that Richard might easily decide to fly to Pula and from there, would come and find us to tell us he had made a huge mistake, I thought this very unlikely. For a start, I didn't think he would be that adventurous, not on his own. And exactly how would he find us? At that time, we didn't have mobile phones.

One evening we enjoyed an impromptu street party at a crossroads just outside the flat in which Pat and Chris were staying. We were all dancing in the road with some of the local residents until it was too dark to see. I also remember swimming across a sea inlet, with Lallo clinging on my back. And Pat and Chris's older girls making friends with a couple of local lads, whose names sounded to us like Doodah and Stinko.

On my drive back to Britain from our weeks in Yugoslavia, we crossed into Austria where we stayed on one particular site with a natural pool with water the colour of diluted instant coffee. The soil twinkled underfoot with what I assumed to be fine-grained mica. I asked a lady in the campsite post office where the post box was. I had the children with me at the time and they wanted to send Richard a postcard.

'There's a post box very close outside, not in front,' the post office lady told me, 'You need to put the postcard in the back side.'

At her advice, Keir sniggered uncontrollably, Nell too.

'If we do that, it may never get there,' said Nell to me, almost wisely. Sometimes they seemed to share my father's lavatorial sense of humour.

In Austria, we encountered a problem but in the process of dealing with it, I was impressed by Keir's or Nell's spelling and phonic knowledge. We were playing I-Spy at the same time as exploring the Austrian Alps. One of the children wanted to see what the top of a mountain looked like.

'Is it all pointy, like we do in our drawings? Or purple-headed? Because that's what we used to sing at school when we sang 'All Things Bright and Beautiful'.

So, as one never to waste an educational opportunity, I was heading in the car, already laden with the tent and all our equipment, up the windy road towards the highest mountain in Austria, the Grossglockner. We had very little petrol in the car and I knew the brakes were doubtful, the whole car needed either a major service or soon to be scrapped.

The road was so steep that the only way the car would tackle the gradient was by my weaving it from side to side across the road. Fine when there was no on-coming traffic but difficult with a bus coming up behind me. I tried to stop. We were on a hill. It was steep and the brakes wouldn't hold.

'Oh look, kids,' I said, hoping to distract them and myself from the situation, 'I spy with my little eye something beginning with g.' Nell got it; it was 'glacier'.

'Keir can have my go,' she said.

At this point the car stuttered and came to a standstill. I was able to pull it into the left-hand side, with the rear wheels against some sort of curb stone or bollard to hold it there.

'I spy something beginning with 'p',' Keir offered. No one guessed it correctly.

'I'll give you a clue,' he said, proud of his word. 'It's very close, it's not on Mum's side, it's on my side. And it's something we might go down soon.'

We came up with suggestions, sensible ones and silly ones until 'Do you give up?' he asked. We did. And I had more worrying things to think about at the time rather than playing a game.

'It's precipice,' Keir shouted in triumph. 'It's just behind our back wheels,' and then 'Do our brakes work yet, Mum?'

We managed to reach the top of the alpine road and park in the car park. I took a photograph of the three children, wearing anoraks, with the ice in the background. We had a short walk on the glacier and a longer stop in the visitors' gift shop.

Keir was very taken by a large stuffed marmot. I had told the children that we might see marmots scampering about or hiding among the rocks on the mountainside but I don't know if we ever did. But Keir wanted a stuffed marmot toy.

To me, he seemed too old to be given a new soft toy, whether a teddy bear or a marmot, until I realised that he had 'lost' his father so of course he wanted something to cuddle in bed.

It was far more than I could afford but I bought the marmot. Keir had it, talked to it and loved it, until the later house fire singed its fur, making one side of it too abrasive to be cuddled against.

I drove back down the mountain very slowly and carefully, choosing which gear might be the most effective on each bend or straight section. A mist had hidden the sun and was making driving even more difficult. Without effective brakes, we needed to be very cautious.

As we had come out of Yugoslavia, a country with huge constraints on the type of food that we could buy, there were bananas for sale on the Austrian side of the border. It had been several weeks since we had last seen bananas. I bought a bunch.

What the children said they now wanted was something else to eat, something that wasn't nasty meat paste or tough grey bread.

In an Austrian village in a valley, a village with red geraniums planted in hanging baskets and green mown grass beside the village street, I found a bakery. There I bought the nicest looking loaf, a loaf that the shopkeeper said had seeds in it, and half a dozen rolls. I had thought we might enjoy them that evening until Nell quite suddenly asked, as I started the car engine again, 'What's Switzerland like?'

'If you hold on for a few hours' I replied, over my shoulder passing each of them a plain white roll, 'I'll show you.'

I needed the children to be safe, happy and to be experiencing and wondering at new things. There were times when I needed familiarity and other times when I longed for adventure. After Yugoslavia with its limited choice of food, and the problems of driving on an unfamiliar mountain road in a car lacking fuel and adequate brakes, I wanted both but familiarity more. Familiarity was comforting.

I headed towards Lucerne, skirted the lake and took the mountain road towards Engelberg. I could show the children the place that had started my longing for travel, a place I knew well, had visited when I had been a college student and had led a student group there at the end of my second year.

I had seen in my camping and campsites book that there was a campsite at Engelberg, not a fully-equipped site with electricity and all amenities but a field just outside the village that had been set aside only for tents.

We would stop there for a few days, I thought, and explore both the village and the mountain areas. It would be safe but, I hoped, still exciting. There would be tastes of cheese, chocolate-and-almond cake, and hot chocolate. And it would look and smell the same as it had smelled when I had been a teenager, of fresh grass, cows, ice, wild flowers and carved pine.

Despite the culinary restrictions that the children partly imposed on themselves – they refused to eat the Austrian loaf I had bought for the equivalent of nearly a pound, the first bite telling them that the seeds it contained were caraway and that caraway was something that none of them liked, not at all, and my slow realisation that a child will not necessarily eat whatever you provide even if he or she is sufficiently hungry; that taste buds and hunger are sometimes at odds with each other – I was able to make a meal of something that they would eat, even though we were fast running out of money and I knew we would need money for petrol soon.

Cheese proved to be a good stand-by basic - and fresh fruit, although not cheap, was available.

Once fed, together we pitched the large frame tent with its integral groundsheet and laid out the Lilos, the sleeping bags and erected the cooking stove. I was pleased that we still appeared to have plenty of gas left in the bottle. In Yugoslavia it had been so hot that we had rarely wanted anything cooked, resorting to whatever cold food we could buy. Much of it had been matt grapes and occasionally when the hotels didn't require them, olives.

Venturing out from our tent, we did manage to find the fare to travel by funicular, a transport system that fascinated Keir, from the village to Gerschnialp, then around the lake to travel by either cable car or chair lift to Trübsee.

From Trübsee, I thought we might go as far as the Jochpass and head towards Jochstock, but by then a cloud was coming down and it was growing too cold to venture any higher.

Instead, I was able to offer the children a choice. We could either travel back down to the village by gondola or walk back down through the trees after having a drink each at the café of warm Ovaltine. We couldn't afford both.

They chose the Ovaltine. With small rucksacks on our backs, we walked back down the alpine slopes, across the hay meadows, among the cows, and through the pines. Nell told me as we were walking and despite that part of Switzerland predominantly having cows, large brown Jersey-looking cows with soft noses, soft ears and large cowbells attached to leather collars hung around their necks, 'I want to be a goat herd when I get older.'

'A goat herd or a goat herder?' I asked, thinking Nell had read too much Johanna Spyri and Heidi; or seen 'The Sound of Music' film too often.

'A goat herd,' she said. 'Definitely.'

'Well, you can be whatever you choose to be, but please be good at whatever you choose when you are older' I replied, adding 'But there aren't all that many goats in Norfolk.'

'Then I'll go to where there are goats,' she said, as we listened to the cheerful ringing of the cow bells.

When we returned to Britain and Norfolk, the barn was up for sale.

I don't recall the price we were asking, nor who the estate agents were. Richard and Jayne had moved into a terrace house in King's Road, Dereham. I don't know whether they had bought it or whether it was rented; nor, if they had bought it, which of them had managed the purchase.

I only know that when I had asked Richard where he thought the children and I were going to live, he told me 'I don't see why that should be a problem, anyone can buy a house for about £10,000.'

There didn't seem any point in my telling him I did not have that amount of money, how out of touch he was, or asking him 'where exactly?'

I talked to Moo and Dad about our living situation, asked Dad's advice on property prices and locations. Moo offered that we could move into their house in Quebec Road, be with them.

'There's plenty of room,' she said.

I remembered how TCP Grandma and Grandpa had lived with us in Letchworth for a while for what they called 'the worst of the winter', and how, after Grandpa had died, TCP Grandma had had a room with them in Owl Cottage in Wootton; and how exhausting Moo had found that to be.

'Thank you, Moo,' was my response, 'it's a very kind offer and in many ways, it would solve a problem. But it would always be your house and not mine. And. .' seeing Keir at that very moment trying to leap over the central rose bed in their front garden and in doing so, knocking the head off one of Dad's best roses, 'it might damage our relationship. We need somewhere of our own.'

'You're far too independent,' Moo told me.

'And whose fault might that be?' I asked her with a smile, 'Take it as a sign that you and Dad have done a very good job as parents. And as grandparents,' I added.

It was a generous offer on the part of my parents but not one that I could envisage as a long-term solution. Short-term, maybe, but it would have to be very short term, which would probably cause more disruption for the children. I had to think of another way of providing them, myself too, with a home.

People in the village, those who didn't live in houses that they owned, lived mainly in Festival Road council houses. I had heard of people being offered council houses so why, I wondered with incredible naivety, wouldn't I be offered one?

I made an appointment at the local housing department. After explaining the position, I asked if there would be any council houses that I could use.

I hoped we wouldn't need it for very long but 'At the moment we appear to have nowhere to live, except with my parents in their house in Dereham. They have room but they are both pensioners and I don't think that would work well for very long. They are lovely but . . no.'

The official told me, after I had explained that I wanted at least two of my children to be able to continue attending their current schools, that they did not have any spare council houses in my area. He mentioned that sometimes a house in Thetford might come up for exchange, but there were none of those at the time nor in the foreseeable future.

I had started to leave the room, when he added 'One of the problems you have is that, technically, you have made yourselves voluntarily homeless by selling the family home you have, or had. That may disqualify you from being offered . . . ' His voice tailed off as he saw the look on my face. Then I had an idea. I needed to ask a further question.

'It's just a thought, but if I and the children slept in the building that is currently a workshop, would there be any objection to that on the council's behalf? It is sound, fairly recently built with full planning permission for a workshop – and it does belong to us, well, to my husband and me. It would avoid us having to be rehoused at public expense, should we even have qualified, and it would disrupt no one. Two of the children could, if you would be satisfied with our doing that, continue at their current schools while my eldest is due to start next term with an assisted place at Wymondham College.

Or would we be evicted from our own property?'

I left the question hanging there, hoping that he might think of the possible headlines in the local press if there were to be any talk of eviction.

Having, I hoped, satisfied the man in the housing department that this suggestion of mine was not a convoluted way of applying for change of use on the workshop, I returned home. But with a plan.

I have no memory of the actual move of our furniture and possessions from the barn, nor of its sale. I do recall that the family who bought it had a daughter about Nell's age but that is all I can remember. Perhaps, when the barn kitchen had had to be redecorated after the fire, we had moved the chairs out of there, and the pendant glass lampshade that Richard had liked so much, that had hung over the island worksurface.

I do know that the corner bath that Richard had bought so far in advance disappeared from where it had been stored at the far end of the barn. As far as I know, the new owners didn't buy it and there was nowhere I could imagine that it would have fitted in Richard premises in Wellington Road. It had been expensive, 'an expensive luxury', Richard had said. Perhaps he sold it back to the suppliers.

Before Richard left, we had fitted the floor of the reception area of the workshop, an area not much bigger than the average bathroom, with brown carpet tiles and we had fold-down seating there too, covered in a brown corduroy fabric. There were two or three other small rooms, each with the floor still bare concrete.

One, which we had intended to use as an assembly area, had a hatch through to the main workshop space and a built-in wooded bench running along the wall. Another room, opposite the main entrance door, was to have been used as the office. There was also a loo with a washbasin, that led back into the intended reception area. The window of the third room looked out onto the main drive.

The two single beds that Keir and Lallo had used were originally bunk beds. There were sections of royal blue wool carpet that had first belonged to Nenna, then became the floor covering for the sitting room in the house at 100 Broadway. I used parts of that, cut as near as I could to shape, for the room opposite the workshop entrance and I erected the bunk beds there, one above the other.

The square-shaped windows looked out onto the corner field where nobody went, so the lack of curtains wasn't important. It made a small but adequate bedroom for Keir on the bottom bunk so he could easily get to the loo if needed, with Lallo on the top bunk.

I made a bedroom for myself in the room facing the drive. It was just large enough to take the double bed if I pushed one side hard against the wall and there was also just enough space to allow a small chest of drawers. I covered the concrete floor with another section of the blue wool carpet, it didn't quite reach into the corners but it was good enough.

That room and the reception area had vertical blinds at the window. I don't remember clearly where Nell slept but it must have been either in the 'jewellery assembly' room with its hatch and wooden bench, or on a fold-down bed in the reception space – where we also stood a Christmas tree for our first Christmas there.

As somewhere to live, it had one big advantage over the barn. It was warm. And so far, dry. There was a huge industrial heater that ducted warm air into the reception and small-room area as well as into the main workshop. It proved warmer and cosier than the barn had ever been. The only disadvantage was the lack of anywhere where Keir could shower.

With a wet bed every single night, there was no way he could go to school without first having had a shower, he would smell of urine and the other children in his class could not have failed to notice.

A strip-wash relied on Keir being sufficiently thorough and when he tried to wash his bottom and back, his front, and both legs that way, the loo concrete floor was left very wet, too wet for the girls to use.

No, what he needed, at least on a weekday, was a shower. Moo was more than willing for each of the children to have a bath at her house but first thing in the morning, she and Dad would be using the bathroom. Either Keir or I needed to devise a better solution.

There was nowhere in the workshop where Keir could stand and have me pour clean water over his head from a bucket. So, if not inside, then outside would have to do.

It was on an in-built wooden bench in the workshop that I placed the electric kettle and the Baby Belling gas hob, just next to the main sink that had been inset into the wooden bench.

Now we had bedrooms, somewhere to entertain any visitors should we have any, a place where I could also stand the upright piano, and somewhere where I could prepare and heat food. I shoved the fridge under the wooden bench, close to the sink in the workshop part.

But there were two other problems with living there, apart from the lack of bath or shower. Both of these we could overcome but not very easily.

One of these was due to the fact that the workshop had not been completely finished. The water and electricity had been connected, as had the telephone. By finding and laying carpet pieces, we had overcome the lack of comfort from the concrete floors. The lack of curtains or curtain track hardly mattered and certainly not in the rooms facing the corner field. But it would have been handy had Richard fitted handles to the internal doors.

The doors were in place and quite nice ones too, the holes halfway down were already there ready for the handles to be added, but we had no easy way of opening each door or closing it again, other than by pushing it shut.

I tried inserting my middle finger but it was almost too fat and there was the possibility of my finger becoming stuck in the hole, swelling and becoming really really stuck.

One of the children came up with the answer.

'If you get your toothbrush,' either Keir or Nell suggested, 'hold the brush end in your hand,'

'With a clean hand,' I put in -

'and poke the toothbrush handle through the hole, there's enough grip there to open the door. Look, watch,' and he or she demonstrated.

'So,' someone else advised, 'we ought to always keep our toothbrushes . . . .'

'You mean always to keep,' I corrected, somewhat pointlessly because it was the solution that mattered rather than the grammar

'. . . . our tooth brushes with us, on whatever side of the door we are on.'

'That's right,' I said, 'or almost.'

As a solution, the toothbrushes worked well.

There was a less comfortable method for keeping Keir hygienic and odour-free.

'There's no easy way to shower you indoors' I said, 'so I'd like you to try something else.

'If I put this outside on the grass, just behind the rear doors of the workshop,' which fortunately were the only doors in the workshop that did have handles - and I produced a tall yellow plastic swing-bin, the sort that is often used in kitchens for rubbish – 'and you step into the bin, it will come as high as your waist, possibly even a little higher. Then I can pour water over your head, hand you some soap and stand by with a bath towel.'

Lallo giggled, she was beginning to like the idea of her brother being washed like this.

'And it doesn't need to be cold water,' I told him, trying to soften the prospect, 'I can boil the kettle and add some hot to the bucket if there isn't already enough warm water in the tap. Can we just try it?'

There was a good reason why performing this operation at the rear doors of the workshop didn't work but I don't know what it was. Perhaps it was because the ground there was so muddy, beside the tall red gas bottles. We ended up doing the same shower process with the bin standing on the grass verge beside the drive and Keir inside it, just outside the main door and nearer to Keir's and Lallo's bedroom inside.

If I propped the main door wide open, Keir's dash back indoors to a towel, to his bedroom and to his clean clothes could be quite quick.

The downside of this shower arrangement came one Saturday morning. Keir had had a very wet bed the night before so after stripping off his sheets and pyjamas and putting them into the washing machine, which I had stationed somewhere in the workshop end of the building and close to the tap, I positioned the swing bin outside the front door.

Keir climbed into it. I had poured water over him and he was covering his body with soap, when the paperboy from the village came whistling down lane and into the drive with the weekly Dereham and Fakenham Times, and stopped.

I went to meet him, holding out my hand to receive the paper – and to take his eyes off Keir. I thanked him and he went on his way, looking slightly puzzled.

Keir wasn't very pleased.

'It'll be all round the village,' he said.

'Well, why didn't you hide,' I asked, 'at least your face?'

'And what would have been the point of that?' he asked. 'I couldn't have been anyone else, could I? I don't look like either Nell or Lallo and it was unlikely to have been anyone else.'

I had to agree. I wasn't sure whether it was his dignity that he was safe-guarding or his private parts. But he was much cleaner and sweeter smelling.

A third disadvantage of living in the workshop that we discovered later, was entirely due to Richard. Richard had decided that the bakelite doorknob on the door of the Wellington Road computer centre lacked style.

'It let the place down, gave customers quite the wrong image,' he told me, much later, when I confronted him.

I told him what we had to do, what adjustments we had had to make to our daily living and how it might have affected our security.

Apparently, Richard had come to the workshop on a day when we were all out and had unscrewed the modern green D-shaped door handle so that he could use it on the showroom door in Wellington Road.

That left us with no easy way of opening the main door to where we were living. We could shut the door and lock it from inside but not open it from the outside. We tried using the handle of a large spoon which nearly worked in some way.

In the end, we had to resort to leaving the key somewhere outside and near the front step, that was accessible but hidden, inserting it into the lock and opening the door by pulling on the key after turning it.

A lighter side of life, certainly for Nell and for me, was provided in the summer of 1983 by Masque, described as Community Theatre for Norfolk. I don't know how I got to hear about it but perhaps that was through TIE Break. Masque were hoping to put on a play with music entitled 'With Orphans' Tears' involving more than fifty participants from communities throughout Norfolk in the production.

The production was planned to take place at Norfolk Rural Life Museum in Gressenhall, just outside Dereham, on several evenings in late June. I mentioned this to Nell and she was interested. I thought that Gressenhall was sufficiently close to where we lived for me to be able to drive Nell to and from the evening and weekend rehearsals and that the final performance would fit well before she began at Wymondham College.

For Nell, this was her first excursion into the world of musical theatre and she loved it. She was one of the youngest performers on stage.

Nell began her more formal education at Wymondham College in September 1983, joining Fry House. With a mixture of new and second-hand uniform, I managed to fit her out with the current clothing as well as buy all the kit she needed for games, and still provide money each half term for a small amount to be withdrawn each week and spent at the tuck shop.

I missed her tremendously but I felt she was safe, being nutritiously fed, although perhaps not on the things she would have most enjoyed, and had her own space in a dormitory with about nine other girls.

In a letter, she wrote 'Dear Mum, having a great time made lots of friends of all different years, us first year get called ticks but it doesn't bother me. The foods quite nice and the lessons aren't too bad. I'm the only one in our dorm that cried having a great time bye for now, Nell XXX PS: give my love to the other two. Sorry about my scruffy writing. I'm playing the trombone.'

I tried to visit her in school each weekend and to ask Mr Brand or Miss Rackham how Nell was settling in and getting on. Nell told me everything was fine, that she was enjoying the sport and going across to the music block for music lessons or practice. Many years later, when I was staying in her room in her digs in Rochdale, Nell said 'I've told my friends that I don't get on with my mother.' That comment punctured like a sudden wasp sting. I could see no reason for it, so rather than damage the relationship further by trying to discuss any cause for this unexpected statement, I let it pass, unchallenged. Since she had invited me to her digs, to her room and stay for the night for us to share her very small bed, it made no sense to me. Someone, I thought, either is or has been playing mind-games – and that person might not be Nell.

Very occasionally Richard would come to Wymondham College if there were some special function, an event or a performance. On one or two occasions, he turned up wearing an old shirt, a pair of very baggy denim shorts as well as his sandals, and Nell said how embarrassed she was. But she had seemed pleased to see him, all the same.

At the same time that Nell began at a new school, I started teaching again at Toftwood Middle School, just outside Dereham. I was offered a longer-term post, this time teaching what was then described as Year 3, a class of ten-or-eleven-year-olds that would now be classed as Year 6. I was employed to teach general subjects including French and games. I also took on the day-to-day co-ordination of the school library.

I enjoyed working there, I was well within my comfort zone but there were also new challenges and new experiences which I needed on a regular basis in order to be happy in any job. I could drive to Dereham, drop Lallo and Keir at Dereham Church

Middle School (D.C.M.S.) and continue on to park at Toftwood Middle just in time for staff briefing before school started.

It was during this time that Moo, then in her early eighties, had her first stroke. Nell remembers it as having been in March, around the time of Nell's birthday. I visited Moo in a bed downstairs at my parents' house.

For general convenience, they had moved their twin beds and furniture from an upstairs room to downstairs in the room that they had previously used as a dining room. Just beyond the kitchen and the chest freezer was a downstairs loo and shower room so they had all necessary convenience on the same level. Moo told me 'I woke up in the night and felt something cold where my right leg should have been. I wondered why Leslie had slipped a joint of cold lamb in the bed beside me until I realised that the lamb joint was actually my own right leg, that it had no feeling in it at all.'

Asking her how she felt in general about having had a stroke, she said 'Well, I knew it was likely, it's what my mother had had so it was what would probably happen to me too. But I had hoped I could put it off for a little while longer.' She had no feeling in her right side, her right hand didn't work, so rather than expressing any further regret over her condition, she said 'Isn't it lucky that it struck my right, and that I'm left-handed?'

Moo always looked on the bright side of life, she could see the positive in almost any situation.

She was moved into Norwich Hospital for a week or so. According to the ward nurse, in the middle of one night, Moo had roused many of the other patients in the ward and had tried to form a choir. I suspect she wasn't very successful, and that the nursing staff weren't best pleased either. Either Moo or one of the nurses told me that Moo had thought the alarm cord hanging over her bed was there to dispense vodka. I doubted the veracity of the story: not only was Moo brought up to be tee-total but also, I couldn't imagine when or where she would have even heard of vodka, let alone ever tasted it or wanted any. But her mind was beginning to wander.

When Val had travelled down by overnight coach from Scotland to visit Moo in Norwich Hospital, Moo thanked her politely but then told Val 'It's nice to see you, Dear, but are you all right leaving your family to be here? Because I saw you yesterday as well as today.' As Val said quietly to me, 'If I'd known she could imagine I've been here when I haven't, I needn't have bothered coming all this way.'

It was difficult for Dad, who had given up driving his Dormobile several years earlier, to get into Norwich by bus during the day to visit Moo. Quite soon after the choir incident, Moo was moved to a room in Dereham Hospital. I visited her there every day and tried to encourage her to use both her hands to play an imaginary scale on her bedside table but the fingers on one hand wouldn't obey her.

She was unable to walk so she had to use a bedpan. Her appetite seemed to be normal but her mind was on a path of its own. One day, I asked her what she had eaten for lunch. Looking down at the headlines of the Daily Telegraph newspaper she had been reading, she said 'Leon Brittan. I had Leon Brittan for lunch.'

Moo also told me 'I'm sharing a room with Princess Margaret. I think she should be given a room of her own, she's a princess and she doesn't need to be sharing with anyone, let alone with me.'

It was less ideal for Lallo and Keir to walk after school to Quebec Road any more. Although it was good for them to see their grandfather and for him to see them, four o'clock in the afternoon might be the very time at which he would be walking back from Dereham Hospital. After that, he needed a rest and also to consider Moo's condition, and what he might expect in the near future.

Instead, Keir and Lallo would walk from DCMS to Toftwood, to re-join me after I had finished in the classroom, or wait quietly inside the building if there were an after-school staff meeting. As an arrangement, it seemed to work quite well.

There was only a potentially hazardous corner of the road for them to cross and I was confident that they would look after each other. They had a good relationship. Keir would sometimes help carry Lallo's cello and she would help him when needed with any school work.

Aunty Dorothy had died while Richard was still living with us. We arrived late for the funeral and Moo was upset by our late arrival. I was cross too, because it hadn't been my fault. Thinking she was rather too young to take there and back to a funeral being held in Hertfordshire, we had left Lallo in the care of someone living across the road from Moo. After dropping Lallo there, I couldn't get Richard to hurry. He needed to stop on the way to fill up with petrol, then he chose the wrong route and we had to double back to find the better road. By the time we arrived, everyone else was gathered in the church.

I was annoyed with Richard. Whenever he didn't see a need to hurry, he would take this time and I felt that just because

Aunty Dorothy wasn't his aunt, then our visit had had low priority in his mind.

He also seemed to resent spending money on the petrol because 'our being there won't make any difference, will it? She's already dead,' he said which, although true in part, wasn't the point of our visit to Northaw Churchyard. I felt I had let Moo down by being late, by not being sufficiently supportive or being on time.

Aunty Dorothy's Will was read many months later, after probate and after Richard had left me to start on a life of his own choosing. Bless her, she had left me sixteen thousand pounds. It was enough for me to consider buying another house, if I could get another mortgage. It gave us the possibility of moving out of the workshop and finding a place of our own. I started looking almost as soon as I had the good news. By then, at Toftwood Middle School where the previous head had left and a new head was appointed and in post, I was co-ordinator for languages - which meant English and French - Drama and the Library and I was given an addition point on the teachers' salary scale.

I had reorganised the system that the previous teacher in charge of library had used and I brought in the Dewey decimal system for organising non-fiction so that the books were in order by subject, using numbers from 000 to 999 as in most public libraries. I went through the fiction books and reclassified them on a g.r.o.w. system of using the colours of green, red, orange and white to indicate not only the difficulty of reading level but also of sentence structure and the content of the material.

I took out all the old or damaged books, mostly with hard covers, and was given a budget to order new copies and other paperbacks by new or popular authors, because paper-backs proved more popular than hard-backs, even though they lasted less well. This meant that I needed to use almost every spare moment to read a wide range of children's fiction.

One evening, after a huge delivery of new books had arrived, I was determined to catalogue these and introduce them into the library before the next day. I made up beds for Lallo and Keir at the back of the estate car, opened the school gates which Ernie, the school caretaker had locked earlier that evening, drove the car round the school to the back of the library windows, and parked it there on the playground so that I had the car and the two children in full view, as they had of me.

After relocking the entry gates, I felt the children were safe enough and if either of them needed the loo, then they could tap on the school window and I could let them in. I worked in the library consistently until 5am, when I felt it was time for me to drive back home, grab an hour or two of sleep and transfer the children into their own beds, before setting off again for our schools later that morning.

I was pleased with the night's work. What felt to me as slightly unfair was that, as it was raining, I was asked by Mr Appleby the headmaster to cover 'wet playtime' in the hall the following day. I managed it, with all the noise and excitement from the children in such a confined space, but I could feel my eyelids drooping. I was pleased when 'home-time' came.

I told Mr Appleby that I was hoping to move house and asked him, if he were in my position, where he might move to. He suggested that, if I wanted to stay in teaching, I might look at houses in the Wymondham area, where he had once lived before he had moved to Dereham. It would, he told me, give me the opportunity of applying for posts on the Suffolk border as well as in Norfolk, should I need another job or be looking for promotion. That made sense to me.

However, before looking at the Wymondham area, I saw a barn conversion for sale not far from the village green at Gressenhall.

I contacted the Dereham estate agent and made an appointment for myself and Dad to look at it. I mentioned it to no one else. Having had to leave the barn, I suppose I was hankering after some sort of replacement and I already had some minor attachment to Gressenhall through our activities at the Rural Life Museum.

We went upstairs in the converted barn that was for sale. Dad thought there could be a problem with a main beam running across the upper storey, especially if I needed to cut or alter it in any way by inserting a r.s.j. (rolled steel joist). I made further enquiries and I would have pursued the matter, had the estate agent not contacted Richard directly.

Richard told me the estate agent had contacted him and had asked him whether I was serious about buying the property. I was furious. I went into the estate agent's office and asked why he had contacted my husband, who no longer lived with me, to ask about my intentions.

The estate agent gave some lame excuse about wanting to check that I had the finances, said he needed to know about 'the man of the family' and so on.

I told the estate agent I wanted nothing more to do with his business, he had not respected my privacy or my rights and he had no business contacting anyone else about my intentions or my finances.

Feeling very brave, the next day I drove to Wymondham and contacted various estate agents there.

I was still teaching at Toftwood Middle School when Moo, aged 84, died. I was in the middle of a lesson when I received the message. Paul, another member of staff with whom I had been in competition for a post at the school with more responsibility and higher salary and whom I had beaten, said to me and in front of others in the staffroom 'Well, what did you expect at her age?'

Mrs Macquire, another member of staff, comforted me with 'any death is tragic, however much you expect it.' And later, quietly, 'the death of a mother is a particular loss. She is someone you have always known, the only person to whom you have never needed to be introduced.'

Chapter 18

Travellers

'I've a slight problem with your mother's funeral,' Dad confided. 'We don't have a church that we regularly go to so there's no minister in the town who knows Moo. I'm not sure how best to proceed. I need someone who can say a few words about your mother, someone who knew her well but not anyone who might get upset, or who can't address a congregation.'

Dad had stopped going to many things locally. He no longer travelled to London to his Freemason Lodge, he had pulled out of Rotary meetings and he had long ago ceased to attend church and other meetings where lots of people would all be talking at once because, he said, 'I can't hear what people are saying and I don't want to have to ask them to repeat whatever it was.'

He discussed the idea of asking Reverend Charles Johnson who had married Moo's cousin Jocelyn. Uncle Charles was a canon of Chichester Cathedral and previous head of Seaford College, a private boarding school near Petworth in Sussex. Although Dad had done Jocelyn and Charles a favour by drawing the plans for the extension to their cottage in the grounds of Lavington Park, he felt it was too much to ask Charles to come all that way from Sussex.

In the end and through Rotarian contacts, Dad asked the Dereham Methodist Church minister to hold the service there and to address the congregation. Although the minister hadn't known Moo personally, he was able to gain quite a lot of information about her from her work as President of Dereham Inner Wheel and her involvement with local charity organisations, as well as from friends and family.

To my surprise, Richard arrived at the funeral. I had told him that Moo had died and he would have heard about it from the children. I had not told him any particular venue because at the time, Dad was still unsure where it might take place. When Richard did arrive, just as the last people were entering the church, he was cross with me. 'I went to the wrong church because you told me a different one,' he said. I left it at that, a funeral was no time for an argument. He didn't stay or come back with us to Quebec Road. He looked and probably felt, out of place.

The coffin was brought in to the church with a dozen red roses lying on top of it from Dad. I thought what a pity it was that he hadn't given them to my mother earlier, when she was still alive, when she could have appreciated them. Moo had at some time told me that she wouldn't want people to be dressed in black at her funeral because black was so depressing: she would rather people wore white, like mourners at funerals in eastern countries.

She had been brought up in a time when there was an expectation within the wider family and her social class, of ladies being involved in charity work, philanthropy or becoming a benefactor. Moo had helped raise money or items for various local and national causes and had been a willing hostess to young students coming to Britain from abroad.

She had welcomed a house full of my various friends and had been a second mother to my friend Fiona.

Losing my mother was like getting rid of a soft pillow or a comfortable armchair. I might have taken her for granted – I expect I sometimes did - but she had always been welcoming, would wrap herself around me and hug me as a favourite armchair might. I could rest my head against her, I felt safe and loved with her. There was a strength there, a firm structure as well as a softness.

I was always aware of her presence in a room even if she was sometimes hard to shift out of the way. Like an armchair, she had a solid frame that had been well-upholstered over the years, and in a fabric that would absorb life's stains but not show them. She seemed to understand me, to empathise while not always agreeing.

When I had been younger and more impressionable while we were living at 100 Broadway, I had been nervous of going up that wide sweeping staircase and near the top, seeing the blank black glass of the curtain-less window that looked out onto the garden during the daytime, but who knew who or what was there, looking in, once it grew dark? It was a huge black square near the landing, I didn't know what might be behind it or what might come pouncing through.

To help me overcome my fear and get myself upstairs at night, Moo would stop whatever she was doing, stand at the bottom and sing the beginning of a hymn,

> 'Looking upward every day,
>
> Sunshine on our faces;
>
> Pressing onward every day.
>
> Toward the heavenly places'

by which time I would have reached those ‘heavenly places’, my bedroom or the upstairs bathroom.

I missed Moo tremendously but I was resigned to her death, even to the extent of welcoming it when the time was right.

She had said that she hoped she would die before Dad because she couldn’t imagine living contentedly on her own, whereas she thought he would cope with living alone far better than she would. And it was becoming too much for him, walking all that way every day to visit her at the hospital.

He told me, when she was first admitted to hospital, ‘I feel so guilty. She looks at me in a strange way, a way I have never seen before with those hazel eyes of hers, almost as if she is saying ‘Why are you putting me in a place like this? I’m your wife, so why aren’t you looking after me, like you said you always would?’

What could I say to make him feel any better. Only that I thought he had done the right thing and that Moo would have agreed, with hindsight. But Moo was the woman who, when he had had a hard day and needed to relax, would read to him each night in bed, usually a chapter or two from a novel or even a children’s story, until he went to sleep. Only then would she put the book down and switch off the light.

Dad was grieving, it was premature bereavement and deep down, he knew it. On her death certificate, the causes of death were recorded as being cerebral thrombosis and diabetes mellitus. Moo knew about the diabetes only because the hospital had diagnosed it. I was glad she hadn’t known that before, otherwise it might have stopped her from enjoying the occasional slice of cake. And a mince pie.

She had once told me that when she and Dorothy were girls, she had been given the nickname 'Skinny' by her cousin John, Jocelyn's brother. I found a skinny Moo hard to envisage.

I said my mental goodbyes to her, standing by the water of the creek at Burnham Overy Staithe. We had had such good times there, difficult ones too occasionally but times we either enjoyed or managed somehow. We had taken Kim there, when he and I were both young. I had been there with my close friends Fiona and later John B., both of whom had been welcomed on holiday with us, by Moo.

With a one-pint metal churn, Moo and I had fetched milk together from the farm that overlooked the upper reaches of the river that gave rise to the creek. Overy Staithe was my special place, a fitting place to say goodbye, and a silent 'thank you' for being my mother.

With minimal discussion, I bought Dad a puppy, called Sam. I didn't think it would ever take the place of Moo but it was company for him and I thought it would give him structure to his day, provide a reason for him to get up and go out, if only to walk the dog. But before too long, Sam proved too much for him.

Sam was a Pointer crossbreed and grew large and strong. The local doctor saw Dad struggling to take Sam for walks around the town, teaching him to 'sit' or 'heel' and not managing it. He talked with Dad and with Dad's approval, arranged for Sam to be given to another family, one with young children and adults younger than Dad.

I was sad for Dad and for Sam but also relieved. Giving Sam to Dad had been well-intentioned on my part but a poor decision.

At the same time as I had acquired Sam, I had bought a springer spaniel puppy whom I named Muffin, because he looked like the children's television string puppet from my childhood. Muffin's face had lopsided markings which might have been why he was cheap, only £40 rather than the other puppies at £45.

We bought him from a breeder in a house near Reymerston, between Dereham and Wymondham. Keir wanted to call him 'Gooch' for some reason but I settled on Muffin. I'm glad I did because it was calling him 'Muffin' that partly led to my next serious relationship.

It was an in-between time, a state of limbo for me as well as for Dad. I had 'lost' Nell, who had been my best buddy and a huge support, to Wymondham College, even though I knew it was the right thing to have done.

I had lost my husband and my mother, as well as the building we had hoped would become a family home. I knew we could not continue living in the workshop for long, it lacked the facilities that a normal house in this country would have and sooner or later, I thought, someone would object to our living there.

What I did have, and felt secure about, was three children who kept me busy, entertained and occasionally worried. What they were not, ever, was boring. I also had a job that I enjoyed and where I felt valued, as well as having a regular income through my salary. Things were not so bad then, I assured myself. And I still had Moo's motto to cling to, her saying, whenever something was not as she would have wished or chosen, of 'I'll cope'.

There was only one house for sale in Wymondham that interested me. It was half of something that had been bigger. When I had first picked up the details and located the house, I looked up at it from the other side of the road and said to myself or whoever was with me at the time, in wonder, 'Oh, my goodness.'

To me, standing there, it looked huge. It had a black and white façade and judging from the jettied first floor, was obviously quite old. The estate agent's details of the side that was for sale, described it as having exposed timbers, three floors and a small enclosed garden.

It also had a right of way running through the land at the rear of the house and an additional area of land that lay behind the current Methodist Church. It was priced at just over £38,000.

I made an appointment with the estate agent to view it.

I went into the property through the front door and immediately thought 'Wow!'

Where, as I later discovered, there had been an internal wall dividing the hallway from the main room, were now only the main upright and diagonal timbers that had once contained clay lump or the daub part of wattle-and-daub.

The large gaps in the structure made the main room seem light and spacious. There was a large open fireplace and fringed by a window seat, a bay window looking out onto the street.

'The kitchen at the back is a later addition, probably nineteenth century,' the estate agent told me, 'It may require a little updating but it is perfectly serviceable.' By that time, I had spotted the bread oven beside the chimney stack in the kitchen and I was hooked.

I must have asked Dad to come and look round the house before I made an offer but I knew I wanted it, even before going upstairs to the first floor and then on, through the doorway at the top of the stairs that led up a winding half-spiral wooden staircase to the next floor that could become, I thought, the children's area.

'Those stairs will require a strong hand rail' Dad observed 'and although I can see there's a lovely view from the upstairs room that looks out over the main road to Dereham, it leads straight onto the tiles of the house next door and there's a steep drop.'

I made a mental note to consider installing a fire escape. This house had history and character: I felt I could fall in love with it.

Dad gave it his approval along with some cautionary comments about death watch beetle.

'I haven't seen signs of any,' he said 'but in a house of this age, it's always a possibility. That and woodworm, and of course, dry rot.'

Whereas Moo had always looked on the bright side, had a positive disposition, Dad would be far more cautious. He worried about things he didn't know were there, things that he might be alarmed to find, once he poked around a little longer. 'There are indications of damp near the bay window' he advised, 'so you might need to mention that too to the vendor'.

But in general, Dad approved of the house.

'It stands there with a certain confidence,' he said, which was indeed a high accolade.

I put in an offer that day and within a month or so, with the mortgage agreed, it was mine. The name of my side of the house was 'Westview.' I thought the name lacked distinction.

Through enquiries at the local public library, I discovered that its previous name had been 'Culyers' because it had belonged to a man whose surname had been Culyer. As an alternative name, I liked 'Culyers' more that 'Westview' but not enough. As Dad said, 'What would the name 'Culyers' mean to anyone who didn't already know?'

Fair enough, I thought. And the number 16 was also indistinctive. I would need to conduct more research if I were to come up with a suitable name that I liked.

I celebrated my purchase during a small end-of-summer-term gathering of Toftwood staff and a few parents, at the Upper School Co-ordinator's house.

I remember wearing a dress in red, black and grey stripes, with laces up the front; and thinking what an unusual purchase it had been for me to have made; and having a long conversation about the school 'Adventure Week' with fellow teacher Sean.

We didn't move into our house straight away. There was no rush, no one was badgering us to get out of the workshop and there was decorating to be done in the house, as soon as I could manage it.

Matt, Richard's son from his marriage to Doreen, came to stay for a couple of days and helped me with a few things. He was strong and had long ago left school. Casper, who had had the small printing firm in Stoke Ferry, came to stay with us in the workshop and helped with the packing. He also came shopping for groceries with me and bought some treats for the children.

Colin and Dad wallpapered in the bathroom of our 'new' house – a pretty strawberry print from Laura Ashley – and for the walls in the L-shaped room that was to become my bedroom, I had chosen 'Country Garden'. In a moment of extravagance because I already had sufficient bed linen, I bought matching 'Country Garden' curtains and a double duvet set.

There was a small room leading off from what was going to be my bedroom. The estate agent had shown it to me and had started to say 'That would make a lovely nursery' until I gave him a look from under my eyebrows. Couldn't he see that I was viewing this on my own and well into my forties?

I hired a Luton van to move our furniture from the workshop to Wymondham. I had driven a Luton before when I had cleared out the interior of Aunty Dorothy's house in Northaw so I had a rough idea of how much it would hold.

The hardest thing to move was the walnut upright piano that had once belonged to Moo. I could not imagine living in a house without a piano, it didn't seem right somehow.

Peter B. and Philip, two other colleagues from Toftwood Middle School, helped me move in. Philip was puzzled by my choice of house. He asked me how much I paid for it and after I told him, he remarked 'But at that price, you could have bought a new one.'

It was difficult to explain to someone who had moved into a newly built house on an estate, that a new build wasn't what

I most wanted, that I liked having an old one, a second-hand one. Or in the case of this house I had bought, a probably fiftieth-hand one.

'You might like to see a vacant property that I've considered buying,' I suggested to Richard, and I arranged when he might come to view the house.

I collected twigs and small dry logs from the area beyond the abbey known as 'Becket's Meadow' and piled them into the fireplace with crumpled newspaper. I lit it and watched the smoke slowly crawl its way up the chimney. I watched out of the bay window and saw Richard drive up and park his car almost opposite. He knocked on the knocker and I let him in.

'What do you think?' I asked, adding 'Of course, it would need quite a bit of work and the ceiling plaster in this room. .' as he walked through the entrance and into the main sitting room '. . looks as if it might fall down at any minute.'

He stopped. Looked at the fire.

'But someone is still living here,' he remarked, frowning. 'Do the owners mind if . .?'

'No, they don't mind your having a very brief look at the downstairs,' I replied. 'What do you think, so far?' He began to give me advice as to what I might need to do until I cut in with 'Because I've already bought it.'

It took him a minute or so to digest that. And then 'But you didn't ask me first,' he stated, in some annoyance.

'Why would I ask you?' I responded, almost enjoying his protestation and bewilderment. 'I don't need your permission to find somewhere for me and the children, your children, to live, do I?'

I watched while the whole new situation between him and me sunk in. And I enjoyed it, I gained strength from it. Because there was no doubt in my mind, and as far as I could see, in his either, that I had come off better from our split than he ever imagined. I remembered another of his parting shots to me that had been 'but you've never suffered like I have. Maybe one day you will. And I hope you do.'

Was that, I wondered, what all this had been about? Some form of competition about who can be, or has been, worse off than whom, a desire for some levelling down on my part? I had done all I could to be supportive. There was nothing I could have done about his loss of parents in his earlier years, that was just the way it was.

There had been a possibility, according to the historian at the local library, that my house had once belonged to Robert Kett, a local hero for many in the town and surrounding villages, a man who with his brother had fought against land enclosure.

I had been told that the Kett family had owned a house in the centre of Wymondham and mine, which was certainly standing there by 1615, might have been it.

I borrowed a copy of a book showing the inventory of articles in the house at that time. There were only two houses still standing of the right age so my house might have been the one. But I knew from records that my house had belonged to a local yeoman so I decided to cover a range of possibilities by renaming it as 'The Yeoman's House.'

I continued to teach at Toftwood Middle School. I enjoyed the job and I enjoyed the pupils, seeing them gain in ability and self-confidence. The new headmaster, a fairly strict Baptist in his practice and beliefs, seemed more willing than before to trust his staff. I was allowed to take a group of Toftwood children, including Lallo and Keir because I couldn't very well leave them at home, to Holt Hall and Howe Hill Residential Centres, and Keir handled this well despite his nightly bed-wetting.

After I had taken the top class for a day to Boulogne, I led a school group for a successful week in the Alps and I was able to make a visit to the Haywood Gallery with a coach-load of the older children, when I had almost to prise one artistic eleven-year-old lad away from gazing at the Renoir painting of 'Girls at the Piano', because the coach was due to leave. As we came away from the Haywood, he said to me, in tones of awe, 'Isn't that painting incredible! I wish I could paint like that.'

'Maybe you will, one day,' I replied, 'if you keep at it and don't give up.'

Back in school, each class took it in turns to lead morning assembly once a month. At the beginning of December, when my class comprised some of the oldest children in the school, it became our turn to present and lead something suitable for Assembly. I asked the children what they would like to do, whether they wanted to put on something connected with Christmas.

Together they said 'Yes, but could we write it ourselves? Because it is supposed to be our assembly, not something that someone else has thought up or comes out of a book.'

That seemed fair to me. I wanted the children to take ownership. I had already had a slight *contretemps* with the Head regarding behaviour during assembly and my involvement.

He had said that everyone, including the staff, was to join in the hymns and prayers during assembly, because it was meant to be an act of corporate worship.

I had argued privately with him that I was more than willing to supervise the children but that he could not demand that I join in, because worship, by definition, had to be voluntary since it meant a feeling or expression of reverence and adoration.

I wasn't even prepared to feign further involvement because, as I told him 'That would be pure hypocrisy. The children will see through that in me and probably in each other, and I think that teaching has a lot to do with trust and honesty. I will supervise such that the children do not disturb any of their colleagues who genuinely are worshiping, I'll join in the hymns but only because I enjoy singing, as long as you understand that that is all that I am doing. But I will not shut my eyes, as you ask, during any prayer because I am there to supervise and I cannot supervise if I cannot see.'

I didn't add that Toftwood was not a church school, that as a local authority establishment it should be non-denominational, acknowledging and respecting all faiths and none, because I thought that I had already said as much as he could take.

When it came to the children writing their own pre-Christmas assembly, I wanted it to reflect what the children thought was important about Christmas rather than produce, unless they wanted to do so, a standard Nativity play.

As it happened, that was almost what they did want to put on, although not standard. They chose Chris B., an articulate black lad who had told me he wanted to be an international lawyer when he grew up, as the Angel Gabriel. They didn't want to dress each other or themselves in robes, they wanted to wear their normal clothes.

I can't remember whether we had a Baby Jesus but I think not, they probably pretended there was a baby - or perhaps their production didn't get as far as Jesus' birth. But I do remember Gabriel announcing that a baby would be born, and 'shepherds' coming and actually saying in their lines that 'we don't wear striped tea-towels on our heads, and we won't be having any 'Santa's grotty'.

When one of the shepherds was carrying a chemistry set to present to the Baby Jesus, someone, possibly Gabriel, told the shepherd 'Jesus will manage miracles and that sort of thing on his own, he won't be needing a chemistry set.'

At that point, two of the staff walked out of Assembly halfway through and later I was called into the Head's office where I was asked to stand in front of his desk as though I were a naughty child.

'What' he asked, "was all that about? Two members of staff were so shocked that they felt they had to leave the room. I was pleased none of the governors were present, whatever would they have thought? It was like the sort of thing you might see on television.' I took that last remark, privately, as a compliment. What seemed most to have upset him and the others, was that I had allowed a black lad to be the Angel Gabriel.

'Chris B,' he said more than once, 'I ask you! Whatever made you choose him! In future I shall ask that the Head of

Religious Education has to approve the content of any assembly before it is presented.'

'I had told Miss Manly, as the head of R.E., that I was a little anxious, that it might be a trifle unorthodox,' I informed him, 'but she didn't seem concerned at the time. And it was the children's own work and they selected who should play which part. If you show or express your disapproval, then it should be to me and not to them, because they worked hard on that, and practised it time and time again.'

I began to wonder whether, with the new head teacher and a few changes of staff, I really fitted in any more at Toftwood, whether I belonged. We were required to submit written lesson plans for each day of the week – not a problem for me, I always planned rather than relied on what was known as 'doorknob planning' – and I produced a written detailed summary of the week, describing what our teaching aims and objectives had been and whether the children had achieved them.

I had my doubts as to how carefully the Head read these each week from every teacher. One week, in the middle of my report of what I had done for one of the days, I wrote 'ate the caretaker', to see what the Head's reaction might be. There was none.

It was shortly after that, perhaps at the end of the Autumn Term or the beginning of the Spring one, that a friend of a friend, hearing of the Christmas Nativity Play debacle, alerted me to an advertisement in the Norfolk Education Bulletin. It was an advertisement for a two-year secondment for a job as 'Liaison Teacher for Travellers Children'. One teacher had been doing the job for the previous two years and she was due to return to her substantive post.

Citing, as well as my general class teaching, my special needs work, my previous experience at Edenbridge of teaching Gypsy children and my proven self-motivation and self-discipline in being able to write a radio play that was good enough for the BBC to broadcast, I submitted my application. A couple of weeks later, along with one other person, I was called for interview.

The Area Education Officer David Felton and his deputy Mr Gough interviewed me, with Pauline W., the current post-holder, also present. Mr Gough several times used the expression 'if you survive it' in connection with the two-year post, which I found interesting. I thought, if I am applying for this post and get it, I shall make sure I survive it, there will be no 'if' about it. I was up for a challenge, but it did make me wonder what the general impression and attitude within the county was of the job I was being asked to fulfil.

I was soon to learn. The successful candidate was to work only in 'Central Area' of Norfolk, supporting children in school and liaising with their families.

There were two recognised Traveller sites run by the local authority, one at Mile Cross and another at Roundwell in Costessey. There was a third site, the Showmen's site at Hooper Lane in Norwich where families involved in the Fairground would over-winter and restore their rides, as well as the children attend local schools.

The need for a liaison teacher had been, I was told, Central Area's response to the Report by Lady Plowden that praised child-centred approaches to education.

I had not heard of this report, as far as I could remember it had never been mentioned during a staff meeting at

Toftwood, but it was published in 1967 on 'Education in England – Children and their Primary Schools'. The particular part of this report that concerned the Area Education Officer and his Deputy had been in Appendix 12, where it was stated:-

'Successive generations of gypsy children are deprived of the education that would enable them to compete on equal terms with the rest of the community. Extreme as they are, the needs of gypsy children cannot be effectively met by measures of the kind we recommend for the more general problems of urban deprivation. They will require special attention and carefully planned action.'

Hence the need for me, were I to be appointed, and previously for the person whose role I would be taking over. She and I would work in tandem for a term until she returned to her substantive post and I took over full responsibility. She would introduce me to various families, their children and particular schools, explain what had been done so far and then hand over to me.

Although I was officially appointed as from April 1986 on a salary of £9,639 per annum. it was a staggered start. I was due to spend further days at Howe Hill for Toftwood Middle School, while David Felton wanted me to attend a five-day residential course run by the Department of Education and Science at Chester College, called 'Planning and Providing Education for Travellers including Gypsy, Fairground, Circus and Other Traveller Children'.

There was also a question of my secondment requiring my return to Toftwood after two years. I was fairly sure that the Head didn't want me back but would have preferred me to resign my post there outright. He was reluctant to grant me the secondment but for me, having this as a secondment from my substantive post, guaranteed me a job after my two-year stint was over.

After considerable discussion and wrangling and some advice from John Knowles, the previous head of the school, the Head of Southern Area offered me a secondment from the Area rather than from Toftwood Middle as the specified school. I was happy to accept that.

I was also asked to keep a low profile from the Norfolk County Council point of view. Norfolk was a Tory-run council and, I was told, might not approve part of its education budget being spent in this way on this particular group of children. I was to stay within Central Area and not undertake any liaison or teaching work outside those boundaries.

Within less than a year of being appointed, I was contacted by the Head of the King's Lynn and West Norfolk Education Area. There had been talk of a new Traveller site being established on an existing unofficial site beside the Saddlebow factories in Kings Lynn. Would I please drive across to St Margaret's House in King's Lynn to discuss with him the possible implications for neighbouring schools?

I had to ask permission from David Felton, which was granted, for me to cross over the different Area borders and I was asked, once I had had those discussions about Travellers in Western Area, to report to Mr Bradford, an Education Officer at Norfolk's County Hall.

I had a similar conversation with Len Ricketts, the Head of Yarmouth Area, about a proposed site at Gapton Hall in the industrial area of Yarmouth.

I remember parts of that conversation, telling Mr Bradford that it seemed likely that Norfolk, as an agricultural county dependant on seasonal labour, would always attract Travellers and that it seemed 'silly to me to appoint someone for only two years, and then have to start all over again with training and raising awareness'; and 'since the same Traveller families are often moving from one side of the county to another, there seemed little logic in having to ask permission to move from one Education Area to another. It might be more sensible to have a county-wide approach and I would recommend that,' and then thinking that I was being very presumptuous, that it was not up to me to recommend anything and certainly not a course of action at a county level.

However, within a very few years, the positions of Area Heads disappeared and I was managed at a county-wide level and able to operate across the whole of Norfolk. My having made a case for it, several more liaison teachers were appointed to work with me and Mrs Steynor, the Assistant County Education Officer was able to write to me to 'confirm that your seconded position may be made permanent from the 1st of September 1988.'

In March 1990, following the revised structure of the Traveller Education Service, I was confirmed as the Co-ordinator with the status of Headteacher Group 3. By now there were some twenty-five people working within the Traveller Education Service under my management, as either teaching assistants or liaison teachers.

By November 2004, I had joined the County's Advisory Service and Children's Services as an Advisory Teacher. My revised salary was the equivalent of point 12 on the Leadership Group Pay Spine.

I had been told, by both my predecessor and other people working in Traveller Education in the region as well as by the families themselves, that Traveller children did not transfer to secondary school, they regarded the primary school as the source of their formal education and considered that, if a child had not learned what was required by the time he or she left the primary school, there was no point in the youngster moving to a secondary school; he or she was required at home, either to help the mother with younger siblings or to help the father in whatever the trade or occupation might be.

There were a few exceptions to this. One or two of the lads from the Hooper Lane Fairground Site would attend at Blyth Jex School for the winter months and a housed Traveller family sent their lad to Costessey High School for a term or two but in both cases, attendance was irregular. It appeared to depend on the state of the weather, the state of the family vehicle for transporting the child to and from school, and what other tasks the family required the child to undertake that day.

There was a Scottish Traveller lad called John Burke, with an older sister named Claire who used to hide in a downstairs cupboard whenever I or one of my colleagues called at her house on an estate in the Mile Cross area, to see why she was not in school - again. John was quite a bright eleven or twelve-year-old lad but his parents seemed set against him moving on from his middle school to a secondary school.

I thought that, before taking John and one of his parents to look over a secondary school to see what huge opportunities it had to offer him, I should talk to the Headteacher first. I asked my line manager which school and therefore which Head she thought would best accept the idea of a lad, with minimal prior schooling and minimal parental backing, transferring to his or her school the following September.

My line manager Mrs Steynor said 'I suggest you go and talk to Mr D., the Head of Earlham School. He would probably see this as not a problem.' I asked her his surname and initials. 'His initials are I.E.,' she said 'as in 'Ivor the Engine', although he is generally known to colleagues as Danny. Make an appointment with him and let him know I sent you.'

Before I did so, however, I thought I would attend the school's open evening when the parents of prospective pupils could look around the building and talk to staff. And I would invite John and his parents to accompany me because, as I explained to them, 'I know you have an idea of what a secondary school is like and what goes on there because you've told me. But it really isn't all drugs, swearing, smoking in the bicycle sheds or misbehaving with the girls. I'd like you to see for yourselves, see what John might be able to do. And what, if you turn this down, he might be missing that he might have enjoyed. Practical things such as science and vehicle maintenance, not just reading and writing.'

I was slightly amused to be standing with them in the same school as the one in which Richard had once taught pottery at an adult education evening class but with me now in a completely different role, and in the very same hall in which I had once, when I lived in St Giles Street in the city, played badminton.

On the current occasion, the hall had been set out with rows of chairs for prospective parents and their offspring to occupy. I don't remember whether John came with us or whether I went only with his father. What I do remember was that while we were sitting there, waiting for someone to welcome us and explain what was due to happen next, someone, possibly one of the older pupils, set off the fire alarm.

I watched to see what the Head would do, how he would react. Whether he would tell the assembled prospective parents that there was 'no need to panic', get cross with the perpetrators or just in case there were a real fire, organise everyone to 'leave the premises in an orderly fashion'.

He did none of these. Dressed smartly in a dark suit, white shirt and tie, he stood there on the school stage, upright and still, arms folded, silent, looking calm, self-composed and totally in control. 'Now there,' I thought, 'is a man in charge of a well-oiled machine.'

Within less than half a minute, the members of his senior staff had switched off the alarm and signalled to him that everything was then in order. With a slight nod of his head in their direction, he took a breath and, making no reference to the fire alarm situation, began 'Ladies and Gentlemen, welcome to Earlham School.'

Two weeks later, I made an appointment to see Mr D., the Head of Earlham School, to discuss the possibility of John being admitted there in September. I remember very well that meeting with Danny in his office at the front of the building.

I had been in meetings with a number of head teachers, some who stood on ceremony and others, generally those in charge of primary schools, who were more relaxed. I explained to Danny who I was, what my job was and why I had come. We talked about the local Earlham estate and beyond, about children who were held back from achieving as well as they might, because of family circumstances.

I talked about John, explained how if he were to transfer from his primary school to a secondary one, it could have huge consequences not only for him but also for the entire Traveller community, how he would be a pioneer in that respect, could show other Travellers that secondary school was not all bad and had much to offer. During this conversation, our basic philosophies and values must have revealed themselves, our attitudes towards formal education, towards other people and to life itself.

I remember Danny also referring to the pile of videos he had on one of his bookcase shelves and how we had both smiled. 'Those are not that kind of videos,' he said with a slight grin, 'they are for education training purposes.'

He showed me out of his office, walked with me to the main entrance on Earlham Road and to my car. Then, 'I'd like to see you again' he said, smiling. Not quite understanding, I responded with 'Well, I hope to be bringing John myself for the first couple of days, just to reassure him that he is safe and in the right place.'

Danny explained. It was me he would like to see, not just me the Traveller Liaison Teacher, but me, Lorna, the individual. I suppose I must have given him my contact details, a telephone number or something: I don't think at that stage we had email addresses, whether in the workplace or private.

Then I climbed into my car, drove back to my office and thought no more about it except that I had met a man, a headteacher, who was not much taller than I was and beginning to lose his hair, but a real person with an intelligent face, whose eyes twinkled and who seemed genuinely alive.

Chapter 19
Chinar

Danny invited me to join him for a drink and suggested I might meet him early one evening near the bar in The Arlington Hotel, just off the Newmarket Road.

Although I was fairly familiar with certain parts of Norwich, the area between Newmarket Road and Unthank Road wasn't one that I knew. Richard and I had not been accustomed to drinking in hotel bars, nor anywhere else really.

I checked it out by driving there the day before, found the hotel tucked down a side street, established whether it had a private car park. Then I arrived on the agreed day, feeling slightly nervous because I wasn't sure what was expected of me, nor who I really was without the job to wrap myself around with.

Not long before he had left, Richard had dismissed me with the words 'You'll never attract another man, you're far too capable.' But I wasn't there at the Arlington to attract another man, I was there to have a sensible intelligent conversation with someone with whom I thought I might have something in common.

Richard had also told me, in giving his unrequested advice as usual and assuming that I needed someone 'You need someone who can use words, someone like a lawyer or a solicitor. I can't find the right words when I talk to you.'

'Not my problem', I thought but didn't say. I had had several encounters with different men after Richard had left, some I had known previously and some as new relationships. Whatever the attraction had been of me to them, each of them had appeared to me to be seeking sex, including those who, as I later found out, were married.

One, according to what he had told me, had been a professional footballer, playing for Norwich City and other clubs. I had continued a relationship with him for a couple of years, not because I especially liked him but because I didn't dislike him and he was helpful with any building maintenance tasks. And mainly because I sensed that Keir needed a male role-model, someone who could teach him to do practical things that Richard didn't want to involve himself in, not with us anyway, not with Keir.

Richard had James, Jayne's boy, at home and the idea of spending his precious time with his own son instead, with Keir, didn't seem to interest him. I did once ask Richard whether he wanted to see more of his children. His reply? 'Well, they know where I live'.

My 'being capable' had been the reason why I had continued the relationship with Ralph, the ex-footballer who had told me he was 'a boffin', sometimes needing to travel away to Bacton or Easington, because his expertise, he had said, was in fuels and energy usage as well as having a financial interest in cement.

Ralph had come on a camping holiday with us a couple of times to Padstow and the Lake District, he would treat the children to things or show Keir how to weld, help him to build a go-kart, let him cut plasterboard. Ralph had been the builder who had been working on the side of the house adjoining the one I had bought, and who, with my encouragement and assistance, was employed to take down the plaster ceiling in our main living room and expose the oak timbers beneath.

By the summer of 1986, I had saved sufficient money to book a fortnight in Sicily for myself and the three children, staying in a holiday complex on the coast. I thought we all deserved it. I had seen photographs of it in the travel company's brochure; the swimming pools and water slides looked amazing.

Ralph was a bit annoyed that we were excited about it and that he wasn't going with us. He complained 'It's not very kind of you to be discussing it and talking about where you're going, when it doesn't include me.' I had never considered his coming along too.

My involvement with him had gone relatively well until I discovered him implying to Keir that he should not be seen walking down the street beside his mother, that Keir should be walking some distance in front of me 'to maintain credibility among his friends', Ralph had said, and later telling lies not only to me but also to two of my children about a paid holiday job with his son-in-law's printing firm that he said he had arranged for them.

It turned out there was no such job, and the children had been relying on it to earn some extra money for themselves.

Ralph disappeared from the scene after that, after I had told him 'I know you have lied to me, made your age seven or eight years younger than you really are, but I'm not prepared for you ever to lie to my children. Or to show off again by driving them along the dual carriageway at over 90 miles an hour.' Whatever, he got the message and that was the last I saw of him, or he found someone else more gullible.

There had been, from my side, no emotional involvement other than a working relationship regarding my house, although he had once, before I knew he already had a wife, suggested marriage and said, with minimal romance, 'because otherwise you might die on your own, as a lonely old woman.'

He told me that his wife had left him, that he had a housekeeper at home but I was never invited to his house in Hethersett.

I suppose, with hindsight, I should have been more suspicious. But I was trusting at that time and had not encountered many men, apart from Richard, who regularly told lies. I think Ralph was flattered by having a much younger woman to visit, and Keir and I had enjoyed having a practical man around the place.

I wore a Laura Ashley multi-floral tiered skirt and a pale-yellow cotton jacket that evening to meet Danny. I kept those clothes for almost twenty years afterwards, they no longer fitted nor suited me but they were a reminder of Danny, of our first meeting.

He asked what I would like to drink. No one had asked me that since I had left college and I wasn't sure what it would be best to say. I settled for 'a half of lager, please' and Danny ordered one for himself too, with low alcohol. I was struck by that; this wasn't a man who would show off about how much he could drink; this was a man who was restrained, who had nothing to prove.

I had been impressed too, either then or before at the school, by the car that he drove. Nothing big or flashy like Ralph had driven, no 'little man, big car' statement. Danny's car was a small red Citroën, with a number plate very similar to mine.

Our next meeting was a walk across heathland and along the Suffolk coast. I remember the sign saying, 'Beware of adders' and telling Danny, rather reluctantly because I didn't want to appear a wimp, that 'snakes are the one thing in the world that I am afraid of, although I've never actually seen one.' And 'my mother told me that they are more afraid of you than you are of them, but I don't think that's true because I'm much more frightened. Although she also told me that they would disappear if they sensed someone coming. So, would you mind if we stamped our feet a bit and deliberately make a noise?'

Despite my having owned up to my fears and vulnerability, there was no sign of an adder and the path we had taken through the heath and bracken led us to a tarmacked road running parallel to the coast.

Here Danny told me that he and his ex-wife, whom he had divorced some years previously, had a son named Mark who was only eighteen months older than Nell, and who was at a selective English independent day school in Norwich.

'On a scholarship' he explained, 'because he was offered it. And, as the son of a local headmaster, I felt that his choice of secondary schools in Norwich was somewhat limited,' and he ran through the list of other possible secondary schools and why they would not have been suitable.

When talking about his previous life, he told me that he had owned a springer spaniel but that 'we had to get rid of it after six months because it kept going after the neighbour's chickens. Its name was Muffin.'

Well, I thought, that settles it. Similar cars with similar number plates and a preference not only for the same breed of dog but also with the same name. What more in common could we possibly need?

He told me how he and his wife, who was part-German, had lived together and had married in a registry office 'almost because it seemed to be what was expected of us. We lived in Zambia for a couple of years after that, in order to help Zambians after independence.'

Apart from my stamp-collecting as a teenager, I knew nothing about the different countries of Africa and had to admit some ignorance. So, Danny explained, 'At independence, despite its mineral wealth mainly in copper which was much in demand across the world, Zambia faced major challenges. Within the country itself, there were few educated Zambians considered capable of running the government, and the economy was largely dependent on foreign expertise. I was invited by the Foreign and Commonwealth Office to go there and assist in establishing a structured system of secondary education.'

He also told me, 'Before reading English at university, I went to Finland for a couple of years, where I struck up a friendship with a Finnish dentist. I told her I would go back there one day and see her, but so far, I haven't done that. I won't now, I've left it too late.'

As we were walking, I thought of Ralph, of how he had recounted to me that he had had a verbal argument with someone who was black, how Ralph had been pleased he had gained the upper hand and his horror and disgust when the black fellow had responded, so Ralph told me, with 'One day we will rule this country and then you'll see.' Ralph had then gone on to refer to 'those people'.

I reflected again on those words and the determiner pronouns of 'those' and 'these', which had indicated, certainly where Ralph was concerned, his desire for total separation from 'those people', his disgust and complete dismissiveness of anyone who was not white or like him. I ruminated to myself, as I listened to what Danny was saying, on how much words can tell you about underlying attitudes and probably background as well.

I was interested in the extent of Danny's foreign travel and in particular in his attitude to people of other nationalities, in the language he used when talking about them. I had just completed, as part of my TES training, a four-week day-release 'Ethnic Diversity in Schools' course at Homerton College in Cambridge. I had been one of two attendees nominated by Norfolk Education Authority for the training.

As a result of the course and of confronting myself with the attitudes with which I had been raised, particularly by my father and his parents and their suspicion of all things foreign and therefore unknown, I realised what a colonial attitude I had absorbed, prior to that course, a puzzled 'why don't you go back to where you came from?' approach towards anyone with a dark skin.

I silently wondered, as Danny and I walked together, where my 'white first' attitude had come from, particularly as Moo had been so welcoming towards anyone and everyone, British or not. Had it come from Dad, who had always been reluctant to venture abroad, or was it a remnant from his family having been at war with other nationalities?

I had felt quite ashamed of my earlier attitude and had confessed this during the course; that I had been prejudiced without knowledge, had subconsciously believed in white dominance and assumed white supremacy. Being with Danny was making me think, quite deeply.

At home with my parents and siblings around the meal table, we used to listen to 'The Navy Lark' on the wireless and were discouraged from meaningful discussion, particularly from talking about money, religion or politics or given the opportunity within the security of the family to form our own beliefs and make choices. There had been no encouragement of individual thought, no genuine respect for contrary expression at home with my parents and siblings, only the likelihood of being put down with 'you'll understand when you grow older' or 'what do you know, at your age?' and ridicule from Val.

Learning that I was interested in the theatre, a week or two later Danny suggested that he and I might go to see a play together at Norwich's Theatre Royal.

We were walking beside the Broad at Salhouse on the boardwalk, which skimmed the edge of the Broad. 'I see' he said, 'there is a production next week of 'The Inspector Calls' at the theatre. Would you like to see it with me? I could get a couple of tickets. Is there any evening that you couldn't manage or should I just see what tickets are available and when?'

After our walk, we went back to his flat in Plantsman Close that he shared with Mark when Mark was not at his mother's house not far away in College Road. I was wearing an apricot-coloured jump-suit; I had grown hot and slightly sticky after the walk.

Danny made me a drink of something and suggested I might stretch out on the settee while he put on a 'Dire Straits' tape.

He came and sat beside me, stroking my arm. I avoided contact that was any more intimate; I suspected my armpits didn't smell their best after my exertions and the marsh humidity of the Broad. Looking over my shoulder, on the cream-painted dining table I noticed a bunch of fresh flowers standing in a vase.

Thinking that they suggested a woman's touch, another woman, I remarked 'Those flowers are very pretty. Do you have an area of garden where you grow them?'

'No' he replied, 'I have only the few pot plants that you see in the communal hallway just outside my front door. I sometimes buy a bunch of flowers for myself and Mark, they make the room seem more cheerful.'

We went on to discuss the importance of nature and wildlife for both of us, Danny telling me about the grey squirrels that had jumped from the trees and onto the roof, entered the loft of his flat and other people's too from under the tiles. 'They'd started to chew on the electric wiring there. I had to get someone in to deter them but I wouldn't want them harmed. Nor to electrocute themselves.'

We ate in the theatre restaurant before the play. Danny had taken a chance and pre-ordered fish and chips with garden peas for us both. I left the three children at home on their own. I recall Lallo having made some witty remark about the title of the play so the children knew where I was and with whom, where to get help from the neighbours should they need it.

Nell was at home from school either on holiday or an exeat. By then she was rising sixteen and well able to keep an eye on the others, even though Keir could be a handful. Lallo, aged thirteen, was more reliable than her older brother, and sensible.

My father was now living on his own in the house in Dereham. I would visit him regularly and take Nell with me each time she came home. Dad was very fond of Nell; he would sometimes address her as 'Tuppence' and was very interested in how she was doing at school. He had come with me, and Ralph, to listen when Nell was giving a solo singing performance in a Norwich church of Fauré's 'Pie Jesu'; he seemed very proud of her.

I wondered whether Keir would do well at the same school as Nell and sought the advice of the Senior Education Welfare Officer. According to a letter from her, addressed to the County Education Psychologist and with a copy to me, Keir 'was accepted . . . for admission to the school in September 1986. It was not possible for Keir to be given an assisted place, and as Mrs B. was not in a position to pay the fees herself, she declined the placement.'

The letter went on to say Lallo 'is a naturally homely girl who tends to take over the responsibilities of the home when Mrs B. is working. Mrs B. would like to relieve her of some of this responsibility and she sees the possible admission to Wymondham College as a means of developing Lallo's social needs. If Lallo is granted an assisted place at the college, Mrs B. is unsure how this news will affect Keir as he is very dependent on Lallo. However, she feels this situation should not jeopardise Lallo's chances of a possible place at Wymondham College.'

My father asked me 'Do you think Lallo would do as well as Nell at Wymondham College?'

I told him 'She'll probably thrive anywhere because she's that sort of person. But now we've moved out of the workshop and into 'The Yeoman's House', I can't see a case being made for her to go there, not on the grounds of 'boarding need', which was the reason why Nell was offered a place.'

However, I did try.

Lallo was invited for interview at Wymondham College in early March 1987 but I was informed by letter that 'this interview plays no part whatsoever in determining boarding need and that decision will be made entirely independently of this interview.'

Within three months I was informed that Lallo could be offered a place at Wymondham College but not an 'assisted place', that the boarding fees for 1987/88 would be £2,469.

I knew I couldn't afford that, I tried working it out by dividing the sum by twelve but £205.75 each month was quite out of the question on my salary. I told Dad the news.

To my surprise he offered to set up a trust that would pay Lallo's boarding fees, he had done something similar for Val's eldest son, Peter. Neither of us thought that it would ideal for Keir to go to Wymondham College, he had already transferred in September 1986 to Wymondham Secondary School but hadn't settled down and didn't appear to be receiving the help he needed with his reading and spelling. At his Middle School, Keir had been diagnosed by Doug S., the Educational Psychologist, as suffering from dyslexia.

'He doesn't score well on either the language or maths test that I've given him' Doug said, 'but my gut instinct tells me that he is likely to be quite good, even gifted, at things I can't test.'

'Like what?' I had asked.

'Tree-climbing, solving practical problems, things like that,' Doug replied.

'So, not an ideal candidate for Wymondham College,' I thought.

Nor could I have afforded a place for him at Wymondham College, had I even considered it ideal. Instead, I investigated the possibilities of changing Keir's school to Notre Dame High School in Norwich. However, he seemed to need to be at home, he appeared happy repainting his bicycle or fiddling about with his model aeroplanes in the shed. He and I both thought there might also have been a problem at a boarding school with his nightly bed-wetting.

Lallo wrote a letter home, headed 'Fry House, Wymondham College', and dated 18 September 1987.

'Dear Mum + Keir + Muff, I miss you but am enjoying myself very much. But I get on very well with the people in my course. Matron is brilliant because she does everyone's washing and lets you have Choc Break in her room opposite my dorm'. She continued 'When we had prep, I was told off by some teacher for doing nothing wrong, so I went into Mr Brand's office and he said 'seeing as you haven't done anything wrong, you can go'. The girl T. is a real Sharon: you know, denim jeans and jacket. I cried one night about being homesick but Nell comforted me. Chloe is only a first year but is kind of my best friend because she doesn't moan or anything. Hope you're getting on well. Lots + lots of love, Lallo xxx'

Danny suggested that he and I might spend a day together in Cambridge. 'I could show you my old college' he said with some enthusiasm, 'and perhaps we could go on the river, go punting.'

The dress I wore to Cambridge that day was white with blue flowers and green leaves, I had cut it out from a Clothkits pattern pre-printed on the material and sewn it myself.

We ate lunch at a pub near the river. I had visited Cambridge with the children, we had even climbed the inside of the tower of Great St Mary's Church near the market place. But I had not been to Cambridge before with anyone who knew the city well, who had lived there for three years as an undergraduate.

Danny seemed to rejoice in the place, treat it as an old friend. He knew the best place to park the car and how much it would cost if we went over our allotted time. We did go punting on the river, with Danny telling me about each bridge we passed under, getting past the porter at the porter's lodge and showing me which stone stairs had led to his room in Trinity Hall, and even going a couple of steps up them.

After he had reclaimed his car, he drove up Bridge Street, over Magdalene Bridge, turned right and we talked, slowly pottering along beside the river. He told me 'I used to row quite a bit. Not for the university, I wasn't a Blue or a half Blue. But rowing was the sport I liked best.'

I was finding Danny good company. He had interests that he would share and he was happy to look around places with me, to show me things and explain them.

Several years earlier and as part of a project that another teacher at Toftwood Middle School had set up, I had accompanied a group of children to some event near Peterborough. I had been at first surprised, then ashamed and lastly embarrassed by the older Toftwood pupils' reactions and behaviour when they saw children of their own ages, black children, taking part in another school group. There had been pointing, staring, sniggers and comments aloud, both to me as one of their teachers and to their peers.

I felt for the other children, how they must feel being stared at by a bunch of white kids who thought that being black, seeing people with a darker skin all together, was something completely out of the ordinary.

Having attended the 'Ethnic Diversity in Schools' course, I began to wonder how my three children would react if I were not there with them, whether I had given them a sufficient range of experiences while they were still growing up.

I had provided them with ballet lessons, classical for all three plus jazz ballet for Nell, ice-skating with them on my fortieth birthday and driving us all home with what I thought was a broken left arm; horse-riding for all three, violin lessons, brass instrument lessons, music and acting, sailing and kayaking, hill-walking, foreign travel, and camping.

I had even covered girls' rugby for Lallo, mackerel fishing with Ralph for Keir in Cornwall and hosting a French student for three weeks. But what I hadn't done at all was to take the children completely out of their comfort zones, put them in the position of being the outsiders, the ones who were stared at, or expose them to completely different norms and cultures.

I thought, especially as Richard had been told that his mother was half-Indian or Pakistani or from that part of the globe, perhaps an accompanied visit to India might be necessary to help augment their wider education, develop their understanding and their abilities to empathise.

Well before I met Danny, I had begun to investigate this. I had paid the deposit to Bales Worldwide, a travel company, for a trip for week or just over, touring the Indian 'Golden Triangle' of Delhi, Agra and Jaipur, followed by a further week's extension on a houseboat in Kashmir. The dates fitted well into the Easter school holidays.

Being with Danny was such a welcome change. The Royal Shakespeare Company were due to perform several of the history plays at the Theatre Royal. Danny asked me if I would like to go with him. There was never, with Danny, any suggestion of my paying for my ticket or a meal or even a drink. He was always quick to reach into his pocket or wallet.

Richard had had a small leather purse for change, which I felt signified something although I wasn't sure quite what, but whatever it was, I found it embarrassing. I wished he wouldn't do it; it was, I thought, a bit feminine and penny-pinching.

I didn't want Danny for one moment to think I was with him because he would pay for things. When and where I could, I would make sure he was reimbursed in some way. I also wanted to maintain my right to be independent, I didn't want him to think he had 'bought' me, that I was duty-bound to repay him by performing a service that I might not like or choose.

I don't think I ever expressed this in so many words but I think he got the message, that I was capable, - there, I've said it myself - independent and could be, if I chose, self-contained, reliant on no one else.

After visiting the theatre in Norwich, we had been walking side by side down towards the street corner by Debenhams, when quite suddenly, out-of-the-blue, Danny said 'we won't ever argue about money.' I thought at the time, the word 'we' was a trifle presumptuous, that there was, too, the assumption from him after four or more dates, there would be a 'we' in both the near and longer-term future.

It took me some time to realise that, for Danny as a Headmaster, there was money still left at the end of each month, whereas I usually had part of the month left at the end of the money. While I would collect any 'money-off' grocery tokens, he had once said 'I can't be bothered to keep all those' and advised me to put them in the bin. I didn't.

I told Danny that the children and I were already booked on a tour of Northern India. Danny came with us for the Golden Triangle part of our visit to India. He had to return to Norfolk to start a new advisory job in the Summer Term so didn't feel it would be right to join us for the Kashmir part.

On the plane, I was surprised to see how many Indians there were and I wondered why they would travel there by plane, wondered why they didn't choose to go to somewhere different on holiday, somewhere that they didn't know so well. Then it slowly dawned on me that they weren't on holiday at all, they were going home or to see relatives in their home country, that for some, this could be their first ever flight.

That became apparent when I saw one family getting out what looked to me like a primus camping stove and setting it up in the side aisle with packets of various foodstuffs. I don't think that was a dream, although now, with safety and luggage checks being so rigorous, that scene seems unlikely. A stewardess came along and explained, very gently, that they wouldn't need to be cooking for themselves on board the plane, that the meals were provided and there was a choice of menu.

Either before or soon after we went to India, Danny decided that it was time his son and I should meet, and that Mark should meet my three. He arranged it with Mark, for Mark to be available. I don't expect he mentioned the reason to Mark's mother. Danny rarely told anyone anything unless he considered it essential, he was always a very private person. Perhaps it was to protect that privacy, that he never, ever, told me what he was feeling, only what he thought. It was almost as if feelings or emotions were unmentionable, something not quite socially decent and about which he was embarrassed.

I met Mark with Danny first, for lunch at a new hotel just off Boundary Road and Whiffler Road. I don't remember what we ate as our main course, only that for dessert there was pear crumble topped with chopped hazelnuts, a combination that I hadn't tried before but thought well worth repeating when or if I ever invited guests to my house for dinner.

Not long after that, Danny invited Mark to meet my children at my house. Danny and Mark had lived in Wymondham a couple of years before he and I met. Danny and his wife had bought a house called 'Mill Cottage' in Barnham Broom Road, near where the smock mill had once stood. It had had a barn, Danny said, which had been sold off when he had sold the house after he and Mark's wife had split up and they had each moved into smaller separate accommodation off Newmarket Road in Norwich.

Mark, when he was not at school, would spend half the time living with Danny and the other with his mother and her partner John, who had been the main cause of the marital split.

'In case you ever see any Christmas cards addressed to me and Pam,' Danny once told me not long after we had met, 'Pam was my previous, erm, female friend. I met her. .' and then he went on to tell me about their first few meetings, and how they had 'split up after Pam quite suddenly told Mark that she and I would probably get married soon. Poor lad, he looked aghast, didn't know what to think. I got rid of her soon after that.'

I suspected that Mark was gently advised on some occasions by Danny to spend the night at his mother's because 'Lorna will be staying over tonight.'

I stayed at Danny's flat many times. On one occasion, I was told afterwards, Keir had been exploring how a circular hole had been cut in the glass of the building opposite our house. He had been thought by a neighbour of theirs to have been attempting to break in: the neighbour had informed the police.

Keir got into trouble and Nell, who was also at home looking after him and Lallo, decided not to contact me about it because, Nell told me afterwards she had said 'Mum is enjoying herself and I don't want to upset that.'

I don't know whether that was the first time I had stayed the night with Danny but it was one of the first. I remember us being together in his double bed, Danny making a few intimate moves and saying with humour and relief 'Well, it seems to fit,' then climbing out of bed again, grabbing a book from his bookshelf and tossing it straight into the waste paper basket.

'Well,' he said, with a satisfied grin, 'I don't think we'll be needing that.' I didn't see or recognise the cover but it was some sort of 'Sex for Beginners' manual.

At some time during our early relationship, Danny had told me that he was attracted to women who were well-dressed, well-groomed, who did not keep touching their faces and who did not laugh too often. I thought at the time, 'That's never going to be me.' I had been told by Moo that, after seeing my first school photograph, with my hair flying at all angles and wearing a second-hand blouse made of cream-coloured Shantung silk, with loving approval my mother had nicknamed me, and the photograph, 'Little Scruffy'.

I noticed huge differences between the ways in which Richard, Ralph and then Danny treated me and which aspects of this treatment I professed to enjoy, then really liked.

Richard had always taken the view that I was as capable as he, that I did not need to be treated in any way differently because I was female except, perhaps, during childbirth. As he said on more than one occasion, 'You are perfectly capable of opening a door for yourself so why should I open it for you?' and 'We no longer have carriages driving along the road and splashing your long skirts with water from under their wheels, so why would I walk on the outside of the pavement?'

Richard did not suggest I might need any physical protection. On the contrary, on the one occasion when he saw those two men approaching the cottage on foot from the road, two big, hefty men whom he assumed to be debt-collectors or somebody's 'heavy brigade', he had hidden upstairs in our bedroom and sent me outside to deal with them. This may, of course, have been an indication of his confidence in my verbal negotiation skills but at the time, it didn't feel like it. They went away, eventually.

I never had the impression that Richard thought I was worth spending time or money on, certainly not making jewellery for me that he could otherwise sell. Richard's focus seemed to be on money, his own pleasures, and his safety.

Ralph appeared to regard me as a mini-trophy that he could parade to only a few people. He had archaic ideas of what a woman was for, he would spend time and a little money on me and on the children but his focus was on sex.

Danny seemed to regard me as an intelligent and capable human being who, very occasionally, needed physical protection or assistance while respecting my expressed wish for independence. He also thought I was worth spending time, effort and money on, as long as it was something he considered important and worthwhile. But he appeared to have little understanding of what I might be feeling, of where, apart from in any aspect of education, I might appreciate having some emotional as well as practical support, such as in the case of the death of a friend. Emotions, for Danny, were an unnecessary distraction, something slightly unpleasant that, in his ranking of things, came far below intellect and intelligence.

When we were in Jaipur and waiting to ride on the backs of the elephants up to Amer Fort, I had been shifting my weight slightly and stepping backwards. Danny put his arm round my waist and ushered me forwards towards the roadway. I wondered why, where we were going.

'It's all right,' he assured me, 'but you were stepping backwards. I didn't think you'd noticed but right behind you, next to the man with a flute, was a basket with a cobra rearing up from it. I didn't think you would like that, I thought it might alarm you.'

Danny was also quite forthright to a chap in Delhi who was hassling me and the children outside the Red Fort.

'Go away,' he told him 'We don't want your postcards. Stop bothering us, you are standing in our way.' I remember being surprised that he hadn't said 'please'.

It was when we were in India and viewing the Taj Mahal that Danny suggested that he and I should get married. He said, after I and the children had safely returned to Britain 'I would like to buy you a ring. Can we go together at the weekend and choose one?'

This was, for me, completely new territory. Apart from Richard who, long before we were married and while he was still married to Doreen, had given me a delicate pearl-and-gold necklace, no one had ever bought jewellery for me before. Danny and I went in to Norwich and looked in the windows of jewellery shops. I was used to looking at semi-precious stones but those, set in rings and on display, were facetted rather than cabochon. And the price!

Most rings had two extra noughts at the end of the prices at which our rings were usually sold. How was I to know what Danny could afford, how much he had expected to pay? I had no wish to embarrass either of us by choosing the wrong thing.

In a hurried conversation with myself, I decided it would be best to look in the windows of high street shops rather than expensive jewellers, that it was the symbolism of the ring rather than the basic value that mattered, and I didn't want anything big and flashy, because I didn't think I was that sort of person.

I was aware of the general opinion, including Richard's, of H. Samuel and Ratner jewellery companies, although it may have been a few years after this that Gerald Ratner made his famous gaffe by describing the jewellery in his shop as 'total crap.' But I suggested to Danny, 'Shall we looking first at the window displays of H. Samuel because I really don't know what I like in terms of rings?' because doing that would give me an idea of prices. The look on his face might do the rest.

I chose a simple design of ring, set not with rubies and diamonds in case I might lose it, but with tiny alternate garnet and spinel stones. I felt comfortable at Danny spending the amount asked and I wore it at the next conference at which I was speaking, feeling very conscious of the sparkles on my left hand catching the light, trying to hide it. A colleague noticed the ring as I was standing and talking at the front of the audience and afterwards, she remarked on it.

I told my three children that Danny and I would get married but that we didn't know when or how soon. Although I had had a legal separation from Richard years before, I had not made any moves towards applying for a divorce. I had been fairly sure that I did not want him back but I was also fearful, should he request that we got together again, that the children would put me under pressure to 'have Daddy back' and he was, after all, the children's father.

I didn't want him back because I couldn't stand his indecision, his disregard of me and my feelings, his attitude and constant sexual approaches to other women. He had once said almost proudly to me, after he had left and moved in with Jayne, 'I think my problem is that I am over-sexed'.

I replied 'Believe me, Richard, you are not. I have been around a bit since you left and you are certainly not over-sexed. In fact, quite the opposite,' which wasn't very kind of me but nevertheless, I felt it was true.

One of the things that I hope the children realised from our week on Chinar, the houseboat moored on Dal Lake in which we stayed in Kashmir, was that tensions between different groups of people were not always based on skin colour or race. We had heard gunfire but I had assumed it was to mark some sort of celebration. From the veranda of the houseboat, we had even watched a shikara being slowly paddled along, with something big placed horizontally along it and everyone else standing up at one end.

It was later that I knew about the religious tensions between Muslims and Hindus and realised that the shikara scene and the people that I had seen were the result of a death. The people standing had been mourners on their way to a funeral, with the coffin.

When an Islamic insurgency had begun in Indian Kashmir that year, the Hindus living in the area became an early target. Muslim militants directed a systematic campaign of assassinations and intimidation against Kashmiri Pandits, the scholarly Hindus who performed rituals in temples. Most of them were forced out of Kashmir.

Fortunately, no one disturbed us in our houseboat nor during our visits across the lake to the Shalimar gardens. It was in those gardens where we saw the most enormous snowflakes the size of saucers falling and realised that on that day at least, we were inadequately dressed. Later during that week, we travelled in two hired cars, Keir in one and the two girls with me in the other, to Gulmarg higher up among the mountain pastures.

There we went sledging. I found the local people slightly intimidating but we sledged across and down the snow, stopping only before a metal fence topped with spikes that looked as if they might be sharp. Lallo told me that when she had returned to school and told the class she had been sledging that Easter in India, she was apparently told not to tell lies because India didn't have snow.

It most certainly did that year, and in that region. Did the class-teacher not know where India and Kashmir were, in relation to the Himalayas?

On our way back from Dal Lake's landing stage to Srinagar airport in a three-wheeled rickshaw, known as a tuk-tuk from the sound of the engine, we avoided an altercation with what I assumed were the local police. The two tuk-tuks in front of ours were approached by two or three men in uniform and repeatedly beaten with baseball bats. I don't know about the occupants and whether they were hurt or frightened, I was too busy shielding the children. I waited and hoped we looked sufficiently blond and British.

We did. They ignored our tuk-tuk and let us proceed on our way to the airport and home. We were some of the last British tourists that the travel companies allowed into Kashmir that year.

Not long after we had returned from Kashmir via Delhi, Danny moved some of his things into our house and we began to make plans for the future.

Danny's first consideration was Mark, and how Mark would react. Mark was taking his 'A' level exams that summer and, subject to results, had been offered a place at Cambridge to study natural sciences with mathematics, at Trinity Hall like his father.

'I don't want to upset him in any way,' Danny said. 'He had quite a rough time when he was younger, going between his mother and me and never being sure whether what his mother had promised him in terms of treats or outings, whether even going each week to Scouts, would actually take place. He developed a stammer which it took a long while to cure so it's important that Mark feels settled and happy with whatever we decide to do.'

I had been told that Mark's mother's friend John had children of his own, girls I believed, and Mark got on well with them. Privately, I thought Mark would probably cope quite well, especially as, if everything went as he hoped, he would be spending the next three years living in Cambridge.

As a temporary measure, Danny hired a touring caravan and had it placed in the back yard of The Yeoman's House, in front of the shed in which Keir was accustomed to do whatever Keir did involving paint and some sort of glue for his model aeroplane, as well as my forks, which he used as tyre levers, my knives and my teaspoons. I have no idea what he used teaspoons for but they would slowly disappear from the cutlery drawer.

The caravan was to provide Mark with a space of his own, somewhere to sleep or study within the family precinct. I had pointed out to Danny that it would be quite unfair for Mark to have to sleep in the same room as Keir. Mark was an only child and he hadn't chosen Keir to be his younger brother.

'Nor' I explained 'is there room for two in Keir's bedroom, because it's long and thin and has the water tank taking up space in it as well, hidden behind a curtain. And sharing a room with someone who habitually wets the bed every night is not, as I well know, very pleasant. I think Mark needs his own space; having another family suddenly thrust into his life is enough for any growing lad. And I'm not sure that Keir would leave any of Mark's possessions undisturbed, not if they looked interesting.'

After taking his 'A' levels, Mark left school and was spending two months working with 'Camp America'. It was difficult for Danny to contact him personally but we had news from time to time of what he was doing and what his plans might be for the period between finishing 'Camp America' and the time when he would be due to start his university course in Cambridge.

Danny and I were unable to set a wedding date well in advance. We both wanted to get married after the end of the school term and Danny was especially keen that none of his staff should know about it in advance; I'm not sure why. It was another example of his desire for personal privacy, his rather than mine. But I told no one either, except my three children and even then, I didn't give them much notice. They were to be our only witnesses.

I was still technically married to Richard. Although I had been granted a decree nisi, I had not applied for the decree absolute, because until then, there had seemed no point. Now, with the idea of marrying for a second time, it became not only desirable, the decree absolute was essential.

I think it was a simple form-filling exercise. Danny had long since been divorced from his first wife; now I needed to complete my divorce process. Until I had the decree absolute, it was impossible to fix a wedding date anywhere.

The date of my decree absolute was 15th August 1989: Danny and I were married on 23rd August 1989 at Broadland Registry Office. The only reason for it having been at Broadland office was that that was the one registry office that had a space that month in its calendar and Danny was also trying to avoid being at a registry office immediately after one of his staff had booked her wedding there. I remember the words of the civil service and hoping that I wasn't asked to promise to 'obey', a promise which I considered to be archaic and demeaning.

This was no white wedding. I managed to buy myself a blue and white floral Liberty skirt with a matching top in a not very pleasant but serviceable fabric, and to find a navy straw hat that I could wear without it slipping forward and covering my eyes. Keir wore a suit and tie while both girls had skirts that I made from pretty Liberty material, and white blouses. When our full names were given out, I heard the children snigger. I thought they giggled on hearing my middle name but I was told by Lallo much later that they didn't know that Danny's real name, the one he was given at his christening, was actually Ivor Edward. And yes, they too had thought of Ivor the Engine, Lallo told me.

When Mark came back from America, after he had finished at Camp America and travelled around the States by Greyhound bus and then in a car he had bought and later sold, Danny told him that we had planned to marry and had done so while he was in America. According to what Danny told me, Mark was a bit put out that he wasn't invited and asked 'Weren't you going to tell me?'

Danny tried to explain why we couldn't invite Mark to the wedding or give him prior notice, because until a week before hand and the decree absolute had been received, we simply weren't sure ourselves when and where our wedding would take place.

We had a three-day honeymoon, travelling by car around Normandy and Brittany and staying in bed-and-breakfast accommodation recommended by Brittany ferries. It was a short break, only because Danny thought he should be back in school in time to learn the 'O' and 'A' level exam results and perhaps to offer students advice on their next steps.

In our hotel bedroom in Bayeux, a notice on the carpet-textured walls instructed us, in the event of fire, to 'manifest ourselves at the window'; we sniggered at that. And somewhere near Rouen in a hotel attached to a garage, the shower water became cold every time a car went through the car wash.

Now that we were married, having a hired touring caravan in the back yard for Mark wasn't what either of us wanted. We wanted to provide him with his own room. He might be at Cambridge during term-time but we both felt he needed somewhere to return to when he came down. The house I had bought was ample for the five of us but totally inadequate for six. So, we started to look for somewhere else to live.

I didn't want to leave The Yeoman's House; it had been a refuge for me and a solution for each of the children. I felt emotionally very attached to it and grateful that we had had the privilege of living there in something so beautiful and a part of Wymondham's history.

Together we looked for a house within reach of Norwich so that Danny could continue working at Earlham, and sufficiently close to Wymondham so Keir and the girls could get to and from their respective schools easily enough. There was a pleasant end-terrace house advertised for sale on the Newmarket Road that we viewed and two others in Wymondham with sufficient bedrooms. But in order to afford any of these, it would be essential for Danny to sell his flat in Plantsman Close.

He put this on the market almost immediately and waited. Fortunately, he had a potential buyer from out-of-county almost straight away, a woman not much younger than Danny. She and Danny exchanged contracts.

They completed the sale as Danny was moving the last of his and Mark's possessions, just as the Plantsman Close buyer's son also realised that his mother was suffering from dementia and should not be living on her own. Unfortunate though this was for him, we were both very grateful that the sale of the flat had gone through before the buyer's diagnosis had been known.

The owners of the adjoining side of my sixteenth century house in Wymondham quite suddenly decided to sell their half, the number 14 side of the main house. It was a godsend - although Danny said he didn't believe in God and I was becoming unsure. Our accommodation problem was solved but with plenty of work for us both to do.

We decided that Danny should buy the number 14 side with the proceeds from the sale of his flat, that I should pay off the mortgage on my half, the number 16 side, and that we should bring both sides of the property together to form one six-bedroom house and restore the two halves to one whole. Together we did just that.

It wasn't easy because we had assumed that the two sides would have upstairs floor boards at the same level and they didn't. Some on one side had been renewed and replaced, but making it one family house again was a labour of love, and much of my skin, blood and perspiration went into that house. I didn't regret one single minute of it. For the second time in my life, I fell in love with The Yeoman's House, it provided just what we needed.

During this time but quite out of the blue, a card came addressed to me from Her Majesty's Lord Chamberlain. I was invited by Her Majesty, along with my husband and my two daughters, to 'a Garden Party at Buckingham Palace on Tuesday 13th July 1993 from 4 to 6pm.' Danny didn't wish to go, he said something to the effect of 'I don't believe in having royalty, they have gained their position not by election but through inherited wealth and position or, quite often, as the result of war and conflict, with a little murder thrown in.' It was several years afterwards that I realised he was, as Richard had been, a staunch member of the Labour Party.

I still don't know how I came to be invited. It wasn't through my line manager or Norfolk County Council, Mrs Steynor told me, so I assume it was because I had done some work for the Department for Education and Science. I had pointed out, when Nursery Vouchers were first proposed, that having a voucher sent required having a permanent address and that many British citizens, such as the parents of Gypsy and

Traveller children often didn't have a fixed address. Nevertheless, they were entitled to receive the voucher.

I didn't suggest Lallo might come with me to Buckingham Palace because she was still at school, and neither did I mention it to Nell, because I thought Nell might make some disparaging remark or behave in a way I and other guests would consider inappropriate and discourteous. She had done so once or twice during broadcast royal events as well as during ceremonial events at the local war memorial.

No one in my immediate family that I knew about had had any direct involvement with the armed services and although both daughters attended Wymondham College, a site which had once been used as an air-force hospital, both had limited respect for the Armed Forces as institutions. I assumed Nell was just being a teenager and against anything and everything that represented authority or position.

I went alone, travelling to London by train and catching a taxi to Buckingham Palace. I carried an umbrella because the clouds threatened drizzle. I had met Her Majesty once before, when she had been in Canterbury to distribute the Maundy Money and had come on afterwards to open Christ Church College.

I had been advised, when I accepted the invitation, to enter the palace grounds by a side gate off Constitution Hill and from there to proceed as directed, through the outer courtyard, in and through the building itself and out into the gardens behind. I met one or two other guests who introduced themselves and who followed that with 'and where do you come from?' and then 'so why do you think you are here, have been invited?'

When I mentioned to anyone who asked that I worked with Gypsy and Traveller children, I would watch the distance between them and me gently increase as the questioning guests moved discretely backwards, presumably fearful of some sort of contamination.

I looked askance at the carefully planted flowers in regimental rows, before being offered Earl Grey tea and cucumber sandwiches with the crusts removed and thinking how Moo would have loved all this. She would have given it her total approval, even if my current husband wouldn't and didn't. I had the feeling of being on some mid-stream stepping stone that belonged to neither bank but stood there on its own, wobbling in the water.

Chapter 20

Seroxat

Much of our life together, with my three children and from time to time with Mark, was peaceful and relaxed. Danny had once told me 'I don't really understand teenagers,' a remark I considered rather strange from the headmaster of a secondary school. I don't know to what extent he really realised what he was taking on by marrying the mother of someone else's teenage children.

I thought he managed the situation quite well, with one or two exceptions. And should there have been a question of fault on anyone's part, then it was either more often the fault of one or more of the children who did not realise what having an adult working male in the family involved, or the result of a clash of expectations or domestic cultures.

I did, once or twice, try to reassure them by saying 'I love Danny very much but if it ever came to my having to make a choice between you, then I would stick with you because I'm your mother. But if there's any disagreement in the meantime, that doesn't necessarily mean that you are in the right'.

By this time, Nell had completed her GCSE exams and become a day-pupil at Wymondham College, living at home with us and studying music and English for 'A' level.

On more than one occasion, Danny would come home from school at about half past five in the afternoon, tired and needing a rest, only to find Nell and two of her male friends slumped across the settee and in the armchair, leaving Danny nowhere comfortable to sit. Rather than make a fuss in front of Nell's friends, he mentioned it to me quietly later and as far as I knew, the situation did not occur again.

During our weekends - Danny drew the line at attempting anything as demanding as building work during the evenings - we spent time reorganising rooms, especially our bedroom so that until both sides of the property could function as one house, we were able to live and sleep in warmth and relative comfort.

Brick by brick, we took down the outhouses on either side of the property and stacked the cleaner bricks for future use, throwing away any covered with too much mortar or whitewash. The area would, we thought, make a sizeable garage for one car and a hard stand for the second one. We also needed to develop the small area at the rear into a compact but attractive garden.

We intended to turn the former kitchen of the number 14 side into a utility room to house the washing machine, ironing board and any spare crockery. I chose dark green tiles to cover the space immediately above the work surface.

'Would cork tiles be sensible as a floor covering for the utility room?' I asked Danny. 'I thought they would offer warmth if we went in there with bare feet, but how good are they at dealing with any moisture, just in case the washing machine ever leaked?'

With Danny's approval, I chose the cork floor tiles and had them delivered. I also contacted a firm that would lay the tiles with a special adhesive and seal them, once they were stuck down. The company sent a chap round to inspect and measure the floor area and deliver a sealed tin of the correct adhesive.

'Be very careful with this,' he warned 'because the adhesive is highly flammable. Store it somewhere sensible, out of the sun and away from any direct heat.'

I did just that, placing the tin on the concrete floor in a far corner of the utility room, ready for when the flooring man was due to return the next day.

The flooring chap had just started to smooth the adhesive onto the underside of the first two or three cork tiles, starting the tiling at the gas boiler and intending to work from that point across the floor.

There was a loud whoomph, and in a moment the room filled with black smoke. The timer on the boiler had ignited the pilot light. That ignited either the adhesive on the few tiles already on the floor or the tin of adhesive which the flooring man had placed right beside the boiler.

Hearing the sound and seeing the smoke, I phoned the fire brigade, told them ours was a listed building in the centre of Wymondham and it was timber-framed.

Within five minutes and just before the whole crew arrived, I was able to phone them back, tell them it wasn't a gas leak and that I thought the fire was under control.

I don't remember who put the flames out or how. But the adjoining room that we used as a library, which had shelves of books from floor to ceiling, was completely black.

The walls that I had so carefully decorated only a matter of months before, were black. The ceiling was black. All the books were covered in black soot. And I and the people around me had black faces and filthy clothes.

Kevin and the rest of the men who had arrived to install the kitchen units in the utility room were there too, looking slightly dazed by what had happened.

Danny appeared from somewhere the other side of the house. But what I remember most, apart from the black and our need to make a claim on the house insurance, and all the books needing to be sent away to be cleaned, were the emotional reactions, or lack of them from Danny.

I felt relief that no one had been hurt, and an equal amount of relief that the whole house hadn't gone up in smoke.

I was annoyed at the flooring guy who should (I thought but didn't say) have known better than to work that close to a gas boiler with a pilot light. I fought back my tears and feelings of exhaustion, both physical and emotional.

After all my pleasure and excitement at finishing the utility room, the last stage in bringing together both sides of the house, our family home, I felt completely disembowelled, hollow inside.

I stood in the garden, just outside the utility room, watching the faces of the kitchen fittings people and in particular Kevin, who had done some work for Danny in Earlham School.

Kevin and his men seemed unsure of what to do next for the best, whether it was appropriate for one of them to put a comforting arm round me in front of my husband, or what to say.

But Danny made no effort to console me; he went completely into practical mode and looking at the damage, he ignored me. He looked shell-shocked. At the very time when I needed reassurance, emotional support and some comfort, he was totally out of his depth or too embarrassed in front of people he knew in a different context to show any emotion, either towards me or towards anyone else.

That was when I saw most clearly that he didn't have the skills or the will to deal with emotion, whether mine or his own.

I re-entered the concrete world by trying to reassure the flooring man that 'nothing too terrible has happened, the house is still standing and you weren't to know that the pilot light was on and might suddenly ignite. Please don't worry, everything can be restored or repaired, it was just an unfortunate accident and no one was at fault.'

This wasn't completely true, but there seemed no point in making the poor guy feel any worse than he already did, by heaping blame on his already-cowed shoulders.

I had told Danny various things about my life with Richard, about the fire in the barn, how it had been, although accidental, nevertheless caused by my error and our need to have the whole kitchen in the barn redecorated.

I told him how, as I understood it, Richard had never really got over behaving like a teenager and kept trying to fill in the gaps in his development.

'He just didn't grow up,' I explained. 'If you ever have an affair, Danny,' I said, 'please don't tell me - or if you feel you have to, please keep the details to yourself. Richard seemed to derive real pleasure from going into the details in front of me, perhaps it was his way of reliving the whole experience and enjoying it all again.'

'That's not going to happen,' Danny assured me and I had no reason to doubt him. I knew he was an honourable man and that he had been through a very difficult time when his first wife had left him several years previously for one of her university colleagues.

With both Danny and me leaving home at almost the same time to go to work and returning home around 5.30pm, whichever one of us parked the car and got indoors first would then put the kettle on and wait for the other to return.

One of us would ask the other, as I or he came through the back door and into the kitchen, 'Kettle's on. How was your day?'

We would both go to our work places at the weekend as well, it gave each of us time to focus without needing to deal with phone calls or staff.

To get to my office in Turner Road, I had to drive past Earlham School so if I left home after Danny, or left Turner Road before he left his office, then I would see his car parked outside his school.

Quite often at the weekends, there would be another car parked as well, a member of the senior staff would be there too.

I was pleased for Danny that he wouldn't be on his own, that other staff were also working on a Saturday or more likely a Sunday; I hoped he wouldn't be disturbed though. I would have my base in Turner Road to myself and could get on and concentrate on what needed to be done before the Monday morning.

I once collapsed with laughter before pulling myself together, when a teaching assistant, very new to the job, asked me 'what bonus do we get at Christmas?'

I, and the others in the team, explained that she was no longer in the world of industry or commerce, that in education, the word 'bonus' was unknown.

'Teachers' someone explained to her, 'are required to work a minimum number of hours but there is no maximum or overtime. The higher up the management line teachers progress, the more they can work until they drop or till they are off work with stress or illness. There is no maximum. The biggest bonus you are ever likely to get is the use of a school pencil at home, and even then, you could be in trouble for taking Education Department property home.'

The Traveller Education Service increased in size in line with the budget and the need.

In March 1990, following the revised structure of the Traveller Education Service, I was confirmed as the Co-ordinator with the status of Headteacher Group 3. By then, there were some twenty-five people working within the Traveller Education Service under my management as either teaching assistants or liaison teachers.

Norfolk being an agricultural county, it had long been dependent on the casual labour that the Traveller community was accustomed to provide, starting the seasonal harvesting first with rhubarb, then strawberries, and then apples before potatoes.

Whereas most teachers in infant schools were used to knowing how to deal with children who were late to learn to read or write, many classroom staff in junior or middle schools had fewer resources at their finger-tips for teaching those skills and needed additional support from members of my team.

With the high number of 'virtual' pupils which was increasing every year – 'virtual' because they were usually on roll at other schools as well as on our list of Traveller children requiring support or contact - I was placed on the Headteacher's earning scale and joined NAHT, the National Association of Headteachers.

By November 2004, I had been subsumed into the County's Advisory Service and Children's Services as an Advisory Teacher. My revised salary was the equivalent of point 12 on the Leadership Group Pay Spine.

So as a Service we grew, so did my need to oversee what was happening across the entire county and in the hundreds of

Local Authority and church schools. It was not uncommon for me to be working for more than sixty hours each week in term-time, and Danny did the same.

It was important to both Danny and me to get completely away from Norfolk and from Britain, to go somewhere else that would provide mental and physical stimulus of a totally different kind and also offer relaxation, somewhere where we could flop and read if that's what we wanted, or walk around a different environment, enjoying the sun, the food or the architecture.

'I've been looking at what seems to be best value as a holiday destination,' Danny said one day, pushing any remaining hair back from his steadily-balding head 'and Cuba looks to be a good bet. It's somewhere I've always wanted to go and now it's become a possible travel destination for a British citizen.'

That is where we went a few months later, taking with us the things that we understood to be shortages in Cuba, items light in weight and easy to pack such as soap or lipstick or tee-shirts; and trying hard, until we could stand it no longer, to eat only what the Cubans could buy to eat, which was mainly rice and beans.

Then we ate the chicken that we as tourists were offered, and felt mean and greedy about doing so.

After Cuba and snorkelling off the coast, in 1993 we spent a week at Easter in Sri Lanka, returning there a year or so later for a tour around the island by private car. Keir and Lucy were engaged on Lucy's eighteen birthday in April and in October 1996 they were married, with Lucy being several months pregnant. Their wedding in a local hotel may have been the only time that Richard and Danny met. Lucy's parents arranged and paid for the wedding.

Keir found a house in Belvoir Street in Norwich that he could afford to buy and he asked Danny's advice.

'Would you mind looking at it with me, Danny, before I commit myself to the mortgage? Because you've bought houses before and I haven't had your experience,' which was both sensible and surprisingly tactful of Keir.

It was the sort of thing that my father would have enjoyed doing and would have been very useful with his knowledge and experience, but by that time, Dad had moved from the house in Quebec Road in Dereham and had bought a flat in a sheltered complex in Exmouth, not far from where his friend Frances was living with her friend Bett.

I was at a meeting in Birmingham when Danny phoned me. 'There's nothing to worry about,' he said in the way people do when you know perfectly well that you are about to hear bad news, 'but Keir's had an accident in his car. He's in hospital at the moment, I've been to see him because he asked for me.'

'How is he, is he all right and what happened? Shall I come home?'

'He's fine. When I saw him this evening, he was having parts of his head glued together. He wanted me to make sure that he was still in the running to buy the house in Belvoir Street.'

I heard later that Richard was cross that Keir hadn't asked to see his biological father, Keir had asked for Danny instead. Tough, I thought.

When on one occasion I was camping in Wales with the children, I had asked each of them what they thought about their father and about his leaving.

Each of the girls had gone into some length to tell me how they felt, which was mixed.

Keir, on the other hand, was a lad of few words.

'Dad?' he asked. 'Disappointing.'

That was his only description.

Danny was due to retire in 1997 at the end of the summer term and said that he would like to go to Estonia in May. He gave me a video camera 'to thank you for being such a supportive wife during my headship.'

I thought our forthcoming visit to Estonia would be an ideal time for me to use the new camera, to record our trip.

He told me that his staff seemed quite upset at the thought of his forthcoming retirement and that one senior member of staff, Miss S., a woman he had once described as 'rather odd', had also been close to tears in his office 'because someone she had once lived with had died' he recounted to me 'and she didn't know where he was buried. She was still in tears so I gave her a hug before I asked her why it mattered where he was buried.'

'That was kind of you,' I told him. 'And I too would have wondered why someone's burial site matters. Surely, it's the time you have together that matters, not what happens after you're dead?' and I thought no more about it, except to notice how often, when Danny's car was parked outside the school on a Sunday, Miss S's car was also there.

'Is she like you, working every weekend, preparing for when you leave?' I asked.

'I don't know,' he replied. 'I don't see much of her when I'm there; she's up in her office and I'm downstairs in mine.'

'Well, I hope she's helping you with the preparations you need to make before you leave the school for good,' I said and then 'Who will take over once you've left?'

'That's not up to me,' Danny replied 'maybe one of the three Deputies may have to hold the fort until the authorities can advertise for a new Head. I think one of them will make a poor job of it but it's not up to me.'

Once we had arrived in Estonia and had walked through Tallin airport, Danny told me he thought he ought to make a phone call.

'Is there a problem?' I asked.

'I haven't heard from Mark for ages,' he responded 'and I don't think I mentioned we would be away. I'd just like to let him know where we are.'

'Shall I come with you to the phone booth, or shall I stay here by the airport exit?'

'Stay there, I shan't be long.'

And I thought no more about it until months later.

Danny had booked for us to spend two weeks that summer after he retired, in Bulgaria, where he had once been before, skiing with Mark.

I vaguely remember his retirement event. I knew he wasn't much looking forward to it.

He had been Head at Earlham for over twenty years so the school had become a large part of his life. When he was giving Geoff, the Education Officer, due notice that he wanted to retire at the end of the Summer Term rather than the following December when he would have reached the proper retirement age, he told Geoff 'because it could be very disruptive for the school if I left part-way through the academic year. It seems to me to be much clearer for everyone for me to leave at the end of the school year, to have a clean break. Then new staff and new pupils can grow accustomed to a new head without having to get used to someone else being only temporarily in charge and needing to learn another name only a term later.'

Danny went on to share with me 'I had wondered whether Geoff would ask me to stay on for a further term, until he and the Governors could appoint someone new rather than ask one of the deputies to take the reins for a term. I was all ready for him to do that.'

'So how did Geoff react to that?' I asked.

'Not as I expected. He said he had already gone back to the Governors and told them it would be no use them trying to persuade me to stay on because I had already made up my mind.'

'And had you? I mean, have you?'

'Almost. But I would have stayed on for another term, if it were for the good of the school and he and the Governors had asked me to. But as it is, I think they quite wanted to see how

Miles my Deputy would get on if he were temporarily in charge. I've already had to warn Miles unofficially about certain aspects of his behaviour but Geoff doesn't know that, so I fear for the school with Miles if he becomes Acting Head. But what's done is done now and I'm out of it.'

Danny's mother had moved into her own room in a Nursing Home in Bournemouth, with Danny paying the extra weekly costs. During this time, she died. It was not unexpected and Danny and I, with Danny's sister Irene, her husband Phil and their daughter, all went to the funeral.

As the hearse with the coffin drove slowly up the driveway to the crematorium, Irene muttered 'Oh, that's Mother in there' as if it had only just hit her that her mother was dead.

I pondered then, and again years after, on the wise words of Mrs MacGuire at Toftwood Middle School; and on what she had not added, about one's mother having instinctively provided protection to her child before birth and afterwards, sometimes at her own expense; about how and when those roles may become reversed, about the effect on sibling relationships of that loss of maternal love, physical and emotional protection, and about loss and death sometimes becoming the catalyst for establishing and affirming other reliable loving relationships.

Danny and I were due to spend one week in a well-known Bulgarian ski resort and another in a different part of Bulgaria.

Irene had given Danny a subscription to the RSPB as a retirement present, it was something he said he had always wanted. I knew he had always been particularly interested in birds, although Irene teased him by telling him 'Surely bird watching is something that only old people do.'

He said he was hoping to see a wallcreeper in Bulgaria and told me what to look out for on the rock face, that its wings were carmine red with black and white spots. But we didn't see one although Danny spent a long time in the right place, peering through his binoculars.

He looked quite sad and thoughtful.

I tried to cheer him up by suggesting a walk along the ridges of the Rhodope Mountains but in the end, I went alone with a guide, leaving Danny to read or watch other birds back at our hotel, or take another walk through the local village.

I had bought myself a new yellow bikini and I went swimming in the hotel's indoor pool. Danny didn't join me, he seemed withdrawn and quiet.

One night, he woke quite suddenly and sat up in the bright moonlight that flooded our bedroom.

'I'm sorry, my Darling,' he sleepily said, 'I am so sorry.'

'What's wrong?' I asked, waking up. 'What are you sorry about?'

There was silence for ten seconds, then 'I don't know,' he replied. 'It was only a dream.'

But a night or two later, he woke up suddenly again, saying out loud to someone or to himself, 'But that's just stupid. It's a stupid thing to do and I'm not doing it.'

'What is?' I asked, waking up. 'What is stupid?'

When he understood where he was, he explained.

'I dreamed I was being asked to drink some milk from a carton. But instead of opening the carton, I was told to swallow the carton whole. I told them, it was stupid, a stupid thing to ask me to do. Because I'll choke and then stop breathing.'

He was hot and sweaty.

'It's all right,' I said, trying to calm him, 'I love you and I'm here, so try to go back to sleep. I will deal with the carton of milk and with whoever is telling you to swallow it whole. And you're right, it is a really stupid thing for someone to tell you to do.'

In the morning, Danny could remember little about the previous night. But he was quiet, appeared withdrawn, didn't want to go with me in a cable car to ride through the tops of the dark pine trees to the summit of the nearest mountain.

He said he would prefer to stay quietly in the hotel. I noticed how often he would want to go to the gents' toilet which lay round a corner from the main lounge, next to the public phone booth. I watched him disappear, then reappear some ten minutes later.

I wondered about his general health, whether he had an upset stomach. But he said not.

I was concerned about Danny's depression. He looked unhappy, rootless, almost lost.

It was hard to get him to smile whereas previously, he had found fun and joy in so many things.

He had been the ideal travel companion, researching the places we should visit, places we should not miss, and passing on to me little bits of interesting information.

When we returned to England, I was sufficiently worried to contact his doctor by telephone, said I would like to talk with him because I was genuinely worried about the depression that Danny had told me that the doctor had diagnosed.

'Might be something else more sinister?' I wanted to ask.

Dr Thurston phoned me back when I was at work, and confirmed that Danny did appear to be suffering from depression.

I didn't tell Danny that I had phoned his doctor, he would have considered that a huge intrusion into his privacy, but I did ask him whether he would be getting private treatment through his health insurance.

I had even asked the doctor what the treatment might be. I was told that normally, both husband and wife would attend if private treatment for depression were offered.

There was some suggestion of Danny having counselling but he dismissed the whole idea, saying 'I don't see what good just talking about something can do, in fact it might even make it worse.'

I have no idea whether he ever went to see someone for counselling.

If he did, he wouldn't have told me anyway, he would have considered that to be too invasive, a loss of his authority, an intrusion into his privacy, a questioning of his ability to deal with matters himself.

But he did tell me that he had been prescribed a course of 'Seroxat' tablets and I saw the pack myself, with his name on.

He told me that he had been warned that taking them could cause changes in his mood, but also that he had fears about self-harming.

On one occasion when he was looking completely black and I asked him what was wrong, he said 'I just don't want to be here any more.'

I checked on the side effects of 'Seroxat' and read that the tablets worked 'by relieving the symptoms of depression and any associated anxiety in the brain. These tablets are not addictive. This medicine works by bringing the levels of serotonin in your brain back to normal' and 'You should take extra care when you are driving or operating machinery'.

During our house-conversion time, my scatty but much-loved dog Muffin died.

He developed some sort of brain tumour that caused him to walk into walls or bump into furniture. It was slightly amusing until I realised he had a serious health problem.

Then it became decision time, before he did some irreversible damage to himself or anyone else. He was suffering.

I took him to the vet and had him put down. Muffin had been a good friend but I knew I was doing the right thing, making that horrible call that sometimes any pet owner has to make.

I didn't cry, I just felt empty and almost lonely.

I wanted to come home from work and be immediately greeted by a wagging tail and a lolling tongue and the unconditional love that a dog can offer.

Danny was lovely during this time. He seemed to understand and perhaps also share my sense of loss.

He found a springer spaniel breeder living on a farm near Coventry and made an arrangement to go there to look at her latest litter of puppies.

'I don't want one with its tail docked,' I said, 'because I don't think docking a dog's tail is natural and it isn't necessary for a non-working dog. My next puppy is going to be an obedient friend and a family pet rather than help set game birds up into the air for someone to shoot, and probably not even eat afterwards.'

Danny agreed with this, he and I held similar values and principles so we agreed over most things.

About a week later, he told me 'I've contacted the springer spaniel breeder who has puppies for sale. They don't have their tails docked so I've arranged to go to see one tomorrow.'

I don't know why I didn't go with him; I expect I was busy or at work.

He came home that night, he was tired, it had been a long drive there and back to Coventry and he came almost straight to bed. In the morning he said 'I've something to show you. Come and see.'

He had taken the video camera with him and had taken a video of the puppies, focussing on one in particular.

'I especially liked this one,' he said. 'It seemed to have more go about it than the others. At the moment, its name is 'Winston' but the breeder said we could change that if we bought him and once we started training him. What do you think? Does he look right to you?'

Danny collected 'Winston' as soon as it was eight weeks old and ready to leave its mother. Without too much discussion, we settled on calling it 'Chaucer' because he had a magnificent long fluffy tail, and I liked how its proposed name was maintaining my connection to Canterbury and English literature.

Danny was good at teaching him to go out through the dog flap in the kitchen wall to relieve himself and very soon Chaucer was house-trained.

Danny offered to take him out each night on a lead 'just around the block' and Chaucer seemed to settle very well with us and with Kwai, our Burmese cat. We also had Romany, a cat that had come from the Roundwell Gypsy site that we had acquired to celebrate Nell's successful five GCSEs.

We had been going to call it 'Fiver', but 'Romany' suited it better. Unfortunately, it had a miserable disposition and didn't purr or enjoy anyone's company.

It didn't think much of Kwai and Chaucer either.

Danny was accustomed to hanging his coat up in a cupboard in the kitchen or, if he were planning to go out again, over the knob at the bottom of the stairs. For some reason I was cold one evening and I slipped his coat on while I went outside to fetch some wood for the fire.

Without thinking, I slid both my hands into his coat pockets to keep them warm.

In the left-hand pocket I felt something hard.

Thinking Danny had left his car keys there and forgotten, I pulled out the hard object.

It was a key, but not car keys. It was a key I had never seen before.

I wondered if the key I had seen was the key to a shop in the town that Danny might have taken on, it was the sort of thing he might do as a project, and only tell me afterwards.

I encouraged him to take regular exercise, continue to walk Chaucer as far as the post office and through the park to get back home again.

'Or swimming,' I suggested. 'That might help, it would be good for you – if you would like that, of course.'

'I think I will go swimming,' Danny told me, a couple of Sundays later. 'I've looked out my swimming trunks but I'm not sure which towel to use. I could take my bath towel but I'd rather not use that.'

From before the children were little, I had assigned different coloured bathroom towels to each person, a reflection of my mother's drive for personal hygiene. Keir's had been dark red, mine were cream and Danny's brown.

'Take my swimming towel,' I suggested. 'It's a bit harsh because it's often been dried in the sun but perhaps it will do for today.'

I went off to work in my car, leaving Danny to lock up.

As I came home by the back route, I saw no cars parked outside Earlham School. But when I came through the kitchen and into the sitting room, my multi-coloured beach towel was stretched out to dry along the hall radiator, with Danny's swimming trunks beside it.

'I decided not to go swimming in Wymondham,' he said. 'I wanted to avoid bumping into anyone I knew, so I went down to Diss Leisure Centre instead. It's quite a nice pool there.'

He was sitting by the bay window on the Number 16 side of the house, still looking gloomy. 'What's wrong, Danny?' I asked. 'Even after a swim, you still look so unhappy.'

He nodded in agreement, then said 'But I can't tell you' with slight emphasis on 'you'.

'I appreciate that you consider counselling to be a waste of time,' I said 'but talking to someone might help. Would you even consider talking to someone, someone you trust who wouldn't be judgemental? Because at the moment, you look as if you're having an affair or something but if so, it isn't making you very happy.'

I left it at that, to give Danny time to think about counselling or talking to a friend.

But I was worried, he had talked about self-harm, had told me that he and his doctor had mentioned that as being a danger or a possibility.

The only time that I ever lied to Danny came the next day. He had been drinking at home, not excessively, only a glass or two of sherry but sufficient that I thought it unwise for him to drive, in case he had an accident or got caught by the police.

I knew he valued his reputation as a respectable law-abiding citizen just as much as his regular use of a car and at a time when he was already feeling low, a fine or headlines in the local press would only do him harm.

When he said, quite suddenly, 'I think I'll go out, I need some fresh air so I'll drive around for a bit,' and went upstairs to fetch something, I took his car keys that he had in a small leather pouch, went outside with them and dropped them behind the wood pile in the back yard.

Then 'I can't find my car keys,' Danny said in annoyance, 'they aren't where I left them in the kitchen. Have you seen them anywhere?'

'No,' I replied, hoping to sound convincing, 'whereabouts did you leave them?'

Then, compounding my untruthfulness, 'Well, Chaucer was sniffing around in the kitchen earlier. I suppose, if they were in the leather pouch, he might have picked that up thinking it was part of his lead or something to chew.' I continued the dissimulation, 'I'll look in his basket or outside.'

I can't remember when I 'found' the keys but I suspect it was several hours later as I was collecting wood for our open fire from the wood pile outside, that I 'remembered having seen' Chaucer jumping on the wood, had thought to look behind where I had seen him and 'goodness me, look what I've found,' I said to Danny while thinking that it would be a miracle if he believed me - and that it mattered neither way whether he did or not, 'losing' his keys had prevented him from doing something rash that he might have regretted.

I apologised quietly to Chaucer afterwards.

Danny's friend Paul suggested that we might have a meal with him and his wife Carole, whom I had known at Toftwood Middle, in a local public house called 'The Wildebeest' in Stoke Holy Cross. It was a good meal and the pub atmosphere was convivial. The tables were oak with solid wooden bench seats on either side.

We sat, discussing life in general, the Local Authority in particular, and current events.

Mentioning events in America, Paul talked about the inappropriate relationship that President Bill Clinton was reported to have been having that year with Monica Lewinsky, a former White House intern, and the political fallout.

Paul was saying 'I think it's a lot of fuss over nothing. Clinton's private life is nothing at all to do with his ability to be President.'

'I disagree', I said. 'How can the American people trust someone who can't be loyal to his wife and who then chooses to lie about it? As far as I can see, that's totally destroyed all credibility he had. Even if he wanted to stand again, he wouldn't get re-elected with that as a track record.'

The conversation moved on then, to discussing the food and current changes within Norfolk schools and the County Council, and Danny's reputation as having been a good reliable Head, a 'safe pair of hands', Paul said and considered to be an overall 'OK guy'.

Danny excused himself for a few minutes and went off in the direction of the pub lavatories.

I took the opportunity to thank Paul and Carole for inviting us for a meal because, as I said to Paul 'Danny has been very low since he retired. Does he seem all right to you?'

Paul said he hadn't noticed any change, and at that point, Danny returned to the table.

I was still worried about the possibility of self-harm, of suicide and thought I ought to keep an eye on Danny in case he attempted to do something that he and others around him might later regret.

Not long after this, Danny told me 'I've had a phone call. From Miss S., who is still teaching English at Earlham. She and one of my other senior staff would like to meet with me. Apparently, they think the school is going to pieces with Miles the Deputy in charge and they want my advice.'

He was gone for several hours. I knew Miss S. had been looking at properties nearer to Earlham and had moved, before Danny retired, into a rented flat near Park Farm in Hethersett.

She had asked his opinion more than once about buying accommodation and from what he had told me, he had been to look at one or two houses with her. I had told him at the time 'That was kind of you, it does no harm to have someone else looking at houses or flats at the same time, because they might spot something or ask questions that you haven't thought of.'

Sometime afterwards, Danny told me that this member of staff had found somewhere that she was hoping to buy, not far from Park Farm so she could still go swimming at the Leisure Centre there.

He didn't say exactly where it was and I didn't ask.

I was coming back from my base in Turner Road one weekend when driving past Earlham School, I saw Danny's staff member Miss S. coming out of the school drive in her red car about a hundred metres in front of me.

She and I were clearly going in the same direction, and taking the same turning.

As we came to the main road and had to wait for traffic, she is able to pull out before I could, and then turned left after a mile or so.

I noticed which road she had turned her car into but I went straight on; I had planned to have a quick swim at Park Farm before going home.

Returning home from work a week later, I don't know why but I took a completely different route home from Norwich, through Mulbarton and hoping, on my way back home, to stop *en route* for a swim.

Aiming to reach the main road again near Hethersett, as I slowed near a corner, looking both ways to see that the road was clear, I came past a chalet bungalow and saw Danny's white Nissan parked outside.

At that very moment, just rounding a corner from a different direction, Miss S's red car came nose-to-nose with mine.

We both saw each other and she knew that I must have seen Danny's car there, parked at what I assumed must be her house.

Realisation dawned.

I shouted aloud to myself 'No, no, no' and pulled into a driveway, then into the Park Farm entrance not to swim, but to think.

Both slowly and suddenly, everything slipped into place. I don't know for how long I sat there in my car, thinking. Wondering what to do next, knowing that sooner or later both Danny and I would have to face something that was looking very unpleasant and difficult to deal with, sensibly.

When I reached home, Danny's car was back in the garage. Danny was sitting on the settee looking thoughtful and gloomy. He must have heard my car arriving, the back door opening, then closing.

I confronted him with 'You're having an affair.'

He didn't seem to know what to say, I don't remember whether he stood up and went upstairs, or what happened next.

There was no verbal explosion, nothing sudden, just a chilly silence from each of us as, I suppose, we each gathered our thoughts and protected our feelings.

Regarding what to do next, I had only one role model to go on and that was Doreen's.

At the very time when I wanted to shrink, I knew I had to face something I feared and to do so quickly, before I had time to change my mind.

Still wearing my dark green anorak, the same colour and style that Danny had for his Berghaus waterproof, I drove straight to Miss S.'s house, parked the car and rang the bell. She must have seen my shape and the colour of my clothes through the glass of her front door because she opened it before looking and said 'Well, this is a surprise. I thought . . .' and then realised it was me.

'I think we need to talk' I said, and stepped inside her house.

She was drinking what might have been brandy in a glass and smoking a cigarette.

I didn't realise she smoked and I wondered whether Danny knew that - he disapproved totally of smoking – or whether she smoked only when under considerable stress.

I knew I had to take charge of this conversation, the one that neither Miss S. nor I wanted to have, but I needed to do it, I needed to know where I stood.

She asked me to sit down and I did, while she sat crouched near the hearth in her living room with her arms folded around her knees.

I don't remember much of the conversation, except that she said 'I am in love with Danny' and I replied 'I can understand that, he's a very nice person.'

I explained that he had been prescribed medication for depression and she commented only that 'he seems very happy when he comes to see me.'

Echoing the words of Mandy Rice-Davies[xii], I responded with 'Well, he would, wouldn't he? He's not going to come to see you when he feels depressed or down in the dumps.'

I told her that according to the doctor and the side effects of Seroxat, Danny was in danger of harming himself. I don't think she took that in and I was certain that Danny hadn't told her that.

She said something such as 'I told him it was Earlham he was missing but he said, 'No, it's you, it's you.'

'It's Earlham,' I said, perhaps rather unkindly, 'it's not about you at all. He's lost his status, his position in the community, his whole identity.'

'But he can't just stop seeing me,' she almost wailed, 'I won't let him.'

Big mistake, I thought, you can't tell Danny what he may or may not do, he'll decide that for himself but he needs time to sort himself out first.

'No, he can't,' I replied 'because he can't suddenly break off a relationship like this. It will take time to phase itself out.'

While I was there in her house, the phone rang. Miss S. picked it up.

I assumed, from what she said into the receiver, that it was Danny calling to tell her what? . . That I had returned home but left again soon afterwards, driven off to . ? That I knew?

'It's all right,' she said to her caller, 'she's with me now.'

I had invited Keir and Lucy for a meal at our house that evening. I had prepared monkfish with steamed vegetables which had been what I had chosen to eat at a restaurant on one of my first dates with Danny, when I was sitting opposite him and he had spent time stretching his legs under the table to put his toes up my skirt.

But on this particular family occasion with Keir, I couldn't eat, I couldn't swallow properly, my throat wouldn't open. I had to leave most of my meal and put it in the bin.

I felt I was letting Keir down by not explaining what was wrong but to have done so, to have explained, would have been disloyal to Danny and shown him in a bad light.

After the meal, we said our goodbyes to Keir and Lucy at the front door. Then came the 'what do we do next' question.

I thought I had better take the lead again, because Danny seemed very unsure what to do.

'We must both be feeling very tired,' I suggested, 'you especially because, one way or another, you've had quite a difficult day. I suggest we go upstairs very soon after I've settled Chaucer, and that you curl up in Mark's double bed in his room and try to get some rest. Then in the morning, I'll bring you a cup of tea and we can talk much later, if you want to, when you feel ready.'

I remember Danny saying, 'Good God, you're strong.' What did he expect, I wondered? That I'd throw him out, pack a case for him as Doreen had for Richard?

No, if he was going to leave and move in with Miss S., then it wouldn't be with my help, he wouldn't be able to tell other people 'My wife threw me out and I had nowhere to go, until that kind member of staff, Miss S, took me in', as if he were a stray cat or dog standing outside in the rain.

I was terribly hurt but I wasn't stupid. I needed to think as clearly as I could, and leave my emotional side out of the matter for the moment.

Moo's training came to the fore. 'Don't react because it probably won't help and it might even do more harm.'

I went to bed in our bedroom as usual and although I was turning things over and over in my mind, I knew the best thing I could do at that time would be to get some sleep.

Taking Danny his tea in the morning and bringing his towel with me, I suggested he might like to use the shower in Mark's en-suite.

Then, when he was ready, 'I'm here to listen and to talk, if you would like to do that,' I offered.

About a week later, after Danny had told me 'I won't see her again,' and while Danny was out bird-watching, I went to see Miss S. once more at her home, to impress upon her the seriousness of Danny's mental condition. She didn't seem to believe that Danny was on anti-depressants so I showed her the dated Seroxat packet with Danny's name and address on, and warned her about the possibility of Danny harming himself. She didn't seem to realise what mental turmoil he might be going through, only to assure me 'We didn't talk about you at all.'

Why would they, I wondered? Why would she think that was what might bother me?

'Mostly we talked about books, poetry, the things we had read,' and later, after I had mentioned that Danny and I still slept together 'But we always used a condom when he was . . we . .,' she told me.

As I told Danny a few days later after he knew I had been to see Miss S. again, 'So why would she tell me that you always used a condom if she didn't expect you to be back making love to me again? Why would she think that mattered to me?'

And then, 'You and I both know that you may say you won't see her again and even intend to keep to that. But usually, when someone says the 'affair is over', it isn't, not entirely. And one party or the other makes every attempt not to let the other person go. So, whereas I believe what you say and I believe that you believe it right now, I also believe that Miss S. will make sure you feel in some way under some moral obligation to see her again.'

Unfortunately, I was right. I had to behave rather sneakily but I needed to know.

In the boot of his car was a book that I knew was a set book for the examination that year so I assumed that Miss S. had accompanied Danny somewhere and while he was either birdwatching or taking Chaucer for training in Poringland, she had stayed in his car and read.

When he had visited the BUPA hospital for some minor surgery to remove lipomas on his arm, he had been most insistent that I shouldn't visit him there or collect him from the hospital. I guessed that Miss S had already arranged to meet him, to offer him sympathy and comfort.

I decided to let that go, that she or he could come to little harm in a BUPA hospital waiting room and it was no place to have a stand-up snarling match between two women.

Over a month later, Danny needed minor surgery on a growth near his mouth. Again, this was to be done privately at the local private hospital. I offered to collect him after whatever anaesthetic he might be due to have but he was most insistent that I shouldn't, that he would come home on his own.

I didn't take this as personal rejection, only that he was afraid of a meeting at the hospital between myself and Miss S. and of what each of us might tell the other.

I had warned, even before we were married, 'If you ever have an affair, Danny, then you are out on your ear, on principle. My husband having an affair isn't something I would tolerate, I tried doing that with Richard and it didn't work.' But despite my principles on the matter, I realised I didn't want Danny to leave.

I wanted him to put an end to the affair but not to leave, I loved him too much. I told him this.

'I will end it,' he assured me, 'I have already ended it. But you are going to have to trust me on this.'

'That will be hard,' I said 'but I will try. I will try to trust you but I don't for one minute trust Miss S. I think she will do everything she can to make life difficult for you if you stay with me. And you may find that difficult too.'

Danny signed up for Adult Education bird-watching evening classes at Wensum Lodge and also, I later discovered, for massage classes. Massage classes and Danny seemed such an unlikely combination, it made me giggle. There had to be an ulterior motive, or pressure or coercion from Miss S. So, I signed up for similar massage classes for myself during the afternoon so that I could be one step ahead on technique and massage oils. I even persuaded Keir to let me practise on his back.

Quite soon Danny stopped attending the classes for massage, he said 'They aren't quite what I thought they would be, I can't see when I would use the skills I was being taught.'

'A wise decision,' I replied and left it at that.

He was still attending the bird-watching classes. I had my doubts that that was where he was each week, or at least for the whole two hours of the lessons. I wondered whether he would stay until coffee time, then meet Miss S. somewhere until he was due to be back home. One week I decided to check.

Taking Danny's spare car keys with me, I drove to Wensum Lodge and circled round the car park. I felt very sneaky. But to my dismay, there was no sign of Danny's car there, although there were spare spaces. So where was he? He wouldn't risk parking outside Miss S.'s house, his car would have been too easily spotted there.

I was just coming back up Music House Lane when, to my left, I saw Danny's car parked alongside the kerb in Rouen Road. I drew up in front of it, got out and used Danny's spare keys to open the boot. I wanted to know what he was keeping there, whether there was, as there had been previously, evidence that he had been meeting Miss S again after he had promised not to do so.

There were no set books this time, only Danny's sports bag in which he kept his binoculars, his Thinsulate beanie hat, several bird identification books, a small telescope, and the dark green woollen gloves I had bought because he had complained of having cold hands and I had given to him quite recently.

But right at the back of the boot was a box, a box of chocolates, a big box of Thornton's white chocolates, the sort that Danny would never have bought for himself, the sort that might be intended as a present. I didn't for one moment think they were meant for me, I assumed they had been given to Danny. Given, I guessed, by Miss S. after Danny had had the minor surgery on his mouth.

But if that were so, how was he going to eat so many chocolates on his own, I wondered? Or were they for the two of them to scoff together? No, I decided they were a present from Miss S. and he was now stuck with it.

I would watch and see how he handled the situation, whether he made himself sick with chocolates - which would serve him right - or ate one each day.

Putting everything back exactly as I had found it, I closed the boot of Danny's car, locked it and climbed into my own and started to drive away . . . but something was niggling at the back of my mind.

I wasn't sure whether I had reset Danny's car alarm.

I didn't remember turning the alarm off when I had opened the boot. Had he actually set it himself or had he left the car not-alarmed? Surely not, parked on a public street?

I drove back and parked again in front of Danny's car. I spent almost ten minutes in indecision, wondering whether to set the alarm, whether Danny had left it unset, what to do if a policeman came and saw me fiddling with a car that wasn't mine, delving into the boot, playing about with locking and unlocking, setting and un-setting the alarm.

I began to laugh aloud at myself, what a poor detective I was if I couldn't remember whether an alarm was on or off. Finally, before Danny was due to emerged from his class, I decided that the best thing would be to set the alarm, drive quickly back home before Danny realised that I had been out for much of the evening.

I felt amused by my own lack of skills while also wondering what to do, if anything, about a large box of chocolates in the boot of a car that wasn't mine.

Despite his assurances that he had 'finished' with Miss S., I had a very strong feeling that he hadn't, or that Miss S. hadn't accepted that the affair was over. Apart from the box of chocolates, I thought it more than likely that 'finished' and 'over' were words that Danny might say but either didn't mean or couldn't stick to.

He was normally a man of his word, a man that people would rely on. I considered that if there were further involvement, it would be because Miss S. wasn't prepared to let go, that she would have insisted that he maintained or upheld some sort of commitment that he had made to her.

On one occasion, I was outside Miss S's house and I called 'I know you're in there, Danny.'

I wanted to throw stones through her windows or set fire through her letter box but common sense got the better of that. It would be stupid. Common sense told me that if I did any of that, however much I felt like it and it would break the tension I felt inside my body, then they would call the police and I would no longer have the moral high ground.

I also considered harming myself on the railway track so that then, whenever they heard a train rushing past when they were snuggled in bed together, they would remember me and what their behaviour had led me to do.

But then I thought of my three children, and I didn't think they would be happy living with either Danny and Miss S, or going to live with Richard and Jayne's two children.

I was silently angry with her, not for the affair itself although that was bad enough, but because she had been prepared to let Danny throw away the excellent reputation that he had built up for himself, both professional and personal, while being in Norfolk.

She would not, I imagined, have seen it as such. She would have seen their being together as a case of 'don't they make a lovely couple, so well matched with their joint interests in literature and shared backgrounds by having lived in parts of Africa.'

At a Heads' and Partners' dinner, I had heard several of her colleagues, teachers in positions of responsibility, describe her as 'a complete non-entity.' I was pleased to hear that and wondered whether Danny saw her in that way too, or whether he thought she just 'hadn't yet reached her potential', to use an expression so often used in school reports of those whose results proved disappointing.

I considered her an unprincipled opportunist and potentially predatory. This may have been harsh, but it was what I thought and felt.

On some occasion when Danny was at home, I decided to tell him 'Despite my principles, I want you to stay with me because I still love and respect you tremendously. If you decide to leave and divorce me and team up with Miss S., then I genuinely hope you will be happy although I think it unlikely, for long. If you do leave me, I intend to keep your surname rather than revert to my former one, because it is as important to me as you are. But I am not prepared to be an occasional wife and partner or to share you with Miss S.

What you decide to do from now on, is up to you.'

This was not any game-playing on my part. I knew what I felt and what I needed now was peace of mind rather than the limbo, mental turmoil and domestic uncertainty in which I found myself. I needed to hold my nerve and think before reacting emotionally, to see what Danny and Miss S. would do next.

There were a few other seemingly-isolated things about that time that related to Danny's affair with Miss S.

On one occasion I made some reference to the fact that it would be almost heartless of him to stop seeing her completely, even though she knew he was married. and he replied, almost dismissively, 'Well, she knew the score.'

On another, he told me 'Whatever happens next, I will continue to pay the mortgage.'

For some reason which didn't seem to me to be financial, Danny decided to offer his services for supply teaching.

On one occasion, he told me, he was offered a Reception class in a small school on the other side of the county. On his way back to Wymondham, he told me that he would call into the Little Chef restaurant on the A11 dual carriageway, just before taking the turning back to the town. I knew there was a public phone box there, so I decided to go there myself on some pretext and to wait for him.

He arrived as I expected, but on seeing me, he decided 'Perhaps I'm not as hungry as I thought, I'll wait until I get home.'

On another trip away, either for bird-watching or supply teaching, he told me that he might call into a Little Chef before he reached home that evening. I thought that that might most likely be a time when he would meet with Miss S., so I decided to opt for the Little Chef near the Thickthorn roundabout on the A11.

I drove there, parked my car out of direct sight beside the petrol station, and went on foot as far as the entrance to the Little Chef café.

I looked careful in through the window. There was no sign of him in the café - but his car was parked outside. After allowing time for him to have been in the loo, I walked back to my car and sat there, in the dark, waiting.

He had to be coming back to his car somehow, I thought, and from somewhere.

Within half an hour or so, Miss S's car drove up alongside Danny's and out stepped Danny. He walked in front of her car bonnet to wish her or kiss her good night through the driver's window. I thought that that was enough.

I got out of my car, called out 'Danny, I'm here.' He looked at me, turned to say a few words to Miss S., then walked across to my car and got into the front passenger seat.

'I'm not going to leave you,' he said, 'I've told her.'

I felt very relieved but that was when I realised there are two types of truth: there is truth for now, and truth for all time, and I wasn't sure which truth 'I'm not going to leave you' was from Danny.

Some weeks later, I found he was phoning Miss S. again from the public phone box outside the main Post Office. I asked him why.

'She needs my help,' he explained. 'She's doing an NPQH course, the National Professional Qualification for Headship. I said I would help her.'

'Fine' I said, while thinking it was far from 'fine'. 'But that should be the last time you get in touch.'

When Miss S's request for Danny's help occurred again and he told me about it, my response was 'But surely, if she's good enough for headship, she ought to be doing this alone without anyone else's help. Or is she really not up to it and can't prove she has the required leadership skills without having you at her elbow? Other people will be completing the course without your help, so why can't she?'

He seemed to take the point. Or to see that he was being used for someone else's potential benefit.

We started to try to rebuild trust and belief in each other. I have no doubt that Danny felt very ashamed of himself, of his behaviour although he didn't say so. I did on two occasions ask him why he had had the affair with Miss S.

On the first occasion, he was standing in the kitchen of The Yeoman's House. His answer was 'I thought I was in love with her.'

'And are you?' I asked, then modified it to 'And are you still?'

'No,' he replied, 'I thought I was, but I'm not.'

The other occasion was some nine months later, after our life together had begun to settle down. We were walking beside a railway line near Exmouth, having been to visit my father, and were on a bird-watching visit to a marsh. We saw what we each thought was a sparrowhawk sitting on a branch of a tree and after some doubt in identifying it,

'Can I ask you a question?' I asked.

He nodded, still gazing towards the sparrowhawk.

'Why did all that stuff with Miss S. start?'

'I don't know,' he said, 'I really don't know.'

I decide to leave it at that, not to offer him possible reasons that he might cling on to such as 'perhaps because you were depressed?' or 'was it because you had lost your identity?' or even 'Did I do something wrong?'

I left him to look up a picture of the sparrowhawk in the RSPB book and we walked on from there, side by side across the marsh, pointing out the best path to take and jumping over drainage ditches.

The last of his supply teaching was for a term at a secondary school in Suffolk, where he taught English. I watched him grow in self-confidence and gain the respect and confidence of the Head and other teachers in the department.

At the end of the term, he wondered what to give the English department staff as a leaving present. I suggested taking something that they might all enjoy.

'Depending on how many of them there are, how about taking a bottle or two of wine, something they could all share. And perhaps get hold of a really nice big box of Thornton's chocolates, something special? That should solve any problem.'

Chapter 21
Wildlife

Danny continued to pursue his interest in bird-watching. I frequently wondered whether he was spending the whole time with the group at Holkham or Titchwell or Minsmere, or whether he would sneak off somewhere to meet Miss S. - but from the various phone calls and emails from the group leader that I knew about, it seemed unlikely.

Sometimes I would go with Danny to the places he had visited the previous fortnight, to see whether we could see a lesser-spotted whatnot on a different occasion, especially if the sighting had been poor during the previous visit.

He had heard that there were some interesting birds to be seen in the Picos area of Spain, birds with names that sounded almost fictitious to me, such as griffon vultures, lammergeiers, bee eaters, thekla larks, alpine choughs, red shrikes and black redstarts.

We travelled there by car and ferry, staying in small selected bed and breakfast places in the areas that Danny wanted to visit, and eating out every evening.

I enjoyed gaining the ornithological knowledge that he was able to pass on to me and very occasionally, I might be the first one to see something in the hedge or on a rock, point and say, 'Look Danny, over there on the top branch.'

Then I would glow with pleasure when he said 'Oh, well-spotted,' or commented on my sharp eyesight, despite my need for contact lenses, with spectacles on top if I were reading.

On one occasion as Danny was driving across the Zaragoza Plain towards our next stop, I had a sudden panic attack. I imagine I must have been looking out of the car window while thinking about Danny's affair with Miss S., when suddenly I had an urge to open the passenger door, hurl myself out and get right away.

I didn't say anything at the time but I broke into a hot sweat and needed to grip tightly onto the sides of my seat, hoping the feeling would pass and I could calm down again.

Other than that occasion, I tried hard to put the matter out of my mind, while remaining alert for Danny's behaviour to become in anyway unusual or out of the ordinary. I knew that we were both trying to build and maintain trust, and to stay away from subjects that we thought might prove sensitive for either of us.

We laughed a lot together at anything that amused us, and shared problems such as when Danny got locked in a restaurant toilet and couldn't get himself out, or when his little red Citroen car developed a problem with a gasket, causing the engine to overheat and needing us to stop frequently to allow the engine to cool down.

Neither of us was prone to becoming irritable; we each took a philosophical approach to problems, especially if they were ones we couldn't easily solve.

Neither of us spoke any Spanish but when it came to needing to ask for something, to order something in a restaurant or check into our accommodation, Danny would usually let me take the lead to use my French.

Both of us had a reasonable knowledge of French but mine was probably more current than his and with him taking the lead on bird identification and driving, and me on our planned accommodation and shops or restaurants, we seemed to make a good team.

In October 1998, my first husband Richard celebrated his sixtieth birthday. He and Jayne invited a number of friends. I don't know whether his first three children had been invited or whether they chose to attend. If they did, they didn't stay with me in Wymondham.

Nell, Keir and Lallo were also invited but I'm not sure if all three of them went.

Someone reported to me that Richard wasn't looking very well at his party although I had heard that he and Jayne had been to the South of France that summer.

I also heard that he had had a kidney transplant not long before travelling abroad, but I either didn't know or didn't take it in that he had P.K.D., polycystic kidney disease; I had written him out of my life.

It was, then, a shock to hear that later that month, Richard died.

Apparently, he had been on dialysis for some months before receiving his kidney transplant and the dialysis had weakened his heart. He had been waiting in the car outside Sainsbury's while Jayne was inside shopping, had suffered a heart attack and died almost as he reached the hospital.

Despite not being a relative, Jayne registered his death and collected his death certificate so I did not have the details.

Along with our three children, I was invited to the funeral which took place at St Peter Mancroft Church in Norwich, the same church that Richard and I had attended each week when we had first arrived in Norfolk and lived in the flat in St Giles Street.

I found it a strange funeral. Ruth, Doreen's elder daughter was there as also was his son Matt, I think. I don't remember if Lizzie came but I suspect she didn't. She would have been very tearful and I'm sure I would have remembered that. Whenever she and Ruth had come to stay with us in the cottage and they had had to return to Doreen on the train, Lizzie had always been very tearful at having to leave us.

Jayne, James and Rebecca were side by side in the front pew with the rest of us seated in rows behind. Rebecca read something, and Jayne had asked Nell to write and read something about her memories of her father. Afterwards, Ruth told me that from what Nell had written, she didn't recognise her father at all, the person Nell had described didn't fit with Ruth's knowledge and memory of him.

As the coffin was brought into the church and borne towards the altar, Jayne rose to her feet. Quite slowly and deliberately, she removed the hip-length fur coat she had been wearing . . . to reveal she was dressed only in a dark brown basque. She was carrying a pair of Richard's old leather sandals which she then placed, almost reverently as if they were a final floral tribute, onto the lid of the coffin.

To me, this final tribute had all the decorum of a rehearsed strip tease. Or a farce.

Although I had asked Danny whether he would come with me to my late husband's funeral, he said 'I think it isn't really appropriate so I'll stay at home.' I was glad he had, although I could have done with the support. He had already told me 'I'm not good at coping with tears and a lot of emotional stuff. I suspect Nell will become quite emotional.'

I suppose he assumed I would have no emotional reaction at all. He would have been correct. I felt no sense of loss at the time: I had experienced all those years before.

My purpose in being there was to support our children and any of Richard's other children. Danny would have been totally out of place, I thought afterwards, and bemused, shocked or bewildered by the sight of the basque.

The sandals too, probably.

I did not know exactly where the Norwich Cemetery was, nor the main entrance in Rosary Road, so I approached it from a side road and went through a side gate. I could see where people had gathered.

Richard's coffin was lowered into the freshly dug hole. We were asked to sprinkle a handful of earth onto the coffin.

As we prepared to do so, Ruth, looking sadly down at her father's coffin with soil in her hand, whispered to me 'Silly old Sod.' Barney, one of Richard's male friends from his 'Grassroot Computers' days, turned to me and in recognition said, 'Oh, I didn't think <u>you'd</u> be here' with the emphasis on 'you'd'.

'Why wouldn't I be here' I responded rather than asked and Barney said no more. Perhaps he had forgotten that I had been Richard's wife and that Richard and I had three children of our own.

Jayne had also invited me to the Wake, which I found a surprise and kind of her.

It was held at the Cumberland Hotel, almost opposite the house where she and Richard had lived in Thorpe Road. The Wake was a surreal occasion for me, partly perhaps because the only time I had been to the Cumberland Hotel previously had been for a meal with Ralph.

There were various nibbles and titbits, Jayne's husband Jeff was there with James and Rebecca. He recognised me although I didn't recognise him until afterwards, I suspect we had both changed since the days of being parents at King's Park Infant School.

Either Rebecca or James read something from T.S. Eliot's 'Old Possum's Book of Practical Cats'.

I didn't feel I belonged, although it was good to see Richard's other children and to talk with them as well as with my three, who were in their own personal stages of grieving. I left for home.

Returning to the cemetery only a few days later, I planted three crocus bulbs by Richard's name on the grave site, one corm for each of our very able and much-loved children.

Late that December, I received notification that a friend's funeral was to be held on the 29th, the same day as Danny's birthday.

I had known Jock for several years in various capacities. He was the father of a girl in Nell's year at Wymondham College, she and Nell knew each other but weren't close friends. I had come to know Jock through a friend in the village who, like Jock, had been a supporter of the 'Compassion in World Farming' organisation.

Jock had had a small holding in Southburgh near Dereham and after his first wife had left him and between Richard's leaving and my meeting Danny, I got to know him better.

During one harvest, I had helped him to stack the bales of straw that his baler created and ejected. The string cut into the skin on my hands as I lifted each bale but it had been fun, working together outside in one of Jock's fields and after we had finished, returning indoors to the farm house to enjoy the roast lamb that Jock had cooked, a lamb that he had also raised and had had humanely slaughtered.

I had departed early the following morning, leaving Jock to milk his few cows on his own. We treated each other cautiously but he and I got on well together, we seemed to have similar interests and attitudes. Jock used to supply various delicatessen shops with soured cream and cuts of meat; Moo had also bought some lamb and pork direct from him for the freezer. Jock had sent me flowers when he heard that Moo had died, with a note which read 'I hope these will help brighten your day.'

I had liked Jock. He was a gentleman who knew how things ought to be done, which was probably why Moo took to him so well and who stuck, as far as I was aware, to his upbringing and his principles. He had moved in social and farming circles very different from mine but there was a common understanding of how things were and ought to be.

Apparently, he had been related to Rab Butler and had been very cut up when Lord Mountbatten was assassinated in August 1979 by a bomb, planted in his own boat during the Irish troubles.

Leaving Danny at home and explaining that I needed to go to the funeral of an old friend only slightly older than I, I made my way to St Andrew Church in Southburgh and joined the rest of the mourners. There was no one there whom I knew well. Jock's previous girlfriend Janet wasn't there and I don't remember whether his first wife Christabel and their daughter attended. From the address given by the vicar, I assumed that Jock had remarried or had been hoping to do so.

The vicar had obviously known Jock well or had been well briefed, because he referred to Jock seeking female companionship after his first marriage ended and mentioned in his obituary that, in his search for a soul mate, Jock had 'pursued various different avenues'.

From my place in the pew, I smiled at that. I have been called many things during my life but I never regarded myself as an 'avenue' for Jock or anyone else, more of a bridle path, a side track or even a cul-de-sac. Jock had helped me over a couple of difficult times in my life but never overstepping the mark.

I felt a strong urge to say a mental 'goodbye' and a private 'thank you' to him at the graveside. Our relationship had been an uncomplicated friendship, caring but undemanding, it had been as much as either of us could handle at the time.

Jock had made it clear that he wished to avoid any emotional involvement, not so much for his own protection but for the sake of his daughter. 'I don't want her to have to make relationships with the different women in my life, for her to get used to one woman brushing her hair each morning, only to find that that relationship gets broken off for no fault of her own, and she has to start all over again with somebody new.'

Each year, Danny and I continued to travel as often and as widely as we could, almost as a secondary way of rebuilding trust between us, as well as furthering our joint interests in bird-watching, wildlife in general and for me, ancient history.

I don't remember him ever offering to fund these travels for both of us, but I made sure I paid my way, it was important to me to do so and I felt that my being self-funding for any holiday or visit abroad, was some sort of statement: that I had stayed with Danny because I wanted to, not because I couldn't afford not to or because I experienced any financial gain.

Danny said he would like to revisit the Orkneys, make a second visit to Iceland – we had stayed at a hostel near Reykjavik several years previously – and from Iceland, to travel by sea to the Faroe Islands, then to Shetland, returning to Aberdeen and back by plane to Norfolk. He thought that travelling by public transport around Iceland, car ferry, bus and boat in the Faroes and hiring a car in the Shetland Islands, would offer us the best opportunities for exploring the different landscapes and seeing the widest species of birds.

I still felt a strong need to write down my thoughts and my feelings about various things. I do not know who it was who once said that 'a writer is a frustrated talker' but I certainly felt that was true, that I had to make a note of the thoughts I really wanted to express aloud but either couldn't or shouldn't because it might prove unwise.

I found the writing process to be cathartic.

When 'The Daily Telegraph' advertised a competition for mini-sagas in fifty words, neither more nor fewer, it offered me the opportunity for it to become a dumping ground where I could say something and then leave it. I told the story of my realisation that Danny had been having an affair. I counted the words and submitted it without too much thought.

Weeks later though, I grew increasingly concerned. The newspaper had said that the best mini-saga would appear on the front page. What would I do if I won, if Danny bought his usual copy of the Daily Telegraph that day and read it? I knew he would be angry with me for telling the whole world, or those parts that 'The Daily Telegraph' reached, about his indiscretion.

By that year I had acquired a small Nokia mobile phone and before we left for Scotland, I explained my concerns to my younger daughter.

'Please, Lallo,' I asked 'would you nip round early to 'One Stop' and look carefully at the newspaper headlines and front page? Then, if my story called 'Breaking Links' appears there, phone me and leave a message. If the story is there, I shall have to decide what best to do.' I thought that, if it did appear, Danny would be so displeased or mortified that I might need to jump off a cliff and onto the rocks below.

I am not good at handling it when people I love are cross with me.

I picked up Lallo's message on our way to visit Skara Brae. I hadn't won first prize and the newspaper didn't have Danny's indiscretion printed all over the front page or any other page, because Lallo had taken the trouble to buy a copy and to trawl through the newspaper from beginning to end. It was such a relief.

When my free copy of 'Mini Sagas 1999' arrived by post as had been promised to the winners of the best two hundred stories, I hid it.

I don't know if Danny ever read it. But not long afterwards, he did change his car as my mini-saga had proposed.

During that holiday, we were able to continue focusing on hooded crows and great skuas, or 'bonksies' as they were locally known. And discovering that arriving by boat into Tórshavn harbour at 5am on 30th July in the morning after Ólavsøka or St Olaf's Wake, was a new experience. Broken glass, empty beer bottles and recumbent male bodies everywhere.

Our hotel, the one we had booked for the next three or four nights, had a notice on its locked-and-bolted door to tell us, and anyone else inebriated and keen to gain entry, that it was 'Gestonkt' or something similar. We assumed that meant either 'Full', 'Closed' or possibly 'Bugger Off.'

This was the holiday when we saw minke whales from a fishing boat from Húsavík - where Danny turned slightly green from the movement of the vessel, - were amazed by the microclimate and botanical gardens at Akureyri in northern Iceland, stunned by the high cost of the bus journey from Reykjavik to Husavik and debated good-heartedly for several minutes about the origin of the Scandinavian ending 'vik' and its similarity to Norfolk and Suffolk town-name endings of 'wich' and 'ich'.

We agreed to disagree, Danny saying that the Scandinavian ending denoted a bay and I held the view that 'ich', 'wich' and also 'wick' marked ancient crossing places over an expanse of water, such as a river.

Danny displayed his lack of sea-legs again in the Faroe Islands, when we took a spectacular boat tour through the Vestmannabjørgini, the Vestmanna 700-metre-high sea cliffs that were home to so many of the local sea birds. He and another passenger both needed to focus on the scene straight ahead and look neither up or down, nor from side to side.

I was sympathetic without, I hope, drawing too much attention to Danny's discomfort but as we navigated narrow straits and sea grottos along the way, I did wonder whether Miss S. would have enjoyed this holiday or would she have much preferred to have been sunning herself on a beach in Lanzarote while reading a copy of Wilkie Collins' novel 'The Woman in White.'

But everyone appeared to have moved on by now from playing his or her part in that rocky period in our marriage.

Each year we decided which countries we wanted to visit, with Danny, perhaps because he was retired and had the free time to conduct the necessary research, making most of the suggestions. On one occasion he expressed a wish to visit China.

With that in mind and my limited budget as well as limited time because I was still employed and leading the Traveller Education Service, I asked for a day's leave on either a Friday or a Monday in mid-February. I had found a weekend package offering a flight to Beijing and a hotel.

'Would you like to go to China for just a few days,' I suggested to Danny 'as my belated birthday present to you? Because I think I can arrange that, if it's what you would like.'

We both went, wondering to what extent our time and exploration in Beijing might be restricted by the Chinese government.

It proved to be a cold winter in that part of China. The lakes were covered in ice so thick that people could walk across it, although they were told not to do so. When they ignored that, they were summoned to return to the banks by local officials blowing shrill whistles, almost as if denoting 'off-side' or a penalty.

One advantage of our visiting China at that time of year was the lack of tourists. Tiananmen Square and the Forbidden City were almost deserted as were the Ming Tombs, a few miles from Beijing.

From a stall in the Ming Tombs car park, Danny managed to buy himself a furry Cossack hat with a star at the front, making him look, on the few occasions on which he dared to wear it, rather like a Russian railway engine. It went to the charity shop a few years later.

We also managed to spend a couple of hours at the Great Wall, where Danny was excited to see azure-winged magpies, which I at first thought, from the way they flew, were enormous dragonflies.

A couple of years later we visited Tanzania. Danny had always said 'One day, I'll take you to Africa' and he did, though not to Zambia, a country which he knew far better. We toured in

Tanzania, staying at various lodges. I remember my shock at seeing zebra and wildebeest wandering about freely in an area not far from Nairobi, where we first landed before proceeding by jeep into Tanzania. We had time before moving on, to visiting Nairobi Zoo, where a notice on one of the reptile cages warned visitors not to tap on the glass cages and advised them that in the snake pit, 'Trespassers will be poisoned.'

We continued to make the occasional trip away at weekends. Danny said that he would be interested in visiting Bratislava for a few days so in 2002, we spent a long weekend there. It gave us the opportunity to visit the City Museum beside the River Danube which we each thought was excellent, and to see the amazing street sculptures. I particular liked the one in bronze of Cumil, the sewer worker who appears to be emerging from a manhole cover in the pavement.

Exploring the city streets, we came to the Primates' Palace and although we had no tickets for entry, we decided to investigate whether there were any toilets inside that we could use. We met each other outside afterwards, both of us greeting the other in amazement with 'I don't know about your loos that you've just visited, but the ones I went into were absolutely enormous' and then going into details as to the palatial size of the wash basins.

Later that day, we walked alongside the river on the side opposite our hotel. I looked at the giant white trumpets of convolvulus or bindweed on tendrils entwined among the brambles that colonised the edges of the footpath on the flat ground below the tree-covered mound on which Bratislava Castle stood. Despite our earlier visits to the Primate's Palace toilets, Danny wondered if there might be a convenient place where he could stop to pee among the bindweed shrubbery but he decided it was not sufficiently private and he had relieved himself quite recently anyway.

From there and having sufficient energy, we decided to climb the path at least as far as the castle's outer defence walls.

From the castle's outer walls, we walked down the path again quite quickly towards the River Danube, found the steps and the footpath on the bridge that separated pedestrians from the vehicular carriageways above.

Danny walked hurriedly across it, not even stopping to look up at the viewing tower shaped like a flying saucer. I called out as he strode forward 'Aren't you going to wait for me?' but he hurried on, now almost running, down the steps on the far side, across the road, towards our hotel, in through the main door, to the reception area.

'Couldn't stop, got to go, now' he called over his shoulder as the door to the Gents closed behind him. I found an armchair in Reception, sat and waited.

'What was all that about?' I asked when he emerged, looking much happier.

'Sorry about that, I needed to pee quite urgently and I didn't think it was wise to stop.'

That evening, there was a promotional wine-tasting mounted by a wine company and organised through the hotel. Since there were so few people staying at the hotel and only one other couple participating in the wine-tasting with nibbles that gave me my first ever taste of caviar, we were happy to accept the offer of a glass of red.

We were interested, on hearing the explanation from the vintner, to discover for ourselves that the shape of the wine glass really did make a difference to the taste of the wine. But we didn't place an order, it hadn't been that spectacular and we had arrived by plane with only hand luggage.

We went to bed instead and the next day, we flew back to Britain.

For over a year, Danny had been regularly paying maintenance to his ex-wife. It was around this time that he discovered that she had remarried and therefore she already had someone who was supporting her financially. I don't remember how Danny found out but I know it wasn't Mark who told him, although Mark had known what had been going on for several years and had said nothing. He would have had divided loyalties, I suppose.

I was quite shocked at how unethical that had been of Mark's mother but Danny appeared to swallow without complaint the fact that he had been financially cheated, took it almost as if he should have expected no better. But he put a stop to those payments to his ex-wife.

My father decided to sell his flat in Exmouth and to move to Scotland to live with Val. Dad had become worried that he might one day leave the gas on in his flat or do something stupid. Val had offered to care for him and to provide one of the downstairs rooms in her B&B for him on a permanent basis. In exchange, Dad had paid for Val's extension that offered a better entrance and an enclosed sun room.

Dad also, Val told me, was paying regularly for his room to make up for any loss of finance that Val might have earned, had she been able to use that room for other B &B guests.

Dad was good like that, apart from Danny he was one of the most ethically-driven men I had ever met.

On several occasions as he grew older and less and less able, I would drive to Scotland to visit him and would stay with Val as a B&B guest. I know he enjoyed living there, helping Val pluck a chicken or perform a simple task while able to remain seated. He would often be either in a wheelchair in the garden or sitting at the kitchen table with a pencil, sharpened to a point at each end, placed above and behind his ear, ready to tackle the Daily Telegraph cryptic crossword each day.

Dad had told me, 'I enjoy looking out for birds from the windows or my chair, and occasionally I might see a dipper going past along the river, hopping from stone to stone and then diving down to find something else to eat. It's amazing how it can do that, when I can neither swim nor can I now walk without help. All my life I have been used to seeing water coming towards me and going away again but here, I see it only going in one direction, as it flows past towards Callander.'

Dad never seemed to stop enjoying what he could see around him but I didn't see him even attempt to paint with watercolours in his final years. In 2002, Val called to say that Dad appeared to be likely to die quite soon. He was eating little and existing on teaspoonfuls of food enhanced with a glass of port.

A month or so later, he was living on 'After Eight' mints that Val would divide into four bits and flick to the back of his throat for him to digest, as well as sipping hot chocolate with cream on top and the occasional glass of fortified wine or when he could get it, his favourite tipple called Atholl Brose, made from oatmeal, honey, whisky and sometimes cream.

So much for sticking to a healthy diet! Val told me the doctor had said that it would do Dad no harm now at his advanced age and if he enjoyed it, why not?

Dad died on 28th August 2002, only a week before we would have celebrated his 97th birthday. His funeral took place at Callander Kirk on 3 September.

Danny came with me for the funeral and afterwards, Val, Danny, Colin and I went for an evening meal at the Lade Inn in Kilmahog, almost opposite Val's house. At the end of the meal, I felt I had good reason not to have followed Dad's solicitor's suggestion that Val should be named as one of Dad's executors in my place.

Dad had loved Val a great deal but he and Moo both knew that her ideas about money, honesty and the law, could be flexible and in accordance with her perceived need.

At the end of that meal in the Lade Inn, Val said she would pay for the dinner with Dad's cheque book. Although Dad had given her Power of Attorney, which had been quite sensible as he had become less able to make decisions for himself, I told her 'You can't do that, Val, he's dead. His bank account will need to be frozen and closed down as soon as possible.' Val looked surprised and a little cross with me for being such a stickler to the law. Her response was 'But he would have offered to have paid for it if he could.'

'Yes, he would,' I agreed, 'but he can't do that now, can he.'

In the end, with questioning and understanding looks being exchanged between myself, Colin and Danny to make sure that we all agreed but with no one offering to pay from his or her own funds, Danny said, 'It's all right, I'll cover this,' and produced his cheque book.

I thought that was very decent of him, it wasn't his father who had died.

It may have been later that year that Danny expressed a wish to travel on a Naturetrek trip to see the wild bison population that were in the forest and National Park in western Belarus. Our visit there took place some years after the Chernobyl disaster; we were able to enter the forests in Belarus but were advised not to eat the bilberries or smaller wild blueberries.

At the start of that visit, not long after we had boarded the coach at Minsk airport that was to take us to our accommodation, the coach developed a fault. It pulled into the side of the road and the driver opened the bonnet. We passengers climbed out and stood waiting on the grass beside the coach. There were mosquitoes, plenty of them. We weren't dressed or equipped, in our hand luggage, for mosquitoes. With British expectations, we waited for a replacement coach to arrive. It didn't, nor did any roadside mechanic.

It slowly dawned on me that in Belarus, there was no fall-back emergency provision, each person had to handle the situation as best he or she could and cope with the outcome. I do not know how the driver got the coach going again nor what the problem had been, I don't read or speak any Russian.

Very few people whom we met spoke any English, or French or German or, for Danny, any Finnish, although I don't think he even tried using that. This was a completely new situation for each of us; we became totally dependent on our Naturetrek naturalist and group leader.

Our accommodation just outside the National Park was some sort of hostel that might once have served as a convalescent centre, barracks or local hospital. It must have been quite close to a railway line because I remember seeing a railway coach being used for some sort of livestock housing but with 'ресторан', the Russian word for restaurant car written on the side.

The hostel manager appeared quite unused to having visitors or guests. There were no bottom sheets on the bed; instead, we lay on rough bath towels. Our meals were substantial but repetitive. Dessert, when we didn't have a picnic and at either lunch or dinner and sometimes both, was what appeared to be a choc-ice with the ice part factory-made of either dried milk or curd cheese. Strange but not unpleasant, once we got used to it. There were other small dwellings in the vicinity but only one shop to speak of, about a mile and a half away that stocked basic foodstuffs and hardware.

Toward the end of our visit there and before spending a day in Minsk prior to our flight home, I bought a 'waterproof' at the village shop. The waterproof was akin to the sort of emergency covering that a British visitor might buy on a visit to Warwick Castle in unexpected rain. It was flimsy plastic, shaped like a poncho, a square of thin orange plastic film with a hole cut in the centre for my head.

It was quite unlike me not to have brought a waterproof in my luggage. I had inadvertently left it in the car and forgotten to retrieve it at the airport.

Prior to the discovery in the village shop and seeing I might be in difficulties, one of our local guides had lent me a long khaki trench coat, such as might have been worn by a Russian on patrol along the enemy border. It gave Danny and others in our group considerable amusement to see me in it, with shorts or trousers and a tee-shirt underneath but it was serviceable and didn't attract unwanted insects or distract other wildlife.

We travelled on tracks through the virgin forest in two dark green Russian ex-army mini-bus vehicles with unsprung seats and windows that rarely opened. Seated towards the rear, I wondered how we would get out, should the vehicles overturn, but fortunately I didn't need to put any plan into practice.

We moved from location to location, seeing no signs of bison. I felt sorry for the guide, it wasn't his fault that the bison had moved on that year from their normal habitats, to graze in different parts of the forest.

In desperation, our guide pointed out where, on the bark of a tree, a bear had been sharpening its claws recently and beside a pond, we knelt down to see minute frogs that had recently changed from their tadpole state.

Our guide checked every nest box he came across for mice. On one occasion he discovered something that he identified as a northern striped birch mouse, only to drop the nest box and see the tiny mouse scuttle through the grass. As this was the only mammal we had seen so far, our guide was concerned that we should stand absolutely still, in case one of us trod on it by mistake and completely flattened our only sighting.

While others in our group were delighted by seeing something, anything, alive, this warning not to squash it had me in fits of giggles. I enjoyed the irony of a situation I could only imagine, of the guide picking up the flat dead mouse by its tail and the others squeezing past each other to take photos of its corpse.

One member of our group, a butterfly enthusiast, was delighted when, on the following day, our guide took us to where the birch forest opened out into a field of wild flowers beside a slow flowing river. Our guide led us through the field as far as the river because 'there are beavers here and we might see a sign of where they have tried to dam a stream that leads into the main river.'

'Are we likely to see a beaver?' one of the group asked.

'Very unlikely, in daylight. Your best bet would be to take a boat out along the river at dusk, you might see one then. Or hear the splash of its tail as it dives under the water.'

The butterfly enthusiast wasn't very interested, he was in his element taking photos of butterflies, butterflies such as the Camberwell Beauty that were quite rare in Britain, he told us. His wife was more interested in the variety of wild flowers in the meadow and in plants on the banks beside the river.

In one forest opening, standing in a field of long grasses and nettles, we came across a wooden hut, made of greying wood that looked as if no one had been there for a long while. Walking carefully through the long grass, our guide approached the hut until 'Look, quick, there's a male adder,' he said in a loud whisper. I held back but then decided that it might be my only chance to get close to an adder, with Danny there to protect me, more from my fears than from the reptile.

With its black zigzag pattern showing against the grey background scales, it slid gently and assuredly along the length of the wooden hut, then disappeared into a patch of nettles. It was then that the guide mentioned the Bielski Brothers Tuvia, Asael and Zusya, who had grown up in Eastern Poland, now Western Belarus, which had been annexed by the Soviet Union in 1939. Belarus became an independent country on 25 August 1991. The brothers had lived in the village Stankevich, located between the towns Lida and Nowogródek in what had been the Belorussian region of tsarist Russia.

Although I didn't have a map of Belarus or the region, I assumed that we were in that same area. The guide told us that the Bielski family home stood on the other side of a small lake fed by a river. The Bielskis had been the only Jews in Town and the Bielski home had stood separate from the main section of the community. In 1941, the three brothers witnessed their parents and two other siblings being led away to their eventual murders. Instead of running away or giving in to despair, these brothers had fought back, waging a guerrilla war of wits against the Nazis.

By using their intimate knowledge of the dense forests surrounding the Belarusian towns of Novogrudek and Lida, the Bielskis evaded the Nazis and established a hidden base camp. They then set about convincing other Jews to join their ranks and they provided shelter and protection to some 1,200 Jews[xiii].

On hearing this, some of our group wanted to know more. I didn't like to ask the guide in our hostel in case the hostel manager understood English, his family had had some involvement and he might get upset. But when we returned to Britain, I found that the story of the Bielski brothers had been made into a movie called 'Defiance', starring Daniel Craig.

Before we left Britain, we had been warned by the travel company about the possibility of getting tick-born encephalitis from the ticks that lived in the long grass. At the local surgery I had had an injection of the vaccine to protect me against this. We learned that the ticks usually got picked up on the lower legs and would then travel upwards in search of a meal. Ticks, we were told, prefer areas of the body that are warm and moist, they may be found in the armpits, scalp or groin.

Back in our room and after one picnic lunch in a grassy clearing in the forest, I felt slightly uncomfortable in my lower regions and asked Danny 'Would you mind checking my groin, because I can't see for myself if there's anything there that shouldn't be?'

He was hesitant, looked slightly uncomfortable but he did as I asked. There was nothing there that he could see but I sensed that he found looking at my groin was a step too far in intimacy. It reminded him of his indiscretion with Miss S.

Still hoping to see a beaver, Danny and I found someone who would take us one afternoon along a river. We spend several hours in that small boat, being punted or rowed along but the only wild life I saw was a grass snake swimming in the water. Half way through the afternoon, our boatman pulled into a small island in the river to allow us all to get out and stretch our legs or pee. But even as it grew dusk, we had no sign nor sound of a beaver.

Towards the end of the holiday, we were to realise that Belarus wasn't equipped for foreign tourists who weren't Russian, to such an extent that our group visit featured on local television as being something completely new. We were asked to make a short one-sentence comment on how we found things in Belarus, what we liked about the country, to be broadcast across the nation. Fortunately, everyone was complimentary.

Before our return flight to Britain, we spent a day in central Minsk, visiting Gum, the only department store we could find and an interesting reminder of the fading Soviet era. We were looking for a traditional wooden box decorated with woven straw. Our guide told us that this might make an interesting souvenir of our visit to Belarus.

Minsk and Gum appeared not to have public toilets. Deciding that thirst was more pressing than principle, we went into a branch of McDonald's near Gorky Park, ordered an orange juice for each of us and having drunk that, found the toilets near the staircase.

We explored the gardens as much as we wished until Danny said 'I need the loo again. Can we walk quite quickly back up the street to McDonald's?'

No one appeared to object to our using those facilities again and we had, we told ourselves, been customers there only an hour before.

Our flight and journey back to Britain was uneventful. Arriving home, we unpacked our suitcases and made a pile of the clothes to be washed.

Danny went out while I sorted out our mail. I was in The Yeoman's House utility room, stuffing clothes into the washing machine when he returned. He came into the room and I looked at his face. He looked glum.

‘What’s wrong?’ I asked, and then ‘Where have you been?’

‘I’ve seen the doctor,’ he replied without his usual smile. And without any lead up or warning,

‘He thinks I may have prostate cancer.’

Chapter 22
Cancer

I gulped. I felt there was something I should say, a helpful way in which I should respond but my mind again refused to instruct or co-operate. I had no idea what or where anyone's prostate was. It was the word 'cancer' that hit me.

I had no experience of cancer, neither direct nor indirect, it wasn't something that had ever affected my family. My parents and grandparents suffered strokes almost to the point of specialising in them but cancer had not, to the best of my knowledge, occurred in any of my relatives. Cancer was something remote, not connected with me in any way.

I didn't even know what the symptoms might be, other than a lump somewhere in the breast, and I only knew that from television programmes and because I had had breast examinations as part of a general health check.

Any response of 'Oh dear, what a shame' or 'Is there anything I can do to help?' would be misplaced, totally inept, wrong. Danny, I knew, was more comfortable dealing with facts rather than an emotional reaction, whether mine or his.

So, I sought information, from him.

'Whereabouts in your body is your prostate? And do men have only one, or do you have two prostates, like testicles?'

I felt almost embarrassed, not by my questions but by my ignorance of the male body.

Why, I wondered, was none of this mentioned when I was gazing at the line drawing in the 3rd form biology text book of the reproductive organs of the rabbit?

'The prostate is a walnut-sized gland located between the bladder and the penis' Danny explained, himself sounding like a textbook. 'The prostate is just in front of the rectum, so a doctor's examination can sometimes determine whether there's a problem.'

I realised we were both having to come to terms with the news and the likely implications, although in different ways.

'What's it for, the prostate?' I asked, sounding even to myself like a four-year-old.

He explained, 'The urethra runs through the centre of the prostate, from the bladder to the penis, letting urine flow out of the body. The prostate secretes fluid that nourishes and protects sperm. One of the signs that there might be a problem is the urgent need to urinate and the urge to do so many times during the day or night.'

'But I don't understand. Why does the doctor think it might be cancer?'

'He doesn't yet, he only mentioned it because it is a possibility. I'll need some tests before I know whether it is cancer or not.'

'What sort of tests?'

He explained about levels of PSA, prostate specific antigen that is found in a man's blood and produced exclusively by prostate cells; that high levels of the PSA enzyme can be helpful in diagnosing issues with the prostate, such as cancer or infection.

By then, my mind had taken in sufficient information for one day. What I really wanted to know was 'Are you in any pain? And how is this likely to affect life from now on?'

I hadn't got as far as thinking how, further along the line, it might affect my own life. That didn't cross my mind.

Within only a couple of months of our return from Belarus, Danny was talking about how amazed he was, retrospectively, that he had managed the boat trip along the river to look for beavers. 'I don't know how I managed that for so many hours without having to stop for a pee,' he said, 'so perhaps things won't be as bad as the doctor suggested.'

Only much later did I remember that we had stopped on that island, got out and relieved ourselves into the long grass beside a small tree; and I didn't remind Danny of that, it seemed unkind to shatter what hope he still had. But within the following week, he woke me in the middle of the night, he was in pain and pacing up and down the bedroom.

'Something hurts,' he told me. 'I want to go to the loo, there's a burning sensation inside but when I try to pee, nothing happens, nothing comes out. But the burning feeling is still there, it hurts and I don't know what to do in case I do suddenly go, in case I wet the bed and we have to have the mattress cleaned.'

'Danny,' I said, 'I've dealt with more wet beds than most people and one more wouldn't make any difference. But if you are really worried, I can slip one of Keir's incontinence pads under the bottom sheet – I think I still have some somewhere, they're so useful if I'm decorating – and that will save the mattress. I suggest you climb back into bed and try to get some sleep. Then, in the morning, you can try to get an appointment with Dr Thurston.'

Within the month, Danny was in hospital, having stents inserted through his back, to relieve the pressure on his bladder and provide an outlet for any obstruction. That seemed to help for a while.

Since his retirement and his period of supply teaching, Danny had undergone training as an Ofsted Inspector.

'Not so that I would ever want to act as an inspector, but so that I would know exactly what Ofsted would be looking for,' he told me.

From that, he had been trained as an external assessor so that he could professionally assess the performance of individual members of staff as well as schools or education services. On the face of it, he was well-paid as an external assessor but there seemed to me to be a tremendous amount of paperwork involved, both beforehand and after each visit.

He was employed in this by Cambridge Education Associates or an organization with a very similar name. This would involve him setting up appointments to visit the secondary school, usually in Britain but a few times in Germany, in schools connected to the British Armed Forces.

He seemed to enjoy the work, it made use of his knowledge and prior experience as a head teacher of a large secondary school.

'It's something I feel I can do,' he said, 'it brings in additional income for every visit and at the moment, I can't see any reason not to carry on working. But it's short-term. The doctor has told me, if I feel all right to work, then there's no reason why I shouldn't. But he says I might feel quite differently in eighteen months' time. From what he says, it looks as though there's a limited window in which I can work and we can still travel. But it will come to an end and, the doctor says, when it does, I will certainly know about it. But by then, he says, I probably won't want to work anyway.'

Prostate cancer was confirmed. We had both read that men did not usually die <u>from</u> prostate cancer, although they might die <u>with</u> it. We were both hopeful and positive in outlook.

Danny decided that he ought to tell Mark the diagnosis, and in person rather than by a phone call. We had not been invited to Mark's wedding to Claire, whom he had met while in Cambridge and whom we had both met in Mark's flat in Oxford. We were told they wanted a very quiet wedding beside Niagara Falls.

Danny called Mark.

'Now I've retired and as I'm obviously growing older, I'd like to spend some time with you fairly soon. There are a few things that I would like to discuss with you. Could I visit you sometime this summer, only for a couple of days? I can easily occupy myself while you are giving a lecture or conducting supervisions, I would enjoy looking around Kingston. I could perhaps even travel across Lake Ontario if there is some interesting wildlife to be seen.'

'I hope' Danny told me 'that will give Mark the message not to include Claire. I need to talk to Mark alone and I find Claire quite sharp.'

Having arranged that with Mark, Danny booked return flights for himself to Toronto and onward to Kingston.

We thought that this was a visit to Mark best paid by Danny on his own and that Danny and I would explore Canada together at a later date, perhaps flying to Vancouver, taking the Rocky Mountaineer train across the Rockies and spending several days in Toronto.

Danny was away for only a few days and returned tired, but pleased that he had seen Mark and Claire, their house and their Rhodesian Ridgeback dog.

I kept a diary of this time, I don't know why except that I wanted to make a note of it, to write it down. Perhaps, although Danny appeared to be in reasonable health, I was picking up on something underlying and otherwise unexpressed.

I wrote 'On Saturday 19th August 2006, Danny drove us both to Stratford-upon-Avon for a matinee performance of Julius Caesar. We had set off early and arrived in time to order a quick pub lunch before the theatre. Danny's appetite was minimal.

We had had a breakfast of blueberry muffin and coffee on the way to Stratford and ordered something very similar on the return journey. Danny refused ice-cream but had an apple when we got home again at 7.30pm'.

The following day I wrote 'Weather reflects mood rather. Grey, heavy rain, briefly clears then rain again. Discussed the finer details of how the Trust might be set up with £XXX of Danny's estate to be in Trust. Couldn't easily settle to work – lacked involvement and enthusiasm. Just want to be pottering about in my nest – almost sorry there wasn't much to iron.

Danny went for a hot bath mid-day, says it relaxes him and his back aches. The hot baths in the middle of the day have only started this week. Psychological? Didn't have these in Belarus so perhaps the walking was helpful whereas now there is too much sitting around. Feels a bit like Christmas without the fun - a lot of waiting around for the next thing/meal/event to happen.'

A former Education Adviser and colleague offered Danny some work at £300 per day.

'That's provided me with quite a dilemma,' he said, his mouth twisting with uncertainty. 'I'm stuck between constant tiredness, the need for financial gain and the pressure to do certain essential jobs around the house.'

Apart from that, Danny's condition didn't immediately affect either of us except, perhaps, to ensure that we each knew that our time together was probably limited, in one way or another. In the following months and years, we still pursued many of our interests.

Danny drove a couple of times to the Isle of Mull. We had found a very pleasant inn in Dervaig in which to stay, and from there we saw golden and white-tailed eagles, and on each of those visits, otters swimming in the sea lochs.

We had planned in advance how and when we might ask the minibus driver on any organized wildlife day trip to stop for a comfort break. By catching a ferry, we ventured as far as Iona to try to hear and see a corncrake.

We managed neither but I collected some lovely sea-polished stones from the beach. On our drive to Fionnphort and a walk towards the pink granite rocks, we came across two hares that appeared totally unafraid of human beings. They scampered right across our path, so close that we could have touched one of them. Their acceptance of us and their lack of fear gave each of us unexpected pleasure.

Other visits to Scotland tended to focus on the mainland and in particular, the Cairngorms National Park.

Being based in Kingussie, Newtonmore, Aviemore or Grantown-on-Spey offered us, particularly Danny, the chance at dawn to see black grouse lekking, a female capercaillie in the ancient Abernethy Forest, tree pipits and sometimes osprey as well as red deer, red squirrels and other mammals. It also offered the opportunity to visit whisky distilleries.

Danny enjoyed the occasional whisky at the weekend and on one occasion, he almost worried me when he announced 'I'm in love with twelve-year-old Glenturret,' I thought for a moment he was announcing a change of sexual preference!

It had been on a walk towards the Glen Ogle Trail a couple of years before the diagnosis of a prostate problem, that I had wondered whether he was in the best of health. As we had climbed up to the old railway line from Lochearnhead, ready to follow the former track through Glen Ogle and high above the floor of the glen, his face had turned white and I feared he might faint. I had even looked for a place where a helicopter might land, should that prove necessary.

That was the last long walk that we attempted to do together. From then on, I made sure that we were no more than a mile or so away from the car or other assistance.

It was after our return to Norfolk that we discussed the possible dates on which I might retire. I loved my job. I had been given an almost free rein to develop it. I enjoyed the Gypsy families I had got to know and often through several generations of children. I was proud of the innovations such as an interactive fiction book for children that we produced titled 'Sean's Wellies', the establishment of a stand at Appleby Horse Fair, aimed at showing Traveller parents some of the things that children were taught in school and the culturally-reflective materials that might be used in the classroom.

I was also pleased and proud of the development of an educational activity programme for schools at Gressenhall Rural Life Museum. I had been offered the chance for the Norfolk Traveller Education Service to work on a further project in closer partnership with the Department for Education and Skills.

But I considered my conversation with the Chair of Norfolk Women's Institute as one of my most successful and necessary initiatives, although both presumptuous and provocative on my part. I was aware that the purposes of the Women's Institute were to 'revitalise rural areas communities', 'providing women with educational opportunities and the chance to build new skills'.

'Why then', I asked, 'was this voluntary and well-meaning organisation not regularly approaching the women living on Gypsy and Traveller sites across the country?'

To the credit of the local W.I., they did invite Gloria, the warden of a local Roundwell Gypsy site, to be the main speaker at one of their meetings. I was told afterwards that members had found her to be an entertaining and informative speaker, as I was sure she would prove to be.

My work was exciting and I had plenty of further ideas. I had advanced from being paid on the Head Teacher's Salary Scale to Soulbury Scale for Advisors and Education Improvement Professionals. After over twenty years leading the Service, I had had ten different line managers, most of whom had displayed real commitment to the work we were doing and I wasn't yet ready to give up work.

After a further visit to the doctor, Danny told me 'We need to have a serious discussion. Although I am managing well at the moment with the assessor work, there will soon come a time when I won't be able to do it, certainly not to the same extent any more. I don't see how we will be able to manage the running costs of The Yeoman's House on two pensions alone, not if you still hope to retire just before your sixtieth birthday. As I see it, either one of us will need to be still bringing in an income or we will need to move house, to down-size to something smaller and easier to manage financially.'

'So, you are saying that The Yeoman's House will be too expensive to run on two pensions so we need my income until the house is sold? Which means, as I understand it, that I need to continue to work until we could sell the house and downsize? But we've worked so hard on bringing both sides of the house together and making it into one house. And the half I bought in the first place offered me security, it was very much my refuge away from Richard, his lifestyle and all his debts. Buying it was my way of keeping my family safe and giving them somewhere where they and I could feel emotionally and financially secure.'

I gulped.

'This house has been put together with a great deal of my blood, sweat, tears and skin, not to mention energy and sheer hard work. I've stroked its beams with love and teak oil, and

I've plastered over its cracks. I've watched it develop and change, reaching its potential as one whole house again, almost as if it were a child. To me, it's ideal, it's everything I've ever dreamed of having and living in.'

I needed time to think as well as to feel, before responding further. Quite tentatively I said 'I had thought, Danny, when it looked as if you were going to leave me, I would run the house as a B&B. But now I realise that that would be financially impossible either if I were working or if you became more unwell. If I am going to retire, which I shall sooner or later, then we need to decide quite seriously where we would like to live. What ideas do you have? Where do you fancy spending the rest of your life?'

Together we chewed over the advantages of buying a small house on Mull, as well as the disadvantages which were unknown to us, apart from the 'blind bidding' system and the different legal process of purchasing a house in Scotland.

We had never spent a winter there. In fact, whenever we had visited Scotland, we had had good weather on each occasion; it hadn't even rained.

We also considered Devon and Cornwall, particularly the area around Bude or Kilkhampton where Danny's family had had its roots. But that part of the country seemed a long way away from my children and where they might decide to settle, and a long way away from a major international airport, which seemed a drawback, were we to continue to travel.

Once we had thought carefully about these options, we agreed that there appeared to be no clear reason for us to move from Norfolk nor from Wymondham itself; on the contrary, there was a clear advantage in our remaining in the same town as the one in which we were already living. We would have the same doctor, could continue the same friendships and pursue the same interests as we previously had.

Realising that Danny might become further incapacitated, it was clear that we needed to live in a house with a downstairs loo, otherwise Danny would be trapped upstairs or needing a bedroom on the ground floor. Since The Yeoman's House was a Grade Two listed building, we could not easily convert any of our current rooms to provide a downstairs toilet and shower room, not without a great deal of fuss and upheaval, especially since we had only just finished bringing both sides of the house together.

That being the case, I reluctantly had to accept what Danny said, 'We need to move to a house we can maintain more easily, and a garden we could also manage.'

By September that year, Danny resigned from being a governor at one of Thetford's secondary schools and was no longer actively seeking work. He went to the hospital for an MRI scan and a bone isotope scan. Advanced cancer was confirmed but it was not known how far it had travelled through his body. He would wake every hour and a half at night and needed to get up for the loo.

On account of this alone, he was growing very tired and was clearly not comfortable. He had lower back pain. Nevertheless, each day he painted the outside window frames at the rear of the house but for a limited time only, before taking a rest.

He had lost a great deal of weight, although partly through a change of diet; the fear of straining meant that he was eating a considerable amount of fruit, with pear and muesli and granary toast for breakfast and plenty of plums.

From time to time, I was aware of feeling very alone, not just for the future but also in the present. Having lost my management team at work, I could easily feel isolated. I was aware of the conflict between my need to continue the routine of work, which provided social contact and a focus quite divorced from illness and no future, and the irony of my working while I felt the need not to waste the precious time I had with Danny.

I had toyed with the idea of resigning at Christmas. Danny knocked that on the head with a perfectly logical argument that it could take up to two years to sell the house and that every month during that time when I was not earning would result in drawing on his retirement capital. However, he was emphasizing a July 2007 final retirement date for me, which totally undermined his own argument.

Mark suggested that he might pop over to the U.K., once Danny knew how extensive the cancer was. Danny got very low sometimes, partly brought on by physical pain or discomfort. There was so much I would have liked to have said or asked, but I felt it might be intrusive. Danny seemed to think that if he could make decisions without discussion, he could maintain control. I reasoned that maintaining his privacy gave him a protective shell from loss of emotional control.

I still didn't know what Danny's relationship was with Miss S, or continued to be. We had each made our Wills with personal bequests and I feared some reference or token for her in that, or coming across some gift or a letter she had given him. By that time, I could never ask what or why about his affair.

My own insecurities were coming right to the fore. I sheared the grass near the water feature at the weekend and inadvertently chopped into the face of a frog sheltering in the long grass. I felt I'd betrayed its trust and just kept crying 'I'm so sorry, Froggy.'

Danny hit it over the head with something heavy in a polythene bag because 'it was the kindest thing to do.' My emotions clearly needed an acceptable alternative outlet.

I felt a measure of guilt that, when I was at work, I had no mental space nor the time, to give Danny much of a thought. That I could laugh and joke with people involved in the new Gypsy Life project we were planning at Gressenhall Rural Life Museum. I logically accepted that this was OK but I was aware that I had that as an escape and that Danny hadn't.

After a hard but generally happy day in my own separate world, I would return to our shared one which was brooding and seeking any new development, even a negative one, just to inject some high or low stimulus or occurrence into what otherwise was a slow, downward line towards Danny's death. I gave Gressenhall much of my time, thought and energy. One Saturday morning I got up early with Chaucer and was gathering heather on Bawdeswell Heath at 6.30am, ready for the visiting groups of school children to construct sprigs of 'lucky heather'. Everything there a light grey – no colour, dew, light or cobwebs stretched across the bushes of heather.

Diffused light, muted. Very like home life then. Premature bereavement, they call it. Silent sadness.

It appeared that we might uphold our current quality of life for as long as possible, but that in the meantime we should complete and sell The Yeoman's House, find and buy a smaller house in the same town. It sounds simple when put into words but the words masked a great deal of heartbreak for me, heartbreak that I knew I could not avoid but that would need all my inner resources to deal with successfully on my own.

Danny didn't want other people, apart from his son and Irene, to know that he had any health problem. More than once he told me 'I cannot deal with their emotional reactions as well as my own.'

That was all very well in theory but adhering to Danny's wishes left me with no support, no one other than him with whom I could talk or discuss issues. I did hint to David, my latest line manager, and to a couple of my staff that Danny was not very well but they didn't press the point. I knew that David chose very carefully what to pass on, and what not to pass on, to Terry, his line manager.

Judith, one of my teaching staff had told us that her son had a finger that had been diagnosed as cancerous and how worried she was that it might metastasize. Such was my ignorance of cancer that I had to ask her 'What does that word 'metastasize' mean?' She explained.

I did not realise at the time just how important it would be for me to know that. Neither did I know sufficient to ask Danny whether any prostate cancer that he might have was invasive or non-invasive. I didn't ask at the time and I don't know whether Danny did, but I expect he would have asked the doctor, he would have wanted as much knowledge as he could get on which to base any later decisions he might need to make.

Danny decided that before advertising our house for sale, the rendering at the front needed to be repainted, as did the external doors onto the pavement and all the window frames.

He requested a quote from a painter and decorator who had done some jobs for him in the past but even before we received the estimate, he decided it would be too expensive to employ someone to do the work.

Instead, with his usual decisiveness, he resolved 'I think, rather than pay out a large sum for little return, I'd rather repaint the entire frontage myself, including any repairs to the decorated brackets that support the jettied first floor. I'll hire some scaffolding; it will have to stand partly on the pavement.'

We had already had the upstairs rear wall of the house insulated and re-rendered the previous year. That had been the same winter that I tore the ham string of my right leg and had to be brought home from a walk in some stranger's car. I had spent my Christmas meal in a restaurant with my leg raised and supported on a chair seat.

I chose an estate agent that I thought would do a reasonable job of advertising our house and within a few weeks and several internal photographs, our house was on the market.

'I don't think it will sell very easily,' Danny doubted 'so we may be left with it for months, even years.'

We had extended the mortgage by a small amount in order to pay for the installation of a dormer window at the rear of the top floor so that it no longer became necessary on the number 16 side to walk through one bedroom to reach the second. I knew Danny was worried about that extra amount we were having to meet each month.

Our house appeared in the estate agent's window that weekend. A couple of families looked round the house on the first Saturday but were concerned either that the garden was not big enough or that the stairs were too steep for their young children. Danny had not wanted to look at other properties that we might buy, until we received a reasonable indication that there was a keen purchaser for our house, unless he became disappointed, I suppose; or until we knew what we could afford, based on the price we might be offered for The Yeoman's House.

'I would like a house with a productive garden in which I can grow fruit and vegetables' I told him 'so that might rule out newer houses that have been designed with busy working families in mind.'

Danny was adamant. It was only after he voiced his concerns with 'I don't want anything with lawns that I will have to spend all my time walking up and down, mowing the grass,' that I understood that the possible short-term nature of his living in whatever we might buy, hadn't occurred to him.

He remained focused on a belief that he could deal with any prostate or bladder problems and remain in good health; and for a while, he was correct.

After two other viewings in that first weekend that it was advertised, we had an offer from someone who told us he had always wanted to buy our house. He told us 'I'm hoping to bring my children and those of my new partner together, therefore I've been looking for a six-bedroom property in the town. Because that would allow my partner's children to attend their current school.'

Once we could verify that this potential purchaser was indeed a firm buyer, Danny agreed that I could give notice of my proposed retirement and suggest a provisional date a couple of years after my sixtieth birthday.

We continued to plan further foreign travel, with me mapping out the toilet possibilities in advance. We flew to Riga for a weekend in Latvia, where Danny was keen to see the old Jewish quarter before making for a café and ordering a coffee, so that he could legitimately use the café's toilet facilities.

We were able to spend a week in the Gambia. Danny had managed to find a local bird guide online and was able to get in touch with him by 'phone once we had arrived. As a result, we spent a couple of days travelling in the country with our guide in his dark green car. It had no safety belts for passengers and rear door locks that would open only from the outside, such that we travelled for most of the way to bird-watching sites with our windows wound down, ready to extract ourselves in case of an emergency.

We were offered the asking price for The Yeoman's House and once that was assured, began looking in earnest for somewhere else to live. On the other side of the town, we found a house that was large enough to accommodate visitors but with a downstairs loo and separate bathroom, as well as a bathroom upstairs. The house had a wrap-around garden and fields at the back, reminding me of where I had lived on the edge of the town in Letchworth. I gave the Local Authority an indication that I definitely intended to retire within the next year so that they might find someone who was willing to take on my job and replace me.

I packed all our possessions into boxes, Danny ordered a removal van and in September 2007 we moved house. I mentioned at work, quite briefly, that I had moved house. I didn't go into further detail, gave just my new address.

Kwai, our Burmese cat that Danny had bought when he moved in to live with me, appeared to manage the transition between houses quite well but soon died. Kwai had been accustomed to making a nest for himself in the void created by the cooker hood in The Yeoman's House kitchen and would happily sleep there for much of the day. He and Chaucer had got on without apparent rivalry, innate fear or resentment. Kwai, though male, had treated Chaucer as his kitten and the pair would play together.

I hated moving from The Yeoman's House. I don't think Danny ever understood how much that house meant to me. It had provided safety, a refuge, comfort and consolation, and a measure of status. It had been unique. It had been a dream realised and moving from there was akin to losing my identity; it was like losing my mother, or both my parents because, several years before I knew Danny, Dad and Colin had both helped me wallpaper the bathroom and my bedroom.

The house we decided to buy was a chalet bungalow on the other side of the main railway line. It could not have been more different from The Yeoman's House. It was slightly reminiscent of Owl Cottage that my parents had bought after Dad had retired.

With the main mortgage paid off, Danny said 'You won't need to worry about maintaining that place, even if a tile slips off the roof. It's not like The Yeoman's House, you can even reach the ridge tiles with a couple of ladders. It's a house that you'll be able to maintain quite well on your own, when I can't be there any more.'

I appreciated his confidence in me, although at that time I was in my early sixties and well able to do most physical things required of me. Neither of us could envisage how things might be when I grew older. I was, as Richard had described me, still very capable.

Danny decided that a house without a cat couldn't possibly become a home. Online he found a breeder of Burmese cats, living on the Norfolk/Suffolk border. Leaving me waiting outside in the car, he went into the breeder's house, chose a kitten and came out with it in a cat basket.

On the way home and the following day, we discussed a suitable name for our kitten. Kwai had been named after a river in Burma, known locally as the Mae Klong River (or the Kwai Yai River) in Kanchanaburi Province. We wanted to follow our tradition of selecting a name that reflected its ethnicity but felt that calling a cat 'Irrawaddy' after another Burmese river was unkind and downright silly.

Naming it 'Rangoon' was somewhat reminiscent of a 1950/1960s radio programme and it was not until the 1980s that Burma became known as Myanmar.

After considerable research, Danny proposed we might give the kitten the name 'Chin', not chin as in facial feature but to reflect the Chin State in western Burma. Chaucer bonded quite quickly with Chin, he had grown used to having a cat around the house, and nicked its food when he could.

During the first winter in our new house, we contacted a garden designer, hoping to change the front and rear gardens into something that better suited our needs. I wanted a vegetable patch that was more interesting in shape rather than the dull rectangle established by the previous owners. Jamie, the garden designer, had also planned a water feature that was safe enough for small grandchildren to enjoy. Working together in the frost and ice, Danny and I laid the necessary cabling and pipework to enable water to trickle up through a small millstone.

Danny was still able to stand, look, consider and give me directions, so long as I did the bending or digging and any heavier work. He also invited his sister and brother-in-law to come to stay, so that they could see that he was still able to function almost as he had done previously.

Irene was anxious that I should contact The Royal Marsden Hospital, where various clinical trials into prostate cancer were being conducted, to see whether we could get Danny onto one of those trials. But I didn't contact The Royal Marsden, I thought it would be pointless, we lived too far away from London.

Internally, the house was indicative of old people having lived there, and people with taste quite different from our own. The furnishings were pink, frilly and fluffy. I set about choosing stronger colours for emulsion paint and checking with Danny that he approved my choice.

The existing carpeting would have to stay but I chose quite different curtains. I took the earlier ones to the recycling centre or the charity shop. Those thick dark red velvet curtains I had had in the sitting rooms in The Yeoman's House, we left there. There seemed no point in doing otherwise, they would never have fitted our new windows and I thought they would have looked totally out of place, hanging in a 1960s bungalow.

So much happened in the subsequent two years and yet the picture didn't change much, except for a downward slide.

There had been a grievance case at work, my line manager's lack of following the County Council recommended procedures, his clumsy approach to performance review, my foggy memory due to being overwhelmed by work, the move and Danny's deteriorating health, the financial queries, selling The Yeoman's House, buying the smaller house on the other side of the town, Danny in Canada while I did the packing, the moving process, the death of Kwai our elderly and arthritic Burmese cat, and Chaucer's insecurities.

We needed a change of focus and some enjoyable time together.

On my birthday in February 2008, we visited Jordan for a week or so. I have no idea what Danny did regarding any travel insurance. Snow lay on the ground as we entered Petra to locate our hotel but by the following morning, all snow had vanished and the sun was blazing. We walked through the Siq, the narrow sandy gorge that leads to the Treasury, Petra's most impressive monument and from there, we walked up the rocky pathway, stepping aside to allow mounted donkeys to pass us, to climb to the gigantic 1st Century AD monument of the Monastery.

It was at the Monastery that Danny had another urgent need to pee, despite having visited the toilets at the café at the bottom of the rock-strewn cliff where we had had lunch. He couldn't find anywhere that was completely out of anyone else's view and became almost panicky.

I tried to reassure him. 'People haven't climbed up all this way, in the heat, just to see you peeing. They are far more interested in the Monastery or the view over the mountains across towards Amman.'

I reminded him of a similar occasion a year or two earlier, when we had been visiting Glastonbury Tor and I had had to keep watch on the path while he hurriedly peed into a bramble patch.

After Petra, our tour guide took us to Wadi Rum, where our group joined a series of jeeps that were to take us across the desert sands to a Bedouin encampment (erected, no doubt, especially for the tourists) where we were due to have a meal.

Danny and I shared the rear passenger bench seat in the jeep but it was difficult for us to see through the windscreen past the driver and the other front passenger. Even before we got out to make our way to the black Bedouin tent and the waiting buffet, Danny was complaining.

'Sitting on that unsprung utilitarian rear seat of the jeep and having to crane forward to see what lay ahead, was hurting my back. Were you all right, could you see properly?'

He rarely complained about discomfort so I thought that having some food and sitting down somewhere more comfortable in the shade might help.

It did, but not a great deal.

However, that evening in our 'hotel' room that had been created from what had apparently once been a Bedouin village, Danny appeared to sleep comfortably, despite being woken early by the muezzin calling the people to prayer from the minaret.

Danny seethed for a few words over what he thought about religions in general but I don't think the muezzin's calling had disturbed his sleep too much, it just gave him the chance to make his views known, to repeat that he was an agnostic verging on atheism, to rail 'How on earth can intelligent people such as so-and-so and my niece believe in a loving god who is all-seeing and all-knowing?' and so on until it was time for breakfast.

When we returned home from Jordan, Danny's back was still hurting. There were his trips to the loo almost every ten minutes through the night and he was obviously unwell, with visits to the hospital, stents, the TURP[xiv], the catheter, phlebitis, and his loss of mobility.

By September 2008, he was unable to negotiate the stairs and had been having his meals upstairs. He managed to drive himself to and from the surgery for the Zoladex implant and to the dentist but he couldn't contemplate ten minutes in the local barber's chair for a swift but necessary haircut. I suggested he might have damaged or pulled a muscle and proposed 'Why not make an appointment to visit our local 'Back in Motion' clinic and see a physiotherapist who might be able to give you some exercises to help strengthen those back muscles?'

Danny did just that. When he returned from his appointment, he told me 'The physio looked at my back, took down a few details and suggested I should visit the doctor again to see what he thought the problem was.'

I shall always be grateful that the clinic had recommended that. After pressing the doctor really hard, Danny was referred to a neurologist to try to ascertain why the lower back and leg pain was so bad. Within a short time, the diagnosis of prostate cancer was further confirmed by a consultant. However, the cancer appeared to have spread from the prostate into Danny's bones and around his spine.

He was offered radiotherapy and chemotherapy at our local Norfolk and Norwich University Hospital. Danny declined the chemotherapy.

'I have no wish to spend my final days being sick and feeling uncomfortable,' he said while also telling me and Irene that he had signed a DNR, a 'do not resuscitate' notice.

He allowed me to load him into my car and drive him to the hospital, push him in a wheelchair as far as the Colney Centre main reception desk and the radiotherapy waiting area.

From there he would be taken away for about fifteen minutes, then returned to me in the wheelchair.

We didn't talk much on our way back home. Danny was tired after each session and needed to sleep. For further doses of radiotherapy, we ordered and paid for a private ambulance so that Danny could lie down and travel in greater comfort on a trolley in a private ambulance rather than a hospital one, so that he didn't need to wait for other patients to have been seen by other departments before he could be brought home.

After various spells in hospital, the longest being for three weeks in the autumn of 2008, Danny was finding it too uncomfortable to climb the stairs to reach our bedroom upstairs. I moved him and his immediate belongings permanently downstairs into his own room where there was a single bed that I had bought for any of my older grandchildren to use.

While he was away in hospital, I repainted the previously pink walls with 'honey-drizzle' emulsion and fixed some voile as well as honey-coloured curtains at the window. Since Danny's return from 'Mulbarton Ward' (the cancer ward), Chaucer slept every night in Danny's room.

I was aware of a shortage of finance for the Traveller Education and other pupil support services. From July 2007 and for the following six months, I had been on sick leave from work until my sick pay ran out. None of my staff contacted me to see how I was.

Although on sick leave, I was still technically at work and receiving emails from other TESs about Traveller pupils, their education records, professional training or regional meetings. I would forward these emails to my temporary replacement but received no thanks or acknowledgement that matters had been dealt with. The gap that my absence had caused had soon closed over.

I experienced some gentle pressure from my line manager to retire as soon as possible because the Service needed to make staffing reductions, but he carefully avoided anything that could be taken as constructive dismissal. The grievance at work from other staff had been brought about partly by possible staff losses. I had evidence that would address the grievance and various underlying allegations regarding undue work pressure but my former line manager instructed me to destroy the records I was holding.

Norfolk County Council did not follow their normal published procedure of settling a grievance by a face-to-face meeting: on the contrary I was instructed not to talk to or contact the complainants. I had not the energy to contest any of this at the time, I was too involved with looking after Danny, he was my priority and everything else could wait.

I gave notice in September that I would tender my formal resignation to take effect on 31st December 2007. Under the County's counselling scheme, I had been seeing a professional counsellor where I could offload. I found those visits helpful and reassuring.

Once I could leave the pressures of Norfolk Traveller Education Service behind and with Danny's agreement, I applied to go onto the County's list for supply teaching. I needed to fill in various questionnaires so that The Education Department could determine whether I was fit to work again and establish that my earlier vagueness and general feeling of walking around in a daze had been attributable to a complexity of different and often opposing stresses.

I didn't tell any of the children that I had been on sick leave for six months, they would only have worried.

While Danny was still ill, Lallo had been living and working in parts of Russia. Through her work as a teacher of English to foreigners, she had met Sergey, a professional diver in the Caspian Sea and she had shared her flat in the Kazakh city of Aktau with him. After two years of living together, they were married halfway up a snowy mountain in Eastern Russia.

Although invited, I couldn't go to the wedding, I couldn't leave Danny on his own. I offered to pay Keir's fare for him to go instead but he decided against it. As a result, none of Lallo's family was present to witness her marriage that winter. Nor did any of us speak or read Russian - or Kazakh.

To keep Danny interested and his mind active, I rented a portable television that stood on the chest of drawers in that room, with a portable aerial perched on top of the wardrobe.

He enjoyed watching 'Judge Judy', described as 'a reality show about a female judge that had made a real impact on the American justice system' and would often suggest that I should watch the programme with him, to see whether we agreed with Judge Judy's handling of the case.

Danny had the remote on the side table beside his bed, as well as one of our cordless phones so that he could make and receive calls. After meals and before bed, I would give him the medication that had been prescribed. I also bought a baby monitoring system with a listening device that I could have by my bedside upstairs.

That was so that I could hear if he called out or was in distress during the night. It allowed me to remain on duty while also getting some much needed, if shallow, sleep.

Danny was experiencing increased pain and was taken to the Priscilla Bacon Lodge in Colman Road that was known as the Centre for Specialist Palliative Care Services – the very same building that had once been the Jenny Lind Children's Hospital where I had had to take Keir after the metal five-barred gate at the Wild Life Park had fallen across his chest and head when he was only two years old – so that the nurses there could assist Danny's level of pain and prescribe appropriate pain relief.

Danny was amused and impressed to find that before lunch each day in hospital, he was offered either a glass of wine or a tot of whisky because, we were told by the nurses, that generally improved patients' appetites. Whatever it did, it had a beneficial effect on Danny and improved his general mood.

I had bought him some new pyjamas for his visit there. Previously with his urine problems, he had requested nightshirts in order to remove the need to fiddle with pyjama trousers when he was in a hurry. The new pyjamas, now that he was provided with a catheter and a urine bag, were woven through with a silver thread that, according to tests, could reduce the spread of infections. It didn't reduce the smell of urine, though.

When Mark and Claire came to visit Danny in the Priscilla Bacon Centre, I was very aware of the pungent urine smell coming from under Danny's bedcovers. For the sake of his pride and self-esteem, I hoped he remained unaware of it.

After he'd returned home from his stay at Priscilla Bacon Lodge, a Macmillan nurse came to see Danny a couple of times. She didn't ask to talk to me at all but I may well have suggested to her that she should spend all her visit talking with Danny in private. I don't know how much help he found her visits. On one occasion as she left the room, I saw that he had been crying but neither she nor he made any comment about that to me.

It was someone else who mentioned the Big C Centre to me. 'It's at the hospital, you might find it helpful to visit someone there,' she said. 'They can give you advice about finance, about things you can legitimately claim for. They will also probably offer you a cup of coffee and a biscuit,' she added.

The nurse at the Big C told me that Danny and I might well qualify for receiving money for additional support, and that any alterations to the house considered necessary by the doctor would be exempt from VAT. I can testify that the Big C biscuits were delicious.

While he was suffering pain and having difficulty walking to the loo, Danny had been sitting on the edge of his bed to pee, using a bucket which I would then empty. On one occasion, he either caught the full bucket with his foot or Chaucer knocked it over. I suspected the former but either way, the result was the same. I mopped the wet patch on the pink bedroom carpet, sprayed disinfectant and resolved, when this was all over, that the first thing I would do would be to have a new carpet fitted.

But I was also pleased that we hadn't done that before, the pink shaggy carpet could stay for the time being.

I decided to ask a painter and decorator to paint the walls and ceiling in the hallway. I didn't think I could sensibly manage an energetic Springer Spaniel with open cans of emulsion paint lying around on the floor and wet paintwork, as well as a frisky kitten or being at work and looking after Danny all at the same time.

I also asked a builder to alter the loo and the shower room doors such that they would open outward rather than the normal inward into the room. I did that in case Danny should ever make his way to the loo or washing facilities and fall, thereby blocking access to the door and any hope of an easy rescue.

With Danny's endorsement, I accepted bouts of supply teaching to give me short-term finance and a way of getting away from focusing on illness all day. I told my children of the situation regarding Danny's cancer, Keir particularly because he was the nearest geographically. Telling him provided me with support and I appreciated that a great deal. I felt I was going against Danny's expressed wishes for secrecy but also knew I needed the support of my children. I owed them the truth.

Danny had become very uncomfortable in the bed. Social Services provided a water bed for Danny that would automatically inflate; I was told that it was intended to prevent bedsores. I wondered how automatic any deflation might become under my care and how best to deal with it, should that happen. Danny was provided with a catheter, and I had the telephones changed to provide four cordless phones, each on its own housing; one in the study, one in the hall by the front door, one in the kitchen and one upstairs beside my bed. I could easily unplug the study one and place it in Danny's room beside his bed, if necessary.

When Danny became doubly incontinent, Social Services also provided a commode on a chair and a seat for the shower. I was able to collect a huge box of urinal pots, each one made of egg-box type material that would hold liquids for only a brief amount of time, as I was to discover.

Irene was unhappy about Danny having stents inserted in his back. 'You wouldn't do that even to a dog,' she protested to me, almost as if I had sanctioned and done the operation myself. Her remark had also made me wonder about her knowledge of canine surgery and her attitude towards dogs in general.

One day, as I was watching Chaucer standing on the back lawn in the garden, I saw his legs buckle. He slumped down onto his chest and lay there, his mouth open, panting. I had taken him only a fortnight previously to the vet because he appeared off-colour. The vet had not given him an X-ray but had checked him all over and found nothing obviously amiss. I had attributed that to Chaucer having picked up on Danny's cancer and the resultant change of doggy mood.

I went over to him to try to help him up but he couldn't stand, he collapsed again. This was so unlike him, so sudden and unexpected. I felt very guilty, I had been so busy looking after Danny, checking that he was all right and keeping him occupied, that I had rather taken Chaucer for granted. It had never occurred to me that there might be something seriously wrong that the vet had not detected.

Unable to bundle Chaucer into the back of my car, I called the vet and asked her to visit as soon as possible. I put Chaucer into his basket and covered his back with a fleecy rug, not because he appeared cold but to show him that I cared and was doing something, anything, to help him feel loved and better. By this time, he was panting but otherwise unresponsive.

I was still talking to him when the vet arrived, telling him that everything would be all right, thanking him for taking such care of Danny each night, thanking him for being such a wonderful dog. I led the vet straight into the kitchen.

She examined Chaucer, listened to his heart, peeled back his top lip and looked at his gums. 'The gums are very pale, I think he's bleeding inside,' she said, 'I suspect some internal injury or organ failure. There's nothing much I can do for him now.'

I think that's what she said or something very much like that, because by that time I was in tears. I held his front paw while the vet gave him a lethal injection. I told him, jerking the words between my sobs, that I loved him very much and thanked him for being such a super dog, for taking care of Danny. The vet removed his collar and asked if I would like her to take his body away. I think I said 'yes', took the collar from her hand and watched her carry and load Chaucer's body into the boot of her car.

I wept buckets of tears that night and all the next day, so much so that I felt I had no more tears left inside me to weep. Along with Danny, Chaucer had been fun, been my happy, loyal friend and companion that Danny had chosen. He had been keen and enthusiastic to do whatever I suggested or asked. And now he was gone. For ever. I felt totally empty, totally drained. Of everything.

Chapter 23

Ash

Because I wanted to remember and record what was happening during that period of my life, I kept a diary in an old notebook.

<u>'Wednesday 28 January 2009:</u>

This is the pattern of a fairly typical day right now: -

06.40 My alarm goes off. I need to be up right away to be ready for the bathroom fitter, who arrives promptly at 08.30.

07.00 By now I've fed Chin, our Burmese cat, made myself a cup of tea, switched off the house alarm and decided that my hair is sufficiently OK to skip having a shower this morning – it saves nearly half an hour. I check whether Danny is awake. He is, having had a rather broken night. I remove his duvet, replace it with a cellular blanket and a stripy fleece throw, and encourage him to have a pee.

07.30 Danny's had his tea; I empty his pee bucket and note that this morning, it's not as bloody as it sometimes is. I get dressed, having had a quick wash, and begin to get breakfast. It's not complicated; 2oz porridge oats to 300ml milk and water. Danny tells me he won't want much.

08.00 By now we've both had a bowl of porridge in his room, with sugar and single cream. I've helped him to sit up by holding his hands and pulling; the occupational therapy bed does only so much. I've put out Danny's tablets (3 Gabapentin; 1 Lansoprazol; 1 pink Stilboesterol; 2 Naproxin; 8 Paracetamol and 1 asprin in a separate eggcup so as not to take it at the same time as the Naproxin) and he has his morning dose. He looks rough this morning and is obviously hurting. Everywhere.

08.10 I phone Wymondham Medical Centre and ask the receptionist (I get through the first time. Miracle) to ask Dr Thurston to ring Danny after morning surgery. She takes the details. Danny is having real difficulty now in self-catheterising. The district nurse tried on Monday to fit an in-dwelling catheter . . . and failed miserably. And on Tuesday evening he dropped the pee bucket again, making a large area of the carpet wet. I cleared it up OK and was truly thankful that I'd made the decision not to change the pink carpet for a new one.

08.30 Steven the bathroom fitter arrives. Today it looks as though he'll get the bathroom floor tiled. I get Danny's clean pyjamas from the washing machine and dryer and put them in the airing cupboard. Although they had been clean on last Saturday, they got wet when Danny dropped the bucket, so needed a wash. I take Danny his after-breakfast cup of tea and wash up the porridge saucepan. I put a load of whites into the machine, including Mark's soiled dress shirt and I look at how to mend his dinner jacket. I cancel next Tuesday's teaching, as it will be the day after Danny's radiotherapy.

09.30 And it's raining. I drive into the town and get the paper and some bread. I take Danny The Daily Telegraph.

10.0 I make Danny and Steven drinks and phone 'Simply Doors' to check on various items before I put in an online order. I start to mend Mark's ripped jacket lining.

10.55 The phone goes. I hear it via the baby alarm which I've put on the table while I'm mending in the dining room. I try to get to the hall phone in time to pick it up but it rings only four times before going onto answerphone. The caller apparently withheld his/her number as well as leaving no message. I assume the missed call is from Irene rather than from Dr Thurston. Danny is not best pleased at my not reaching the phone in time. I ask him why he didn't pick it up, as he has a phone right by his pillow. He says he thought I'd do it.

11.15 Toftwood Juniors ring and ask if I can cover Thursday and Friday this week. I say no to Friday, as we are due to go to the hospital. I offer to let them know about Thursday but not until 1pm-ish after (hopefully) Dr Thurston has phoned – he may suggest Danny goes to the Norfolk & Norwich to have the catheter inserted. But Pam at Toftwood would prefer to get Thursday's cover sorted this morning, which is fair enough. The post has arrived and I sort it. Danny reads his and I deal with it as necessary.

11.30 I make Danny and me a cup of coffee and ensure that he has the commode ready if necessary. I deal with my mail.

12.30 I go into his room to ascertain what Danny would like for lunch . . . . and he is fast asleep. I have my lunch while talking to Steven until Danny wakes up. I make him (i.e., I get from the freezer) some spicy tomato, bean and pork soup with a fresh white roll. I wait for Louise, the palliative care nurse, who said last week that she would call in today. No call from Dr Thurston. Danny wants to use the commode so I get that ready for him and check that he has pads, wipes, loo roll etc.

And light the perfumed candle. I overcome my frustrations re a) Dr T. not phoning and b) Louise not arriving, by chipping the purple paint off the shower room wall. It comes off very, very gradually. I see Louise pass by the window to ring the backdoor bell. I fill her in briefly but honestly about Danny's condition and general mood. I take her in to his room. No, she wouldn't like a cup of tea and Danny hasn't drunk his after-lunch cup either.

16.00 Danny has obviously been in tears during his conversation with Louise, as the two wet tissues evidence. He looks red-eyed. Louise and I discuss increasing the pain relief by increasing the two Fentanyl patches from 12mg and 25mg, to two 25mg. She bravely washes her hands in the almost-clean bathroom, neatly avoiding the flakes of purple paint all over the white sanitary ware. She says Dr Thurston will call in, after his afternoon surgery, to try to fit the catheter himself. I check what miscellaneous supplies we have in the intended en-suite and bring them all downstairs. Supplies seem to comprise lots of tubes, bags and various sorts of pads. I continue scraping, while Steven leaves at about 5pm.

19.30 Dr Thurston arrives, plus medical bag. No, he can't get the catheter in either, so he arranges for Danny to go up to Edgefield Ward at the N&N tomorrow to have it fitted there. Dr T. also accepts my offer of the wash basin – the towel was clean – and I'm pleased that Steven replaced the hot tap last week so that it now turns off as well as on.

20.00 I prepare cold chicken and oven-ready chips, followed by yogurt. Danny watches some TV and then nods off.

23.00 I wake him, having removed his cold, untouched cup of tea, and bring him a cup of hot. I bring him a bowl, toothpaste and brush, cold water in a measuring jug and a towel so that he can brush his teeth. He catheterises himself again – some old clots of blood and a little capillary fresh blood as well as some fairly dark pee. I administer the Oramorph – 7.5mg – cover him with the duvet, check the baby alarm, switch off the light and kiss him goodnight. He looks fed up and disinterested.

23.45 I sort out Chin, the washing and drying, leave the washing up which is minimal, set the alarm, check the doors are locked and go upstairs. The best part of the day is then to come – climbing into a warm bed and reading for half-an-hour or so. This is my 'Me Time'.

It is early July 2009. I hear a car door open. Voices, as it closes. I grit my teeth.

Irene and husband Phil have arrived from Southampton. Expected but not invited. They have come to stay for a few days. Not by my request, certainly. I could really have done without this. But Irene, as my sister-in-law, has felt that it is her right, her 'duty' even, she said. And to some extent it is. And perhaps her last opportunity to say . . . well, whatever she might want to say to her brother. I feel in no position to object or deny her, or them, this visit.

Danny seems genuinely pleased. When Irene phoned her elder brother and announced that they would be coming, he appreciated her unspoken comprehension of what is going to happen, quite soon. 'Irene knows', he tells me, as if I don't. When Irene says that their whole family is riddled with cancer, Danny has contradicted her in his familiar forthright manner, always willing to spar with his sister when he thinks she is wrong, being ridiculous. 'Like whom?' he asks. Then a long debate ensues about what and when Aunty Mary or their father died of.

'All Father's relatives are at risk of cancer, it's in their genes,' Irene again asserts. Danny turns his head away; listening to Irene requires energy. He knows what happens once she gets an idea into her head. And anyway, Great Aunt Mary was on their mother's side of the family.

I have prepared the spare bedroom for them, and the bathroom. Danny is still occupying the single room downstairs with his own loo and shower room just across the hall, but which he is no longer able to use, cannot access. Even with the walking frame, he is unable to take more than a couple of steps without intense pain. He has a catheter and a portable commode.

Irene has said 'Don't bother about a meal this evening. We don't know what time we will arrive, it will all depend on the traffic on the M25. So, we will eat out or get soup and sandwiches. We don't want to be any trouble,' she says.

He isn't eating much by now. A spoonful of porridge for breakfast with his medication; an egg, perhaps, at lunchtime. Very little in the evening, just a slice of apple, his tablets and a double dose of Oramorph to help get him through the night without pain. Each night I wash his face and body parts with a warm damp face flannel, bring him a bowl and water so that he can sit up to brush his teeth.

I turn his pillow so that it is soft. I set up a baby alarm that picks up any sound from his room and relays it to wherever I decide to place the monitor, my bedroom upstairs at night, downstairs in the kitchen during the day. That way, I can tell that he is asleep and breathing normally. Or hear any sounds of distress.

He has a phone by his bed. He is alert and sometimes amusing. I enjoy our conversations and there is a completely different level of intimacy now. Until now, his brain has seemed to be the only part of him that the cancer has not reached. Prostate first, then legs and back, stents inserted towards the kidneys. He has had radiotherapy on his bones but resists chemotherapy. 'There is no point, not now,' he says. He is prepared. I hope I am.

Today he mutters a welcome to Irene, tries a smile. But then he says something odd to her about his only son Mark, about Claire and their new daughter. A *daughter*? His son and wife Claire *are* expecting a baby but it isn't born yet, not due until next week. They live in Canada. The couple have decided not to find out the sex of their unborn child. It would be like unwrapping one's Christmas present early, they have said. Irene and I exchange glances. *A daughter?* Has Danny forgotten? Is he confused?

Mark has visited his father a couple of times when he was in hospital, having his pain level assessed. Danny is always very pleased to see him; and Claire too, he adds politely. Danny says that it is really good of Mark to come so far, when he is so very busy; and he finds it hard to get away from the university, he assures us, where he is a professor. Danny is genuinely grateful, totally uncritical, almost adoringly.

We move to the kitchen, I put the kettle on to make Irene and Phil a cup of tea after their long journey. I nip back to Danny to see whether he needs a drink.

But he doesn't answer, his mouth looks dry, he cannot open it. There is dark sticky stuff between his lips.

I place my hand across his forehead, fetch a fresh damp flannel and try to dampen his lips, wipe the stuff off. I can't. It stays stuck. Black. Glutenous. This has nothing to do with the last thing he had eaten.

I decide to call the doctor, who has visited quite regularly. Doctor Thurston is not available but a palliative care nurse will come as soon as he can. I explain this to Danny and hope he is able to understand.

Irene and Phil wait in the kitchen. I realise that they can hear everything that I am saying, through the baby monitor. And everything that Danny might say, were he able.

This is probably going to be my last time to say . . . anything. Goodbye, I think. And thank you. For everything. Nearly everything.

And I am quite suddenly pleased that he cannot speak. There are things that I would like him to say. Like 'Sorry about . . . you-know-what.' And I would say, I hope, 'It doesn't matter now'. Although it does. It still hurts terribly, acutely and I try not to visit those memories, to distance myself as much as I can. Not let my mind lick around them, the taste is still far too sharp, bitter. Better to switch off feeling, not to feel, not to react or slash her tyres, not throw stones at her window nor wish her dead. Stay in control.

But if he were to say anything like that, apologise, thank me for staying with him, not telling him he had to leave, looking after him, then Irene would probably hear. She regards him as such a wonderful person; says so, and I see no reason to shatter that, not at this late stage. It gives her something to hold on to.

I can, if nothing else, protect his reputation.

The palliative care nurse arrives. He decides that the black on Danny's lips is blood. Clotted. That he is bleeding from his stomach. And that I have to make a choice. Now.

'Very soon' the nurse tells me, 'your husband will be in intense pain. The previous medication that you gave him at breakfast will be wearing off . . . and because he is unable to swallow any morphine or any other pain-relieving substance.'

I take this information in, in small gulps.

'You can allow your husband to die in agony,' the nurse tells me 'or let me give him a large injection of morphine. I'm not sure quite what amount, but sufficient that it will be enough to lessen the pain . . . but it might possibly finish him off'.

'Can Danny hear this? Does he know what is happening?' I ask the medic.

The nurse is not certain, but thinks that it is quite likely. And I wonder what choice Danny would make?

I am uncertain as to what choice I need to make. For him.

Irene is in the room by this time. She has heard all this. She says that that is what happened to her mother, in the end. To Danny's and her mother. That after that last injection, she had died.

'Peacefully', Irene says. I hope I can believe her. Although this might be another of Irene's 'ideas'.

The nurse injects him. And Danny dies, quite quickly.

I find this hard to accept. That, though I know he is dead, he is no longer in the room. He looks the same. Pale. Dry skin. But his blue eyes are lifeless, no focus.

I ask the palliative care nurse to double-check, to call a doctor, just to make sure. And I am not sure what to do next; what needs to be done.

On Irene's and the nurse's suggestion, I contact an undertaker.

Suddenly I am pleased Irene is there. Not for comfort, not for me anyway. But because she can tell Mark what happened, that we, I, did what we thought was best, what Danny would have wanted. And, as an afterthought, I ask about organ donation.

'Only his eyes would be worth donating,' I am told. But I give the undertaker and the transplant co-ordinator the go-ahead on that.

Irene and the doctor suggest, quite strongly, that I shouldn't be in the house on my own 'at a time like this'. I tell them that this is nonsense, that I am going to have to get used to being on my own. And Irene and Phil leave, return to Southampton until the day of the funeral.

I have very few tears left to shed. Most of my grieving has been premature, when I first learned that Danny had cancer, that it had spread and that my best friend, my confidante, companion and ally would be leaving me for good. And when I had Chaucer put down, only a week ago.

I have never wept tears like those. They hurt my throat. And again I feel guilt. Again I know I focused so much on Danny that I had taken Chaucer for granted.

I believe that I have let him down, let them both down. I am totally bereft.

But I have to face up to another loss, however much it was predicted. Life without Danny is now real.

Over the phone to Irene, we talk about the funeral. Danny had stipulated that he wished to be cremated, that there was to be no religious service or reference to God. 'None of that nonsense', he had said, 'no cross or hymns or anything'.

I would like some sort of occasion to say goodbye, formally.

Irene tells me 'You won't be in any fit state to arrange anything, nor able to hold it together once the reality hits you. And certainly not to speak at his funeral.'

I resolve to prove her wrong, that I am not going to let any grief, tears or emotional response show. I know Danny would expect no less.

Danny could never deal with any expression of emotion; he simply didn't understand it. He considered it was something childish, like infant teething or bed-wetting, that people should have grown out of.

I decide that he would have told me to 'just get on with it', that's what he would have said.

I settle for some Sibelius for the introductory music, 'Going Home' by Mark Knopfler which was the music to the film 'A

Local Hero'; 'Days' by the Kinks as representing what I would like to have said to Danny, and to read 'You Can Shed Tears', a poem by David Harkins.

I am determined to be in control and matter-of-fact and positive about this occasion.

Irene writes and sends me something that is to be an address at the funeral.

It's all about how she and Phil had lent Danny money after his flat was burgled, how helpful they have been during his first marriage and how they have looked after Mark when Mark was little.

I reject this tribute as tactfully as I can. Danny would have hated it, especially the mention of money which, at the best of times, he would have considered distasteful. But Irene is grieving too, I tell myself.

Mark composes a tribute to his father which he will read, something to do with 'Watership Down' and the unfairness of death.

He has been undecided as to whether he can get away from Canada for the funeral but at the last minute he thinks he can.

He can, for just a couple of days, leave his wife who has only that past week on 9th July given birth to a son, and fly to England.

Cars are arriving, one after another at a respectful speed; they are being parked wherever their drivers can find a gap. Vehicles hunch up in the increasing row against the sombre green trees and border of leggy perennials.

Within minutes of her arrival at the crematorium, Irene is in tears. Not just tears of grief, it turns out, but because there are so many mourners here.

'Who are all these people?' she asks me, 'I don't know them. Who are they, why are they here? What has my brother's death got to do with them?' and there is a note of resentment in her voice.

'He wouldn't have wanted that, he would have wanted . . .' and her words become less firm . . . 'just his family'.

At that, I wonder whether my sister-in-law considers that I, as her late brother's second wife, am really not quite *family* enough.

'Yes, he might,' I agree, assuming more authority than I had thought possible, 'but I take the view that a funeral is not just for the deceased. It's also for the living, for them to pay their final respects and to say their individual goodbyes.

Especially,' I add with more apparent certainty than is actual, 'as he chose not to let anyone other than his immediate family know that he had cancer. I understand why that was what he wanted, he said he could deal with his own emotion and loss but not with theirs; that was his choice.

But now he would understand. .' and I try not to think that I am talking about a man who professed not to believe in any form of after-life, '. . that there are a lot of other people to be considered: people who worked with him, who respected, admired and even loved him'.

So there, I think. I don't wish to appear brutal, but Irene has been at home with me in the room when Danny had been pronounced dead and she has been there, when I would have appreciated having a few last words with him in private, there more by her self-assumed right than by invitation - and she has had the golden opportunity to say goodbye to her brother.

So why, I ask myself, would she be upset because other people want to pay their respects?

'But I don't know them,' she bleats and I wonder, not for the first time, whether she quietly resented her brother's prominence in the local community, his career success, his financial security and his good relationships with a range of friends, colleagues and acquaintances.

There can be a time and a place for saying 'but it's not about you' and this isn't it.

But afterwards, after the ceremony – which I shouldn't call a service because Danny was adamant that there were to be no crosses, hymns, prayers or references to God at his funeral – afterwards, once the wake is over, when the cups and glasses have been washed, any left-over food has been covered with shiny foil and put in the fridge, the guests have departed – then I wonder to what extent Irene had been almost possessive over her brother.

Wanting to influence him regarding his first marriage, his choice of where and in what house to live, his choice of me as his second wife, his attitude towards my children, his choice of school and career, illnesses, funeral, speeches, his son, the lot.

And the house and what she thinks should be done with it, who should benefit from his Will and so on. She has already implied to Mark that our house, my house, is now his.

Presumably Mark has some idea of English law and will ignore that. But Irene is . . not exactly controlling because no one could have 'controlled' Danny but . . . she had wished to have her say, certainly. To influence him. And, I reflect, has probably done so quite often in a quiet but insidious way.

In his Will, along with making a few monetary gifts to the children, Danny says that he wants me to do the things that I want to do; that these, had circumstances been different, might include the things that he and I would have done together. I assume he means travel. And perhaps write.

Danny was a keen walker and with that codicil in mind, I decide to take a break abroad, do something active, stay occupied. So, after I have been to Nepal with Saga Holidays and walked in the foothills of the Annapurna range, for Summer 2010 I book an alpine 'Ramblers' holiday to Austria, a country where I have been before, but to a different area. And on my own.

I need to show myself that I can do this, that I don't always need male companionship. I choose a guided walking holiday in the Stubai Valley, where the walks are graded from 'moderate' to 'challenging' according to difficulty. I decide that I will start off gently and work towards something more strenuous, when I feel I can manage it.

The group consists of about fifteen people, including the two leaders and three married couples. Everyone else appears single. I am not a fast walker. I am tall but my legs are quite short so while others are striding out, I try to keep up with my lower limbs working ultra-fast, like a clockwork chicken.

The others on this walking holiday are similar in age and despite a mix of gender, we each seem to find the altitude and the constant changes of gradient a challenge to our more senior or middle-aged lungs and leg muscles.

I meet Rosemary and Barry, who live on the Norfolk/Suffolk border; they gel well as a couple and I say so. Barry, it transpires, is Rosemary's third husband.

Rosemary and I swim together in the hotel pool after each long walk and enjoy each other's company. She tells me that this is her third marriage and that the other two had not been successful. And she seems to understand when, on the 6th of July, the first anniversary of Danny's death, I take myself away from the group, to sit quietly on a hillside and watch birds through my binoculars.

As I would have done with Danny. And to remember him.

A month or so later, the Association for International Cancer Research contacts me. Would I be willing to raise general public awareness and money for cancer research by getting people to sponsor me to climb Mount Kilimanjaro in Tanzania? I have just returned from the holiday to Austria. I found it hard going, partly because of the altitude, but I completed the ten days without any ill effects. So yes, I tell them, I will give it a go. Danny would have approved. And I would try to raise several thousands of pounds in sponsorship money.

I do not approach Irene and Phil directly. It seems rather insensitive so soon after the cremation, even though, as I am tempted to remind her, Irene had been adamant that cancer runs in her family, which presumably would include herself, her own daughter and Mark.

In 2011, I spend a wet Spring weekend of training in the Lake District and being assessed by the coach and administrators as to my suitability to manage the three- or four-day hike, up to an altitude of 19,341ft above sea level, to the rim of the crater of the dormant volcano.

Although by now I am in my late-sixties, no one mentions my age. A slogan on someone's tee shirt reads 'Success is more a matter of attitude than altitude'.

I do not really accept what the internet tells me, that climbing Kilimanjaro is probably one of the most dangerous things that I will ever do.

Instead, when I tell Irene what I am going to attempt and why and make no mention of sponsorship, she tells me that I should manage it easily, that she knows that school parties go up there and quite often, the children run up.

I don't inform her that every year, approximately a thousand people are evacuated from the mountain and approximately ten deaths are reported. Nor do I mention that the actual number of deaths is believed to be two to three times higher, that the main cause of death is altitude sickness, due to speed of ascent.

When Irene believes she is right, she is right and no amount of information to the contrary will change her mind.

But I do wonder about her general level of awareness - and common sense.

Even now, I don't think about that trip much. It wasn't fun.

I didn't do it because it was some long-held aspiration.

I try not to recall the run-down hotel in Moshi where we spent our first uncomfortable night before loading our bags onto the big truck that would laboriously take us to Marangu Gate and the entrance to Kilimanjaro National Park where we were instructed to register.

Nor our slow plod up a red cinder path through the rain forest, the mist and drizzle, sweaty in our clammy waterproofs and the unaccustomed African heat, almost tripping over a mongoose near the make-shift toilets.

Nor having lunch cooked for us by our cheerful porters and continuing on, damp, sticky and uncomfortable, to Mandara Huts for our first night: unrolling our down sleeping bags onto badly-sprung bunk beds.

Nor the ever-upward tramp over heath and moorland, seeing unfamiliar yellow plants until we arrive through the cloud at Horombo Huts, over twelve thousand feet above sea level. And arguing our way out of the women having to share a hut with strange men who are not from our group.

Next, a day of necessary acclimatisation and our daunting first sight of Mawenzi and Kibo's summit. We are acting more as a team now, supporting each other and making sure that we are each safe and cheerful. Sharing my bag of boiled sweets helps.

A second night in the Horombo Huts while we acclimatise, that ghastly porridge and Milo for breakfast; then a climb through dwindling heathland that blends into a moonscape as we enter the sweeping saddle that connects Mawenzi and Kibo.

The last water point between Horombo and Kibo Huts, the reassuring sight of a helipad that we hope we will not cause to be used, and the very sobering view of Kibo across the high desert.

Kibo Huts at fifteen and a half thousand feet, the nose bleeds starting, the headaches, the buzzing noise in our ears, the foul long-drop toilets with a door that will not close.

And the cold. The gripping, cheek-numbing, are-my-fingers-still-in-my-gloves cold.

Two hours sleep until I am woken just before midnight, given a hot drink of something unrecognisable and a ginger biscuit.

I grasp my walking poles and down jacket. We have to set off in the dark, up the steep ashy outside wall of the crater to the summit of Kibo.

Only the moon and a headtorch to guide me. And the walking boots of the guy in front. Can't see who it is. Doesn't matter anyway. We are a straggly group and I feel totally alone. If I feel anything at all.

Up, breathe. Up, breathe, up, up. Stop on the path. Get my breath.

Water in my camel-pack has iced up. Mouth dry. Need to pee.

Might be more than a pee. Can't leave the ash path, don't know where the edge is. If there is an edge. But still need to pee – or poo. Tissues? Somewhere, probably in a pocket. Forget privacy. It doesn't exist, not here among the group and the porters.

Bugger the moon. Safety more important. Roll down layers of clothing. Aim away from my boots. Cold. And hot. But better now.

Pull up, start walking again. Slowly, slowly. In Swahili, 'pole, pole.'

Finally, and hours later, summit in sight. But look. Rocks, not just ash, huge jagged rocks. At the summit. At Gilman's Point. I'm nearly there. Relief, not elation.

But enormous rocks I have to clamber over, poles no use here, a damned nuisance. Not only now, but on the way down. If there is a down.

Some of my colleagues are talking absolute gibberish. I think. Unless it's me. Snow on Uhuru peak. I don't care. Seen snow before.

And sunrise. Now sunrise. Yellow sky. Cloud below.

Can't see the whole of Africa below me from here. What nonsense. Too much cloud.

My porter says that's enough, not to walk around the crater rim. I agree with him, I'm done in. Shaking with cold. Or fear. Or exhaustion.

Want to start down again. Nervous. Frightened. Shut that out. Left ankle has no brakes, no balance. Deep breath . . .

Ash in my hair, up nose, in eyes. Dark glasses help protect contact lenses. Start down again. Go carefully. Very gently. Rock. Ash slope. Steep. Too steep. Might start running; not be able to stop.

The doctor accompanying us on this trip has handed me his bottle of water. What is his name? What's mine?

Ash over the top of my thick socks, over and into my boots. Long strides, slide. Long stride, slide. Again. Like scree hopping.

Cover the distance, leave a grey gritty cloud sweeping behind. Ash. Ash.

Ash. In my lungs. And between my toes and fingernails, on my tongue, more dark grey grit. Keep going.

At last, at the end of a snaking path, I spot Kibo Huts far below. Keep going and I can get there. I can see someone else from our group. Cascading, blazing a trail.

Can taste ash. I have ash in my pockets, in my hood. I pull that up over my balaclava, to keep heat in and ash out of my ears. Pull it down again, too claustrophobic.

I am growing quite warm as I head steadily back towards the rising sun, nearly four thousand feet back down to Kibo Huts.

Walking poles not needed now and useless in the depth of ash.

After a drink outside the huts and a brief rest, too brief, the further long walk back to Horombo. I have been walking almost non-stop for over twenty hours. I am too tired to sleep. Too tired.

Once home in England, I leave unpacking my bag and rucksack for as long as I can. Still tired. But I put my poles away.

Irene contacts me to ask if I have chosen the urn for Danny's ashes or collected it from the undertaker. I assure her that I have.

She suggests that, whenever Mark is in England again, we should all get together and have a joint sprinkling of Danny's ashes over their mother's grave, each say a few words, that sort of thing. But I know, because we discussed it when we each wrote our Wills, that this is absolutely not what Danny wanted.

Danny wanted his ashes, so he said, to be flushed down the loo and then go out to sea.

I had balked at part of this suggestion, the plumbing is recent and I had told him, jokingly, 'I don't fancy having our lavatory pipe blocked by your remains.'

I unpack, empty all that Kilimanjaro ash which has collected in my boots, bag, pockets, hood, into a small glass jam-jar and screw the lid on.

Shove a pile of clothes into the washing machine. I download my photos and put them into a folder.

I label the jar 'All I have left from Kili' and put it on the downstairs shower-room window sill. I check to see whether I am anywhere near the goal I set myself to raise for AICR in sponsorship. I am, and just above it.

Almost two years later, Mark and Claire ask if they and their young son may come for Christmas. Mark tells me over the phone, 'I'm lecturing in Paris this semester and the next, and it makes no sense for us to return to Canada for just a few days.'

I agree to their visit. With my children and their families too, there will be fifteen of us for Christmas dinner, if Keir returns from Antarctica on time.

I find Claire hard work but Mark is fine. He was a bit helpless at his father's wake but he was grieving, so his lack of initiative was understandable.

I mention to Irene that they are coming for a few days. Only a few days, I stress. And that I would find Claire hard to accommodate, to understand. Not just her accent, which is heavily Canadian but her attitudes on sexuality, her comments about men and their apparent dominance. She lectures in Women's Studies and English Literature.

Irene suggests that Phil drives her to Norfolk so that she can see Mark. And his two-year old son. And do anything that Mark wishes to do.

I assume she is referring to some joint sprinkling of Danny's ashes. Imagining each saying a few loving words about her brother; my husband; his father. But there was no common relationship.

Grief separates rather than bonds. Danny was someone quite different to each of us.

I tell Irene that I have already taken Danny's ashes to Cornwall, to Morwenstow where the family had come from some five hundred years ago. Danny and I had not been able to trace further back than that.

I have thrown some of the ashes into the gentle stream that runs around the churchyard, across a field of sheep, over a steep cliff and into the sea. Said my own thoughts. Not all the ash, though.

I keep some in a plastic jar in my bedroom. I do not offer these to Mark. Nor Irene. They could ask, could request.

But neither does.

Bundling up sheets and towels to wash after Irene, Phil and Mark have each gone their separate ways, I see that the jar on the shower-room window sill has been turned round, the label dampened and the last part of the writing smudged.

There is less ash than there had been. The level of grey has dropped.

Not much. But a bit.

Someone, I imagine, has helped himself or herself. Has taken the matter into their own hands. To hold their own ceremony.

I smile and pat the lid of the jar, wink at the ceiling. Danny would be smiling too, I think.

Chapter 24

Likewise

When Danny died of cancer, I anaesthetised myself emotionally. There were things to be done, duties to perform, legal stuff to get through. Other people's emotions, mine too, can be embarrassing. Danny's advice to himself and to other people when faced with anything difficult, was always 'Oh, just get on with it.'

But I miss him. I miss his intelligence, his interests, his sense of humour, his understanding, his caring, his love.

Being married, being close to someone is like being one of a couple of semi-detached houses. You sit comfortably side-by-side, sharing a combined structural frontage onto the road. But if one of you is demolished, then ideally the adjoining wall should be sliced down the middle, leaving the remaining property intact.

But in our case, Danny seems to have claimed the party wall, leaving me with a roof and only three outside walls, open on one side to where there previously has been warmth and protection. Open to whatever influences or intrusion that might arise. This is the first time for many years that I am living alone, without the children. I feel empty, unsure, vulnerable.

Mainly for company, I buy a Retriever puppy. I think it will give me a reason to get out of bed each morning, take regular exercise and provide a structure to my day.

On account of its colour and because it loves rootling about in the banks of the nearest willow-edged pond, I give it the name 'Butterworth'.

Rosemary and Barry, the couple I met on the holiday in Austria, were kind enough to sponsor me on the A.I.C.R. Kilimanjaro climb. I met Rosemary several times afterwards, in a café in Norwich not far from the John Lewis store.

Telling her a little about the trek and the problems that the group had encountered, I asked her how she and Barry met. Apparently, Barry had known Rosemary from way back when he was the sailing instructor for her two daughters, so he was familiar with the family set-up.

'When Barry retired and his marriage ended, he made contact with me again and found me unattached, although I was dating various people,' Rosemary explained.

Rosemary was more than ten years younger than I and employed in the National Health Service. She was small, bubbly, energetic and a born worrier.

'I was worried' she told me quietly, 'about my two girls reaching puberty without any positive male influence in their lives.'

'So how,' I asked her, 'in your situation, were you able to meet other men, men who weren't coming to the surgery as patients, let alone be asked out on a date?'

'It was fairly easy,' she said, 'I advertised myself.'

Over a second cup of coffee and a cheese scone, I asked her exactly what she meant by 'I advertised myself'. She explained that she placed an advert in the local 'Lonely Hearts' section of an East Anglian daily newspaper but found this, considering her job, too local for comfort. So, she explored various dating sites. 'It was interesting,' she said, 'I met a variety of people, some from quite a long way away.' And then, 'But men lie, of course.'

So, it was purely on account of the likely age range that I decided to look at 'Likewise', an online dating site for the 'Over 50s' - although I hesitated before signing up and paying for a six-month membership. Logging on and deciding what to press, I wondered what I was getting myself into, it all seemed a bit too technical. I did not realise, until much later, that the 'Likewise' site was linked to several other national newspaper and media dating sites. And that link showed me just how much some men are either very forgetful, or prepared to lie.

I saw that some chap, about my age, calling himself 'Hawkeye1947' had signed up to 'Likewise'. He said he was a college or university student, ex-RAF, single, aged 70, of average build, lived in Nottinghamshire and 5 feet 10 inches tall. He said he was looking for 'friends/let's see what happens'.

On the same page, with identical photographs, was 'Hawkear1947'. His profile said that he was widowed, lived in Nottingham, educated at university, financially 'comfortable', 5 feet 11 inches tall, stocky, 69 years old and looking for a 'long-term relationship' There was no mention of the RAF.

I deduced that 'Hawkeye1947' and 'Hawkear1947' were the same person; that 'Hawkear1947', not realising that the sites were linked, had signed up to one of the other dating websites and paid two separate subscriptions. But this chap seemed to have altered age and height between the two sites.

Were I interested, I would have to wonder what else he was inaccurate about, what he believed in, what his aspirations really were?

I could only assume that many others, like me, were experiencing some confusion about their identity. It isn't easy, when you've been one half of 'us', to know exactly who you are when you are just you. Or when there's no one around to measure you.

I asked Lallo for her advice on what I should say about myself.

She was mildly helpful but she knows me as her mother, not as some strange man's prospective date. But she took my photograph, with me standing against the neutral-coloured curtains in the hallway.

Using the name 'Susan 2324' to provide a measure of privacy, I began my narrative for the 'Likewise' dating site with 'My second husband died six years ago; whereas I'm OK on my own, there's someone vital missing, a soul-mate.'

I went on to describe my interest in wildlife and the countryside and as I did so, I became increasingly aware how I was echoing those interests that both my father and Danny held. I described my taste in music as classical, mainly Bach and Beethoven, which were my mother's preference and the composers I was brought up with.

Or, as my mother would have insisted that I should write, up with which I had been brought. And I decided not to mention that I could be linguistically pedantic.

I specified the sort of books I enjoy reading, my liking for the theatre – I started to put 'well-acted Shakespeare' but then considered that it sounded a bit too highbrow - and my dislike of technology as well as thinking how best to complete the tick-box questionnaire about my height, age, politics and religion.

I needed to consider the last two carefully because I was not really sure whether I knew what I thought or believed. Nor accurately answer the question as to what my party behaviour might be, because without either Richard or Danny at my side, I really didn't know. But I did know what my retirement plans were, so I opted for 'Finally writing that novel', while recognising that my plans might possibly change.

Under 'politics', I suspected that my upbringing and the values of my parents were Conservative – my mother in particular had implied that she considered the ideal education would be at a good private or recognised public school; it would not only enhance one's learning, she assumed, but also develop one's culture and promote good manners.

Even though they couldn't afford private school fees for me, my parents managed to do so for my older brother and sister until we moved to Hertfordshire, where I was enrolled at Local Authority schools.

I knew my mother had been brought up by my grandmother, uncles and aunts as 'Liberal' so I suspected some of that had been grafted onto me. But my first husband Richard had been a socialist, had stood as a District Council Labour candidate and I had helped deliver his Labour Party pre-election leaflets around that ward. Not because I was particularly interested but because I thought that was what a wife was supposed to do, offer support to her husband; just as my mother had provided tactful support to my father in his local government post in which he was required to be politically impartial.

Politics was a subject avoided for discussion within the family home, in case any political leaning on my parents' behalf were detected and might inadvertently be quoted by us children.

Endeavouring to complete this form accurately, I was mindful of the 'nature v. nurture' debate and I regretted that this controversy lacked mention of 'later influences'.

I recognised how I had become a product not only of my upbringing but also of the values of people who had been important later on in my life. This had happened by exposure, in the way that exposure to the sun might bring out one's freckles. Or as shrapnel from a major event, marriage even, might penetrate the flesh and lodge itself within one's body, to be carried around for life and accepted as being an integral part of oneself - or re-emerge, years later, breaking the skin when long since assumed to be buried.

But now this shrapnel might prove to conflict with my own choices, or the expectations of others.

When I bought the cottage in a field in 1969 – and I was the one who bought it, supported by a £300 loan from my father - I was granted a mortgage because I was the one with a teaching job that the Woolwich Building Society recognised as being a reliable source of income.

I furnished it with redundant items from my parents. In that first couple of years, my husband Richard stuck a Labour Party poster in our bedroom window facing the road and I had fixed a Tory Party poster beside it, to indicate domestic debate. I still didn't know which party I thought preferable.

Danny had been a member of the Labour Party. And I respected and upheld his attitudes and behaviours towards less fortunate people. So, had I also become a socialist by association, had that somehow been grafted on to me? In the end, I wanted to write 'liberal' with a small initial letter to show that I had a range of views and could not wholeheartedly agree with any one political party. But the website wouldn't allow me to insert my own word so in some doubt, I ticked the 'Liberal' option.

I was trying to be honest on the website and to any future 'date', while at the same time attempting to please everyone whom I have valued in my life by being the person they would like me to be and be proud of. It still rankles that Richard's parting shot to me had been 'but you never made a home for me'. I still wonder why I didn't bite back. Mother's advice, probably.

I opted for a match with an age three or four years either side of my own. In that way, I hoped, we would share a common history regarding what was going on in the world and what affected us as our lives progressed.

The star sign under which anyone was born appeared to me to be irrelevant, but I did stipulate that having a photo is 'non-negotiable'. On reflection, I asked myself why a person's face really mattered? But then I decided that it did, because a face and how it is presented can tell you a lot about a person.

I preferred to see someone's eyes so I was initially disinterested in anyone who chose as his main photograph an image in which he was wearing sunglasses or looking away from the camera or parading himself in surroundings that he considered might look impressive. But I was curious about shots taken inside people's homes; the pictures on the walls and the things on the bookshelves could tell you quite a bit.

Another heading that I considered to be important is the one on 'Income'.

It wasn't that I was interested in the amount of money that one's date might have, but in his attitude to it. I didn't want to link up with someone who continually mentioned money, his lack of it or the rising cost of things.

Richard had made a point of not earning sufficient to pay Income Tax or National Insurance. He considered it 'clever'. But he would drive several miles out of his way to find somewhere that sold a cup of coffee five pence cheaper, just to show what a smart fellow he was.

While I was a single parent, I coped surprisingly well on very little income. Since then, living with Danny and his legacy had shown me how having sufficient money allows you to do together some of the things you would each like to do. So, I opted for 'solvent/enough/comfortable/managing' as being 'decidedly important', leaving aside 'struggling' or 'wealthy'.

Discussing and focusing on money can become undignified. I wanted anyone I might meet and who had a shortage of funds, to keep quiet about it and to 'manage' the situation appropriately. At least until we knew each other better.

I was viewed by my parents as being the 'good' one of their three children. This was due to my basic disposition rather than it being my choice and it was also fortunate, because being good was the only niche left unfilled by either of my siblings.

I was innately well-behaved and obedient, in contrast to Val who, before I was born, had been referred to the Tavistock Clinic on account of her wayward behaviour.

My mother, after one of Val's misdemeanours, said in desperation to me 'If you ever behave like your sister, I shall just leave.' My brother Colin, nine years older than I, was scared to go into the garden during the summer because, he said, 'there might be wasps'. He was considered by our parents to be rather 'wimpish', intellectually very capable but lazy, unmotivated. But I trusted him, he was kind and protective towards me.

The question on 'religion' should have been easier. My parents and grandparents worshipped at their respective 'Free' or 'Congregational' churches so I have been brought up with strong non-conformist Christian values such as honesty, kindness, forgiveness and meekness.

At the girls 'Crusader' class on a Sunday afternoon, run by a couple of Baptist women, we were taught the values of 'The Sermon on the Mount'[xv] where, in the case of Val who took great delight in being annoying and blaming me for some misdeed that she had done, I would be encouraged by my mother not to react, but to cling to 'Blessed are they who are persecuted for righteousness's sake; for theirs is the kingdom of heaven'.

By failing to achieve high enough marks in my 'A' level exams, I missed being accepted at university and instead was offered a place at what had been my 'fall-back' choice, a newly-established teacher training college in Canterbury.

The fact that it was run by the Church of England particularly concerned my non-conformist father but his disapproval was lessened by its being placed in Canterbury, the city in which he had gone to school a generation before. I enjoyed Evensong at the Cathedral and regularly attended sung Eucharist in St Martin's Church, where our presence or absence was noted by the Principal. And Christ Church College was where I met Richard, the man who became my first husband.

So, although my desire to please, to be accepted, to do and be what people want did not changed, it was my religious beliefs that I had to reconsider rather than my personal code of conduct. My second husband said that he didn't believe in God, that he considered Christianity to be a religion founded in the Iron Age.

Looking more recently at the creed and the teaching of the Bible, I had my doubts over some of what I had been taught as 'fact', and therefore, on the website, I thought describing my religious belief as 'agnostic' was closest to the truth.

Under 'My match' and the question asking what level of education I was looking for in my dating choice, I was offered a choice of 'student/F.E./University/Postgraduate/Private school/Secondary/' and lastly 'Any'. I selected the 'university' and 'post-graduate' boxes and rated my choice as 'very important'. But I added 'F.E.' to cover any potential match with skills more practical than academic. However, I didn't think I would be sufficiently patient with anyone who could be described like the city of Canterbury's walls – as 'ancient and thick'.

I would, I thought, find it hard to relate positively to someone who couldn't use scissors or a saw properly, who had minimal general knowledge or no practical ability despite having a brain. Danny, a Cambridge graduate with a good degree, knew the best way to cook asparagus, played the piano by ear and could manage basic household tasks such as plumbing and electrical wiring.

Under the question asking what sort of relationship I was looking for, I selected 'activity partners; friends; let's see what happens; a long-term relationship'. I rejected the 'a fling' option. I was not sure what that word meant to other people but for me, it suggested some sort of relationship that had no warmth, was temporary, had no care or concern for the other party. Richard had been too keen to have his flings with some of my female associates and I ended up being flung out. There wasn't a way of inserting 'close male friend' but that's really what I wanted. I missed the sensible, practical, protective male aspect of mixed company.

When it came to completing the 'Qualities Important to Me' section, among those I identified were 'charity; compassion; contentment; devotion; faithfulness; forgiveness; honesty; hope; humility; humour; kindness; mercy; patience; self-control; sexiness'.

Having had two husbands who, for different reasons, were unfaithful, I didn't think I could cope with another relationship that didn't include faithfulness, exclusivity or loyalty. And a keen sense of humour was fundamental. Not slapstick humour or anything puerile, I preferred an irreverent approach to humour: and I do need to laugh because life is essentially very funny.

Having done all that, I pressed the 'Complete' button. I waited to see whether anyone had looked at my profile. Then, an email arrived. From 'Likewise'.

'Exciting news, Susan2324. Scudamore has added you to his Favourites. To check out his profile, log into your 'Fans' area.'

Chapter 25

Reginald, aka Scudamore

Scudamore
Reliable, cultured country-lover.
Widowed, 75, near Woodbridge, Suffolk.
Two-way match = 89.3%
He is a 82.7% match for you. You are a 96.0% match for him
Photo supplied

When I log on to the 'Likewise' site, a flag shows that 'Scudamore' has sent me a message. He writes that he thinks we may have common interests and a similar background but that he would like to talk to me over the telephone. He signs his name 'Reginald'. I scroll down to his profile.

He describes himself as 6'2" tall, slim, active and healthy, confident without being too assertive. He says he lives near the coast; his interests include natural history and bird-watching, he describes his income as 'comfortable'.

I realise that that last one, having a compatible income level, is more important than I previously thought. There is no point in one of you wanting to do something or go somewhere if the other one cannot afford it; it becomes embarrassing and creates tensions.

He writes that he likes to travel and does so extensively, is involved in local affairs. He is, according to the website, looking for someone who is active and healthy, critical in a sensitive way, trustful, honest and reasonably tolerant, sociable but not over-exuberant, who also appreciates living at home in a comfortable house near the Suffolk coast, who could accompany him to official functions, share meals and outings, entertain at home etc.

What a long sentence he writes!

He then adds 'Ideally I am looking for someone who is optimistic, positive and not too seriously minded; who I am able to confide in, to discuss and maybe argue issues with, to bounce ideas off and ultimately possibly share aspects of my life.' Lots of words again. And he is happy to end with a preposition, up with which my mother would certainly not have put.

OK, although I can feel quite shy, I suppose that, with a bit of effort, I could just about fit the bill. I loved travelling abroad, I'm a country person, my income is adequate for most of the things I want to do, otherwise I just stop wanting to do them. I've had dealings with local councillors in the past and my childhood has taught me the delicacy of local politics, with both sizes of the letter 'P'.

I'm not so sure about the cooking, though; my cuisine is more 'country-style' from necessity than 'cordon bleu'. So maybe I'm not as optimistic as I think I am. Just a realist.

I decide to ask him for a convenient time when I might 'phone him rather than have him call me, out of the blue. I am not struck by his photograph – his head and face seem a bit lop-sided, reminiscent of an irregular sweet potato that might prove awkward to peel – and when I get through and say who I am, I find his voice harsh and increasingly unpleasant, like tyres scratching on gravel. His very first question is about my politics.

Apparently, he is concerned as to whether I am 'a rampant Guardian-reading socialist' as he describes it. I explain why I have put what I have put, that I may be in agreement with certain aspects of each political party but cannot, in all conscience, sign up to the complete package of any one of them.

Having got that political bit in our conversation out of the way, I agree to meet him, although I am not very hopeful. He suggests somewhere on the Norfolk/Suffolk border that he thinks is midway between our two homes, which is thoughtful. He proposes a day and time, selects a pub called 'The Castle' and gives directions as to where it is. I deduce that he has no trouble in making decisions.

I arrive ahead of time, to be sure of finding a place to park and arrive looking unflustered. I have decided to wear my white linen trousers and a blue-and-gold Indian cotton top. There was a time in my life when lack of money meant that I had little choice of clothing but now things are different, I can sometimes afford to purchase new.

I enter the pub garden from its nearly empty car park and go into the rear entrance of the yellow brick building to check that he hasn't arrived before I have. No, no sign of him, no sign of anyone except the bar staff.

I walk outside again, sit at a wooden picnic bench and wait. It is June, mid-day and airless; it might thunder later, the honeysuckle smells oppressive, clings to the garden.

I hear a car engine, shingle crunching, motor cut, hand brake applied, car door opening? Closing.

As he steps through the leafy archway, I recognise him from his photograph. The sweet potato is wearing pale cotton trousers and a long-sleeved blue striped shirt. He looks older than I have imagined. A small part of me knows immediately that this isn't going to be the love of my life but good manners and curiosity require me to stay put and smile, he has invited me here, after all.

A barmaid brings us a menu – I have already looked at this when I went into the pub before, in case he might tolerate my company for long enough to suggest lunch, so I know I am going to opt for the crab salad – and he asks me what I would like to drink, while he studies the lunch choices.

Once we have confirmed our names – his as 'Reg' with 'Please, not Reginald, that sounds far too formal', mine as Lorna rather than 'Susan' – in conversation he tells me that he is a Major, retired from the Armed Forces several years ago, now a local councillor and acts in some sort of liaison capacity with the emergency services, especially flood defence. We talk about our various interests. I struggle to find his sense of humour, it isn't apparent and once lunch is over, I am sure we are unlikely to meet again.

But he emails me the following day, thanks me for my company and invites me, in ten days' time, to a production of 'Twelfth Night' by a local theatre group that produces a well-known play every year in the local forest. He, as a local dignitary, has two complimentary tickets. A friend has spoken about these open-air productions with some enthusiasm so I accept, it might be interesting. He gives me directions from the main trunk road to his house, 'white clapperboard, almost beside the church and the village green', he says, 'with 'Scudamore', that's the name of the house, on a post by the front path.'

At the agreed time, I pull up onto the mown grass verge alongside his BMW. He comes out of the front door of his house and crunches along the gravel path to meet me. Good heavens, his footsteps sound exactly like his voice, I can't tell whether he's talking or . . .yes, he is, he's saying hello and . . . kissing me on my cheek.

He shows me into his house, through an oak front door and carpeted hallway, out through the glazed study door and around the garden, which is big and mainly lawn. He tells me he is considering selling the house because he doesn't need anything so big now and although we have met only once, he would like my advice on colours for redecoration; so, what would I suggest in the kitchen, where I see that the Aga cooker is vanilla-coloured and the walls are currently a shade of crushed raspberry?

With such tact as I can muster, I say that I would leave it as it is, partly because I like it – well, sort of; and more importantly, it was or is his choice, or his wife's; and also because, as I tell him, if any prospective purchasers don't like it, they would change it anyway and probably enjoy doing do, making it their own. He seems content with that.

We go in his car to the performance venue; he drives quite fast along the narrow lanes to the woodland theatre. Here he collects his special visitor tag on a blue lanyard and hands a second one to me. Good grief, from what it reads, I am now considered a V.I.P!

We are offered a glass of dry white wine, which he accepts despite being a driver, and a refill and some pretentious nibbles that prove difficult to eat tidily. He spots a couple of other local dignitaries, makes eye contact, gravitates towards them. He responds to their 'Good evening, Major' with a nod of his head and after exchanging a couple of sentences about mutual acquaintances who may or may not be expected, he introduces me to the dignitaries as his 'friend'.

Later we discuss this or rather, he refers to it. He cannot, he says, describe me as his 'partner' (well, thank goodness for that) because that would imply a different relationship - nor his 'dating site match' because that would be 'embarrassing' (for whom, I wonder?).

At this point I look down and feel rather more embarrassed by noticing that my sheer nylon foot socks - I could find only black ones in the tights drawer- that prevent my newly bought shoes from rubbing the skin off my toes, provide a visible dark error of judgement at the hem of the white linen trousers (worn to ward off mosquitoes - we are in the woods, after all) and the Indian cotton long-sleeved top. Sensible, but hardly chic.

Once the reception is over and our glasses have been returned to the refreshment table, we are shown to our seats, high up on a tiered rack and I settle to watch 'Twelfth Night' in the woods. I tuck my feet under my seat.

I wonder how the company will cope with the scenes set on the sea coast. Once characters Sir Toby, Sir Andrew and Fabian have hidden themselves behind the trunk of a pine tree augmented with additional leafy branches, Malvolio appears in yellow stockings, cross-gartered and wearing a crash helmet. He is riding a motorised disability scooter and hooting. An interesting take but will it descend into farce?

I realise, from snippets and remarks, that this is the first Shakespeare performance that Reg has seen since studying at school for 'O' Level exams. The innovative production is proving quite entertaining and I find Shakespeare's familiar words reassuring. Despite the need to smack the occasional insect against my freckled skin, I find I can concentrate and am not be put off by small unlikely portrayals. But is Reg taking it in, is he enjoying it?

At the end of the evening, driving back through the lanes edged with young oaks, silver birch and bracken, I attempt to discuss the production. My companion has, he says, enjoyed it but makes no further comment.

Instead, Major Reginald mentions a forthcoming concert at a converted malt house, says he always supports local Youth Orchestras and would I like to come too?

Suddenly a deer leaps out of the Suffolk woodland and into the road, its eyes picked out by the car headlights and shining with apprehension. Reg says it often happens around this part of the journey and how many near misses he's had.

I wonder why, in that case, he doesn't slow down; I don't mind if he is careless with his own life, that's up to him, but I have grown-up children, grandchildren and a dog at home that relies on me to feed and walk him. In fact - and I look at my watch - when we reach Reg's house and he offers the likely coffee, I plan to decline and head off for home as soon as politely possible.

A week or so later in an email that starts 'Dearest Lorna', (Dear<u>est</u>? A superlative? How many Lornas does he know?) he reminds me of the concert on a Saturday evening and suggests that I might like to come for the weekend, bring the dog, there are plenty of good places to walk him around the heath or the marshes; 'and you like walking, don't you' he states.

I have a brief mental picture of my Retriever Butterworth, his normally pale cream fur emerging black and smelly from a stinking salt marsh and wonder how this neat and organised Major would cope with that all over his Persian-rugged study. Butterworth and I have never been away together to someone else's house, so I don't know how this would work; where would he sleep? He is usually in his basket on an old rug in the kitchen at home where he can get in and out of the garden through a large dog-flap.

Butterworth and I arrive on the Friday afternoon, the dog full of inquisitiveness and trust. I am curious but more reticent, even guarded. I have been offered an upstairs room 'with your own bathroom, Dear'.

Having been greeted with a perfunctory kiss, I am shepherded to the first floor, shown the Major's room where he and his late wife Margaret slept. Their bedroom carpet is dreadful, a patterned mixture of circles in oranges and green that don't go and smack of public house flooring in the 1960s. The room I am to use is less dramatic.

It's smaller, lighter, has a double bed with a cream duvet cover, a bedside table and light with a switch that almost works, some harmless watercolours on the walls. He tells me that he has 'a girl from the village' in for three days a week to 'help me in the house, change the linen and so on'.

Downstairs again, I remark that the garden looks lovely. He has someone come once a fortnight to help him there, he confesses, not with cutting the grass though, no sense in paying someone to do something he can perfectly well do himself, just the heavy stuff and a bit of weeding.

There is a wide sweep of green lawn, punctuated and shaded near the centre by a tall stout silver birch growing out of more moss than grass. In one corner, nearer the house, is a small pond, concrete lined with various forms of aquatic vegetation. I eye it and consider Butterworth, who is presently chasing after a tennis ball thrown by Major Reginald demonstrating his cricketing skills. Better keep him away from that pond area or he'll be in, then out, covered in green pondweed and slime, making his way into the Major's house.

We sit drinking Earl Grey tea ('Do you take milk, Dear? Or lemon') outside on a teak seat that wobbles slightly on the stone patio where alpine strawberry plants and gone-over forget-me-nots peep between the cracks in the hotchpotch of York stone slabs.

I notice how the white gloss on a side window frame is peeling into those little wigwam shapes you get from pencil shavings. The Major remarks that he will need to redecorate some of the exterior paintwork before the autumn but that it's a job he doesn't enjoy. I tell him that I quite like decorating; but that I'm not much good when it comes to wallpapering. Major Reginald picks a tiny red strawberry and offers it to me. He says he leaves the plants, doesn't weed them out because they look so pretty.

He throws the ball again across the grass for the dog.

Butterworth, in his enthusiasm, makes a straight dash to catch it, colliding with a terracotta pot that had been perched on top of a low stone wall. It crashes onto the paving, breaks into shards. The Major picks up the bedraggled remains of whatever plant had been growing in it, tells me that that had been Margaret's favourite herb pot but that, in response to my expressed sorrow, 'it really doesn't matter.'

I ask him how long ago his wife had died. I don't like using the gentler 'passed away'; it sounds indecisive, which death isn't - and too close to 'passed out', which I imagine she probably had anyway. People, once dead, are issued with a 'death' certificate, not a diplomatic 'passed away' slip.

He tells me that it had been quite sudden the December before last. She had been preparing the icing for the Christmas cake and had said she felt quite tired, had gone to lie down. An hour later, he had found her dead. 'From a heart attack', he adds. Local people thought he had 'taken the news quite well' because 'you have to put on a good face, don't you, especially at that time of year'.

After a respectful minute or two of silence, suppressing the wish to ask him whether the Christmas cake icing was ever finished and in order to move the subject on, I ask him why he subscribed to the 'Likewise' website. He tells me that his holiday tour operator had suggested it the previous year when he had been on a 'singles' winter holiday to the West Indies.

I try to imagine a conversational context in which a manager of a tour to Cuba or wherever, would suggest such a thing to a solo traveller. He explains, appearing slightly embarrassed, that he and she, the tour manager, had 'got on quite well'; that in fact, after the holiday, she had met him again by arrangement and had come to stay for a week at his home – 'in the room you are currently occupying', he adds. They had shopped locally for particular foodstuffs for her stay and 'I noticed she always went for the most expensive option', he says rather disapprovingly. I conclude that the week had not proved a total success.

'And she told me at the end of the week that she thought I was very controlling' he confides, slightly sadly. He pauses. Then, 'I wonder if I am.'

I feel that I ought to comment on this, that my silence might indicate that I am in agreement, so I assure him that I have not found him to be so, so far. And I suggest that, if the unnamed 'She' had selected the costliest items - he offers further information on this, it had been about which brand of mustard to choose, the well-known, the store's own make or an unknown - perhaps she knew that he recognises good quality. His response is a 'humph' sound.

I ask him if he has told anyone, his children perhaps, that he has tried using a dating site. He tells me that he hasn't. I ask him why not. 'Because it would be so . . demeaning' he says, then falls silent.

'Yes', I respond after time while not knowing to quite what my affirmative 'Yes' has referred. 'However,' I suggest to Major

Reginald, 'a dating site such as 'Likewise' can prove to be a forum for failure; one sets up expectations, describes ideals and the likelihood is one of falling short.'

I don't think he sees what I'm talking about. He says it is not really a 'dating' site, more a way of getting to know people of the opposite sex, without upset or embarrassment.

'Because' he says, indicating the engagement and wedding rings on my fingers 'seeing those, if I didn't know you were a widow, I would be careful about what I said or did. I would naturally assume there was a husband or fiancé somewhere in the background and back off.' He pauses.

'Anyone who I form a relationship with, will have all this' he says, waving an arm at the house and garden. 'And if you were living with me, or came to live with me,' he speculates, 'I would expect you to do all the cooking.' Ooops. The 'I would expect' flashes an amber warning light in my head about controlling, negotiation, and the lack of any mention of it.

And much as I envy his having an Aga to cook on – we had a coal-fed Rayburn when I was a child, my mother referred to it as 'the poor man's Aga' and having one is still an aspiration – lovely though having an Aga might be, it's the rest of the package at which I am balking. We hardly know each other.

He has bought, from the village shop, some broccoli, green beans and an uncooked beef pie 'that, according to the label, just needs putting in the oven. Only I'm not quite sure for how long. Could you be in charge of that?'

I feel I am on trial. However, I am hungry too and it can't be too difficult to pop a pie in a cooker, however unfamiliar, and take it out when the shortcrust pastry looks done. So, I accept it as my job, while he copes with the vegetables which, we both agree, we prefer on the crisp side rather than mushy. He also asks me to make some gravy. He has some Bisto or similar in the cupboard, he thinks, so it isn't a problem.

There is a photograph of a woman whom I assume to be Margaret in a frame on the dining room sideboard. I take a quick glance at it. She is dressed smartly and is wearing a hat. Was that taken at a family wedding or an army event, I wonder? He sets the polished table with placemats, silver-plated cutlery and wine glasses and I put the plates in the lower oven to warm. He cannot find any linen table napkins, so would I mind paper serviettes?

The meal, if not a rousing success, is far from a failure and Butterworth gets any left-overs. Once fed and patted, I settle him for the night into his basket in Major Reginald's study, leave the garden door slightly ajar as instructed, so Butterworth can relieve himself during the night.

I note that the Major is not concerned about anyone entering his house from the garden, which is very secluded and now guarded by a large cream dog.

Major Reg and I finish our wine. He tells me that his daughter Rachel who had also joined the army, is now married with two children and living in Portugal; but that grown-up son Andrew is still a worry, doesn't seem to know what he wants to do with his life, doesn't discuss it much with his father, and might return to more studying if he can find someone else to pay for it.

I listen, commiserate with the Major and his disappointment, while feeling that poor Andrew is choosing to do something that interests him and makes him happy. Brave lad, I guess that taking a different path has taken some courage.

I ask a few more questions about nothing special until I can reasonably head for bed. The Major indicates where the clean towels are and which ones I should use, how the bathroom locks, that the loo needs only a gentle push to flush it. I feel he has been through all this before.

I have packed my best cream silk dressing gown and long nightie, not because I think it will be needed or on view but just, well, just because. I use the bathroom, have difficulty flushing the loo which seems to have an idiosyncratic handle with a mind of its own, call out 'Goodnight' and head for my designated bedroom. I draw the curtains to shut out the view of the church and am just turning down the bedspread, revealing the covered duvet and getting into bed when there is a gentle tap on the door.

'Oh no', I think and then, bringing my eyes and eyebrows down from the ceiling 'but perhaps there's a problem with Butterworth', so I respond with 'do come in'. The Major is standing on one foot in the doorway. He has a tartan dressing-gown covering his blue-striped pyjamas. He wonders whether I have everything I need (like what?), can find the bedside light switch (?) and could he come into bed for a quick cuddle?

Deep sigh. But since he has demonstrated minimal physical affection so far except for the welcoming peck on the cheek, I assess it unlikely that this so-called cuddle will progress to anything further; so, thinking both 'if you must' and that any such contact is probably to be regarded as a courtesy on both our parts, I assent.

He climbs in beside me with more confidence than I have expected and puts his arms mechanically around me. I wonder who is to make the next move, should there have to be one. Without asking for permission, he kisses me on the lips and moves his hand to my breast. Not for the first time, I wonder why many men just don't 'get it', don't understand that my prior requirement is for some verbal expression or demonstration of general affection for me as an individual rather than regarding me as just a person with the appropriate female bumps and warm apertures, a potential repository for excess seminal fluid.

A hug or caress goes a long way but unless I feel love and that I am loved in return before progressing to anything more overtly sexual, then a hug is all it is - just a hug, a greeting, a reassurance or a farewell. It's important to me that sex is more than some game of tennis to be played for one's personal physical pleasure with any willing player who owns a racket. I have been brought up to believe that it has something to do with giving oneself, of caring and some sort of commitment, ideally not short-lived. I guess I have been conditioned rather than inhibited by that.

What's the saying - that a man 'may profess love in order to get sex while a woman may offer sex in order to get love'? Something like that, anyway. And I'm very uncertain as to whether now I am capable of feeling that sort of love for anyone else. But I'll never know unless I am open to it.

From past experience, I deduce that the Major is likely to demonstrate minimal finesse in the sexual department, the limited repertoire that so many apparently happily-married men seem to possess and possibly (even probably, considering his age and blood pressure) limited ability and erectile dysfunction. I make a gentle move across the front of his pyjama trousers with my forearm. I am not wrong. All is as soft there as his Winceyette nightwear. This, should it be even worth his bothering on either of our behalves, would be akin to trying to shove blancmange through a keyhole.

But he progresses from my breast to my lower regions. While he is unromantically trying to locate the keyhole and missing, I am hoping he has clean short fingernails; and assessing that any condom, should he present one and should it have crossed his mind on sexual health grounds to keep us both free of any unknown nasties – and I'm thinking here of the tour manager, his previous date - is just not going to go on.

Although a free weekend away on the Suffolk coast is lovely, I don't feel any obligation to 'give myself' in return for his hospitality and a set of clean sheets. In fact, the bottom line is that I just don't feel anything much towards him. Curiosity, perhaps. Certainly, no deep emotion or physical attraction towards this man whose head and face are shaped like something in the Waitrose 'reduced' vegetable aisle, nothing other than a small amount of appreciation and the empathetic caring that one human being may have for another who finds himself in a similar domestic predicament. I wonder if I am just rather shallow; isn't it one's personality that should really matter rather than one's appearance?

Thus, to avoid hurting his feelings or his manly pride, I suggest that we probably both need our sleep after having drunk quite a bit of excellent red wine – and that we'll see each other in the morning unless Butterworth barks and disturbs us first. He returns to his own room. I try to sleep.

Major Reg offers a breakfast of coffee, toast and marmalade – and he thinks he has some cereal somewhere, left from when his grandchildren last came to stay.

Over a search in the fridge for some butter, he tells me that he is trying to teach himself Portuguese from a BBC grammar book, because he plans to drive his car to his daughter's house in the Algarve and will need to make himself understood at motorway petrol stations and so on.

And then, 'How would you feel about coming with me? I know from your profile that you enjoy travelling. We could stay in bed and breakfast places across France and Spain; then you could meet Rachel and my two grandchildren. We'd unload all her stuff that she's asked me to bring, her books and things, stay with her and her husband and the children for a few days - and then head back to Britain. We wouldn't be away for more than a fortnight or so. It wouldn't cost you anything and I know you speak some French so we'd find that useful on the way. And' he adds 'I'd really like Rachel to meet you.'

I quickly mentally calculate the cost of putting Butterworth into kennels for two weeks; and the cost to my mental health of maintaining an equitable relationship with this man from whom I would have little relief, little break; and the possible impact on my physical safety, for while his driving appears competent, he doesn't take much care over either possible roadside hazards or his alcohol levels. I tell him yes, it might be fun, that I will have to think about it, consult my diary, talk to my children – and ask what approximate dates he has in mind. I am hoping that I can honestly say I shall be busy doing something else at that time; we have only just met and a pre-planned meeting with his family seems several steps too far.

After a light fish lunch at a local pub, some brief polite words with people from the village who regularly eat there on the once-a-month reduced-for-pensioners lunch session, and a walk on the beach for Butterworth, we prepare for the concert.

We discuss leaving Butterworth in the Major's study, once he has had his dinner of meat and kibble and relieved himself outside. The Major says that he will be quite safe, he can leave the door from the study to the garden ajar, the garden is enclosed and that he can't get through the garden fence. I am more concerned. First, there is a house security issue. It's not my house, but it's still an issue or should be.

Then there's Butterworth, he's my very best friend and I would be totally distraught if he were to get lost, if anything were to happen to him. And I am still mindful of the pond. Butterworth loves water and will be in, given half a chance. And I doubt that the Major will welcome pond-slime indoors.

The compromise is to set the intruder alarm to secure the main part of the house, but give Butterworth the study and the run of the garden, with all gates to outside securely fastened. I give Butterworth his favourite teddy that he loves to chew. And put his basket on the Major's study floor, lined with his red fluffy rug with the black paw prints. And offer a chicken-and-carrot dog biscuit. And a tennis ball, that he will inevitably wreck. And a last-minute ear-rub at which he grunts with ecstasy. But I am still anxious.

We are shown to our reserved seats in the concert hall. It's the first time I've been here and it's impressive. Once an enormous warehouse, it stands by the side of a tidal river. Outside are the marshes, the purple-headed green reeds whispering and gently swaying, the air slightly salty and smelling of tide water, a sense of harmonious change and a relaxed but mindful acceptance of the 'now', the 'what was' and the 'what will be'.

An old bare-masted wherry is moored to a heavy rust-pitted iron ring set into the harbour wall. The converted building is brick and weathered wood, our chairs have cane seats that sag slightly, the whole place might well have risen from the mud, the reeds and the sea itself. Nothing is superfluous, everything functional and indigenous. On stage, the metal music stands and chairs have been set out for the orchestra.

The Major, and I as his guest, have been invited for pre-performance drinks in an upper room. He is greeted and welcomed, the organisers with red lanyards hung around their necks supporting identity badges to indicate that they are official, are appreciative of his interest and support. Of mine too, they say as an afterthought. I realise that my function here is to be a sort of consort, an accessory. Once I have grasped this, I feel rather like a second-hand crocodile handbag. And that I don't quite match his Russell and Bromley suede shoes. Might even have been handmade.

Regardless of his needs or preferences in the kitchen or the bedroom, it's an acceptable accompaniment that he is searching for, a 'Margaret' who knows what to say and dresses appropriately, a female appendage who can participate in conversation that is pertinent, interesting and generally uncontroversial.

At this point I again regret last week's misjudged black foot socks and am pleased that today I am wearing a dress from John Lewis in Liberty's material, patterned with small turquoise and tan-coloured flowers, medium-heeled shoes and a 'seconds' Jaeger jacket in peacock silk (the silk trousers to which, I regret, no longer fit because I have put on weight.) Not quite Margaret, no hat, but I guess I'll have to do.

The concert is good. I particularly notice a girl cellist who is clearly in love with her instrument, nurtures it, plays it with passion. And the dark-haired lead violinist doesn't look much over eleven but he commands with his eyes and his bow and has the respect of the other players. They cope with the Elgar and the Britten pieces very well. And that percussion player at the back of the staging is spot on every time, never takes his eyes off the conductor, is just waiting to crash those cymbals again. Oh, well done, Youth Orchestra, wherever you are from!

There is a brief interval. A group of spectating primary school-aged children who have been sitting cross-legged at the front on cushions on the wood floor, shuffle their bottoms and wriggle their shoulders. They have been absolutely quiet throughout the first half of the programme. One of them offers a tube of sweets to her friends. A boy slowly stands up and walks towards the exit door. But most of them remain still, waiting for the next half to begin. I guess that their older siblings are in the orchestra and that their parents are seated on chairs somewhere nearby.

Major Reginald excuses himself from my side and disappears for a while. I wonder if, while the Elgar is being played, he has been thinking of his army service and how often he has been called upon to lay wreaths at memorials. Or reflecting on his near-adult son Andrew, who has apparently decided against the armed services and so seems to have disappointed his father; but who has had the guts to follow his own path and not be controlled by parental expectations.

One of the advantages that Major Reg explained he was hoping to find through the dating site, was someone with whom he could share his concerns and aspirations. I had been more than willing to listen and to empathise with his concern for Andrew but also to suggest that his son would probably turn out fine. I wonder, as I sit watching the children at the front of auditorium, whom the said Andrew has to talk to, to share with. Probably not his sister Rachel, who has done the right thing by her father and joined the army.

I move from that to reflecting how lucky I am to have my three grown-up children of whom I am very proud, who are all quite different, who had a far from text-book model childhood that some people might have considered materially deprived but who have all grown to be lovely, caring, hard-working people whose company I enjoy.

Major Reginald returns to his seat. He makes some comment about how hard he has always tried to encourage music tuition and development within the local area. I guess, from that comment, that he imagines that his presence at the concert is encouragement enough. I suspect that the members of the orchestra and the audience couldn't care less who else is in the audience, or what their ranks and professions are, that the people that they most want there are their friends and families.

So, I deduce, it is officialdom, the management whom he is encouraging, endorsing music development by his appearance and occasional council vote. I wonder, and then ask, what kind of music and which composers he prefers.

He appears floored by my question, isn't sure how to answer. 'I like all this sort of thing,' he says, waving his hand towards the staging. We settle in our seats as the players return for the second half.

On the journey back to 'Scudamore', to his house, I ask whether Reg plays any instrument himself. There has been no sign of a piano. I have been brought up with both an upright and a baby grand piano in the home and I find it strange not to see one. He tells me that he tried to play the clarinet but that he found it too difficult; and he doesn't read music; his wife used to sing in the church choir but he. . well, he doesn't sing. 'But I enjoy listening to music', he assures me.

Butterworth greets me enthusiastically as he hears us switch off the house alarm and open the study door. I have tried to encourage him not to jump up but he is too excited this evening to remember. I am licked and nudged; he tries to put his front paws on my shoulders until I tell him sternly to get down. He seems pleased to see Major Reginald too, recognises him as 'tennis-ball man'. I take the dog around the garden, play with his teddy for a while, then head indoors again.

The Major has offered me a coffee - and do I take milk? I do. We sit at the table in the kitchen, Butterworth's head on my knee. He is eyeing the crisp sugary Nice biscuit that the Major has offered me from a packet that I notice is well-past its sell-by date. I am wondering where we go from here, how to handle what might or might not become another bedroom situation, what approach to take.

The Major yawns, then apologises. I wonder how spontaneous, how genuine the yawn was, then accuse myself of being a hypocrite for being simultaneously suspicious and grateful. Whatever, it has introduced the idea of being tired and we can each resort to that. I suggest that I should lead Butterworth back to the study and settle him down again for the night. The Major tacitly nods.

Then, to my horror, he asks if I was warm enough last night, whether I need another blanket. I tell him I was fine, that everything was very comfortable – and that I shall go to sleep still hearing the music. We say goodnight to each other and each heads up the stairs for our own rooms.

Chapter 26

Scudamore continued

It is Sunday morning and I see through the bedroom window that the smaller metal arrowed hand on the church clock has hit eight. At breakfast, I ask the Major whether the bells are rung every Sunday, or only at weddings. He tells me 'Only on special occasions' and that as he is one of the holders of the key to the church, someone will come to the front door very soon to collect the key.

I wonder how he, as a recently widowed member of the community, would explain my presence and, should anyone have noticed, my car having been outside all night. This doesn't seem to have occurred to him or if it has, to bother him. He suggests that we take Butterworth across the fields to the river this morning, to give him a good run before he has to go into the back of my car.

This agreed, we clear and wash up the plates. The Major dons a pair of well-used walking boots 'To protect my ankle, it's a bit dodgy sometimes,' he confides. I hang the dog whistle around my neck on its silky ribbon and attach the stretchy lead to Butterworth's red needlecord collar.

We leave the main road that leads into the village and head off to the left, towards a tarmacked path that apparently leads to a now-defunct railway track. There are dew-spangled cobwebs on the gorse bushes and a few damp spiders are apparent, although last night was dry and almost cloudless. The grass is wet underfoot. Butterworth rolls in it, he is happy. Happy to be out and to investigate new smells. I feel in my pocket to check that I have a plastic bag handy.

The Major sees a group of geese feeding on the fields beside the marsh. They take off when they see Butterworth. Major Reginald has not brought his binoculars but he thinks they are Greylags or possibly Barnacle Geese, it's too far away to be sure.

Standing on a patch of hard ground beside the river is a man with an easel and a pallet of paint. His brush is poised towards the canvas. The Major tells me that people 'come here quite often, set up their easels, that sort of thing, but they generally don't like it if you try to look at their work, pass comment even if it's positive, or distract them in any way.'

As we approach that area, I keep Butterworth on a tight lead just in case he should show artistic interest or cock his leg against the easel. I love him to bits but he can prove quite a responsibility at times. Fortunately, Butterworth is more interested in the water. It's quite fast-flowing but clean. Once we are clear of people, fishermen and bystanders, I unhook his lead and let him go in at the edge. He loves it, ducks his head under the surface, brings it up again, opens his mouth and takes in water. He'd really like it if I had a ball to throw so that he could swim towards it and retrieve it. But I haven't.

The Major questions me as to why I called him Butterworth. I tell him that it has something to do with the yellow colour of his coat but mainly because I find particular enjoyment in traditional English music. 'Like yesterday's Elgar', I add. 'Or Butterworth's.'

'But I enjoy Purcell - and Bach too,' I quietly reflect, rather tongue in cheek, 'so I could have named him 'Purcell' if he'd been completely white. Or 'Bach'. Or even 'Offenbach. Because he does.' I am getting rather a blank look now; I wonder if the Major is slightly deaf. Or just not amused. I decide to shut up.

We walk back to the village in silence, apart from my occasional need to call Butterworth to heel. Although I am not, I don't think, what the Major is looking for and he is certainly not my ideal, nevertheless I have developed quite an appreciation of his gentle kindness. I feel I may be a disappointment to him or perhaps he is disappointed in himself. I would like to remain friends with him, despite the huge differences between us. We have little by way of shared background; I have no idea about military service, Sandhurst and who can go there or what they do. He has had no experience of university life and the state education system.

I try to think what might constitute the attributes and qualities needed to make one whatever is meant by a soul-mate. I guess it's about feeling fully comfortable and really relaxed with that person, as if you have known him or her for a long while, far longer than you really have, that you can say or do anything you could as with an old friend. Like I had felt with Danny. Almost right from the very beginning we had both felt a deep connection, had said things to each other at our first meeting that we couldn't later quite explain but that somehow assumed that we would always be together, have the same ethics. I feel wistful.

As I encourage Butterworth to jump into the back of my ancient blue hatchback Fiesta, load the car with my belongings and say goodbye to the Major whom I still find hard, as everyone else seems to, to address simply as 'Reginald', 'Reg' or, and I feel tempted here, 'Raj', I thank him for what has been an enjoyable and genuinely interesting weekend.

He takes my hand, kisses me again on the cheek and waves through the rear window glass to Butterworth. He tells me that he is likely to have to come to Norfolk some time, he has to attend a meeting just outside Norwich that is something to do with combined county services and he would be in touch 'so that perhaps we can meet up. And when I have some more definite dates,' he adds as my car pulls out and onto the road, 'I'll be in touch about the Portugal visit.'

I receive an email unexpectedly soon: Reg must have sent it almost immediately I left his house.

Dearest Lorna,

I mean it; but I am not being presumptuous or assuming anything - I don't know any other Lorna's!! (sic)

Today was our opportunity to talk to each other for as continuously as we wanted for as we said the other night it is not that easy to have intimate conversations at the theatre or in the concert hall! Today (Butterworth permitting, the lovely boy) we were able to talk and discuss things. I was so glad that you came and brought Butterworth, he is a beautiful hound and I judged that he and I got on well, although I doubt that there are many people he does not get on with - he is fun. So that just leaves us, and I thought that we got on quite well! I have to say in your understanding of the natural environment; walking and talking are amongst my delights and you were the perfect companion and you didn't roll your eyes up at Barnacle Geese or when we saw sea lavender!

We talked a little about ourselves and I guess that we will have to explore those aspects a bit more. I don't want to appear overtly clinical but I am a pragmatist and I do not ware (sic) my heart on my sleeve. You seemed to accept that I might 'call the shots' and what a previous girl-friend described as 'my controlling instincts as unattractive', but you severely rebutted them and I am grateful that you did - I like people who I can talk straight to.

Let me be blunt, I don't find it difficult, but how do you think we measure up to the expectations we expected from Likewise, or is it too early days?

Sorry, yes, it is early days to ask these questions. See you soon I hope and we have some dates in the diary.

With love,

Reg xx

To which I reply:

Dear Reg,

I have just returned home after visiting you (more of that later), grabbing a yesterday's Waitrose chicken sandwich from the 'fridge before taking something to my daughter Lallo, then straight on to my son Keir's house to discuss the viability of arranging a Maths tutor for my grandson. So, it's now past ten o'clock and I can spend some time at the computer.

You ask how I think that we measure up to our expressed 'ideal'. I can answer only part of that, that being how you measure up against my 'wants' list. Presumably you will be doing something similar regarding me. Yes, it's a blunt question but one that each of us needs to consider. Of course, I have been weighing that up on my drive back to Norfolk, while trying not to be too clinical about it. So, taking a dispassionate item-by-item approach, I'll try to answer your 'how am I doing so far?' question.

Here goes. You get high marks for the following, in no particular order: getting on well with Butterworth, understanding his needs without being soppy about him; in return, he recognised your authority and responded to it. All good.

More good stuff - the physical importance of walking, the understanding and appreciation of the natural environment, the birds, plants – very important to me, I'm not an indoors person. Not fussing about getting wet or muddy, being able to deal appropriately with it; also mentioning but not dwelling on physical problems, (I am thinking of your ankle here) excellent.

I wouldn't see 'calling the shots' as controlling, I like it when people can make decisions – and I can always object, negotiate or opt out. My late husband often made the important decisions, I was quite happy about that because he had done his research or whatever and his decisions were usually informed and very sound. We appear to share an annoyance at those who make judgements based neither on knowledge, experience nor understanding.

You don't shy away from any physical contact and often initiate it. So high marks again. I enjoy your different handling of different situations - simple lunch, teabags in the mugs, instant coffee etc. but also enjoy a good restaurant meal.

And, if we are being absolutely clinical about this, you appear to have sufficient resources to be able to enjoy the sort of activities and general life-style that I enjoy. The travel element we have briefly discussed and we seem to share a preference for exploring interesting places.

As you say, it is yet early days and there is much yet to discuss and discover. And I wonder where, in the profiles, do feelings, emotion and all that stuff fit in?

I have had a lovely day today, Reg, thank you for that. I'm still thinking about it – and looking forward to spending time with you again before too long.

Lorna

By the weekend, I receive a response to my message.

I have had plenty to do the second half of this last week but have reflected on your critique. I am quite pleased with my 'half term report'. I recognise something of the 'school ma'am' here which in the past I was not altogether unfamiliar with.

Your comments are very useful but in my badly expressed e-mail I was trying to ask how you thought that you and I got on together, rather than what you thought of me and what I thought of you. Oh, the joys of e-mail which having revisited what I said I can see that it was easy to misinterpret my question; it also reminds me to use the spell check more regularly!

I suppose what I really wanted to know was whether it was worth us pursuing this friendship and your response seems to me to be pretty positive in this respect. As you say we have only explored the more material aspects of our characters and perhaps confirmed what Likewise bases suitable matches on. The one observation I will make and it certainly is not a criticism, is that you appear quite reserved and serious minded. That is fine by me up to a point as I don't much care for 'fluffy headed' people of either gender. I did make you laugh on two occasions while we were talking on the patio but that was probably because of the absurdity of what I said rather than anything particularly funny!

I suspect the emotional side of each of us will take a little teasing out. I guess it is what is called the 'chemistry' between us (however you define that and just what it means I don't know?). Just to start the process, I certainly do have deep feelings and sentiments but am not the most, nor do I want to be, outwardly demonstrative person - maybe military training has taught me to keep much within me.

When my wife died, people remarked how steadfast and resolute I had remained and they were either impressed or horrified but believe me I had my moments. I will leave that there for now.

You said that you would come to two events at the Orwell Arts Festival at the end of the month. The first is on Saturday at 7.30, Percussion Ensemble - Mussorgsky; Tchaikovsky; Saint-Saens - and includes some of the kids from the local school where I am a governor.

The second event is the final night President's Concert again at 7.30 in St George's Church - Ravel; Strauss; Rider; Brahms. We have now been invited to the Last Night party afterwards at 10.pm in the workshop but we can play that by ear. My offer for both evenings is a late-night bed but I know that you can't stay Friday, instead bring Butterworth Saturday and spend at least the afternoon and stay till Sunday.

With love,

Reg xx

This is quite a tricky email to reply to. I work at it for some time, trying to be accurate and honest, not always easy. I ignore the kisses.

Hello Reg,

Oh dear, how the school teacher side of me keeps poking out! I do apologise; I guess it's in the blood. I would like to pursue this friendship, as you put it, if you are happy to do so. The 'Likewise' process of getting to know each other is painfully artificial and takes me some time to break through.

I hope I haven't disappointed you too much so far. I thought we got on well on a first day together and had time to talk and explore common interests. I can be reserved initially, and appear quite serious when I'm trying to behave properly and play the Head's wife. I'm afraid there is also a ridiculous side to me, which shows itself through verbal banter when I'm relaxed and more secure in the relationship. And I also have a maverick streak.

As for emotions, your handling of your bereavement appears to have been very like mine. I held it together because my husband would have expected no less of me. Public front and all that. Privately alone and in my own home it was different, I allowed myself that.

To recap, I think that the best way forward for us – well, for me at any rate – is to try to establish a friendship based on mutual respect and any common interests and to see where we go from there. We hardly know each other and this can all get a bit scary when we have no idea of the outcome, only the current process.

There are bound to be times when we misunderstand each other or do something that the other one finds irritating. I guess the best thing then is to talk about it sensitively and honestly. How does that sound to you?

Best wishes,

Lorna.

It is only a week later when Reg sends me another email. It is interesting how, having had our first conversation over the telephone, we now appear to prefer email as a way of conversing. I wonder privately whether I prefer to see the written word rather than to listen to Reginald's voice, and if so why. Is it because, until I get attuned to it, I find the tone of his voice, regardless of his use of standard English, grates so unpleasantly and sets my teeth on edge.

He writes that he has been invited to 'a harvest-type supper do' next Saturday by members of his local political party - and there is to be a short recital to follow, in a local church. He would be very pleased if I would go with him because he would rather not go on his own, he says, and to stay for the night rather than drive home late.

This statement about not going on his own, is something that I understand.

I am normally perfectly happy attending things on my own except for the arrival and departure parts of the event. Arriving on one's own, that 'walking in through the door' business, can make one very self-conscious.

There are two, sometimes three options as to what to do, once in the room. To stand there looking lost; to make immediately for someone whom one recognises while trying not to butt into an existing conversation or hover on one leg feeling excluded and looking rather like a naughty child; or to find some notice or menu or picture to look at with assumed attention and interest until it's safe to move forward.

None of these is guaranteed to be successful.

Dear Reg,

Thank you for your email. I have just returned from a day trip to London, responding to my 15-year-old grandson's request to take him to see the Globe Theatre and to go to a Prom concert at the Royal Albert Hall. All went well, apart from the difficulties of attracting and acquiring a vacant taxi late at night to take us back to Liverpool Street Station.

I should like to attend both the events next weekend, i.e., the harvest supper and the concerts, if the offer still stands.

I can see a difficulty if I were to bring Butterworth on Saturday – it would be only his second visit and I fear for him and your study if we left him alone there all evening. My daughter

Lallo has offered to take him for his afternoon walk, feed him and the cat, and later put them to bed and give them their breakfast on Sunday morning if I were to stay the night at your house. It's a *quid pro quo*, at this time of year and with her husband abroad, I keep her amused and in cherry tomatoes.

Thus, it is time for bed and a little reading before switching the light off - I'm about half way through the book you lent me set in Woodbridge and am enjoying it.

How has your weekend been?

Best wishes,

Lorna

At the agreed time, I arrive, minus dog, at 'Scudamore'. I hope I am appropriately clad for what Major Reginald has described as being a harvest supper, in the barn belonging to one of the local political party farming members. We are likely to be sitting on prickly straw bales placed around the edges of the room, 'well, we did last year,' he recalls. 'And there will be wine for sale on site', he tells me, 'with a buffet set out on trestle tables in the centre of the barn.'

I transfer from my car to his with minimal further information given, and off we go. On the way, he advises me that the local constituency parliamentary and possibly the European parliamentary candidates will be present and probably anxious to talk to everyone to gain their votes. I deduce that for this event, I am to act as his consort on his suggested 'just be your very pleasant self and tell them what they want to hear' basis.

I wish I had read more about Prince Albert, gained a hint or two on how to be a consort. I don't enjoy limelight but this being a matching accessory or appendage is really not my scene. I feel like a child. Or a French poodle.

After a twenty-minute journey along main roads, he turns towards a village, a country lane, then to a farm drive, then through an open five-barred gate on to a green field, and parks alongside a line of what he cynically refers to as Chelsea tractors, all sporting number plates from this year or last. Gingerly, I open the front passenger door.

I lower my feet onto what I hope is firm ground. I keep my eyes open for possible cow pats. The air smells rural but not particularly of livestock. The grass around the car is long, too long for comfort walking through it. It has rained here recently, the hems of my trousers are becoming damper with every step, long blades of lush grass lick my ankles like cows' tongues and my shoes are liable to sink into the damp earth. That normally wouldn't matter to me, I walk Butterworth around the fields at home every morning - but for that, I am sensibly dressed, not all poshed up in heels and trying to remain presentable.

I have a small handbag with me, not a designer one, I don't do designer bags. But it is leather. It's somewhere to keep my spectacles, contact lens case, lip salve, lipstick, tissues, a mobile phone that I rarely switch on anyway and that my children and grandchildren consider laughably archaic because it doesn't receive emails, an address book and my purse.

I take a deep breath and hope that I am equipped for what is to come. And to remember what my purpose here seems to be. I refrain from muttering to myself 'Remember, Lorna, you are just a handbag'.

The Major and I pick our way towards the barn. I notice that he doesn't take my hand or my arm to help me surf the soggy grass and I'm uncertain as to how I feel about that. Relief, certainly. But it might have been nice to have felt looked after, just a bit. It would have shown some caring - although I know that we have only recently met, so ask myself what reason he would have to display any caring for me. But although it can feel intrusive and chauvinistic, nevertheless I do appreciate the more old-fashioned courtesies, such as walking on the outside of the pavement or taking a woman's arm or a hand. It makes me feel female, protected.

The tile-roofed barn appears quite old, it seems to have been a wooden construction with some later red brick infill walls, some of which appear to have had lime plaster between the upright timbers. And yes, stacked like benches against the walls on three sides are bales of straw, the horizontal surfaces covered with cotton cloths in a variety of checked patterns so that guests can sit in rural comfort.

Slightly incongruously at this time of year, festooned just above head height and hanging from rusted nails are looped garlands of fresh green ivy and very dry, ochre-coloured crisp hops interwoven with stalks of wheat, barley and the occasional wilting cornflower and orange nasturtium. I surmise that the hops may have been left over from a previous year. Nevertheless, someone has been to a lot of trouble to do that, it's fiddly work. I begin to consider the event in a slightly less negative light.

The Major is set to mingle and takes my hand, drawing me from just behind him and to his side. He introduces me as Lorna to his friends. One man, standing by the bottles of red and white wine that are lined ready for guests to purchase to have with their meals, shakes and holds my hand for a second longer that politeness deems necessary, his pupils dilating and eyebrows raising slightly with approval. So, I gather that I'm looking reasonably OK then and not my 71 years - not quite.

I hold my stomach in, look him in the eyes for an equally unnecessary length of time, raise my left eyebrow quizzically and smile knowingly. I consider that a little admiration will do me no harm – or is he wondering to himself what an old codger like the Major has to offer and thinking that he could better it? Maybe. But I am not interested. Not really. Just mildly flattered and reassured.

I ask the Major if he would prefer red or white wine and offer to collect and pay for a bottle. He seems happy about that, not affronted. I feel more comfortable covering half the costs where I can; it's about my financial and personal independence, not wanting anyone to presume that I am under some sort of obligation to provide a physical or sexual service.

With a wine glass in my hand and at the heels of the Major, I circulate as best one can when one knows nobody, has apparently little in common with other guests and doesn't come from the area. The man with the raised eyebrows approaches me, offers me a slice of asparagus quiche made, he assures me, 'by one of the women' and talks to me about the structure of building, the farm and its previous owners. I speculate on the age of the barn and whether the beams are oak or elm.

Raised Eyebrows wants to know if I've known Reginald long. I am tempted to tell him that we met quite recently on an internet dating site but that to do so would be unkind and serve no purpose other than to make his jaw drop. It would be fun, though.

His view of the Major is clearly one of being an upright member of the community, not as a person who goes around picking up strange women. Raised Eyebrows places a hand gently upon my shoulder and is ushering me towards the side room where the wine is arranged. Fortunately, the local constituency parliamentary candidate comes over to join us and introduces herself to me, exchanges a few pleasantries about the venue and the food and, with her agent alongside and Raised Eyebrows making himself scarce, asks me whether she can count on my vote.

I tell her I will consider it carefully but that I don't think it will be possible, that I don't think that it would be allowed. She looks confused and I decide to help her out. I tell her that I live in Norfolk, not even just across the border and that I'm only here in Suffolk because a friend invited me. Very quickly, she loses interest in me. I am a non-entity, not worthy of her prolonged attention; I have the wrong address.

Major Reginald tells me a little about the concerts that he mentioned. One is part of the Orwell Arts Festival with a Percussion Ensemble playing Mussorgsky; Tchaikovsky; Saint-Saens; it includes some of the kids from the local school where he is a governor.

The other he refers to as the President's Concert, - whatever that might be - will be in St George's Church. Both are taking place at the same time after the harvest do and in totally different venues. He asks me which I would prefer.

Rather than selecting an evening of percussion, I opt in total ignorance for the nearer one in a village church.

'Bernard Rider, the composer', Reg assures me, 'of one of the pieces of music is a local chap and will be present.'

However, I am concerned that by making this choice, I have discounted his attendance at the concert involving a number of the children from the school where he's a governor.

'Will that be a problem, become an issue?' I enquire. He thinks not.

The church and part of the graveyard are illuminated by floodlights. I can see dark figures making their way up the path from the lych-gate, between the dark tombstones, to the church porch. Major Reginald aims to park his car on the left-hand side of the road as near to the church as possible, if he can find a suitable space.

He curses quietly as his front nearside hub cap scrapes along a kerbstone and one or two people in the line progressing up the church path turn slightly to see the cause of the noise. I open the passenger side door, avoid a second scrape as the underside of the car door meets the pavement and, picking up my pashmina shawl in case the air temperature has dropped, swing my legs out. The Major joins me by my side.

Looking at the back views of the queue, I guess that not everyone present has been at the harvest supper. Some have opted out, gone elsewhere while other people have joined us. A woman with a very sparkly silver metallic top is two in the line in front of us, she is carrying a long slim instrument case and no handbag. The Major gesticulates towards it and informs me that Sparkletop is tonight's flautist, he thinks.

We file into the small church and step on to the tiled floor. We present our tickets and, with a whispered greeting directed at the Major, are handed a folded sheet of white paper and ushered toward a partly vacant pew on the right-hand side of the aisle. Metal music stands and wooden chairs have been set up in front of the altar rail. We are to hear Ravel; Strauss; Rider; Brahms.

The first orchestral piece of the concert is to be Richard Strauss's opening theme to the film '2001 Space Odyssey'. The folded A4 programme sheet tells us *'Richard's father Franz was a professional horn player who taught his son about music from a very early age. Richard was composing at the age of six, and his first symphony composition was performed when he was only 17!'* So, having read that, I expect we all now feel incompetent.

As seemed likely, the music by Ravel is to be the 'Pavane pour une infante défunte'. The computer-printed programme notes inform us that *'Ravel was at pains to point out that this piece of music is not a funeral lament for a dead child, but rather an evocation of the pavane that might have been danced by such a little princess as painted by Velázquez'*. I am almost surprised that it doesn't go on to say *'Now hands up all those of you who've got that wrong before.'*

Someone sitting on the pew directly behind us whispers to her companion that 'the composer, Bernard Rider, is sitting in the pew two in front. With the dark jacket on.' I don't think Major Reginald has heard that. Or maybe he already knows. The Mistress of Ceremonies moves from the side of the chancel to stand in front of the small orchestra and, taking a deep breath, she announces the next piece as a 'Concerto for Flute and Orchestra written by Bernard Rider' and that she is 'delighted, as are we all, to welcome Mr Rider here today to hear his music played publicly for the very first time.'

If I were Bernard Rider, I would be having kittens at this point. But he appears calm and confident as all heads turn towards him, he smiles wanly in acknowledgement and there is spontaneous applause. Even though we haven't heard a note yet; a bit previous, I think. However, it's polite to welcome him.

SparkleTop gleams and glides to the front, stands, takes a slight bow (not too low, dear, or we'll all see your boobs) and fingers her instrument. I suppress a giggle. The music strikes up. It is reminiscent of a dawn chorus and appears to me to lack melody or structure. But what do I know.

Only that the programme so far has struck me as exclusive, it seems to have been assembled in order to appear intentionally cultured and educative rather than enjoyable and, together with the typed notes, to be putting the audience in its place.

Having heard the Rider piece, the last item on the programme is Brahms Lullaby. The programme notes do not give us much more information about this, only that '*Brahms used variations on this melody for much of the first movement of his Symphony No. 2 in D major, Op. 73.*' A fitting end to an interesting programme.

The evening ends as the sky is getting dark. We return to 'Scudamore', me to my car and I drive carefully and thoughtfully home. Butterworth recognises the engine sound of my Fiesta as I pull up by my garage and he barks a greeting, just the one. He is pleased to see me, as am I to see him. He sniffs my clothes to check who I've been with and detects that somewhere along the line, there's been food involved. I rub his furry back for a minute just above his thick wagging tail, and tickle his tummy. Smiling fondly at him, I settle him into his basket with his duvet and a chicken-and-carrot bedtime biscuit and say goodnight.

In the morning, I email my thanks to the Major, tell him that he lives in an area with plenty going on and lots of opportunities to become involved. In his reply, he expresses his pleasure at having had my company and at the way I was 'able to mix with everyone, talk so well and with such confidence to so many different people, Dear'. I ignore the opportunity to respond either sarcastically or with humour, he doesn't mean to be patronising and I'm genuinely glad that I didn't let him down in front of his party colleagues, that from his point of view the evening was a great success.

But although I feel that I have to be on the level with him, be honest without hurting his feelings, allow him to plan ahead, I do not refer in any detail to his suggestion, repeated at the harvest supper, that we should travel to Portugal together so that he can introduce and show me to his daughter Rachel and his grandchildren.

I understand how he feels, I do much the same to Lallo when I have a pair of new shoes. But spending a couple of weeks with him, confined together in the car and relieved only by time with his family, is just not what I want to do. So, I have been procrastinating by not mentioning it while simultaneously trying to think of a truthful way of getting out of this while being sensitive. In the end, I settle for this: -

> Dear Reg,
>
> It was a really lovely harvest supper, thank you so much for inviting me to join you for that. I hope I didn't disappoint your local parliamentary candidate too much by being unable to give her my vote. She did seem very pleasant.
>
> You talked about travelling to visit your daughter, son-in-law and your grandchildren whom you haven't seen for some

time. I hope you will understand when I say that I don't think I ought to come to Portugal with you. It was a lovely idea and very kind of you to have asked me but I have promised to spend quite a bit of time with my three eldest grandchildren out of term time, there's so much I would like to do with them before they grow much older and get involved in examinations and career choices.

As I think I have told you, their parents both work and they are unlikely to be having a family holiday this summer so we have places to visit and a host of activities to get involved in.

I hope I can take them to Stratford to see a production by the Royal Shakespeare Company, I think it would counter any negative impression of Shakespeare that they may gain in future from reading one of his plays around the class.

You did mention that you might need to travel to Norwich for a meeting sometime soon. If so, please do let me know when. Perhaps we could meet for coffee or a bite to eat somewhere, I think it's my turn to take you out for lunch?

With best wishes and thanks again,

Lorna.

And I hope he will understand. I feel a bit of a rat. And I then rationalise this by remembering that he probably hasn't seen his family since . . . his wife's funeral? And although having my company across France and Spain might seem, in theory, fun to him, helpful even, father and daughter probably just needed to be together, talk over old times spent with Mum and Grandma, Nanny, however she was known, re-establish family relationships and identities - without having to be polite to some strange woman whom they had never met before; and about whom and whose future role Rachel might be wondering.

I understand that Major Reginald wants me to see the very best in what he has to offer but . . there's something vital missing. I may meet some of his needs . . . but where and to what extent does he, would he, can he meet mine? No, I decide that I have made a sensible decision. I just hope Reg would see it that way too.

He doesn't. His next email comes rather too quickly. It starts: -

Dear Lorna,

I was surprised by the contents of your last message. I must say, I am deeply, deeply disappointed. . . .

I have hurt his pride. And also ruined his plans. Because, unless he can find a partner to help him run the house and garden, he intends to downsize, to move within the village or even outside it, lose his friends, his contacts and perhaps his status.

I understand that. Three times I have been in that position, have found myself abandoned and in charge of what was to have been a joint project of converting, renovating or extending a property. And, I guess, Major Reginald had hoped that I would be a way of his avoiding having to do all that, by being his 'Margaret'. Hence Rachel and Andrew would need to accept me as their father's – what – carer? A step–mother?

He felt he was being so generous, offering so much, and I have spurned that. But his email goes on to say: -

> . . . I have to attend a morning meeting of the East Suffolk & Norfolk River and Broads Authority on Wednesday 23rd, being held at a conference centre just north of Norwich. It should be over by noon so I wondered, could we meet for a pub lunch somewhere of your choosing? I could pick you up from your house, if you give me the address; or I could meet you at the pub.
>
> Best wishes,
>
> Reg x

A 'lower case' x? So not too much rancour then. A meeting at the pub seems preferable. My house lies off a side road off a narrow country lane that leads to a farm and then the next village. It might test the Major's army orienteering skills to find it. So, I suggest, not 'The Feathers' which would be my local if I ever went to a pub on a regular basis, but 'The Railway', because the restaurant reviews are quite good.

I arrive at the pub before Major Reginald, order myself a gin-and-tonic, possibly for courage, and within ten minutes or so he arrives in the bar. He looks almost pleased to see me but - something has changed. He is reserved. Maybe he still has the meeting on his mind.

I ask about it but he dismisses my enquiry with a wave of his hand, instead drawing my attention to the blackboard with 'today's lunch suggestions' chalked on it. There's whitebait on the menu, which I'm keen on and that I opt for. Major

Reginald does the same. We talk about mundanities, he doesn't mention Portugal or his forthcoming trip. There aren't many people in the pub, certainly none whom I know, but I want to avoid any disagreement or a scene.

I would like to relax and enjoy my lunch but I can't. I can feel I've done, said, written the wrong thing, that I am the target of some disapproval.

I want to say 'So I said 'no'. Aren't I allowed to say no? I do have a choice, you know' but I don't. There is tension at our bar table, I can almost see and touch it, it circles our plates like impending thunder.

To distract myself and lighten my own mood, I silently wonder whether Margaret was met with this disapproval and distain when she 'decided' to die. How thoughtless of her. Then, while he finishes off his lunch and ignores the accompanying green salad, I ponder upon my possibly having had what might be termed 'a lucky escape'.

Trying to show that we can still be friends, I suggest that, rather than ordering coffee here, we might go back to my house. I will put the kettle on and he can say hello to Butterworth. Major Reginald agrees, though without much apparent enthusiasm. His BMW tails my car home.

Suddenly I feel as we approach the driveway, if not quite ashamed of my house, that it doesn't match up to his - although the setting in the middle of fields is one I prefer, as does Butterworth. However, it's home, it's mine and I have fresh ground coffee available.

The Major sits in my kitchen, looks out of the dining room window and at the patio. He asks if I enjoy gardening. I tell him 'It's not a question of enjoyment. It's something that needs to be done so I do it. End of story.'

Unconvinced, he sips his coffee; he seems uncomfortable here and soon starts to make tracks, asking how best to get back onto the main road to Norwich.

I don't hear from Major Reginald again for several weeks. Then, quite unexpectedly because I rarely use my ancient Nokia mobile phone, I receive a text. From Major Reginald. It reads:

> DEAREST LYNDA, (who on earth is Lynda?)
>
> HAVE RECEIVED AN INVITATION FROM THE BRIGADIER TO ATTEND A SOCIAL FUNCTION NEXT MONTH NOT FAR FROM WHERE YOU LIVE. WILL YOU DO ME THE HONOUR OF BEING MY PLUS ONE? COULD MEET FOR A DRINK BEFOREHAND, NOT AT THE RAILWAY BECAUSE HAVE FOUND SOMEWHERE FAR BETTER AND UPMARKET THAT THINK YOU WOULD PREFER. WHAT DO YOU SAY? LOVE REGGIE.

After a moment's puzzlement - ('Dearest' Lynda? So, the 'deeply, deeply disappointed' feeling has worn off quite quickly then?) – and some relief because I hadn't wanted to hurt him, I text back to Reginald quite kindly, I think, to explain that he appears to have sent me this text in error, that it was meant for someone called Lynda; and I emphasise the Y.

His message back, not thanking me for pointing this out, is verging on the abusive. He tells me that he did not feel welcomed, only by Butterworth, when he came to my house;

that I am too serious, have no sense of humour and 'absolutely no charisma.'

I am uncertain as to what to do about the last, I might try placing an order for charisma from John Lewis or Waitrose. Otherwise, it isn't a very helpful remark and I try not to take it as anything but a subjective response made by a man whose nose has been put out of joint. He goes on to write that when I am his age, I may also make mistakes so I am not to laugh at him, he is not one of my delinquent children. And I am too strict with 'Poor Butterly'.

I bridle at the 'delinquent'. My offspring, none of whom he has ever met, are far from delinquent; or perhaps was he referring to my teaching children with particular needs? In which case, I bridle again twice as much on their behalf. Traveller children who have specific needs may have these because their pattern of schooling has often become disrupted and fragmented, they are rarely delinquent, not in the state educational system anyway; otherwise, they would be in a different specialist sort of establishment.

I give him a mental and unexpressed lecture, then calm down and rationalise. I have turned him down. And then, to add insult to injury, I have pointed out that he has sent a text intended for 'Dearest Lynda' to me in error. He has faults, no wonder he feels exposed and wounded. He has been seen, in the face of adversity, to be soldiering on but has let down his guard. I decide to delete his text and all his emails. It's time for me to move on.

Chapter 27

Duncan aka Sandyman

> **Sandyman**
>
> You can see my photos – do I look my age?
>
> Widowed 69, Stibbard, Near Fakenham, Norfolk.
>
> Two-way match = 89.3%
>
> He is an 82.7 % match for you. You are a 96% match for him

Within the week, I receive a flag on the Likewise website, indicating that I have a message from 'Sandyman'. I wonder who that is, whether I have looked at his photos and his profile. The name 'Sandyman' doesn't ring a bell; and isn't that a brand of sherry?

I check on his profile. It reads:

> 'Honest, reliable, young at heart and genuine. Do I look my age? You tell me, you have seen my photographs. If you are smart, intelligent and of average build I

> should like to meet you. An ideal timeline would be to meet over coffee then next have a day out together.
>
> Beauty springs from within and it shines through despite the covering. I am fit and healthy, don't smoke and my teeth are my own. My hair has almost gone though. Anyway, what I want is to love, care and share. Could it be with you? Good friends are made slowly and it can all start over a coffee. I am IT and DIY competent and have a number of interesting hobbies. Have an interest in wildlife and nature which I would like to share. Would like to explore the UK more. Why not contact me to find out more?'

He describes his ideal match thus:

> 'Honest, fair and fun. In other words, just normal. Just be yourself. I hope you are interested in walks, holidays, eating out and all the normal things in life.'

Judging by his photograph, which I guess he chose himself, he is no film star. But there is nothing off-putting about his profile, though he records his height as what I would call 'a trifle on the short side', but otherwise – well, he might be OK. So, what does he say in his message to me?

'Sandyman' writes:

> Hello, Susan2324,
>
> I liked your profile and your photo very much.
>
> I live not very far from you, I moved into the village a few years ago after my second marriage.

If you are interested in writing to me, I would like that very much and promise to reply.

Best wishes

Duncan - followed by his telephone number

Well, nothing ventured, nothing gained, so I might as well respond; it can do no harm.

Hello Duncan,

Thank you for getting in touch, I'm glad you liked my profile. Quite apart from the question of whether or not we have anything in common (and we do seem to), your email is heartening as it's very easy to be considered invisible when one is female and in one's seventies!

I've been in Norfolk since the 1960s. I love the coastline and the countryside; it isn't hilly but it certainly isn't flat either. The dog enjoys it too.

I would be interested to hear more from you, if you're not too busy. And I always reply to emails, unless they are from someone trying to sell me something.

With kind regards,

Susan2324

And then I phone him. Well, what was the point of including his number otherwise? Fortunately, when we speak, he doesn't pose his written profile question of 'You can see my photos – do I look my age?' If he had, I would have answered it truthfully – I'm not very good at being tactful and I don't do lying – and as a result, we probably never would have met. But we did meet. And he did. Look his age. And grey. I decide to tell him my real name. 'The '2324' bit', I tell him, 'relates to my birth date. My first name is Lorna.'

It was my suggestion that we should arrange to meet away from my home area and his village, to give ease of conversation away from neighbours, friends or interruptions. So, we meet mid-morning outside the local building society offices in East Dereham. I park my car, check my hair and make-up – a little lip gloss wouldn't go amiss - pay for an hour's parking and walk towards the shops. He is leaning, with his back to the road, on a metal fence that prevents pedestrians from stepping off the pavement and into the path of cars. He is the only man of his described height waiting there, so I know it must be he.

'Are you Duncan?'

His face is not unlike his photograph, slightly on the thin side and with a rather blotchy complexion. Sandy hair and not much of it. Pink striped shirt and grey suit. Does the occasion, do I, really merit a suit?

He nods. 'Yes. Are you Laura?' I correct him, tell him my name. He has an Essex accent. Oh, well.

Another nod and 'Hi' and a whatever-do-we-say-next pause. I feel the need to move things forward. So, I offer 'We can't talk here, we'll block the pavement. Shall we see if we can get a coffee somewhere?'

We cross the road to a pub on the opposite side of the road, he pushes at the oak door and holds it open for me. Manners are OK, then. So far. Seeing the lounge bar empty, we make our way to a padded bench seat, covered with green patterned William Morris material in the window and sit ourselves down. I had cushions at home in fabric like that. He goes up to the bar to check whether coffee is being served and turns round to look at me. Yes, he is quite short, his trousers could do with being turned up an inch. He asks what I would like and orders a cappuccino 'with chocolate sprinkled on top? Or cinnamon?' for me and an Americano for himself. Returning with the coffees and sitting down again, he jogs the table so that my coffee slops into its saucer. Nerves, I wonder? Or just a bit clumsy.

'What can you tell me about yourself that I don't already know?' I ask. And in a low voice, 'And why a dating website?' He hitches the cloth of his grey trousers at the knees, delves into an inside pocket of his grey jacket and pulls some photos from his wallet. 'This is my house', he says. 'Honeysuckle Cottage. And this is my Cynthia, my wife.'

I make all the right admiring noises and his wife is, or had been, very pretty, her hair bleached blond. And young, younger than I would have imagined.

'It was taken several years ago' he explains 'before she became ill. Tell me' he adds without pausing for breath, 'when your husband passed away, did you feel that part of you died too?'

I am taken aback and my eyes prickle with unexpected tears. This perceptiveness isn't quite what I had expected and I feel a mild kinship towards him; because he understands. We talk for a while about how it has been, those times, for both of us. I ask him how long ago she died.

'Two years. It was quite sudden. She hadn't been ill or anything. It was only afterwards that I learned that she had had a heart condition.'

He asks me about my interests and then 'What are you doing tomorrow? Because there's an antiques street fair on in Fakenham. Would you be interested in coming with me?' and he gives me his address. 'If you came to my house at about 11 o'clock and left your car there,we could go together in my car.'

As it happens, I have nothing planned for the next day; and although I am not an avid collector of antiques, there might be something unusual and of interest. So I agree. He goes on to tell me how he and Cynthia had bought the house together, just before they had got married and that it had been a second marriage for both of them. 'And we bought a piece of land, not for anything special, but just because, well, it was land and land has value. We leave it natural. It's in the village too, not far from the cottage,' And knowing I am interested in wildlife, 'and I put up some nesting boxes. On the trees. For owls. Or squirrels.'

Not wanting to appear to be one of those women who gets men to buy their drinks for them, I offer to pay for my coffee but he refuses. 'Then it's on me, tomorrow', I say.

Once home, I feel slightly uneasy about what I have agreed to, especially about meeting him at his house. I decide to check on what little information I have about him. How do I know he is really a widower? And really lives where he said? Opening up my laptop, I put 'Cynthia Green' into Google and wait. Yes, there is a brief report on her death, from the local Mercury paper. And there had been some report of a drainage problem which included properties in his lane in his parish and mentioned Honeysuckle Cottage, though not who owned it. So far, so good.

Using my satnav, I find my way to his house relatively easily, recognising its white painted façade from the photograph he showed me and park my little blue Fiesta sensibly just off the narrow road and on to a patch of gravel beside what I hope is his garage entrance. Pushing through a small stiff garden gate to get to his front door, I realise I have arrived five minutes early and hope that won't put him out in any way. But he opens the front door before I have time to knock, and invites me in.

After a few pleasantries in his pamment-tiled hallway, he leads me into the garage at the side of the house and to his car. It is smart, last year's model and as far as I can see, spotless inside and out. He opens the front passenger door for me and I clamber in as he positions himself in the driving seat.

We sit, side by side in the dark facing the closed garage door with the road on the other side and I wonder just what is coming next.

'It's electric' he explains, pressing a device on his key; the garage door swings up and over our heads. 'It was a present that my wife and I gave to each other a couple of Christmases ago', he explains. 'We discussed what we each wanted and really, there was nothing. So, we decided on this.'

'It seems more useful than a self-indulgent luxury.' Then I wonder whether using the term 'self-indulgent' implies some sort of criticism on my part. So, to endorse what I have said and genuinely feel, 'I can imagine coming home on a cold wet day with a week's worth of groceries in the boot and how good it must be, not to have to get out of the car and fiddle with the garage lock in the pouring rain.'

'There's a similar benefit when I leave the house and don't have to stop the car in the lane to get out to close the garage doors' which he demonstrates as he pulls out alongside where

I've left my Fiesta, turns his car immediately to the left and sets off towards the town.

We chat as he drives to Fakenham. He seems quite easy to talk to, though I have the gut feeling that we are both making an effort to make the day as easy as possible. On the outskirts of the town, he pulls into the grassy field designated for parking, stops alongside the line of vehicles and we get out.

I make a mental note of the model and registration number, I am out with a perfect stranger after all. And the website has stressed the need to be mindful of one's safety, to meet in a public place, that sort of thing.

'The antique fair is all along the main streets. If we go this way,' as he presses my elbow, 'it leads to the main square.'

Plastic multicoloured bunting hangs across the roads and on either side of the street are tables and make-shift stalls displaying china mugs, glassware, clocks, a heavy flat iron, several pairs of children's spectacles with pink National Health frames, an old yellow AA badge like the one my father had fixed to the front of our Austin 16, black telephones with the finger dials and old fashioned handsets, a black and gold Singer sewing machine, mugs heralding the names of long ago wound-up companies, tarnished foreign coins, even a rusty Dunlop bicycle repair kit tin. So much junk.

I ask Duncan – his name is Duncan, isn't it? Or is it Douglas? – what his main interest is.

'Watches. Especially old pocket watches. Though I think we'd be lucky to find any here. Often, they were made of silver. And we certainly wouldn't find a gold one. Or if we did, it would be quite pricey. What about you? Has anything taken your fancy? What are you mainly looking at?'

Actually, I'm not looking at anything much, it all seems to me to be the sort of stuff that people clear out of their attics and take straight down to the local refuse tip. There are some sherry glasses that I quite like, though I already have plenty of sherry glasses and entertain nobody for sherry, except perhaps at Christmas. And they probably aren't cut crystal anyway, more likely to be moulded glass and a petrol company's give-away. I don't want to pick them up and examine them, because doing that will show interest and might get me into a conversation with the stall holder and I would end up having to buy them, rather than being the sort of woman who shows interest, then says 'no' and walks away.

'The pictures are very varied,' I observe. 'Some of the prints are quite interesting. But one or two of the oil paintings are very . . .' I don't want to appear a snob but ' . . . well, amateurish. Colours too bright, no technique and little to say. But' I add, though not actually believing it 'I guess it's all a matter of taste.'

Duncan – by now I am pretty sure his name is Duncan; it certainly begins with a letter D and I'm sure it isn't David – nods, in what I take to be agreement. Or resignation. Perhaps I'm not quite the date he was looking for. Perhaps he wants someone to show much more enthusiasm. Changing the subject might help.

'Gosh, I'm quite thirsty. How about a coffee? And it's my turn to . . .' I don't want to use bald terms like pay or cash or money ' . . . pick up the tab.'

In a small courtyard off the High Street, there are more stalls set out selling ribbon, buttons and white linen goods. Or they have been white, once. Nothing of real interest; although one of those crocheted things with beads around the edge that you put over a milk jug to keep the flies away might come in handy. But there doesn't seem to be one. And I don't want to stop and rootle through the bundles of stuff. We push past the tables, through the crowds and make our way to the entrance of the Fox and Goose.

'Are you happy to have coffee? Or would you rather something else, something stronger?' He is driving so I hope he won't say yes thank you, a double scotch would be great.

'Coffee would be fine', he assures me.

I pray we won't bump into anyone I know; I do know a few people in the town, people who have been friends of friends. And I don't want to have to introduce . . er, Duncan as my . . . what? As someone I've only met once before, on a dating site? Oh, heaven forbid.

Once we have had our coffee and gathered our thoughts for a few minutes, I realise two things; first, that I need to go to the loo and second, that it is nearly lunchtime. When I go to the bar to ask where the Ladies is, I pay for the coffees and then make my way along the stone-paved corridor to the toilets. It is good to sit down, if only for a moment and I try to avoid trailing the bottoms of my trousers on the loo floor. Whatever am I doing here? And why?

I had asked myself that usual question that morning when stepping out of the shower; what should I wear? Did I really want to look special? Or did I want to be warm and comfortable? Did I think, from what I had read, heard and seen, that this was the man for me? No, I didn't and I still don't; it was just to be a pleasant day out and that at the end we will probably call it a day. So, I should look good but not stunning; not that there was much hope of that, not at my age; but I should make a reasonable effort. In the end I have opted for the pair of white linen trousers with flesh-coloured pants underneath and a white bra under a red and white patterned Indian cotton long-sleeved blouse that fastens all the way down the front with a series of bobble buttons. And I decided upon a red pashmina wrap to carry or fling casually around my shoulders in case it grows chilly. And a small handbag.

Through the pub window we can see passers-by, eating hot dogs or bacon rolls. More important than that, Duncan can see them. Hopefully they remind him that it is lunchtime. I haven't wanted to mention food. I know, although I'm tall, I am on the tubby side and hefty with it – what my father kindly termed 'Juno-esque' - so much so that people, by which I mean men, imagine that I can help lift something heavy like an upright piano with one hand.

One of my previous 'acquaintances', whenever we met, would visually weigh me; in fact, he once told me his weight and had the cheek to ask what I weighed. I don't do lying and not often avoidance but neither did I want the acquaintanceship to end just because he was a couple of pounds, well, maybe a stone, lighter.

So, it's a sensitive area, my weight. Maybe that's why I tend to prefer taller men, so I don't feel so . . big. I noticed right from the start that Duncan is only an inch or so taller that I. And slimmer. No, that's a comparative term; he is just slim.

But he doesn't give the impression of raw health, his teeth are quite yellow and his skin is a bit grey; I feel he should get out more often into the fresh air. And do something physically active. I'm always on the move, walking the dog, swimming, pottering about in the garden. What does Duncan actually do with his time? I shall ask him later. Reading someone's profile tells you only so much.

'If you've finished your coffee,' he suggests, to my relief, 'let's walk along the other street that runs parallel to this one, see what there is and then think about some lunch.'

The next street is rather like the first, though there seem to be more people zig-zagging slowly in the middle of the road, taking their attention towards the mix of stalls on either side. Duncan is gesticulating to me; he has seen a group of ancient pocket watches clustered in a small plastic basket.

He goes closer to gain a better view and I follow him, realising that it would be easy to lose him in the crowd and he is my main form of transport back to my car and then home. Have I forgotten what sort of car he drove? It was a white something.

'The watch I fancied was over-priced', he tuts, 'I thought it looked like one my grandfather used to have, but it would need a lot of cleaning and a lot of work.'

'Was it still going?' I ask and immediately feel naïve.

'Didn't notice. Don't expect it was.'

'What would you, what do you do with old watches? Do you just, well, collect them? For fun?'

'It depends. I might keep them and see if I can get them going again. They're intricate things, watches. Lots of tiny parts, cogs and levers, each bit depending on another. Or I might sell them on to a retired watch-mender I know, who still does it for a hobby.'

Before we reach the food stands, the smell of cooked meat reaches us. We come to two stalls almost opposite each other in the main square, that have people crowded around them. The one with blue-and-white striped awning is selling burgers and hot dogs. On the high counter are yellow and red plastic bottles of mustard and tomato sauce that customers are seizing by the waist and squeezing on to their food. I am prepared to settle for a burger, with or without onions. But from the stand opposite wafts a slightly different aroma. The sign 'Crispy Duck' above the awning attracts me straight away; so much more up-market and tastier than a hot dog. It comes with optional lettuce dressing and some sort of oriental sauce.

'Which would you prefer?' I ask. 'Or does neither appeal to you?'

Duncan appears undecided so I feel it is time for one of us to make a decision and I move towards to the duck stand. 'This is what I'd prefer, I can have a hot dog any day. And I don't really like them, I'm a bit fussy about my sausages. But I'm quite happy to have a burger if that would be easier' I say, eyeing and comparing the length of the queues, 'so long as it's made with reasonable quality beef. Or would you like the duck too?'

There are three people in front of me when I join the line, Duncan standing beside me, and we move forward quite quickly. By the young lad behind the counter, we are given our duck, brown crispy flakes, in a long white split bread roll with a bed of lettuce in the valley. I hand over some coins. I don't want Duncan, or anyone else I meet on a dating site, to think I am just in it so that some guy will treat me to a lunch, even if it is only from a market stall.

Duncan says he thinks there might be something of interest in the Corn Exchange but it turns out to be a collection of old hats and the sort of lace-up stack-heeled shoes into which my grandmother would have inserted her bunions. After a little more browsing, we decide that we have seen all there is to see of antiques and bric-a-brac and make our way slowly back to the car park. As we turn into a narrow alley, there are people coming in the opposite direction, people who have presumably had lunch at home and are out for an afternoon of looking, fingering, bargaining and buying. The field seems further away than when we arrived but I try, almost as an intellectual exercise, to spot and identify his car before Duncan does.

I fail and walk past it.

Nearly back to his village, he says, 'I'll tell you what, I'll show you the piece of land we bought. See what you think of it' and almost immediately he stops the car in a narrow lane somewhere remote from any houses, and gets out. An area of apparently waste land is hedged from the road by overgrown hawthorn except where a metal gate blocks a hardly-used entrance. He fiddles with a padlock and chain on the five-barred gate and pushes it open.

The long grass swishes against the bottom metal bar. He drives us in through the gap, through long grass to a spot where the ground is stony and the grass shorter and he parks the car.

I wonder whether he will, or needs to, shut the gate behind him. He doesn't.

We get out of the car and walk quite slowly, because I'm not too keen on nettles or reptiles, through the vegetation towards a small pond - for a brief moment, I wonder whether the 'wife' is still in there – a pond which, he tells me, he has had pumped out and cleared out that spring. Around the edges are emergent flag irises which would look quite pretty in spring and early summer.

I silently assume therefore that 'she', Cynthia, is not still in there, her body drowned and bloated in the black water; and then wonder why I am feeling uneasy about where we are and why we are here. Perhaps it's because it is quite dark in this enclosed area, the thick oak trees overhead shut out much of the light and there's no one around.

Duncan has constructed nesting places high up in two of the trees, 'for owls', he says.

In one corner there is a large long compost heap, 'for nettles and hedge clippings' from his own garden. I silently hope I won't end up on or under the compost heap. So, we must be quite near his house and therefore near other houses; I feel a certain relief - and then smile to myself that here am I, the one who goes off travelling across the world on her own, worried about being with a man with whom she's quite pleasantly spent several hours, in a small Norfolk field and with a mobile phone in her handbag.

Although it isn't switched on and probably not charged. Duncan or Douglas is just pointing out to me his two upright compost bins, when something glides through and is moving the dark green grass blades towards the base of the bins.

'There are snakes in there usually' he tells me. I dislike snakes, even the thought of them. I try not to respond, endeavouring to assume a disinterested, careless air and arrange my face accordingly.

But half-jokingly to myself, I hope, if he is about to strangle me – and I know nothing about this man, after all – and bump me off in some way, he won't dump my body under the compost with the snakes – just in case I'm not completely dead and die all over again, of fright.

Then, because it's getting quite chilly, it's back to the car and to his house to collect my little blue Fiesta. But first, I am invited indoors for a drink and Duncan thinks he has half a bottle of wine open.

I decide he is not a linguist and therefore not to tell him that he may have a whole bottle of wine open (unless it had been a 35cl half bottle or the bottom half has been severed from the top), or what has been a whole bottle, but that there is apparently now half of the wine left. It would be wasted on him; the observation, not the wine.

I accept a seat on the sofa and a small 'small, please, I'm driving' glass of red. He asks if he may kiss me. It seems a harmless request, so why not. He does. As kisses go, it's not bad. But then his right hand goes towards my red cotton Indian blouse.

I sigh with what is almost boredom; he's not very subtle. The blouse has globe-round knot buttons and they are hard for him to undo. Oh, good.

He suggests I put down my wine glass, in fact he takes it from me, takes my right hand and places it on the crotch of his trousers. This seems a trifle pointless if it is meant so that I can feel his train of thought – does he think I'm mentally slow or something? - a train of thought which is becoming, unless I intervene and deflect, increasingly clear.

He moves my hand to his desired spot; I am nearly seventy, does he think I don't know what part of a man's body lies where? And tells me he is becoming quite damp, wet even. I find this a less-than-attractive image. Am I becoming damp too, he asks?

To my slight annoyance, I might be and I'm not even going to think about it; so much for the menopause.

'Would you like to go upstairs, to lie down beside me on the bed, just lying, side by side?' he asks me.

'I think it would be a bad idea', I tell him. With an apparent quick change of mind and subject, he asks me 'What are your plans for the rest of the day?'

I jump at this redirection and hurriedly say 'I've got several emails to answer, I need to have a sensible conversation with my son before the evening, I have a disciplinary code of practice to write, and I must take the dog for a walk before it gets dark,' all this to accentuate that I have responsibilities and people at home who expect me back for an evening meal.

'OK,' he says, 'you're busy. . . . so, no chance of a quick shag, then?'

I take a deep gulp of air and laugh pathetically, probably with nervousness. I notice that my jaw has dropped and my eyes have become wide, wide open. I try not to choke or say 'Oh, perleeeze'. Who, or what, does he think I am? I seem to remember something he wrote in his profile about good friends being made slowly. Slowly? This man is taking things at an ultrafast pace.

'No, absolutely no chance', I assure him.

'A pity,' he mutters; then 'Another time, perhaps?' And after a very, very long silent time lapse, he says 'My wife would have liked you; you'd have had a lot in common. She loved taking her clothes off.'

There isn't anything I feel I can sensibly reply to this.

'Tell me,' he enquires, 'how do you feel about oral sex?'

Whatever dumbfounded means, I'm close to it. Whatever did I do or say to get into a conversation like this?

Then, 'Do you like it? And tell me, do you swallow – or spit?'

I am amazed at the speed at which my mind and mouth can work in a tight spot, without any intended instruction from me. My mind decides, faster than my brain can assemble itself and make a decision, that a deadpan reply is probably the best response to what I intend to regard as an academic enquiry; and regardless of what his enquiry relates to, of whether oral sex is within my preferred repertoire, I hear my voice tell him 'I am a lady – and ladies do not spit.'

I wait until the blanket of silence has dropped politely to the floor, after which I ask 'Any chance of a coffee before I hit the road?'

He makes me an instant coffee, suggests meeting again for a day out next weekend in Woodbridge. 'Perhaps, I will need to check my diary,' I assure him, hurriedly finish my coffee and I offer a courteous goodbye 'and thanks for a –' and I am stuck for a word here – 'an interesting day out.'

Driving home, I reflect on the day. Will I see Duncan again? Perhaps. But probably not. He appears to have coped with – no, 'accepted' would be a better word, I think – the death of his Cynthia. But now he is seeking company for events. Outings that he used to enjoy with her. But what he seems to miss most, is the sex; or any form of sexual stimulation. From what little I have seen and deduced, he appears quite capable in the kitchen, with his laundry and the garden.

We seem to be wanting, expecting even, completely different things from this online encounter. Have I totally misunderstood, got the whole thing wrong? Perhaps I've had another fortunate escape, it could have gone so badly, with or without being composted.

Back home, I am happy to be greeted by the dog, whose needs and wants are pretty clear and who provides affection, protection and consistency. Even a gentle woofed reminder sometimes. I know where I am with Butterworth. And that will do very well for me, for now.

Chapter 28

Olive Branch

It was September 2012. The large building in front of me seemed familiar although I didn't think I'd ever stayed there before. When I had come to Canterbury in 1962 as a student, my first year had been spent in digs in Ethelbert Road while the student blocks were being built. Six of us living together there, the only mixed digs because Mrs Stevens refused to have students unless the genders were mixed.

When I had arrived for interview at the Priory, wearing a navy winter coat and a pork-pie basket-weave hat that I had borrowed from my mother and in which she used to keep the previous day's eggs from our chickens, I had come just for the day; and we certainly wouldn't have afforded a hotel room for me.

But wasn't this building the former Chaucer Hotel? But now displaying a Travelodge sign? And where I had booked a room online, for three nights?

I had returned to Canterbury only once before and with some reluctance because, just before I left some fifty years ago, I was treated almost as *persona non grata*, regarded by some as a Jezebel, a marriage breaker; one or two of my former colleagues were reluctant even to talk to me because of what they considered I had done.

I felt shunned and wounded; but it would have been quite wrong and unnecessary of me to have explained the whole situation to them at the time, that would have done far more damage; and part of the unspoken accusation was true, but only part.

But I still regarded the place with mixed feelings, so I had been tentative about accepting the invitation for this weekend.

But the college had recently become a university and Education was now only one of the different Faculties. The current students probably had a wider perspective too.

When I had applied for a place over fifty years ago, the only main subjects on offer for prospective school teachers were English, Maths, Geography, Divinity or Science. And we all had to study something else as well, something called 'Civilisation'. Along with many other students, I had opted for English as my main course. I had wanted to take English as a fourth 'A' level; but, as it was gently explained to me by the school and my mother, the amount of study necessary for four separate subjects would have been enormous and possibly beyond me. There was more to it as well, involving Valerie.

Much in my life had involved Valerie or been influenced one way or another by her, by her behaviour, her exam results, her resentment, her mental health and her temper. I had suggested dropping Latin; but that, I was informed, would militate against my being accepted for Cambridge, so, I had been strongly advised to stick with French, German and Latin.

Not that I thought there would be much chance of my applying for a place at Cambridge University, let alone being accepted. I knew I wasn't that good, not that academically capable. But Moo, my mother who had no personal experience of university herself, was ever hopeful.

I remembered the Chaucer Hotel because it had been in one of the downstairs rooms there, when I had only just started at the college, that I had an embarrassing situation involving Mrs Ramsey, the wife of the then Archbishop of Canterbury. I had no idea why we were assembled there or who she was, standing among a few dignitaries and looking around her for someone to relate to or recognise. As far as I knew, she might have been someone's parent or a new lecturer.

'Have you come far today?' I asked her, my pitiful attempt at small talk.

No wonder she had looked surprised. She explained who she was. And where she lived. Not so far away, then.

My room in the Travelodge this time was on the first floor at the very end of a long corridor. I heard someone sneeze in the room next to mine and wondered if it were a tourist or another 'one of us'.

Coming into Reception from the car park, I had bumped into Brenda and recognised her, but I had very little idea who else would be coming to Canterbury for this occasion. The whole invitation coming from the college authorities had been a huge surprise.

Strolling through Canterbury around lunchtime, I had found myself smiling wanly at people, a rather pathetic gesture of intended greeting towards anyone who looked about my age, in case it turned out to be someone from my year whom I didn't immediately recognised.

I noticed where the city had changed in the last fifty years, which shops had disappeared, wondered where my favourite outdoor café was, where the department store called Riceman's had gone. I had worked in Riceman's kitchen department down in the basement during the summer after I left college, selling bath-chain and saucepans for the first few weeks, then in the office dealing with invoices.

I remembered having someone explain to me what an invoice was and where to file the copies in alphabetical order of supplier. 'Invoice' was a word that I hadn't heard before: in my family, we only had 'bills'.

Walking down Burgate towards the cathedral main gate, in the distance I spotted a group of people standing talking together and making their way slowly towards the Buttermarket.

Without any pre-thought, I recognised Peter immediately, not from his face which was too far away for me to see in detail, but from his confident stance and walk. How strange that that information should have remained lodged in my memory, unwanted and unneeded for all these years.

Hilary may have suggested that we all meet at 'The Olive Branch' before the big event the next day. Did we eat an evening meal in that pub or did I get myself something at the Travelodge?

I didn't remember having a meal that first evening. But I recalled being in the former Olive Branch which had become renamed as something else, and walking up the entrance steps and into a crowd of elderly people all about my own age, meeting other people I should know and with whom I had kept in contact, although sporadically. A few I recognised instantly.

And someone else, a tall man with fair hair that was now almost white, who said 'I'm glad you're here, I hoped you would be.' I had no idea who that was. His looks reminded me of the younger years of a well-known naturalist celebrity and television programme presenter.

Then he helped me out by saying 'We met a couple of years ago at an earlier reunion. There weren't many of us there then, I think many of the others couldn't attend, for some reason.'

I remembered it vaguely. It had been only a few months after Danny had died so the world had still been hazy. Those who knew I was recently bereaved had been especially careful about what they said to me, probably afraid that they might set off a flood of tears.

'There were so few that year that five or six of us had breakfast together in a local café round the corner,' he reminisced and I then remembered his name as Robert or something like that.

We sat down as a group on wooden benches and ordered drinks from a long menu or wine list. Someone else came in, I didn't recognise her but she introduced herself to me as 'Barbara W' and told me, when I looked blank, that she had been in the year below mine.

She reminded me that she had stood against me as a candidate in the Students' Union 1964/65 election for Vice-President. She hadn't gained many votes; I had completely forgotten her and the whole election process. I wondered how many other people from the year below mine lived in the area and would turn up, just to see what we looked like after so long, and whether we remembered them.

In the general exchange of information about who was doing what, who had married whom and how many children they had had, Robert quite suddenly announced in a matter-of-fact voice, 'My wife is asking for a divorce, says she doesn't love me any more.'

Sudden silence, intakes of breath. Christ Church is an establishment founded and underpinned by the Church of England, an institution in which marriage is sacred and divorce simply didn't happen. Or if it now does, is severely frowned upon; and I should know. Perhaps to fill the gap of silence or to move the conversation on to something more positive, one of the men asked Robert 'So what are you going to do?'

'I'm going to travel,' Robert replied 'probably to India.' And then, perhaps because he knew from a previous conversation that I had been to India a few years before with my children when they were teenagers, to my surprise he looked directly at me and asked 'So, are you coming with me?'

The next day was the 50 Years Golden Anniversary of Christ Church as an institution. A few years before, the college had been awarded University status so was now currently known as Canterbury Christ Church University rather than C4, the term that we used to use as an abbreviation for Christ Church College, Canterbury. As a mark of respect and an acknowledgement of the contribution made to the University by us, the students in its foundation year, those of us who had been granted a Certificate of Education in 1965, were to be awarded honorary degrees.

I wished Danny could have been there to be present, to see the place that was so important to me but of course he couldn't, he was dead. And perhaps, for him anyway, having an honorary degree from Canterbury wouldn't have compared all that well with his 2.1 degree from Cambridge or his son's First, also from Cambridge. Father and son had both studied at Trinity Hall, Danny reading English and his son Natural Sciences.

But I was very proud to be awarded this honour, regardless of other people's qualifications, and was very grateful, even though I hadn't had to do any further work to deserve it. I thought how pleased Moo would have been that someone in the immediate family had gained a degree, even if the comment I imagined she would have made, her 'Well, you got there in the end, Dear, and that's what matters' would have been laced with faint praise, praise in which she would also have basked, from the side lines.

We gathered together at the appointed time the following day in the main drawing room in St Martin's Priory, with its oak panelling that I loved so much and its large windows and window seats. I nipped out into the corridor with Robert to look at a long black-and-white photograph of our year group and the year after ours, it was hanging in a frame on the wall under the main stairs.

Enid made a comment - she hadn't changed, her remarks were quite often barbed – while Sue raised a questioning eyebrow at me. Referring to the two of us pairing up outside the throng, however briefly to Robert's current situation and in the light of my own recent sad marital history with which Sue was acquainted, I shook my head and referring to Robert's announcement, I explained 'It's nothing, just that I can recognise a wounded animal when I see one.'

No one had asked in advance for our measurements but in the adjoining room, the one we, during our time there, called the library, there was a tall cheval mirror, several tables laid out and draped with red-and-purple robes and mortar boards.

A woman, an official, eyed us up and down, presumably to assess our height and possibly girth.

She asked us to try on a robe from this table or that table, ready for the graduation ceremony, our graduation ceremony, in the Cathedral later that afternoon.

I heard that some of my colleagues, after leaving Canterbury, went on to study at various universities and had been through a graduation ceremony before.

I hadn't, there had been neither the time nor the money, certainly not the need. But for me and for many of my colleagues, that event that afternoon appeared to be the culmination of our adult careers, an endorsement of the energy and dedication that we had put into our lives as teachers and as former students going into unknown territory, taking on a pioneering role.

A few of my colleagues, one or two of the women including Enid informed us that they taught for only a few years before leaving teaching and getting married, living abroad.

We were taken by coach from St Martin's Priory to the Cathedral precinct. We were told that we would be led in, in twos, and who our 'partner' was deemed to be. I suspected there was some alphabetical order involved but I was aware that Robert was walking just behind me. For some strange reason that I could not explain to myself, I knew I would feel more at ease with Robert beside me, which was strange because we hadn't known each other at all well during our three years at C4.

I felt as if I had been in an alien country for a very long while but that now I was coming home to warmth that was familiar and where I could relax.

Either before or immediately after the ceremony, we gathered together on a patch of grass towards the side of the Cathedral, to have our photos taken, as a group.

Once inside the Cathedral nave, we were handed 'Orders of Service' booklets, because ours were not the only honorary degrees being awarded that day.

Edwina read the lesson and Hilary gave a very brief description of what it had been like in each of those first years of the university; of being spread out in digs across the City and wider, of living in halls on campus, of the spire being placed by helicopter on the top of the C4 chapel - she tactfully left out the incident of female underwear being draped around the spire by a group of daring students - of the deep snow, the intense cold in 1962/63 and of the sea freezing at Whitstable and Herne Bay.

Back at The Priory and having handed back our robes, we were asked to gather on the rear lawn and divide ourselves into two groups according to height, so that together we might form the shape of a figure 50 if viewed from above. A man with a camera stood on a chair to take the photograph and we were told to wave. Then there was tea and cake indoors.

It was surprising to me how many of us had kept in touch with each other over the previous fifty years, who had shared a flat with whom, who was godparent to whoever else's children.

Robert suggested quietly that he and I might have dinner together somewhere in the city. We agreed to meet at the other end of the city, outside the Falstaff Hotel because I remembered that they usually served meals. Only on this occasion, they did not, something to do with refurbishment of the property.

Seeing a fish restaurant on the opposite side of the road, Robert and I headed over towards it and glanced at the menu. We discovered that we both enjoyed fish, and the food seemed to be within our price range. No longer students, instead we were both now careful pensioners and on pensioners' incomes.

We climbed upstairs to the restaurant and the waiter brought us a menu. We settled for mackerel which we found we both enjoyed. And we talked, exploring what teaching we had each done in the years before and between when we had last met, Robert abroad as well as in the U.K. and me in Kent and then Norfolk.

We talked about our families and about Italy, where Robert told me he had a house.

'I have been to mainland Italy only once,' I told him, 'The first time was a school trip run by the Latin staff to Rome, Naples and Pompeii. I had a holiday in Sicily with the children and this last summer I went on a Ramblers holiday to the Aeolian Islands, where the walking was unexciting but the swimming from the Lipari hotel was fun. Do you speak fluent Italian?'

Robert confessed he didn't, that languages were not his thing and 'anyway, where I live, there's no need, nearly everyone speaks English.'

On the way back to the Travelodge and walking past Westgate Tower, we saw a man squatting on the ground against a wall, begging for food or money. We didn't react or respond, he looked as if he might be drunk or become aggressive. Once we had passed the beggar, to my surprise Robert asked 'May I hold your hand?'

Although there was no traffic along the High Street because it had become a pedestrian area, he took my hand and walked on the outside of the pavement. It had been a long time since anyone had treated me like that. Richard would have frowned at what he would have regarded as old-fashioned manners, would have said I was perfectly capable of looking after myself; and Danny, knowing how I valued my independence, would have responded in a very similar way. But I appreciated Robert's caring attitude and his request, it struck me as respectful.

I was no more vulnerable than anyone else, regardless of gender but I enjoyed being respected, not taken for granted, being cared about, someone having concern for my welfare - someone other than my children. The children always show concern for my welfare, they are very good to me, two of them especially keep in touch with me regularly, and with each other.

We reached the Travelodge safely, walked upstairs and along the same corridor. It transpired that Robert's room was next to mine. We said good night, he kissed me lightly on the cheek and thanked me for my company. I heard him preparing for bed as I prepared to go to sleep. For a brief moment, I was tempted to tap on his door but I didn't. And if I had done, I didn't know what I would have said, or done, or suggested.

But I knew I liked him, I found him respectful, intelligent company. I felt that somehow I had not been starting from scratch in getting to know Robert and sharing a meal with him. It felt more like having been away for a very long time and that now I was coming home to something warm and familiar.

In the morning just before breakfast, we met by chance in the corridor. Robert gave me a warm hug. We stood face to face looking at each other, feeling slightly unsure.

Robert asked 'Did last night really happen?'

'It did' I responded, 'we had dinner together. And I'm very glad. And we talked. And now we are going to have breakfast together, as well.'

After breakfast at the Travelodge, those of us staying there had various things to discuss including how we might best show our thanks to Christ Church for bestowing honorary degrees on each of us. Once we reached an agreement, many of the others headed back to their modes of transport and their homes. Robert told me he was thinking of catching a train to Broadstairs that afternoon.

'Why?' I asked 'Were you in digs there during your first year? Weren't we all in the student halls during our second and final years?'

'No, it's not for any nostalgic reason but I haven't ever been there and I'd like to see what it's like – and because Charles Dickens used to go there. You probably know that Broadstairs was Charles Dickens' favourite seaside town, it was while he was staying in a house in Broadstairs that he had the idea for 'Bleak House.'

I didn't know that at the time, I was more of a Jane Austen fan and I had only recently, thanks to one of my Likewise dates, become familiar with her writing. I had read only a few of Dickens' novels and the main ones that I could remember were 'Hard Times', 'David Copperfield' and 'Great Expectations'. Having been an avid reader as a child and having studied English at Canterbury, I felt embarrassed to admit my limited knowledge to a fellow colleague whose main subject had been Maths.

'Would you mind if I came with you?' I asked, hoping that he would not reject my suggestion.

The hotel named 'Bleak House' stood on the cliff overlooking the Broadstairs beach and the sea. We went inside to the tea room and Robert ordered two cups of tea with scones and butter.

The proprietor told us that Dickens House Museum had been closed recently but Robert thought it was worth going to find it, just to see whether it was open.

I felt slightly lost in the Museum and wanted to be close to Robert, I felt very comfortable with him, but I tried not to let this show by following him into every room, trotting after him as if I were an annoying younger sister, a stray dog or had no mind of my own. Clearly, Robert had read more Dickens that I had and I felt slightly naïve in those surroundings.

After spending time in the Museum and looking down at the people on the sandy beach, we walked back to the station together and waited for the next train back to Canterbury.

On the way back to Canterbury, I plucked up courage and asked Robert 'Did you mean what you said about going to India? And me coming with you?'

He said he did, but 'My sister-in-law says it's not worth spending more than a day or so in Delhi.'

'Oh, I disagree, I think it is. I think, if you haven't seen it before, you'd be bowled over by the range of colour and the vibrancy of that part of India, especially compared with London in winter. And if you are serious about going, then you might find it sensible to spend a couple of days in Agra and Jaipur because each is well worth a visit, they can be quite mind-blowing.'

On our return journey, Robert and I talked further about our lives, our teaching experiences, our families and our homes. We had both experienced two marriages and we both had step-children, as well as having in common our shared experiences of student life in Canterbury. We seemed to get on quite well together and I made a conscious effort to help raise his self-esteem, because he told me 'I feel battered and bruised, after all the unpleasant things my wife has said, her wanting a divorce because she says she no longer loves me. And if we are no longer together, I suppose we will need to sell the house. We have only just finished renovating it, making it into one house whereas before it had been two.'

I could sense the huge similarities in our two different positions and circumstances. But although Danny had hurt me with his affair with a fellow member of staff, I had picked myself up as best I could and felt I was managing to deal with life again - whereas for Robert, it was all still very new and raw.

I felt a deep empathy for his situation. He had been a fellow student, we fellow students stuck together, we shared a common past and from some of what he had told me, we shared much of our present situations as well.

'It sounds to me as if a trip to India might do you good,' I responded. 'If you like, I could look in the travel companies' brochures for the details, the ideal dates and the different prices. Although I've been before, that was with my children and years ago, before I married my second husband.

If you are really willing for me to come with you, I would be interesting to see if anything I remember about Northern India has changed. If you don't think you'll get fed up with me too quickly. But I already have a visit to Patagonia planned, with my travel companion Rosemary, for next February. So, we would need to discuss possible dates - because I suspect that that part of India, the part known as the 'Golden Triangle', would be almost unbearable in the summer.'

To save him from having to catch a train, I drove Robert part of the way back to London. I was wearing a linen shirt, a brown skirt with white spots and a grey cashmere cardigan that I had bought that very weekend from Marks and Spencer in Canterbury. Robert commented on my clothing and asked 'what material is your blouse made of?'

When I told him that it was quite old and linen, he responded to my quizzical look with 'because I like it, I like the texture.'

At his suggestion, we stopped on the way for a cup of coffee at a petrol station, it was the only place we could see on the main road that sold coffee. I dropped him at a tube station, kissed him goodbye and made my way back to Norfolk.

Robert and I were in contact that autumn and winter by letter, email and telephone. I sent Robert the details of Newmarket Holidays, a company running a tour called 'Tigers and the Taj Mahal' that seemed the best for price and itinerary.

We booked two places on the tour leaving Britain only a short time after I was due back from Patagonia – and to check our final arrangements, we agreed to meet at the Heathrow departures concourse in February 2013, a couple of hours before Rosemary and I were due to catch our flight to Buenos Aires.

Robert had been able to get his visa for India quite easily but it presented more of a problem for me.

In those days, it necessitated sending away one's passport and I was unable to do that in advance; I needed my passport with me to enter Argentina and Chile on my Patagonia visit. As there were only a few days after my return date before Robert and I were due to fly to Delhi, I needed to pay extra to have a courier rush my visa application through the necessary formalities and return it to me.

Robert had no working camera in Britain but I had two identical digital Pentax cameras, one had been Danny's. I suggested Robert should borrow it and he accepted gratefully.

I hoped that I wouldn't feel nostalgic on the trip, that if I missed Danny, I wouldn't let it show too much. I wanted to retain and preserve my memories of the time I had spent with him in India, I didn't want to smother one memory by superimposing a more recent image involving someone else.

When I, Danny and my three teenage children had arrived in Delhi, we had been greeted by having garlands of orange marigolds placed over our heads and around our necks. This time, when Robert and I arrived in our first Delhi hotel, the same thing happened. Robert was very surprised and said how endearing he found it.

We both hung our garlands up in the hotel room; they didn't survive, of course, but it was a lovely way to be welcomed.

The bathroom facilities and fittings surprised first Robert and then, when I became aware of them, me. I heard him say 'Well, that's very public. I'm glad I know you quite well and that we are not total strangers.'

I was not sure what he was referring to at first, but then I noticed, after he came back into the bedroom and I went to use the loo, that there was only a sheet of clear glass between the bathroom and the bedroom so that anyone using the loo, washbasin or bath was in full view of anyone in the adjoining bedroom. It was, as I later discovered, possible to pull down a wide blind to obscure the view through the glass but the room cleaner had left the blind in the 'up' position for Robert. I wondered if the cleaner had either been forgetful or possessed a wicked sense of humour, and I thought of my father.

Most of our party took rickshaw rides along the narrow lanes of the Chandni Chowk. The shop fronts on either side glistened in an array of colours with the sparkling merchandise but we did not stop to admire or buy anything. Stopping there would have been too risky with so much rushing about of pedestrians, bicycles, carts and other rickshaws, both behind and in front of us.

When we visited Jaipur and were invited to ride up the hill to Amber Fort on the back of an elephant, one of the other women on our tour who had also come from Norwich, told the guide 'I can't do that, I'm far too frightened. I don't want to go anywhere near those elephants, I might fall off.'

Having drawn the attention of everyone else who tried to reassure her with 'You'll be absolutely fine. It's quite safe and those howdah things are strapped on under the elephant's belly,' the yellow-dressed woman was persuaded by the rest of the group to join us rather than walk up the hill beside our guide.

For much of the rest of the tour, she would sit on a front seat and while the guide was explaining something, she would turn round to face the group, pull silly faces and make fun of what the guide was saying.

I felt embarrassed for him and strangely also for me, because she and I both came from East Anglia and I felt that she was letting Norfolk and the rest of Britain down by being so unappreciative and rude.

After several days of putting up with this, the guide told her 'I'm doing my job, and I also have feelings. Please let me get on with my work and show some respect.'

I was tempted to clap when he said that, but to have done so might have been equally impolite towards the woman in yellow. And I did not really want her to know that we lived quite close to each other; being on the same tour with her was proving embarrassing enough.

As we travelled through the countryside, our Indian guide wanted to show us a typical street market so as the coach passed through a town, he asked the driver to pull in and stop. We all got out and wandered about, looking at stalls and displays of fruit and vegetables, as the cows ate the rubbish and anything else lying on the ground. To separate myself from 'The Yellow Peril' woman, as Robert named her, I walked slightly ahead of the group. I came to a food stall and the owner offered me a cooked chilli to try.

A small group of other stall holders gathered round me; I assumed it was because they either wanted to see my reaction or were fascinated by my fair hair.

Robert hovered in the background, keeping me in sight but not intervening. I felt he was being protective while also giving me space. I appreciated his care and his confidence that I, as a well-seasoned female traveller, could handle the situation in whatever way it might develop.

I offered to pay the stallholder for the chilli I had nibbled, before clambering back onto the coach.

At Ranthambhore National Park, sitting in one of the large safari vehicles with no roof and no protective side barriers, I thought it unlikely we would see a tiger, except in the distance. I hadn't ascertained how interested Robert might be in Indian wildlife or whether he would just enjoy the experience of riding along tracks through the Indian forest and dry undergrowth, to see what there was to see.

We did see tiger paw prints on top of the tyre marks made by vehicles that had set off earlier that morning but there was no other sign of a live tiger, even though our driver took us to all the places that he thought might be the most promising.

One of the sites I had not seen before was the step well at Abhaneri. I thought it an amazing construction, mathematically ingenious and practical in an area short of fresh water.

Just at the entrance to the step well, a young girl approached Robert and engaged him in conversation. I was interested to see how he would relate to her, what her body language might convey. Having learned from him that he had been a teacher, she was anxious to show him one of her school textbooks.

There appeared to me to be interest on both sides, and respect.

Our guide realised that Robert and I were both retired teachers and asked what we felt about schools and teaching as a career. When each of us was enthusiastic, he asked 'Would you like to see an Indian school in progress?'

The coach stopped on the road beside what looked like a set of concrete garages with the communal roll-down metal door raised. A teacher came out and spoke to our guide.

It proved to be a girls' school, or a school where girls were being taught that day. There were rows of desks or tables and the girls, aged between perhaps ten and thirteen, were seated with their books open. Our stopping was obviously a chance for the school teacher to encourage the girls to practise their English on us.

I knelt on the bare concrete floor beside one of the girls, who appeared quite unabashed; she wanted to read to me and asked me to look at what she had written in her exercise book that day. I started to talk to her but the driver of the coach wanted to leave.

I could feel my eyes beginning to prickle as I climbed back onto the coach. I suddenly realised how much I missed teaching and engaging with young children.

We were both amazed by Agra and our first sight of the Taj Mahal on the other side of the garden and the water. A man who had been working in a side garden came up to us and by miming taking a photograph, gesticulated where he considered we could take the best pictures.

He did that several times, using his arms to beckon that we should follow him to get the best views, before holding out his hand for a tip. I did not give him one, I had not needed nor requested his services.

Inside the Taj, we were encouraged to 'please move quickly, not stand, stay quiet, not talk, just view and make space for other person'.

Our guide whispered to us and after shining his torch on one of the inlaid precious stones around the tomb, handed the torch to Robert. The stone must have been carnelian or something very similar. Under the light, it was translucent and gleamed as a vivid dark orange colour.

Outside again, Robert was anxious to take photos of women or girls in their brightly coloured saris, and one or two of those young women wanted to take photos of us. As we made our way reluctantly back to the entrance gate where our guide was waiting, Robert turned to me and said 'I'm enjoying the company.'

'Good,' I replied, 'I've travelled with them only once before but they were quite reliable then and seemed good value for money.'

He had to explain that he was referring to me, not to Newmarket, the travel company although 'that's pretty good too.'

Chapter 29

Beyond Pescasseroli

'Why didn't I get to know you better, about fifty years ago?' Robert had asked me, back in 2012 when we were relaxing together on my bed in the Canterbury Travelodge.

'It wouldn't have worked,' I told him with more assurance than I had actually felt, I didn't want to feel regret about something in the past that I could not change.

'I was going out with Anthony at the time and he was so possessive. Sometimes he could be quite violent, not towards me but towards things that he would smash or sweep off a desk with his arm, it seemed to relieve his frustration or annoyance. I wasn't allowed to talk with any of the other men, let alone dance with them. He was even jealous of my female friends. He resented the time I spent with Tasha and not with him.

And later, my being with Richard gave me my three children who are very special to me and whom I love very much. I expect you could say the same about your marriages and various offspring.'

Robert made no response other than a grunt.

Not long after our visit together to India and while Robert was staying for a few days at my house, he mentioned that he wouldn't be able to keep the house that he and his wife owned in Italy's Abruzzo National Park. This was, he told me, because his wife had paid all the renovation costs from money she had inherited from her father, and she needed that money back, now they were no longer living together.

They had contacted an agent and the house was up for sale, although no one had shown any interest. Robert explained that he couldn't afford to buy his wife out, although living in Italy had always been their intention. He couldn't live in it on his own and behave as if it were his house, because only a small fraction of it actually belonged to him.

'I feel trapped,' he said sadly 'both financially and as regards finding a place of my own. I still need to pay all the bills whenever I visit our Italy house, for water, bottled gas, electricity and the telephone charges, plus anything else that needs doing. I could ask to have those services disconnected but they are essential for anyone living or staying there – our children have used it quite often during the school holidays and it would cost far too much to have services reconnected again, whenever anyone wanted to stay there.

I still pay someone to keep an eye on the place when I'm not there, otherwise if there was any damage or anything that needed attention, I would not know until I arrived there from Britain.'

'I wish I could help,' I responded, 'It doesn't feel fair that I can manage financially better than ever before, while you feel so stuck or, as you say, trapped. Couldn't you find a rich Italian woman who already has a house, and propose to her?'

'Quite apart from the doubtful ethics of that, exactly what would I have to offer? I am close to penniless and although

I have a pension, I have minimal prospects. And I want to avoid any complications. With my wife leaving me for another man, at the moment I feel I have the moral high ground so I'd like to keep it that way.'

During further conversation that evening, it seemed to me that it had been Rob's intention to live permanently in Italy and that his ex-wife had gone along with the idea. He didn't actually say this but it was the impression I received.

He might not even have realised this himself, I thought. I considered how unfair life was, although we had both started off from college in Canterbury with very similar prospects.

How, although we had both lost our more recent marriage partners, I had benefitted greatly from the pension and small but sensible investment income that Danny had left me, whereas according to Robert, life had left him with only his teacher's pension, his old age pension, and a small slice of a house an international journey away - plus, as he later explained, far-distant prospects of inheritance from his aged but currently healthy parent.

In principle, I didn't believe in inherited wealth, I believed that financial gain should come only from personal hard work, applied skill and knowledge, although I had been happy enough to receive what Danny had left me. So, was I a hypocrite, I wondered, to hold such principles about inheritance, yet behave in a contradictory way?

I hoped I was not, that I recognised how theory and practice did not always tie up and that in my case, they hadn't.

But I still felt a degree almost of guilt, at not needing to struggle financially when a valued colleague with whom I shared a common history appeared to be under financial pressure. Struggling financially was something to which I had grown accustomed since birth and my first marriage, and I was hugely enjoying the freedom that the current lack of struggle now offered.

Moo had impressed upon me that in itself, money had no intrinsic value, its value lay in the doors that it could open, the horizons and prospects that it could extend, the stress and worry it could alleviate. 'Money,' she had told me 'needs to be put to work to improve lives.' She could be quite puritanical at times.

'Couldn't you take on another teaching job?' I asked Robert, 'perhaps somewhere still in Italy? Just something part-time or on a temporary contract so that it would give you an income?'

'But I'm retired, I've moved on from that stage of my life.'

'I suppose I might continue with supply teaching,' I suggested, knowing that I felt as reluctant as Robert about returning to something I thought I had finished as a career 'or I could try to write something. That's what my mother used to do when she ran short of house-keeping money. She wrote articles for women's magazines, the sort of magazines that she would never normally choose to buy or read. A radio play wouldn't bring in enough money but I could try to write a novel. I've already had an idea for one, I just need to get on with it. Then, if it proved successful, you could use the money from that to help you.'

We had been talking together about relationships and I mentioned to Robert that I missed having Danny and that I felt I was lacking a soulmate, someone with whom I could confidently discuss issues. I told him that I knew someone who had been recommended to join an online dating site, and that I had done the same thing, aiming to find that missing soulmate. I even showed him my profile on the computer, it had been a flattering photo that Lallo had taken of me and I was quite proud of it.

Robert however displayed no interest whatsoever in looking at it, he dismissed the whole idea.

'I'd have thought it would have been better to get to know someone through an organisation or a club you belonged to,' he said.

I didn't like to tell him that I didn't belong to any clubs, that any organisation to which I belonged consisted of single women or married couples – and that I had no close friends living near where I lived.

'When you were working at the International School in Rome,' I asked Robert, 'where were you living?'

He told me where it was, there may have been on-site accommodation allocated to the school staff.

'And your wife, was she living there with you?'

'I found her a flat nearby,' he said blandly.

'So, you didn't live together as a married couple. How did you each feel about that?'

'Well, most of my time and energy was taken up by my role within the school. I don't think I thought about much else at all.'

'And when you were teaching in Vicenza, were you living together then?'

'I had a small flat in Vicenza and I found very similar accommodation for my wife. She didn't complain. I think she enjoyed shopping in the market,' and then, after a moment of two of what I assumed to be him picturing his time there, 'I thought Vicenza was a delightful town. In fact, quite recently when I was travelling through London, I bumped into a couple of my former students: they recognised me and came over to say hello.'

We talked for a while about his need to sell his house in Pescassaroli; looking after it as well as regular return flights to either Rome or Pescara was costing him too much.

'If I could sell it, I would still like to live in Italy,' Robert said, rather wistfully, 'but I would never want to share my house with anyone again. Getting out of that sort of arrangement is far too difficult. And it is nice to have the bathroom to myself, without the female members of the family leaving their bras and skimpy G-string panties draped all around the room.'

Then he asked 'Would you ever consider getting married again?'

I had to think for a few minutes before answering, because I wanted to be clear in my own mind about where I stood on what I took to be an academic enquiry.

'I wouldn't rule it out completely, but it would have to be a really good relationship. I wouldn't be prepared to settle for second best, just for the sake of companionship or because, as one male married friend once told me when I was turning down his advances 'or otherwise I will die a lonely old woman'. My marriage to Richard had been because I thought it was the right thing to do in the circumstances.'

I paused while I refilled Robert's wine glass and passed him the bowl of salted peanuts.

'My second marriage, my marriage to Danny, was because I loved him very much. We shared a great many interests; he was practical as well as creative and he showed initiative. He also had a keen sense of humour which I found essential, in addition to having a sharp mind. I felt very safe with him. He taught me a great deal and I shall always be grateful for the time he and I had together. We had some really good times and we travelled to some fascinating places.

He usually made the major decisions as to where to visit next, and because I respected his ideas and choices, I would generally go along with whatever he proposed because he would have done his research. I supposed I was used to agreeing and he was used to being in charge, because of his job. I suspect I'm a natural deputy rather than a leader. I follow, I'll suggest and improve on an idea. I'm not an 'A' rated person, I'm more of a 'B' or on a good day, even a B+'.

'My eldest daughter says the same,' Robert observed, 'She says she's a 'B' person too. That's how she rates herself.'

'I'm not an initiator,' I continued. 'According to psychometric tests, I'm more of a completer finisher once someone else has kicked off an idea. I don't normally have original ideas, instead I copy, I plagiarise or I follow. Like I borrowed the idea of signing up to an online dating website, I suppose.

But if there were to be a 'next time', which I think is highly unlikely, then I would hope that it would be someone who would be faithful and stick to his marriage vows. And who appreciated that I sometimes have an opinion which might be quite valid. And someone who could appreciate that having feelings and emotional responses is perfectly normal for either gender - and even healthy'.

I paused before continuing, remembering some of the comments and how I had not refuted them. Then I went on.

'I was amazed by Danny when, after the death of Princess Diana, he referred to the country's grief as 'hysterical nonsense' and asked what use she had been to anyone. I think his socialist politics clouded his opinion. And he hadn't responded or even looked thoughtful when my older son-in-law Rik pointed out that she had been a mother, a sister and a wife, among other things; that she had left two young children who would be desperately feeling the loss. At the time, I was quite shocked at Danny's comment, at his lack of perspective.'

As I thought about what I had said to Robert half a conversation ago, I asked 'Why, would you? Re-marry, I mean?'

'No, I don't think so,' was his reply. 'I would not want to be hurt that much ever again. For a start, remarriage would adversely affect my children's inheritance.'

It was several years after this exchange that I realised that had I remarried or chosen to have a live-in partner, I would have to declare it and would no longer be eligible to receive Danny's teachers' pension - and without that extra income, that would seriously curtail much of my foreign travel.

'And if I were to move in with someone,' Robert hypothesised 'as you described Richard and then Danny had into your house, to where you were living, where would I put all my stuff, my furniture and the things that are important to me? I might always feel like a guest. As it is, whenever I return to Britain now, I spend most of my time moving from relative to relative, living out of my suitcase. My family are very kind but I have no real home of my own, not in Britain.'

I said something intended as empathetic such as 'I expect you find moving from relative to friend or relative quite difficult at times. And awkward.' I could see that talking or thinking about his marriage break-up was appearing to cause Robert some discomfort.

He made no comment but went on with 'But I do have the offer of a plot of land not far from my house in Gioia Vecchio, that's the name of the village where we live, it's quite near Pescasseroli, which is our closest town. I've measured the available plot, it's large enough to take a house. It belongs to an acquaintance; at the moment he only has a few unproductive olive trees growing there. Only I don't have enough money to buy the materials to build a house as well as meet the cost of the land. I did wonder if I would put a wooden house there, if it didn't infringe local byelaws.'

He paused and looked thoughtful for a minute before continuing 'I've looked online for wooden houses but I haven't actually seen one for real. I wouldn't want anything that looked like a garage or a garden shed when it was finished, in case my children poked fun at it or found where their father lived an embarrassment.'

Then, taking a deeper breath than normal, he asked 'Would you like to see the plot I'm thinking of buying? I would appreciate hearing your thoughts.'

Rob used my laptop for further online investigation. His computer was still in Italy, although he could read his emails using Yahoo and my laptop. This remote access to one's emails was new to me; ever since leaving my job with the Local Authority, my I.T. adviser and reference point had been Danny. I enjoyed talking with Robert; by giving me his view point, he made me think about things I had not previously considered.

Was it Danny himself that I missed, I wondered, or the things he offered and provided for me? Robert provided a measure of familiarity and also stimulus for thought. I realised how much I needed that mental stimulus. And how much foreign travel can offer to a thinking person.

After breakfast the following day, I suggested 'Why don't we look online and see what wooden houses there are available? If you get an idea of the prices in this country, that might give you an indication of whether your idea is viable or a non-starter.'

Robert nodded and opened up Internet Explorer.

We looked together at images of wooden buildings, some appearing more like Swiss chalets and others similar to cricket pavilions.

'It's difficult to know from the website,' he said, 'I can't tell the thickness of the wood - the specifications say that the timber they use is slow-grown conifer or spruce but it's difficult, from the plans, to envisage the layout of real rooms. I would need to know about the insulation and the roofing material. And how I could get it shipped to central Italy from Scandinavia, which is where much of the wood seems to come from; unless there are similar companies already in Italy producing timber buildings.'

'Well,' I suggested, 'since many of the companies you've looked at have their headquarters in either West Norfolk or somewhere in the Fens, I could drive you over in that direction later this morning and you can see for yourself? I expect the timber is imported through King's Lynn docks, which may be why those companies are based where they are.'

We visited several timber-building companies that day. One company was quite helpful, letting us spend time inside one of their preconstructed buildings and giving us time to discuss the layout of any proposed kitchen and bedroom.

Looking around it raised the question in Robert's mind of plumbing, drains, heating and the gradient of whole platform on which such a building might sit, as well as the internal and external height of the roof and its general visibility from the road. He gained a vague idea of the initial cost if he were to buy something similar in Britain and on our way back after visiting two more companies, he mused about importing a timber building direct from Estonia or Latvia because 'that would probably be cheaper coming direct from there.'

As arranged, I met Robert at Stansted a month or so later, but only just in time to catch our flight to Italy. There had been a long delay getting from Wymondham to Stansted. There was an early autumn gale and trees on the line had halted the train at Thetford. I had got out of the train at Thetford, as everyone had been required to do, and I looked for a public toilet. Shut. I weighed up the chances of being seen peeing behind some hoarding at the station and decided against it.

A taxi from the company that I had called and that had told me that they were too busy, unexpectedly arrived, having completed its school run. It took me to straight to Stansted.

No time to ask the driver to stop at a service station on the way.

I went through security, checked my messages on my mobile and found Robert already waiting in the queue to board the plane.

Robert's acquaintance Troy met us outside Rome's Ciampino airport and drove us through the centre of Pescasseroli and up to Gioia Vecchio. Troy had a few words with Robert about the state of the house since Robert had last visited and showed him a minor repair to plasterwork that had been done to the kitchen ceiling. Then he left. Robert checked the cupboards to see what dried goods and tins he had in stock; he saw that the fridge needed a clean.

Because I had already asked him to give me some jobs to do while I was staying in his house, he suggested 'If you wouldn't mind spending a few moments wiping down the inside and removing some of the mould that has built up since I was last here, I'll call the chap who owns the land he's hoping to sell me, and ask when it would be suitable for me to visit, look at it again and discuss it'.

He picked up a small personal telephone directory, to check on the number.

'Then on the way back, we can go to the supermarket in Pescasseroli and pick up anything else that we need, including some wine from the wholesalers. The local wine is one of the reasons why I like living in Italy, it's good quality and so cheap. Fresh fruit and vegetables are also so much less expensive than in Britain. And this evening, I thought we might go to Ristorante Peppe Di Sora or A Cavu't; they both open quite late, they're where the local residents choose to eat.'

The plot of land that Robert had been offered stood on a slope, just down from a ridge within two valleys between mountain ranges. A road ran along that ridge. I made a mental note of that and to ask whether the owner ever got snowed in in winter when this became a skiing area. We spent some time talking indoors to the owners who fortunately both spoke English. They were very hospitable and I wondered how Robert heard that they had land to sell, what the local planning regulations might be and whether established olive trees ever had tree preservation orders on them.

I had toyed with the possibility of buying Robert's house myself, partly as a way of helping an old friend out of a difficulty and also as somewhere for my three children to spend their holidays each year. But after due consideration, I abandoned that idea, it was totally impractical. And it had no swimming pool, which I and my grandchildren would have wanted.

Nevertheless, it was, I thought, a lovely house, split on two separate levels and with views of the mountains from nearly every window. I had seen it only briefly but it felt to me like home. I told Robert this. 'Even to me, it feels like home. I'm amazed that your wife felt able to leave it and make off instead with the electrician. Whatever did you do to make her do that?'

'Nothing,' he replied 'nothing that I know of. She just said she didn't love me any more. Her sister said she thought she was regretting growing older, that she wanted her youth back again.'

'Did you suspect that she and the electrician were having an affair?'

'It didn't really occur to me. They used to spend quite a bit of time together. My wife was overseeing the house renovation to start with, and then the two of them set up a joint business enterprise.'

Within a matter of a week, Robert had rejected the idea of buying the plot of land and managed to tell the owner that, without landing himself in any unpleasantness or embarrassment. 'It all got too complicated,' he explained.

I stayed at his house for two or three nights, helping to make a bonfire to burn any of the olive branches that had become damaged or broken in the previous year's heavy snow.

'If there is anything else I can do to help and earn my keep, please let me know. I'm quite capable at most things,' I said.

He suggested 'If you really don't mind, you might like to pull up some of the weeds growing around the property.' I was relieved that there was something useful that I could do, I wanted my visit to become a help rather than a nuisance.

'I could saw some of the thicker olive branches into log-sized pieces,' I proposed, quite keen to use up some of my energy.

'That's kind of you, but you mustn't overdo it,' he said, while I wondered what 'overdoing something' actually meant; or whether he found the idea of a woman capably using a saw offensive or even threatening. No one had ever said that to me before.

My father had expected Colin, Val, me and Moo all to help in the garden, to tackle the weeds and each of us children, regardless of gender, age or height had to pull up the sapling elm trees growing in the part he intended to make into a sunken lawn.

In my married life, it would have been, from Richard at least, 'You don't need me, you're quite able to do that yourself.' Or Danny would tell me 'Just get on with it.'

What Robert had said sounded, and felt to me certainly, protective and caring. It reminded me of my brother Colin and how he would have taken care of his younger sister.

But I wasn't Robert's sister and I was six weeks older than he was. As he quite often mentioned, with a wicked grin.

Robert kept his car parked in a layby opposite his house. I expressed surprise and some concern when he told me 'Just get in, it isn't locked. I never keep it locked, there's no need, it's so easily recognisable that no one would be silly enough to steal it. And it's right-hand drive. We need to drive to reach the supermarket,' he said, as he locked the front door of the house and hid the key.

I was glad to see that he took some precautions against an intruder or a break-in, I could see that if people knew that he was often away, they might take advantage of that and do some damage. We went into the supermarket together.

Robert asked me to fetch some milk while he was busy buying bread. 'You buy bread here by the weight,' he told me. I didn't read Italian so I was not sure which milk was whole milk, semi-skimmed or skimmed. I brought two different cartons and showed them to Robert. 'That's the one we want,' he said, 'I recognise it by its label.'

I placed the one Robert indicated in the basket he was holding and put the other back, thinking again how difficult it must be to spend most of one's time in a country while being unable to speak or read its language.

I was not sure how Robert felt about me. I had had only that one comment in India, 'the company's not bad either', to go on. Judging by his willingness to share a room with me, I obviously had some physical effect on him. He certainly attracted me too, physically as well as intellectually. He was tall, his previous fair hair was turning white, he had blue eyes and a voice with a standard English accent and deep rich tone that could make me go weak at the knees.

I had retained one of his calls on my message answer machine, purely so that I could hear his voice which was the aural equivalent of dark-brown velvety chocolate. He read fiction and non-fiction keenly, especially if the subject matter had a historical slant and he sometimes recommended to me books in which he thought I might be interested.

He was still happy, he had said, to spend time camping on his own, whereas Danny had told me he had 'grown out of that years ago.' I had thought at the time that camping had been an economic necessity for us as a family, rather than a preference.

I realised I was very fond of Robert; in an unguarded moment I had even once said 'I love you' as a term of approval after some celebration in Canterbury, but I was not sure in what way, whether my love was, in Greek terms, 'agape' or 'eros'. I suspected it was a bit of each.

I was glad that I felt like that, because if I were enjoying that level of intimacy with anyone for whom I had no emotional feeling, what would the sex make me apart from an unprincipled alley cat who displayed no sense of discrimination? What I most wanted was his continued friendship because I valued that above anything else.

After Danny, his prostate cancer and general disfunction, I had learned to manage quite well without the closeness of sex itself, so long as I felt loved and appreciated. A little care, consideration and human warmth would be good too, I thought. Only Robert did not do hugs or cuddles. After I had once asked about this, he had told me 'Hugging isn't something we have ever done in my family.' I did not know whether that applied to his parents and particularly to his mother when he and his brother were children, or to his interaction with his different wives and children.

But either way, a hug, a cuddle or an arm round me was important to me and I regretted the absence of such. And wishing other goodnight when we were in bed was something that Robert didn't do either. I felt the loss of that too. I might gently call out 'goodnight' but I would be met with silence, leaving me to feel that I had fulfilled my required purpose and that rest and sleep were all that were now needed.

During my stay, I helped Robert to take some of his wife's clothes out of cupboards in their bedroom, bundle them into black dustbin sacks and carry them to the touring caravan that was parked alongside the house.

'That caravan isn't mine, it belongs to the electrician,' Robert told me. 'He actually comes from New Zealand. He was working in the area and someone recommended him to us when we decided to renovate the house. He did some of the plumbing, too. He asked if he could park the caravan there until he needed to use it. I think he now intends to sell it, or perhaps he's handed it over to my ex-wife. She has asked me to try to sell it and give her the money for it.'

'And will you?' I asked.

'I can try,' he responded 'if anyone around here wants a caravan.'

A day or two later, Robert mentioned that someone was coming to collect the caravan so 'perhaps we should put my wife's clothes back in the spare bedroom again.'

I wondered why, if she had dumped him, he didn't choose to do the same to her clothes. He also said he would give her the money he was paid for the caravan.

I thought then of what Richard would have done after he had abandoned me and the children and moved in with Jayne. Richard had even walked off with some of the volumes of Bach and Beethoven piano music that had been passed on to me by Moo. I never got them back.

I was not sure whether Robert was being extremely hospitable or had found himself just stuck with me and was unsure what to do with me next. In the evenings, he would play 'patience' on his laptop computer, while in the same room I sat on the settee and either read or wrote ideas in a slim notebook.

A day or so later, he suggested 'I wondered whether today we might drive to another small town that I like. It's called Sulmona, it's up in the hills and it has an open-air market in the town centre on Wednesdays and Saturdays. The market in Pescasseroli is only on a Wednesday so at the weekend I often drive up to Sulmona to do my fruit and vegetable shopping. If I could choose to live anywhere in Italy, I might well choose

Sulmona. There's also a good supermarket on the outskirts of town, it's more like a cash-and-carry and the prices are lower than in the town itself.'

As Robert drove us out of Gioia Vecchio and turned to go down the hill, I saw several cars parked behind the church and groups of two or three people standing together, holding binoculars in front of their faces.

'Is there a wedding?' I asked. 'Because I've seen an Italian wedding once when I was on holiday near Sorrento with Phoebe, my eldest granddaughter, and the bride and the groom both looked slightly embarrassed, perhaps because they were drawing a large crowd.'

'Unlikely,' Robert observed, 'they are probably from some nature group looking for wild boar or bears down in the valley. We see wild boar and bears sometimes if they are hungry and make for our dustbins. But that's only occasionally. They can be a real nuisance though.'

'What other wildlife do you have in this area?' I asked. 'I've seen bears in Finland near the Russian border when I went there with another of my granddaughters; and polar bears in Svalbard, but only from a distance.'

'There are plenty of deer and I am told there are wolves but I haven't seen or heard any. Once or twice a year, parties of school children from Pescasseroli come out at dusk, go into the forest and try to hear wolves. I don't think they are very successful. I think it's part of their normal curriculum at least once during the year to visit a wild area. The idea of keeping an excitable group of children silent for more than half a minute seems to me close to impossible. It's hard enough in a classroom.'

I got the impression that wildlife did not hold any particular amount of interest for Robert. I remembered our time in India, where he had been particularly interested in the saris that the women were wearing, and not especially in the wildlife – which was just as well; he hadn't seemed at all disappointed at not seeing a tiger, he had been more absorbed by absolutely everything else the country had to offer. I thought wildlife might not be his thing, having been brought up, as I understood it, in a flat in Kensington.

I thought how interested Danny would have been in the local wildlife, how we used to go for long country walks together with Muffin and then Chaucer - how neither of us was in any position to enjoy long walks any more, me because of my increasingly arthritic knees, hip and back pain and Danny because . . . well, he just wasn't around any longer.

'Before we get to Sulmona, would you like an ice cream? If so, we'll stop *en route* halfway and I'll take you to one of the best ice cream parlours that I know.'

Robert parked his car close to an ice cream shop and ushered me inside. He greeted the owner, who seemed to know him quite well.

'Which flavour would you like?' he asked me, 'There's . . ' And then the owner took over, describing, in her best English, each of the flavours on display in the glass-fronted cabinet. I opted straight for lemon.

The large car park in Sulmona contained a coach and several local cars. Once parked, Robert's Peugeot was, I agreed, quite distinctive, not because it was an unusual make but because it was obviously a foreign car. Robert had told me that he and his wife had brought it all the way from Britain.

'Wouldn't it have been easier to buy a second-hand car once you had moved here?' I asked.

'Buying a used car in Italy is a complicated procedure with certain unavoidable legal formalities,' Robert told me. 'For a start, EU nationals must supply a Residence Certificate, known as a *Certificato di Residenza*. Then you need the vehicle documents and the car registration certificate. But what puts most people off is the *Codice Fiscale* or the personal tax codes of the buyer and seller. People don't like giving that to anyone, let alone anyone in authority. And it's even more complicated.

So,' he went on, gesturing that we should climb the upward flights of stairs that nestled within an enclosure that looked more like a lift shaft, 'I suppose this all helps the Italian car market, people prefer to buy a new Fiat rather than go through such a palaver. If we manage to sell the house, then either I or my wife will probably drive our current car back to Britain rather than try to sell locally. And now, here we are, up and into the town of Sulmona.'

We both stopped at the top of the steps to get our breath. The climb had been slightly demanding, as we had needed to look down at our feet to avoid any chipped or broken tiles on the steps and Robert had been talking for most of the way. I found him interesting, he knew things that I didn't and he was prepared to explain in as much detail as I wanted. It was practical knowledge that he imparted, things that explained how life in Italy might be, especially for a foreigner.

I was still toying with the idea of offering to buy his house but becoming increasingly aware what a stupid idea that was. Was it, I wondered, a way of my having a small part of Robert for myself? Because his house already felt like home to me. Or was it because I needed the stimulation of living somewhere different that would require all my mental and physical resources to deal with satisfactorily? Or somewhere that I would invite him as my guest to visit and stay for some time? Was I trying, almost like some infatuated teenager, to maintain a connection with him, or with my earlier self?

'I like Sulmona,' Robert stated. 'It's in a healthy area, surrounded by mountains; it has interesting architecture, a lively market and a sense of history. What's not to like? You'll see when we come to it, there's a Roman aqueduct just before we reach the market place. It was also the native town of the Roman poet Ovid - there's a bronze statue of him on the town's main road. And the other interesting thing about the town,' he said, ushering me from the main road and onto the pedestrianised streets, 'is that it's where real confetti comes from. You're familiar with confetti, aren't you?'

I was tempted to make a slightly caustic reply but I nodded in agreement.

'Well, sweets have long been part of the Italian culinary tradition. I am told that the ancient Romans covered fruit, flowers, nuts and kernels in honey to make sweet treats. In Italy, paper confetti – in the English sense – is still called coriandoli, while the word confetti is related to confection or confiture, meaning stuff with sugar in. Apparently, in the 15th century, the nuns at the local monastery in Sulmona wrapped pieces of almond candy in silk and gave it to noble brides.'

'Nuns?' I interrupted, 'at the monastery rather than at the nunnery? So, naughty goings-on, then.'

'Very likely. According to what I'm told, including the stuff about the local church which was of course Roman Catholic, bishops and royalty were given dragées, made with imported luxury sugar from Persia, as welcome gifts. Ordinary people's only chance to taste the sweet was during the Ferragosto processions, when the magistrate threw confetti to the crowds.'

Imagining the scene, I felt I had to say 'So I suppose those who were being pelted with honey came to a sticky end? Not my idea of fun.' Robert ignored my comment and continued telling me 'As sugar became more commonplace, so the number of confectioners in Sulmona increased. In the mid-19th century, there were about a dozen confetti producers in Sulmona. They competed against each other to make the most spectacular and ingenious presentation of their products. The sugared almonds were wrapped in paper or coloured film and used as mosaics to create decorative flowers or pictures. If you see in this shop and that across the road,' as he waved his hand in each direction, 'there are what look like artificial flowers displayed in the shop windows and just outside the shop in those window boxes, things that look as if they are made from what we in Britain used to call 'chocolate beans' or 'Smarties'. I don't know what they taste like but those are Sulmona's confetti. But I don't think they use almonds any more, not whole almonds, anyway.'

'I might buy a confetti flower or two later,' I said, 'to tell my family about them and see what they taste like. And whether Smarties would be a better bet. But the chocolate in Smarties might melt.'

I felt I had lost Robert's interest by now. I remembered that more than one of my Primary School teachers had told Moo that I talked too much. I fell silent for a moment, thinking how important I thought words were, especially the right word to describe something, and its correct usage.

As we approached the aqueduct and the busy market place, I asked 'Is there anything in particular that you are planning to buy?'

'There's a stall toward the back of the market where the woman who owns it sells really fresh plaits of garlic. I am running short of garlic and there's no point in buying just a corm or two. The plaits look pretty, hanging up in the kitchen. Braiding or plaiting helps garlic to last longer and is a more aesthetically pleasing way of storing it than keeping the bulbs in a mesh bag or a jar. Buying some fruit would be sensible, as well as cheese and ham while we are here. You might want to take some local ham home with you too. If you do, when we get to that stall, if you just mention it, we can buy some and have it packed so that it will travel well. And if possible, I would also like to buy a new watch strap. It's not worth my paying the price in a local shop so if someone in the market can sell me one, so much the better.'

We wandered around the market for several minutes, looking at the different stalls. Some sold fruit and vegetables while others were displaying socks or underwear, presumable made in the Far East. I wondered who would buy underwear from the market, especially a bra, without trying it on first.

After making several enquires by using a mixture of gestures and English, Robert was directed to a stall selling belts, wallets and a combination of leather items including watch straps. When the stall holder turned his back to get Robert some change, I was surprised to see how hairy the stall holder was. Thick dark hair protruded from the gap between the bottom of his shirt and the waistband of his low-slung trousers.

I wondered how comfortable it might be to be covered with all that hair, what basic function it fulfilled on either a hot day or a cold one, whether it was a Neanderthal throwback or perfectly usual in a dark Italian man. I didn't find it the least bit attractive and looked up at Robert with approval.

Robert bought a plait of garlic from a stall holder who seemed to recognise him, and a kilo of tomatoes from a different stall.

'The ham's very good here,' he told me as we walked round square and back towards the aqueduct. 'I'm going to buy a small amount. If you like it and wanted to take some home with you, we could get some and have it wrapped properly so that it would stay fresh. Why not try a sliver?'

I nodded so the ham stall holder produced a small slice on the tip of his sharp knife and held it out towards me. I decided to take it in my fingers rather than straight into my mouth, that knife looked really sharp.

The ham was delicious and I told Robert so. He asked for an amount, placed his purchase into his bag and spoke to the stall holder before turning back to me.

'In Italy, we ask for ham and cheese by the *etti*. An *etto* is a tenth of a kilogram so *due etti* equal 0.2 of a kilo, or just under half a pound. I've asked him for *due etti* for you, unless you want more?'

I shook my head, took out my purse and handed Robert some euro, which he waved away and handed me the ham package. Rather than clutch it, I placed it in Robert's bag too.

'Would you like a coffee or something stronger?' he asked. 'Because there's a café in the corner of the square close to the aqueduct. We can sit down there and have it in comfort while watching the crowds go by.'

I felt Robert was behaving rather like Danny, my brother Colin or a caring holiday guide, explaining to me the things that he thought I might be interested to know or utilise in the future.

Robert ordered the drinks and we were enjoying them when a female voice called out 'Robert. I didn't know you were back. How are you?'

Robert rose to his feet, looked into the market-place crowd and seeing someone he recognised, held up his hand in greeting.

'Christina. It's good to see you. Are you back in Italy for long? Come and join us.'

I felt a minor pang of irritation, I was enjoying having a quiet cup of coffee with Robert and I had no idea who this Christina person was. She greeted Robert with a kiss on each cheek, which he returned.

He introduced us, me as his friend for the past fifty years and slim tanned Christina, with her long greying hair, as a friend who spent most of her time in the United States but whose close relatives lived in a village on the other side of Pescasseroli. Those relatives, it turned out, were good friends of Robert's and would sometimes give him advice on his olive crop or tree management.

My old shyness returned. I felt awkward, I wasn't sure what to say to Christina. She spoke good English with a slight American accent and she obviously had less interest in me than in Robert. I wasn't sure whether to find an excuse to go somewhere else and leave the pair of them to talk together, or whether to stay and wait for Christina to take the hint and continue on her way. She and I squared up to each other through narrowing eyelids as only women sometimes do.

Having stood my ground for long enough, I looked around for the classic excuse, a public toilet, but there didn't seem to be one. I wanted Robert to think I was being kind and tactful by giving them space but I didn't feel like giving Christina an inch.

I was quite shocked by how possessive I suddenly felt towards Robert as an 'old friend' and I could almost see Christina's claws. And my own. So, I sat there and hoped I appeared appropriately interested in what Christina was saying about her fantastic new job in The States. This was, I tried to tell myself, purely a chance meeting. Or had Robert, I wondered, hoped he might see her? It had been his idea to come to Sulmona on market day. And his idea for us to sit in the café in the corner of the market place, in full view of anyone and everyone who also happened to be shopping that morning.

Then I told myself I was simply reflecting the experiences I had had of other women and my husbands' behaviour during both my married lives, that I should get a grip of myself.

Eventually Christina stood up. 'Goodbye', she said 'or perhaps I should say *arrivederci.* I hope you enjoy your time in Italy,' she wished, insincerely, to me as she kissed Robert goodbye, and taking a backward glance at him or perhaps at both of us, with her right hand she flicked her long hair behind her neck and over her shoulder. It reminded me of Miss S. with Danny.

'She fancies you,' I told Robert, once she had disappeared from sight back into the market. 'That flick of the hair said it all.'

I waited for him to refute this with 'Nonsense', but he came back with 'But she has a boyfriend in America.'

'What's that got to do with it?' I countered. 'It doesn't stop her from fancying you.'

He shrugged. I hoped my mentioning Christina's gesture would have a positive effect on his self-esteem rather than encourage any follow-up advances he might make, especially once I was out of the way and back in Britain.

On our way from Sulmona to Pescasseroli and Gioia Vecchio, Robert stopped at the cash-and-carry.

'Do you have a list or are you just seeing what's available?' I asked.

'No list,' he replied, 'I don't do lists. I try to remember what I need instead; I think it's better brain training to do that.'

Taking them from a chilled cabinet, he put some mussels, salmon and rump steak in his basket and just before joining the queue at the checkout, he grabbed a bottle of Aperol and some tonic water. At the checkout, I tried to pay for it with euros but he brushed aside my attempt and used his bank card instead. I was not sure whether he thought he was being unmanly if he allowed me to pay for anything or whether I was being patronising.

I was also not sure whether to remind him that I didn't normally eat meat, but realised that I was assuming that the steak was intended for both of us sometime during the next couple of days. Then I wondered whether the meat really was rump steak. If it was, then it would have been one of the few times that anyone had treated me to a meal of steak, and I felt flattered and valued if it was intended for the pair of us. But it might, I thought, have been intended for his freezer.

'We're eating out this evening so perhaps we should keep the salmon in the fridge for tomorrow. The mussels too, if we pack crushed ice around them.'

We had driven extra slowly through Pescasseroli and were on our way up the incline towards Gioia Vecchio when I saw, in the twilight and in the distance, a dark shape coming from the forest on my right towards the open meadows that bordered the road. It was followed by a lighter similar shape. Both shapes crossed the area faster than a man walking briskly.

'Look!' I cried, 'Isn't that a bear? Two bears. I think it might be. Could you stop, please? I'd like to watch them in case they come this way.'

Robert indicated to pull in to the side of the road although there was no one behind him and he turned the engine off.

'I won't get out in case I scare them or startle them by closing the car door. I just want to watch. It's quite exciting, isn't it.'

But Robert did not seem as excited as I was.

'I assume one is female and the other male but I have no idea which is which, whether the male is chasing the female or perhaps it's the other way round,' I muttered, almost to myself.

'If you really want to see a bear close up, then there's a mini zoo in the town.' Robert advised. 'It's called the Centro Visite Parco Nazionale d'Abruzzo. My grandchildren have been there and according to them, there is at least one bear there. I think it's quite expensive to get in, though.'

'Is there any reason why there's a zoo in the town, when there are already wild bears in the vicinity? Is there a breeding programme or something? Because unless it's an endangered species or there's a need to promote breeding, I don't see the point of zoos, except to make money out of captured animals, which seems all wrong to me. They should be left in the wild, which is where they belong.'

Then a thought occurred to me. 'I assume they aren't hunted here?'

Robert assured me that the main hunting in that region was for wild truffles. The Italian government had, he said, recently begun to stress the need for the conservation of the bears. Hence the park had become a sanctuary dedicated to animals such as the Marsican or Apennine brown bear, with hopes of rekindling the bears' once-thriving existence, since in prehistoric times, hundreds of bears used to live in these mountains.

'Thanks to the presence of bears as well as deer, wolves and wild boar, tourism for wildlife viewing has helped the whole Abruzzi region to develop economically,' he said. 'Like that group of people you saw near the church. They are probably staying at a hotel somewhere in Pescasseroli, eating out each evening and spending money locally.'

'Couldn't you use the fact that your house is situated in The National Park area as a selling point? Pretty it up a bit with hanging baskets on the metal railings at the side of the entrance, with red geraniums, something white so that the colours reflect the Italian flag?'

'I'm not sure it would be worth the expenditure' he said doubtfully 'because it would be me who had to buy all that, arrange it and keep it watered. I've already told you, houses in Italy don't sell very easily unless they are on the coast or have a swimming pool attached.'

I thought Robert was being a trifle defeatist, but I assumed he knew more about the Italian property market than I did.

'Have you thought of reducing the asking price of the house?' I asked, feeling that I was beginning to tread on his toes or being annoying by making suggestions about something that had nothing to do with me.

'My ex-wife has determined the asking price' he said "so that she can get back all the money she's spent on the renovations.'

That seemed to close the conversation until we arrived back at Robert's house.

Often during the following two or three years, if Robert had flown to Italy and was due to return by the late evening flight to Stansted, I would drive from Norfolk to the airport to meet him, usually with sandwiches and a flask of coffee in case he hadn't been able to buy any food, either before or during the flight.

'I can hardly roll up after midnight at my son's flat in central London; and by the time I got into London, the last train from Paddington or Waterloo to the West Country would have gone so there's no hope of me spending the night at my parents' house. I might have to find a cheap hotel in London . .'

'Why don't you come home with me, spend the night at my house and then set off for London the following morning?' I suggested. 'The train fare from Wymondham to London might cost you a bit more but you could travel off-peak, you'd save on a night's hotel room and you'd be sure of getting a bed. And breakfast.'

Put like that, my suggestion seemed to make sense to both of us. On several occasions, I met Robert at Stansted from the low-cost flights from Rome or Pescara and either brought him back to Wymondham or booked a room for us both at the Stansted Airport Hilton Hotel. Either way, it gave us time to talk, to reminisce, eat and discuss ideas for our different futures.

Robert was very supportive towards my idea of writing a novel. He even gave me some advice such as 'Try not to make the first chapter too long. Keep it short so that the reader isn't put off or puts the book down before reading any further.'

In the banter and in retaliation toward someone whom I knew wrote neither fiction nor non-fiction but used watercolours as his creative medium, my reply was 'Then if it ever gets published, in the acknowledgements I will thank you by name for all your encouragement and advice, 'only some of which I have followed'.

Touché.

Chapter 30

Tiles, Dates and Sand

Having so much enjoyed my time in India and later in Italy with Robert, by 2013 I was feeling a strong urge to travel somewhere exciting again. I looked at the places on offer from the company with which I and three friends had gone to Mongolia to see the eagles in the Gobi Desert that my son Keir had traversed and talked about, and at the right time of year to watch the Mongolian Naadam Festival.

The Exodus Travel Company trip called 'Highlights of Morocco' looked interesting and more or less affordable. Bearing in mind the Moroccan weather and temperatures in summer, I wanted to see if there were still a place available in October that year.

I asked Robert if a visit to Morocco would interest him too. He was undecided for a while but I offered to cover the cost for him, if finance were a problem. In the end, I believe he was able to pay for himself and he agreed to come with me. Apart from our visit to India together, I gained the impression that his previous experience of travel had been as a sole traveller going to and from a specific destination, and that he had never participated in an organised and guided group tour.

Since a winter visit to Norway by travelling up the coast on a Hurtigruten ferry six months after Danny had died and signing up for the Ramblers visit to Austria, I had not travelled abroad on my own since participating in a French Exchange school visit when I was aged thirteen and I was slightly reluctant to do so now that I was fast approaching my seventies.

It wasn't that I was in anyway nervous of travelling alone but I had hugely appreciated having Danny as a travel companion, having someone to talk to particularly at meal times and someone with whom I could discuss what we had seen and done during that day. It made the whole trip so much more vivid and memorable.

I had revisited Jordan with Lallo in 2011 and the following year Jaki, whom I had met during a Saga walking trip to Nepal, had invited me to join her on a visit to Svalbard in the summer of 2012, so I was aware of the benefit of travelling with a sensible companion who would value the whole experience.

So, in October 2013, Robert and I landed under a blue sky in Casablanca and were met by Omar, our Moroccan guide.

The Hassan ll Mosque in Casablanca was the first place that we visited on the tour. It had been built only twenty years before and we both marvelled at the exterior tile work at the top of the tower and the way that the huge painted cedar ceiling and roof could apparently slide back mechanically to reveal the sky. I stood for a while, gazing at the ceiling roof and wondering what happened to the chandeliers when the roof was slid back.

The high chandeliers bathed the lower part of the interior of the mosque in a blue light that reflected off the metal barrier posts that held lengths of the cordoning rope in position, showing us where we could walk and where we should not.

I was surprised that I, as a woman, was allowed to enter the mosque along with the men in our small party. No one at the entrance objected and Omar told us that it was permitted.

I think it was the first time that either Robert or I had seen such intricate decoration on anything that was not designed for Christian worship. Neither of us realised that we were visiting Morocco during the Islamic festival of Eid-Ul-Adha.

It soon became more obvious when in the streets we saw cars pulling small trailers containing a couple of sheep destined, we assumed, for sacrifice and festive consumption. I think we both felt some sympathy for the sheep.

From Casablanca, we were taken to Rabat, Morocco's capital city. We explored the unfinished Hassan Mosque and gazed up at the 12th century minaret that soared high above the mosque ruins. Omar led us into the Rabat Kasbah, where the lower outside walls of the lime-washed houses, the bollards in the narrow cobbled streets and even the tubs for flowers were painted a dazzling saxe blue.

The day was growing quite hot and in the Andalusian Garden, we were directed towards a tiled café that was overlooking the sea. It served both of us with excellent mint tea. From the ramparts of a former fort, we both looked out over the estuary.

Through my binoculars, I could see what looked like a cemetery on the other side of the harbour. There appeared to be multiple tombstones between the modern buildings and the water's edge, thousands of them, shoving against each other and tumbling all the way down to the sea.

I asked Omar about them because I had assumed that the Muslim faith required a dead body to be buried as soon as possible and I did not know whether they had special burial places. Omar said he thought that the graves might be for Christians, or possibly Jews.

He explained that Morocco had been a destination for the Jewish who arrived in the country following a law in 1492 which expelled all Jews from nearby Spain.

'There were also many Christians living in Morocco, so the graves could well be Christian. If we could see the tombstones much closer, we might be able to tell by reading any inscriptions. But we don't go that side of the estuary on this tour,' Omar said as he turned away from the view.

Robert and I spent a few minutes discussing our personal beliefs and preferences regarding death and cremation versus burials, and what each of us might want written on our gravestone. I quite fancied a paraphrase of words I had heard in the film 'The Most Exotic Marigold Hotel' and had taken to heart as my mantra – and had often quoted to Robert. 'It will be all right in the end and if it is not yet all right, then it is not yet the end,' with the outline of a snowdrop engraved underneath the words.

It was in Meknes that both Robert and I had to amend our former ideas about Muslim gender relationship taboos, particularly among its young people. It was early evening and our guide recommended any members of our group who fancied a stroll 'to walk around the huge water tank and visit the stables and granary. They are well worth seeing. They were created by Moulay Ismail, who you remember was . . .'

Neither of us had any idea who Moulay Ismail was. I suspected that Omar had told us, possibly more than once, during the coach journey to Meknes and that I had nodded off. Robert too, possibly.

We did visit the huge granary. I asked Robert 'Why do you think the townspeople needed to store so much grain? Were they expecting a famine?'

Fortunately, we found an information board that told us. 'The location and construction of the stables were both carefully considered to accommodate the large number of horses. The building itself has massive walls, original cedar wood doors, arched ceilings, very small windows, and a brilliant system of underflow water chambers. The high ceilings and small windows kept the stables cool in the summer and warm in the winter, while the canal constantly fed the stables with fresh water. The royal horses were always kept at an ideal temperature and never lacked clean drinking water'.

On another board, we read more about the granary that had been built adjacent to the royal stables. I wondered why I had bothered to buy and pack the hefty guide book that I hadn't yet had any time to read.

We took photos in the diminishing light and began making our way back to our hotel by walking alongside the water tank that served as a reservoir. Sitting side by side on a concrete bench overlooking the reservoir were several young people who looked about fifteen or sixteen. One girl with dark hair not covered by a scarf or hijab was studying what appeared to be a text book with various line illustrations. A boy of about the same age came and sat beside her, quite close, and together they looked at the book and seemed to be discussing those pages.

It could have been a scene from a British park or common, with both young people talking together and sitting side by side. There appeared to be no chaperone, no segregation, no reticence involved in the close body and eye contact, and no embarrassment with schoolmates all around.

Jerking his head towards the young people, Robert remarked quietly to me 'Well, there goes another of my misperceptions. Not at all what I would have expected.'

'Me neither,' I responded. 'So why, in Britain, are we told something quite different? They look no different from any other Western European school pals. I wonder if their parents or grandparents would object.'

Almost as soon as we returned to our hotel, we met Omar as arranged in the hotel lobby. 'I would like to show you some more of this royal city,' he proposed proudly 'so we will visit the city walls, the enormous doors and see people out shopping in the street market.'

Gathering us in a group outside the city walls in the evening light and pointing to a flock of birds in the sky, our guide said 'Look, many swallows. They go back south.'

I hadn't the heart to tell him they were swifts.

Very soon Omar left us, saying he was giving us time to look around that part of the city and that he would meet us back in the same place in an hour's time. Others in our group wandered off to look at the decoration on the walls and Moorish gates.

In the open area where Robert and I were standing, a small crowd had formed a circle around a street performer.

We moved closer to get a better view. Seeing me standing among the onlookers with my fair hair and no veil or hijab, the man who appeared to be compering the performers walked across the circle towards me, grabbed me by the hand and pulled me into the centre. He said something to me, then to the crowd who laughed. I began to feel rather uneasy.

Robert was on the outside of the ring of people; I wondered if he would come to rescue me – because what I most wanted at that moment was to be rescued.

Instead, the compere placed a wooden box down on the ground, put a half-peeled banana into my hand and turning to face the crowd, said something else in Arabic to his audience. Images came into my mind of being like an animal in the zoo, I didn't want to be their amusement, I didn't know what the compere was going to expect me to do with that banana. I looked over the heads of the crowd surrounding me, where on earth was Robert? I felt suddenly very vulnerable, uncomfortable and embarrassed.

I was neither Robert's partner nor his responsibility but I was a woman in a country that did not particularly respect or value women and I remembered how protective he had been when we had been in the vegetable market in India. I couldn't see him and my thought of being protected and rescued by him transformed into the realisation that it was up to me to get myself out of this situation, whatever it was, ideally with good humour and British good grace.

I smiled at the compere and at the crowd, with no understanding at all as to what had been said or suggested. I withstood the situation for five minutes or so, then walked across to the compere, handed him the banana, stepped over the wooden box and pushed my way out of the circle.

The men parted to let me through. I found Robert standing somewhere on the outside, looking around at the car park and photographing the sun setting behind the palm trees.

'I didn't enjoy that,' I told him.

'I knew you would handle it,' he responded. 'Shall we go and investigate the street market before we have to meet Omar?'

'Fine,' I replied 'but this time, please don't lose me. I thought the proceedings, when I was in the ring, could go in one of two ways and I didn't fancy being the butt of either. But neither did I want to lose my temper or appear unsettled. We British are supposed to be calm and patient.'

Although I did not feel in the slightest bit cold and Robert was still wearing short sleeves, we noticed that the local women had slipped full-sleeved djellabas over their lighter clothing and were shopping for household goods among the many stalls which were by then lit by street lights. We wandered among the crowd; there was nothing either of us wished to buy and many of the cleaning items looked exactly the same as in any British or Italian market.

Just for fun, I bought a box of dates and shared them among the group when the coach and Omar turned up to take us back to our hotel. I did wonder about the wisdom of eating those dates with my fingers and without being able to wash either my hands or the dates, but I hoped it was all right. The sticky dates were sold ready boxed rather than loose on a market stall.

The following day proved to be a real delight for me and I assumed for Robert too. On our way to Fez, where we were to spend two nights, our coach stopped at Volubilis. We had left

Meknes straight after breakfast and after a short drive, the morning sunlight was gentle and welcoming as we climbed off the coach.

Neither Robert nor I had known what to expect in terms of Moroccan history and yet here, among the plains and soft hills, was Volubilis.

Having once been a large Roman town, Volubilis had become a UNESCO World Heritage site with the most extensive and best kept Roman ruins in Morocco.

Both of us were amazed by the extent of the ruins and their preservation; the mosaics were better and brighter than any I had seen previously in either Italy or Britain.

'How did the Romans get water, out here?' I asked Omar.

'There is an aqueduct that brought water from the mountains,' he explained, 'it is dry now but I expect it gave plenty of water when the snows melted.'

Both Robert and I were interested in history so the unexpected introduction to Volubilis was a huge bonus. Some of the others in the group, however, were not as impressed and climbed back onto the coach before the scheduled departure time.

I spent the journey to Fez thinking how good it was to travel with someone whose interests I shared and who was neither surprised nor disappointed that I had not read all about the area in a guide book before setting off, as Danny would have done. Or been disappointed in me.

We trailed in a line around the narrow alleyways of the medina in Fez, visiting several workshops and both seeing and hearing the metal workers making huge copper bowls that were larger than a baby's bath.

In one workshop, we saw how the Aloe Vera plant leaves were stripped to produce a fibre that could be dyed and woven. Pony-tails of this coloured silky fabric were hanging from struts across the roof of the medina. Several of our group bought shawls or scarves from the weaver, bargaining for what they took to be a fair price. One woman with fair hair and a broken nose who had told me her name was Selina and that she was born in Canada, bought a pink scarf for herself with Omar's help, and another grey one with a silver thread.

Further along in the medina, we were led into a leather workshop and upstairs to the sales area. 'My daughters wanted me to buy them some slippers' Robert told me, 'and I know exactly the sort of thing they had in mind, but I can't see any like them here.'

He tried to explain to me what he was looking for; I assumed they were rather like ballet shoes but many of the slippers we saw for sale had pointed toes.

'What sizes are you looking for?' I asked.

Most women's feet are smaller than mine and narrower. I have grown used to apologising for having feet that are larger than average. When I was growing up, having to squeeze my feet into Val's outgrown or unwanted shoes was always rather unsatisfactory and I would end up with either having to have the toes cut out, as had happened in a pair of Clark's white leather sandals, or in considerable discomfort because Val's feet were two sizes smaller than mine.

That might have been the start of the bunions that I now have on each foot, like TCP Grandma used to have, and upon which Robert had commented. Clothes rationing and lack of finance were the underlying causes for me. Or poor circulation. It was only after Danny had died, that winter did not automatically mean having cold wet hands and cold damp toes. By then, I could afford to buy good gloves and leather shoes that actually corresponded to the shape of my feet.

The leather workshop was fascinating. Because the sales room was upstairs, we were able to look out over the yard below. The windows were open and a pungent smell of urine hit our eyes as well as our noses. Some of the group complained among themselves and scurried back down the stairs again.

In the backyard below were huge open vats, each filled with a slightly different coloured liquid. The man in the leather workshop informed any of the group who was still listening that when the hair and flesh had been removed from the animal skins, they were soaked in the vats. Then the skins were dried and rinsed before being dyed and handed over to the leather-workers.

'But what causes that strong smell?' one of the men in the group asked.

We were told it was ammonia: that ammonia in water breaks down the organic material, making urine the perfect substance to use to soften and tan animal hides. Soaking animal skins in urine also made it easier for leather workers to remove hair and bits of flesh from the skin.

Robert whispered in my ear 'So those men with their feet in the vats don't need to ask for a toilet break, they can just pee where they stand.'

'Very convenient,' I agreed 'but I might not buy anything just yet until I can get rid of that thought - and the smell from my nostrils.'

Looking around at all the leather items on racks and shelves, Robert pointed to some leather things on the floor that looked like the dry empty skins of huge fruit, with the flesh extracted.

'They even make dog baskets,' he observed. 'Do you want to buy one for Butterworth?'

I looked where he was pointing and thought for a moment.

'Those aren't meant as beds for dogs,' I said, 'they are pouffes or floor cushions without their stuffing. There would be no point in stuffing them until after getting one home. And, much as I love Butterworth, I am not going to buy him a leather bed that he might chew - or a pouffe for myself.'

The next place on the itinerary was Merzouga. By this time, I was becoming resigned to not knowing what lay ahead and was almost excited by it. I hoped I had packed and brought anything that we might need for any eventuality, including things that Robert might not have considered or even known to be useful, such as various items of medication and first aid. I felt a certain responsibility towards him, to make sure that he was well cared for during the trip; it had been my idea and I felt I should take ownership of that, and that I had, I had assumed, the greater experience of participating in organised tours to unknown places.

Or was I treating him as one of my children and covering every possible eventuality as if I were still heading up a one-parent family, I wondered. Had catering for the possible needs of other people become a habit?

As our coach drove through the town of Erg Chebbi, the land looked flat. Any soil had become sandier and palm trees grew in isolated clumps. Once through the town and into open land again, the coach stopped outside two tall square-sided towers that reminded me of a castle entrance. A sign on each of the towers offered three words of explanation; 'Sahara' and underneath 'Auberge - Camping.' A man appeared and opened the gates that were blocking the way. Our coach drove in.

It was dusk and by the light of the camp and a rising full moon, we were shown to our room rather than to any tent. A low sandy wall separated the block of bedrooms from whatever lay beyond but Robert and I planned to investigate all that the following morning. That evening we were too tired and too full of thoughts and the day's memories to do anything other than head for a meal and bed.

The following day, as we stepped out of our hotel room and onto a sand-trodden path, we were met by a lad in a loose cotton garment like a nightdress and with his head and neck wrapped in soft blue material. He explained that he was one of the local Berbers and he would like to show us around.

'But first,' he said with considerable authority, while sitting down on the sand and dumping his canvas holdall beside him, 'I show you what things I have in my bag.'

He spread out on the sand a row of brightly-coloured open geodes and items of black marble. Robert picked up one of the geodes and asked what it was.

'Is lava bomb,' said the Berber boy. 'Outer shells of lava go hard and silica is on inside walls in bomb.'

I had seen something similar in Iceland but not with the bright colours of the open 'bombs' or grenades that the local boy had displayed.

'Are those natural colours?' I asked, looking at the bright magenta and Prussian blue geode crystals.

'All natural,' the lad assured me, without blinking.

'If you say so,' I responded, looking askance at Robert. I had my doubts.

Years of working with natural gems had made me more sure about what I was seeing and the vivid colours of those bombs bore no resemblance at all to the gentle purple of the larger natural amethyst geode that I had once had, and from which Keir, as a boy, had hacked off fragments and sold them, as he had later admitted, to his friends at school.

'And what are these?' I asked as Robert and I each picked up something that looked like a dish, with the shape of an ammonite embossed on it.

'Is good and very rare' was the reply. Then, 'Desert was once floor of early ocean. In ocean, many plants, fish and sea animals remain when water is gone. Stone is black marble, animal you see is ammonite. Is all natural and very old. You like? You buy?'

Robert had told me, when we had only just re-met in Canterbury the previous year, that he had started a business, acting as an agent for items produced in Italy to be exported and sold in Britain.

As I paid the lad for a black marble-and-ammonite dish that I intended to use at home as a soap dish, I was not surprised when Robert said to me 'I've had an idea about some of that stuff. I'll tell you more when I've thought it through. But I might need to come to Morocco again.'

We followed our young Berber guide by stepping over the low wall and there, rising some quarter of a mile in front of us, enormous and totally unexpected, was a huge sand dune. And another. And behind it, another. Not yellow sand dunes like those at Overy Staithe or Holkham on the north Norfolk coast, but wave after wave of orange dunes stretching, as far as we could tell, into the distance.

The lad led us across a patch of flatter sand to where there was some sort of brick or stone construction that looked as if it were the top of a wishing well or the start of a squat ventilation shaft. As he explained, it was one of several such constructions and the top of something that turned out to be both a well and a shaft to an underground water system. The lad pointed out a series of these, running in almost a straight line into the distance as far as we could see until the flat land stopped and the dunes began.

Across one of the well shafts was a metal bar like a scaffolding pole and from the central point of the bar, a rope had been tied that descended into the compressed sand. I could not see, the light outside was so bright against the darkness of the shaft but I assumed that at the end of the rope was some sort of bucket.

'Long water system under ground. Natural.' our guide explained before taking his leave and refusing any reward.

The group was invited to gather after a late lunch and take a stroll outside the sand 'castle' walls. I did not think to take an umbrella with me for shade, Omar had said 'No need for coach, we will walk.' He was correct, he pointed to a cluster of low buildings not far away at the side of our hotel in the opposite direction, away from the sand dunes.

When we approached the buildings, we saw on two metal poles a blue sign with white letters that read 'Laverie' and underneath 'Laundry'.

I could not image a more unlikely place out there in the desert for a laundry and thought of how, when the children and I had no washing machine, we had had to find sufficient cash and bundle everything – clothes, towels, Keir's wet sheets and pyjamas – into the back of the car and drive into Dereham to the laundromat at the back of the market place. Surely this place couldn't be the same? But perhaps it might be, but without the need for the drying machines, I thought, because our desert hotel would need to have the bed sheets washed very regularly.

I did not manage to find out, because among those flat-roofed buildings, just behind a solitary tree with a man's bicycle lying on its side and three or four cane stools left in the shade, was a carpet warehouse.

We were led in and offered something cool to drink. I refused mine, politely, I hoped. I took a seat next to Robert and watched while a carpet salesman told his soft-shod men to spread out carpets, one by one, in front of us on the tiled floor with arabesque gestures as if taking part in some sort of impromptu ballet.

When we had been in India, Robert had bought himself a rug with elephants depicted on it and I had bought a turquoise green one for my bedroom.

'They're wasting their time on us,' Robert whispered 'but some of the others look quite interested. Shipping a carpet home might prove quite expensive but I expect the carpet company would arrange all that.'

I remembered then how, just after I had first met Danny, he and his son Mark had been going on a holiday to Morocco at the end of the summer term.

'It will probably be the last foreign holiday I ever have with Mark,' he had told me.

Danny had brought two rugs back with him. One I have now as a wall-hanging in the house in the otherwise empty space above the stairs. Danny gave the other rug to me, he had chosen one with wools in a mix of natural colours because 'I thought it would be the sort of colour range that you would like,' he had said.

One of the rugs being spread on the floor was quite unusual. It was brighter in colour than I thought I would like – an intricate design incorporating red, orange, oatmeal and sage green hexagons. Without giving it much more consideration, I decided to buy it, if it were not too expensive. It would, I thought, hang beautifully on the dining room wall between the two raffia and banana leaf baskets brought back from the visit that Danny and I had made to Tanzania and opposite the Moroccan garden print left over from an exhibition from when Richard and I had an art gallery.

'Robert, if I asked you, could you lend me any dirhams towards that rug? I can pay you back this week when I cash some of my Travellers Cheques. I could pay in sterling on my credit card but I would rather not. I am very particular as to who gets my card details.'

'Not a problem,' he replied. 'How much do you need?'

I bought the rug. It folded up beautifully in my suitcase and I guessed that if I wore my coat with the books in the coat pockets, my luggage would still be under the permitted weight.

The following day, we are asked to pack into a bag or rucksack anything we might need for a scheduled overnight stop in the desert, some water and a hat. Pre-warned by the tour itinerary, both Robert and I had brought three-season sleeping bags and I also had a silk liner that I had used during the Kilimanjaro climb. Robert was wearing a tee-shirt and light trousers; he had no hat nor any covering for his neck.

Acknowledging my tendency as a single mother accustomed to planning for a camping trip with three children to bring extra 'just-in-case' items, I lent Robert one of my neck buffs and a spare hat with a cord for his neck.

We were led to the flat land with the well shafts, where we were confronted by a string of camels. 'Choose what camel you like,' a Berber man called out, as he held tightly on to the rope of the front camel. I walked towards the camel bearing a number 2623 in its yellow ear tag and spoke to it. It viewed me with what I took to be distain and fluttered its eyelashes in disgust.

One of the Berber guides helped me into the saddle and indicated that I should take my rucksack off my back and carry it in front of me to one side of the saddle, which proved to be minimally upholstered and made mainly from angle iron. I had the feeling that, were I to fall off, the angle iron would knock my teeth out even before I hit the ground.

Slowly at first, the line of camels and their novice riders progressed from the flatter sand area towards the dunes. There was grim determination on Robert's face as he gripped the central iron bar of the saddle, pressing the heel of his walking boots well down into the stirrups.

In convoy, we spent a painful and nervous hour trying not to disgrace ourselves by falling off and hitting the sand dunes at speed, as the camels slipped and slid as they tried to maintain their footing on the shifting wind-whipped corrugated dune slopes. At last, and to my relief, as the sun began to drop below the tallest dune, we came to the black coverings of a Bedouin or Berber camp.

Most of the group had opted to spend the night in the shelter of the camp and once the camels had been secured for the night by having their legs tied together, several of the group took their belongings there. A few of us, Robert and I included, had chosen to spend the night out in the open desert.

After a meal in the Bedouin camp, we were handed foam plastic mattresses and shown where best to place them on the sand, not far from a pile of sticks that looked as if it could become a bonfire.

Having done that, several of us scrabbled our way to the top of the nearest and highest dune to make the most of the failing light. One of our party was having difficult in reaching the top so I went half way back down to meet her and offer her one of the dextrose tablets that I keep with me, for when my blood sugar level appears low and I am lacking in energy.

I left Robert sitting at the top of the dune with the full moon behind him, smiling broadly and looking very happy, almost smug. So smug that I was very tempted, at that moment when I came back and reached him, to say 'Will you marry me?' and then push him in the chest to shove him backwards down the dune – but I resisted the urge. I feared he might either take me seriously and accept, consider I had lost my mind, or even break his neck as he fell backwards. None of these would have been what I wanted.

We spread our sleeping bags on the mattresses, brushed our teeth with what little water we could spare, peed where we were told to near the bonfire sticks, and wriggled into our sleeping bags. I zipped mine up as far as it would go, I was not sure what else lived in the desert but I did not want any snake to slide in and spend the night beside my warm body.

I left my contact lenses in. I wanted to see the stars properly even though I knew that not taking the lenses out would probably make my eyes sore in the morning. I said quietly 'Goodnight, Robert. Sleep well' and gazed up at the twinkling stars until my eyes shut themselves.

The sun rose early the next morning and I went only a few steps from my bed before crouching down and having a pee. There was no sign of anyone else around. As I stood up and adjusted my clothing, I saw animal footprints in the sand. They looked like paw prints, similar to Butterworth's prints except smaller. We had not seen any dogs in the vicinity. I mentioned them to our guide.

'That will have been a fox,' Omar said, 'you can sometimes catch sight of them in the starlight. They come near the camp to look for food.'

I was glad that the fox had decided not to try to bite me and pleased that my arms and toes had been well covered within my sleeping bag.

Robert did not seem at all concerned about the fox.

'I often slept outdoors when I was with the army cadets' he said. 'All sorts of creatures and insects would appear then.'

I was pleased by what he said, that he appeared to cope even better than I could with outdoor life and that he did not seem to regard me as a wimp. I didn't want to be a drag.

Leaving the desert behind, the group was moved to a hotel in Tineghir. There were two options on offer from which we could choose, a five-hour walk in Todra Gorge or a gentle perambulation through the local allotments. I chose the Todra Gorge walk, mainly because it offered the chance of meeting local nomads, some of whom lived, we were told, in troglodyte homes cut into the mountain sides.

I thought it would also give Robert some time on his own without me, since he had opted to view the vegetable crops and the layout of the allotments.

The walk was quite energetic and I was slightly unsettled to discover that Omar had not asked anyone to act as back marker. On all other organised walking holidays I had had, either abroad or in Britain, there had always been a back marker who could ensure that no one got left behind, or alert the leader to any problem.

This particularly mattered to me because I tended to be the straggler towards the back of the group, sometimes because I walked more slowly than other people but usually because I liked to pause from time to time, sniff the air and take stock of everything around me.

Once we were clear of the gorge and well into the mountains with the paths of loose stones, we came across an elderly

Berber. There were only five or six of us walkers in this group and the man emerged from a man-made tunnel into the rock, just outside which he had been boiling a kettle of water. He invited us to sit down on carpet-covered palliasses under a thin canopy of printed cotton material, and drink tea with him from small drinking glasses - I hoped they were clean - for which we felt obliged to offer him some money.

Since everything was laid out ready, apparently for any passing stranger who happened to be wandering thirstily through the mountains, I guessed that this was a regular arrangement set for a specific time and established between the Berber and Omar.

If so, I felt it was safe also to assume that the glasses had been hygienically washed somewhere in the gorge and the water drawn from a safe source. Suitably refreshed, although I noted that each one of us in the group was sensibly carrying his or her own bottle of water, we descended and walked along a roadway until we arrived at a restaurant.

I had the feeling that Omar was slightly impatient with me, that I wasn't walking as quickly as he would have wished. I wondered whether he had some sort of time-scale to meet and whether I was causing him an unscheduled delay.

There, when we reached the restaurant, sitting at a long table outside and in the shade, was the rest of our group, the ones who had been on the lower allotment walk. Plates of food arrived as we were pulling our chairs to sit down and join them, so I assumed they had already chosen and ordered what they wanted for lunch.

I noticed that a plate of mixed green salad arrived for Robert and I wondered about his choice. Should I have warned him about the dangers of eating anything abroad that had not been recently peeled or very recently cooked, despite all assurances that it had 'been washed in very clean water'?

No, I assume he was a grown man and could use his own knowledge and common sense. I have no recollection of what I chose from the menu but it certainly was not the salad. Fried aubergines, probably, with a hunk of local bread.

We ate in the hotel restaurant that night and having been out exercising in the fresh air all day, went to bed quite early. At some point during the night, Robert woke and went to the bathroom. After he had come back, I wriggled over to his side of the bed, put my hand out across the bottom sheet to feel where he was, encountered something tacky, switched on my torch and 'Arrh, I think you've sprung a leak. And it's not just wet, I think you've had a slight bout of diarrhoea.'

He looked, moved out of the bed and still half asleep, looked at where he had been lying and asked 'Oh, what shall I do?'

'Don't worry, I'll deal with it. You go and wash whatever part of you you think is necessary while I deal with the bedding.'

While he was out of the room, I stripped the lower sheet from the bed, bundled it up with its messy contents in the centre, and placed it beside the bedroom door. I went to the bathroom to wash and dry my hands, then stripped off the top sheet, spread that across the mattress and pulled the duvet over ourselves. That done, we went back to sleep.

Early in the morning, carrying the sheet bundled in front of me, I padded along the corridor in my nightclothes and found a maid. I handed her the bundle, telling her, while rubbing my stomach and making the appropriate gesticulations, 'very sorry, upset stomach, not well.' My miming must have done the trick because she took a moment to understand the problem, then handed me a complete new folded white sheet. I thanked her, apologised again and returned to our room. Robert was in the bathroom. I re-made the bed and restored everything to its proper position.

Later that morning he thanked me and told me 'I thought you were really heroic, dealing with that as you did and without any fuss.'

At the 'really heroic' I felt my face glowing and I swelled with pride. No one have ever said anything like that to me, and just for changing a messy sheet. My actions just seemed sensible, to me. But I did wonder what Robert's previous experience with his wives had been, whether they would have done as I did and if not, why not?

Later that day, we were due to visit a deserted fortified village so I kept an eye on Robert in case he should still feel unwell. We were told that the Kasbah of Aït Ben Haddou was a UNESCO World Heritage Site, one of Morocco's most impressive historic landmarks and a popular film location. At the entrance to the site, Omar pointed out certain buildings and areas, saying 'I expect some of you recognise this as the location for part of the film 'Gladiator'. There were nods among the group but it meant nothing to me.

Omar explained that the ksar was a fortified village or a group of earthen buildings surrounded by high walls, and a traditional pre-Saharan habitat. The houses crowded together within defensive walls, which were reinforced by corner towers.

'Ait-Ben-Haddou is a striking and well-known example of the architecture of southern Morocco,' he said. 'If you look here. . ,' and he pointed to blocks of mud bricks lying on the ground, 'you can see what the walls were made from and how these bricks are still laid out to dry in the sun.'

It was very windy that day. We had to shield our eyes from the flying sand and after admiring someone using guar gum, painting what he called 'sand pictures' and trying to sell them to us, we were led up some steps to where there was a canopy made from bamboo that shaded a long table and chairs. This was where we were to have lunch.

'If you like,' said Omar 'some of you can go down and visit part of the village. Only part of it, as it is not open to the general public. But it is windy and you may find the sand stings your legs as it is blown against you.'

I was glad that Robert did not take up this offer. His stomach was still causing a slight problem and being stuck in a film set, deserted or not, and without toilet facilities, seemed to each of us to be a bad idea.

Our next overnight stop on this holiday could be reached only by four-wheeled vehicles and mules. We had been advised to bring soft-sided luggage rather than hard suitcases and had even been sent long green kitbags for us to use and keep afterwards. The coach we had been using as transport, dropped us on some land between brown hills studded with juniper bushes.

Waiting for us was a group of mules or donkeys and their owners. Our kitbags were loaded onto the donkeys, with one bag attached to each side of a thin saddle, and the donkey train set off up the track towards something that was out of view.

'Follow behind please,' we were told. 'You walk, is not far.' This unusual method of transport was slightly reminiscent of the time Robert and I had spent in India, when our group had had to sit on pillows to cushion the planks of a wooden makeshift wagon that was initially pulled by an ancient tractor; the shafts had then been transferred to a camel which pulled us the rest of the way to Geejarh, where Robert had been persuaded good-naturedly to wear a turban and pretend to 'ride' a large red-and-silver toy horse around in a circle.

I would have been far too embarrassed but he had risen to the occasion in good spirit. Danny, I had thought, would have declined in horror even at the request. Danny would have clung to his dignity and not taken part at all, would have regarded such play-acting as rather puerile and a totally unnecessary part of the tour.

Clutching, as instructed, any valuables in a separate bag, we walked for an hour gently uphill to reach our gite, with the mules carrying our heavier luggage. The sun shone the whole time, we were not carrying any bottles of water and as a village and what we hoped was our gite came into sight, Robert, having been unwell the previous day, was losing energy and beginning to tire. I thought he was struggling.

The final hundred metres of track to the gite was steep. I grabbed hold of Robert's hand, and tried to pull him along and up the final few steps.

He brushed my hand away and although I thought that this was where we most needed Omar, Robert walked the last steps on his own and reached the cool inside entrance of the gite. There we sat, waited for our luggage and to be told about our rooms, while I pondered on the nature of 'male pride'.

The gite did not offer meals but a local widow from the village supported herself financially by offering tea and cake to parties of foreign visitors. Judging by the things she had in her house, as Robert said quietly to me, 'it would appear that she does very well out of the arrangement.'

There were limited individual rooms in the gite and I have no idea what happened to the married couples but Robert and I were allocated a mixed gender room. I was the only woman in the room that I shared with Robert and three other men, nearly all of whom snored quite loudly. I hoped I did too, it would be a chance for those men to know what they sounded like.

After our stay at the gite, we rejoined our coach and were driven towards Marrakech over the Atlas Mountains, over the Tizi n'Tichka which, at 2,260 metres, was the highest road pass in Morocco. Wherever the coach was able to pull in to allow us to take photographs of the winding road a mile below, there would nearly always be someone by the side of the road, selling those lava bombs or some other souvenir at a price far above that asked by the Berber lad at our 'Sahara Camping' hotel.

Along the road, we stopped at a centre established for unmarried local women and widows to use their skills to extract argan oil from the kernels of the argan tree, which is reputed to cure facial wrinkles. The argan tree is endemic to Morocco and Omar told us that goats frequently climb the trees.

'Why?' I asked him. He explained 'The goats are attracted to the pulp of the fruit of the tree. The goats will keep all their hooves firmly on the ground and graze on fruit hanging low but when they have gobbled the fruit they can reach, they will scramble up into the tree in search of more.' He also told us 'The argan oil is supposed to reduce the effect of diabetes but I do not know how.' I made a mental note to check on that when I returned to Britain.

The last place we visited before Marrakech was the walled city and old Portuguese fishing port of Essaouria on the coast of the Atlantic Ocean. The smell of fish fresh from the sea pervaded the air in the central square.

Having had a long coach journey, once our luggage was trundled to the Beau Rivage Hotel and taken up the stairs to our rooms, we gathered in a group to walk together to the harbour.

Silver fish were spread out on a white board that rested on a wooden box turned on its side to offer the correct height for the buyers.

'Mind where you walk,' warned Omar.

The concrete under our feet was wet from sea water and from the daily hosing down of the area with fresh water to get rid of slivers of gut, bone, fish heads and any spilled oil. Gulls cried overhead but most were standing on the wet shore just above the wave limit, their shapes reflected in the damp sand and mud under their feet. They looked to me to be immature glaucous gulls in summer plumage but I could not be sure.

A few, I thought, could have been lesser black-backed gulls on their way south. A couple were certainly herring gulls, I could see their yellow beaks with the red dot at the end. . . and I remembered how and where, on a road trip to the Orkneys, Danny had explained to me how to tell the difference.

Bringing my gaze back to the present, I noticed how only Robert was waiting for me, the others had moved on. We took the opportunity to explore the harbour on our own. I knew Robert was interested in boats and sailing for pleasure so when we came to what appeared to be a very small boat-building yard, we peeped through the fence.

Sure enough, lying on the ground like the bones and spine of a filleted fish, were thick planks of wood, splayed out on each side from a central beam.

'It looks to me as if they're using mahogany,' Robert observed.

One of us pushed against a gate, which swung open, and 'Let's have a look inside, we're not doing any harm and I'm sure the owner won't mind,' I suggested.

Robert hesitated with 'Are you sure that . .?' and we went in.

We were gazing at the half-finished construction, when there was a voice and a man with a beard appeared, wearing a loose blue shirt over his polo shirt. He must have realised from our voices that we were English or certainly not local, so he spoke to us first in French and then in halting English monosyllables.

'You look, see. Boat. Big boat. Boat, me. Come.' And he beckoned, by which we assumed him to be either the owner or the boat-builder or both, and that he was inviting us to view the boatyard and his construction.

He showed us around the hull of the boat with its huge metal rudder and slightly rusty-looking propeller, put his arm around Robert's much taller shoulders, smiled into Robert's face and said 'Is good. Yes?' We both made all the suitable complimentary remarks. The man continued to smile, showed us to the other side of the hull that was not visible from the perimeter fence, and through a gap in his yellowing teeth, said 'Money!'

'I don't think he's asking you to make an offer for the boat or guess at its current value,' I told Robert, 'He's asking for a reward for his services that we neither needed nor requested. However,' I said, looking down at the number of heavy metal tools lying carelessly around on the floor of the boatyard, 'it might be wise to thank him, give him a few small coins and get out of here, as safely and as soon as we politely can.'

I had the strap of my red shoulder bag across my chest so there was no way that we could pretend that we had no money on us.

I smiled as best I could at the man, who was looking expectant and pointing to my little Pentax camera.

'Yes please,' I said, 'Photos please. You. And us' and handed the camera to him.

While he was snapping Robert and me standing beside the rudder and I was positioning him with the same backdrop looking proudly into the distance, his arm still around the back of Robert's neck and on his shoulder, I was able to grab a few loose coins from my bag.

'Thank you,' I said, holding out my hand for my camera again, 'very good boat. This for you' and I dropped the coins into his still-outstretched pink palm.

'Goodbye,' I called and we made our way back through the gate in the fence and onto the main harbour again.

Behind me, I heard the sound of the gate being closed, bolted and a padlock being locked.

Essaouira's Hotel Beau Rivage did not have a restaurant so we would take our continental breakfast each morning in the café on the pavement outside that looked onto the main thoroughfare from the port to the town. On one particular morning at the end of the week, the bookshop opposite the hotel entrance appeared closed and there was not the usual number of clerics going into and out of the entrance to the mosque, on the other side of the road.

Nor did anyone appear to serve us with rolls and cake, and take our order for coffee or tea for breakfast.

We wondered whether we had overslept and where the others in our party were. Had we missed some announcement from Omar while we were inspecting the boat yard? We sat at one of the wicker tables which, unusually for that day, was not covered by a small table cloth, and waited for a further fifteen minutes.

While we waited, we wandered across to the other side of the thoroughfare to stretch our legs. Looking back at our hotel, Robert appeared to be in full planning mode and announced 'What this hotel needs is a lift. If you and I clubbed together to buy the place, we could install a lift shaft there,' and he pointed to the façade 'where the stairs are now, and develop the downstairs with a restaurant open also to the public. Then there'd be no need for all these tables and wicker chairs outside.'

We went back to our table to wait. Five minutes more. Still no sign of anyone to bring us a drink or take an order.

Slightly bemused, we decided to take ourselves for a walk along the thoroughfare, as far as a small park that we had discovered previously. It was only ten minutes away and if we had made some mistake over the timing that morning, then by the time we returned, we supposed that someone would have appeared.

We reached the park which was encircled by a metal fence, with metal gates for access.

But that morning the gates were not only shut but locked. With padlocks. We speculated about why the gate would be locked but then decided that it was to deter anyone from either spending the night on a park bench or using the park as a discrete place for courting couples.

'I could climb over the gate?' I suggested.

Shaking his head, Robert looked doubtful.

'Breaking the law in a strange country isn't usually a good idea,' he advised.

We had been getting on very well together during this holiday so far, so I did not want to put him or me in a difficult position if I were caught.

'Look,' he said, 'there's a café over there that looks as if it is just opening up. Those clerics or Mullahs . . ' and he nodded his head towards two men in long white robes approaching the cafe ' . . might report you if they see you, a woman, lifting her skirts to get over a locked gate.'

I had to agree with him.

'So, let's go to the café, queue behind the clerics and sit outside with cups of coffee while we try to discover whether this is some special religious weekend, with most places closed.'

We did as he suggested. I spent a few moments gazing down at the Mullahs' footwear. To me, the bright yellow pointed-toed leather mule-type slippers on their feet appeared a little incongruous below the white robes. Another Mullah appeared, wearing tan mules, and joined the queue.

I remarked to Robert 'The Mullahs nearly all seem to prefer yellow. The bright green mule-type slippers that we saw yesterday would be just as jolly but perhaps a little too distracting. They might make them appear more like Moroccan leprechauns.'

Robert reached the café counter and put his finger to his lips; he was telling me to 'sssh'.

We sat drinking our rather strong coffee at a table outside the café.

I was talking to Robert about Danny being a secondary school headmaster and how I had been uncertain, once Danny and I were married, as to what a Head's wife was expected to do or how to behave, when Robert remarked 'I never wanted to be a Head of a school, I was far happier being the Deputy. I enjoyed that.'

Then, after a moment or two of mental reminiscence, he came out with the statement 'But I would never want to work under a female Head. Because women are so disorganised, they are incapable of planning.'

I blinked, took a deep long breath and thought how best to respond. Was I, I wondered, going to empty my coffee cup over his head at that daft remark, or talk more generally about the danger of prejudice, generalisations and jumping to conclusions without any supportive evidence? Was he stuck with some historic social perception of women as lesser beings, with how they should behave – or was he deliberately trying to start a discussion or an argument?

Or was he simply teasing, knowing how I was likely to reply?

I decided, within a couple of seconds, not to rise to what might have been intended as bait, but to wait, observe and take note in future. I thought that Robert and I had been getting on very well so far and I did not wish to upset that, but at some point quite soon, I knew that I needed to challenge his comment, especially as it had been I who had helped organise this trip to Morocco and bring things that he might require.

I did not want him to be grateful but neither did I want to be taken for granted nor for Robert to assume that I was any less able to plan and organise than he was.

And perhaps also to remind him that, when we were both students in Canterbury, it had been I who had planned, arranged and led a party of fellow students to Switzerland and back by train, and had booked rooms at Engelberg Youth Hostel and arranged for a birthday party for our colleague Wendy. Or remind him that he and I were jointly responsible for the former students' part of an annual event at Canterbury University, and that I kept everyone informed as to what was planned and expected, while his role in this seemed far less involved.

No, on this occasion I would let Robert's remark ride but if ever . . .

We made our way slowly back to our hotel in Essaouria, talking all the time and looking at the locally-made items for sale. I did stop at one place and tried on a djellaba. I thought it was not well-made and would probably shrink when I washed it but I bought it, nevertheless. I also bought one or two items made from Moroccan wood that I thought I might either give as Christmas presents, or keep for myself. One was a wooden box with a clever way of opening it.

I bargained for this and managed to get the price considerably reduced but I think that both I as purchaser and the seller were content with the outcome.

To celebrate our 'success' as a group (or because either he or the hotel had made a mistake regarding our breakfasts), Omar suggested that we should all go out as a group for early evening drinks and then move on for our evening meal in a local restaurant that he recommended and which, he told us, 'overlooks the sea and the marina.'

I was unsure about the 'marina', which may have been his word for a fishing port but we all went along with his suggestion and met at the appointed time just outside the hotel entrance.

From there, he led us along the main thoroughfare until we arrived at what he termed a 'bar', where we went inside and ordered what we wanted. I asked for a small dry white wine and Robert chose something very similar. Several of the others were into spirits and seemed very relieved to be able to drink alcohol so openly, and profusely.

We spent about an hour and a half there, chatting together, looking out of the open window and appreciating the sea breeze that was helping to lower the bar temperature.

'Please finish your drinks and follow me again,' called Omar and we obediently did as he asked. He suggested that for our main meal, we would proceed to a restaurant on an upper floor overlooking the harbour and the dock. Further along and avoiding tripping over any bollards and ropes, we turned a corner and behind an open door, came to a flight of stairs. The restaurant lay at the top, part open to the air and part covered by a roof.

Omar helped us choose from the menu. I chose local fish of some sort with roasted vegetables, while others went for local delicacies or chicken. I was drinking bottled water while most of our party had ordered more wine, beer or cocktails.

Once we had finished our choices of main course, a waiter presented Omar with the dessert menu which he read aloud to us, while the waiter made notes as to each individual preference.

Selina shook her head, to turn down the chance of a dessert.

'I don't feel very well,' she said quietly to the people sitting beside her. 'I'm very tired and I want to lie down, so I think I'll walk back to the hotel now, on my own.'

Omar looked concerned at this and when none of us offered to walk back with Selina, he said 'I will walk back with you because I am responsible for your safety,' and to us 'I will not be long, I must make sure that Selina gets back to her hotel room. I will return before you have all finished and paid for your meals, then I will lead you back to the hotel and tell you about the arrangements for tomorrow morning, when we will leave the hotel and will go to Marrakech.'

By this stage in our holiday, my perception of Morocco as an alcohol-free country had totally disappeared.

In one town, after Robert had visited a chemist and managed to buy some Imodium or other anti-diarrhoea medication to replace the packet of mine that he had used, we had been led by Omar to a general store, which had a backroom refrigerated store, full of bottles of alcohol. While we were there, making our own private purchases, one or two local people had appeared in the backroom doorway and they too went away with full shopping bags.

The following day, we loaded our luggage bags onto the coach. I chose to sit on the left-hand-side row of seats behind the driver while Robert decided he would prefer the more shaded right-hand side, to spread out a bit. Selina came and sat on the seat beside me. We started to talk.

I asked her whether she felt any better after the previous evening and she said that she did. We chatted gently about our lives and families, I asked her about herself, when she came from Canada to Britain and what had made her choose to make that move. I gained the impression that she was lonely and missing part of her family.

Almost as if in return, she told me she worked for a book-publishing company, was an aspiring writer and asked me about Robert, about my relationship with him and then surprised me with 'I thought you and Robert were married.'

'No, we are just good friends, we've known each other for ages. What made you think we were married?'

'Nothing really, except you appear to get on so well together. It was only when I heard you ask to borrow some money from him that I had my doubts as to whether you were married. So, what is your relationship with him?'

I felt Selina was asking out of more than politeness or idle curiosity. She appeared to be checking on his availability.

'I really don't know apart from what I've said. We are good friends; we've known each other for about fifty years but never particularly well until fairly recently. I like him, I think we get on quite well together, we have quite a lot in common but I have no idea what he really feels about me.'

Then she suggested 'Would you like me to try to find out?'

'You can certainly try but you probably won't find out, even if he knows himself.'

I assumed that was the end of that part of the conversation. But later, as Selina and I were coming out of a Ladies toilet on the way to Marrakech, she asked for my help to raise her profile in Omar's eyes. I was puzzled by that and I must have frowned because I didn't understand the reason for the request.

She went on to tell me that she, accompanied by Omar, had returned to her room the previous evening, after we had all enjoyed a meal together on a terrace overlooking the harbour. She told me his body was almost bony and she had found it quite uncomfortable.

I assumed they had sex, possible unprotected but she was not specific. I felt quite shocked. I had heard of English tourists and foreign guides of being thrown together for a short period of time and taking advantage of the situation and of each other, but I had never knowingly encountered it.

'So, could you' she asked 'say to Omar something like 'I really like Selina, she's a lovely person, isn't she'? I want him to think really well of me.'

Whatever the reason for this strange request which I found to be almost beseeching, I told her 'I will do what I can if I find an appropriate opportunity, but I can't promise.'

In Marrakech, the coach off-loaded us at our hotel with our luggage. Once we had been given our room keys, Omar suggested that we should all catch a bus to the town centre to explore Marrakech.

From the bus stop near the town centre, we followed Omar in a line through the cobbled back streets, stopping from time to time at stalls and shops to buy natural spices and various healing ingredients.

Robert had told me 'I want to return to Morocco for business purposes, so perhaps I could sell 'the best of Morocco' both in Italy and in Britain. I would like to commission someone to make soft suede leather pouches for mobile phones. I've already designed them,' and he broached the subject with one or two leather purveyors, in the narrow cobbled lanes.

'Well, I'd be quite happy to return with you to Marrakech in a few months' time and help you negotiate if you like, because I think my French may be slightly better than yours.' Robert did not contest that nor agree, but he nodded.

After making a few last purchases, we had a series of local snacks, sitting as a group at a stall in the central market place of Place Jemaa el-Fna.

Rather than return to our hotel early with the rest of the group, Robert and I decided to make the most of our short time in Marrakech and wander freely through the market place. But we had difficulty finding our way back in the dark to the area of the city in which we thought our hotel lay.

We tried to catch a bus that seemed to be going in the correct direction but we could not read the Arabic script and no one appeared to understand English. We walked most of the way back, using various landmarks that we had seen during the twilight on our bus journey into the town centre.

Almost as we reached our hotel, I tripped and fell flat in the middle of the tree-lined road. A man came to see across from the pavement to see if I was hurt, while Robert appeared less concerned. I told the man 'Je ne suis pas blessée' and picked myself up.

Our own hotel had stopped serving meals by the time we reached it, so Robert and I ordered an evening meal for ourselves in the restaurant of the next hotel. After our walk back from the centre of Marrakech to our hotel, we were both quite hungry.

At the airport, Robert managed to lose his boarding card although 'I had it just now, I must have dropped it' he said, as he rummaged unsuccessfully through his papers.

'Don't worry, it will turn up', I told him while wondering quite what to do if it didn't. Fortunately, someone found it and handed it in at an enquiry desk, from where Robert was able to retrieve it.

I did find an occasion to commend Selina to Omar, just before we all said goodbye to each other and made the promise that we knew was unlikely to be kept, that we would all keep in touch with each other.

In the airport shop, Robert bought me a silver teapot. Selina whispered to me 'That silver teapot says 'I love you'.

I responded quietly with 'That silver teapot says nothing more than I'm a silver teapot that Lorna might like.'

Once back in Britain, I repeated my offer to accompany Robert if he really wanted to commission and import goods from Morocco to sell elsewhere, but he was non-committal.

I placed the silver teapot on a shelf in the dining room, just beside a brass teapot that Danny had brought back from his holiday with Mark, in Morocco.

Three weeks later, I heard from Selina that Robert had returned to Morocco on the identical scheduled trip and been recognised by the same guide Omar, who had obviously kept in communication with Selina.

Robert seemed surprised to know that I had heard about this from Selina and Omar and told me that his mother had suggested he needed a holiday. Since he had not long returned from our visit to Morocco, this seemed to me to be complete nonsense. Apparently, he had returned to Morocco with Elena, another long-established female friend.

I felt slightly hurt, then resigned. Despite calling me 'heroic' and my lending him essential equipment, I assumed that Robert did not find me a compatible travel companion.

Within six months or so of this second visit to Morocco, Robert also travelled to Turkey without mentioning it in advance or suggesting that we might go together. That visit too had been with Elena, he told me long afterwards.

My rational mind could accept this as being entirely reasonable and his choice to make. I had met Elena once when she had come to an event in Canterbury with Robert as his 'plus one'. She was a divorcee with several adult boys, Robert told me. I found her to be a very pleasant and knowledgeable person and I had warmed towards her, and to her appreciation of Robert. My emotional self, however, felt it more keenly: I assumed I was being given a message to 'back off'.

Chapter 31

'Michael', Cinque Port

After feeling rejected by Robert as either a soulmate or a travel companion, I decided, as Keir put it, that I was 'looking in the wrong shop window.' Or, if not the wrong shop window, that I was seeking the wrong item.

So, in the light of earlier conversations that I had had with Robert, I amended my 'Likewise' profile so that it then read 'Happy traveller seeks global travel companion'. I did not want anyone to move into my house, nor I into his. I was just looking for someone with whom I could reasonably share travel costs, a twin room, a meal, and a conversation about the places and things we had seen each day. I had had one or two false starts with this.

One of those was with a chap called Ben, whom I met through the website and briefly on a walking holiday in Spain. He told me he had written an account of a walking trip he had made across the Dales. I didn't ask him whether he had published it.

After we had met and spent a week among other company, Ben planned to visit me and stay nearby in his mobile home. I had even found a camping-and-caravan site for him within three miles of my house, where he could park his vehicle. Just before he was due to arrive, he emailed me to say that he had sold his mobile home and wondered where he could stay instead.

I wrote back and told him that, as we had met only as fellow-participants on a walking holiday and we did not know each other at all well, I would not be inviting him to stay with me but perhaps he could find somewhere local where he could get a room for a few days. As a result, he booked into a hotel on the outskirts of Norwich.

I met him each day and showed him around Norfolk for almost a week. He had told me he had not been to Norfolk before but as the days wore on, he mentioned more than once 'Oh, I stayed here once with my last wife and we. .' and made several other references to places he recognised. As it was, I was already finding him rather dull and during the walking trip in Spain, he had shown he could be quite forgetful.

We had little in common, he talked a great deal about himself but asked me nothing about myself, and I paid the parking and entrance fees for both of us at every place to which I took him. At the end of the week, we said goodbye politely and I heard no more from him. I was not sad.

When I last looked, his profile and photo were still on the 'Likewise' website.

My first meeting with Michael took place at Snape Maltings in the summer of 2015. Judging from the map, Snape lay about halfway between his home near Frinton and mine in Wymondham. I suggested that we met at the 'Plough and Sail' Public House in Snape, so that we could park on site and get a coffee - and if necessary, each make a quick exit in case, despite our long emails and chats online, we decided that we really didn't much like each other.

I walked through the bar and checked at each of the wooden tables around the corner to see if he had arrived already. I wondered whether I would recognise him from his photograph, according to which and judging by his profile, he was in his mid-seventies and almost bald.

When he did appear, almost on time, he recognised me first and spoke my name, in order to be sure.

He was not as tanned as I would have expected. I knew from his emails that he had only recently returned from a not-so-enjoyable couple of weeks on holiday in Cuba and a week in Spain before that, on a course about male/female relationships. But we selected a table, he ordered a couple of glasses of house wine and passed the lunch menu to me.

'So how did you find the final week in Cuba?' I asked, although I already knew most of his answer.

'Only couples remaining for the second week and one single man, who was very boring', Michael told me. 'And that message from Miranda that I told you about. That cast a gloom over the whole trip.'

After attending a week-long relationship course in Spain and before leaving for Cuba, Michael had decided that he had fallen in love with Miranda, another participant on the course. He had taken things at a very fast pace indeed. He had sent her an email, told her that he found her very attractive, invited her to come to stay, to be his guest at his younger daughter's forthcoming wedding.

Miranda, once back in her native Ireland, had initially responded very warmly, but had then got cold feet and decided to tell Michael that they had no future together – or something of that sort. And that had ruined his holiday in Cuba, made him totally miserable, apparently.

According to my reckoning, Michael and this Irish lady had known each other for only a week and even then, just as fellow participants on a course.

'So,' he mused as he sipped his wine 'I am still wondering whether to write a long reply to Miranda, or just to draw a proverbial veil over her and move on.'

I could understand his dilemma. I mentioned that I was attracted to a fellow student whom I had met again recently and with whom I thought I got on very well. But that his wife had recently abandoned him for the electrician and had moved out of the home they were renovating, declaring that she no longer loved him. This had left him emotionally battered and bruised and I thought that he needed time to heal before considering any new relationship.

After we had enjoyed a light lunch, we sat on a bench outside the Maltings and chatted, looking out at the purple reeds until the air began to grow chilly. Michael was easy to talk to and I learn quite a bit more about him.

I told him I had changed the heading on my profile on the 'Likewise' site. Although most of my travels abroad had been either alone or sharing a room with friends Jaki or Rosemary, there were many places that I would like to visit – southern India, for example, or the Silk Road – where I thought that having a man along would be helpful for personal security as well as company.

Michael and I met a couple more times, once in Cambridge where he introduced me to Leonie, his elder daughter and a violinist; and Michael and I met again at his house just outside Frinton. Here I met Gemma, who had recently married and lived only on the other side of the village green across from his house.

Michael had recently moved from Herefordshire to be closer to his daughters. I wondered whether they enjoyed having their father nearer than he previously had been - and in particular, how newly-married Gemma felt about him being able to look across the green and see who was visiting, and at what times of day her curtains were drawn. Both daughters, I suspected, might be summing me up as a potential carer, for when or if their father became ill or incapable.

I wondered whose idea it had been for me to meet each of them.

Michael's main interest was music. I knew from what he had already told me that before retirement, he had been a church organist and choir master. As a young man, he read music at Oxford.

Michael knew from my online profile that I was interested in creative writing. Quite quickly, he mentioned a book he had written, which were his memoirs as a choir master but he regretted that he had not sold many copies so far. I ordered a copy from the local distributer; it seemed a supportive thing to do. I tried to engross myself in the book.

The blurb on the back cover sounded exciting enough, but much later, when I set aside time to read his account, I failed to become sufficiently interested and chose to watch television instead. The author, I thought, spent too much time complaining about how poorly he was treated by the choir-school authorities and how little he was paid. Nevertheless, he and I did seem to share some interests, including foreign travel.

When we met in Cambridge, he suggested that we went to Evensong at Kings College Chapel before enjoying a local orchestral concert although, he told me, 'I have totally lost what Christian faith I ever had. But I enjoy singing. And I would like to return to South Africa sometime soon, where I went a few years previously as a music examiner. If I returned there, I would hire a car if I could find a fellow driver, and explore the wine-growing area and the South African coastline.' I was quickly aware of what he was thinking.

Apart from his inability to reverse his vehicle competently, as he demonstrated as he tried to park outside the concert hall where Leonie was playing in the orchestra, a shared trip by road through South Africa sounded interesting, especially with someone who knew the area.

'But first,' Michael said, 'we would need to know if we could compatibly spend several weeks together.'

So he had, we both had, an idea.

If we were to rent somewhere on a self-catering basis for between five and seven days, then by the end of that time, we would know whether a longer holiday together were feasible.

We discussed, as much as was possible at that stage, the ground rules. I stipulated that 'anywhere we rent must have two separate bedrooms, a reasonably equipped kitchen, a bathroom with a shower, if possible; somewhere comfortable to sit, and parking fairly near the property - and we should share all the costs. I am not concerned one way or another about having a television.' Michael seemed quite content with this.

He sent me details of two possible properties, one in Rye and another somewhere in Gloucestershire. We agreed that, wherever we chose, it should have no previous connotations, no earlier emotional connections. It should also be in an interesting area with places that we could visit together during the day and discuss afterwards. From our frank conversations on line and during our time in Snape, I thought he understood that any suggestion of sex between us was completely out of the question. We might have corresponded quite a bit and got to know each other that way but we had, in person, only recently met.

In conversation, Michael had also introduced me to Cortijo Romero[xvi], a centre in southern Spain near Orgiva that ran week-long courses and where he had met Miranda. He had got to hear about Cortijo Romero through another female singer acquaintance of his.

Of the two places in Britain that Michael suggested where we might spend a few days together, I preferred Rye. Both properties were about the same price but, judging from the map, Rye seemed easier for each of us to get to - and I suspected that Gloucestershire might not be completely unknown to Michael. Over the phone, I stated my reasoning to Michael. He seemed to be in agreement, although he asked me what there was to do in the area surrounding Rye.

I wondered whether he thought I was more able to Google than he was, or whether he assumed I already knew - which to some extent, I did, from my association with Kent. I suggested a list of foodstuff and cleaning materials that we might need to bring between us and asked him what meals he would like to suggest and provide for.

I left it to Michael to make the arrangements with the owner of the property; to discuss dates, keys, access arrangements and any restrictions. Neither of us smoked and I was not planning on bringing the dog, although I knew I would miss him.

After much deliberation about who should drive whose car, I said that as I would be coming from Norfolk with my luggage and basic provisions in the boot, it would make more sense for me to pick him up on the way rather than transferring items from one car to another.

I also knew that my little Fiesta used less petrol than Michael's car and would therefore be more economical since we agreed to share the petrol costs. I could hear that that appealed to Michael. I also suspected that I was probably a better driver than he was, although I had no wish to put that to the test.

The house in Rye was old, mainly oak-framed and when the owner showed us his section of the building as well as around the part that we would occupy, I was interested in its architectural history. Michael wasn't very enthusiastic, not even about the ancient wall painting and crest that had been uncovered in the owner's living room.

Upstairs, Michael said he would leave me to choose which bedroom I preferred. Both rooms had a double bed but I went for the one at the top of the open staircase, leaving Michael the one at the far end of the narrow landing and beside the upstairs bathroom. I suspected he might need to get up during the night and I did not want to be disturbed by any flushing.

We made a meal. I provided the main course and Michael constructed the dessert. After we shared a bottle of wine and sat in the comfy armchairs, he took off his socks, saying 'My feet hurt'. He placed both feet on the coffee table and asked 'Do you think there's anything wrong with them?' They looked quite red but I had no wish to handle his feet so I suggested that we had a quick game of Scrabble.

Having beaten him twice, we decided that, after the drive from Norfolk and over the Dartford crossing, an early night might be wise so that we could explore the town and the castle in the morning. I left the landing light on, because it was dark there and I told Michael 'I will also leave my door slightly ajar so that any creaking, should I need the loo in the night, won't wake you.'

He thanked me for my thoughtfulness and suggested, equally kindly, that he would close his door so that I would not be disturbed by his snoring. I thought that this already indicated a measure of care and trust between us, it seemed to bode well.

As an afterthought, as he was closing his bedroom door, he asked me if I would like him to wake me in the morning. Thinking 'cup of tea', which was something that my previous travel companions Rosemary and Robert both liked to have, I thanked him and added 'milk but no sugar, please'.

Daylight is filtering through the drawn curtains as I hear Michael padding along the carpeted landing to the bathroom.

A flush and then some more padding. As I open my eyes, I see him standing in his striped nightshirt by my bed and I wish him 'Good morning'.

I am just about to ask whether he has slept well when he moves my duvet aside and clambers in beside me.

I say 'No' quite sharply but he takes no notice. He moves his hands around my waist and starts to ruffle up the hem of my warm nightdress. I shove him in the ribs with my elbow but he complains 'Your nightie isn't very glamorous; it's more like a dress. Take it off and we can get to know each other better'.

I decide that this is no time to justify why, for a stay in a cold draughty unknown house, I have selected the sort of nightwear that a respectable granny might wear.

Instead, I look at his unbuttoned nightshirt and the bit, surrounded by grey whiskers, that is poking hopefully out of it.

'And you can put that away,' I say crossly, 'I've thrown better looking things out of my fridge!'

He looks crestfallen. And I ask him 'What do you think you are doing, especially as you say that you are still in love with Miranda.'

'I don't see that my feeling for Miranda is in the slightest bit relevant, as she isn't here,' he responds.

We carry on this rather pointless conversation until I suggest that he should go downstairs, put on a dressing gown or something, and switch the kettle on.

He does so and by the time I reach the kitchen, he appears to be back to normal. His previous day's socks are still draped over the sofa.

We spend the afternoon looking around Bodiam Castle. Michael is quiet, a little withdrawn, almost sulky. I note that he makes no apology, instead I feel that I have spoilt his weekend. As we clear up our stuff and load our possessions back into my car for the drive home, we do not talk as much as we did on our way down to Rye.

Back in Frinton, he unloads his luggage and says goodbye with a few pleasantries. Back in Wymondham, I realise that Michael has left his rather grubby trainers in the footwell of my rear seats. I email him, tell him that I have them and ask him if he would like to come and collect them; or meet me somewhere and I could hand them over.

Michael replies:

> 'Hi Lorna,
>
> Many thanks for your comprehensive reply. I am sorry not to have replied earlier, but I have been much occupied by arranging a series of holidays with new friend Barbara - yes, already!
>
> We were at Snape Maltings on Saturday and Monday evenings last weekend, and at Blythburgh church on the Sunday afternoon, listening to three very different but very engaging concerts in the Aldeburgh Festival.
>
> Next week we are spending a few days in Herefordshire to see some of my own haunts. Next month we are both

retracing my own steps in the Isles of Scilly, renting the house where I have stayed for the last three years. And, becoming ever more adventurous, we are doing a conducted tour in Morocco in October!

So, I'm sure you are right that you and I don't need to meet again, but I do thank you most warmly for your friendship, both as a 'date' and as an 'agony aunt', over a good many months. I see our first actual meeting was last September. Here's wishing you well, and hoping things work out as well for you as they seem to be doing for me.

Michael x'

I take Michael's trainers to the local charity shop; they seem pleased to accept them. I have no wish to have them any longer in my car.

Chapter 32

Verdi in the Wet

The next time I saw Robert was at a formal event at the University in Canterbury. 'What are you planning to wear?' he asked me, a week beforehand, over the phone.

'I have no idea,' I told him 'Probably anything that still fits.'

'And what are you wearing now?'

'My jeans, a stripey top and as I hope to work in the garden this morning, my red zip-up fleece. Why do you ask? I can hardly wear jeans to a formal dinner.'

'And what are you wearing underneath all that?'

'Right now, it's a bra and a pair of navy travel pants in a soft material that is easy to wash and quick drying. Why?'

'Why don't you wear a dress more often, it's far more feminine.'

'Because I'm going to be in the garden today and the circulation on my legs is so poor that I need jeans to protect them. I've had quite enough wounds and leg ulcers over the years. I'll probably wear a dress to Canterbury, though.'

'And how's the novel writing going?'

'Slowly. I think I need some professional help with it, it's turning out to be something else.

I had told Robert that I had recently stayed in Rye for a few days with someone I knew, but I did not tell him any more than that.

Oh dear, I thought as I put down the phone. Does Robert still have old-fashioned ideas about women, their limited organisational abilities such as those he mentioned in Morocco, and what they should do – and wear? I appreciate his interest, his caring attitude and gentlemanly good manners but will he expect me, when we next meet, to be embroidering a sampler or playing Couperin's barricades mystérieuses on the harpsichord?

Two particularly important things happened to me during that weekend in Canterbury. I was in St Martin's Priory to meet a current student at the University and also Dr John Moss, who was Head of Faculty of Education. In general conversation with Dr Moss while we were both waiting for the female student to arrive, he asked me where I had travelled from that day. I told him 'I drove down from Norfolk yesterday so I stayed overnight in the city.'

He asked me whereabouts I lived in Norfolk and I told him, explaining that Wymondham was an ancient market town only nine miles from Norwich. He nodded, then asked 'And how do you spend most of your time now, when you are not driving to Kent? I assume you have retired?'

'Apart from running a home and a large garden, I'm struggling to write a novel or something very similar. As I was walking up to the Priory, I wondered, does Canterbury Christ Church University offer a Masters course in creative writing? Because I think I need some help.'

'Yes, we do,' he replied. 'But my daughter has just finished a degree, although not in creative writing, at the University of East Anglia; and she said she thoroughly enjoyed her time there.'

He paused and then 'But why would you come all the way to Canterbury for a Masters course in creative writing, when you have U.E.A. on your doorstep? U.E.A. is known world-wide for its creative writing so, despite any loyalty factor that you might feel towards Christ Church, why not apply to UEA, if that's what you want to do?'

It was so obvious that once Dr Moss had suggested it, I could not imagine why applying to UEA had not occurred to me. But it hadn't, perhaps because it was too obvious and almost too local. Thanks partly to that conversation with Dr Moss, I did apply to UEA, managed to find two referees who knew me and my abilities sufficiently well. I was interviewed and accepted on a part-time two-year Masters course, starting the following September 2016.

During that weekend in Canterbury, I mentioned to several other music-loving colleagues that Danny had been very interested in opera.

'Danny and I had both been to the Royal Opera House in Covent Garden to see various productions,' I said 'but what I would most like to do would be to see an opera in a totally different setting, rather than on the stage in a theatre. I did see La Traviata once in the Albert Hall but I was feeling miserable at the time; I had only just realised that there was something seriously amiss with Danny and that rather spoiled the occasion. I heard the music but there wasn't much going on to see and there was no atmosphere to speak of.'

Robert was party to that conversation and he mentioned that he had been more than once to Verona specifically to see the opera. It may have been later that weekend that he suggested that if he were in Italy at the time, he could meet me and take me to an opera in the Verona Arena.

'Only you would need to pack a l.b.d.'

I had to ask what an LBD was.

'Little black dress,' he explained, amazed at my ignorance, 'I thought every woman knew that.'

'Well, this one didn't but she does now. But I don't have a black dress, whatever the size; I never wear black. It drains all the colour from my face and makes me look as if I've died. But if you really mean what you say, I would love to do that. I have been to the Roman Arena twice before; the first time was with Danny when we spent one Christmas at a hotel in Bardelino on the shores of Lake Garda. We decided to have a break from festive pasta and one day caught a bus to escape to Verona for a few hours. I remember going inside the amphitheatre to where the animals would have been held, and I walked up to the top row of stone seats, just to look at the view, both inside the Arena and outside across the city.'

I paused to see whether Robert was still listening or waiting to withdraw his suggestion. 'And I came again, not so many years ago, when I was taking Phoebe and Mollie, two of my granddaughters, on a 'Northern Cities of Italy' tour, when we stayed in Lake Garda and visited Verona, among all the other cities. Since they would both have still been at school, I suspect that would have been either at Easter or during the summer holiday period. Summer, I think, because I bought us all an ice-cream in the centre of San Gimignano, although it was raining at the time and Phoebe hadn't read any E.M. Forster until much later.

In fact, Robert, didn't you phone me on my mobile when I was at the Lake Garda hotel? Just to say hello, because you were in Italy, staying at your Italian house at the time? And you asked how my trip with the two girls was going.'

Robert frowned, he looked as if he were trying to remember.

'So yes, I liked Verona as a city and I would really like to see an opera being staged there in the Arena. Aida especially. I hope to go to Egypt one day.'

Far cheaper and probably better than booking myself onto a prearranged tour, Robert suggested that I should fly to Venice; he would meet me there and the next day we would travel together by train to Verona.

'Then in Verona, we can go to the Information Centre - I know just where that is - see if we can get tickets for Aida and the older staged version; ask them to find us a hotel and we can view the opera from whatever seats we can afford, that are available. Does that sound OK?'

Thank goodness, I thought, for someone who can plan and sort things out where travel is concerned. With certain arrangements agreed in advance and others in outline only, I caught the train from Wymondham to Stansted Airport.

As I was changing trains in Cambridge, Robert phoned me on my mobile.

'When the plane lands at Marco Polo airport, that's in Venice, could you try to get off the plane and get through security as quickly as possible?' he asked. 'Because the transfer bus from the airport to Venice city goes only every so often and you won't want to miss the last transfer of the night.'

I had only an orange carry-on luggage bag that I had borrowed from Lallo because it was lighter than my more solid cabin bag. Robert had booked a hotel in Venice, for which I had agreed to pay because this trip was for my benefit. He met me as I got off the bus and trundled my carry-on bag across Venice, trying to find a way across the canals and through the streets to get to our hotel which, he thought, was on the other side of the main canal, opposite a church with a dome.

We had to ask the way more than once to the hotel but the people we asked were very helpful.

'That's why I like living in Italy,' Robert told me as we followed the way that the man had pointed and found the bridges that he had advised us to cross, 'I find people are far more friendly than the French I've met, who always appear rather annoyed at being asked anything.'

It was a very pleasant hotel, looking onto one of the smaller canals and we ate breakfast in a small courtyard at the side of the hotel, with the sunny inside wall of the courtyard covered by purple Morning Glory. Once we had finished and checked out, Robert led the way to the gondola station.

We took a gondola across a wide canal and from there, walked across the Rialto bridge to a café directly onto the water front, where we stopped, had a coffee and a tooth-challenging biscuit flavoured with amoretto.

Robert led me from there to St Mark's Square which I remembered from when Phoebe and Mollie had refused to leave their rucksacks somewhere, in order to enter the basilica.

After Robert had pointed out the carved lion on the pinnacle of St Mark's Cathedral as symbolising Mark the Evangelist, we stood and admired the chiming clock above the archway and he described the bell tower as being almost a hundred metres high and which, on a less focused occasion, I might have wanted to climb.

From there we made our way to the train station and caught a train to Verona.

I had used a ticket machine only once before to buy a train ticket abroad but Robert knew exactly what to do, how to select the correct train and its time, and where to insert the required amount of money.

After all the times I had spent shepherding my grandchildren through stations and airports with their luggage, it made a very pleasant change to have someone else take charge, especially someone who clearly knew what he was doing and upon whom I felt I could rely.

We walked from Verona's train station, passed an arch that I remembered having seen with Danny and up a long dual carriageway street towards and under another arch across the road.

I recognised the main square or piazza. Robert, still trundling my suitcase, led me toward what I assumed to be part of the ancient city wall, then stopped for a moment and gesticulated with his head. 'It's just over there, the Information Bureau. Which would you like to do first, check what's on tonight and see if we can get tickets, or find a hotel room?'

We went in, saw that Aida was the performance for the next few evenings and asked whether there were any tickets available. The person behind the desk showed Robert various plans and maps while I stood guard over my case.

Robert turned to me, 'It's the older version of Aida tomorrow night and we can have a couple of places in the seats five or six rows up, almost directly opposite the stage. They're quite hard so we might need to hire a cushion. Are you OK with that, because there isn't much choice left?'

I grinned. 'Excellent,' I replied. 'And is there a budget hotel near the Arena that has any spare rooms?'

Robert turned back to the woman behind the Bureau desk, who made a phone call, wrote something down on a piece of paper and gave it to him.

We walked back down the way we had come. Almost halfway down the Corsa Porta Nuova was a small hotel or Albergo on a corner of a side street; we had already walked past it on our way from the station. The entry door was right on the corner of the building. Robert held the door open for me and we went in.

The lady behind the desk spoke little English but she was obviously expecting us and said that her daughter who, she told us, spoke excellent English, would be there very soon. We were shown past the lift and up the stairs to Room 7. It was not a very big room but it was large enough with en-suite facilities and a small wardrobe in which I hung my equivalent of the l.b.d., a dark green calf-length dress with short lacy sleeves.

Having unpacked as much as was necessary, we came down the stairs. The hotel manageress offered us both a cup of coffee and introduced us to her daughter Francesca, explaining that we would 'take our breakfasts' at the same tables at which we were sitting. Then we went out for Robert to show me around the city.

He obviously knew Verona quite well. He led me to the outside of the Castelvecchio that overlooked the river but we decided not to go in; I thought that I might do so on another occasion but it seemed a waste of my time with Robert if he had already been there.

We walked along on the far side of the river until we came to a bridge, the Ponte Pietra, that I vaguely recognised from my time here twenty years before with Danny.

Robert told me as we walked on to it, 'This is Roman, it's made up of several arches with the base of each arch standing in the river. It's the oldest stone bridge in Verona and at one time it formed part of the main road from Genoa to Aquileia. Aquileia was founded by the Romans as a colony and a fortress, to defend the faithful people who were Roman allies, from hostile tribes such as the Istri. This region, which we now called the Veneto, was linked to the Roman world by two main roads and the Via Postumia, where you are standing, was one of them. During the Second World War, four of the arches were blown up by German troops as they were retreating but it's been rebuilt since then, with original stone materials.'

'How did the Romans manage to start to build the feet for the arches, if they were always standing in the river?'

'I really don't know, perhaps they waited until the end of the summer when the river would have been at its lowest – or devised some sort of shutter system to block off those parts of the river where they planned to erect the arches.'

He also took me to the Roman theatre on the other side of the river with a slight hill behind. There was some scaffolding in place and a couple of workmen while we were there.

'It's still used as a theatre so perhaps they are getting ready for another production,' Robert suggested. 'It's quite different from the arena of the amphitheatre with quite different proportions. If you stand where the stage would have been and say something dramatic to me, I will move about and wave to show I can hear you.'

I stood where Robert suggested and started quite quietly to recite 'Odi et Amo', a poem by Catullus that I had learnt at school.

'I could hear you speaking perfectly well,' Robert called to me from where he was standing between the seats, 'but I couldn't understand what you were saying.'

'I'm not surprised, it was in Latin.'

'Oh. I assumed you would branch into something from Shakespeare. Would you like to try that again with something I might recognise?'

I shook my head; other visitors were beginning to enter the theatre area and I had no wish to command an audience.

'Since it's quite a warm day, what about a glass of wine at a nearby bar or cafe? One of the nice things about having a drink in Italy is that they always bring you some nibbles to go with it. Crisps, nuts, olives or even carrot sticks and celery,' Robert said.

I thought this sounded a good idea so we left the theatre and set off again to walk along a pavement on the far side of the river.

I rejected Robert's invitation to see Juliet's balcony. Phoebe, Millie and I had seen it before and been unimpressed with it then, although Phoebe had been fascinated by the padlocks that other visitors had left, attached to various messages or photographs of their loved ones.

After visiting the Piazza delle Erbe market place which I had also visited twice before, at the end of the afternoon we returned to the Albergo Trento to shower and change, then to find a restaurant where we could have dinner.

Half-way up a side street from the piazza, Robert found a small restaurant with two or three tables standing on part of the road that had been partitioned off and incorporated into the pavement. I ordered a tuna salad, Robert had something similar that included prawns and he asked for a bottle of red wine.

The wine proved to be excellent, so Robert asked to see the label. I do not drink wine on a regular basis but even I was impressed by its smoothness. We did not finish the whole bottle between us so we asked the restaurant to cork it in some way and we carried it back to the room with us.

Walking through the ancient streets of Verona the following morning, Robert pointed out the statue I was looking up at, asked me if I knew who that was and when I shook my head, said 'It's Dante Alighieri, I thought you would already know that.'

I stuck my tongue out at him and asked 'Why do we get on so well?'

Robert paused to consider. 'Trust,' he said. 'I think it all comes down to trust.'

'And honesty?' I suggested.

'That too,' he agreed 'and a little mutual banter. It helps too that we have many of our interests in common and neither of us is totally stupid.'

'I think that's the nearest you've come recently to paying me a compliment,' I responded. 'My mother would have called that either 'back-handed' or 'being damned with faint praise'.

That evening, we changed into our clothes for the Arena and ate early in the street restaurant in the Piazza Bra before the performance, explaining to our waitress that we need to be served quite quickly with our main course, as we would be going to the opera.

'No problem, because I also sing tonight in the chorus at the opera,' she told us, smoothing her apron with pride and anticipation, before dodging back into the restaurant kitchen.

It had not occurred to either Robert or me that local residents would be asked to participate and contribute to the performance. Judging from what the waitress had said, I suggested to him that it might make a very pleasant change from serving at tables those diners who considered themselves to be privileged and culturally superior.

We took the remaining part of the previous night's wine with us to drink during the performance. When we collected and paid for our cushions, we were each handed a small 'birthday cake' candle in a card holder.

Climbing the steps to reach our entry gate onto the Arena, I asked 'What's that for?' referring to the candle.

'Wait and see,' Robert replied, as an attendant was searching our bags.

The attendant challenged him about the half-bottle of wine. 'You may not take glass into Arena,' he said slightly aggressively. Robert explained that it was a warm evening and we would need something to drink during the performance.

'You can buy drink inside Arena,' was the response. 'You must leave bottle with the attendant at the entry gate. You can collect bottle after the performance is finished and when you leave.'

We located our seats and with nothing to lean back on except the legs of the person behind, made ourselves as comfortable as possible. The weather was hot and there was no breeze. 'What's with the candle?' I asked. 'It won't give us very much heat and I'm warm enough already.'

'In a little while, when everyone has sat down, we light our candles. Then we can see them all flickering around the arena. It's pretty and it's probably also a way of getting everyone to be quiet and stop talking, ready for the music to start.'

Since neither Robert nor I carried matches, feeling rather presumptuous, I asked the chap behind me if he had a light.

He lit my candle for me, then I lit Robert's from mine. Within a minute or two, the orchestra tuned up, there was clapping and the strings began to play the overture to Aida.

Actors began to filter on to the stage area from either side and take up positions across the stone stage. I could feel my spine tingling. I shivered with excitement.

There was a slight drop in temperature and a sudden breeze.

I looked across the arena, at the tiny lights from any candles still flickering. And at the lost sunset, at the sky. The sky had turned navy-blue behind and above the stage, a broad indigo blanket of cloud rather than an isolated bruise.

Another sudden breeze. The first drop. Then the second. And the third. The rain began gently at first, then within ten seconds grew heavier.

As some of the spectators rose to their feet, there was an announcement over the tannoy. The performance would be stopped, it was impossible for the string instruments to play in the rain and too dangerous for the actors to move and dance on the slippery stone. The stage was too wet. And even if the rain stopped soon, the performance would not restart.

It did not stop. There was a rush for people to get to the stairs, to get out of the rain. Cushions were being flung back at the attendant, people pushing and jostling. Robert asked the cushions attendant for our half-bottle of wine but the attendant shook his head, he did not know anything about a bottle of wine, had we come in by a different entrance?

We had not, but our delicious wine was gone. As was the money we had spent on our tickets.

Once outside the Arena, there was little point in running or even trotting, we were already very wet. No point in avoiding the puddles on the cobbles that had become wet furrows and were now becoming streams.

Across the piazza, past the restaurant upturned tables, across the road under the arch, paddling and splashing down the pavement of the Corso Porta Nuova until we reached the closed door of the Albergo Trento.

The owner's husband must have seen us approaching. He opened the door and we stood drenched and dripping at the reception desk, our saturated clothes clinging to our bodies. He made some obvious remark about the weather, handed us a key and before we had even started to squelch in our shoes up the stairs, had poured us two cups of coffee and set them down on the one of the circular breakfast tables.

I do not remember whether I returned the next day to the airport in Venice, or whether I travelled with Robert back to his home in Pescasseroli and flew home from Pescara.

What I remember most about that visit to Verona was the trust and warmth that was established between Robert and me, how he had not once complained about being soaked through, almost to the skin, by doing something that I wanted to do and that he had gone to some trouble to arrange.

I decided during that occasion that the very best way to get to know anyone really well, to appreciate their strengths and their weaknesses, was to travel with them, preferably somewhere abroad and out of one's comfort zone.

Chapter 33

Room with a View

I was walking with Butterworth along a muddy track and close to the railway line when, just as a train was applying its brakes and whistling before entering Wymondham Station, I heard my mobile phone ring.

Above all that noise, it was neither possible to answer nor hear who was calling me but I pressed 1471 to find out who it had been. That missed call had been from Robert, on his mobile. As soon as I reached home, I phoned him from my landline.

'My mother has just died,' he told me.

'I'm so sorry to hear that. Losing a mother is very special, and often can be extra difficult to deal with,' I commiserated. 'One's mother has always been there in one's life; so, your life will probably be quite different from now on.'

I realised I was almost repeating what had been said to me when my mother had died. And how it was true, life was and would be different for Robert now, in so many ways.

I knew, because he had told me previously, that he had moved temporarily into a room in his mother's house to look after some of her needs, as she was well into her nineties.

While he had been out of the family home, his elderly mother had slipped on the plastic wrapping around a weekend newspaper colour supplement; she had fallen, possibly lost consciousness for a short time, but definitely lost the ability to stand, walk, clean or dress herself.

After a short period of time in hospital, the hospital had released her into a Care Home which she apparently hated. She wanted to return to her own house but her inability to look after herself made this impossible. I had talked to Robert as to whether he could look after her himself, but he said 'There are some things that she needs that it would be quite inappropriate for me, as her son, to do.'

'Can you get people to come in to look after her, so that she can return to her own home?'

'They would need to live in, which would probably cost more than the Care Home – and we might still need two separate people, so that whoever had been on duty could get some sleep. And there are no spare rooms. I am using one as my bedroom and Mother has the other bedroom.'

I decided that I had put forward sufficient suggestions, it was nothing to do with me. I asked whether Robert's sister-in-law might help but his reply was 'Mother doesn't like her very much; I don't think they get on. And she and my brother live thirty-five miles away from Mother's house.'

I had never met Robert's mother but I did not like to think of an elderly lady, especially the mother of a friend of mine, having to live among people she had not chosen and with whom she probably had little in common, especially when she still had her own home.

After several months in the Care Home, Robert's widowed mother had, to quote the report in the local newspaper, 'passed away peacefully'.

I felt very honoured that Robert had phoned me to tell me his mother had died. I sent him a condolence card with the David Harkins poem[xvii] rather than any other words. I thought that the poem, which I had read at Danny's funeral, was positive in its view of the departed person and of the future.

Robert phoned me to thank me and to tell me that one of his grandchildren would read the poem at their grandmother's funeral. We kept in touch a little more regularly after that.

Some months later, when I had finished the creative writing course and handed in my dissertation at U.E.A, I told Robert. I even emailed a copy to him, almost as proof to myself that I had done it.

'Good,' he responded by phone, 'I knew you would.'

I glowed at his confidence in me.

Once again, I had very kindly been invited to participate in an event at Canterbury University. On this occasion, it may have been to a formal dinner or perhaps an annual reunion of my year group.

Driving down to Kent by car allowed me, after the main event, to travel on to where my brother Colin lived with his wife, and for me to see them both. I was very fond of Colin and I appreciated his kindness and his abilities, which were anything other than sporty.

Having lost her first child Howard as a new-born baby, Moo had treated Colin very gently and would wrap him up in metaphorical cotton wool whenever she could. TCP Grandma also regarded him as being very special, perhaps because he reminded her of my father, her only son.

My father, on the other hand, seemed almost disappointed that Colin was not physically particularly able and did not enjoy participating in sport of any kind. I got the impression that Dad also thought Colin was lazy, because 'he didn't work hard enough at his accountancy exams. He could have done much better,' Dad had remarked to no one in particular.

Dad was an extremely hard-working man who gave a huge amount of time and energy to his job, and it may be that he felt that the money he had spent on Colin's training hadn't been particularly well used or even wasted. Colin once told me, when we were much older and long after Dad had died, that he did not think that our father liked him very much.

'That was probably a misunderstanding on both sides,' I told Colin. 'But I know he was very proud of you and he enjoyed your involvement in the theatre and amateur operatic productions.'

Colin did not appear very sure of this. I loved my brother because he was kind, thoughtful, caring, never vindictive or keen to make mischief, like Val. He would tease me but only kindly and he treated me with respect, even when he thought I was being over-optimistic.

He had once been very upset because he had accidentally shut the index finger of my left hand in the door of the car while I had been standing between his legs as he was sitting in the front passenger seat of our Austin 16, holding onto my knees and allowing me to look out of the sunroof of the car. I was about five or six at the time. I lost the nail of that finger as a result and it never grew back again properly.

When I told him that in my first teaching job, I had agreed to take the recorder class, Colin's ironic response was 'Well, if you're the recorder teacher, then I must be the football coach,' which very slightly hurt my pride as well as making me laugh.

But there was a great deal of truth in what Colin had said; he was far better at music that I could ever be, while I was better on the sports field and I probably worked harder. What we had in common was our enjoyment of words, standard English grammar, an appreciation of standard U.K. spelling and a similar sense of humour.

For this forthcoming occasion, I had been in contact with Robert, who would be travelling to Canterbury by train, 'by the cheapest possible route,' as he had told me. I had offered to book a room for us both, partly because it would almost halve the cost of a hotel stay. Although I might have preferred a room in the Canterbury Premier Inn, because I could park very close by and it was marginally nearer to the University venue, Robert favoured a different hotel.

His choice was the Cathedral Gate Hotel. It had once been a café where, when Anthony and I were students and going out together, at the weekend we would often ask for hot buttered toast with anchovy paste.

'I like seeing either the Cathedral or the Buttermarket cross from the window,' Robert told me, by way of justification. So, I had booked a double room with en-suite in Robert's chosen hotel that stood right beside the main gates into the cathedral.

The proprietor checked my booking and led me, with my holdall, across a few stairs, along a short corridor, through a door, across a walkway over the roof that overlooked the Cathedral Precincts and into one of three rooms close to each other. 'The other person arrived some time ago,' she assured me, 'I think he is in the room now.'

When we knew we would both be coming to Canterbury that weekend, I had offered to pay for the room in return for Robert taking me from Venice to Verona. After Robert had told me 'One of the places I would like to go to, when I can afford it, is Malta,' I offered to treat him to a joint visit to Malta as a way of celebrating my being accepted by UEA and of thanking him for his continued support for my writing.

I had requested and brought with me brochures from two different travel companies and I told Robert I would be bringing them. Lallo had even lent me the book about Malta that she had bought only a few years before, during her honeymoon there.

As I walked into the hotel room, Robert was sitting in an arm chair, reading. He looked up but did not rise to his feet nor say anything other than rather tired 'Hello,' followed by 'I wondered when you would arrive. I've unpacked already.'

I was wearing a linen dress in several pastel colours, not to please Robert particularly or because, to use his words, 'it's more feminine' but because I knew it would be a hot day, especially if I were travelling the 150 miles to Kent by car and without a break.

Robert made no comment on seeing me in a dress, he merely said 'If you want a shower before we go out, then you had better get a move on. I've already been in the bathroom.'

That evening we did whatever we had come to the city to do, we joined friends in a pub for a drink after dinner and returned to our room. Robert talked happily to our other friends but towards me, he was quiet and almost dismissive.

Robert woke me just after six o'clock the following morning. 'Come on,' he cajoled, 'we need to get on, we can't hang around here all day.'

After breakfast and feeling rather puzzled, I asked 'Would you like to look now at the information I have brought about Malta? Lallo has lent me her book about it, you might find some of the information interesting. Or do you need to catch an early train back to London?'

'No,' he replied.

'Is that 'no' to looking at the stuff about Malta, or 'no' to catching an early train?'

He did not answer. Instead, he folded the suit he had brought and packed it into his bag. At reception, I paid for the room on my debit card – Robert offered to give me half but I turned down his offer.

'You paid for everyone's gin yesterday evening', I reminded him. Then I asked, 'Would you like me to give you a lift to the station? It's quite a walk from here.'

He made no reply but at the foot of the hotel stairs, I said 'Come on, it will only take me a minute to fetch the car and you could be looking after my holdall while I walk to the car park.'

He seemed to agree, reluctantly. On the way to Canterbury West station, he told me he was planning to meet one of his step-daughters at Sturry railway station, only about three miles away at the most. 'Then I'll drive you there and drop you, before I head back to Norfolk,' I said.

I did just that. There were no farewells, just a curt 'goodbye' from Robert in Sturry as I turned the car round and headed for the main A2, the M25 and the Dartford Crossing.

On the return journey, I turned over in my mind what it might have been that had gone wrong. I asked Hilary, one of the friends with whom we had spent the evening, if she knew of anything I had said, or should not have said, that might have upset Robert.

She gave it some thought, then offered 'I saw Robert on the platform at Ashford Station as I was travelling down here. He must have recognised me but he looked as though he wanted to avoid me. In fact, he looked as if he didn't want to come to Canterbury at all this weekend.'

'So, it wasn't just me, then? That's a relief.'

I abandoned any idea of visiting Malta with Robert. It was a shame, I thought, because we would both have been interested in the history and in all the places that I would have liked to visit. But I also remembered Rosemary's words of caution, 'but men lie, of course.'

Instead, I spent the money I had saved for us both for Malta, on a Saga ten-day small-group visit to Uzbekistan.

Looking at the tiles and decoration in Samarkand, I imagined how much Robert might have enjoyed the tour, had he wanted to travel with me. Perhaps I would have to look for a different travel companion.

Only two other women in the group to Uzbekistan that I had joined were travelling as single people, they were both about my age. One was effervescent in character and behaviour, she enjoyed dancing and being in the centre of things. The other complained for much of the time 'I'm afraid of tripping or falling over,' or 'The steps are too high', or too steep, or too something else. I was walking through the streets with one walking pole to give me increased stability and I offered to lend the Complainer my other stick.

She turned my offer down, holding out her hand or arm instead for someone to take hold of and help her.

I did try to be friendly and I suspect she may have had a problem with her eyesight that she decided not to mention. I wondered that, when I first noticed that she had maroon eyebrows; or rather, I assumed she had used a maroon lip-liner instead of an eyebrow pencil to enhance her thinning eyebrows.

I guessed it was a mistake but maybe not, I considered her rather strange in other ways too. She may have become unsettled by viewing the memorial to the damage in Tashkent caused by the 1966 earthquake with a magnitude of 7.5 but she did seem very uncertain as to where, when and how to place her feet.

However, she did not appear particularly worried when our guide told us 'Tashkent and its immediate vicinity is prone to earthquakes. In the years since 1914, there have been more than 75 earthquakes in the area of magnitude between 3 and 6, and as a result of the earthquake in the Ferghana region that had lasted for about three minutes and the damage caused to houses, 13 people were killed.'

I am not sure that she joined the rest of the group on our night-time tour of Khiva. I really enjoyed that and felt personally quite safe, wandering about in the dark.

The fortress in Khiva and its basic architecture reminded me of the Sahara Auberge camp in Morocco, which then brought Robert to mind, as did the towering minarets, turquoise domes and tiled decoration in Bukhara. I imagined how much he might have enjoyed this visit, or even one with me to Malta.

However, I tried to tell myself, his apparent disinterest had not necessarily been all about me as a travel companion; he had had his reasons and I had to respect that, even when I was exploring in Samarkand and seeing the variety of tile decorations there, as well as the amazing array of shawls and tablecloths, gifts that he might have bought for his daughter and granddaughters, and watching bread being baked in a tandyr or tandoori oven until the crust became brown and crisp and delicious.

Then, when I saw the array of fur hats for sale in the streets, I thought of Danny and how he had bought that ridiculous furry hat with a star stuck on the front at the Ming Tombs in China, and how fortunate I was to be able to travel to such incredible places, even if I had no personal travel companion for this particular visit. Danny, I thought, would always be with me wherever I went, because I was carrying him in my mind and my thoughts. Robert too, sometimes. But Richard, only very rarely.

On my return from Uzbekistan, I reported on the trip to Rosemary, who had covered much more of the Silk Road a couple of years previously with the 'Ramblers Organisation'. Meeting in a café in Norwich, we discussed whether we would like to visit western Canada together in July the coming year. Rosemary volunteered to investigate the possibilities further.

I had also offered one day to take Phoebe to India and with her 21st birthday coming up, that year seemed to be the ideal time to introduce her to the parts of India with which I was more familiar. I did suggest we might go for two weeks during the Easter holidays as I knew the weather would probably be suitable at that time of year but Phoebe told me that with her finals approaching, she would need to be studying during Easter.

'But unless I am called to re-sit my final exams, I would be free any time from mid -July onward.'

'July in India will be too hot,' I advised her 'and very likely wet as well. It might be sensible to arrange only a very short time in Delhi and the Golden Triangle, and instead to head for the hills and mountains further north. How would that suit you?'

I contacted a company that was running an escorted small-group trip to Ladakh and Kashmir. I had been to Ladakh two or three years previously with a couple of female travel companions, Jaki and Hazel. We had stayed in Leh, the historic capital of the Himalayan Kingdom of Ladakh, sharing a twin room and having an additional single room, and in Kashmir with a one-week stay on a house boat on Dal Lake.

I thought the mixture of those two places, with a first day in the heat and humidity of Delhi, would give Phoebe an idea of the wide variety of situations and cultures in India.

I had checked the UEA annual timetable for the previous year, to try to ascertain when the 2019 Graduation Ceremony might take place. If I were correct in my estimation and I was conferred with Master of Arts in Biography and Creative

Non-Fiction, the Ceremony should occur in the week between my return from Canada to Heathrow on 11th July and Phoebe's and my departure from Heathrow to Delhi on 19th July. After all my hard work during the previous two years, I didn't want to miss the Graduation Ceremony.

Graduation was held on the Thursday after I returned from Canada with Rosemary and the day before leaving from Heathrow for India with Phoebe. I had asked for three tickets for the UEA Graduation Ceremony, one for Lallo, one for Phoebe and the third for - I wasn't sure whom but if it weren't needed, I could always return it.

Robert hinted and I invited him. I really wanted him to be there, he had been with me and very supportive from the very beginning, but I did not want him to feel under any obligation.

I responded 'If you really want to come, I would love to have you there. You have been such an encouragement, kept me on track. But Lallo will be using the spare bedroom upstairs so I can offer you only the smaller downstairs bedroom with its single bed and the shower room. But I will have to shoot off very quickly the following day because Phoebe and I are due at Terminal 3 at Heathrow to get through security and catch the 21.20 departure to Delhi.'

When I had heard that I had been granted my Masters, I had left a message on Robert's phone to tell him.

He rang me only a day or two later when I was out, greeting my answer machine with the words 'Good morning, Qualified Writer.' I kept Robert's greeting on the answerphone rather than deleting it.

I liked the sound of Robert's deep voice, it was another thing about him that I found very attractive. When I rang back and several times since, I had to tell him 'The postgrad. qualification is only the start; now I need to write something 'for real', something longer and meaningful, and without UEA's back-up. The prospect is slightly scary.'

Robert accepted my invitation for an overnight stay. I was pleased and flattered that Robert wanted to be there, he had hinted heavily about coming but then was concerned that I would be allocated only two tickets and he didn't, he said, want any other members of my family to forego their place in favour of him. I had, however, already requested three tickets in the hope that . . and he came, all the way from the West Country, with a stick and a patch over one eye, the result of his recent stroke.

He arrived by train and I met him at the station. He had had some health problems that he had told me about.

'I'm losing my sense of balance and my eyesight is limited. I often fall backwards and can't get up again, I don't have the strength any more in my arms to be able to push or pull myself up,' he said, without any self-pity. It was just the way things were.

The next twenty-four hours were all a bit rushed. I had to be at UEA by 09.00 the following day to pick up the three tickets. Lallo drove me there in her car, then returned to collect Robert from my house and pick up Phoebe from her home in a nearby village, then made her way back to UEA with her two passengers. I had asked her to show them both into the Hayden Morris Hall at the far end of the UEA Sportspark.

Robert was still walking with a stick and showed difficulty in maintaining his balance. 'Don't offer to take his arm or help him,' I advised Lallo 'because he's as independent as I am. Just be on hand and take your cue from him.'

I was very touched by Robert wanting, asking even, to be present at my graduation. I was aware that it was not physically easy for him to travel and the return fare to and from the South West was expensive. I admired his determination, he was not going to let his disabilities control him, nor to be defined by them. So, he came - because he wanted to and perhaps because he knew it was important to me too.

Once I had collected my robes, I made my way past a long line of waiting people, into the hall and along the allocated row of seats beside my fellow postgraduate students. After being handed my dummy certificate with its ribbon on stage – I had already received mine by post a month beforehand with the words 'with Distinction' printed on it - we assembled in a marquee outside the Sportspark for formal congratulations, drinks, nibbles and official photographs.

As there were many more graduands waiting to receive their certificates that afternoon, we needed to vacate UEA so after Lallo made a phone call to book a table at a sensible time, she drove us all to 'Bird in Hand' in Wreningham for lunch and a bottle of wine.

'But now, having got the official stuff out of the way,' I said as Robert and I finished our main course and looked at the dessert menu, 'I have to produce something far more than a dissertation. I need to produce something longer, a biography or a memoir, that says something that is important to me, something in which I genuinely believe. It will probably be based on past experiences and perhaps a bit of travel.'

Once he had caught his train back to the West Country, that was the last time I was to see Robert for many months. He phoned me to make sure that Phoebe and I had got out of Kashmir safely, because the Indian army had been moving into Kashmir as Phoebe and I flew home and that had been reported in the international media. And he also called again to say that he had moved out of his mother's house and it was up for sale, that his ex-wife was ferrying him around the county to help him find somewhere that he might wish to buy rather than rent, once his mother's house was sold and he had inherited a proportion of the selling price.

I had been correct about Delhi in July; it was hot and uncomfortably humid. Phoebe as a travel companion was delightful. She was friendly and caring towards the only other person on the tour apart from me; she was appreciative, looked very happy and interested in everything we saw and were being told. I had taken Phoebe to Sorrento when she was a few years younger and she had been an alert, keen and caring companion then.

While in Ladakh, we both bought a number of curiosities in Leh, visited several monasteries and had the basics of Buddhism explained by our guide.

From Leh, we were taken to the Nubra Valley, where we stayed in two separate camps, one under canvas with its own en-suite in a separate compartment at the back of the tent. This set-up had good plumbing and excellent drainage, while we stood either in the flip-flops provided or barefooted on the bed of smooth pebbles. The other accommodation was a more permanent structure surrounded by apricot trees and familiar flowers such as cosmos, chrysanthemums, roses and dahlias.

From Ladakh we moved on to the houseboat in Kashmir with its own manager who seemed to do the cooking in a nearby house on the lake shore. He was kind enough to get up at dawn one morning from where he slept (almost like a guard dog) on the houseboat's carpeted floor, so that he could paddle the shikara and take Phoebe and me to the floating market. Phoebe, slim and sitting in the shikara with her long dark hair not covered by any scarf and looking almost Indian herself, attracted a great deal of polite attention and some excellent bargains of plant seeds which we hoped would grow, back in Britain.

It was on this trip that we discussed religion with our guide. 'I do not understand,' he said 'why most beliefs in the world start with a God who tells people what to do, what he considers to be good and what is bad. Why do people not accept the world simply as it is, without needing to believe in an initial Creator, who then gives them instruction on their behaviour. Can people not work this out for themselves and treat each other properly?'

Mulling this over in my mind, I thought it made absolute sense to me and I wished Moo could have still been alive to have heard that.

It made me question many of the things that I, brought up as a 'Christian' child, had been told. I thought that the behaviours described in the Beatitudes were beneficial but I dismissed the concept of an all-seeing and all-knowing God with a personal interest in me, Old Testament teaching about heaven and hell, and certainly the idea of divine intervention.

As a child I had been offered very few choices. I had been told what to believe, how to behave, what subjects at school to study or not study, and what to wear. – and what would happen if I didn't. It was almost compulsive control, which it has also been while I was married to Richard.

While I still wanted to maintain and uphold what I considered to be basic virtues, I was now edging gently towards Humanism and the need to respect and protect the planet, and everything and everybody in it. And to understand that the concept of 'fair' and the childlike complaint of 'it's not fair' showed a lack of acceptance that there is nothing at all fair about the world and that most living creatures accept that. Life and death have nothing to do with whether it is fair or not fair, nor even 'sin' or being 'unworthy'. It is neither just nor ironic. It is just the way it is, it's how the world works. All we need to do is accept what we cannot change, and to change where and what we can, for the better.

Once I had been back from Ladakh for several months, I was starting to think again about travel and where to go next. After looking at what was available and during which months, I booked two holidays for 2020, one entitled 'Highlights of Lebanon' that was being run by the company with which Rosemary and I had previously travelled, and was scheduled to depart on 25th April 2020. I was interested in Lebanon, partly to be able afterwards to talk to Colin about where he had lived for two years and to help him to remember and relive some of his earlier experiences. I also wanted to visit the Roman remains, which Colin probably would not have seen while he was living and working for those two years in Beirut.

I also paid the deposit on a 14-day escorted tour of Crete which was due to start on 19 May the same year, not long after I should have returned from Lebanon. I wanted to visit Knossos and also enjoy the Greek food and relaxing in the sun. Both these trips had a bias toward history and each was described as a 'small group' tour. I hoped that on each of these tours I would not be the only single person.

On the other hand, I had been told by more than one person, that booking oneself onto a holiday described as being for single or solo travellers meant being in a group with only one or two men but a much larger number of competitive and probably predatory women, most of whose aims seemed to be, I was told, 'to latch on to any available heterosexual man, and as quickly as possible'.

This was not at all what I wanted to do and certainly not, at my age. I was too old for competition with anyone other than myself and I was not willing to compromise neither my current way of life nor my ideals.

I did want someone to talk to if I were on holiday that was somewhere different and interesting but if that were not achievable, then I preferred solitude. I had no close or single female friends living in the county but I was not willing to regard myself, nor to be viewed by others and especially not by my children, as 'a lonely old woman.'

I still had my independence and some pride and I was not prepared to be on the receiving end of anyone's pity. But I knew I was missing intelligent 'companionship' rather than simply 'company', and someone with whom I could successfully travel and perhaps share a room.

I wanted to do things while I could, because I knew, sooner or later, that there would come a time when I was no longer able to travel, or drive, or get about on my own – or even look after myself.

At the service of Thanksgiving at Barham Crematorium after Colin, aged 85, had died at the end of May 2020, the music for the Committal, which he had apparently chosen himself, was 'The Slow Train' by Flanders and Swann. For a brother who was a railway enthusiast, a lover of music and of the true meanings of words and with an accomplished bass-baritone singing voice, there could have been no more fitting farewell.

'They all pass out of our lives, on the slow train.'

From time to time, I look at Youtube, look at the wood-engraving picture that illustrates the recording of Flanders and Swann's 'Slow Train' as a way of remembering my brother - and I occasionally feel a tear. I suspect my relationship with my brother was the bedrock, the caring, sharing, companionship and familiarity in the true sense of the word, of what I have wanted since, in any close relationship with a man. As well as exciting, there can be something very comforting about travelling with close members of my family who care about me and I about them.

Chapter 34

Cornflakes without Milk

I had paid the deposit for two separate weeks at Cortijo Romero in southern Spain, as well as the seven-day visit to Lebanon and a similar week in Crete, to look at the historical remains. I planned to be out of the country and exploring for much of the summer 2020. But in the spring of that year, the media reported on a new virus that appeared to have started in China, spread to Italy and parts of Europe.

It was causing a continuous cough, high fever and severe breathing difficulties, leading in some cases to death. Anyone with these symptoms who also lost the sense of taste and smell was asked to 'stay home' and self-isolate. Schools were told to cancel trips abroad and by mid-March, the U.K. Foreign and Commonwealth Office was advising against all but essential travel to Spain. Coronavirus was declared a pandemic.

But somehow my membership of 'Likewise' had been automatically renewed. Before a lockdown had been declared and after I had logged on and viewed the men that 'Likewise' considered as 'My Matches', a chap called Larry got in touch with me. I was mildly interested because he had been a foreign reporter and correspondent during recent conflicts in the Middle East.

Since I had visited Oman, Egypt, Iran and Jordan, and was due to visit Lebanon later in the year, I thought he and I might have something in common and enjoy some interesting conversations.

According to what he had written on the Likewise website, he frequently travelled, which was one of my criteria and he was obviously also interested in the written and spoken word. In his online profile, he described himself as 'a nice guy seeking friendship' but also, against the 'Relationship Status' question, he had selected the 'it's complicated' option.

I was both intrigued and deterred by 'it's complicated', because I had deduced that that expression usually meant 'I'm with someone else who doesn't know I am on this website and who would wholeheartedly disapprove if she did.' But at least he was being honest, with me.

I was interested in his choice of meeting place. It made sense with my interpretation of 'it's complicated'. Meeting someone in a café in Waitrose could be defended as having been completely by chance especially, I assumed, if one shopped regularly at a branch of Waitrose.

I arrived there ahead of the agreed time, so that I might feel settled and comfortable by the time my 'date' Larry arrived, even if he were slightly late. He texted me again with 'I'm outside in the car park' which seemed to me rather pointless, as I didn't read the text until much later that evening. But he arrived, we saw each other and after exchanging names and Larry fetching a coffee for both of us, we settled down to talk.

Almost my first question was 'You wrote 'it's complicated' against your current situation. Would you like to tell me more about that or is it either private or painful? And you wrote that what you are looking for is friendship, with intelligent and thoughtful conversation. So?'

'The 'it's complicated' is because I am married to someone with whom I have no physical relationship - because she doesn't want one.'

'Does she, your wife, know that you have subscribed to the 'Likewise' site? And what you say you are hoping for?'

'She does. I've told her that we both deserve to be happy and to have meaningful relationships and she seems to understand that. We have children in common and living on the other side of the Atlantic, so we have every reason for living together under the same roof, and as harmoniously as possible.'

'And what can you tell me about yourself, your interests and hopes for the future? I apologise if I sound as if I am interviewing you, I suppose I am, really, but I can't think of another way of getting to know each other better.'

'I'm looking for a close friend, someone whom I can trust. I'm not looking for a sex only friendship.'

I noted Larry's application of the word 'only'. So he was, or is, expecting sex. I thought as much. However, the conversation was worth pursuing, I thought.

'And the friendship part? How do you see that developing?'

'That's more difficult. In theory, I have retired. Retired from being the war correspondent that I was for several international news companies. You asked about my hopes and plans for the future. What I would like to do, if I can get the funding, is rather what I was doing before – set off with basic equipment to absolutely anywhere in the world, to look for interesting stories that don't usually get day-to-day news coverage. So, I could never be guaranteed to be available for a visit to the theatre, or to travel anywhere with anyone, I don't want that sort of commitment because it would interfere with what I really enjoy doing. And what, although it may sound big-headed, I am very good at doing – as you can see if you google my name and details.'

Just then, one of the attendants from the café came across to the table at which we were sitting, carrying a small plate.

'Would you like one of these?' he asked, proffering a couple of bread rolls. 'We will be closing in about five minutes and I can't offer these for sale tomorrow, so are they any good to you. With our compliments?'

I declined but Larry took first one of the rolls, then the other.

'That will do very nicely on my way home or later for supper this evening,' he assured me, before jumping to his feet with 'but if they are just about to close, then I must have a quick look at one of the financial papers. Leanne, one of my daughters, is the financial correspondent, so I'd like to see if there's anything in today's copy. Leanne writes very well.'

He came back without the desired newspaper. 'Sold out. Never mind, I'll look again tomorrow.'

Larry and I met a couple more times before he was due to fly to the States to stay with one of his daughters, ready for the birth of another grandchild. Although my profile had mentioned that I was trying to write a novel, he asked nothing about me, my family, my interests, my writing or anything else.

On the third meeting at an earlier time in the evening than usual, I suggested that if he were really hungry, as he had appeared to be on previous occasions, he might follow me home, where I had some duck spring rolls that I was never likely to eat, that I could put in the oven and have ready in half an hour, since he had each time treated me to my coffee.

He took me up on this offer very readily. I was interested to ask him more about Lebanon before I went there, whether there is anything I should look out for or be aware of.

Over this light snack in my kitchen, he asked me in which Beirut hotel I will be staying. I was not sure but 'it will be in the travel itinerary' I said, 'I could look it up now, if you are that interested.'

'I expect it will be the Commodore Hotel,' Larry stated 'that's where all the war correspondents stayed when we covered the Lebanese Civil War conflict. If you do stay there, perhaps you could send me a photograph of the door to room 620, which was my room?'

'I'll do my best,' I responded.

Once we had polished off the duck spring rolls and a glass of wine, there was Larry's unspoken expectation of sex. I turned this down as politely and as tactfully as I could. Despite a little mental fiddling around at the edges, I was neither flattered nor interested. It felt intrusive. I did not wish to expose myself to him emotionally or in any other way. I was far more interested in finding an honest, close friend. My reticence towards the sex offered had, I decided, no left-over Christian ethics behind it. In theory, if sex between two consenting partners hurt no one and broke no rules, then, as Lallo had recently commented, why ever not? I had no declared loyalty to anyone else and if Larry was to be believed, neither had he.

But I didn't know him, the most we had shared was a coffee; we had done nothing else together and been nowhere together so what exactly would the sex be for, or achieving, or ratifying? Judging by his age, I guessed that he might have some erectile disfunction and if that were the case, it would probably be up to me to follow through on any initiative he might attempt to make. I felt that sex without love and caring was like cornflakes without the milk, or any sweetness. OK maybe, if one were desperate, but far from ideal and for me, now, almost pointless.

When we had discussed it recently, Lallo had offered me a different point of view which might be fine for her as a younger woman but not for me. I was not interested in sex toys or 'rabbits' or masturbation. I believed and I still do, that sex was about relationships and love, not about personal gratification or, heaven forbid, power.

I thought very briefly of Richard and his desire to use me as some sexual bargaining chip, a pawn, so that he could exchange me for something or someone he wanted for himself.

I now set my own boundaries and having a stranger ejaculating in my bed and making my bed linen all wet, I consider almost akin to his blowing his nose on the sheet, then wiping off the snot on my pillowcase. It would be decidedly distasteful.

In the past, I have had some excellent and very fulfilling sexual relationships with people I loved and cared deeply about. But now, without receiving love and a demonstration of caring and exclusivity, and without my feeling love towards the other person, then I would reject the offer of sex – and opt instead for a back-and-shoulder massage. Or shared travel, intelligent conversation, honesty, a comforting arm round my shoulders and a helping of battered whitebait.

Due to the Covid-19 pandemic that was sweeping across the world, my planned, booked and paid-for holidays to Lebanon and Crete were both cancelled. No photograph for Larry of the Commodore Hotel in Beirut.

Infantile paralysis, or poliomyelitis as it became better known, had arrived each summer throughout the first half of the 20th century, striking without warning. No one seemed to know how polio was transmitted or what caused it, despite the wild theories. There was no known vaccine or cure at that time. But unlike the coronavirus that targets adults and especially older people of my age, poliomyelitis had targeted children. Children would be taken from their families and isolated in sanatoria or sanatoriums, which is how I first learned the word 'sanatorium'.

There was no official lockdown in the decades after World War ll, only my parents' fear of losing yet another member of the family.

Thinking further about Larry and his wants as he specified online, I recalled the uninvited comments that four different and apparently happily married women, each about the same age as I am, had made to me in the past about their response to sex. I wondered why I had inadvertently committed them to memory.

C. had offered, just before a staff meeting that I was chairing, 'Do you know, the most hurtful four words in the English language that you can say to a man are - 'is it in yet?'

K. commented that for her 'Sex is sometimes a matter of gazing at the wallpaper.'

S. said 'When you are with someone of a certain age, it's the woman who has to do all the work.'

And a married fellow student at UEA whose name I have forgotten, told me 'I think sex is wildly over-rated.'

I cancel my membership of 'Likewise' forthwith. I am, and shall remain, Lorna Felicity rather than Lorna 'Facility'. I am not prepared to be anybody's facility. Nor an exchangeable commodity, as Richard had hoped to regard me.

There is nothing wrong with solitude, it allows me time to think. I am better off travelling with members of my family, or on my own, and with Butterworth who is fast ageing but who at least loves me, protects me and cares about me, wants to be with me rather than with someone who wants to spend time with me, only for what I can do for him.

I wonder how my dear friend Robert will react to that. And whether I will stick to it. I want him to be happy in whatever way he is able to choose. Whether knowingly or not, he helped me over a tricky period in my life and stood me on a better path, I am very appreciative of that. I care deeply about him, he has been part of my life across the past sixty years, he is good company and we have shared some fascinating times together. I regard him almost as a younger brother in part of my wider family.

My two quite different marriages and my foray into online dating has been a learning experience, one which I would advise anyone against repeating. I can only assume that there are things about which my mother, who always thought the best about other people, never warned me.

Judging from my encounters, what most men on a dating site and elsewhere are wanting and expecting is free, uncomplicated and convenient sex, pure (or not so pure) and simple. And in my case, sex with a widowed woman in her mid-seventies avoids any chance of fathering an unwanted child and unwanted commitment.

It also appears to engender an accompanying feeling from them that I should be grateful, 'at my age'.

It's insulting and downright irritating, quite apart from the fact that I have recently suffered from breast cancer and appear to have lost my libido (although Lallo says that the word 'libido' refers to a small training blue, mauve or white plant that elderly people plant in pots and window boxes. I think she means lobelia).

I am Lorna Felicity, not Lorna 'Facility' for anyone's sexual, financial, political, domestic, consort, social or career purposes.

Bugger that.

‘Snowdrop’ postscript

With the imminence of the pandemic, my own likelihood of suffering a stroke like my mother and maternal grandmother (who died as a result aged 84 and 76 respectively), my arthritis and the confirmation in January 2021 that I had stage 2 breast cancer, I have written this account more as an autobiography or a memoir than a cautionary tale. I hope it may provide background information for my children, (two of whom are currently on dialysis, pending organ transplants – all the result of a genetic disability unwittingly passed on from their father Richard), and for my grandchildren and great grandchildren.

The events in this account are non-fiction, based on fact as I remember it and have described.

People cross our paths, come and go out of our lives, all the time. If a relationship does not survive the passage of time, it does not mean that it lacked something, was in some way deficient or was not worthwhile. Not all encounters with people last for ever. Sometimes the people in our lives teach us something; sometimes what lasts is not the relationship but what we have gained from it - and given to it.

In case some of the people mentioned here do not wish their part in my story to be told, I have changed the names of the main people still living, as I mentioned at the beginning. I have also altered some of the places referred to that might help a reader to identify particular individuals.

I have changed the name and colour of the main dog in my account, and the title of the online dating site. As far as I am aware and at the time of writing, there is no site currently known as 'Likewise'.

In all other ways, the events and accounts on a differently-named site are exactly as I encountered. What I value most from the Likewise and other life experiences are my family and friends. I have gained Ryan B. aka Brian as a friend and also Robert, I hope, who has been consistently supportive and interested in my wish to write. I have also gained better knowledge of myself.

I wanted to have a better relationship with my older sister but I was wary. Experience had shown me that she could spread dissent and would undermine any positive experience if she could. The last time I saw her was by chance at Jocelyn's funeral – and at the Wake, we had no angry or deflating words over the cups of tea and slices of carrot cake, we almost began to share something. That is how I would like to remember her – pleasant, polite (if not actually welcoming) and sharing pleasure in hearing music by Bach.

I did graduate and was very pleased, surprised even, by my result and by some of the comments that tutors at UEA had written regarding my dissertation.

From now on, and despite having limited mobility, I intend to travel on my own, in a small group of strangers or close friends, or with members of my family.

Unless, of course, I get a better offer.

LFD/LFJ, 8th July 2021

Notes

i The Beatitudes sum up Jesus' teaching about what it means to live as a child of God's kingdom. They can be found right at the beginning of a long passage of teaching by Jesus in Matthew's Gospel, known as the Sermon on the Mount. Just as Moses taught the people of Israel from the mountain after he had received the Commandments, so Jesus begins his ministry by going up a mountain and teaching his disciples.

ii I referred to this in my radio play 'Gloria's Baptism', which was broadcast on Radio 4 in 1980.

iii The Tavistock Clinic saw its first patient, a child, on 27 September in 1920. Its name was taken from its original location at 51 Tavistock Square. The Clinic was established by Hugh Crichton-Miller, with contributions and pledges from wealthy donors and started off with seven doctors. The Tavistock Clinic originally had two departments: Adult and Children's. At the time, having a separate children's department was quite revolutionary and anticipated the work of Child Guidance Clinics by several years.

iv Fairfield Hospital in Fairfield Park, Stotfold, Bedfordshire was a psychiatric hospital from 1860 until it closed in 1999. The main hospital buildings are Grade II listed. They have been renovated, developed for housing, turned into luxury flats. I have a copy of the death certificate which, when I look at it now, I find intensely sad. My grandfather's occupation is described as 'Commercial Traveller'. He died aged 54, much younger than I am now. In a photograph of him, which I saw for the first time only after Moo had died, he looks very much like my brother Colin.

v ECT or Electroconvulsive therapy or electric shock treatment, was a treatment which was not uncommon in those days and considered to improve the mental state by increasing antipsychotic responses, although official guidelines in other countries were cautious in prescribing ECT for schizophrenia. It was believed at the time to be the safest and most effective treatment to relieve symptoms in severely depressed or suicidal patients although it was also known that ECT could result in temporary or permanent memory loss and general confusion.

vi At the age of 18, Inès appeared for the first time in photos for Elle magazine and began a modelling career. In 1983, she became the first model by fashion designer Karl Lagerfeld to sign an exclusive modelling contract with the haute couture fashion house Chanel.

vii Construction site forbidden to the public.

viii On April 20, 1968, Enoch Powell, a leading member of the Conservative Party in the British parliament, made a speech that would imprint itself into British memory—and divide the nation with its racist, incendiary rhetoric. Speaking before a group of conservative activists, Powell said that if immigration to Britain from the country's former colonies continued, a violent clash between white and black communities was inevitable. 'As I look ahead,' Powell said, 'I am filled with foreboding. Like the Roman I seem to see the River Tiber foaming with much blood,' which was an allusion to a line in Virgil's Aeneid. He maintained that it would not be enough to close Britain's borders—some of the immigrants already settled in the country would need to be sent home. 'If not,' he declared, attributing a quote to one of his constituents, 'in this country, in fifteen or twenty years' time, the black man will have the whip hand over the white man.'

ix Karlovy Vary is a spa city in the Karlovy Vary Region of the Czech Republic. It is named after Charles IV, Holy Roman Emperor and the King of Bohemia, who founded the city. It lies on the confluence of the rivers Ohře and Teplá, approximately 130 km west of Prague.

x The Sainsbury Centre was not completed until 1978.

xi Sharpies are a type of hard chined sailboat with a flat bottom, extremely shallow draft, centreboards and straight, flaring sides. They are believed to have originated in the New Haven, Connecticut region of Long Island Sound, United States. They were traditional fishing boats used for oystering, and later appeared in other areas. With centerboards and shallow balanced rudders, they are well suited to sailing in shallow tidal waters.

xii Rice-Davies was a central figure in *The Trial of Christine Keeler*, a BBC drama about the Profumo affair which told the story of the sex scandal that rocked 1960s Britain and helped bring down the Conservative government. The script of the drama ensured that the line, 'Well he would, wouldn't he?', was presented correctly, in the showgirl's own words.

xiii The Bielskis stayed hidden in the woods for two and a half years before emerging in July 1944 to learn that the Germans, over run by the Red Army, were retreating back towards Berlin.

xiv TURP, a transurethral resection of the prostate, a surgical procedure that involved cutting away a section of the prostate.

xv The Sermon on the Mount is a collection of sayings and teachings attributed to Jesus Christ which emphasizes his moral teaching found in the Gospel of Matthew chapters 5, 6 and 7. The name and location of the mountain is not stated.

xvi Cortijo Romero is a smallish centre, not far from Orgiva in southern Spain, with 20-30 guests most weeks, split between 2 courses during the summer months. There is a friendly, intimate feel there, and although some people come with a partner or friend, many travel here alone. The group, however, is central to the courses, and for many, it turns out to have been one of the most important aspects of their stay. For those who want to embrace community and meet others, the pool and surrounding area, as well as the dining area and the roof-top, provide more social and lively places for connecting with the other guests on the chosen course.

xvii 'She Is Gone/He Is Gone' poem by David Harkins

CPSIA information can be obtained
at www.ICGtesting.com
Printed in the USA
LVHW111633220822
726589LV00012B/207/J